CREDIT AND COLLECTION HANDBOOK

Michael Dennis

Prentice Hall

Library of Congress Cataloging-in-Publication Data

Dennis, Michael [date]
   Credit and Collection Handbook / Michael Dennis
      p. cm.
      Includes index.
      ISBN 0-13-082783-5 (cloth)
      1. Credit—Management.   2. Collecting of accounts.   I. Title.
   HG3751.D46   1999
   658.8´8—dc21   99-048409
                                                                        CIP

© 2000 *by Prentice Hall*

This publication is designed to provide accurate and authoritative information in
regard to the subject matter covered. It is sold with the understanding that the
publisher is not engaged in rendering legal, accounting, or other professional service.
If legal advice or other expert assistance is required, the services of a competent
professional person should be sought.

—From a Declaration of Principles jointly adopted by
a Committee of the American Bar Association and a Committee of Publishers and Associations.

Printed in the United States of America

10 9 8 7 6 5 4 3 2 1

ISBN 0-13-082783-5

ATTENTION: CORPORATIONS AND SCHOOLS

Prentice Hall books are available at quantity discounts with bulk purchase for educational,
business, or sales promotional use. For information, please write to: Prentice Hall Special
Sales, 240 Frisch Court, Paramus, NJ 07652. Please supply: title of book, ISBN number, quantity, how the book will be used, date needed.

PRENTICE HALL
Paramus, NJ 07652

On the World Wide Web at http://www.phdirect.com

CONTENTS

8 CHANGE

9 WORKING WITH REPORTING AGENCIES

12 GETTING INFORMATION FROM PUBLICLY HELD COMPANIES   *201*

Contents

18   FINANCIAL RATIO ANALYSIS   *281*

26   HANDLING DELINQUENT COMMERCIAL ACCOUNTS   393

27 REDUCING CREDIT RISK   *415*

30 CREDIT AND THE LAW   *457*

31 COLLECTIONS AND BANKRUPTCY LAW   479

32 CREDIT FRAUD   497

33 FRAUDULENT FINANCIAL STATEMENTS   *519*

38 CREDIT AND COLLECTION AND INTERNATIONAL LAW   *591*

INTRODUCTION

Credit is not intended to allow companies to purchase goods they cannot pay for. Trade credit, and specifically open account terms are intended to make it easier and more convenient for companies to purchase the goods and services they need and can pay for.

Consumer credit is defined broadly as credit granted to an individual by a retail store, a bank or a finance company for the purpose of purchasing goods or services for personal or household use.

Commercial credit is defined as credit granted from one company to another for the purchase of goods or services that are to be paid for at some point after delivery to the commercial buyer.

As a general statement, despite the increasing complexity of federal and state regulation of certain aspects of the economy, commercial credit granting and collection remain lightly regulated. In contrast, credit granting to individual consumers and collection of past due balances from consumers is highly regulated.

Used properly, open account credit benefits both the buyer and the seller. If the credit granter is unskilled or the collection staff is untrained, the use of open account credit terms can result in expensive mistakes made by the seller. That cost will come in the form of increased delinquencies and higher bad debt write offs.

Both the buyer and its creditors bear some responsibility when debts become overwhelming and the customer cannot retire them as they come due. Specifically, the buyer is accountable for not planning ahead, and the seller is accountable for not looking ahead. Having said that, even the best credit manager will lose a certain amount of money to bad debt write offs each year. Bad debts are a cost of doing business, and are not necessarily an indication that anyone in the credit department has made a mistake.

Business credit is extended from one company to another for the purpose of acquiring goods or services based on a commitment from the buyer to pay for those goods or services at a specified point in the future. Literally billions of dollars of goods are sold each day on open account credit terms between businesses. Open account terms are the most popular method of doing business with commercial customers. Open account terms encourage customers to buy more and to buy more often than they would if they were required to pay for the product on delivery.

Credit management is a difficult profession. Credit professionals must make unpopular and controversial credit decisions on a daily basis. Decisions to approve and release orders pending and on credit review are difficult and stressful because they often must be made quickly and with limited information. Negative credit decisions [decisions to hold orders, to refuse to offer open account terms or to reduce or withdraw a customer's open account terms] are stressful because the credit manager is often prevented from explaining why the decision was made because of formal and informal agreements to keep certain information confidential.

Many companies seem to consider their credit departments to be a necessary evil. The sales department sometimes refers to the credit department as the sales prevention team. If the credit function is ever going to receive the recognition that it deserves, credit managers are going to have to work harder to elevate people's perceptions about the credit department. All too often, the sales department is convinced that the credit department makes decisions on a whim rather than based on sound judgement backed by relevant and factual information.

Historically, companies have found it difficult to find ways to properly measure the effectiveness and efficiency of their credit department. As a result, the credit department's performance is sometimes more easily measured in negative rather than positive terms. For example, many companies use bad debt losses as a way to measure the credit department's performance. One problem is this: bad debt losses are often influenced by decisions made by senior management relating to accepting higher risk accounts in order to increase sales and profits.

Credit allows individuals and companies to acquire goods and services without having to pay the full cost at the time of the transaction. As such, credit terms are part of the buyer's cash management cycle. In most instances, trade creditors become a source of short-term working capital financing for customers experiencing cash flow problems.

Credit managers are fond of saying that a sale is not complete until the product or service provided is paid for. This is not quite accurate. It might be more accurate to say that there is no profit in a sale until the customer's payment is received. Few people recognize how critical the credit department is in collecting the payment and the profit from the sale.

Credit managers are finding their work environment to be changing rapidly. Today's credit manager is expected to find ways to do their jobs better, more efficiently, faster, and with less errors. In addition to collection and order approval, many credit managers are also actively involved in:

- Developing and updating credit policies
- Performing credit risk analysis
- Setting credit terms
- Meeting with applicants in order to establish large, open account credit terms more quickly
- Representing the company in bankruptcy proceedings
- Managing the cash application function
- Maintaining and strengthening business relationships with key customers
- Analyzing vendors for the purchasing department
- Managing cash flow, and forecasting cash

Credit professionals who cling to old ideas, or to outdated technology will soon find themselves obsolete. Credit managers must be able and willing to respond to new challenges, or they will soon be considered replaceable. Credit managers must be technically proficient as well as being good managers or they can relatively easily be replaced

Most credit departments are working harder than ever to improve efficiencies, reduce costs, and strengthen customer loyalty. This book is intended to help credit professionals to prevent problems by:

(1) shortening the learning curve in areas new to the reader,

(2) by reducing or eliminating the necessity to learn on-the-job by trial and error

(3) by presenting ideas as clearly and as concisely as possible without being superficial

(4) by differentiating between business credit and consumer credit, and explaining the differences in the laws affecting consumer and commercial credit granters

Most credit managers have been in the credit field for less than five years. With that single fact in mind, this book was written to help fill in as many of the blanks as possible. The material in each chapter is *not* cumulative, so the reader is free to "jump around" to a particular chapter of immediate interest to them. I encourage each reader to do so.

This book is intended as a practical, user-friendly guide to credit and collection principles and practices. The intent of the book is to address all the following areas of credit management:

- how to address day to day problems with domestic customers
- how to deal with the globalization of business
- how to improve overall productivity
- how to reduce bad debt losses
- how to reduce delinquencies and maintain an acceptable DSO
- how to make more sales, safely to marginal customers
- how to get senior management to listen to the credit manager's ideas and recommendations

Unfortunately, the future for many credit managers is not bright. In large numbers, companies continue to centralize their credit operations, reducing jobs and opportunities for advancement. Mergers and acquisitions often result in the elimination of certain positions including that of the credit manager.

Credit managers who do not find themselves unemployed may find that more of their duties are being automated. Some of the more common software programs already in use in some credit departments include:

- Software that determines which past due customers are to be contacted and in what order.
- Software that tracks deductions and determines the next step in the deduction management and resolution process.
- Software that performs financial statement analysis and interpretation.
- Credit scoring software that predicts default and delinquency both in applicants for credit and in existing customers, and then recommends credit limits or terms changes in response.

This book was written for the working credit professional. A complete table of contents and a useful index are included for easy reference. Within each chapter are numerous sub-headings to help you find the information you need as quickly as possible. And what's more, you don't have to read the entire book. Read only those chapters that interest you. Getting started is the hardest part of any project. All you need to do at this point is scan the table of contents to determine which chapters hold the most interest for you immediately—and start there. Good luck and let's go!

CHAPTER 1

THE ROLE OF THE CREDIT AND COLLECTION MANAGER

Business credit involves the extension of credit from one firm to another for the purpose of (a) acquiring finished goods that will be sold, or (b) acquiring raw materials that will be used to manufactured goods for resale, or (c) providing services to a company. The key element of business to business is that the extension of credit does not involve an immediate payment for the product or service. Instead, the credit grantor relies on the recipient will pay the balance due at the agreed upon due date.

The credit department is a part of [and not apart from] the rest of the company. The credit approval process, and all of the processes surrounding it must function smoothly within the larger business environment, and the actions of any company's credit department must generally be consistent with the actions of competitors' credit departments. This is in no way intended to suggest that companies collude in formulating credit policy or worse in establishing terms of sale. Consistent credit department activities would the following:

- Requiring that applicants complete a credit application and sign it.
- Requesting or requiring bank and trade references.
- Requesting that customers pay within terms, and calling customers when they do not.
- Holding orders when necessary to force customers to address past due balances.

The credit function is only one step in a long process that begins long before the customer issues a purchase order and ends long after the goods are received and paid for by the customer.

It is the credit manager's responsibility to plan and direct the activities of the credit department so that the credit department remains responsive to the needs of both internal and external customers. Internal customers include sales, operations, and the shipping department. External customers include direct customers and the ultimate end users of the merchandise sold.

The company's overall goals and objectives must be kept in mind when establishing the company's credit policy. Equally important, the company's goals and objectives must be operationalized; they must be considered while handling the day to day activities in the credit department. Inconsistencies between the stated policy and the actual practice are hard to explain and even harder to justify to senior management, to sales, or to customers.

For example, assume that the stated goal of the credit department is to maximize sales while maintaining a sound and collectable accounts receivable balance. Operationally, this requires that the credit department look for ways to approve every order. If the credit department routinely rejects orders from marginal accounts, then the way the credit department acts is different from the policy established, and inconsistent with the goals of the company.

THE ROLE OF THE CREDIT DEPARTMENT

Contrary to what some people might say or think, the credit department does far more than harass customers for money and make it difficult for salespeople to earn a living. One of the most important tasks of the credit department is to protect the company's investment in accounts receivable by releasing only those orders that the credit department believes have a reasonable chance of being paid on time.

The credit manager must strive to find the appropriate balance between risk and reward when reviewing orders, when updating active accounts, and when evaluating applicants for credit terms. The only way to effectively manage risk is to do so proactively.

Companies must sell to marginal credit risks on open account terms in order to achieve certain sales volume, profit and market share goals. Leading companies have developed companywide risk management strategies in order to help them remain competitive and profitable. Specific to credit risk, the two sides of the coin are:

(a) That credit risk can result in delinquencies or bad debt write offs, and...

(b) Credit risk creates opportunities for generating additional sales and profits.

In trying to strike the right balance between risk and reward, a prudent credit manager will be on the alert for indications that a customer's financial condition has deteriorated significantly. However, an experienced credit professional will not overreact to unsubstantiated rumors that a customer may be in financial trouble. Credit managers must remind themselves and counsel their subordinates not to become paranoid about credit risk. Unfortunately, some companies make controlling bad debt losses the litmus test for the credit department and the credit manager. As a result, some credit managers can become overzealous in their attempts to reduce or eliminate bad debt losses. In doing so, they may reject good business in their efforts to avoid write offs. One of the tests of a credit policy is that if losses are too low, the policy is probably too conservative.

INDICATIONS OF DELINQUENCY AND DEFAULT

Since customers are unlikely to announce that they are experiencing cash flow or other financial problems, credit managers are constantly looking for indications of problems. The early warning signs that a customer may be experiencing cash flow problems and that its ability to pay vendor bills is worsening may include any or all of the following:

- lawsuits are pending
- tax liens have been filed
- There has made a significant change in its payment pattern—for example, the customer has stopped discounting, or the customer was paying on time but now is seriously past due.
- the debtor has lost market share and/or the debtor is losing money
- the customer has established a history of slow payments with its other trade creditors
- The customer has failed to meet its bank loan covenants.

THE CREDIT DILEMMA

Every day, credit managers are faced with a series of contradictory goals. Here are a few examples:

- Credit managers are expected to maximize cash inflows, but can be criticized for being too assertive in their collection efforts.
- Credit managers are expected to have systems and processes in place in order to minimize bad debt losses, but at the same time they are

GUIDING PRINCIPLES FOR THE CREDIT DEPARTMENT

The credit department needs certain guiding rules or principles. The following is a recommended set of guiding principles:

The credit department must focus on finding ways to meet customers' needs.

Credit department personnel will be as flexible as conditions permit in releasing orders and extending credit to customers.

Credit department personnel will be receptive to suggestions, and will remain responsive to inquiries from sales department personnel and from customers about the status of accounts.

The credit department will strive to anticipate future credit requirements to proactively manage credit risk.

The credit department will work with the sales department to pre-qualify prospective new accounts.

The credit department will work in partnership with the sales department and the operations department to ensure that as many orders as possible are approved without unnecessary delay. The credit manager will periodically review the criteria used to place accounts on credit referral and modify them when appropriate.

The credit manager will make certain that only those orders that require individual review and manual approval are forwarded to the credit department.

The credit department commits to open and honest dialogue with customers and salespeople.

The credit department is committed to complying with the letter and the spirit of all applicable federal and state laws governing credit granting and collection.

Sales personnel will be given as much information as possible about the decisions made by the credit department—except when providing this information would violate a commitment to confidentiality made by the credit department to the information provider.

The decisions made by the credit department will be based on facts and good judgment, not on opinion, guesswork, or personal bias.

The credit manager should be certain that everyone in the credit department and everyone in sales management receives a copy of the principles that have been adopted.

expected to extend credit to marginal credit risk accounts, provided it can be done safely. [Few people outside of the credit department understand the irony of trying to make "safe" open account sales to marginal credit risk accounts.]

- Credit managers are expected to accelerate cash inflows, while at the same time they are discouraged from holding orders as leverage to force a delinquent customer to clear past due invoices.

- Credit managers will be criticized by sales management for being overly conservative in credit granting, and equally harshly criticized by executive management for taking too much credit risk.

The appropriate steps for the credit department to take in order to achieve the contradictory goals they face include:

(1) Promptly and diligently following up on past due accounts. The more quickly and professionally that a past due balance is addressed, the less likely the sale will result in a bad debt loss. [Quick collections also help ensure that the creditor company has enough cash on hand to meet its cash requirements.]

(2) Scheduling periodic updates on all active accounts.

(3) Differentiating between customers with temporary cash flow problems and customers with serious and long-term problems representing unusually high risk. Once identified, high-risk accounts must be managed more carefully than the rest.

(4) Holding subordinates accountable for the decisions they make, for the actions they take, and for the errors they make. Credit managers should emphasize to subordinates that with autonomy comes accountability for their actions.

(5) Developing a thorough understanding about trends in the industry—and how they might impact the company in general and on the credit department in particular.

(6) Finding out what the company's long term goals and objectives are, and then making certain the credit department's policies and procedures will help the company to achieve its goals and objectives.

LEADING AND MANAGING SUBORDINATES

Leadership demands a unique combination of talents and traits including tact, diplomacy, honesty, coaching skills, charisma, self-confidence, empathy and discretion. Leadership in the credit department also requires an under-

> No one is irreplaceable. Consequently, there is no such thing as job security. The best advice is to constantly upgrade your skills in order to make increasingly more valuable contributions to the company. How? Many people concerned about their jobs volunteer for extra work; in addition to working longer and harder to make certain their own work is completed on time and is entirely satisfactory.

standing by the credit manager of corporate goals and objectives and the ability to explain the seeming contradictions inherent in these goals to subordinates. [An example of the contradictory nature of these goals would be a requirement to sell safely on open account terms to an account identified as a marginal credit risk.]

Leadership requires that the credit manager understand each of these points:

(a) People are the most important factor in determining how successful the credit department will be—not the technology the department uses and not the policies and procedures that have been written.

(b) Everyone has a specific role to play in the success of the department. For example, the ability to build rapport with customers will help a collector be more effective.

(c) The ability of the credit manager to communicate confidently with all levels of sales and sales management will make the credit department's decisions more readily accepted.

(d) The ability of the cash application specialist to persuade customers to provide information missing from the remittance advice quickly will make the cash application function and the credit department more efficient.

(e) Working in the credit department is stressful. It requires a special type of person to be comfortable working in that environment.

(f) Credit managers need to be alert for symptoms of stress or burnout and need to find a way to address the problem—even if that means removing the employee from the credit department.

One of the keys to managing people involves making certain that there is mutual understanding between the employee and the manager as to what is expected of each employee. The goals established with and for each employee must be specific. For example, a goal of keeping accounts as current as possible is not specific. An example of a specific goal is:

The collector shall manage his/her accounts so that, on average, no more than 10% of the total accounts receivable balance on accounts assigned to him/her are past due on the month end summary due date aging report.

DEVELOPING EMPLOYEE SPECIFIC GOALS

Employees are more likely to accept and embrace goals that they have helped to develop. Their active participation in the goal setting process helps ensure that the goals set are achievable, and relevant to what they do. For these reasons, credit managers should insist that subordinates help to formulate their own performance goals.

Good credit managers coach their employees, and offer comments, advice and encouragement throughout the year, not only during the annual performance review. Good managers conduct quarterly reviews with employees. They discuss the progress that their subordinates have made toward achieving their goals.

Credit managers can make these quarterly reviews easier for themselves and more meaningful for the employee by asking the employee to gather the relevant information in preparation for the meetings. If it becomes apparent that the goals need to be modified, or if new goals need to be added, the quarterly meetings are the proper venue to discuss these proposed changes.

APPRECIATION

Good credit managers express appreciation to their subordinates for a job well done. They do so in public. Good managers evaluate and critique performance, good and bad, throughout the year. Good managers address performance, attendance, tardiness, and morale problems in private. Good credit managers encourage subordinates to talk with them about problems rather than allowing small problems to grow into major issues.

ANNUAL PERFORMANCE REVIEWS

Annual performance reviews should contain very few surprises. If an employee is caught off guard when a performance problem is presented, it is an indication that the credit manager has not been as effective a communicator as they could have been during the year. Credit managers should seriously consider re-writing an annual performance review if they believe the employee will be surprised by the contents of that review.

CREDIT MANAGERS AS PROBLEM SOLVERS

The best credit managers are excellent problem solvers. They have the ability to look at a situation, assess alternatives and options quickly, determine which alternative is best, and then follow through on their decision. The trick is for the credit manager to be decisive, but not opinionated. Decisiveness is an appropriate and necessary skill, given the volume of decisions that must be made on a daily basis. Credit professionals need to remember that opinionated credit managers may be considered as reckless.

CREDIT DECISIONS IN THE ABSENCE OF PERFECT INFORMATION

The ability to make good credit decisions quickly and decisively requires experience, knowledge and self-confidence. It also requires a willingness to make the decision in the absence of perfect information and subject to significant time constraints. Experienced credit managers learn to accept the consequences of their decisions recognizing that mistakes are inevitable.

For credit managers, the key is to learn from their mistakes and not to dwell on them. Experienced managers understand that the most expensive mistake that any credit professional can make is one that no one learns anything from.

HIRING

The expression "garbage in, garbage out" is as applicable to computer programming as it is to hiring new employees for the credit department. Recognizing that the credit department is only as good as the people it employs, the importance of hiring the right people cannot be overemphasized. The steps in the hiring process include:

- Developing a profile of the ideal candidate, in addition to a profile of a candidate that meets the minimum standards
- Recruiting, including networking and advertising
- Screening the résumés received

- Pre-screening applicants by telephone in order to eliminate those that do not match the profile
- Interviewing applicants using a structured interview process and a panel of interviewers
- Verifying the background of the candidate selected before making any job offer
- Extending the offer of employment

The credit manager, not the human resources department, has the primary responsibility for hiring decisions within the credit department. Credit managers should accept input from human resources, but they cannot allow the H/R department to be overly influential in the decision-making process. The credit manager has the most insight and information about what skills the ideal candidate for the position would have, and the credit manager has the most to lose if the new employee does not work out as planned.

Credit managers should take their time in selecting the right person, and learn from any hiring mistakes they may have made in the past. Applicants that pass an initial screening process should be carefully interviewed by a core group of interviewers. Ideally, each person will ask each candidate the same questions to permit easy comparison. The credit manager should discuss the strengths and weaknesses of each applicant with each interviewer.

Credit managers must also stay focused on the future. They should hire people with the potential to accomplish more than the position they are being hired into. At the same time the credit manager should not hire someone clearly overqualified in the hope that a position will open up that the new hire can migrate into.

TRAINING

Training is motivating. It demonstrates a commitment by the employer to its employees. Training is a perk, especially training that is conducted off site and on company time. Training need not be conducted off site to be valuable.

One of the most important things a credit manager can do is to take the time necessary to train subordinates properly. For example, credit managers may do a fairly good job of explaining how to complete a task but do not take the time to explain why the task must be completed. As a result, employees who might be able to make a bigger contribution if they understood more lack the information needed to make recommendations and suggest improvements.

TRAINING NEW EMPLOYEES

Embarrassing and potentially costly mistakes can be avoided if trainees [new employees and employees being cross trained] are encouraged to ask questions any time they are unsure of how to handle a situation. Credit managers should explain to their subordinates the risks and costs associated with guessing at answers in the credit department. Credit managers should instruct their subordinates to interrupt them any time they have a question about a task assigned to them.

The kind of training that seems to work best for credit department personnel is on-the-job training. The normal process is as follows:

(1) The new employee watches their trainer perform the task.

(2) After a period of time, the employee performs the task while the trainer watches.

(3) When the trainer believes the employee has been adequately trained, the trainee is released to perform this task with minimal supervision or oversight.

(4) New employees are told that, if problems or questions arise, they are not to guess at the answer. Instead, they should refer the matter to the trainer or the department manager for clarification.

Credit managers have only themselves to blame if an employee is not given adequate training and then makes a serious mistake. New employees learn at different speeds, and the training process is too important to be rushed.

USING THE CREDIT POLICY MANUAL AS A TRAINING TOOL

A well written, up-to-date and detailed credit manual can serve as a teaching aid. Even if such a credit manual is available, new employees will need extensive on-the-job training.

One common mistake is to inundate a new employee with information. New employees must be allowed to assimilate new data at their own pace, since providing them with too much information often results in a poor outcome in which new workers become confused, frustrated and stressed by the experience.

USING OFF-SITE TRAINING AS A MOTIVATIONAL TOOL

In addition to on-site training, employees should be rewarded for their efforts by being offered opportunities to attend company sponsored off-site training on company time. with pay. Examples of this type of training include credit group meetings, conferences, seminars, speeches, and evening classes [all designed for working credit people].

THE BENEFITS OF CROSS TRAINING

Credit managers should also seriously consider cross-training people within the department so that if an employee leaves, another employee can be slotted into the new position with as little disruption as possible. Whenever possible, involve employees in special projects. Special projects are an opportunity for employees to demonstrate their unique skills. Also, special projects and cross training are a way to break the monotony of doing the same tasks day after day.

THE PROBLEM WITH RETRAINING

Poor performance does not always mean that an existing employee needs and would benefit from additional training. Before considering training, the credit manager must try to find the reason for the poor performance. If the poor performance is due to a lack of attention to detail or a lack of enthusiasm, then additional training is clearly not the solution.

Credit managers must remember that training is only one tool for increasing and improving job performance. For example, a lack of motivation will not be cured by training. If the credit manager determines that a lack of training is the culprit, then training should be scheduled as soon as practical. If it is not, the problem should be addressed with the employee and if the substandard work continues the employee should be terminated.

DOWNSIZING

One of the most devastating things that can happen to a credit department involves downsizing—an involuntary layoff of one or more employees. Assuming that the credit manager is allowed to keep his or her job, the credit manager will be part of the team to notify the affected employee(s). Perhaps the most difficult role for the credit manager after a layoff is to keep the rest of the employees' morale and productivity up. Rather than simply dividing the work of the laid off employees among the remaining workers, instead, the credit manager must prioritize the tasks and eliminate as many low-value-added tasks as possible.

REDEFINING THE CREDIT MANAGER'S ROLE

There are many changes occurring in the credit profession and in businesses in general. In order to survive and prosper, credit professionals need to constantly redefine their roles. If possible, credit managers should try to break out of the narrow range of actions and activities they are normally limited to. Credit professionals can begin to redefine their roles by embracing the following concepts:

- The goal of the credit manager, and the credit department, should be to meet or to exceed customer expectations.

- Only make commitments you can keep, and always keep all the commitments that you make.

- Make review of pending orders a top priority for the department. This will demonstrate the department's commitment to customer service, and will help the company to schedule orders and shipments more efficiently.

- Embrace new technologies. Employees and especially managers who fail to keep up with new technologies will be viewed as eccentric at best, and expendable at worst.

- Investigate technologies such as credit scoring and deduction management software that show promise for the credit department

- Work with the sales department to ensure that every option is considered before an applicant is rejected for open account terms, and before any active customer's open account terms are withdrawn.

- Acknowledge that there is value in inter-departmental cooperation, and that the credit department has an obligation to work with other functional areas including production, shipping, order entry, customer service and marketing.

- Meet periodically with other department heads to determine how the credit department can assist other departments to make the company more efficient, more responsive to changing market conditions, and better able to satisfy customer needs.

- Recognize that the credit department must constantly strive to improve efficiency because rapid approval and on time delivery is essential to customers. As companies reduce their inventory levels and require suppliers to provide goods on a "just in time" basis, a delay in approving an order can result in orders missing their delivery date.

Credit managers can further recast their role in the organization by accepted or requesting additional assignments. Credit managers have been successful in many new or additional areas of responsibility including managing:

- Accounts payable
- Order entry
- Customer support
- Cash application
- Cash forecasting and treasury related functions
- Contracts management
- Purchasing

WORK ASSIGNMENTS

Frequently, accounts are assigned to collectors either geographically or based on some type of alphabetical distribution. Why? Because this was the simplest way to assign accounts and to divide accounts prior to the widespread use of computers in business.

Another option involves assigning accounts based on their level of complexity. Specifically, more complex accounts would be assigned to employees that have more experience; more routine accounts can be assigned to employees with less experience. This way, the most complicated problems are assigned to the personnel with the best chance of resolving them.

Regardless of whether accounts are assigned alphabetically, geographically or based on their level of complexity, one thing is certain: From time to time the workloads among collectors will become unbalanced. The credit manager must be alert to this problem. He or she should reallocate workloads as soon as it becomes apparent that one employee is overworked. Failing to reallocate work so will demoralize employees.

DELEGATION

Most credit managers have too much to do and not enough time to do it in, but often they are reluctant to delegate. Rather than taking shortcuts credit managers need to learn to delegate more of their work. The reluctance to delegate stems from a number of concerns, including:

■ loss of control over important tasks

■ fear that the task will be done incorrectly

■ a concern that the task might not be completed on time

■ the difficulty in finding the time necessary to train subordinates to perform the new task

By failing to delegate, credit managers frequently wind up with more projects than they can successfully complete. This results in a lack of focus, an inability to prioritize, and a fragmentation of the credit manager's efforts. Delegating work allows credit managers to distance themselves from the day-to-day activities of the credit department and to narrow their focus onto what is truly important rather than what is simply urgent.

Many employees like additional responsibilities because they want to demonstrate their capabilities. The credit manager's role as a delegator is not to overload employees. One key is to make certain the subordinate understands the relative priority of the task being assigned to the tasks previously assigned, and has the time to complete the task and is prepared to commit to doing so.

One of the principles of delegation involves delegating work to the lowest level at which it can be competently performed, and one of the best ways to delegate is to ask for volunteers. Employees who volunteer are likely to be highly motivated. They may be seeking promotion, and volunteering for extra work is one way to demonstrate both commitment and some unique skill.

THE CREDIT MANAGER'S ROLE AS A DELEGATOR

If the credit manager takes the time to do some preparation and planning, the chances of delegating assignments and having a satisfactory outcome increase dramatically. Some of the steps credit managers should take in delegating tasks include:

■ The manager should develop an outline of the project

■ There should be an agreement about how and when the subordinate will report progress

- If the assignment is complex, the tasks should be outlined in writing
- The credit manager must make it clear that his or her goal is not to see if the employee will sink or swim. Instead, it is to help the subordinate to succeed.
- Subordinates must be encouraged to ask for advice when [not if] problems arise, and cautioned against guessing at the proper course of action when they experience problems.
- If, prior to the deadline, the employee indicates that the project will not be completed on time, the credit manager should be willing to take the assignment back.

All too often, credit managers cannot see the forest for the trees because they are too busy with the minutia. Delegation improves a credit manager's productivity by allowing him or her time the time needed to plan, to prioritize, to train, to coach, and to evaluate individual performance. Delegation also gives the credit manager the time necessary to study the overall performance of the credit department and make the changes necessary.

TIP: Many companies have employee recognition programs. Their intent is to let employees know that their effort and hard work are important to the company. The rewards offered to employees in these programs vary widely.

It really doesn't matter much how employees are rewarded, provided they understand that their individual efforts made a difference for and to the company.

THE HIDDEN ADVANTAGES OF DELEGATION

The hidden advantage of delegating work to subordinates is that doing so improves their problem solving skills, their decision-making skills, and their project management and time management skills.

The major reasons delegated tasks are either not done or not done properly include all of the following:

(1) The employee was improperly trained, or
(2) The employee was not motivated to doing the assigned task properly.

Providing employees with the appropriate training prevents the first of these problems. The second problem is far more complex than simply an issue of training. Analyzing the motivations of employees and developing strategies to increase their drive to succeed or to compensate for a lack of motivation is a complex process.

Probably the single most important thing that credit managers can do is to remind subordinates that with responsibility comes accountability. Once subordinates are fully trained, credit managers should hold them accountable for the mistakes they make—just as credit managers are accountable to senior management for the mistakes that are made by the credit department as a whole.

REDUCING COSTS

For credit managers, activities that increase the cost of doing business but provide no benefits to the company or to the customer [called non-value-added activities] should be eliminated. Credit managers must search out and eliminate such non-value-added activities so that assets [including employees' time] can be put to good use.

Credit managers need to change or eliminate:

- Obsolete and inefficient processes
- Unnecessary rules that create bottlenecks
- A lengthy and overly complex order review and approval process
- Multiple handling of the same document

ELIMINATING SURPRISES

Senior management does not like surprises from the credit department. Therefore, one of the roles of the credit manager is to make certain senior management is aware of the types of credit risk the company is accepting. The types of credit risk the credit manager accepts should be compatible with both the short term and the long-term goals of the company. For example, if the goal of the company is to double sales and increase its market share, the credit department may need to liberalize its credit granting process. If the company has cash flow problems, the credit department may need to put more restrictions on marginal credit risk accounts, and will probably need to place delinquent accounts on credit hold more quickly.

CREDIT RISK

Credit managers would be well advised to confine themselves to making sound credit decisions. There is an old expression: "Not every good credit decision is a good business decision." Unless credit managers are expressly authorized to make business decisions they should confine their activities to making sound and defensible credit decisions. Admittedly, there is sometimes a fine line between taking action that is good for the company and making appropriate credit decisions, but generally companies rely on their credit department to fulfill these roles:

- Safeguard the company's investment in the accounts receivable asset, and
- Maintain the company's cash flow by monitoring and managing the types of customers that are offered open account credit terms.

Creditors who make business decisions rather than credit decisions are unlikely to find either sympathy or support for their actions if and when collection problems occur.

REMEMBER YOUR ROLE

Occasionally, a credit manager who has referred an account to his or her manager for review will be asked what to do if it were up to them to make the decision. This is a trick question! By offering an opinion the credit manager will have crossed the line between credit decision making and business decision making. Credit managers can sidestep the question by indicating:

"I don't think I am qualified to answer that question. There are too many variables that I do not know about. There is no valid credit reason to release this order pending, but because of the unique nature of this problem I thought it should be referred to you to see if you wanted to override my decision."

MANAGING AND TRAINING CREDIT DEPARTMENT PERSONNEL

Credit managers should expect excellence from subordinates. Excellence requires training, and attention to detail. Credit managers cannot expect excellence unless they recognize their role as a trainer.

Credit managers should acknowledge subordinates for the good work they accomplish, and counsel those who do not meet your expectations. Every time work does not meet the credit manager's expectations, it should be looked upon as an opportunity for the credit manager to counsel or train subordinates to make certain that their work meets the credit manager's standards and customers' expectations.

COACHING REQUIRES CONSTRUCTIVE CRITICISM

In their roles as a trainer, teacher, leader and mentor, credit managers need to offer constructive criticism from time to time. It is important to know how to give constructive criticism in order to correct negative behaviors without creating a situation in which the subordinate feels demoralized and de-motivated. As a general rule, constructive criticism should be presented calmly, professionally and in private. Specific examples or issues should be given to the employee whenever possible.

MANAGING CUSTOMER RELATIONSHIPS

In this highly competitive business environment, customers increasingly are demanding superior service. One of the roles of the credit manager is to make certain credit department personnel understand that a large part of its job is customer service and support—particularly as it relates to dispute resolution and problem solving.

For example, if a particular customer complains regularly about being shorted on shipments, rather than simply issuing credit for the shortages the credit department should notify the shipping department manager about the recurring problem and ask what can be done to solve the problem.

GOAL SETTING

Many credit managers unilaterally and arbitrarily assign goals and objectives to each of their subordinates. A more enlightened and effective technique involves asking subordinates for their ideas about goals and building on them.

The concern that some credit managers have about a cooperative approach toward goal setting is that it might result goals being set too low. Clearly, if the individual goals would not cumulatively meet the departmental goals there is a problem. The credit manager would need to explain the additional work must be done. By explaining the shortfall to subordinates and asking for their comments and ideas most managers soon find the discussion going in the direction it needs to go.

PERFORMANCE EVALUATIONS

Employees expect and deserve regular performance reviews. Performance reviews allow the manager to point out differences between the employee's actual performance and specific performance expectations. Performance evaluations allow the credit manager to establish more realistic goals if that is appropriate, to determine if and when additional training is required, and to discuss shortcomings.

In the credit manager's roles as leader, manager, trainer, coach and mentor to his or her subordinates, regular performance evaluations are one of the tools that can be used to improve the overall effectiveness in each of these overlapping roles.

DEALING WITH PERFORMANCE PROBLEMS

When problems arise, concerns and disciplinary action should be expressed directly, discreetly and in private with the employees involved. Subordinates should be allowed to express their opinions—but the discussion should never be permitted by the credit manager to turn into a debate.

After the credit manager has explained the problem, he or she should ask what steps the subordinate thinks are appropriate to correct it. The goal is to solve the problem cooperatively. If the subordinate is unable or unwilling to make any suggestions, the credit manager must be more direct. If sufficient progress is not made toward a mutually agreed upon plan of action, the credit manager may have to mandate such a plan.

Once corrective action has been agreed upon [or once the subordinate has been given specific instructions], the credit manager must track the progress being made and follow up periodically to make sure the subordinate has taken the necessary steps to correct the problem. If significant progress is not made, the credit manager must take additional steps to correct the problem.

DEALING WITH ON THE JOB STRESS

Credit and collection work is inherently stressful. Recognizing this fact, there are a number of things that a credit manager can do to reduce on-the-job stress, including:

- Acknowledging to your subordinates that the work can be stressful.

- Providing subordinates with sufficient training so that they are not overwhelmed by the complexity of their tasks.

- Helping subordinates to prioritize their work so they get a "bigger bang for the buck" by allocating their time in the areas and with the customers that offer the most promise.

- Helping subordinates learn when to say "when." There is a point of diminishing returns when continuing to pressure delinquent accounts for payment is no longer productive.

- By meeting regularly with subordinates to discuss the status of outstanding issues and past due accounts. After a reasonable effort, a subordinate should be encouraged to pass along a delinquent and uncooperative account to a more experienced person.

- By encouraging subordinates to develop a support group at work that they use to focus on problem solving and stress relief. Unfortunately, some credit department personnel get caught up in a cycle of gripe sessions with like-minded peers. This can be damaging to their morale, and to the morale of the entire department.

CONTINUING PROFESSIONAL EDUCATION AND TRAINING

Successful credit managers understand the importance of continuing education and training for themselves and for their subordinates. Some training can and must be done on-the-job. Training should be scheduled at least once a quarter for credit department staff members.

In their role as advocates for their subordinates, enlightened credit managers also support and encourage continuous personal development through ongoing evening educational courses through their local credit managers' association, through coursework at local colleges, and by establishing a budget to allow subordinates to attend company sponsored training seminars and credit conferences.

CONTINUING PROCESS IMPROVEMENT

Process improvement is not a one-time exercise. The credit manager must accept their role as champion for continuous process improvement in the credit department. A manager that redesigns a major process cannot afford to sit back and admire their accomplishments. Instead, the manager should continue to improve the process, and look for other opportunities to improve credit department policies and procedures.

This may require a paradigm shift in thinking. The credit managers must adopt a philosophy that no matter how good something is, it can be made better and more efficient.

EVALUATING NEW EMPLOYEES DURING THE PROBATIONARY PERIOD

One of the biggest mistakes a credit manager can make is to hold onto a marginal new employee beyond the initial probation period hoping that in time the performance will improve. The tough facts are these:

- Credit and collections is not for everyone.
- Keeping a marginal employee, especially one that has a bad attitude, damages the morale of the entire department.
- Additional time on the job is not likely to overcome basic deficiencies such as an inability to get to work on time, a lack of self-motivation or self-discipline, or a poor work ethic.

Marginal performers should be terminated during their probationary period. In the long term, it is probably best for the employee, and it is almost certainly the right thing to do for the department and for the company. It is difficult for a marginal employee to close the gap, and the gap represents the difference between poor and acceptable performance.

RECOGNIZING SUPERIOR PERFORMANCE

There is an unfortunate tendency to take employees who do their work quietly and efficiently for granted, especially if their work is not high profile. [Low profile positions would include cash application, and new account investigation positions.] Acknowledging the work that they do and the contributions they make will help to keep employees motivated, and make it less likely they will transfer or resign. The role of the credit manager is to support every person and every position in the department, and not just the high profile positions such as collections.

REPORTING TO SENIOR MANAGEMENT

In their role as middle managers, credit managers need to know what types of information their manager wants to receive documenting the credit department's performance and how often they want these reports. It is waste of time, effort and resources for the credit manager to prepare reports their manager does not need or want.

Some credit managers meet with their managers daily; others meet weekly and others meet only when a specific situation makes it a necessity. It is up to the credit manager to find out how his or her manager wants to handle this issue, and then to act accordingly. Generally, [but not always] the more confidence a manager has in his or her credit executive the less frequently meetings will be scheduled.

THE CREDIT MANAGER'S ROLE AS PART OF THE MANAGEMENT TEAM

To succeed in business, credit professionals must be careful to present information to senior management in a way that demonstrates they are committed to helping the company achieve its short term and long term goals. Credit managers should at all times demonstrate these traits or characteristics to senior management:

- Integrity
- Flexibility, and a willingness to accept changes and new challenges combined with the ability to manage change within the department
- A strong work ethic combined with a high energy level
- Self confidence and decisiveness
- The ability to contribute in specific and measurable ways to the company's short and long term goals, combined with the skills and ability to get improved performance from the credit department staff
- The ability to build consensus as part of the management team
- The ability to align the operations of the credit department with the goals and objectives of the company

EMPLOYEE RETENTION

No company can prosper if key employees leave. Similarly, the credit department will be less productive and efficient if key personnel leave. Therefore, credit managers must develop a retention strategy for key employees. Conceptually, employee retention is simple: If the best and brightest employees are paid the most, they will stay. Even if that were true, most credit managers do not have the flexibility to make this happen. Therefore, credit managers need to develop other retention tools and techniques. Some useful employee retention strategies include:

- Invest in the key employee's professional development by paying for continuing professional education or for college.

- Give key employees more autonomy and more authority

- Recognize and reward excellence—not only with cash but also with praise, awards, certificates, letters of appreciation, etc.

- Ask key employees about their personal goals, and then look for ways that the company can help them to achieve those goals.

Other techniques to retain key employees involve giving credit managers discretionary budgets and other incentives to reward their best employees. These discretionary awards might be in the form of bonuses, profit sharing, rewards for productivity increases, or awards for new ideas and innovations that save the company time and money. Other discretionary incentives include time off with pay, flexible work hours, a choice of work assignments, and promotions.

Unfortunately, most companies do not have these programs in place, and lack the flexibility to offer this type of program. As a result, companies often lose their best and brightest employees to other companies that offer higher pay. It is not necessarily the higher pay that prompts the best employees to leave. Instead, it is the fact that they have not received the recognition and the rewards they can believe that they are entitled to.

Compensation systems are extremely hard to change because they are normally entrenched throughout the organization. It is fair to say that the idea of flexible compensation will go nowhere without sponsorship from senior management, but companies do have a choice—they can find ways to keep their best and brightest employees, or they can watch them leave.

MAINTAINING A CURRENT CREDIT POLICY

One of the most important tasks for any credit manager is to make certain the credit department's policies and procedures manual is kept current. Sound internal control practices and guidelines are the first step in controlling credit risk. Underlying these practices and guidelines should be the policies and procedures manual. An up-to-date credit manual will help a company to control credit risk and to reduce bad debt losses.

SUMMARY

The ability to convert accounts receivable into cash quickly is critical to every company's financial success. Many companies get into serious trouble because they run out of cash. The credit department plays a vital role in a company's cash conversion cycle, and the role of the credit manager is to ensure that the credit department converts accounts receivable into cash as quickly as possible with as little disruption and damage to the seller's ongoing business relationship with the buyer as possible. Arguably, this is the most important task for any credit manager.

CHAPTER 2

COOPERATION BETWEEN SALES AND CREDIT

Establishing a mature, professional and viable working relationship with the sales department is one of the most important goals for any credit manager. Even when this goal is achieved, maintaining that relationship requires constant attention and effort. Some salespeople still view the credit department and the credit manager as obstacles to be circumvented. At the very least, this is a shortsighted view of the relationship between sales and credit.

If the sales department and the credit department work cooperatively, both departments and the company as a whole will gain. If the "us vs. them" mindset is allowed to prevail, then neither department will benefit—and the relationship will continue to be strained. The two departments in the company, which have the most direct contact with customers, can accomplish more as a team than the departments can work against each other.

THE ADVERSARIAL RELATIONSHIP

Part of the reason that an adversarial relationship may exist between the sales department and the credit department is the fact that the salesperson often wants orders released that the credit department has to hold. Credit holds are considered to be a last resort. The credit hold is normally used only when other methods to convince a customer to address a problem—such as a seriously past due balance—have failed.

Order holds are unpopular with customers and with their salespeople. Part of the blame for an adversarial relationship between sales and credit lies in the fact that many credit managers take a detached, clinical approach credit risk management decisions such as credit holds. This unemotional approach to decision making often spills over into the way in which credit managers inform salespeople and customers about their decisions.

With a little practice, credit managers can improve the way they deliver bad news to customers and to salespeople. Better yet, by working proactively with the sales department to get customers to address problems before they become so serious that orders are placed on hold, both the sales department and the credit department win. By failing to take into account the human element of every negative credit decision, credit managers are creating barriers between sales and credit by being seen as insensitive to the potentially devastating impact on the long-term relationship of decision to hold orders.

On the other hand, salespeople contribute to the historically strained relationship between sales and credit by taking negative credit decisions personally—or by assuming that these decisions are made on a whim rather than on the basis of calm, rational consideration. In this highly competitive business environment, most credit managers accept more risk now than they have in the past. Credit professionals do so in order to help their employers to maintain adequate sales volume, and ideally to maximize profits.

SALES ORIENTED CREDIT MANAGERS

All companies expect their credit managers to be sales-oriented. Essentially, this means that credit managers are expected to look for reasons to release orders pending rather than for excuses to hold them. Being sales oriented requires credit managers to look for creative solutions to problems. For example, rather than holding a pending order until a promised payment is received in the mail, the credit manager might suggest one of the following alternatives:

- The creditor will pay for a courier to pick up the payment
- The creditor will pay the cost for overnight delivery
- The credit manager will arrange for someone [in sales or credit] to pick up the check
- Release orders pending based on the customer's commitment that the check is in the mail assuming that the customer does not have a history of borken commitments.

Salespeople will always try to pressure the credit department to release orders to marginal accounts. Sometimes it seems that the higher the credit risk the more the customer wants to buy. Another observation is that the worse the credit risk, the more pressure the credit manager may get to release an order pending, or to approve the applicant for open account terms.

No credit manager can afford to release an order to an account that is not creditworthy. However, unless the term creditworthy is carefully defined credit managers may be overly cautious.

SURVIVING THE TEST

From time to time, salespeople will test the credit manager's resolve when it comes to a decision to hold an order or to deny credit to an applicant. The credit manager must have the discipline and the self-confidence to stick to the decision, and the maturity needed not to take the salesperson's challenge personally. However, if the salesperson presents the credit manager with additional information that leads to a different credit decision, the credit manager must have the maturity and the flexibility to change the decision immediately based on the new information as presented by the salesperson.

EXPLAIN, DON'T JUSTIFY

One of the best ways to address a challenge to an adverse credit decision is with the facts. For example, if a customer is over its credit limit, past due, with one or more broken payment commitments presenting this information in support of a decision not to release a pending order is fairly compelling and difficult for the customer and the salesperson to dispute.

If they want to improve their working relationship with the sales department, credit managers must take the time to explain their decisions. Unfortunately, credit managers are often constrained from providing the salesperson with all the facts by the need to keep certain information confidential. Credit managers should take as much time as is required to explain their decision, but should not allow the discussion to degenerate into either a debate or an argument. The credit manager is not obligated to convince the salesperson that the credit decision was proper—and doing so would be an uphill battle at best. Instead, credit professionals should concentrate on sharing the facts so that the salesperson knows how to respond if and when the customer calls to discuss the decision made by the credit manager.

CREDIT OVERRIDES

From time to time, almost every credit manager will have a credit decision overridden by senior management. Credit overrides are not personal attacks, nor are they necessarily a criticism of the credit manager's decision-making ability. Senior management is required to make business decisions from time to time, and not every good business decision is necessarily a good credit decision.

A mistake made by some credit managers involves insisting that senior management go through some sort of elaborate process to document their override of the credit decision. This is unnecessary, and indicates a failure on the credit manager's part to appreciate that senior management looks at the company from a different perspective than the credit manager. Documenting management's decision to override the credit manager can be as simple as sending an e-mail message such as this:

> "As you instructed, I have released sales order #12345 for account AB9876. I will inform you of any problems."

The credit manager is free to document the override in the credit file in any amount of detail that he or she feels is necessary. What is important is to demonstrate to senior management that you have confidence and trust in their decision-making ability—even if you as credit manager would not have made that decision.

THE REVOLVING DOOR

Too many overrides tend to undermine the credit manager's confidence, and his or her authority. The more frequently credit overrides take place, the more likely the sales department is to appeal any and every negative decision made by the credit manager to senior management. For these reasons, senior managers should not to overrule decisions unless it is absolutely necessary to do so. Otherwise their office might soon resemble a revolving door with salespeople lined up for approval to override the credit decision. The proper course of action is for senior management to meet with the credit manager if a fundamental adjustment to the credit department's policies is required.

By the same token, credit managers should not overrule the credit decisions made by their subordinates unless it is absolutely necessary to do so. There is a fine line that credit managers do not want to cross. On one hand, they do not want to undercut their subordinates. On the other hand, they do not want to allow an inappropriate credit decision to stand. The best strategy is to use every appeal of subordinates' decisions and actions as an opportunity to review the department's policies and procedures and make certain the people making the decisions know what the kinds of risks the company is and is not willing to accept. If small adjustments are required, they should be discussed and implemented immediately.

LOWERING CREDIT STANDARDS

One of the biggest frustrations that the sales department can have is when the credit department does not understand the changing dynamics of the marketplace. For example, if demand for the company's products or services drops off, one way to offset the reduced demand is by making it easier to obtain credit. This solution is overly simplistic.

The credit manager cannot or at least should not lower the department's credit standards before consulting with senior management. Even if the credit manager believes that the best way to correct a decline in sales would be to lower the credit standards. The credit manager must not make the change unilaterally, because lowering the credit standards will result in increases in delinquencies and bad debt losses.

THE GOALS OF SALES AND CREDIT

Credit and sales tend to have slightly different goals. Typically, the goal of the sales department is to maximize sales. The credit department's goal is to maximize sales while maintaining sound and collectible accounts receivable. When credit and sales work cooperatively, more sales are likely to result. For example, cooperation between credit and sales can improve collection results. This in turn will make it more likely that orders pending will be approved.

US VERSUS THEM

If they are honest about it, both the sales department and the credit department will acknowledge that over time an adversarial "us against them" mindset has developed in both departments. The credit department vilifies the sales department as having the following attitude: Do anything to make the sale. Who cares whether or not we ever collect a dime of it? In many instances, the sales department characterizes the credit department as aloof, out of touch with business realities, and as a department that makes decisions based on whims or emotions rather than based on the facts. Both the credit department's characterization of the sales group, and the sales department's characterization of the credit department are stereotypes borne of a lack of real understanding of the goals and the constraints that each department must deal with daily.

Rather than focusing on past problems and conflicts, both the credit and the sales department need to focus on the changes that are necessary to improve the relationship between the departments.

The relationship between sales and credit would improve if both departments could agree that all of the follow facts and factors influence their views about the role of the credit department:

- Salespeople have a personal financial interest in getting pending orders released. Credit department personnel have no financial interest in either holding or releasing orders. Therefore, the credit department can be more objective about whether an order should be released or held.

- Salespeople have a right to question the decisions made by the credit manager, and the credit department acknowledges this right. Also, the credit department should always be willing to listen to new information presented by the salesperson.

- Credit decisions are not as subjective as salespeople seem to think they are. They are subjective to the extent that credit managers don't have to hold orders, but in many instances the justifications for doing so are overwhelming.

- Personal relationships between salespeople and their customers may cloud the salesperson's ability to look at problems objectively.

- Distance from the customer and limited information about the competitive environment reduce the credit department's ability to understand the dynamics of each sales situation.

- Comments from salespeople such as "I have known these people forever" have little impact on the credit department's decision making process because there is no easy way to place a value on that relationship.

- Every company needs new customers to replace accounts that go out of business, merge, or change suppliers. Salespeople work hard to get to the point where a customer will consider their company as a new supplier. Therefore, credit applications should be handled with great care.

- New applications should be processed as quickly as practical by the credit department. Not every applicant will qualify for open account terms—even if personal guarantees, inter-corporate guarantees, and other forms of security interest back the open account terms.

- Certain applicants will not qualify for credit terms even though other suppliers may be selling to them on open account credit terms. The reason is relatively straightforward: Different companies have different criteria for granting credit terms based on different corporate goals, different profit margins, and different competitive conditions.

- It is impossible for the credit manager of one company to explain to the sales department why another creditor will extend credit while they will not. Therefore, comparisons of this type are pointless.

- Bad debt losses are an inevitable part of doing business on open account credit terms. The goal of the credit department is not to eliminate bad debt losses. Instead, it is to help their employer to maximize sales and profits. This cannot be accomplished without incurring significant credit risk.

- Given its role as a gatekeeper, it is easy to imagine how both customers and salespeople might see the credit department as an obstacle to be overcome. Credit managers must expect challenges to their decisions. Even if the credit manager considers the decision to be obvious, he or she should be prepared to explain it in detail to the salesperson.

- Even if a credit decision seems obvious to the credit department, it is improbable that the customer will agree with the decision.

- Customers often want extended terms as an inducement to buy. For both practical and legal reasons, special terms must be offered to a limited number of customers, for a specific period of time, and only under unusual conditions.

- Prospects and new accounts rarely qualify as "special" and are rarely afforded special credit terms.

- It is up to the sales department to document why a customer needs special dating terms. Sales should understand that the ultimate decision about whether or not to offer extended dating will be made the credit manager's boss with input from the sales department and the credit department.

- Special dating damages the seller's cash flow. For this reason, among others, the sales department cannot unilaterally offer special dating terms.

- The credit department does not arbitrarily place an active account on credit hold, just as the credit department does not arbitrarily reject applicants for open account terms. To do so would serve no purpose, and more importantly it would subject the credit manager to criticism from sales and senior management.

- The financial status, payment habits and overall creditworthiness of individual accounts changes over time—sometimes for the better and sometimes for the worse. The credit department must react to a deterioration in a customer's credit risk profile.

- Certain information in the possession of the credit department is confidential. In explaining its decisions, the credit department will provide the salesperson with as much information as it can.

- Poor communication is one of the biggest reasons for animosity between the credit department and the sales department, and it is also one of the easiest problems to address and correct. The credit department can take the following steps to improve communications:
  - Take the time to explain why a negative credit decision is made.
  - Keep the salesperson informed about pending credit problems.
  - Notify the salesperson promptly any time the credit department holds an order.
  - Welcome information that might change the credit decision.
  - Return calls you receive from the salesperson the same day as you receive them.

CONFLICT RESOLUTION PROCESS

Some disagreements between sales and credit cannot be resolved without the involvement of an intermediary. For example, when sales and credit disagree about the status of an applicant or an order on hold, there should be a specific process in place for the sales department to appeal the credit manager's decision. The process can be likened to a trial. If the credit manager is both judge and jury, and the salesperson cannot appeal a decision that is made against his or her client [the customer], it is easy to imagine how this will cause resentment.

This appeal process could become quite elaborate, but the simpler it is the better it will work. The process may be nothing more elaborate than the salesperson referring the matter to the sales manager and the sales manager could then discuss the issue with the credit manager.

A more sophisticated appeals process involves one in which the salesperson refers the matter to the sales manager, and the credit manager refers the matter to the CFO [or whomever the credit manager reports to]. Then, the sales manager and the CFO would discuss the situation to decide on the proper course of action. In this scenario, both the salesperson and the credit manager are kept out of the decision-making process, and both should be satisfied that the issue has had a fair hearing—regardless of the outcome.

PAYING COMMISSIONS ON COLLECTED SALES

The majority of companies still pay commissions on sales and not on collected dollars, but there is nothing illegal or unethical about making commissions contingent on payment from the customer. Companies often do not implement this policy out of concern about alienating their salespeople. For the same reason, the credit manager should not be the one who suggests this commission structure change. Doing so would tend to increase the animosity between the sales department and the credit department.

Some companies pay commission on collected sales on the mistaken assumption that doing so will guarantee that:

(a) the sales department will want to sell only to creditworthy customers, and

(b) the sales department will help the credit department to collect in the event that an account becomes delinquent.

Experience indicates that only assumption (b) is correct. The reason is simple: If salespeople are paid on collected sales, then they recognize that it is in their best interest to help collect past due balances. However, since there is no disincentive for bad debt losses, and typically no penalty to the salesperson if a marginal account pays late, salespeople have no reason not to play the odds by encouraging the credit department to release every order.

Recognizing this flaw, some companies have gone one step further and only pay commission on involves paid within a specified number of days of the invoice due date. For example, some companies will only pay commission on invoices paid within 30 days of the due date. This will not prevent collection problems for the same reason as noted above—salespeople will play a numbers game as long as there is no disincentive for delinquencies and bad debts. Selling to marginal accounts is like the lottery: You cannot win if you never play.

IMPROVING COMMUNICATIONS BETWEEN CREDIT AND SALES

Ensuring good communication between sales and credit is an important step in improving the level of trust and cooperation. The relationship between sales and credit can easily be strained if the credit department takes action against a customer without informing the salesperson.

The credit department should inform the salesperson about any of the following actions or decisions:

- the decision to hold an order
- a decision to reject an applicant for open account credit terms
- a decision to reduce or withdraw a customer's credit line
- any negative decisions affecting their customers—including but not limited to a decision by the credit department to place an account on credit hold or by actually holding an order pending.

KEEPING IT PROFESSIONAL

There is no need for acrimony or hostility between sales and credit. When disagreements occur, they should occur on a professional level. Emotional outbursts add nothing to the discussion of the facts. Credit and sales should be thought of as the opposite sides of a teeter-totter. Without the sales department, there would be nothing for the company to sell and nothing for the credit department to collect. Without the credit department, anything sold on open account credit terms might never be collected.

If the sales department operated without oversight by the credit department, delinquencies and bad debt losses would skyrocket. By the same token, if not for the influence of the sales department, the credit department would tend to be too conservative in the credit granting process. As a result, the company would not be in a position to maximize sales and profits.

WORKING PROACTIVELY WITH CREDIT

Salespeople can improve the chances of having a new account approved if they can convince the applicant to submit a signed credit application as soon as possible. Salespeople will have a higher success rate with new accounts if they submit to the credit department a list of potential or prospective customers along with their estimated credit requirements. The goal is to allow the credit department can proactively investigate the potential customer and have some preliminary data on file by the time the process develops to the point that the potential customer is prepared to submit an application.

If a new account needs a large credit limit, salespeople can improve the chances of getting that credit limit approved quickly by asking the customer to submit financial statements with the credit application. This is far less stressful than a scenario in which an application is received, an order is placed and the creditor must then go back to the customer and demand financial information as a condition for considering releasing the order pending.

IMPROVING COMMUNICATIONS

Communications between sales and credit can be improved. All that is necessary is the desire to improve the working relationship between sales and credit along with a plan to improve communications. Any company can implement the ideas listed below, almost immediately and at minimal cost, and each will help to improve communications between sales and credit:

(a) Credit managers should meet regularly with sales management to discuss issues and concerns, and to learn from sales management its plans.

(b) Credit professionals should ask what they could do to help the company and the sales department to meet goals and objectives.

(c) When necessary, credit managers should involve the sales department in gathering financial information from customers. Having current information benefits the customer, the salesperson and the credit department. Without adequate information, the credit department has no choice but to adopt a far more conservative posture than if the necessary information was on file. The customer benefits because the credit manager is more likely to be able to release orders pending and offer the credit limit requested.

(d) The credit department should be willing to use its access to information to prequalify potential customers. This benefits the salesperson by allowing them to concentrate their time and attention on potential customers that are likely to be approved. Prequalifying accounts saves money in the form of travel and other expenses.

(e) Credit managers should be certain to meet regularly with salespeople to conduct training sessions. These sessions should make it easier for salespeople to understand how the credit department evaluates risk, sets credit limits, and decides whether or not to release orders pending. Knowledge is power, and providing salespeople with information will help the company, the salesperson and its customers each to get what they need from the business relationship.

(f) The company's credit policy should be made available to the sales department. It should be published and the sales department should be welcomed to comment on it.

(g) Credit managers should invite the sales manager to meet periodically with the entire credit department staff. That meeting should be a give and take.

(h) If the credit manager learns information that may help the sales department [such as information about a merger or acquisition involving a customer] that data should be forwarded to the sales department as quickly as possible.

BREAKING DOWN BARRIERS BETWEEN CREDIT AND SALES

Breaking down barriers of mistrust between sales and credit requires time. Many credit managers believe that most salespeople are willing to put their own financial interests above the interests of the company. Strictly speaking, this is not true. Salespeople do what they are rewarded to do, and do not do what they are penalized for doing. Thus, any actions taken by the sales department in support of the release of orders pending can be characterized as doing what they are rewarded for doing.

Few things erode the sales department's confidence in the credit department as quickly as experiences in which the credit department makes decisions that are:

■ based on inaccurate or out of date information

■ inconsistent

■ not easily explained or justified by the credit department

■ arbitrary

In many instances, trust has been eroded over the years by personal animosity or outright hostility between the sales department and the credit department. In some instances, salespeople have gone over credit managers' heads [and behind their backs] in order to get credit decisions overruled. Under these conditions, it will be impossible to improve the business relationship overnight. However, the barriers between sales and credit will continue to come break down as salespeople begin to accept that the credit department does not exist to hamper sales. Credit managers can accelerate the process of building bridges between sales and credit by encouraging everyone in the credit department to think of the department as being a department that supports sales.

Some techniques that can be used include:

- Not dwelling on past conflicts, and instead learning from past mistakes.

- Discouraging salespeople from stereotyping the credit department staff as bean counters,

- Discouraging the credit department staff from stereotyping salespeople as unprincipled, unethical, lazy, overpaid bullies.

- Asking the salesperson to provide a realistic estimate of a customer's credit requirements, and using this information to prequalify active customers for larger credit limits requested.

- Keep salespeople informed about problem accounts, and give the salesperson as much time as possible to contact the customer before the problem damages the credit relationship or results in a credit hold.

- Work with sales management to make certain that salespeople address rather than ignore problem and disputes that arise between creditors and customers before the credit department must take adverse action to force the customer to address and resolve the problem. As credit professionals know, deductions and other problems tend to get more difficult to resolve over time.

- Unfortunately, the kinds of problems that salespeople tend to ignore that exactly the problems that the credit department wants addressed and resolved as quickly as possible. Why? Because the problems that the credit department cannot address often involve errors committed by the salesperson. For the salesperson, this is a two edged sword. It is difficult for the salesperson to admit he or she made a mistake, and it is equally difficult to confront the customer and inform them that they made the mistake. Consequently, there is an unfortunate tendency to ignore disputes but this only serves to intensify the problem.

- Credit professionals must train themselves not to overreact when a salesperson provides them with bad news about a customer. For example, if the credit department responds by withdrawing a customer's credit limit when they hear the customer is experiencing cash flow problems, then salespeople will quickly learn not to share this information with the credit department.

- Credit managers must take time to explain a negative credit decision in detail, and in plain language. The credit department needs to be sensitive to the fact that the salesperson may have spent hours over a period of weeks or months trying to gain a new customer. What the salesperson needs to know is that the credit department has made an objective decision based on adequate documentation, and not a quick or arbitrary decision about the applicant.

- New salespeople should be scheduled to spend time in the credit department as part of their regular training process. Salespeople who spend time in the credit department will learn the credit department's philosophy about risk and risk management. As part of this training process, it is important that salespeople learn that the credit department has no vested interest in holding orders, and that all credit decisions are made based on the available facts—not on a whim.

PERSONAL GUARANTEES AND SALESPEOPLE

Occasionally, a salesperson will be so certain of the creditworthiness of a customer or an applicant that they will offer to guarantee the sale. It is an understatement to suggest that this is controversial. However, if the salesperson is serious about the guarantee, then he or she must be prepared to sign a personal guarantee form just as any other guarantor would be required to do. The actual process of signing a contract will dissuade some salespeople from making this type of commitment.

Generally speaking, it is not a good idea to accept personal guarantees from salespeople because enforcing such a guarantee might place the creditor in conflict with certain labor laws. In addition, even if there is nothing preventing them from deducting from the salesperson's commissions to clear the debt the idea of doing so is not appealing to most companies. At the very least, the salesperson involved will be demoralized. It is also makes it more likely that they will resign rather than working to pay off the debt.

USING SALESPEOPLE AS COLLECTORS

There is an ongoing debate about whether the sales department can or should be used to augment the credit department's collection efforts. On one hand, the salespeople's proximity to and working relationships with customers may make them excellent ombudsmen for the credit department. Salespeople's personal relationships with customers can be used to leverage payment from reluctant debtors. Other benefits of using salespeople as field collectors include:

- If a legitimate dispute of some type exists, the customer is more likely to explain and to resolve the problem through the salesperson than to want to work with the credit manager to resolve the problem.

- Because salespeople are normally geographically close to the customer, visits can be made quickly and inexpensively. Typically, a visit from the credit manager would take longer to get approved, scheduled, organize, and it would be significantly more expensive. Equally important, the visit might be seen as a threat by or to the customer.

- When the issue of the past due balance is between the credit department and the customer, the customer may be more comfortable than when the salesperson is involved. Why? Because the customer knows the salesperson knows others in the business—in particular competitors. No company wants its competitors to know it is having financial problems significant enough that it cannot pay its bills.

THE DISADVANTAGES OF USING SALESPEOPLE AS COLLECTORS

Unfortunately for the credit department, there are a number of serious problems and disadvantages associated with using salespeople as field collectors. Many of these problems are so serious that if they cannot be resolved then the salesperson should be used as an intermediary. The problems include:

- Salespersons are not trained as collectors. Therefore, they may say the wrong thing to the customer no matter how carefully they are briefed by the credit department before attending the meeting.

- In an effort to preserve the relationship with the delinquent customer, the salesperson may deliver the message but fail to convey the credit department's sense of urgency about clearing the past due balance. As a result, payment may be delayed even longer, further damaging the customer's credit standing.

- However, by conveying a sense of urgency, the salesperson could damage their relationship with the customer—and for this reason alone some salespeople refuse to act as collectors.

USING SALESPEOPLE AS MEDIATORS

If salespersons are uncomfortable in the role of collector, they may be more familiar with and comfortable as a mediator in the process—playing no direct role in the collection or the negotiation process. As a mediator, the salesperson will try to convince the customer it is in their best interest to work out some type of payment arrangement. As a mediator, the salesperson might also share information and insights with the credit department about the account, and about the underlying reason or reasons for the customer's current cash flow problems.

An advantage of using the salesperson as a mediator is the fact that the salesperson can retain their role as an advocate for the debtor—while at the same time helping to get the payment problem addressed and resolved. One way to almost guarantee that the sales department will have an interest in working with the credit department to collect past due balances is to pay the sales department based on collections and not based on sales. While the concept is sound, most companies pay commissions based on sales and not on collections. The reasons are complex. One argument is that salespeople should not be penalized for mistakes made by the credit department in releasing orders to customers that subsequently were found not to be creditworthy.

WAYS TO IMPROVE THE RELATIONSHIP BETWEEN CREDIT AND SALES

Credit professionals should keep the following facts in mind any time they are working with the sales department:

(1) There is nothing to collect until the sale is made. Therefore, the credit department exists in part to support the sales department's efforts, and credit managers must emphasize to subordinates that sales are the lifeblood of every company.

(2) The credit department must try to work in harmony with the sales department. Credit professionals should emphasize to salespeople and sales management that the credit department is an ally, not an opponent of sales. The common opponent of the sales department and the credit department are payment delinquency, bad debt losses, missed opportunities, and mistakes.

(3) Credit professionals should know what sales management expects from the credit department, and try to deliver it. For example, if the sales department needs 24 hour turnaround on credit applications, the credit manager needs to make that a priority. Even if the credit department is not always capable of gathering the required information in time for a 24 hour turn around, it should be simple to track the average amount of time the credit department is taking to process orders. As long as the processing time continues to decrease, the credit manager should be happy with the progress being made.

(5) Give the salesperson as much or more information than he or she needs about a negative credit decision—provided you do not violate any confidentiality requirements in connection with information you may have gathered.

(6) Make sure discussions with sales personnel are candid. If a discussion is sensitive but not confidential, explain why the information is sensitive and get an explicit commitment that nothing said will be revealed directly or indirectly to the customer.

(7) Deliver bad news promptly. If the credit department has made a decision to hold an order, notify the salesperson immediately. A failure to promptly inform the customer of a negative credit decision gives the customer another thing to complain about.

(8) Don't limit communication with the sales department to the telephone. Use a fax machine when you want to send supporting documentation. Use e-mail after normal business hours.

(9) Encourage an open dialogue about marginal accounts. Start these discussions by indicating the credit department is looking for reasons to sell to customers and not for excuses to hold orders.

(10) Describe problems and in detail. If there is something specific the salesperson can do to correct the problem, the credit manager should welcome their assistance.

(11) Any time a collection letter or a dunning notice is sent, the salesperson should be sent a courtesy copy so they are aware of the problem.

HOW CREDIT CAN HELP SALES

There are several practical steps the credit department to help the sales department to achieve its goals, including:

(1) Listen to suggestions and comments received from salespeople and act on the ones that make sense.

(2) Be prepared to change a credit decision on the basis of new facts presented by the sales department, or by any other interested party.

(3) Whenever possible, improve your level of service based on the feedback you receive directly from customers or filtered through the sales department. For example, if you receive a report that a collector was unprofessional when calling a customer, gather as much information

as possible. Then use it the incident as a training tool to make certain that the problem is corrected.

(4) Establish a formal procedure for evaluating any complaints you might receive about collection efforts, new account review, accuracy, timeliness of response to inquiries, etc.

(5) Establish specific standards of responsiveness between your subordinates and the sales department. Emphasize to subordinates that you do not support and that you will not allow an "us against them" mindset to develop between credit and the sales department.

(6) All calls to the credit department must be returned the same day that they are received. Voice mail is a convenience but it is not a crutch. Ideally, calls should be returned within an hour.

(7) The salesperson should be notified of an adverse credit decision before the customer. Often, the first thing a customer will do after being informed of a negative decision is call the salesperson to complain. That call should not come as a surprise to the sales rep.

(8) Make credit decisions as quickly as possible and practical. One way to try to prevent unnecessary delays in the credit decision-making process is to implement a process for reviewing each active customer's credit file on a regular basis so that each one is kept relatively current.

(9) Intervene any time you feel that a subordinate should have handled a problem or a situation differently. Making frequent minor corrections is better for the customer, the employee and the company than making infrequent, major corrections.

(10) Work with your information systems group to make sure that as many orders as possible bypass manual credit review and approval. The more orders that are automatically approved, the more efficient the order approval process will be, and the faster orders will be approved and released.

(11) When challenged about a credit decision, credit professionals should not try to convince the salesperson or the customer that the decision was correct. Customers rarely see their financial problems the same way as their creditors do. Credit professionals should stick to the facts. They list the facts that led to the decision and then leave it at that. They should avoid comparisons and never reveal confidential information.

(12) Don't delay a decision until you have perfect information. Credit professionals have an obligation to make decisions as soon as they have

enough data to make an informed decision—and not to wait for that one piece of evidence that would make the decision easy and obvious.

(13) When you or your subordinates make a mistake, apologize promptly and sincerely. Then fix the problem quickly—and see what can be done to prevent the mistake from recurring.

It is also a good idea to help the sales department to save face in the eyes of their customers. For example, if you must decline to offer terms to a customer you might explain how circumstances have changed, or how your company has a restrictive credit policy. If you decide to release an order after receiving additional information from the salesperson, be certain to mention the fact that the salesperson's intervention was critical to your decision if you contact the customer.

HOW SALES CAN HELP CREDIT

The salesperson is ideally situated to assist the credit department in a number of ways, including:

(1) Making certain the credit application is completed and is signed

(2) Giving the credit department enough time to review the application before orders are placed.

(3) By explaining the terms of sale and the freight terms to prospective customers so they do not come as a surprise when the credit application arrives.

(4) By addressing and resolving disputes including pricing and quality disputes with customers quickly and efficiently.

(5) By promptly processing or forwarding requests for credit memos.

(6) By referring all customer contracts to the credit department [or the legal department] for review and approval before the contract is signed.

(7) Help the credit department to accelerate the collection process by addressing problems proactively rather than reactively. Doing so has the added benefit of demonstrating to the customer that the company is committed to quality, professionalism and attention to detail.

When the sales department and the credit department work together the end result is better customer service. This in turn results in higher levels of customer satisfaction, and a greater likelihood that the creditor will retain the customer.

DEALING PROACTIVELY WITH POTENTIAL CUSTOMERS

Credit professionals should always try to prequalify potential new accounts. The credit department can generate a lot of information from credit bureaus and other sources using only the target company's name, address and telephone number. The prequalification process will not only identify target companies that are unlikely to be offered open account credit terms; the process will also identify prospects that have excellent potential. Using this information, the credit manager can help make salespeople more productive by allowing them to devote their time and attention to the most promising prospects.

One of the most frustrating situations for the salesperson is one in which the credit department refuses to extend credit to an applicant, and that applicant is able to convince another creditor to extend credit to them. It is always difficult to try to explain this discrepancy. However, experienced credit professionals know that there are any number of reasons that one creditor would extend credit to an applicant while another would not. One of the most common reasons is that the company extending credit is willing to accept a significant amount of credit risk in order to increase sales revenue or market share, while the other creditor company is not.

If the salesrep or customer requests an explanation for the company's negative credit decision, the best answer is probably as follows "All credit grantors use different techniques to evaluate risk. In addition, every creditor company has a different tolerance for risk. Therefore, there is nothing remarkable about the fact that another company extended credit and we did not. I cannot explain their decision, just as they would not try to explain mine."

QUICK TIPS TO IMPROVE THE CREDIT–SALES RELATIONSHIP

(1) Return calls the same day as they are made.

(2) Take the time to fully explain your decision. Do so without revealing confidential information such as information received from credit references.

(3) Require your subordinates to be professional and courteous.

(4) Never give the sales department any reason to believe you are hostile toward them, or toward their customers.

(5) Trust salespeople until and unless they demonstrate that your trust has been misplaced.

(6) Speak plainly. Don't try to impress salespeople with your vocabulary or your knowledge of technical accounting terminology.

(7) Recognize that a salesperson or a sales manager challenging your credit decision is not a personal attack. It is a strategy used by the sales department to make certain that a negative credit decision was well thought out and has been well documented.

(8) Allow salespeople to speak to your manager if they want to dispute a credit decision.

SUMMARY

The rift that often exists between sales and credit did not appear overnight and it will not disappear overnight. It takes continued effort for the sales and the credit departments to gain understanding of the other's role and to rebuild goodwill.

CHAPTER 3

MEASURING THE CREDIT DEPARTMENT'S PERFORMANCE

There are a number of widely used methods of measuring the credit department's overall performance. Some are good measures of the effectiveness and efficiency of the credit department, and some are not. Every credit manager needs to know the best ways to measure performance, and the advantages and the limitations of the various other methods used to measure performance.

Armed with this information, credit managers can explain the limitations of some of the more popular methods of measuring the credit department's performance. As with every other employee, credit professionals want to make certain that the ways in which their performance is measured are reasonable and relevant to the work performed by the credit department.

As a general statement, companies do a good job of documenting when collection problems occur and a poor job of documenting when things go right. Specifically, companies are far more likely to document a collection problem rather than a problem that was resolved by the credit department or avoided altogether thanks to the skill and experience of the credit manager. For this reason, credit managers should document the successes they have had throughout the year. That way, they will be better prepared for their annual performance review. The easiest way to do so is to take short but frequent notes—perhaps in a daily planner.

Typically, the credit department's performance is measured based on its ability to control bad debt losses and to limit delinquencies. Since the goal of the credit department is to maximize sales while maintaining a sound accounts receivable base, measuring bad debts and delinquencies seems to be a reasonable way for the credit department's performance to be evaluated. This is not always the case. If the company requires its credit department to liberalize credit decisions, perhaps in an effort to attract more business, then the almost inevitable losses that result should not be counted against the credit department.

CONTROLLING DELINQUENCIES

At its most basic, selling on open account credit terms is similar to making a short term and interest free loan to a customer. The fact that the "loan" is in the form of merchandise rather than money is not particularly relevant since the customer accepts the goods or services but pledges money in return. In theory, because customers realize the economic value of being able to obtain goods and services on credit they are careful not to jeopardize their ability to get open account terms from their creditors. In reality, for a variety of reasons a certain number of customers are unable to pay invoices as they come due. This results in delinquencies and in some instance in bad debt losses.

One popular method to measure the performance of the credit department and the credit manager is to measure the department's ability to control delinquencies. In theory, an experienced credit manager will be able to limit delinquencies using these tools:

- The ability to resolve disputes
- Negotiation skills
- Finesse
- Tenacity
- The proper use of subordinates as collectors
- The effective use of collection tools and techniques

In theory, the more a more experienced credit manager is the better the department's collection results will be.

DAYS SALES OUTSTANDING [DSO]

One of the most common ways to measure the credit department's performance is by using Days Sales Outstanding [DSO]. DSO measures the average number of days it takes for invoices to be collected. It is a weighted average, meaning that small invoices have less of an impact than large dollar invoices on DSO. The concept of weighted average is important because companies are more interested in collecting large dollar past due invoices than they are in collecting small past due balances.

In many companies credit managers are held accountable for changes in DSO on a month to month bases. Specifically, if DSO goes down the credit manager is acclaimed, and if DSO increases the credit manager's performance is considered suspect. If DSO increases from month to month, senior management will normally want to know why. One possible explanation is that the number of delinquent accounts has increased. If that is the case the next question is what can be done to correct the problem. There are any number of techniques to accelerate the collection of past due invoices, including something as simple as adding headcount to the credit department so that additional collection calls can be made each month.

However, an increase in DSO may have nothing to do with an increase in delinquencies. In fact, DSO can go up even if delinquencies go down. How? There are a number of ways. If the terms of sale offered to customers by the sales department increases then DSO will also increase. Unfortunately, in many companies the credit department does not always control the terms of sale being offered to customers.

In some companies, only senior management has the authority to approve extended dating. Thus, in some companies the same senior managers that are asking why DSO is rising are the same people that are causing DSO to increase by approving longer dating terms on open account sales.

When Days Sales Outstanding [DSO] increases, the credit manager needs to know why. If the reason for the increase was largely out of the credit manager's control, then the credit manager must document this information. In the absence of such documentation, senior management is likely to assume that the DSO increase was caused by the credit department. Credit managers should not wait to be asked about changes in DSO. Credit managers should calculate DSO, and they should proactively investigate any increase in DSO. It is a good idea for the credit manager to prepare a monthly analysis of DSO for his or her manager, summarizing the reasons for any change in DSO—up or down.

For example, sometimes it is a combination of extended dating, disputed balances, outstanding deductions, and delinquent accounts that results in an increase in DSO. If that is the case, the credit manager's report should detail the relative impact of each of these factors in the increase in DSO. For example, if DSO increase by five days from the previous month and half of that increase was attributable to payment delays but the other half was attributable to extended dating terms, this is exactly the kind of information that senior management needs on a monthly basis.

THE ADVANTAGES OF CALCULATING DSO

Credit managers should always do their own DSO calculation. They should do so on a monthly basis even if the accounting department also prepares this information. Calculating DSO quickly gives the credit manager additional time to review a problem such as a significant increase in DSO. It also means they re unlikely to be caught off guard by a question or complaint from senior management about an increase in DSO. Not knowing about an increase in DSO makes the credit manager seem to be unprepared and unprofessional.

As mentioned earlier, another popular way to measure the credit department's performance is based on the number and dollar amount of bad debt losses. Once again, in theory a large number or a large dollar volume of bad debt losses is an indication that the credit manager has done a poor job of risk management and loss control. There are any number of potential flaws with the implication that there is a direct correlation between bad debt losses incurred and the credit department's effectiveness and efficiency.

Bad debt losses are impacted by:

- Poor credit decisions.
- Management overrides of credit decisions.
- Orders that are somehow released without credit approval
- Orders released by persons not authorized by the credit manager to do so.
- Actions that were largely unforeseeable, such as losses that occur as a result of credit fraud.

To the extent that bad debt losses result from poor decisions made by the credit department, the credit manager should be held accountable for their mistakes. The other types of losses as listed above are largely beyond the control of the credit manager and therefore should be excluded from any discussion on bad debt losses. The credit manager should review any losses, determine their cause, and what if any action can be taken to mitigate the damage.

In addition to safeguarding the company's investment in its accounts receivable and improving cash flow, most credit departments assist their company in a variety of other ways, including:

(1) Helping to maintain a good working relationship with the company's customers, including those customers that are seriously past due. This

can be accomplished by using flexibility in dealing with temporary cash flow problems with restraint.

(2) By acting professionally with a delinquent account with an eye toward resolving the problem and collecting the past due balance within a reasonable time frame.

(3) By not making any personal attacks on the customer, such as questioning their professionalism, their competence, or their honesty.

OTHER NEGATIVE MEASUREMENTS OF PERFORMANCE

As mentioned previously, the performance of the credit department is often measured in negative rather than in positive terms. Previous examples included measuring increases in DSO or in bad debt losses whether or not either of these problems were directly or indirectly controlled and controllable by the credit manager and his or her department staff. It is far easier to measure the things that go wrong involving the credit department than it is to measure things that went right.

Here is a simple example: Assume one of the criteria senior management uses to evaluate the performance of the credit department involves logging the number of complaints that they receive about it. What is missing from this process is a measurement of the number of complaints registered in relation to the number of calls and letters being generated.

Still another limitation is the number of complaints received that are without merit. In other words, if the company measured the number of complaints that were based on errors committed by the credit department then this statistic would be relevant. In the absence of some formal methodology to determine whether or not the complaint had any merit or was related to a policy violation, there is no way to know whether or not the credit department continues to function in the way the company intends it to.

REPORTS MEASURING CREDIT PERFORMANCE

There are any number of computer reports that can be used to measure the credit department's performance. It is best for the credit manager to arrange for these reports to be generated automatically. Typically, the credit manager would like a week between the time the report is generated and the time the analysis is required.

Ideally, two different types of reports will be generated on a set schedule. The first report would present information for the department as a whole. The second group of reports would present the same information but divided based on how work is allocated within the department. Here is an example:

Assume the report in question was a detailed accounts receivable aging report sorted by due date. The credit manager would need the report for the entire company. On the other hand, the collectors would each want an accounts receivable aging report for their specific customers. Therefore, ideally the system would automatically generate both types of reports on a specified date. The credit manager would analyze the company wide aging report while the collectors would evaluate their individual customers' payment performance.

Some of the most commonly requested computer generated reports include:

(1) A summary of bad debt losses, both month to date, and year to date.

(2) A summary accounts receivable aged trial balance showing exactly how for a past due each customer has become.

(3) A report of DSO for the month, along with historical DSO for the purpose of comparison.

The advantage of these measures of the credit department's performance is that each of these reports is easy to generate, and each is a relatively objective measure of the credit department's performance. Another advantage of these particular reports is that each of them can be prepared quickly, and will present precise and specific information consistently from month to month and from year to year.

Some people believe these three reports are used to measure credit department performance because they are easy to calculate and because they are intuitively attractive to senior management—rather than because they are good tools for measuring performance. Unfortunately, despite their appeal and widespread use weaknesses abound in these reports. In fact, there may be as many compelling reasons not to use these reports as there are reasons to use them to benchmark the credit department's performance.

THE LIMITATIONS OF BAD DEBT ANALYSIS

Assume that the credit manager receives a report showing that bad debt losses rose significantly in the quarter just ended, and year to date. Assume also that this year's bad debt losses have a significantly higher run rate than last year. Assume also that bad debt losses are significantly higher than they were expected to be, and that the company's earnings suffered as a result.

It is true that the increase in bad debt losses might be the result of poor risk management decisions made by the credit manager. The losses might have been compounded by spotty and inadequate follow up once the account became past due. If in fact this was the case then the credit manager needs to be counseled, disciplined, fired or placed on probation.

On the other hand, bad debt losses might have increased because of a decision made by senior management that the credit department should relax its credit acceptance policies in order to increase sales. Or, senior management may have taken a more direct role by approving orders for release that the credit manager had rejected. Senior management might also have been involved in the process of establishing credit limits for customers, over the objection of the credit manager.

Another reason for the losses might have been decisions made by senior management to assign higher credit limits to accounts identified by the credit manager as not creditworthy. The losses might have been the result of shipping errors that the credit manager could not control and against which the customer refused to negotiate a settlement. The losses might have been the result of actions that were beyond the credit manager's ability to forecast or control. For example, the loss might have been the result of a bankruptcy filing entered against a public company following an investigation in which financial fraud was discovered, or a privately held customer might have filed bankruptcy following a natural disaster.

For all of these reasons, DSO is a relatively blunt instrument to evaluate the performance of the credit department. DSO is often influenced by actions or decisions made not made by the credit department or by the credit manager. Outside of the credit manager's control. In fact, some bad debt losses [such as those that occur as a result if shipments denied by the credit manager but approved by executive management] occur despite the efforts of the credit department rather than as a consequence of those efforts.

MANAGEMENT OVERRIDES AND DSO

The comments about the fact that DSO can be negatively impacted by management policymaking, and by management overrides should not be taken to suggest that (a) terms cannot or should not be used to win business from the competition, or (b) that the credit manager should protest or should refuse to release orders when in good conscience they believe the orders should not be released.

Terms are an important tool in the selling process, and senior management always has the right to review and to override the decisions made by its credit manager or credit department—even if that action results in an increase in DSO. The credit manager is obligated to share his or her concerns with senior management assuming management is willing to listen. However, the credit manager does not have the right to delay releasing orders or offering extended dating if they are instructed to do so by their superiors.

DSO, EXTENDED DATING, AND ANTITRUST LAWS

Another problem with offering a special dating program to a specific customer is that the action might violate the Robinson-Patman Act. The Robinson-Patman Act is a federal law that prohibits price discrimination. Therefore, in addition to adding to the credit risk and increasing DSO, offering extended dating to one customer and not to a "like" customer might result in a violation of federal law.

DISPUTES AND DEDUCTIONS AND THEIR IMPACT ON CREDIT DEPARTMENT PERFORMANCE

Delinquent balances will grow as the number of errors made by the seller increase. For example, a simple data entry error in entering an order can result in (a) the wrong product being shipped, (b) the wrong quantity being shipped, (c) the wrong price being charged on the invoice, or (d) any combination of these three problems.

Deductions and disputes must be addressed and resolved individually. It is a highly labor intensive process for both the buyer's and the seller's accounting departments. Unless the seller puts adequate resources into the process of researching disputes and deductions, chances are good that there will be a backlog of deductions outstanding and awaiting review and resolution. Even if the credit department is adequately staffed to review and resolve customer deductions, the credit department must often wait for other departments to gather information or to review the information gathered by the credit department before a dispute can be addressed and resolved.

For example, assume a customer takes a deduction of $1,000 on a $10,000 payment because of a pricing dispute. Further assume that the order was received by telephone and that there is no hard copy of the purchase order to document the price agreed upon by the buyer and the seller. If the seller company does not have a fixed price for the product in question for whatever reason, then the credit department must forward an inquiry to the sales department and await their response before either (a) processing a pricing credit to clear the deduction or (b) contacting the customer to explain that the price was correct, and that the deduction was therefore taken in error and must be repaid.

This process is both labor intensive and time consuming. It is particularly time consuming if the salesperson does not respond promptly to the credit department's inquiries. Unfortunately, in many companies this is often the case. Often, the salesperson has a financial disincentive to approve the issuance of credit memos because credits typically offset sales for the purpose of calculating commissions.

One complaint common to credit departments is that the seller's sales department, order entry, manufacturing and shipping departments have the capacity to make more errors and to create more collection problems than the credit department can possibly handle in an orderly and timely manner. For this reason, creditors must concentrate on identifying the root causes of billing and shipping problems. Trying to correct them after the fact has been likened to trying to hold back the tide with a bucket.

Further complicating the process of resolving disputes and deductions is the fact that many accounts payable departments are heavily automated. Accounts payable automation makes it relatively easy for them to handle routine task such as paying "clean" invoices. Automation also leads to staff reductions—making it more difficult for customers to find the time to review the documentation sent by vendors in support of their request that a deduction be repaid.

Still another problem for the credit department with data entry or shipping errors is that many customers refuse to pay any portion of a disputed invoice until the dispute is resolved and either (a) a credit memo is issued or (b) the customer receives documentation proving the creditor's bill was correct. Even after the dispute is addressed, it may take days or even weeks for the invoice in question to be scheduled for payment. Meanwhile the invoice remains open and past due.

Unfortunately, customers are often slow to inform their creditors about a problem or a dispute. Often, an invoice is already past due before the credit department learns that there is a problem. Often, the credit department's explanation of the problem is complex and must be sent in writing along with supporting documentation and a request for repayment to the customer.

What is clear is that the dispute resolution process is one that can only be partially controlled by the credit department no matter how experienced and skillful the credit manager is. In some companies, deductions and disputed invoices constitute the majority of the past due balance, and despite the fact that the credit department did not create the problem and cannot always control the problem resolution process, the credit department's performance will be judged based on their ability to control [or on their lack of success in controlling] past due balances—including disputed past due balances.

To use an analogy, the traditional role of the credit department was to walk along at the end of the parade and clean up any mess then might find along the way. [This "clean up" would involve investigating the problem and either issuing a credit or demanding repayment]. A more proactive and pragmatic approach requires that the credit manager not simply be an observer. Instead, the credit manager should become an active participant in identifying problems that result in errors made by the creditor company which in turn result in deductions being taken. For example, if the credit manager studies pricing deductions and finds that the company is at fault 80% of the time, then a proactive credit manager would present these findings to senior management and suggest that corrective action be taken to reduce the frequency with which this problem occurs.

Statistics indicate that customers tend to be correct about half of the time when they short pay invoices. The key to reducing deduction problems for the creditor company to make fewer errors.

Some credit managers do not enjoy the role of detective in trying to learn the root causes of deductions. However, as long as the credit department and the credit manager continue to be evaluated based on their ability to control delinquencies [including delinquencies that result from disputes and deductions] this is a job that credit managers are going to need to get accustomed to.

TECHNIQUES USED TO MEASURE CREDIT DEPARTMENT PERFORMANCE

There are a number of other popular ways to measure the credit department's overall performance. Some methods are described below, along with the advantages and the disadvantages of each:

(1) *Controlling departmental expenses.*

Every manager is evaluated in part on his or her ability to manage expenses and to stay within budget. For most credit managers, the largest budgeted item by far is bad debt expense. Ignoring bad debt expense for a moment, the credit manager's ability to control other expenses [such as labor costs] is an indication of their control of the credit department and of its day to day operations.

While there is no direct correlation between a manager's ability to control routine administrative costs and the credit manager's ability to control risk and reduce delinquencies, controlling costs is still considered to be one measure of the credit manager's competence. The best credit managers will continuously improve the performance and results of credit department operations while at the same time controlling expenditures.

The advantage of controlling expenses is that it contributes to the seller's bottom line. The disadvantage of reducing expenses is that it can be done at the expense of departmental efficiency and effectiveness.

(2) *Measuring the time it takes to establish an open account.*

Determining how long it takes to open new accounts is an important measure of how well the credit department is organized, how well the staff is trained, and how high a priority the credit manager has placed on customer satisfaction. In a highly competitive business environment, customers expect fast decisions. In fact, it is not uncommon in many industries for the credit application to accompany the opening order, and for the customer and the salesperson to expect that order to be approved and shipped on open account terms the same day. A fast response to a credit application also sends a message that the company wants the business, is efficient, and is therefore the kind of company the applicant wants to do business with.

(3) *Measuring how soon an account is contacted after it becomes past due.*

It is no secret that the sooner a delinquent account is contacted about the past due balance, the sooner payment can be expected. Therefore, measuring how quickly, on average, past due balances are contacted is a measure of the credit department's overall effectiveness. In this regard, the credit manager must learn to be specific. For example, the statement: "Delinquent customers must be contacted as quickly as possible" does not provide specific guidance to the collector. The statement "Every delinquent account must be contacted within 5 days of becoming past due" is much clearer and makes it easier for the credit manager to measure and evaluate the collector's performance against this standard.

(4) *Measuring the time taken to review orders pending.*

For most sellers, orders in the credit queue are reviewed and approved on line and in real time. Typically, very little programming is required to determine the average amount of time an order stays in the credit queue before it is reviewed. Credit managers and their subordinates should be evaluated on how quickly they review orders pending, and there is no excuse for ignoring orders in the credit queue.

A review is separate and distinct from approving and releasing the order. Measuring the time taken to review orders means the difference between the time the order entered the credit queue and the time it was first reviewed. It is an important and relevant measure of the credit department's overall performance because the sooner a pending order is released, the more efficient the rest of the order fulfillment function can be. Orders that remain on hold too long because no one took the time to review them end up being rushed, and rush orders are costly because they are more labor intensive, require special handling, and are likely to result in more errors.

(5) *Measuring customer satisfaction.*

The credit department has both internal and external customers. Clearly, one way to measure the credit department's performance involves surveying the credit department's customers. External customers deal with a number of suppliers, so their opinions about the performance of the credit department should be of interest to the company and to the credit manager.

Internal customers of the credit department include salespeople and other departments. Salespeople can be surveyed to measure their satisfaction with the credit department—including their satisfaction with the decisions made by the credit department and with the service provided by the credit department.

(6) *Measuring individual performance within the credit department.*

Regardless of what statistics are used to measure performance in the credit department as a whole, each person in the credit department should be given access to information about their individual performance. Each collector should receive a copy of the detailed accounts receivable aging report for their accounts. In addition, each collector should know the DSO in his or her customer base.

It is important to review employees' performance on a regular basis against the goals established with and for them. Every employee should be given access to this information so that there are no unpleasant surprises during their regularly scheduled performance reviews. Access to this information allows individuals to address and resolve problems before they become so serious that the credit manager must intervene.

(7) *Changes in DSO.*

Many companies use Days Sales Outstanding [DSO] to measure the performance of their credit department. Unfortunately, there are a number of factors completely beyond the credit manager's control that impact DSO, including:

■ The terms of sale offered to customers. The longer the terms of sale offered, the larger DSO will grow.

■ A decision by senior management to liberalize the company's credit policy in order to attract new customers. A more liberal credit policy requires the credit department to accept more risk. More risk results in more delinquencies, and more delinquencies means a higher DSO.

■ A decision by senior management to limit the use of credit holds [perhaps to make order fulfillment more efficient] will ultimately cause DSO to increase because it results in more risks being taken.

■ Delays in issuing credit memos will increase DSO. There are many reasons credit memos are delayed. It may be that the creditor company simply does not have the staff to investigate and resolve deductions in a timely manner. It may be that the data entry department is too busy processing orders to enter credits, or it may be a deliberate decision to delay the issuance of credit memos.

■ Seasonal changes in monthly sales volume cause DSO to fluctuate dramatically. Large volume swings up or down in sales from month to month will effect DSO because of the formula used to calculate DSO.

For all of these reasons, DSO is not necessarily a reliable measure of the credit department's performance. It is used because it is intuitively appealing, and because it is easy to calculate.

(8) *Measuring Days Delinquent Sales Outstanding.*

Days Delinquent Sales Outstanding [DDSO] is a better measure of credit department performance than DSO. DDSO measures changes in a company's past due balance irrespective of the terms of sale customers are offered. The credit department has more control of DDSO than over DSO. DDSO is calculated in the following way:

(1) Calculate DSO using whatever standard methodology the company uses

(2) The "best possible" DSO is calculated using this formula:

$$\frac{\text{Average Current A/R Balance}}{\text{Total Credit Sales for the Same Period}}$$

(3) Subtract the best possible DSO from the standard DSO to get Days Delinquent Sales Outstanding.

(9) *Measuring Changes in Past due Balances.*

A variation on the DDSO concept involves simply calculating changes in the total dollars past due. This is easy to calculate and to track. The only limitation to this measurements was discussed earlier: Deduction and disputes are often a major component of delinquent balances, and in many instances the credit department needs the assistance of other departments to review and resolve these problems.

(10) *Using bad debt losses to measure the credit department's performance.*

It is true that increase in bad debt losses might indicate the credit department is not properly controlling risk. On the other hand, it might simply be a statistical abnormality. For example, if the company lost almost nothing in the previous year, a large loss in the current year might place the two-year average exactly where the company would expect losses to be.

Another problem with using bad debt losses as a measure of credit department performance is the fact that the increase may be the inevitable result of a preplanned decision by the company to accept more credit risk in order to increase the company's sales or to penetrate a new market.

Still another problem with bad debt losses is that they do not necessarily indicate the credit department "missed something." For example, a customer may unexpectedly file for bankruptcy protection because a fire or other catastrophe destroyed their business. Another example would be a successful sole proprietorship that fails overnight because the business owner died. Some bad debt write offs are unavoidable. Measuring credit department performance against an unavoidable loss is not a valid measurement.

While it might seem counterintuitive, companies that experience little or no bad debt losses over an extended period of time probably have unsound, overly restrictive credit policies that are costing the company money. A company with no credit losses is either rejecting all but the most creditworthy customers, or it is driving away too many marginal accounts in order to minimize bad debt losses.

The actual volume of bad debt losses is influenced by:

■ The need to increase the amount of credit risk taken to increase sales

- Changes in the overall economic health of the country. For example, an economic recession will tend to cause more businesses to fail resulting in more bad debt losses

- Interest rates. In periods of high interest rates, companies tend to fail more frequently than when interest and inflation rates are relatively low

(11) *Percent of prior month's sales collected.*

A fairly common measure of credit performance involves calculating the percent of the prior month's Accounts Receivable collected. This is calculated by dividing the current month's cash receipts by the A/R ending balance amount for the previous month.

There are several problems with this measurement. The most striking is if the company sells on other than net 30-day terms the value of this particular calculation is suspect at best. Another problem with the calculation is the timing of sales. For example, if a large order shipped on the last day of the previous month, or a large volume shipped during the last week of the previous month, it is unreasonable to expect that customers checks will clear by the end of the following month—even if the terms are net 30 days from the date of invoice.

Another factor influencing this calculation would be whether or not the Creditor Company offers a cash discount. An inducement for the customer to pay its bills sooner rather than later would tend to improve the percent of prior month's sales collected.

(12) *Sales per employee.*

The ratio is calculated by dividing dollar sales on credit terms by the number of employees in the credit department. In theory, the lower the ratio, the better the job the credit manager is doing at managing his or her employees. The old adage about being penny wise and pound fooling may apply to this measurement of the credit department's performance. If the credit manager is controlling labor costs at the expense of not accomplishing other goals such as updating credit files regularly and contacting delinquent accounts promptly, then the credit manager is making poor choices.

Dollar sales per employee is an important ratio. However, the number of employees required to perform the credit function is not simply a function of the sales volume. For example, a company that had $100 million in annual sales on 100 invoices to one active customer would certainly need less people on the credit department staff than a company that does the same annual sales volume but has 1,000 active customers and issued 10,000 invoices.

Based on the use of more sophisticated credit management software, many companies find that they can be more productive with fewer employees. However, it is fair to suggest that the goal of any credit manager is to reduce the ratio between number of employees and annual sales volume.

(13) *Measuring employee turnover.*

Measuring employee turnover is important. There are significant costs associated with hiring and training new employees. Losing talented people results in significant costs to the company and to a loss in productivity.

(14) *Calculating the number of active accounts per credit department employee.*

This ratio is another measure of the credit manager's ability to control labor costs. The number of active accounts per employee is easily calculated—making period to period comparisons easy and inexpensive. However, the limitation of this analysis is that not all accounts are alike. Some customers are higher maintenance and managing accounts properly is not simply a function of how many employees are working. Properly managing an account depends on how many invoices are generated, how many disputes and deductions arise, and how "high maintenance" that account is.

(15) *Number of invoices per employee.*

The number of invoices per credit department employee is another popular measure, but is suffers from the same problems as described above. Specifically, as the number of invoices generated increases, so does the potential for collection problems and so does the likelihood of errors resulting in disputes and deductions. It is not especially relevant what the cost is of the average invoice. Generally speaking, it takes about the same amount of time to address a past due invoice for $1,000 as it does to address and resolve a problem involving a past due invoice for $10,000 or $100,000.

(16) *Controlling operating costs.*

Selected expense ratios can be used to measure the credit manager's ability to control costs while controlling the credit and collection process. The credit manager is expected to strike a balance between controlling discretionary expenditures [such as travel] and failing to spend money when it is necessary and appropriate to do so. It is important that the credit manager keep costs and expenses in line with the department's budget—unless by doing so the credit manager loses sight of the overarching goals of the credit department.

SUMMARY

There are any number of ways in which the credit department is evaluated and measured. Some of the most popular and common methods of doing so are also the most flawed. Credit managers owe it to themselves and to their subordinates to be certain that the techniques used to measure the department's performance are relevant and reliable ways to determine how well credit risk and the collection process are being managed.

CHAPTER 4

AUTOMATING THE CREDIT FUNCTION

Today's credit department is faced with a variety of challenges including these:

- The credit department is expected to make more decisions, faster and more accurately

- The credit department is expected to be equally efficient with fewer employees

- The credit department and in particular the credit manager is expected to be able to sift through volumes of raw data and extract nuggets of information that are critical to the credit department's goals of managing risk and reducing delinquencies

Automation

Automation involves the use of computers and related software to make the credit department more efficient. Automation allows the credit department to handle a variety of tasks more quickly, and with fewer errors—resulting in lower overall costs and higher levels of customer satisfaction [from both internal and external customers]. Automation allows fewer employees to handle more accounts—and to provide the same or better level of control, collection and customer service.

Advanced software applications are being used by most credit departments to perform a variety of tasks. In many instances, the software is capable of doing certain tasks better, faster and more efficiently than a person. There are many different programs available that can automate and simplify various tasks within the credit function. In most instances, cost is not the determining factor about whether or not one program is superior to another.

If the credit department is considering purchasing software, the key is to make certain the purchase is cost-effective. This can best be accomplished by previewing the software on site before purchasing it to make certain that it right for your company—and that it works within your company's unique business and competitive environment.

When considering purchasing any software package, credit managers must make sure the program meets the needs of the company, not just the needs of the credit department. For example, any software acquired must be flexible enough to allow the credit department to respond to the changing needs of internal and external customers. Any software that does not allow changes in the format of the reports it creates, or does not allow the credit department to modify the parameters of the program is probably software that the company will outgrow quickly.

There are a large number of software packages being sold to credit managers intended to automate certain tasks that were previously were largely or entirely manual processes. The most popular software programs:

- are inexpensive
- are intuitive
- are Windows™ driven
- have on-line tutorials

The most popular software automates the following functions:

- Risk management on active accounts using credit scoring models. Credit scoring software programs can be used to evaluate credit risk on commercial or consumer credit applications, and on new or active accounts.

- Auto cash systems that automate the process of applying customers' payments. Automating the cash posting process for incoming payments is a benefit of automation and in particular a benefit of Financial Electronic Data Interchange.

- Deduction investigation and resolution software.

- Automation of the collection management process. Often, this is accomplished by prioritizing collection calls, and automating follow up on payment commitments made.

- Software that automates the pending order review and approval process—eliminating orders from the credit review process orders that clearly do not require manual review and approval. [By eliminating certain orders from the credit review process, credit department personnel have more time to review marginal risks that do require their time and attention.]

- Automating the process of updating credit files by utilizing a software program that identifies accounts are due for periodic credit review. [Unless active accounts are reviewed periodically, bad debt losses and delinquencies will tend to increase. The more current the information on file, the more likely the creditor can evaluate and control credit risk.]

FULLY UTILIZING EXISTING SOFTWARE

Often, the capabilities of the credit department's existing software are not well understood by the credit department and as a result they are not fully utilized. In many instances, the company's information systems department knows about the system's capabilities but no one has asked them about ways to enhance the way the credit department uses the system. In many companies, the existing software could be made more useful to the credit department if minor modifications could be made to the software. Unfortunately, in many companies the information systems simply does not have the time or money needed to make these changes.

Other common reasons that software is not modified include:

- The information systems group no longer possesses the skills required to make the requested modifications.

- The information systems group has the capability to make the requested changes, but does not have the personnel necessary to make the requested changes or the changes requested did not receive a high priority.

- The software was purchased as a so-called canned package and was not created in-house.

- The information systems department does not have the expertise needed to change the software.

- The information systems group is reluctant to modify one part of the software because changes tend to have a cascade effect through the software —and sometimes a change in one relatively unimportant area causes a critical system to fail.

Evaluating Subordinates' Performance

Employees deserve accurate and honest performance appraisals from their managers. To the extent that automation can be used to provide employees with relevant measurements of their performance, the credit manager should make certain that programs are written and reports are distributed to their subordinates. The key is that the reports provided be relevant and timely when delivered to the individual employee.

Often, a minor modification will turn an irrelevant report into a relevant way to measure performance. For example, an accounts receivable aged trial balance generated by invoice date is not as relevant as a report generated by due date. A minor modification to the software may be all that is required to generate such a report. The report would hold every open invoice in the current column until that invoice became past due based on the credit terms.

This simple [but common] situation is an example of what happens when the information systems and the credit department do not work together cooperatively. Unfortunately, since many credit departments only have access to aging reports sorted by invoice date [rather than by due date] collectors often waste time reviewing invoices that are not yet due.

Other situations exists in which the credit department has access to a variety of reports that would assist them in controlling delinquencies, planning their collection calls, and managing credit risk. Unfortunately, credit department personnel may not have been trained to access the programs the system can create. Therefore, they are confined to reviewing standard reports.

Accessing Current Information

Access to current information improves the quality of business decisions being made by the credit department with respect to orders pending, and access to current information makes the collection process more efficient. There is a distinct advantage to being able to pull up-to-the-minute reports whenever they are needed as opposed to using out-of-date information. Credit managers are able to assess subordinate performance more efficiently, and subordinates are able to see for themselves the progress they are making.

If your system does not permit reports to be refreshed and reprinted on demand, this would be the type of system enhancement the credit manager should push for. The goal of the MIS system is to generate the information needed by internal customers.

- Technology Training Gaps

Often, existing employees do not possess the skills necessary to make use of all of the software and all of the technology available to them. For example, employees may know how to send and receive e-mail messages but may be unfamiliar with how to send or receive attachments to e-mail messages. The solutions to the problems that gaps in training present to the credit department and to the credit manager include:

(1) hire new credit department personnel that are more technologically literate,

(2) encourage employees to experiment with the capabilities of software

(3) ask the information systems department to provide the additional training required

(4) hire an outside consultant or recruit an in-house expert to do the training

Forward Thinking Hiring

As positions open up within the credit department, a forward thinking credit manager can raise the hiring standards by only hiring employees who:

(a) have the necessary experience in credit and collection, and

(b) who are computer and technology literate.

CREDIT SCORING

In terms of automating the credit function, one of the fastest growing areas of computer automation involves the use of credit scoring software. Credit scoring, or credit risk scoring is a process in which a customer's credit application is evaluated using a software program that assigns numerical values to various risk factors. Risk factors are those variables that have been proven by statistical analysis to be relevant in determining the creditworthiness of an applicant or predicting delinquency in payment or bankruptcy. The software develops a specific risk score for each applicant after reviewing and scoring the risk factors.

Customized Credit Scoring

Credit managers normally have the ability to customize their credit-scoring program by re-weighting certain risk factors, or adding and weighting certain factors themselves. For example, if the credit scoring software does not evaluate or weight the profit the seller expects to make on the product to an applicant because the scoring model does not believe this number is predictive of payment delay or default, but the seller believes that profitability should be a factor considered in the credit score, then this factor can be added to the credit score. It can be weighted in any way the seller determines is appropriate.

Credit managers should remember that a credit risk score is a recommendation by the software package about whether or not the company or applicant should be offered open account terms of sale. The ultimate decision about whether or not to extend credit to an applicant company, and if so how large a credit limit to offer is a decision to be made by the credit manager. The credit score itself is only a number.

Risk Factors

Risk factors used in credit scoring software to evaluate the creditworthiness of an applicant would typically include all of the following factors, and possibly others:

- The type of business [using the customer's SIC code]
- Number of years in business
- Number of years at present location
- Number of employees
- Payment habits
- Number of suits filed and pending
- Number of suits settled
- Number of tax liens filed
- Any history of bankruptcy filings
- The number and type of UCC filings
- Whether or not the customer has provided financial statements for review
- The company's financial condition as reported in their financial statements
- Whether the financial statements provided are audited or unaudited
- How current the financial statements are
- Whether the business is a C Corporation, a Subchapter S Corporation, a Limited Liability Corporation, a General Partnership, a Limited Partnership, or a proprietorship

Risk Factors Are Interrelated

The theory behind credit risk scoring software is that certain risk factors, or combinations of risk factors, will result in a greater likelihood of delinquency or default. This theory is borne out by empirical testing that confirms the relationship between the risk factors evaluating by credit scoring software and the likelihood of default or serious delinquencies.

The companies that have develop credit-scoring software for commercial customers represent that it can help identify the future credit performance of an applicant.

Consumer vs. Commercial Credit Scoring

Credit scoring software has been used for decades in the consumer credit field, and has proved to be a reliable tool to help evaluate applicants, and to flag applicants that appear to represent an unacceptable risk. Credit scoring software for use in commercial credit applications has already proven to be reliable. In addition, credit scoring software can save the seller time and lower processing and review costs. Credit scoring is particularly useful for creditor companies that review a large number of commercial applications for credit and want each of them reviewed quickly, thoroughly and impartially.

Sources of Credit Scoring Software

There are dozens of companies that sell commercial credit risk scoring software. As with any software program, the buyer must carefully evaluate the features of several competing products before determining which of them would be best for their needs. One of the most important features to review is the output of the analysis. The analysis should not give only a numerical score, it should provide a narrative which explains the factors that the software considered to be the most important [the most heavily weighted] when arriving at a credit score.

Scoring on Active Accounts

Some commercial credit scoring software programs allow the model to evaluate active customers. The goal of active account credit scoring is to determine if the risk of selling to those accounts has deteriorated over time to the point that the credit limit should be reduced or withdrawn, or the terms of sale should be shortened.

Who Needs Credit Scoring Software?

The more of these statements are true, the more a commercial credit granter needs credit scoring software:

- The company handles a lot of new account applications.
- Customers, the sales department and the company demand fast responses to credit applications.
- The company's past loss history, especially on new accounts, has not been good.

- The credit manager or the company is looking for a more objective way to evaluate applicants.

- The company or the credit department is looking for a better way to monitor and manage risk associated with active customers in addition to new accounts.

The Need for Consistency

The advantage of credit scoring software is its consistency. Given the same set of facts and factors to consider, the credit-scoring software will consistently calculate the same score. Unfortunately, the same cannot be said for people and it is hard for the credit manager to explain an inconsistent application of the department's credit decision-making criteria. No matter how well subordinates are trained, each person given credit granting authority will have their own biases. As a result, given the exact same information two employees might come to different conclusions and recommendations.

This is not to suggest that credit scoring decision support software is rigid. If credit managers change the weighting factors, as they can do with most credit scoring software programs, then the scores and the recommendations can change in response to the changing competitive environment.

Companies using credit-scoring software to evaluate new applicants for credit [new accounts] can expect:

- faster decisions

- better credit decisions, and a better explanation of the decisions

- more consistent credit decisions

- increased productivity in the credit department

- increased sales through the process of identifying accounts which at first glance may have seemed to be unacceptable but which the credit scoring software identifies as being an acceptable credit risk

- lower overall credit risk, which in turn leads to higher profits, lower bad debt losses, and fewer collection problems

    In summary, the advantages of credit risk scoring software include:

- It takes some of the subjectivity out of the decision making process.

- Recommendations made by the software are consistent because the rules the software uses are consistently applied.

- The final decision about whether or not to recommend terms can be made more quickly. As a result, there is a less chance that a competitor will "steal" the customer by offering open account terms more quickly.

- The credit manager remains in control of the process and the decision—but the software provides decision support.

- The criteria used in many credit scoring software programs can be adjusted to reflect the creditor company's tolerance for payment default [bad debt losses] and for payment delinquency. For example, if a creditor company decides it wants to take more credit risk in order to increase sales revenues, it is normally not a complex task to modify the credit scoring software so that higher risk applicants will receive a better credit score.

FINANCIAL ELECTRONIC DATA INTERCHANGE

Electronic data interchange is a process in which two companies [the buyer and the seller] called "trading partners" exchange information with each other using computer to computer linkage. An example of electronic data interchange (EDI) would involve the buyer sending the seller a request for quote and the seller sending a quote—both using the computer to communicate rather than using a phone, fax or mail.

An enhancement of EDI is Financial EDI. Financial EDI (or FEDI) involves the computer to computer interchange of payment related information combined with the computer assisted transmission of the actual payment. This process can work in a variety of ways. Two of the most popular are outlined below:

(1) Bank facilitated Financial EDI (FEDI) payment transfers which works this way.

- The customer generates a purchase order which is delivered to the seller via electronic data interchange

- The seller generates a PO confirmation, a shipping notice, a picking ticket, and an invoice to the customer via EDI

- The customer arranges for a payment to be generated electronically via the automated clearinghouse (the ACH) to the seller. Accompanying that ACH payment are electronic remittance instructions to the seller identifying how the payment is to be applied.

- The payment is debited from the buyer's account. When it is deposited, the seller receives from its bank (a) confirmation of receipt of payment and (b) a copy of the electronic remittance advice that the bank received from the buyer.

(2) A Hybrid Bank and Third Party FEDI transaction

- The seller's bank receives payment via the ACH system.

- The payment is deposited, and the seller is informed of the deposit electronically.

- The buyer forwards the remittance advice which has been scanned electronically or keyed manually [or was sent to the bank in electronic form] to an electronic mailbox at a third party service bureau

- The seller contacts the bureau and obtains the remittance advice.

- Using that information, the seller applies the payment it received electronically using sophisticated cash application software that matches up as many items as possible on the customer's remittance [which is now digitized] to the information contained in the seller's accounts receivable database.

The Advantages of AutoCash

The advantages of automating the cash posting process include all of the following:

- Automating the process to whatever extent possible results in less manual data entry.

- Using AutoCash is more efficient than manual posting. It is faster and less expensive. It also frees up time for the cash application department to do higher priority tasks such as identifying and documenting deductions taken more carefully and more quickly.

- Using AutoCash, payment information is available sooner, making the collection process easier by identifying which invoices [or debits] were paid and which ones have been skipped.

After the bugs have been worked out of the AutoCash application process, it is not uncommon for payment application software to identify and automatically post 70% to 90% of each payment received without human involvement and intervention. The "bugs" involve helping the AutoCash system to recognize the unique ways in which certain customers record information on their remittance advice—whether that remittance advice is paper or electronic.

Here is a simple example: Assume a customer truncates [shortens] a creditor's invoice number on their electronic purchase order by leaving off the first digit of a 6 digit invoice number. Until the AutoCash system is told to look for a 5 digit invoice match, it will not recognize [or at least will not post] a 5 digit invoice number resulting in a "no match found" on the AutoCash report. Once the software has been told to accept a truncated invoice number the system will be able to recognize and post that particular customer's electronic remittance.

BANK CASH APPLICATION

Banks offer a variety of services to their customers that are interested in streamlining their operations in order for the customer to concentrate on its "core competencies." Listed below are some of the services banks provide to reduce their customers' workloads:

■ For customers that do not provide an electronic remittance advice with payment, some banks will actually key in remittance information so that the information can be transmitted electronically to the seller [the bank's customer]. This service is particularly useful if the seller has a program in place that automatically posts payments once the remittance advice has been received electronically. This service is expensive because it is so labor intensive. However, the advantages of contracting or outsourcing this particular service include:

   (a) The creditor company's cash application personnel may be put to better [more productive] use, such as reconciling disputes.

   (b) If the creditor's business is seasonal, outsourcing of this process will mean that the company is not overwhelmed by heavy seasonal payments—which often results in delays, disappointments, and errors.

■ A variation on the theme of having the seller's bank prepare information involves the use of imaging software. A growing number of banks use character recognition software to scan the customer's remittance advice, to turn that scanned information into computer readable data, and then to transit that data to the customer for uploading into the seller's accounts receivable system in order to match and clear open invoices and debits.

■ Another use of imaging software involves simply scanning the remittance advice and forwarding that information to creditors so they can begin they can post certain payments even before receiving a hard copy of the customer's remittances [typically via courier] from their bank.

AUTOMATING THE PROCESS OF ORDERING CREDIT REPORTS

Twenty years ago, if credit managers needed a credit report on a customer [or applicant], they would probably either call or write to the credit-reporting agency to request it. If they were in a hurry, the agency might be able to give them a verbal overview of the report, but most creditors waited for that report to arrive by mail. In some cases, before the report arrived the credit manager had no choice but to make the decision. If the order was released, credit professionals would hope that the credit report confirmed that their decision to release the order was the correct one. Of course, sometimes the report contained unpleasant surprises.

Today, creditors can access credit reports on line and in real time. The information can be downloaded and printed within minutes. Some of the largest credit reporting agencies even allow subscribers to access credit reports via the Internet.

Accelerating the process of accessing credit reports has had a profound impact on the credit department, on risk management and on the credit decision making process. Instant access to current information has made it possible to qualify applicants sooner, to approve higher credit limits more quickly, and to avoid losses and delinquencies by having current and accurate information.

Company's expectations have changed. Sellers have come to expect almost instant decisions from their credit department. It is not uncommon for the credit application and the opening order to be received the same day. Unfortunately, the credit reporting agency's database does not always contain the information necessary to approve orders pending, and the sales department should regularly be cautioned by the credit department not to expect instant approvals, and instead to give the credit department as much advance notice as possible.

AUTOMATING STATEMENTS AND INVOICES

Most companies generate and mail invoices on a daily basis, and customer account statements once a month. This process is normally automated [and if it is not automated it should be]. If the company does not have the resources necessary to automate the process, it should be outsourced.

For a processing fee, a company that specializes in printing, processing and mailing invoices, statements and other critical business documents can take over this function permanently, or for a limited time while the company gears up to do the work itself. The advantages of this arrangement are:

How to Avoid Catching a Bug

Most credit departments are highly automated. One of the risks that every automated credit department faces is the risk of importing a computer virus.

Every computer is susceptible to computer viruses, and in particular the types of networked computers favored by credit departments.

New computer viruses are being created at the rate of more than one hundred a month, and more than 10,000 computer viruses have already been identified.

Credit professionals cannot afford to become complacent about computer viruses simply because they have installed an antivirus software program. In fact, some antiviral programs may block as few as 300 computer viruses, and even the best antivirus program will not be 100% effective. Fortunately, more sophisticated antiviral programs are now able to spot the footprint of a virus, without necessarily knowing what virus it has encountered.

- There are things that every computer user should know in order to avoid computer viruses, including these tips:

- Use the most updated version available of a virus detection and prevention software program.

- Consider establishing a policy for the company of not allowing anyone to download any executable program from the Internet.

- Do not share or borrow software programs on floppy disks. Even with the popularity of the Internet, floppy disks handed from person to person remain the single most common source of computer software viruses.

- Do not use unlicensed [pirated] software.

- Do not download attachments to e-mail messages without scanning the software for viruses. If the antiviral software program your company uses does not do this automatically, don't open e-mail attachments.

- Regularly back up important documents. If you store a lot of information, invest in a zip drive.

- Do not allow employees to load onto their PC programs [such as games] brought from home.

- the outsourcing company has the expertise in this area to allow the creditor to focus its time, energy and limited resources on its area of expertise
- if the work is not getting done, outsourcing may be the only viable option for the creditor company
- If your business is seasonal, it may be appropriate during peak periods to outsource these tasks to permit company employees to concentrate on other areas of greater importance to the company.

ELECTRONIC COMMUNICATIONS

An excellent way for the credit department to communicate with customers and with the sales department is by using electronic mail [e-mail]. E-mail allows for almost instantaneous communication in contrast to inter-office mail that can be delayed or even lost. An advantage of inter-office e-mail is that many systems allow the sender to verify the intended recipient received and opened the e-mail message. In addition, the software can provide a permanent record of what was sent and when it was opened, preventing a common problem in which the recipient denies receiving the correspondence.

SUMMARY

Anyone not interested in finding ways to further automate the credit and collection function should consider this fact:

For almost a decade, companies have been selling software referred to as "payment timing optimization software." This software is used to determine how far customers can delay payment before creditors will push back. For example, the software will recommend the buyer pay a creditor 10 days late and take the unearned cash discount. If the creditor does not call about the delinquent balance or complain about the unearned discount, the software might recommend the next payment be delayed 15 days.

Payment timing optimization software programs also test creditors' sensitivity to the size of the unearned cash discount being taken. For example, the software might suggest that a cash discount of $25 be taken after the discount due date to determine if it is charged back. If it is not, the software might suggest the buyer deduct $50 on the next check and so on until the creditor charges back the unearned cash discount.

The software is designed to build a profile of every supplier the company deals with indicating the creditor's sensitivity to:

(1) Delinquencies

(2) Unearned cash discounts

(3) The size of unearned cash discounts

The system is designed to optimize the buyer's cash flow by trying to balance the need to stay off credit hold against the desire to hold onto its cash for as long as possible.

Credit managers working without the benefit of automation are at a competitive disadvantage. The good news is that the prices of all the software described in this chapter are dropping rapidly, while the power of the software continues to increase dramatically.

CHAPTER 5

Consumer Credit Policies

This is a difficult time to be a credit manager responsible for extending credit to consumers. In 1998, there were almost 1.4 million non-business bankruptcy filings. At the same time, consumer spending continues to rise, consumer debt loads continue to set new records, and personal savings are at record lows.

Consumer spending has been the fuel used to continue the expansion of the national economy for the ninth straight year in a row. There is over $1.2 trillion in outstanding consumer debt in the United States. The United States Department of Commerce reported that consumer debt is growing at a rate of about 4% a year. As is the case with commercial credit grantors, credit professionals dealing with consumers are concerned about bad debt losses and with a debtor's ability to pay its obligations as they come due.

CONSUMER CREDIT DECISION-MAKING

By definition, consumer credit is credit extended or requested for personal, family or household purposes. Just as in a commercial credit situation, each potential creditor will make an individual and unilateral decision about whether or not to extend credit to a consumer credit applicant. Just as in commercial credit management, it is possible for two different creditors evaluating the same information to come to different conclusions about the applicant. The differences might involve the size of the credit limit to be granted, or it might involve a fundamentally different decision in which one creditor extends credit and the other does not.

CONSUMER CREDIT—RIGHT OR PRIVILEGE?

One of the most fundamental questions that must be addressed in connection with extending credit to consumers is whether or not consumer credit is a right or a privilege. Consumer credit is a privilege that must be earned, and not a right guaranteed by law. The implications of this simple statement are profound. At its most basic, it means that consumers who do not pay their bills as they come due will find it more difficult to convince existing and potential creditor to extend credit to them. In other words, there are consequences for the actions [or inaction] of consumers with respect to payments owed to creditors.

The most obvious manifestation of credit problems involves a situation in which a consumer applies for additional credit and that request is denied. Rather than looking inward at the problems they may have created, consumers that have been denied credit sometimes become indignant and demand to know exactly why they applications were denied. In this matter, a consumer applicant that has been denied credit terms has far more rights under federal and state law than a business entity that has been rejected for credit has with respect to the creditor company.

INTERLOCKING AND OVERLAPPING LAWS

There are a number of interlocking and overlapping Federal and State laws protecting the rights of consumers with respect to the extension of credit. They were implemented to protect individuals from the abuses of companies on the assumption that creditor companies are better informed and have far more resources than consumers do.

By any objective measure, the consumer credit field is a highly regulated business environment. The two most frequently misunderstood rules about consumer credit granting are these:

(1) Creditors have the absolute right to deny credit to applicants they do not believe are creditworthy, and

(2) Consumers have the right to know specifically why they were refused or denied credit.

THE FORMS OF CONSUMER CREDIT

Consumer credit takes many different forms. Some of the most common forms of credit are charge cards, bank credit, and home loan mortgages.

Another way to look at the different forms of consumer credit does not focus on who is extending credit. Instead, it focuses on the priority of claims against a consumer. There are three basic types of creditors, which are:

(1) Lien or secured creditors

(2) Priority creditors

(3) Unsecured creditors.

A lien creditors is one that has a lien or security interest in certain real or personal property of the consumer. A lien may arise through statute, through agreement between the parties, or by judicial proceedings.

A creditor may have a priority interest. A priority interest arises primarily through statutory law. A priority creditor must be paid ahead of unsecured creditors but after secured creditors in the event that the individual debtor becomes insolvent or files for bankruptcy protection. As in commercial credit, the largest number of creditors of consumers are general unsecured trade creditors who enjoy no security or priority on their claims.

CREDIT CARDS, AND INSTALLMENT DEBT

Most people are familiar with how charge cards work. A consumer is issued a credit card by a financial institution or by a merchant [such as a department store]. The consumer receives a monthly bill and normally has an option of paying the full amount - or making a stated minimum monthly payment in which case finance or interest charges will accrue on the unpaid balance at an agreed upon rate.

Installment credit is used by consumers to purchase big ticket items such as cars. The seller often retains title to the property sold until it is paid in full. When a consumer buys a home, he or she agrees to make periodic payments to the financial institution. Until all of these installment payments have been made, the bank still holds title to the home.

CONSUMER CREDIT CHECKS

When a consumer applies for a credit card, and upon receipt of a completed and signed credit application, the credit department will conduct a standard review of the applicant. Consumer credit grantors have come to rely heavily on credit reports provided by consumer credit reporting agencies for information about applicants. This is normally the most important part of any credit review of a consumer applicant. In some instances, these consumer credit reports also include credit scores.

The largest of the consumer credit reporting agencies are Experian, Trans Union, and Equifax. For a relatively modest fee, these credit-reporting agencies provide subscribers with up-to-date information on consumer applicants. Creditor rely on consumer credit reports to be:

- Factual, objective and reliable.
- Available quickly on-line.
- Well formatted and easy to review.

For a small additional charge, these agencies will provide the user with a credit score in addition to a consumer credit report.

THE PRINCIPLE OF INDEPENDENT CREDIT DECISIONS

Consumers are often puzzled when one creditor grants them open account credit terms and another refuses to do so. From the creditor company's perspective, there is no mystery about the fact that one company might extend credit to an applicant and another company might decline it. All creditors make independent and unilateral decisions about applicants for credit.

Each creditor makes its credit decision based on a number of variables, including:

- The creditor company's sales goals and market share goals.
- The creditor company's profit margins—or the interest rate and annual fee that the credit card carries.
- The company's appetite for additional credit risk—combined with its ability to control risk simply by offering a relatively low credit limit on the card.
- The creditor's cash flow—which is an indication of its ability to absorb late payments.
- The credit policies of competitors

FACTORS IN CONSUMER CREDIT GRANTING

In considering whether or not to extend credit to an individual consumer, creditors normally consider a large number of variables including all of the following:

- How much the applicant earns

- How long the applicant has lived at the present and the prior address
- How long the applicant has worked for their present employer
- Whether they own their home or rent
- How much money they owe to other creditors
- The amount of their fixed monthly payments including rent or mortgages, car payments, day care, food, utilities, etc.
- How well other creditors have been paid in the past
- Whether or not this consumer has been sued by other creditors, or has filed for personal bankruptcy protection in the past

Typically, consumer credit granters rely on credit reports for most of this information. The rest of the information that credit granters need to get a clear picture of the risks associated with extending credit to the individual applicant comes from the credit application itself.

CREDIT AND THE LAW

As mentioned previously, a number of federal and state laws offer strong protection to the consumer against abuses and regulate consumer credit granting by creditors. The two most important laws relating to and controlling the extension of credit to consumers are:

(a) the Equal Credit Opportunity Act, and

(b) the Fair Credit Reporting Act.

THE EQUAL CREDIT OPPORTUNITY ACT

The Equal Credit Opportunity Act (the ECOA) prohibits creditors from refusing to extend credit to individuals on the basis of sex, race, marital status, national origin, religion, age, sexual orientation, or if the applicant receives public assistance. Violation of the ECOA carries stiff penalties for the companies found guilty.

The ECOA requires that applicants that are not granted credit must be either:

(a) told promptly the reason for their rejection, or

(b) told that they have the right to ask for the reason for the rejection - provided that request is made in a timely manner. Specifically, consumers have 60 days from the date of notice of rejection to request a specific and detailed explanation for the reason or reasons they were denied credit.

Under the Equal Credit Opportunity Act, the creditor is required to provide specific reasons for denying credit to the applicant. Examples of acceptable reasons for denying credit would include:

- The applicant's income is too low. For example, the creditor might deny credit to any applicant with annual income less than $15,000.

- The applicant has a recent history of payment problems. For example, an applicant is found to have had a bankruptcy, or was sued or placed for collection by another creditor over an undisputed debt.

- The applicant has not been at his or her job for at least a year, or the applicant is self-employed or has no verifiable income.

- The applicant's fixed monthly payments for items such as rent and car payments compared to their monthly income is too high. For example, the ratio of fixed payments to monthly income exceeds 80%.

- The applicant is not of legal age. An applicant must be at least 18 years of age to form a contract.

- The applicant is neither a citizen nor a permanent resident of the United States.

The ECOA forbids creditors from providing vague and unspecific reasons for denying credit. Examples of vague reasons would include any of the following:

- "Your application does not meet our current criteria for offering open account terms."

- "Your credit score indicated that you were not an acceptable credit risk."

- "You do not meet our minimum standards at this time."

In addition to the federal Equal Credit Opportunity Act, approximately half of the fifty states have their own laws governing access by individual consumers to consumer credit. Many of these laws contain unique requirements for creditors that do business with consumers in those states. The state laws apply to dealings with any consumers that reside in that state, irrespective of where that creditor company is incorporated or headquartered.

THE FAIR CREDIT REPORTING ACT

Another federal law, the Fair Credit Reporting Act [FCRA] controls the use of consumer credit reports. The Federal Trade Commission administers the FCRA. The premise behind the FCRA is that credit granters depend on fair and accurate credit reporting in their credit analysis. Inaccurate credit reports impair the effectiveness of credit granters to evaluate risk. At the same time, inaccurate credit reports impair consumers' ability to obtain the credit they deserve. The Fair Credit Reporting Act acknowledges the vital role of credit reporting agencies in compiling information about consumers. The Fair Credit Reporting Act requires that consumer credit reporting agencies adopt reasonable procedures to make certain consumer credit reports are:

- Fair
- Impartial
- Confidential
- Accurate, and
- Relevant

The FCRA guarantees the following: When a consumer is denied credit wholly or partially on the basis of information contained in a consumer report from a consumer reporting agency, then the creditor who used that information must supply the name and address of the consumer credit reporting agency that provided the report the creditor used in making its decision.

Under the Fair Credit Reporting Act, the requesting creditor must certify to the consumer credit reporting agency that the purpose of the inquiry is one permitted under the FCRA. Consumer credit managers almost always require written consent from the applicant before accessing consumer [individual] credit reports.

All of the companies policies and procedures must be written, and any actions taken by the credit department must be taken with an eye toward these federal laws.

CONSUMER REPORTS

The term "consumer credit report" means any written, oral or other communication of any information by a consumer credit reporting agency bearing on a consumer's creditworthiness, credit standing, credit capacity, character, reputation, or mode of living which would be used as a factor in determining and establishing the consumer's eligibility for credit or for employment.

A consumer credit report is a factual record of an individual's credit payment history. The typical consumer credit report contains data in the following four specific areas:

(1) Identifying information, which includes the individual's name, address, previous address, social security number, birth date, current and previous employers

(2) Credit information, which includes information from some but not all companies the individual already buys from. It also includes information such as the date the account was opened, high credit balance, manner of payment, number of days delinquent, payment history and payment trends.

(3) Public record information, including items such as tax liens, judgments, as well as bankruptcy filing information.

(4) Inquiries, including the names of any company that has requested a copy of the credit report in the recent past.

TIP: Always get the consumer's written permission or approval before obtaining a credit report. Such approval should be explicit rather than vague.

THE FAIR CREDIT BILLING ACT

The Fair Credit Billing Act [FCBA] is another federal law protecting the rights of consumers. The FCBA generally apples to open end credit accounts that include credit cards, revolving charge accounts and overdraft checking. The FCBA details how billing disputes are to be resolved. Creditors should be aware that the FCBA covers the following types of disputes:

- Charges allegedly not made by the customer or by anyone authorized to use the account.
- Charges for goods not ordered or accepted.
- Bills for which the wrong amount was charged to the consumer.
- Computation errors in calculating the amount due; in applying payments; and when issuing credits for returns or other adjustments.
- A failure to issue and to record payments, credits or adjustments.

Consumers have 60 days from the date of the first bill containing the billing error to notify the creditor of the error. Under the FCBA, creditors who receive a written notice from a consumer of an alleged billing error must acknowledge receipt of the customer's notice within 30 days [unless the problem is resolved within 30 days]. Also, within two billing cycles [but not more than 90 days], the creditor must conduct an investigation and either correct the problem or advise their customer as to why the billing is believed to be correct.

Consumers often want to withhold payment of the entire balance until the dispute is resolved in their favor. As a protection to creditors, the FCBA states that the customer is required to pay any portion of the outstanding balance that is not in dispute. A consumer is not obligated to pay the disputed amount, or any late fees or finance charges on that disputed amount. However, a consumer must pay whatever amount represents the undisputed portion of the account balance when it comes due.

Under the FCBA, if the creditor's research shows the consumer was correct about the billing error, the creditor must adjust the account and must remove all finance charges and late fees from the account placed resulting from the dispute. If the creditor's research shows the dispute is invalid, the creditor may then report the balance formerly disputed as delinquent, and the creditor may take the necessary steps to collect the past due balance including placing the consumer account for collection—if necessary.

If the bill is correct, and after the creditor has presented the consumer with a written explanation of why the disputed amount is in fact owed, the consumer should:

- pay the balance due
- pay any finance charges that may have accumulated while the balance was in dispute
- pay any minimum monthly payments missed while the account was in dispute

THE DEBTOR'S RIGHTS UNDER THE FCBA

Credit managers should be aware that if they fail to follow the dispute resolution procedure as described in the Fair Credit Billing Act, the creditor company might not collect the amount in dispute—even if the creditor can prove the customer was incorrect. For example, if a creditor fails to acknowledge their customer's written dispute notice within 30 days, or if it takes more than 90 days [or two billing cycles, whichever is less] to respond to the dispute in writing, then the creditor company forfeits its right to payment—even if it can prove later that the consumer owed the money.

Under the FCBA, the creditor may not take any legal or collection action to collect the amount in dispute while the dispute is being researched. Similarly, the creditor company cannot threaten to damage a customer's credit rating or report the account as delinquent to anyone. In addition the creditor may not:

- close the account because a balance has been disputed
- restrict the account in any way except that the amount in dispute may be deducted from the customer's credit limit to calculate the available credit limit
- discriminate in any way against a consumer who in good faith exercises their rights under the FCBA to dispute a bill they have received

THE THREE C'S OF CONSUMER CREDIT

Similar to the four C's of commercial credit, the three C's of consumer credit are Character, Capacity, and Collateral. These "C"s represent the most important factors credit managers must consider when evaluating an applicant for consumer credit.

The first factor is Character. Character relates to a consumer's willingness to pay. Character is typically measured by reviewing the customer's credit payment history. In particular, the creditors are interested in knowing if creditors have been forced to place the consumer's account for collection or sue in order to get paid.

Capacity is the second "C." Capacity measures the consumer's ability to pay. It is normally evaluated by analyzing current obligations including rent or mortgage, other living expenses, car payments, and debt repayments, and comparing these fixed and semi-variable expenses to the consumer's monthly take home pay.

The third C, collateral, refers to the fact that some consumer debt is backed by the pledge of assets which might include stocks, bonds, the cash surrender value of an insurance policy, or the pledge of real estate.

A creditor's primary concern is about a consumer's ability and willingness to pay debts as they come due. The fact that specific security has been pledged as collateral is an added benefit, but the credit decision is normally based on the consumer's ability to pay and willingness to pay—not what the creditor might be able to do with the pledged collateral in the event of a default. Collateral is considered an additional assurance of payment because it can be easily dissipated, sold, lost, or hidden when a consumer finds they are in serious financial trouble.

A pledge of collateral is not considered by most creditors as a reason to extend credit if the consumer applicant is not creditworthy. However, the pledge of collateral can and probably sway what would otherwise be a close decision involving consumer applicant.

★ **COLLECTION TIP:** When speaking with a delinquent debtor, creditor's representatives should be as polite as they are allowed to be, but as demanding and as assertive as they are required to be.

In addition, collectors should be assertive, but not aggressive. Collectors should pressure consumers for payment, but not harass them for payment.

COLLECTION POLICIES

Thus, there is a fine line in consumer collections between what is acceptable and legal, and what is unacceptable and illegal. The actions and activities of debt collection agencies are heavily regulated by the federal Fair Debt Collection Practices Act [the FDCPA]. Even though this law does not apply to employees of the creditor company itself, many credit managers have elected to draw from the FDCPA in creating collection rules. For example, a creditor dealing directly with delinquent consumers might create the following guidelines for their in-house collection efforts:

- Limit the number of calls made to the consumer's place of business— especially if the debtor informs the collector that their company objects to these types of calls on company time.

- Limit calls to between 9:00 a.m. and 9:00 p.m. local time.

- Limit the number of collection calls to each debtor to one per day.

- If the debtor informs you that he or she is represented by counsel, contact the attorney not the debtor.

- Do not threaten to use violence or any other illegal means to collect.

- Never use profanity, not even in response to the same from a consumer debtor.

- Don't threaten criminal prosecution to collect balance due.

- Treat every telephone call as if the debtor were recording the telephone call or the debtor's attorney was on the call with them.

CREDIT SCORING

Many creditors selling to consumers rely on credit risk scoring software to automate the process of evaluating new applicants for credit. Credit scoring involves the use of specifically designed software to evaluate the creditworthiness of an applicant. Credit scoring is in widespread use in consumer collection and it is extremely popular because it uses sophisticated software models that are accurate at determining which applicants are likely to either default on payment or become seriously delinquent.

Credit scoring is needed in the consumer credit field because there are literally millions of potential customers and normally far too many applications for the credit staff to review manually. Credit scoring allows the credit department the time it needs to review marginal accounts individually. Without automation, the entire process would take too long and the evaluations made would not be as consistent the evaluations performed by credit risk scoring software.

During the last 25 years, credit scoring software has been constantly refined and improved. The database of historical information has grown, and the statistical accuracy of credit scoring software makes it a viable way to quickly, inexpensively, accurately and consistently evaluate credit applicants.

THE CONDITIONAL SALES CONTRACT

Some creditors selling under an installment contract [for example, a contract to purchase furniture for the home on an installment payment basis of—say—$100 per month] create for themselves a mechanism for repossessing the merchandise if the consumer defaults on payment. When sales are made under a conditional sales contract. A conditional sales contract is one in which the buyer takes possession of the goods in question but title does not pass to the buyer until the entire balance due is paid. Thus, if a buyer defaults on even the final payment, the creditor may repossess the goods since the creditor still holds legal title to the merchandise in question. The buyer and seller's rights and duties under a conditional sales contract must always be detailed in writing and signed by both parties.

✶ **COLLECTION TIP:** If a customer makes a payment proposal, the creditor should insist the agreement be put in writing. The more informal the agreement is, the less likely the debtor is to make the payments as agreed.

Ideally, the agreement will take the form of a signed Promissory Note.

RETURNED CHECK POLICY

It is important for credit managers to establish a specific policy for dealing with bounced checks. There are a variety of reasons that checks are returned. The reason a check is returned is as important as the fact that it was returned. For example, a check that is being returned due to insufficient funds, while still a concern, is less of a concern than a check returned because the account was closed. If the customer closed it, why are they issuing checks against it? It is hard to know if there was an honest mistake, or an attempt to commit fraud.

When a check bounces due to insufficient funds, it is important to speak directly to the customer and to arrange for the customer to take the necessary steps so the check will clear when it is re-deposited. Fortunately, most NSF checks are caused by the consumer's recordkeeping errors and not fraud.

Customers notified of NSF checks need the time to correct the problem before the check is presented a second time for payment. This is not to suggest that creditors should ask permission before redepositing the NSF check. Instead, calls about NSF checks are a service to customers to limit the damage to the consumer's credit standing.

CALLING THE DEBTOR

Creditors must be careful if they decide to contact the customer about a returned check. Once again, the maze of federal and state consumer protection laws makes it important that the creditor speak directly to and only to the debtor about the problem. It is normally not a good idea to leave a voice mail message at work for the debtor.

RETURNED CHECK CHARGES

Some creditors impose returned check charges to "encourage" customers not to bounce checks. Bounced check charge fees should be listed on the credit application, which customer(s) should sign. Assuming the application contains a returned check charge clause, creditors should impose those charges uniformly. The credit department must also follow up until the charge is paid.

CHARGING INTEREST ON PAST DUE BALANCES

Creditors must establish a policy concerning charging interest on past due balances. Clearly, creditors may have the right to impose interest or finance charges on the past due balance provided:

(1) The credit application form is completed and signed by the applicant and specifies that interest or finance charges will apply on late payments.

(2) Assuming that any interest charges added are within the legal rates allowed by law—remembering that the maximum rate varies from State to State.

CYCLE BILLING

Cycle billing is a billing system often used in retail operations because it makes the billing process easier to manage, and the collection process easier to control. Using cycle billing, each account is billed once a month of purchases made in the previous thirty days.

The trick is that an equal number of bills are generated each day of the month. This means statements are generated each day rather than once a month when they might overwhelm the computers, the credit department clerks, and the mailroom.

Cycle billing means that account balances come due each day. As a result, the credit and accounts receivable department is not inundated by incoming payments only a few days a month. This also results in payments being recorded more accurately and more quickly.

POLICY REQUIRING CUSTOMERS TO PROVIDE A STREET ADDRESS

Consumers sometimes ask that their monthly bills and other correspondence be sent to a post office box. This has become even more prevalent since private mail box services became popular. From the creditor's perspective, if it becomes necessary to serve legal papers on the debtor, they will need the debtor's physical address. For this reason, creditors normally insist that applicants list a street address listed on their application.

POLICY ON VENUE

The creditor would prefer the venue for any lawsuit to be in the county and state in which they [the creditors] are located. Unfortunately, state laws require creditors to sue consumers in their locale.

CHAPTER 6

Commercial Credit Policies

A policy is a general statement about *why* a company or a department performs a particular task.

A procedure describes *how* a particular task will be performed.

A credit policy manual contains a series of policy statements that describe how the credit department will address specific issues. A credit policy manual describes the work performed by every person at every level in the credit department; it is not limited to routine, clerical tasks. Credit policies provide guidance to credit department personnel about how certain situations should be handled.

While credit policies describe concepts broadly, credit procedures describe in detail how the credit department will or should perform specific activities. Credit procedures provide step by step instructions indicating how tasks are to be performed, and in what order.

THE NEED FOR A CREDIT MANUAL

Some companies have no formal policy and procedure manual. Companies without one often justify their decision in one in the following ways:

- In a cost-benefit analysis, the benefits of putting together a manual do not outweigh the costs.

- The credit manager does not have the time to create the type of document that would prove useful to the company.

- The credit manager does not have the expertise to create a credit policy manual.

99

- Business conditions are changing so rapidly that the credit manager and senior management are convinced that any credit manual written would soon be out of date.

OUT OF DATE CREDIT MANUALS

Many companies have out of date credit manuals, manuals that have not been updated for years. An out of date credit manual is almost worse than no credit manual at all because it may contain incorrect information. One of the best things that can be said about an out of date manual is that at least it is a place for the credit manager to start—when the time comes to update the company's credit manual.

MISSION STATEMENTS AND CREDIT POLICIES

People sometimes mistake a mission statement with policy statements. A mission statement is a single statement focusing on the big picture, and a mission statement makes no reference to how the goals listed are to be achieved. In contrast, a credit manual contains a group of credit policies. In a sense, these credit policies are performance targets for the credit department. The credit procedures provide detailed information about how the credit department can reach the targets.

A mission statement for one credit department is listed below:

"The goal of the credit department is to help the company to achieve its short terms and its long term goals. The credit department is committed to providing superior service to both its internal and external customers. Our objective is to be seen as a facilitator of sales, and a partner in helping to create a profitable, world class company."

Typically, the credit department's mission statement appears at the beginning of the company's credit manual.

IS A POLICIES AND PROCEDURES MANUAL WORTH THE TROUBLE?

There is an ongoing debate about whether a credit manual is worth the time and trouble to create and to update. Two things are almost certain:

(1) A poorly written or out of date credit manual is almost certainly not worth the trouble it took to write it.

(2) An out of date credit manual should not be provided to employees if it contains erroneous information—which it almost certainly does.

There are numerous advantages of having an up-to-date, detailed credit manual. Here are just a few of them:

- A credit manual helps to ensure that everyone in the department performs tasks according to the rules established.

- A current credit manual can be used as a training tool for new employees.

- An up-to-date credit manual can be referred to when dealing with complaints from customers or the sales department.

- Performance can be measured against the policies and procedures.

- A current credit manual makes it more likely that the credit decisions made will be consistent from employee to employee, and from customer to customer.

THE NEED FOR CONSISTENCY

Credit policies should be consistently applied, and this is one of the most important reasons to create a credit manual. It is hard to explain, reconcile or justify inconsistent actions and decisions. There are few things more frustrating for salespeople than inconsistent credit decisions, and when inconsistencies are pointed out they are usually a source of embarrassment for the credit manager and to the credit department.

ADVANTAGES OF HAVING A CREDIT MANUAL

Aside from helping to ensure that the credit department makes consistent decisions, other advantages of a current credit manual include:

- The manual itself can be used as a training tool for new employees both in the credit department and in the sales department

- A credit manual describes how routine situations should be handled—reducing the number of "routine" questions that are asked.

- More importantly, it describes the process for dealing with exceptions or non-routine situations. For example, a credit manual would state who has the authority to override the policies and procedures described in the credit policy manual.

- Individual actions can be evaluated against the procedures described in the manual. If an employee acts in a manner that contradicts the written policies and procedures, the credit manager has the right and an obligation to know why.

SPECIFIC CREDIT POLICIES AND PROCEDURES

As mentioned earlier, a policy gives an overview of a task and explains why it is done. Procedures detail the steps in the process of implementing the policy. It is not uncommon for the credit department to have a series of procedures relating to each individual topic described in the credit manual. Here is an example:

The Policy: The credit department will collect past due balances quickly, professionally, and cost-effectively. The credit department will do everything possible to recover delinquent balances as soon as possible—consistent with all applicable federal and state laws concerning the rights of individual and business debtors.

Behind this policy would be any number of procedures describing how the company will conduct its collection operations. The procedures might detail:

- When collection efforts will commence once an account becomes past due.

- Whether different classes or types of customers will be contacted more or less frequently than others.

- How the dollar value of the past due balances will affect the collection process. Specifically, will customers with large past due balances be called more frequently than customers with small past due balances?

- How international collections efforts will be handled, and if international collections are to be handled differently than domestic collections. For example, will the same collection agency or collection attorney handle both domestic and international collections?

- How and when the salesperson will be asked to assist in the company's collection efforts.

- Whether the company's general counsel will be asked to generate a final demand for payment—even if he or she will not be handling the actual collection process.
- When to use a third party collection agency or collection attorneys
- How frequently to contact delinquent debtors. This specific procedure would answer these questions:

    How soon after an account becomes past due will customers be contacted?

    What form will that contact take?

    If the first contact is not a telephone call, when will the first telephone call be placed?

    What is the schedule for dunning notices?

    When and how can that schedule be changed if it proves to be ineffective?

    At what point will a delinquent account be considered eligible for a credit hold?

    Who will make the final decision about a credit hold?

    When will the salesperson be notified of a credit hold? Who will make that notification? Who else must be notified?

    When and how will the customer be notified of the credit hold?

POLICY ON THIRD PARTY COLLECTIONS

The Policy: Third party collection agencies or collection attorney will be utilized when the credit department determines that an account is uncollectible.

Specific to the use of collection agencies or collection attorneys, specific procedures must address these questions:

- What conditions must be present before the credit manager concludes that a past due balance is uncollectible.
- Who makes the final decision about placing an account for collection?
- What are the minimum qualifications for a collection agency?
- What is the maximum contingent collection fee the creditor company will pay to a third party for its collection services?
- Who selects the collection agency or collection attorney the delinquent account will be placed with?

POLICY ON PROCESSING CREDIT APPLICATIONS FOR NEW ACCOUNTS

The Policy: Consistent with the credit department's effort to manage risk and control delinquencies, the credit department will look for ways to safely release orders pending to new accounts.

One of the procedures typically included in this section would be the procedure for handling and processing credit applications. A procedure for handling credit applications would need to answer these questions:

- Since every applicant is expected to complete and sign the credit application, what happens if the credit application arrives unsigned?

- How will the credit department know if the person signing the credit application has the authority to bind the applicant to the creditor company's terms and conditions?

- What will qualify the signatory as an authorized signer?

- How long does the credit department have to complete its investigation?

- What happens if there is not enough information to make an informed credit decision?

- What happens if the bank reference does not respond?

POLICY CONCERNING RISK MANAGEMENT

The Policy: The credit department will take prudent steps to protect the company's investment in its accounts receivable.

In connection with this policy, specific procedures would describe in detail the following:

- Assigning specific credit granting authority to individuals in the credit department, including the credit manager. [The procedure would typically include a credit granting or credit authority matrix.]

- Specific rules concerning overrides of all policies intended to control credit delinquency, and payment default.

- Procedures for identifying customers as being high risk.

- Specific procedures for managing accounts identified as being high risk.

- Procedures for requesting financial statements from those customers identified as high risk.

- Specific procedures for requiring that certain customers must provide financial statements as a condition of extending open account credit.

- Procedures for evaluating requests for extended dating terms, along with specific procedures when an extended dating request is denied.

- Specific procedures covering the use of personal guarantees and other tools that reduce credit risk including inter corporate guarantees, perfected security interests, consignment agreements, sight and time drafts, and documentary or standby letters of credit.

POLICIES AND PROCEDURES GOVERNING CREDIT TERMS

The Policy: The credit department will make every attempt to offer applicants and customers open account terms. If that is not possible, the credit manager will select the least restrictive credit terms consistent with managing credit risk and controlling account delinquency.

Typical procedures on this topic would address these questions:

- How are applicants for open account terms to be evaluated?

- Who will make the final credit decision about these applicants?

- What information will be considered in the decision making process?

- Who will obtain this information for the credit decision-maker?

- How quickly must the credit investigation process be completed?

- If open account terms are not offered, what are the alternatives from least to most restrictive?

POLICIES AND PROCEDURES GOVERNING DISCOUNT TERMS:

The Policy: A cash discount of 2% of the net invoice amount will be offered to customers that pay bills within fifteen (15) days of the invoice date.

The procedures would describe:

- When discounts are considered earned.

- At how many days past due unearned discounts are to be charged back.

- The steps to be used to collect an unearned cash discount, and who will take those steps.

- Acceptable reasons for paying late and taking the discount anyway.

- If an unearned cash discount is found to be uncollectible, the procedures for writing off the unearned cash discount.

POLICIES AND PROCEDURES GOVERNING OUTSTANDING DEDUCTIONS

The Policy: The goal of the credit department is to address and resolve customer disputes and deductions as quickly as possible.

Specific procedures describing the process of addressing and resolving deductions and disputes quickly would include:

- A policy of neutrality. If the facts indicate that a credit is due, the credit department must insist that the appropriate person or department issue the credit promptly.

- If the information gathered shows the deduction was taken in error, the credit department will demand payment and follow up to make certain the deduction is repaid.

- The procedures will indicate when a credit hold may be used to force a customer to accept their responsibility to repay deductions taken in error.

- The procedure should make it clear to everyone in the credit department that credit holds may not be used while there is a legitimate dispute about the status of a disputed or deducted balance due.

POLICY ON MAINTAINING CURRENT CREDIT FILES ON ACTIVE ACCOUNTS.

The Policy: In order to manage credit risk, the credit files on all active accounts are to be updated at least once a year.

Specific procedures would describe:

- Under what circumstances the account will be updated more frequently that once a year.

- The actions that constitute an update.

- What reports are to be obtained

- Who can initiate an update?

- The events that might trigger such a request for an update, including:

  News of financial problems.

  A general deterioration in the customer's financial condition.

  Slow payments to the creditor company itself, or slow payment being reported by other unsecured trade creditors.

  The departure of key executive managers from the debtor company.

Lawsuits filed or tax liens recorded against the debtor.

A change in ownership or control.

The customer's refusal to address outstanding deductions.

POLICIES AND PROCEDURES GOVERNING WHEN AN ACCOUNT IS REFERRED TO THE CREDIT MANAGER

The Policy: Accounts may be referred to the credit manager for review at any time. Accounts must be referred to the credit manager when: (a) there is serious deterioration in payments, (b) the account is seriously past due or (c) facts are revealed that indicate the account must be considered high risk.

Supporting this policy would be specific procedures describing when an account must be referred to the credit manager. Specific situations would include:

- When account becomes seriously past due.
- When a customer makes and then breaks one or more specific payment commitments.
- When an account bounces a check.
- When the customer ignores two or more collection calls and messages.
- When a particular account's DSO has increased by more than 10 days in the last 12 months.

Without these specific rules, inexperienced credit personnel will tend to hold onto problems longer than they should—making collection less likely.

POLICY AND PROCEDURES REGARDING THE USE OF THIRD PARTY COLLECTORS

The Policy: When necessary, the credit department will refer accounts to a third party collection agency or collection attorney. The third party selected will be the one that is expected to be the most cost-effective in collecting the past due balance.

The detailed procedures will deal with the following subjects:
- When an account can be placed for collection.
- When a delinquent account should be placed for collection.
- When a customer in default on payment must be placed for collection.

- A decision matrix for selecting a collection agency vs. a collection attorney.

THE POLICY ON NOTIFYING CUSTOMERS OF A CREDIT HOLD OR OTHER ADVERSE ACTION

The Policy: Unless there is a compelling reason not to do so, the credit department shall notify a customer promptly about an adverse action—such as an order hold.

Since the adverse actions the credit department takes are intended to force the customer to recognize and to address a problem, it does no good for the credit manager to keep this information a secret from the customer.

The procedures to carry this out would include detailed answers to all of the following questions:

- Who should notify the customer of the adverse action?
- Should the notification be made in writing or by telephone?
- Should more than one person in the debtor company be notified of the adverse decision?
- If the customer is notified by telephone, should the credit department follow up with written confirmation of the decision?
- When and how should the salesperson be notified?
- How should the notification process be documented for the file?

THE POLICY ON USING SALESPEOPLE IN THE ROLE OF A COLLECTOR

The Policy. On rare occasions, it may be necessary and appropriate to use salespeople to assist in collections, but not in the role of a collector. This is not to suggest that the salesperson should refuse to collect a check if it is offered to them. Instead, the salesperson can act as a intermediary and facilitator between the credit manager and the buyer's chief accountant, its chief financial officer or its chief executive officer.

Using salespeople in collections is controversial. The procedures would detail how and when salespeople could be used in this role. The procedures would describe:

- How the salesperson should explore the question of whether or not the customer feels they have any legitimate excuse for delaying payment.

- How salespeople can leverage their relationship with the buyer to gain concessions from the customer's accounts payable department.
- Why it is important for the salesperson not to negotiate with the customer directly. [Hint: The salesperson is not trained in this area of negotiating repayment of delinquent accounts receivable balances].

Unfortunately, some salespeople refuse to offer this assistance to the credit department. They feel that it tends to confuse the relationship between the salesperson and purchasing agent, and that a salesperson's primary responsibility to sell.

Probably the biggest help the salesperson can be to the credit department is by encouraging the customer to communicate with the credit department about the problem.

POLICY AND PROCEDURES GOVERNING FINAL DEMANDS

The Policy: Prior to placing an account for collection, a final demand for payment will be sent to the customer.

The specific procedures would describe the steps to be taken to ensure that at final demand is sent, received, and acknowledged. A final demand letter should:

- Be sent by certified mail,
- With a copy to the President or owner of the company
- With another copy to any guarantors.

POLICY ON PLACING DELINQUENT ACCOUNTS INTO INVOLUNTARY BANKRUPTCY

The Policy. Placing a delinquent customer into involuntary bankruptcy proceedings is a final collection option. It will only be considered in a situation in which there is good reason to believe that the debtor is committing fraud, or that insiders are receiving preferential transfers and payments, if management is incompetent, or when other trade creditors are being paid but you are not.

Choosing to place a delinquent debtor into involuntary bankruptcy is a drastic step. Specific procedures would address all of the following:

- Approvals necessary from senior management to take this step.

- A review of all of the facts with the company's counsel to confirm that the action is legal, and appropriate.

- Contacting other creditors to participate in the involuntary bankruptcy as soliciting creditors.

Occasionally, the threat of an involuntary filing will prompt the debtor to make some sort of payment proposal.

POLICY ON ORDERING PROOF OF DELIVERY ON PAST DUE INVOICES

The Policy: Recognizing that there is a specific time line or deadline for ordering proof of delivery, and recognizing that that older a past due invoice becomes the more likely it is that the company will need to prove delivery, the company will order proof of delivery well ahead of the deadline imposed by the shipper.

The procedure would describe the following:

- Who is responsible for obtaining proof of delivery?

- How is the proof of delivery to be ordered?

- At what point ordering proof of delivery becomes mandatory.

- Steps in tracking pending proof of delivery requests.

- How proof of delivery, once received is to be stored.

RESPONDING APPROPRIATELY TO NSF CHECKS

The Policy: NSF checks present significant risk of a bad debt loss. The credit department will work closely with the customer to try to make certain the check clears and a bad debt write off does not result from the NSF check.

Specific procedures necessary to mitigate risk would include:

- Procedures for contacting the customer to discuss the NSF check.

- Steps in contacting the seller's bank and asking the bank to redeposit the check.

Creditors should also track the number of NSF checks received from any individual customer over time. There is no hard and fast rule, but two or more NSF checks in less than 12 months is a strong indicator that the customer is in serious financial trouble and needs to be evaluated carefully.

- Updating the credit file.
- Placing the account on credit hold.
- Assuming that the check does clear, reevaluating the account before making additional shipments on open account credit terms.

POLICY FOR HANDLING RETURNED CHECKS:

The Policy: If an NSF check is deposited a second time and does not clear, the risk of a bad debt loss is high enough to justify actions that may damage the goodwill that existed between the customer and the seller up until that point.

Specific procedures would address the following issues:

- The need to contact the customer and demand an immediate replacement of the dishonored check with a money order, a cashier's check or a wire transfer payment.
- The procedure for referring the matter to an attorney if the debtor does not replace the check with clear funds.

WHEN TO PLACE AN ACCOUNT FOR COLLECTION

The Policy: Given the importance of the decision and its implications, no customer account shall be placed for collection or referred to an attorney without written approval from the Credit Manager and the CFO. No account may be placed for collection until all other options for collection have been tried and failed, or evaluated and rejected.

POLICY ON SELLING ON OPEN ACCOUNT TERMS TO A DEBTOR IN POSSESSION

The Policy: Recognizing that the majority of Chapter 11 business reorganizations fail resulting in the liquidation of the assets of the company, credit managers will exercise caution, and good judgment in evaluating a debtor in possession for open account terms.

Specific procedures will describe in detail the following topics:

- How to evaluate the viability of a debtor in possession.
- Who in senior management would need to approve sales to a DIP on open account terms?

- How the DIP will be monitored to determine if they remain credit-worthy.

POLICY ON MITIGATING CREDIT RISK IN THE EVENT OF A BANKRUPTCY FILING

The Policy: The credit manager will do everything possible to mitigate risk once a customer has filed for bankruptcy protection owing the creditor company money.

There are a number of standard procedures used to mitigate risk after a bankruptcy filing, including these:

- Request return of product shipped to the debtor company within the "reclamation period" as provided for in the US bankruptcy code.

- Print an account statement

- Reprint all open invoices, credits and debits; and orders proof of delivery on each open invoices.

- If the creditor has a payment guaranty from a third party, the creditor must inform the guarantor of the bankruptcy and demand payment against the guaranty.

POLICY ON FILING PROOF OF CLAIM FORMS IN BANKRUPTCY CASES

The Policy: The credit manager will complete a Proof of Claim form as soon as practical after it is received in order to safeguard the company's right to payment from the debtor.

Specific procedures for this policy include:

- The credit manager must confirm the Court received and recorded the proof of claim by requesting that the Clerk stamp and return a duplicate copy of the Proof of Claim.

- Copies of all relevant supporting documentation should accompany the Proof of Claim filing.

POLICY CONCERNING DOCUMENTING POLICY EXCEPTION

The Policy: From time to time, credit manager must make on-the-spot decisions that violated company policy. Recognizing the importance of following the company's policies and procedures, the credit manager must carefully document the reason for these decisions—and must be prepared to justify their decision.

The procedures would explain:

- How, where and in how much detail as is required of you the justification for the decision would be documented, and
- Who would be responsible for documenting that decision?

POLICY FOR DOCUMENTING MANAGEMENT OVERRIDES

From time to time, senior management will override the decisions made by the credit manager—often in the customer's favor in the form of a release of an order pending. Credit managers are expected to document management overrides.

The procedures for documenting senior management overrides would include:

- A description of what information to include in the report about the management override.

SOLVING THE PROBLEM, NOT THE SYMPTOM

There is an old saying: "Give a man a fish and you will feed him for the day. Teach a man to fish and you will feed him for life." Many credit managers address deduction problems by treating the symptoms rather than looking at curing the underlying problem. The reason is simple: It is much easier to address a specific and easily recognized problem [such as a pricing error on an invoice] than it is for the credit manager to discover the root cause of the problem and to address and resolve that problem. Often, the credit manager is too busy to look for the root causes of problems or believes that the problems are beyond his or her ability to address and resolve.

Unfortunately, this thinking leads the credit department in circles. The other departments in the company are often able to create far more problems than the credit department can address at one time. Each of these problems is a built in excuse for the customer to delay payment. Addressing the problem without addressing and resolving the root causes means job security for whoever must clean up the mess—but in the long term it is more cost efficient to address and resolve the underlying problems.

SUMMARY

The credit department should have a policy and accompanying procedures for virtually every situation that the credit department finds itself involved in. Credit policies and procedures help the credit department staff to focus their efforts and attention on problems in a logical, methodical, and organized manner. As a result, the credit department is more effective and efficient.

CHAPTER 7

SAMPLE CREDIT POLICY MANUAL

Credit policy manuals are essential to any well-managed credit department. Credit policy manuals provide both general guidelines [policies] and specific instructions [procedures] which indicate how work in the credit department is to be performed.

Often, there is a variance between the stated policies and the actual practices followed by the credit department. This is an indication that either:

(1) the practices need to be changed to conform to the policies, or

(2) that the policies and procedures need to be updated to keep up with current practices.

Credit policies should be in writing. A written credit policy can be used as a training tool, and as a reference guide. Written credit policies make it easier to discipline employees who violate these policies. Experience and common sense hold that it is almost impossible to hold an employee accountable for a variance from an established policy or procedure if that process is not in writing. Therefore, a written credit policy tends to prevent errors, and allows the credit manager to hold those who knowingly violate the company's credit policies and procedures accountable for their actions. Error reduction results in faster collections and fewer bad debt losses.

POLICY AND PRACTICE

It is almost useless to have a credit department policy and procedures manual that is out-of-date. An outdated policy will result in and can be characterized by variances between the written rules and the actual practices of the department. An outdated credit manual cannot be used as a training tool or as a reference guide, and credit managers cannot benchmark or evaluate performance against standards of care and of performance if those standards are wrong.

A well-written credit manual will serve as a training tool for new employees, as a reference guide for inexperienced employees, and as a resource to help ensure consistency of decisions within the credit department. From the perspective of senior management, a current credit policy means that if the credit manager leaves for any reason the credit department will be able to continue for a period of time with limited disruption. Even if there were no other value to creating a credit manual, senior management would be well advised to require the credit manual be updated at least once a year—and ideally more frequently. There are both advantages and disadvantages of documenting changes as they occur rather than doing periodic updates to the manual, but the more current the manual is the more of a resource it is to the company and to the department.

POLICY EXCEPTIONS

A credit policy manual should explain what exceptions could be made from the established policies, and it will indicate who in the credit department is authorized to approve such exceptions. For example, a common scenario is one in which an applicant or an established customer requests extended dating. The manual will list the creditor's standard terms of sale and should also clearly state who in the department is authorized to make this type of exception, and under what conditions.

In some companies, no one in the credit department is authorized to offer extended dating. In these companies, exceptions of this type are referred to senior management. In companies in which the credit manager has been delegated the authority to approve extended dating, there may be specific limitations on this authority. The manual might also include documentation requirements and qualification requirements for extended dating requests.

By documenting standard policies and then by specifying who may override these policies, the credit manager and the company have the ability to hold anyone in the credit department who violates these rules accountable for their inappropriate behavior.

CREDIT GRANTING AUTHORITY

Credit granting authority refers to the authority to offer open account terms up to a specific credit limit, to establish terms of sale, to modify the terms of sale or the credit limit, and the authority to release orders pending. It is essential that every person in the credit department be assigned a specific credit dollar authority and be certain of what their authority level is. In some cases, an individual's credit granting authority may be zero—and that information should be documented in the manual.

Any number of problems can be avoided if the credit manager takes the time to evaluate each employee of the credit department and delegate specific credit granting authority based on their level of experience and skill. Failure to do so will almost certainly lead to preventable mistakes.

THE OBJECTIVES OF A POLICIES AND PROCEDURES MANUAL

The objective of having a current credit manual is to provide guidance and direction to the credit manager and the credit department staff in the performance of their day-to-day duties. Without a written credit policy and procedures manual all of the following outcomes are likely:

- Mistakes made in the past are likely to be repeated.

- Limited corporate resources are likely to be wasted, and unnecessary and preventable bad debt losses are likely to be incurred.

- Collection of past due balances will not be done as quickly or as efficiently as it otherwise would be.

- Applicants that should be offered open account credit terms would be denied credit, and customers whose credit limits should have been increased will not receive that increase.

HOW VERSUS WHY

A well-written credit manual will not simply describe how a particular task is to be performed [procedures], it will also explain why the credit department performs certain tasks. Credit department employees should be told how and why a certain task is performed in a certain way. Unless credit department personnel understand why certain tasks are performed in certain ways, it is difficult for them to:

- Explain the credit department's actions to decisions to others including salespeople and customers

- Make recommendations that would improve the process

- Feel that they are a valuable part of the process, and that their contributions and their ideas are valued by the credit manager and by the company.

DOCUMENTING PROCESSES

There is an old adage that a picture is worth a thousand words. Many of the processes the credit department is involved in are complex. Whenever necessary and appropriate, the credit policy manual should include flowcharts or other diagrams to assist the reader in visualizing and understanding the process being described. For example, the process of describing in a narrative form which orders end up on credit referral is complex. A flowchart describing the process is simple. The order approval flowchart would look something like this:

AUTOMATED ORDER APPROVAL PROCESS

The order is entered.

System software evaluates the order to determine if it can be released based on criteria established by the credit department.

Can the order be released?

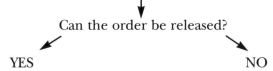

YES

NO

Order bypasses credit and continues until it is picked, packed and shipped.

The order is forwarded to the credit department for review and approval.

OK to release the order?

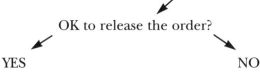

YES

NO

The order is picked, packed and shipped.

The credit manager tries to qualify the pending order for release.

Is the order qualified?

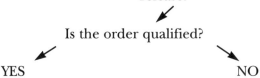

YES

NO

The order is picked, packed shipped.

The order remains on hold until it is approved for release by the credit manager.

POLICY AND OBJECTIVES

The objectives of the corporation have a dramatic impact on the policies of the credit department. The credit department's policies and procedures should be modified when necessary to keep pace with changing corporate objectives, and changing competitive realities in the marketplace, and with changing corporate goals and objectives.

For example, if demand for the company's products surges to the point that the company cannot fill all of the orders that its receives, then the credit department should be more selective in determining which accounts are acceptable credit risks, and which now pose an unacceptably high risk of delinquency or payment default. When demand for a company's goods and services exceeds the company's ability to fulfill the orders it receives the credit department has to become more selective about which accounts are approved for credit. If the credit department does not make this adjustment and sales are made to a high-risk account, then the credit manager may be called upon to explain or justify his or her credit decision-making process in light of the new reality.

More frequently, the business environment in which a company operates has become so competitive that the credit department must be willing to accept more credit risk simply to help the company to maintain its market share.

Another common scenario is one in which a company has decided on an aggressive growth strategy. To accommodate aggressive growth in either sales volume or market share the credit department's policies and procedures are likely to need to be liberalized.

FLUCTUATING DEMAND

A rapidly changing competitive environment can have a dramatic impact on the business and require that the credit department quickly change certain policies and procedures. For example, if a creditor is in the high technology sector and one of their biggest selling products is about to be supplanted by a product that is cheaper, faster and more reliable, then the company would probably want its credit manager to develop more liberal credit policies in order to help "blow out" any remaining inventory of the product in questions before the market for that product disappears.

Credit managers that are slow to react to changing market conditions may be characterized by sales management and/or senior management as out of touch, insensitive, unrealistic and/or uninformed. This is not intended to suggest that the credit manager tries to anticipate changes in the marketplace and act proactively, or that the credit manager should make decisions about significant changes in the credit policy [such as a decision to liberalize the credit policy] unilaterally. Instead, the credit manager and his or her manager should meet to review any significant changes to credit policy. A consensus should be reached before any action is implemented within the credit department, and the credit manager should be certain to document the meeting and its outcome.

The credit manager is often required to perform a balancing act. By liberalizing the credit terms, the credit manager will assist the company to attract more customers and sell more products. At the same time, more liberal credit granting policies and procedures will almost certainly result in more delinquencies and higher bad debt losses. This is specifically why the credit manager must not unilaterally liberalize credit policies, and should take the time to document any agreement made with senior management to do so. Unfortunately, some senior managers occasionally have selective memory loss when it comes to remembering that they instructed their credit manager to liberalize credit policies.

TYPE OF MERCHANDISE

Clearly, the type of merchandise that the company sells will have an impact on credit policy formation. For example, customers buying seasonal products normally ask for and receive extended or seasonal dating. For example, companies selling summer clothing tend to ship the merchandise in the spring [so that it is in the retail stores by the time customers become interested in buying summer clothes] but invoices tend not to come due until mid summer or even later. On the other hand, companies that sell perishable goods tend to offer short dating terms to their customers. The broad objective behind establishing credit policies is to provide the customer with a form of short-term and interest free financing. If the buyer is expected to turn the inventory in question into cash quickly [as one would expect with the sale of perishable goods] then the credit manager should expect payment relatively quickly. On the other hand, if the cycle of converting inventory into collected sales tends to be longer then the seller will be asked to provide longer dating.

CREDIT POLICY IS IMPACTED BY PROFIT MARGINS

Companies selling high margin merchandise tend to have more liberal credit policies than companies with low profit margins. The reason is fairly straightforward: All things being equal, the management and stockholders of a company selling goods or services with a high profit margin are more willing to accept additional credit risk in order to generate additional sales than are companies with lower profit margins.

Companies that sell to a large number of customers in small dollar volumes tend to have more liberal credit policies than companies that sell to a small number of customers in large dollar volumes. Again, the logic is fairly straightforward: Selling to a limited number of high dollar volume accounts means that a single customer default or bankruptcy could have a serious effect on the seller's profitability. On the other hand, the failure of any single company buying in relatively small dollar volume will be of limited concern to executive management and shareholders. Therefore, all things being equal the credit manager selling to numerous small accounts will be expected to establish relatively more liberal credit terms than a company with a small number of customers.

LEGAL RESTRAINTS

Legal restrictions and restraints govern many aspects of the credit department's operations. For example, it is illegal for the credit department to make any agreement with a competitor about how each company will treat a common customer. Legal restraints on the actions and behaviors of the credit department should be explained in sufficient detail in the credit policies and procedures manual that the company's position about violation of these laws is clear and unambiguous. Legal matters that should be detailed in the credit manual include:

- Antitrust issues. Specifically the credit department's commitment to observe the letter and the spirit of federal and state antitrust laws.

- Rules against defamation of a customer either orally or in writing. Examples should be given of what can and cannot be said. Since the greatest risk involves the process of responding to credit inquiries, companies should seriously consider requiring that all such inquiries be made and answered in writing.

- Contract law, and specifically the issues and problems raised for the credit department relating to offer and acceptance should be included in the credit manual. For example, if a customer issues a purchase order with the wrong price and the seller does not challenge the incorrect pricing, is the P.O. an offer and the creditor's shipment an acceptance creating the basic elements of a contract?

- The Equal Credit Opportunity Act, and the implications of this act on the actions of the credit department relating to both consumer and commercial credit applicants and customers.

FINANCIAL STRENGTH AND CREDIT POLICY

One of the most important factors for the credit manager to consider when developing or updating the company's credit policy is the financial condition of their employer. For example, a company that has liquidity problems and is unable to borrow from its bank to cover any short-term cash flow problems will probably need a fairly restrictive credit policy. A liberal credit policy would tend to attract slower paying customers, and a high DSO would put additional strain on the company's already strained cash position.

LOAN COVENANTS AND CREDIT POLICIES

When companies borrow money from their banks, they sign written contracts that contain specific terms and conditions governing those loans that the borrower agrees to adhere to. Many loan covenants deal with the financial performance of the borrower. When loan covenant violation exists, the bank can call the note and demand payment in full.

Certain aspects of the credit department's performance are sometimes included in loan covenants. For example, a loan covenant might state that DSO might not increase beyond 60 days. Another covenant might state that invoices over a certain number of days past due [for example balances over 60 days past due] will not count toward the calculation of the value of the borrower's collateral. Since borrowers are required under most loan agreements to pledge accounts receivable to the bank as collateral, and since accounts receivable is typically a borrower's largest or second largest tangible asset, failure to keep the accounts receivable relatively current may result in problem with the bank.

Consequently, whatever credit policies and procedures the credit department would develop, the credit manager must also be cognizant of the bank's requirements. To the extent that the bank's collateral requirements and loan covenants are important to the company, the credit manager may need to adjust credit policies and procedures to make certain that the company meets the bank loan covenants.

FORMULATING A CREDIT POLICY

The first thing the credit manager needs to keep in mind when formulating a credit policy is that the credit policy does not exist in a vacuum. Instead, it exists as a part of [and not apart from] the company as a whole. It is important that the credit department's policies and procedures fit well with the needs and expectations of the rest of the organization - but only to the extent that such accommodations do not interfere with the primary mission or function of the credit department, which is to safeguard the company's investment in its accounts receivable asset.

PRESENTING THE CREDIT POLICY

As soon as the credit manager is satisfied with his or her draft of the credit manual, the manual should be offered up for comments and criticism. The best way to introduce a new credit policy and procedure manual is to meet with the appropriate department heads, give those managers a copy of the manual and invite them review it, and then schedule a follow up meeting to discuss their questions, comments, and concerns.

Given the dynamics of group interaction, it is often appropriate to meet with key managers after that introductory meeting and before the follow up meeting to get direct input on the aspects of the policy that they would like to see changed. What the credit manager does not want to do is to allow a follow up meeting in which the proposed policy is dissected by the department heads. Unfortunately, these meetings tend to end badly with some attendees of the group become hypercritical about the proposed credit manual.

The goal of this peer review process is to gain consensus among the managers. The proposed policy need not be perfect, and the credit manager would be naive to expect unanimity within any group of department managers invited to review their credit manual.

During the individual or group meetings, the credit manager should avoid arguing for his or her position. Formulating a workable credit policy is a process of give and take. The credit manager should present his or her position succinctly and then wait for other members' reactions and comments. Those comments should be carefully considered and the necessary adjustments made.However, the credit manager should not change a policy simply to avoid an argument or a conflict. Credit managers should yield and modify their credit policies in light of objections that are logical, pragmatic, and fit with the overall needs of the company. When disagreements occur, the credit manager should try to involve other meeting participants. The more active participants in this meeting, the greater the chance that a better, more creative solution to a problem or a dispute will be found.

SAMPLE CREDIT POLICY

(1) Credit Department Overview

The credit department performs all credit functions for the company. The credit policies and procedures are intended to ensure that credit functions are performed properly and consistently. The primary function of the credit department is to safeguard the company's investment in accounts receivable by minimizing bad debt losses through the control of credit risk and by timely collections of past due balances.

(10) Reporting Relationships

The credit department supports the sales activities of the company, but is not accountable to the sales department or to sales management [since this would involve a conflict of interest]. The credit manager reports to the Chief Financial Officer. Only the CFO or the company President has the authority to overrule the credit manager's decision. The credit manager will provide senior management with periodic reports [at least once a month] outlining the status of the accounts receivable and the adequacy of the allowance for doubtful accounts.

(20) The Credit Department's Goals

The goals of the credit department is to maximize sales; minimize bad debt losses; support the sales department in its efforts to maintain and to grow the business; and in a broader context to support the short and long term goals of the company.

(30) Collection of Outstanding Receivables

The credit department performs a key role for the company—it completes the sale by collecting the accounts receivable balance created when sales are made on open account credit terms. The goal of the credit department is to collect past due balances as quickly as possible with as little damage to customer loyalty and to customer goodwill.

The credit department recognizes that it will sometimes be necessary to hold orders in order to "encourage" customers to address past due invoices. Credit holds will be used a last resort, and the credit manager must approve all credit holds. The credit department will try to give the sales department as much advance notice of pending credit hold as possible.

(40) The Credit–Sales Relationship

The credit department will attempt to maintain close working relationships with the sales department, as well as with the operations, order entry and the shipping departments in order to maximize the effectiveness of the company in meeting customer expectations relating to delivery of goods or services. Recognizing the important of salespeople as liaisons between sales and credit, the credit manager will take every opportunity to strengthen that relationship. The credit manager will keep the salesperson [and sales management] informed about the status of problem accounts.

The credit department will attempt to give the sales department as much advance notice as possible about potential problems and pending credit holds. The credit department welcomes the assistance of the salesperson and of sales management in helping to secure payment and resolve disputes. However, the ultimate responsibility for collection rests with the credit manage. The credit manager will have the final decision on the status of any account or the status of any order on credit hold.

(50) Credit and Cash Application

The credit department is responsible for providing instructions and direction to the cash application department to ensure that cash is applied properly, and that deductions and repayments are recorded correctly. Responsibility for resolving disputes and deductions taken by customers remains with the credit department.

Cash must be applied exactly as directed by the customer. Under no circumstances will payments be applied to the oldest balance due on an account without specific written approval of the customer. If no remittance advice is received, the credit department will contact the customer and arrange for the remittance advice to be sent as quickly as possible.

(60) The Credit Department's Function

The credit and collection department is responsible for the extension of credit to and the collection from all accounts owing money to the company. The credit and collection manager will establish credit terms and a credit limit for each account using his or her judgment and experience, and consistent with the specific credit granting authority delegated by senior management.

The credit department's goal is to minimizing bad debt losses—not to eliminate bad debt losses. To eliminate bad debt losses would require the credit manager to refuse to extend credit to customers that would normally be considered creditworthy.

Another goal of the credit department is to collect past due balances as quickly as possible with a minimum amount of disruption to the business relationship between the buyer and the creditor company as possible. The credit department will use progressively more direct and assertive methods to collect a past due balance recognizing that statistically the further past due an account becomes the less likely the creditor will ever receive payment.

(70) *Increasing Sales*

Consistent with the goal of minimizing bad debt losses and controlling delinquencies, the credit department will look for ways to assist the sales department in increase sales safely. In this regard, the credit department will consider every option before denying customer or applicant open account credit terms and/or the credit limit the customer has requested.

(80) *Prequalifying Credit Limits*

The credit department will work proactively with the sales department to prequalify new accounts and to qualify active customers for larger credit limits. To this end, the credit department will notify each salesperson of each of their customers' credit limits. The credit department will encourage the salesperson to notify them anytime a customer is likely to require a larger credit limit than the one assigned to it.

(90) *Credit Investigation—New Accounts*

Credit decisions on new accounts are to be based on factual information received through the credit investigation process. All applicants offered open account credit terms must meet the established credit standards. Credit investigations will be conducted in a professional and ethical manner. The company's credit investigator will obtain the trade clearance or credit bureau reports as ordered by the credit manager, and will contact bank and trade references when requested to do so.

(100) *Signed Credit Applications*

A credit application is a contract between the applicant and the creditor - not simply a method of gathering information about an applicant. Since the application form is a contract, it must be signed in order to be enforceable. The salesperson is normally responsible for delivering credit applications to applicants, and for making certain it is signed by a person with the authority to bind the applicant to the terms and conditions listed on the application.

Credit application [contracts] received without signature should be returned for signature. The credit application contract will indicate the venue for litigation in the event of a dispute. The credit application will provide for interest on the outstanding debt. The credit application should indicate that if litigation were ever necessary that the loser must agree to pay the winner's reasonable legal or collection costs. The credit application should

126

state the terms of sale, and that interest will be charged on delinquent balances.

(110) Initial Credit Investigations

A credit investigation will be conducted before a decision to extend credit is made. Every effort will be made to obtain as much accurate information as possible as quickly as possible in order to develop a profile of the applicant. The credit manager will use this information to establish an appropriate credit limit and terms of sale.

The credit manager will make a decision as soon as there is sufficient information to do so. If the credit department is unable to gather sufficient information to make a credit decision, or if the information gathered is contradictory, then the credit manager will contact the applicant and request additional information or documentation.

Ideally, the sales department will secure a signed and complete credit application before an order is ever received. The employee assigned to do so will obtain:

- a credit bureau report
- trade reference checks
- a bank reference check
- any other reports or information required by the credit manager

Each of these documents should be submitted to the credit manager in a credit file along with the application. Within 72 hours of receipt of the signed application, the application and all of the information gathered in the credit investigation process will be forwarded to the credit manager for review.

(120) Rejecting an Applicant

The credit manager is looking for a reason to extend credit to an applicant, and not for an excuse not to do so. If there is sufficient information and the applicant is determined not to be creditworthy then the applicant will be given the opportunity to purchase goods on terms other than open account. Other acceptable terms include: Letter of Credit, Cash on Delivery, Cash in Advance or on flooring.

(130) Confidential Credit Information

Everything in the credit file is considered Confidential and should remain that way. Credit files should not be reviewed by anyone outside of the credit department. If it becomes necessary to discuss the credit application with the customer, particularly in connection with a decision to refuse to grant open account credit terms, the credit manager will respect the company's obligation not to reveal which of the applicants trade references were contacted and what if anything was said by them about the company under review.

The credit manager will not discuss the contents of the applicant's credit bureau report or trade clearance report. If a request is received for a written explanation of the decision to deny credit, a written explanation that does not reveal confidential information will be provided. After the credit manager has completed their review of the credit application and related documents and a decision about the applicant is made, the credit file will remain in the care, custody and control of the credit department.

(140) Order Processing

It is essential that orders on credit referral be reviewed promptly, and that orders for customers deemed creditworthy be released as quickly as possible. The credit department will make order releases its top priority. Specifically, the credit department should:

- Put order releases ahead of all other credit functions.
- Look for reasons to release orders, not for excuses to hold them.
- Use cross training to make certain as many employees as possible are able to release orders.
- Eliminate bureaucratic rules that prevent credit decisions from being made quickly.
- Work proactively with the sales department to qualify customers for larger credit limits before orders are received which would place the customer over the established credit limit.

(150) Credit Decisions

Credit decisions about new accounts will be based on information received from and through the credit investigation process. Every credit decision must be based on factual information. Credit decisions about active customers will be based on payment history, credit experience with other creditors, credit bureau reports, and when applicable on financial statement analysis and interpretation.

The credit manager will ensure that anyone delegated the authority to make credit decisions, and in particular decisions about whether to release or to hold orders has the necessary skill, experience and training to make proper decisions. The credit manager must also make certain that anyone in this position that is not comfortable about releasing an order understands that they are under no obligation to do so, and that any such issue should be referred to the credit manager.

(160) Credit Limits

The credit manager will try to offer customers the credit limits they require. At their sole discretion, the credit manager may change a customer's credit limit [or credit terms] at any time, with or without prior notice to the customer or to the salesperson. Recognizing that serious problems may occur if and when a customer's credit limit is reduced or withdrawn, the credit manager will not make such decisions arbitrarily—and the credit manager will document these reasons in the credit file for future reference.

For reasons of confidentiality, the credit manager may not be able to provide the salesperson or the customer with a specific reason for a decision to reduce or withdraw a credit limit. In addition, because credit decisions are based on objective as well as subjective information it may not be possible to quantify every decision made by the credit department relative to credit limit increases or decreases.

(170) Customer Master File Maintenance

A specific form, the Customer Master Maintenance Form, shall be used to initiate all changes to customer master information. Some of the more important changes to the customer master file include:

- Changes to the credit limit
- Changes to terms of sale
- Changes to customer billing address
- Changes to the salesperson assigned to the account

Because of the importance of the customer master file, the credit manager must approve all changes to the customer master.

(180) Legal Compliance

Recognizing that applicants for credit are protected by federal and state law against discrimination in credit granting, the credit department will establish and follow policies which forbid discrimination against applicants based on age, race, creed, national origin, sex or sexual preference.

Recognizing that federal laws prohibit a variety of anti-competitive practices including price fixing, and price discrimination, credit department personnel will be trained on how to conduct themselves so that none of these federal statutes are broken:

- The Equal Credit Opportunity Act
- The Fair Credit Billing Act
- The Fair Debt Collection Practices Act
- The Truth in Lending Act

In addition, the credit department will maintain a list of all applicable state credit protection laws in the state(s) in which it does business to be certain that its actions comply with those statutes.

(190) Tax Status

In states in which the company has tax nexus, the credit department will be responsible for making certain that a resale certificate is obtained from all applicants located in those states. If the applicant is unable to provide a completed, signed and dated resale certificate then the account will be coded as taxable and tax will be charged until and unless the applicant proves its tax exempt status.

(200) Credit Interchange

The credit department will exchange credit information regarding accounts in a professional and businesslike manner, and for legitimate business purposes. Special care will be taken when providing credit information to or soliciting credit information from competitors. At no time will opinions about the customer be shared, and in particular no opinions will be offered or sought as to a customer's character, morals or business ethics.

(210) Credits and Debits

Credits and debits represent adjustments to a customer's accounts receivable balance. It is essential that debits and credits be processed with care, and in a timely manner. Anyone may initiate a request for a debit or credit—but typically such requests will come from the cash application group, sales or the credit department. Documentation supporting the request must be attached to the debit or credit adjustment form and forwarded to the Controller for approval. Recognizing the inherent conflict of interest, the credit department may not input a debit or credit without approval from the Controller.

(220) Establishing Credit Limits and Terms

The credit manager will establish a specific credit limit and credit terms for each applicant. Either the terms of sale or the credit limit may be changed at any time at the discretion of the credit manager—based on his or her skill and experience.

New customers will be required to pay in advance, or on delivery, until the credit department has received a signed credit application, reviewed the information contained in that application, and made a decision about offering open account terms.

Depending on the credit limit and terms requested, the customer may be required to submit:

- A credit application and two years of financial statements.
- A resale certificate for each state the creditor is asked to ship to.
- Additional trade references.
- A personal guarantee.
- An inter-corporate guarantee.
- A pledge of security.
- A letter of credit [standby, or documentary].

(230) Maintaining Credit Files

In order to protect the company's investment in its accounts receivable asset, a periodic review of each customer's creditworthiness is essential. These reviews will be conducted in accordance with a specific review schedule based on:

- the credit limit requested
- an assessment of the risk associated with the applicant

The credit manager or his or her appointee must approve any order received that involves an extension of credit above the established credit limit. Any such exception may necessitate the credit file being updated. In addition, at the first sign that a customer may be in financial distress, the credit file should be updated and the account should be reviewed even more frequently.

The actual approval process will be conducted in accordance with the credit approval matrix approved by executive management. Every person in the credit department with authority to approve open account terms and to release orders [including the credit manager] will be assigned a specific limit to that authority.

(240) Financial Statement Analysis

Financial statements will not be required from every customer, however the credit department will take advantage of any opportunity to receive and review a customer's financial statements. Ideally, the credit department will receive the customer's Balance Sheet, Income Statement and Cash Flow

Statement. For the purpose of trend analysis, the credit manager will request reports from two accounting periods.

When financial information is obtained, it will be evaluated in the areas of (a) liquidity, (b) financial leverage (c) profitability, and (d) efficiency. The credit department will use ratio and trend analysis to evaluate the financial strengths and weaknesses of the company under review. In evaluating a customer's financial condition, the credit manager will balance the positive and the negative aspects of the financial statement in arriving at a composite picture of the customer's financial condition as it relates to the company's short term liquidity and long term solvency.

A holistic approach will be taken to financial statement analysis recognizing that every company's financial statements typically reveal both strengths and weaknesses.

(250) Terms other that Open Account

Standard payment terms are Net 30 days from the date of invoice. A cash discount of 1% will be offered if payment is received within 15 days of the invoice date. If, at the sole discretion of the credit manager the applicant company does not qualify for these open account terms, the applicant [or customer] may be qualified to purchase on cash on delivery terms [COD], or cash in advance.

An applicant should always be given options to consider other options when open account terms cannot be offered. Some of the more common options the credit manager may consider include:

(a) a security agreement accompanied by a UCC-1

(b) a standby letter of credit

(c) a documentary letter of credit

(d) a personal guarantee or

(e) an inter-corporate guarantee.

(f) COD terms

(g) Cash in advance

(h) Cash with order

(260) Cash Discounts

Cash discounts may be approved from time to time at the sole discretion of the credit manager. Valid reasons to offer cash discounts include the following:

●   To improve the creditor company's cash flow so that the company needs to rely less on short term borrowing

- To meet or match the terms of sale being offered by the competition
- To increase the frequency of payments in order to reduce the dollar exposure to marginal or high risk accounts
- To improve payment performance

As a general rule, cash discounts should not be used solely to improve DSO by using early payments to offset the effects of other accounts with delinquent balances. An exception to this general rule will be made in consultation with senior management—particularly if DSO is an area of concern for the company's bank or stockholders.

(270) Enforcing Cash Discount Terms

Cash discounts are considered an incentive for customers to pay early. For this reason, cash discount terms will be strictly enforced. Cash discounts will only be honored if payment is received within the discount period plus a three (3) day grace period. All cash discounts considered unearned will be charged back.

It is the responsibility of the credit department to collect any unearned cash discount charged back by the cash application group. Collecting the unearned discount should be handled in the same was as past due balance is collected. The process will begin with friendly reminders of the past due balance, and end only when the balance is cleared.

(280) Extended Dating

Recognizing that offering extended credit terms increases credit risk, the sales department may not offer any customer extended dating under any circumstances without prior approval from senior management and from the credit department. Examples of reasons for offering extended dating include:

- To meet competition.
- As an alternative to arranging for the return of merchandise that was shipped to the customer in advance of the ship date requested.
- When selling to a customer outside of the United States.

Recognizing that offering extended dating is controversial and may damage the creditor company's business relationship with other suppliers if this information were to become known to the other suppliers, the credit manager will not make any unilateral decisions about extended dating. The credit manager's role shall be to qualify the applicant from a credit perspective for the extended dating. Final approval for extended dating will be made by senior management.

(290) Security

Recognizing that certain accounts are high risk and not creditworthy without additional assurance of payment, the credit department will establish policies for:

- perfection of security through proper and timely filing of UCC documents
- completion of personal or inter-corporate guarantees
- completion of credit insurance riders for certain accounts
- consideration of other forms of security for the sale of goods including the use of consignment arrangements, bonded warehouses, sight or time drafts, letters of credit, etc.

The credit department will also establish procedures for safeguarding documentation supporting the security or collateral pledged to the company.

(300) Collection and Follow Up

A collection process will be developed to ensure rapid conversion of accounts receivable into cash in order to maintain days sales outstanding [DSO] at an acceptable level. Delinquent accounts will be contacted frequently and systematically using telephone, mail, fax, e-mail and when necessary through personal visits and through the use of a collection agency or collection attorney. An account will be considered delinquent when any invoice of any size that is not in dispute is past due.

Accounts receivable aging reports will be prepared and printed regularly to help the credit manager and other department personnel to focus on past due accounts. Customer payment histories and payment commitments made or broken will be noted by credit personnel to assist the credit manager in evaluating the creditworthiness of the customer.

(310) Collection Techniques

The credit department will use any and all tools at its disposal to contact delinquent customers to address and resolve past due balances as quickly and as professionally as possible. Some of the more common tools the collector will use will include:

- the telephone
- automated dunning notices
- account statements
- letters, e-mail messages and fax messages
- personal visits

- help from the sales department
- third party collection agencies or attorneys

The goal of these collection contacts shall be to retire the past due balance as quickly as possible with as little damage to the long term business relationship between the buyer and the creditor company as possible.

(320) Documenting the Collection Process

The credit department will establish procedures that ensure that all collection efforts are documented. There are several reasons that documentation of collections is important, including:

- In the collector's absence, anyone can fill in after reviewing those notes
- Notes make it easier to follow up on broken commitments
- Notes make it possible to document the number and frequency of broken payment commitments
- Notes allow the collector to know who to speak to during their collection call.
- Notes allow the credit manager to evaluate orders on credit hold to determine if they should be released.
- The credit manager can review the work being performed by his or her collectors without bothering the collectors for updates.
- Agreements and payment plans can be documented in detail.

(330) Documenting Payment Plans

From time to time, a delinquent customer will report that they are unable to clear a past due balance. In this scenario, the customer may ask the creditor to accept an extended payment arrangement [a payment plan]. The more of the following elements a payment plan contains, the more likely the plan should be given serious consideration by the credit manager:

- Remittances must occur at least once a month, and preferably twice a month or even once a week.
- The first payment must be made quickly as a show of good faith.
- The first payment is a substantial percent of the past due balance [not less than 25%] intended to demonstrate the customer's goodwill and eagerness to work with the creditor.
- The customer is willing to put its payment commitments in writing, or to sign a promissory note documenting their specific payment commitments.

- The customer agrees to provide collateral or other forms of security to the creditor during the extended payment period.

- The customer has identified other creditors that have been asked to accept payment arrangement proposed, and the customer has provided a list of creditors that have already agreed to accept the payment plan.

(340) Payment Arrangements

All customers will be asked to remit payment to a lockbox remittance address. The cash application department will post payments received through the bank lockbox system using facsimiles of the checks and the original remittance advice. Cash postings will be completed within one business day of receipt of supporting documentation in order to provide the credit department with the most up-to-date information about the status of collections.

Regardless of whom the cash application department reports to, the cash application group will work closely with the credit department. Customers should be contacted immediately if payment information such as a remittance advice is not received with the customer's payment. The cash application group will not guess how to apply a customer's payment. When necessary, payments will be placed "on account" and those payments will remain on account until the customer has provided remittance information.

Foreign customers often remit payment directly to the company's bank via wire transfer. The accounts receivable group will notify the credit department as soon as possible after receiving notification of an incoming wire transfers payments.

(350) Reducing DSO

If DSO is higher than expected or higher than acceptable, the credit department will address this problem in two fundamental ways:

- In the short term, the credit department will use more strident and assertive collection efforts to retire delinquent balances—but not limited to the more frequent use of credit holds to encourage delinquent customers to pay more quickly.

- In the long term, the credit department will become more selective in the credit granting process and more conservative in establishing credit limit and terms of sale.

(360) Credit Holds

An account is considered past due any time an invoice is not paid when it comes due. If a customer is past due, any new orders received are subject to a credit hold, if approved by the credit manager, until one or more of the following events occur:

- Payment is received, or
- A reasonable payment commitment is made, or
- Other arrangements satisfactory to the credit department have been agreed upon [For example, the customer agrees to return the merchandise in question, or agrees to accept the order pending on COD terms]

(370) Bankruptcy

Upon notification that a customer has filed for voluntary bankruptcy, or alternatively has been placed into involuntary bankruptcy, the credit manager will take the following steps immediately to limit the company's credit exposure:

- Contact the shipping department and arrange for the return of any shipments in transit.
- If sales were made in the prior month, contact the corporate counsel to review the company's legal rights relating to reclamation as defined in the U.S. Bankruptcy Code.
- Advise the salesperson and sales management about the bankruptcy.
- Review the account's payment history to determine how much in payment was received within the prior 90 days that might be considered Preferential Transfers [preference payments].
- Ask the customer to provide an account statement showing the balance due according to the customer's records at the time of the filing. If a discrepancy is found, it should be addressed in such a way that the automatic stay is not violated.

(380) Participation in an Involuntary Bankruptcy

The decision to place a customer into involuntary bankruptcy should never be taken lightly. As a general rule, the credit manager will participate in an involuntary filing when any of the following events occur:

- Certain creditors are being paid, but we are not
- There is evidence of fraud
- There is evidence of a transfer of assets for less than their fair market value
- The management of the company is incompetent to manage the company

- The debtor simply refuses to acknowledge the balance owed or to explain how it will be paid or cleared.

(390) Compliance with Antitrust Laws

The company will fully comply with the antitrust laws of the United States and of the various States. No employee of the company has any authority, express or implied to engage in any conduct inconsistent with applicable federal and state laws. There is no business justification for any violation of these laws, and any employee who violates the antitrust laws is subject to immediate termination.

Membership in trade associations and participation in group meetings and interchanges is an area of risk. Credit interchanges are lawful activities, however any agreement about future actions taken in unison with competitors is a per se violation of one or more of the federal antitrust laws.

Any activity and any discussion that occurs before, during or after a group meeting that the company representative considers to be suspect or possibly illegal must be reported to the corporation's legal counsel as soon as possible. The employee must leave if any discussion of a suspect nature begins in his or her presence.

(400) The Salesperson's Role in the Credit Function

The sales department will be informed about any acutely slow paying account. The salesperson assigned to the account will be notified as far in advance as practical about an upcoming credit hold. The assistance of the salesperson may be sought in specific collection efforts when the credit department is unable to either:

(a)   Contact the debtor company, or

(b)   Persuade the customer to address the past due balance.

The salesperson's assistance shall generally be confined to contacting the customer and arranging for the customer to contact the credit department to discuss the current status of their account. The salesperson may also assist the credit department by identifying areas of dispute between the creditor and the debtor.

Salespeople may not be authorized to accept compromises, partial payments, payment plans, repayment schedules or any commitment from the customer for any reason. Any such agreements must be made in writing, and approved by the credit manager or his or her superiors. Acceptance of a payment plan will be made after taking into account the customer's financial condition—and based on an analysis indicating that accepting this plan is a better alternative than placing the account for collection, or filing a lawsuit, or participating in an involuntary bankruptcy proceeding.

(410) The Credit Department's Commitments

The credit department makes the following commitments:

- The sales department will be kept informed of credit problems with active customers
- The credit department will attempt to approve new accounts within three days or less
- When problems between the customer and the credit department arise, the salesperson will be given the opportunity to speak on behalf of the customer, or to provide the credit manager with additional information or documentation
- The credit department will change its decision about an account when new information is received from any source that supports a different credit decision.
- Credit will work with sales to pre-qualify potential customers so that salespeople do not waste their time on unproductive potential customers.
- The credit department will not over-react if the sales department shares negative information about a customer or applicant. The credit department's response will always be moderate and measured.
- The credit department will take the time to explain its credit decisions in detail to salespeople—but in doing so will not reveal any information obtained from confidential sources.
- Salespeople as well as customers will be handled at all times by the credit department in a professional and businesslike manner.

(420) Bad Debt Write Offs

A schedule of authority for bad debt write offs will be established. The credit manager will request written permission from his or her manager according to the matrix developed for this purpose.

(430) Third Party Collections

All accounts over 90 days past due are eligible for placement with a third party for collection. Accounts will be placed for collection only on written approval from the credit manager. As a general rule, an account will be placed for collection when the credit manager believes they are no longer making progress toward receiving payment.

(440) Qualification of Collection Agencies

The credit department will establish rules for qualifying collection agencies. Generally, any collection agency considered must be well established, reputable, licensed, bonded, and offer cost effective service to the credit department. The collection agency's rates must be competitive. Collections should be made by the agency on a contingency basis. The agency should provide, free of charge, periodic reports to the credit manager.

(450) Record Retention

Documents including the contents of credit files shall be stored by the creditor according to the retention schedule established for such documentation. The actual contents of the credit file may be purged periodically so that information that is more than two years old [and is no longer of any practical value to the credit department] can be eliminated. Since credit information is confidential, information purged from the customer's credit file must be destroyed or disposed of in an approved manner.

CHAPTER 8

CHANGE

President John F. Kennedy said: "Change is the law of life, those who look only to the past or the present are certain to miss the future."

Organizations exist today in a rapidly changing economic, competitive, regulatory and political environment. Factors such as technological developments; the effects of market supply and demand; prices of raw materials; new domestic and international rules and regulations; decisions and actions of competitors including foreign competitors; among many other factors guarantees that change will always occur.

Change itself is not new. What is new is the pace or speed of change. In some instances, individuals and companies that successfully coped with steady change have been [or will be] unable to cope with the stresses associated with even more rapid change. Individual workers and individual companies that cannot adapt quickly enough are destined to be stepped on and over by the accelerating pace of change.

Thus, the ability to adapt to change is a requirement in every business in every industry, and for every person in the workforce. Individuals that refuse to accept and embrace change will quickly be pushed aside. It will soon be impossible for workers to perform their work without dealing with new technologies, just as it will not be economically feasible for companies to retain workers that are not capable of coping with the changes required.

THE EFFECT OF GLOBAL COMPETITION

One of the key factors driving U.S.based companies to look seriously at the need to better manage change is global competition. As competition

141

increases in intensity, so does the need for change. Change is neither good nor bad. Change can reduce costs, increase efficiencies, and help to develop new markets. In many businesses, constant change is necessary simply for the company to remain competitive. In other companies, changes are initiated to improve overall performance.

SOFTWARE ENHANCEMENTS

There are a variety of new products intended to help the credit department to function more smoothly and efficiently. The products that have most fundamentally changed the credit department are specialized computer software. Some examples of the more popular software programs include:

- Credit scoring software
- Collection planning and collection management software
- Deduction management software
- Financial statement analysis software

This software improves every year. As the prices drop, and the software becomes more powerful, more intuitive, and more user-friendly it becomes more widely accepted.

While the use of these software programs has made the credit department more effective and more efficient, it has also resulted in several fundamental changes. The software tends to further automate the credit decision-making and risk management process making experienced credit managers less critical to the overall business operation. The use of the software programs described above tends to reduce the number of credit department employees needed.

Ideally, the need for fewer employees will have been handed by attrition, but in many companies the enhancements in automation and communication have resulted in centralization and ultimately in downsizing. As a result, a large number of capable and competent credit professionals have lost their jobs.

CHANGE AND EMPLOYEES

As the pace of change within the company and within the credit department continues to accelerate, credit managers will find more employees will have trouble keeping up with the pace of change. Often, it is assumed that older workers will be disproportionately impacted by the problems associated with change and the need to constantly upgrade their skills.

It is fair to say is that workers of all ages will find it hard to handle the requirement to re-invent their positions every few years in response to changing business realities and in response to the introduction of new technologies.

HELPING SUBORDINATES COPE WITH CHANGE

Credit managers can help their employees to cope with this problem by developing strategies and programs that help their subordinates learn new technologies. For example, many companies sponsor in-house training to help employees understand new software and new technologies—and to make the most of what these tools offer.

Many companies try to make this type of training a cooperative venture between the company and the employee. In some companies, employees are asked if they will volunteer to attend a portion of the training on their own time [off the clock]. The reason for the interest in changing from employer sponsored-paid training to cooperative training is that companies have found that employees take training more seriously when they have a personal investment in the process. This is why most employer sponsored tuition reimbursement programs require that the employee pay the tuition and receive reimbursement after the course is completed and the final grade indicates the employee has performed satisfactorily.

CHANGES WITHIN THE CREDIT DEPARTMENT

The credit department is one place in the company [among many] that change has been rapid and sweeping. A quick look at the changes in the credit workplace in the last ten years illustrates this point. These changes include:

- There has been a major shift toward centralization and downsizing of the credit function.
- There has been a migration from mainframe based "dummy terminals" to networked personal computers.
- There has been a widespread acceptance of the use of the fax machine to deliver documents to customers.
- Companies have migrated from DOS based architecture to Windows™ based PC architecture.
- There has been phenomenal growth of the Internet, and the use of the Internet for communication and research.
- Voice mail has become widely used, and widely misused.

- There has been a tremendous increase in personal bankruptcies, along with a steady decline in the number of business bankruptcies.
- Credit fraud has become a growth industry, and the criminals intent on committing this crime are far better informed and educated than ever before.

CHANGING WORK ASSIGNMENTS

One of the most important assets a company can have is a flexible workforce. Flexibility is characterized by people who are comfortable about being moved from one assignment to the next—acting as a resource and going where that resource is needed by the company at that time.

CHANGING REALITIES IN INTERNATIONAL CREDIT AND COLLECTION

Twenty years ago, most U.S.–based companies sold to foreign buyers on Letter of Credit or Cash in Advance terms. Now, according to statistics provided by the Department of Commerce, the majority of U.S. export sales are made on open account terms. While the risks associated with offering open account credit terms have not changed significantly, credit managers are expected to:

- Know how to control risks associated with selling to foreign customers on open account terms.
- To mitigate the credit risk while looking for ways not to require a Letter of Credit or payment in advance.
- To minimize collection problems and defaults without significantly depressing the creditor company's ability to offer foreign customers' open account credit terms.

CHANGES IN FOREIGN BUYERS' EXPECTATIONS

It is a buyer's market for many goods and services. Twenty years ago, foreign buyers expected to pay for goods in advance or against a Letter of Credit—but not now. Often, foreign buyers expect open account terms. As difficult as it was to control the Letter of Credit process to ensure that no discrepancies were created, the risk associated a Letter of Credit is less significant compared to the risks associated with trying to sell safely to foreign customers on open account terms. Unfortunately, global competition has made it far more likely that a foreign customer will be able to find a seller willing to offer open account terms.

Fortunately, the increasing availability of on-line credit bureau reports on foreign companies has made it easier for creditors to gather information quickly—permitting faster credit decisions. Access to the Internet has also made it easier for creditors to access information about foreign applicants directly from the applicant's web-site, and from other on-line sources of information.

Companies intent on capturing a share of the international market know that product quality, delivery, after sales service, reputation and price are not enough to guarantee them the export business they want. Most US exporters realize they must offer open account credit terms to remain competitive.One way to reduce the risk of doing so involves using export credit insurance.

THE USE OF CREDIT INSURANCE

There has been a fundamental change in the way companies look at credit insurance. It is more widely accepted. Credit managers realize that the product itself is not a threat to their position with the company. The ability to offer a buyer open account terms makes the seller's products more attractive than they would otherwise be.

Many European credit insurance providers now have U.S. subsidiaries and have developed new products to attract U.S. based exporters. This has resulted in a growing array of new insurance products being offered. As the U.S. economy continues to globalize, export credit insurance will become more important to companies interested in increasing sales and limiting credit risk. Recognizing that this is only the beginning of a fundamental change in the way companies look at credit management and credit insurance, credit insurance providers are anxious to establish themselves firmly in this marketplace.

Exporting companies that fail to find a way to sell on open account terms to foreign buyers will quickly find their competitors—especially companies located in Europe and Asia ready and able to provide a quality product, and a reasonable price on open account terms. Therefore, many credit professionals are looking at export credit insurance as a viable alternative to open account terms or to strict letter of credit terms.

CHANGING EXPECTATIONS ABOUT THE CREDIT MANAGER

Another fundamental change is management's expectations about the credit manager. The modern credit manager is expected to perform a number of different jobs each day. Among them are:

- The police officer ... To try to prevent credit fraud—which has become a growth industry.

- A lion tamer... To hold the sales department in check and never to lose their respect.

- A line manager... To make certain employees of the department do not waste time or money.

- A negotiator... To resolve disputes and problems quickly—before egos get involves, positions become entrenched, orders are held, and accounts are eventually placed for collection.

- As a risk manager... To assess options, alternatives, and outcomes and selecting the option that should result in the best outcome.

- An international risk manager... To manage both domestic and international credit risk—despite the differences between domestic and international trade credit

- An ombudsman... To deal with the company on behalf of customers with concerns and complaints.

- A cheerleader and motivator... To energize the entire credit department staff.

The credit manager is also expected to be proactive in working with the sales department to manage risk and to maximize sales and profits. Most companies will no longer accept an "us vs. them" attitude to exist between sales and credit departments. The credit manager is expected to look for ways to make sales safely, not for excuses or reasons to hold orders.

CHANGING COMPETITIVE CONDITIONS

Competitive conditions are constantly changing. Credit managers are expected to pay attention to these changes, and to adjust their credit policies and procedures as required to maximize sales while minimizing delinquencies and bad debt losses. This is not to suggest that credit policies should be changed monthly or quarterly, or that small changes in the competitive landscape should result in changes in credit policies.

It means instead that any significant or fundamental changes in competitive conditions should cause the credit department to re-evaluate its policies and procedures. For example, imagine a company that had enjoyed a relatively stable market share and steady sales growth is suddenly faced with a situation in which a foreign competitor establishes a U.S. subsidiary and in an attempt to attract customers begins to offer lower prices and extended dating terms. The U.S. company [and its credit department] can employ the ostrich method of dealing with the threat, or the company can respond with an approach to the problem that would almost certainly involve offering longer credit terms to existing customers.

CHANGES IN EMPLOYMENT, AND EMPLOYEE EXPECTATIONS

The relationship between employee and employer is changing constantly. Here are some interesting facts:

- According to a recent survey, over 53% of employees believe they will be in a different job, or working for a different employer, or will be retired within five years.

- 49% of all workers have had three or more jobs in the last ten years.

- Only 11% of employees have been with their present employer for ten years or more.

One of the most fundamental changes in the business environment involves changing expectations in the workforce. For example, most employees do not expect to work for the same employer for their entire working life. Workers do expect that their employers will offer them a variety of challenging new assignments.

CHANGING EXPECTATIONS OF CREDIT MANAGERS

Almost every credit manager has a friend or a former peer that has been downsized, merged or re-engineered out of a job. Fortunately, because of their unique position in the company many credit managers are in a position to look ahead to determine if their department or even their own position is at risk.

If the company is undergoing fundamental changes such as downsizing, re-engineering, or a merger, it is not likely that the credit department will be excluded from the changes facing the rest of the company. If the credit manager perceives that his or her job may be in danger, they are likely to become active in the job market—because it is easier to look for a new position when you have a job than when you are out of work.

CENTRALIZATION

As mentioned earlier, advances in computer technology combined with improved communications makes it much more likely that companies will centralize their credit operations if they are currently decentralized. Well over 70% of companies now have centralized credit departments, and this percentage is growing steadily.

When a company centralizes its credit operations, chances are good that:

- The credit manager will need to relocate—if he or she is offered a job.

- In a centralized operation, it will be more difficult to get noticed and promoted.

- The centralized credit department's operations will be more tightly controlled than a decentralized operation. The credit manager may find it difficult to adapt to the lack of autonomy.

CHANGING SOFTWARE

Improvements in decision support software have automated and simplified many of the tasks that were formerly handled by a credit manager. For example, as a result of software enhancements, financial statement analysis can be automated, along with credit risk scoring, collection management, and deduction tracking and resolution. Simply stated, decision support software makes an experienced credit manager less critical to the performance of the credit department.

Decisions that were made based on experience and insight are now made [or more precisely recommended] by the decision support software. Every year, these software programs get more sophisticated and at the same time easier to use. As a result, the role of the credit manager is devalued, resulting in downsizing and meaning that raises and recognition for the credit manager becomes harder to earn.

CHANGING THE SPEED OF CREDIT DECISION-MAKING

Customers have come to expect instant gratification. It is not uncommon for the credit department to receive the opening order and the credit application form at the same time—and for the customer to expect the order will be approved and will ship the same day. Established customers expect the credit department to approve increases in their credit limits sufficient to cover orders pending—also with little or no notice. Companies expect the credit department to meet customers' expectations, regardless of the problems doing so creates for the credit manager.

In response to the need for speed, credit managers have fundamentally changed the ways in which certain tasks are performed. For example:

- Credit managers have increased the pace of credit decision-making.

- The pace of change requires the credit department to constantly evaluate and re-order priorities so that the credit department remains responsive to the needs of internal and external customers—and to their company as a whole. In this regard, order review and approval should be the single highest priority for the credit department.

- Credit managers look for reasons to approve terms and release orders rather than excuses not to do so.

- Credit managers communicate a sense of urgency to their subordinates. Customers expect rapid decisions. Credit managers must constantly pressure their subordinates for shorter turn-around times.

- Credit managers encourage subordinates and other employees to recommend changes that would save the department time.

- Credit managers use cross-training to make certain that work does not sit on someone's desk because they are the only ones that know how to perform the particular task.

- Credit managers have empowered subordinates. They have delegated authority to them to eliminate bottlenecks and to make certain the credit department remains responsive to customers' needs and expectations.

RESPONDING TO CHANGING ECONOMIC CONDITIONS

Changing economic conditions affect the creditor company. For example, an increase in interest rates may make it difficult for a creditor company to afford short-term loans. Without these loans, the creditor may not be able to sell to customers that consistently pay slowly. Therefore, as shown in this simple example, a change in economic conditions may necessitate a change in credit policies.

Economic conditions might change for the better. In this scenario, creditors may be more willing to extend open account terms at higher credit limits than when the economy was not as robust or when interest rates were higher. Before re-evaluating credit policies in light of changing economic and competitive conditions, it is important for the credit professional that senior management accept the credit manager's interpretation of the current economic and competitive realities—and for senior management to endorse the policy changes the credit manager proposes.

COMPANIES INITIATE CHANGE

Companies initiate change throughout their organization through a process called continuous process improvement. Continuous process improvement is an offshoot of the pioneering work done by Dr. Deming in post–World War II Japan. Dr. Deming introduced techniques into Japanese industry that revolutionized the way that companies look at the manufacturing process. Without trying to minimize the contributions and the genius of Dr. Deming, the underlying concepts behind continuing process improvement are quite simple. Those concepts include:

- Change is both necessary and good
- Companies should never allow themselves to sit back and admire their own handiwork, believing that a system is perfect stops all efforts at progress
- Management drives process change
- Companies that do not change will not remain competitive
- Every employee can contribute to making processes and procedures, goods and services a little bit better
- Over time, all incremental improvements are cumulative and compounding meaning a company's goods and services improve dramatically—often without any single, dramatic changes to the manufacturing process

A premise of the Continuous Process Improvement movement is that every employee should be empowered and encouraged to recommend changes. If those changes do not work, the employee should be congratulated anyway for their suggestions. The only way to convince employees to offer solutions that improve the company is to create an environment in which employees can try new ideas and make mistakes without fear of retribution, loss of status, or even the loss of their jobs.

Many credit departments have responded to the need for speed by using continuous process improvement to look for ways to:

- Streamline operations
- Eliminate bottlenecks
- Correct inefficiencies
- Reorganize the flow of documents
- Accelerate the order review and approval process
- Streamline the new account investigation process

The goals of continuous process improvement include lower costs, higher productivity and higher levels of customer satisfaction.

ENCOURAGING CHANGE

The suggestion box has been around for decades. The suggestion box is a way that companies recognize that employees, and not managers often have the best ideas for saving money, improving quality and increasing customer satisfaction. Some companies have gone beyond simply requesting suggestions from employees. Some companies make suggestions mandatory. The programs typically work this way:

- Each employee is required to submit at least one suggestion each month.
- An individual whose full-time position involves gathering and reviewing the suggested changes carefully evaluates each recommendation.
- Employees are empowered to spend up to $500 without management approval to implement any suggestion.

The mandatory suggestion program is considered a major success. For at least one company, annual savings are in the millions of dollars. Employees feel they make a difference. As a result, absenteeism and employee turnover are significantly below industry averages.

CHANGING CREDIT MANAGERS

Credit managers who are new to the position face a number of problems. One of the most important challenges the new credit manager will face involves the task of dealing with subordinates. It is not unusual to find employees who:

(a) Remain loyal to the former credit manager.

(b) Are resentful or envious of the new credit manager—in some cases employees might have felt they were entitled to the position.

(c) Are prepared to test their new manager's skill, patience, or resolve.

(d) Hope to see the new credit manager fail, and might even be willing to sabotage the ideas or the work done by their new manager.

(e) Are incompetent, but are seen by the company as being adequate based on previous, inflated evaluations.

(f) Are insubordinate toward the new manager

Experienced managers understand that recognize that many of these problems will be encountered any time they assume a new credit management position. Credit professionals should not be surprised that these problems exist; these exist in one form or another in most credit organizations.

TERMINATION EMPLOYEES

Making a decision that it is time to terminate an employee presents special challenges for any credit manager, but especially for a new credit manager. No manager wants a reputation as being impulsive, or insensitive toward existing employees—especially long-term employees. Experienced credit managers understand that it is often better to work with existing employees than to terminate them. If the credit manager determines that a particular customer cannot be salvaged, this should be the trigger for an immediate change. Failing to terminate a substandard performer tends to:

(b) Demoralize and de-motivate the better workers, and

(b) Lower overall productivity and output

This is not to suggest that loyalty is a thing of the past. However, that loyalty is not unconditional. Most workers are cautious. They want to make sure the company they work for will survive in the long term and that they know where their position with the company is going. If employees believe they do not have a future with the company or that the company may not survive, they will often abandon that company as soon as possible for another position that offers more stability, even if it pays less than they are currently earning.

CHANGING EXPECTATIONS ABOUT EMPLOYEES

In order to remain valuable to their employer, employees must try to continuously update their skills. This can be accomplished through in house training; through off-site training; or through formal college training. Employees who refuse to acknowledge that additional education is important fail to recognize with outdated skills they are good candidates for a lay-off.

CHANGING EXPECTATIONS ABOUT APPLICANTS

The best credit managers are actively recruiting employees who they believe can adapt to change. The best candidates for a position in the credit department will be able to tolerate ambiguity and changing priorities, and must be able to handle the stress of the job in general and managing multiple priorities in particular.

TECHNOLOGY CHANGE

Technology change management is not a new concept but it is taking on increased importance as the rate of change increases. Technology change management involves integrating new technologies into the company in an orderly manner. The objective is to improve the effectiveness of the company by improving the quality of software and hardware in use. The trick is to coordinate the process of re-train employees so that they are fully prepared when the technology is ready to be implemented. Typically, technology change management involves the following steps:

- the organization evaluates new technologies and determines which of them will improve productivity
- the organization creates a pilot project in which new technology is tested to determine whether or not it is appropriate and what the payback for the organization would be for distributing it throughout the company

- if the new technology can be demonstrated to improve effectiveness and it is cost efficient, then training begins.
- after appropriate training, the technology is transferred from the classroom and into the workplace.

CHANGE FOR THE SAKE OF CHANGE

Change is vital to the success of any business. The pace of change is not likely to be constant. Credit managers should remember that change is disruptive enough without introducing unnecessary changes which some employees refer to as "the idea of the month." Changes should be well conceived, carefully and thoroughly introduced. If they are discontinued the employees involved deserve to know why.

If a new program is to be introduced, it should be introduced formally. It should have the backing of senior management. It should be allowed to develop over time, and should only be eliminated if it is demonstrated not to work as predicted. Too often, a program seems to be introduced or changes made to existing programs for the sake of change itself. Credit managers should do everything possible not to fall into this particular trap.

SUMMARY

In the 1940s and 1950s, an employee joining a corporation might expect a career punctuated by increasing economic rewards for hard work and loyalty to the company. At the end of their business careers, these workers looked forward to a gold watch and a healthy retirement plan funded by and administered by the company.

Today, most workers have no such expectations. Most employees do their own retirement planning. Many employees that have seen layoffs and re-engineering [or have experienced it firsthand] have a very different view of the employee-employer relationship. Most realize that without an employment contract or a collective bargaining agreement, an employer owes an employee nothing more than their final paycheck.

Loyalty must be earned both by the credit manager and by the company. One way to earn an employee's loyalty is to keep commitments, to "do what you say, and to say what you do." One way to lose the loyalty of subordinates is to be inconsistent in handling personnel related issues. Surveys continue to point to inequitable treatment as one of the biggest reasons for job dissatisfaction.

CHAPTER 9

WORKING WITH REPORTING AGENCIES

A credit-reporting agency (also known as a credit bureau) is a company that provides credit reports on individuals, as well as on proprietorships, partnerships and corporations. Credit bureaus collect, package and sell the information they compile in a formatted report to subscribers. Generally speaking, the information contained in a consumer or business credit report comes from the following sources:

- The federal bankruptcy courts
- The offices of all 50 Secretaries of State
- From millions of bank and trade references
- From State court records
- From daily newspapers, and other periodicals
- From certain regulatory agencies including the Federal Trade Commission and the Securities and Exchange Commission

As a general rule, credit-reporting agencies tend to specialize in either consumer credit reporting or commercial credit reporting [although there is at least one major credit bureau that offers both consumer and commercial credit reports]. A limited number of credit reporting agencies provide domestic and international credit reports to their subscribers, but many tend to specialize in one or the other.

Credit reporting agencies continually update the information contained in their files. Information for commercial credit reports comes from a variety of sources including these:

- The business itself, in the form of personal visits or telephone interviews.

- Public filings, including filings with the Securities and Exchange Commission.

- Reports provided by credit granters about the customer to the credit reporting agency.

- Other public records such as from various Courts, and from filings made with the Secretaries of State for the various States.

The information contained in consumer credit reports comes primarily from the creditors of the consumer. Creditors provide the consumer credit reporting agencies with trade tapes each month reflecting their experience with consumers.

The three largest consumer credit reporting agencies have approximately 100 million consumer credit files each on record [of course, there are a large number of duplication]. The volume of information being reported every day and every month prevents consumer credit reporting agencies from verifying data.

In commercial credit reports, information may be updated one or more times a day. Therefore, it is possible to receive an updated credit report with a different credit rating on reports ordered even one day apart. The same is true of consumer credit reports. Consumer credit reports might be updated one or more times a day.

Consumer credit reports are not rated in the sense that a commercial credit reporting agency such as the Dun and Bradstreet Company® provides a three digit rating on each Business Information Report™ that it generates for a subscriber. However, for a modest additional fee, consumer credit reporting agencies will add a credit score to the consumer credit reports they provide to subscribers.

CONSUMER CREDIT REPORTS

Credit bureaus provide consumer credit reports to subscribers to that information. Under federal consumer protection law, subscribers must certify to the credit-reporting agency that they have a "legitimate business need" for the information they obtain.

Consumer credit reporting agencies maintain files on more than 90% of all adults in the United States. When an individual applies for credit, the potential credit granteR normally orders a consumer credit report from Experian, TransUnion, or Equifax—the three largest consumer credit reporting agencies. The information contained in the report [along with a credit score if the subscriber orders it] is used by many credit granters to form the basis for their credit decision.

A consumer credit report is normally accessed on line by the subscriber. Creditor companies evaluating a large number of consumer applicants normally request the credit bureau also calculate a credit score and include that with the report. A consumer credit report is considered to be a factual record of an individual's credit history. It includes information from three main sources:

(1) Its subscriber companies who share information with the credit bureau—normally at least once a month. This information consists of data about high credit, balance owed, balances past due and whether or not the past due balance is in dispute.

(2) Information obtained directly from the consumer updating residence address, telephone number, and the name of their employer. This information is normally requested every time a consumer completes a credit application.

(3) From public records and public filings. Information in this category includes tax liens, bankruptcy filings, and lawsuits filed by creditors against the individual debtor.

Typically, a consumer credit report will include personal information about the consumer including their address, telephone number, and current employer, in addition to a list of the consumer's credit card and department store accounts. By federal law, a consumer credit report must list every creditor or entity that viewed the credit report for the last two years.

A typical consumer credit report will include all of the following information:

(1) A list of all active accounts.

(2) The credit limit assigned, high credit, and opening balance on all active accounts.

(3) The current status of each account. For example, whether or not the account is current or past due.

(4) If the account is past due, how far past due.

(5) Whether or not the past due balance is disputed.

(6) A list of the companies that have ordered the consumer's credit report in the last two years.

While the credit report itself is considered to be a factual record of the consumer's credit history—the use of credit scoring remains controversial.

Despite explanations about the relevance of the credit score as a predictive tool, critics typically point to the following examples of the weaknesses of credit scoring:

- If a consumer has a good payment history with a creditor, but that creditor does not report it to the credit bureau then the consumer will not be given credit for their good payment history.

- A credit score is lowered any time an inquiry is received. The reasoning is that the consumer might have recently made a large number of purchases or applied for a lot more credit, but those purchases may not have been recorded yet. Whether or not this is the case, the credit score drops as though it is.

- For example, the credit score would drop if a consumer tried to rent an apartment and the landlord ordered a credit report... even though this may have nothing to do with the debtor's ability to pay its debts.

- Consumers between the ages 36 and 48 will receive lower scores based on their age. The assumption is that people in that age group tend to get into financial difficulty more frequently than older consumers do.

- All things being equal, a person with just one credit card is considered a higher credit risk and will receive a lower score than another individual with three credit cards. Conversely, having too many credit cards increases the risk and lowers the score.

The use of credit scoring models in a sense violates what social scientists call the uncertainty principle. The uncertainty principle states that if it is possible to predict with some certainty the actions of a group, it is impossible to predict the actions of an individual.

SUBSCRIBERS

Credit reports are normally provided under contract to subscribers. Some agencies sell reports one at a time, although it is far more expensive to buy them that way.

Most subscribers to credit reports acknowledge the reports are expensive, but believe that purchasing these reports is cost-effective compared to the cost and quality of information the creditor company would be able to develop on its own. Credit reporting agency contracts are normally for one year. Subscriptions are paid in advance. Subscribers to these reports include:

- Banks

- Collection agencies
- Credit card companies
- Insurance companies
- Department stores, and
- Employers

Credit bureaus are required to keep consumer credit reports confidential. Under the Fair Credit Reporting Act, credit reports can only be provided to parties that have a "legitimate need" and a "permissible purpose" for ordering the reports. Many creditors require a signed credit application with explicit approval and authorization to order a credit report. Under federal law, this is not necessary if the party making the inquiry has a "legitimate business need" for the information—but the practice is widespread and stems from a fear of being sued by a consumer for illegally obtaining their credit report.

The largest consumer credit bureaus are (1) Equifax, (2) Experian, and (3) Trans Union Corporation [not necessarily in that order]. Consumer credit reports typically contain:

- the individual's name
- occupation
- their subject's date of birth
- their social security number
- current telephone number
- current employer, and previous employer
- dates of employment
- information on individual credit card accounts
- bankruptcy records [public filings]
- record of tax liens or other judgments
- the names of creditors that have asked for a copy of the consumer credit report

Contrary to popular myth, consumer credit reports do not contain the following information:

- The individual's race, or religion
- Information about the individual's health
- Data about a person's driving record or any criminal convictions

CONSUMER ACCESS TO INFORMATION

The federal Fair Credit Reporting Act gives certain rights to consumers. The most important of these is the right to obtain a copy of the information contained in their credit file at any time and to dispute any incorrect information in their credit profile.

The Fair Credit Reporting Act also provides that if a creditor declines a request for credit, and even a part of that decision was based on the information contained in the credit report then the consumer is entitled to a free copy of the credit report from the credit bureau that the creditor used.

Consumers have the right to review their files, to add missing data, and to request that erroneous information is removed, and the right to have creditors that have reviewed the erroneous information to be notified if the report is amended. If the creditor providing the disputed information refuses to amend the credit report, then the debtor has the right to have included in their consumer credit report a statement of less than 100 words containing their version of the facts. If the consumer has documentation supporting there version of the facts, the consumer can in their statement invite creditors to request copies of that documentation from them.

Consumers that request a copy of their credit report do not have the right to review their credit score. Credit reporting agencies have convinced legislators that access to a credit score would not benefit consumers because they would not understand the scientific and statistical underpinnings of the credit scoring model. The credit reporting agencies also point out that a consumer's credit score can change from day to day, so providing consumers with their "current" credit score has little relevance to them in understanding why any credit granter denied their request for credit.

If a consumer complains about the accuracy of information contained in a credit report, many creditors will amend the report. Refusing to do so could result in the creditor being sued by the consumer. Consumer credit bureaus go to great lengths to make certain their reports accurately reflect the information provided to them by creditor companies. Credit bureaus have a vested interest in doing everything possible to make certain the information contained in their consumer credit reports IS accurate. Any credit bureau that develops a reputation for providing inaccurate information will soon find itself losing subscribers. Unfortunately, there are any number of errors that can appear on a consumer credit report despite the credit bureau's quality control efforts.

One of the most common errors found on a consumer credit report involves information being added in error to the wrong file—a simple data entry error. Sometimes, the results of this type of error are benign; occasionally the results are dramatic and devastating to the consumer.

In addition to erroneous information being added to a consumer's credit file, sometimes detrimental information is not removed in a timely manner. For example, a bankruptcy is supposed to remain on a consumer credit report for no more than ten years. If a bankruptcy is listed for longer than ten years, the consumer can ask that the information be removed. If it is not, it is a reportable violation of the Fair Credit Reporting Act.

TIME LINE FOR INFORMATION ON A CONSUMER CREDIT REPORT

The length of time that information appears on a consumer credit report is shown below:

Credit accounts paid as agreed.	Up to 10 years
Credit accounts not paid as agreed.	Up to 7 years
Collection accounts.	Up to 7 years
Paid tax liens.	7 years from date released
Bankruptcies—Chapters 7, 11, & 13.	10 years from date filed
Unpaid tax liens.	Indefinitely

COMMERCIAL CREDIT REPORTING AGENCIES

Commercial credit reporting agencies try to provide objective, factual, and impartial information about business throughout the United States as well as throughout the world. In theory, the more information creditors have about customers and applicants, the better the decisions they will make. With this central fact in mind, commercial credit reports are popular because at about $20 each [for domestic reports] these reports are an inexpensive sources of valuable information. The fact that over 10 million business credit reports are in one company's database means almost instant access to critical business information for subscribers.

In many instances, credit reporting agencies gain access to information that an individual creditor cannot get. For example, it is not uncommon for a privately held company to provide financial statements to a credit reporting agency, and to deny requests from individual creditors for this data. From the customer's perspective, the logic of this is fairly simple: "We can provide this information one to a central clearinghouse that most of our creditors have access to anyway, or we can wait waste our time answering dozens of requests for this information."

Commercial credit reports allow companies to process credit applications more quickly, and credit reports increase the department's effectiveness by allowing the department to update active accounts regularly and without a large commitment of manpower. Commercial credit reports allow the credit department to be responsive to requests for larger credit limits by getting up-to-date information within minutes on the customer requesting a larger credit limit.

Credit bureaus have developed a variety of different styles or types of reports recognizing that different creditors have unique requirements. For example, there are payment indexes that provide a summary payment score and detailed trade clearance information about a given customer. There are other reports that provide detailed information about every aspect of a company's business operations. There are so called family tree reports that detail the relationship between one company and its parent company, top parent company, subsidiaries, and affiliates. Credit bureaus are constantly experimenting with new reports that could prove to be attractive to subscribers.

Commercial credit reporting agencies want to make it as easy as possible for their subscribers to access the information in the agency's data base. Commercial credit reports can be accessed using a variety of tools including a mainframe computer, a personal computer, by fax, by mail or by telephone. Several credit reporting agencies have even made their services to subscribers available over the Internet.

DUN AND BRADSTREET

The most widely used commercial credit-reporting agency in the United States is the Dun and Bradstreet Company®. Dun and Bradstreet [D&B] has been in business for almost 150 years. Its database contains information on more than 9.5 million U.S.–based businesses. In addition, D&B provides reports to subscribers international businesses. D&B reports can typically provide the following information about commercial credit applicants or customers:

- A brief history of the company

- The company's payment history with its trade creditors [Approximately 200,000 businesses share their trade payment experience with D&B.]

- The company's high credit with its various creditors, along with the credit terms being offered by those creditors

- A summary of any significant recent events

- A summary of any lawsuits filed against the customer or applicant company, and their outcome if that has been adjudicated [D&B collects data from about 2500 courthouses]

- A summary of any tax liens filed

- A summary of public filings at the local, the state and the federal level including documents filed with the Securities and Exchange Commission; Uniform Commercial Code filings, and business licenses.

- A summary of any changes in management or ownership

- The background of the senior managers of the business

- If privately held, a summary of any financial information the customer shared with D&B.

- A summary of an additional two years of historical financial statements when available.

- The auditor's opinion about the financial statements. An explanation of how the statements were compiled if the statements were not audited.

- Comments on the customer or applicant's relationship with its bank

Often, the summary rating presented on the first page many D&B reports IS misunderstood. Ratings are designed to be a quick reference tool, not a recommendation for or against extending credit to an applicant or to a customer. Credit ratings are not intended to be used as a substitute for human judgment, or to be used to establish specific dollar credit limits. Instead, they are intended to be an important part of an individual decision maker's credit review process. Every day, new information is added to D&B's database. Each time new information is added a customer's credit rating can changed.

THE EXPERIAN COMMERCIAL CREDIT REPORT

Experian [formerly TRW] in making a bold run against the Dun and Bradstreet Company for a larger share of the commercial credit reporting business. The Experian commercial credit report typically contains the following information:

- An executive summary of the company
- The company's history
- Historical payment information including high credit, an industry payment comparison, and a payment trend indicator
- Data on public filings, security interests, liens, judgments, and lawsuits
- Trade payment data
- Number of employees and the size of the facility
- A risk profile

THE FOREIGN CREDIT INTERCHANGE BUREAU

The FCIB, part of the National Association of Credit Managers, offers in depth reports to assist exporters in evaluating the credit risk of international sales. The FCIB has combined with S.J. Rundt and Associates to provide the following reports about foreign applicants and customers:

- Terms of sale offered by other exporters
- Collection experience
- Background of the company
- Political issues involving the buyer's country
- Any regulatory issues the seller should be aware of

   Other international credit reporting agencies include:

- Graydon
- Owens Online
- Veritas

USING CONSUMER CREDIT REPORTS

The Federal Trade Commission has established rules for the use of consumer credit reports. Those rules are codified in a federal statute called the Fair Credit Reporting Act. The Fair Credit Reporting Act [FCRA] deals with the rights of the individual consumer, as well as the responsibilities and obligations of both the consumer credit reporting agency and the companies that use the information provided by these agencies.

   The Fair Credit Reporting Act is designed to promote accuracy, fairness, and privacy of information contained In consumer reporting agency files. Creditors using these reports should be aware that the FCRA requires anyone who takes adverse action against the applicant based on the report—such as denying credit to the applicant—to inform the applicant of that fact along with the name, address and telephone number of the credit reporting agency used.

   Another provision of the Act specifies that access to consumer reports is limited to people or companies with a need to know the information. Entities with a need to know normally include creditors, insurers, employers, and landlords. If the user of a consumer report violates the law by obtaining a report without a legitimate need for that information, the individual may sue them for actual damages as well as punitive damages. Improper use of a consumer credit report is punishable by a fine and imprisonment.

A consumer credit report is not the only information a creditor might use to evaluate an individual applicant, but it is certainly an objective and solid foundation for a more comprehensive evaluation if that is deemed necessary.

CREDIT INTERCHANGES

Many creditors belong to one or more industry credit groups. These industry credit groups are often affiliated with one of the National Association of Credit Managers local affiliates. Often, these industry credit groups include credit interchange reports as a service to members. Credit interchange involves the sharing of one specific kind of information—information about a customer's payment history. Credit interchange reports typically include the following information:

- Each creditor's high credit with the company that is the subject of the report
- The date the account was opened
- The high credit
- The balance owing
- The aging of the balance due broken down by aging category

Typically, a credit interchange works this way:

Once a month, each member provides the association they are a member of with a report of the accounts they do business with showing the accounts receivable balance and aging information. In return, the member is allowed access [for a fee] to the association's database.

The advantages of credit interchange reports include:

- Trade clearance reports are relatively inexpensive. Typically, a credit interchange report can be accessed for $5 or less.
- Information is available quickly since credit interchange reports are available on-line.
- The information on the report will be current since information is gathered monthly.

INDUSTRY CREDIT GROUPS

Industry credit groups are often formed by a local affiliate of the National Association of Credit Managers. These groups cater to creditors that tend to sell to the same types of customers. In fact, in most industry credit groups, it is not uncommon for two or more competitors to belong to the same industry credit group.

Industry credit group meetings usually involves a lengthy discussion of common customers. It is critically important that these conversations do not violate antitrust laws, there is a clear boundary between sharing factual, historical credit information [which is permissible], and any agreement about how creditors and in particular how competitors are going to handle a particular customers. For example, it would be a violation of federal law for creditors to agree to hold orders to a specific customer, or to limit sales to that customer using credit limits, or in any other way to agree or conspire to circumvent the normal operation of the free market economy based on the laws of supply and demand.

Industry credit group meetings typically include an education section in which guest speakers are invited to address specific topics of common interest. In preparation for the meeting, each member of the credit group provides the following information to the affiliate managing the group about the accounts that are to be discussed at the meeting:

- Its member number
- The date the account was opened
- The terms of sale
- Average days to pay
- High credit
- Balance due, and
- Aging of the outstanding balance

Creditors often visit several industry groups before they find the one that is best for them. It is not uncommon for creditors to join more than one credit group in an effort to gather as much information as possible about its customer base. When evaluating an industry credit group for possible membership, the trade creditor should consider all of the following factors:

- How many accounts are in the data base?
- How many of those accounts does the creditor sell to?
- How expensive is the annual membership fee?
- Does the industry credit group offer on line access to trade clearance reports?
- How many trade clearance reports are in the database?

- How much does it cost to access this information?
- How often are the reports updated?
- How many meetings a year are members required to attend, and where are these meetings held?
- Where are the meetings held?

Even after the credit manager has gathered all of this information, it may be difficult to decide which credit group to join.

USING CREDIT REPORTS TO EVALUATE RISK

Credit management is not performed in a vacuum. Credit managers need facts in order to properly evaluate credit risk. Credit agency reports are purchased because they provide the credit manager with factual, unbiased, detailed and up-to-date information about customers. That information is provided to subscribers in an easy to read format. Each commercial credit report comes with a specific credit rating, and each consumer credit report can come with a credit score if it is ordered that way.

Using this information, the credit manager can make a better-informed decision and a better quality decision about the customer or applicant than could be made from information that the creditor could gather by themselves.

USING CREDIT RATINGS

Credit bureaus rate each target company using rules that are consistently applied. As a result, these ratings are objective rather than subjective. Contrary to popular myth, a rating is not a recommendation that an open account should be approved or denied. Commercial credit bureaus do not make any recommendations about whether an individual creditor should extend credit. That decision is always left to the discretion of the individual creditor based on that company's credit policies, competitive position, and tolerance for credit risk.

Similarly, a blank rating is not a warning or a recommendation that open account credit terms should be denied. A blank rating simply means that there was not enough information to the credit bureau to permit the assignment of a rating based on the objective rules the reporting agency creates and uses consistently.

SUMMARY

The ability to manage risk, delinquency and default requires access to information. The more a creditor knows about a consumer or commercial credit risk, the better the decision the creditor can make. Equally important, the more information a credit manager has access to, the more likely they are to be able to respond to the customer's individual requirements.

CHAPTER 10

WORKING WITH BANKS

There are a number of differences between the types of credit extended by banks [and other financial institutions] and credit offered to businesses by trade creditors. The first difference is the most obvious. Banks lend money. Trade creditors sell goods or services for which they expect to receive money. Banks charge interest and certain fees. That interest and those fees represent the bank's profit. Trade creditors sell goods and the markup on what they sell represents their profit margin.

Banks tend to loan money with due dates over a period of years. Trade creditors' bills tend to come due in an average of 30 to 60 days from the date of invoice. Banks are normally secured creditors. Trade creditors are usually unsecured creditors. Banks typically require customers to provide the bank with periodic financial statements as a condition of doing business. Many trade creditors do not have the leverage necessary to convince customers to provide financial statements to them even once a year—much less quarterly or even monthly.

Bank loan officers have fewer customers than the average credit manager, and those customers are normally located geographically close to the loan officer. All of these factors contribute to the fact that the loan officer typically has a much closer relationship with a borrower than a credit manager has with the same customer.

As secured creditors, banks typically require the right to inspect their collateral. Banks sometimes schedule reviews and audits of the borrower's books and records. The borrower will accept such intrusions and inconveniences because doing so is required under the terms and conditions listed in the loan document. Credit managers normally have no such access to information. A credit manager is lucky to get an invitation to visit with the debtor face to face—and rarely is the creditor given access to the volume and the quality of information shared with the debtor's bank.

Because banks lend money for a period of years rather than months, they can demand and normally receive a security interest in most or all of the assets of the debtor company. In fact, it is unlikely that a bank would make a loan unless it can become a secured creditor. Banks prefer to have a security interest perfected in assets of the debtor company that are valued at two or more times the maximum amount the bank is prepared to loan to the debtor.

Often, bank loan covenants will specify that the creditor is to grant no security interests that would be superior to the bank's secured position. For this reason, trade creditors are often unable to convince a debtor to grant a Purchase Money Security Interest in their inventory.

PERSONAL GUARANTEES

Most trade creditors sell without the benefit of a personal guarantee from the owner or owners of a corporation. The reason is simple: Most trade creditors simply do not have the leverage necessary to demand that the individual owners or officers of a corporation personally guarantee the debts of the corporation. In contrast, the majority of bank loans are supported by one or more personal guarantees from the owners or the major stockholders of the corporation.

There are two advantages of personal guarantees. One is the actual ability to pursue the individual guarantor for payment of a balance owed by the corporate debtor. The other advantage is an intangible and psychological. When a guarantor realizes that he or she may be called upon for payment in the event of a default by the corporation, that individual is likely to do everything possible to make certain the corporation retires the debt before the bank makes demand for payment on the guarantor.

BANK FINANCIAL ANALYSIS

Because bank credit tends to be for a longer period of time and for larger amounts than credit extended by trade creditors, banks perform more extensive financial analysis. Before a bank will even consider making a loan it will typically demand several years of financial statements—both fiscal year end and quarterly statements. When reviewing these financial statements, bank loan analysts tend to focus on different financial ratios than do the company's short-term trade creditors. Specifically, since trade creditors' invoices tend to come due between 30 and 90 days from the date of invoice, trade creditors tend to be more concerned about short-term liquidity than they are about long-term leverage and solvency. Banks extending credit for a period of years are interested in:

- the debtor's short-term liquidity
- its profitability
- its long term sales prospects
- the degree of financial leverage
- the quality of its assets
- its choices of accounting methods, its cash flow
- its short term and long term business plans and financial forecasts

THE DIFFERENCES BETWEEN BANK AND TRADE CREDIT

As shown above, there are a number of differences between bank and trade credit. For all of the reasons listed above, trade creditors cannot look at a bank's decision to extend credit and infer any direct relationship between that decision and a decision by the creditor about whether or not to extend credit to the customer. Any trade creditor that extends credit to a customer on the basis that the customer has convinced a bank to loan it money has failed to grasp the fundamental difference between banks and trade creditors.

CHECK PROCESSING

Banks are involved in check processing, and check processing remains the single most popular way for businesses to retire debts owed to supplier companies. Congress created the Federal Reserve System in 1913 to supervise and regulate the banking system, and to provide for smooth transactions within and between banks. About half of all banks are members of the Federal Reserve System. Those that are not are still required to maintain Federal Reserve accounts to enable them to move or to receive funds through the Federal Reserve System. This is essential for the speedy and orderly processing of checks.

Despite the popularity of alternative methods of payment or settlement such as payments transmitted via the Automated Clearinghouse

[ACH] the overwhelming majority of business transactions are settled by check.

Checks are presented for payment to the customer's bank through the Federal Reserve's check processing system which processes billions of checks annually through approximately fifty regional check processing centers. Commercial banks present checks drawn on other banks to these check processing centers to expedite check clearance. At the end of the business day, each bank in the system is required to settle with every other bank. At its simplest, the settlement process works this way:

If bank A has ten checks drawn on bank B totaling $100,000 and if bank B has two checks drawn on bank A totaling $20,000 then bank B must transfer $80,000 [$100,000 - $20,000] to bank A at the end of the business day in settlement of that day's transactions.

The Federal Reserve System also permits real-time electronic funds transfers to occur using the Fedwire system. The Fedwire system is typically used to transfer large sums of money between banks. Commercial banks settle obligations for Fedwire fund transfers through their Federal Reserve accounts.

TYPES OF CHECKS

There are a number of different types of checks that a trade creditor may receive. The most common is a company check, drawn on the buyer's checking account. A company check is a draft, drawn on a bank by a drawer who has an account with the bank and is payable on demand.

Another type of check a creditor may see from time to time is a Cashier's Check. This is a check drawn on the bank itself. A Cashier's Check cannot bounce [unless the bank itself fails]. However, Cashier's checks are forged or stolen every day resulting in losses to creditors who assumed that by accepting a a document that states it is a "cashier's check" that they were protected against loss. Contrary to popular opinion, it is possible for the buyer [under certain conditions] to arrange for a stop payment to be placed on a Cashier's check.

From time to time, a creditor may demand or may receive a certified check. A certified check is drawn on a depositor's account with the bank. A certified check is one in which the bank agrees to withhold sufficient funds from the drawer's account to pay the amount listed on the check. Unfortunately, certified checks are far from secure. It requires little imagination to envision a scenario in which a dishonest customer simply purchases a stamp from a stationary store that reads "Certified Check" and uses that stamp and the company's checks as a mechanism to defraud creditors.

A NOTE ABOUT POSTDATED CHECKS

There is a common misconception that accepting postdated checks is illegal. That myth is false. The drawer for any reason may postdate a check, or a series of checks payable to a creditor. Often, the drawer writes and delivers postdated checks because the drawer does not have sufficient funds to retire a debt and the creditor wants some tangible assurance that the debtor intends to honor the debt.

The bad check laws of the various states do not normally cover postdated checks. For this reason, some creditors are sometimes reluctant to accept postdated checks—but there is a psychological benefit to receiving a series of postdated checks—especially if these checks are delivered to conjunction with a signed Promissory Note.

BANK RATINGS FOR NONBORROWING RELATIONSHIPS

Trade creditors frequently ask banks to provide information about a customer or applicant's relationship with the bank. In addition to the date the customer or applicant's account was opened, creditors typically want to know all of the following information:

- the average balance
- the present balance
- whether or not the account has some form of overdraft protection
- if there have been any NSF checks, and if so how many and over what period of time
- a rating on the account

In response, banks provide ranges rather than specific amounts. There are four basic ranges. They are:

- Low   = 1 to 1.999
- Moderate = 2 to 3.999
- Medium = 4 to 6.999
- High   = 7 to 9.999

Banks list dollar ranges as follows:

- 3 figures = $1 to $999
- 4 figures = $1,000 to $9,999

- 5 figures = $10,000 to $99,999
- 6 figures = $100,000 to $999,999

Thus, if a bank reports that a customer has an average balance in the low five figures, and a current balance in the high four figures the creditor knows:

(1) The average balance is between $10,000 and $19,999 and

(2) The current balance is between $7,000 and $9,999.

BANK RATINGS FOR BORROWING RELATIONSHIPS

If the customer or applicant in question has a borrowing relationship with the bank, trade creditors will be interested in gathering even more information from the bank. Specifically, the trade creditor typically wants to know:

- How long the company has been a customer of the bank
- The types of loans outstanding
- The dollar amount outstanding
- The maximum amount the customer may borrow
- What security, if anything, the bank holds
- A rating of the customer's repayments
- Whether or not the customer is paying as agreed
- Whether or not the customer in question is in compliance with all loan covenants.

REQUESTING BANK REFERENCES

Robert Morris and Associates [RMA] is a trade group representing banks and other financial institutions, just as the National Association of Credit Managers [NACM] represents the interests of trade creditors. RMA is committed to encouraging the exchange of commercial credit information and improving the quality and accuracy of that information.

For decades, the NACM and RMA have worked cooperatively to develop a statement of principles governing the free and responsible flow of credit information between banks and creditors to support the credit based United States economy.

The underpinning of the agreement reached between RMA and NACM is the need for complete, accurate and prompt replies to credit inquiries when they are received. Confidentiality is another of the cornerstones of the agreement of principles between RMA and NACM.

The understandings between NACM and RMA also contemplate that information will be exchanged between banks and trade creditors—not that trade creditors will simply request information which banks will be compelled to provide. When requesting information from a bank, trade creditors should provide the bank with:

- The name and address of the subject of the inquiry, along with the account number
- The reason or purpose of the inquiry
- The creditor's experience with the customer that is the subject of the bank inquiry, including:

    Date account opened

    High credit

    Current balance

    Terms of sale

    Any security or collateral

    Balance past due if any

    Normal manner of payment

- The specific information the creditor making the inquiry would like to receive from the bank. This request would typically include:

    The opening date of the relationship

    For deposit relationships, the average balance, the number of returned checks, a rating of the account [for example, as satisfactory]

    A summary of the borrowing relationship including the type(s) of loan(s), repayment schedule, high credit, balance due, payment performance, overall experience, and the nature of any collateral and the existence of guarantees

Individual commercial banks may receive a dozen or more inquiries a day from trade creditors asking for credit information about the bank's clients. When the number of inquiries is taken into account and the detailed information that trade creditors typically request, it is fair to say that most banks do a good job in responding to credit inquiries.

A bank reference check is essential before a trade creditor can establish an open account—even of terms of cash on delivery. Specifically, a trade creditors need to know enough about the debtor's bank accounts that the creditor is confident that the debtor is able to meet its obligations. Here is a simple example:

Assume that a creditor receives an application and an order for $10,000 from a new customer. The customer offers to pay for the goods with a company check. Without knowing how much the applicant has in its checking account, it would be difficult to approve the order. If the creditor were to reach the applicant's bank and was told the customer had a low five figure average balance, the decision about whether or not to make the sale would be a difficult one. On the other hand, if the bank reported the customer had a medium four figure balance then the decision not to release the order pending would be relatively easy to justify.

Thus, even if a vendor opts to sell on COD terms, the creditor should know to a customer should know:

(1) the average balance in the customer's account

(2) how long the account has been opened and

(3) if there were any NSF checks drawn on that account in the last year.

As mentioned earlier, the most important questions a trade creditor can ask a bank relate to the status of the customer's borrowing arrangements with the bank. From the perspective of the trade creditor, one of the most important types of loans a customer can have with its bank is a working capital line of credit. Working capital lines allow the company to borrow in the short term to make up for any cash shortfall. In theory, a working capital line of credit can smooth out a customer's cash flow and allow the customer to retire bills as they come due.

When a borrowing relationship exists between a customer and its bank, the creditor should learn:

• Whether or not the debtor company has a working capital line of credit

• If a working capital line exists, what is its borrowing limit, and how much is owed at the present time, and

• Whether or not the borrower is or is not in compliance with the bank's loan covenants.

• What security or collateral the bank holds in support of this loan.

The existence of a working capital line of credit and the ability to borrow does not in and of itself guarantee that trade creditors will be paid on time. The fact that a customer could borrow from its bank to pay creditors does not mean it will borrow to do so. Recognizing that trade credit is in a sense a form of interest free short term borrowing, many customers are reluctant to borrow against their working capital line from their bank and pay interest on that money when they can "borrow" from their trade creditors at no charge.

HANDLING A RELUCTANT BANK REFERENCE

Occasionally, a trade creditor will have trouble getting any information from a bank about a customer. Fortunately, there are several ways to get around this problem—none of which are overly intrusive or are in any way unprofessional.

These techniques include:

- Arranging for a bank to bank reference on the customer in question. For whatever reason, banks are sometimes more comfortable sharing information with other banks than they are with trade creditors. The process is straightforward: When a creditor is unable to get the customer or applicant's bank to respond to their questions, the creditor contact's its bank officer and requests that its bank contact the customer's bank for the same information.
- Contacting the customer directly, explaining the problem that the creditor is having in getting the customer/applicant's bank to respond to its request for information, and asking the customer for their involvement or intervention.
- Ask the customer for the name and telephone number of their bank officer or
- Ask the customer to contact their bank officer and arrange for that officer to contact the creditor with the requested information.

AUTHORIZATION TO RELEASE BANK INFORMATION

Frequently, banks refuse to provide information about their customers to trade creditors without the express written authorization of their customer. For this reason, many creditors now include a specific authorization on their credit application form authorizing the release of this information. The need for written authorization is another reason why the creditor should insist that the applicant should sign the credit application form and contract.

A typical authorization looks like the one listed below:

SAMPLE BANK AUTHORIZATION

Date

Bank Name

Address

Attention:

In connection with our efforts to secure open account credit terms from
_____ (name of creditor), the creditor has asked that we sign this
authorization. Please provide the creditor with all customary information
about our business relationship with your bank including but not limited to
information about our depository and our borrowing relationship with the
bank.

Thank you.

_____	_____	_____
Signature	Title	Date

While there is no guarantee that any approach will result in the bank
providing the information the trade creditor has requested, banks have a
vested interest in helping their customers to succeed and if, by providing a
reference, the bank can help its client to secure open account credit, then
it should and normally will do so. In fact, it is in the bank's best interest as
a secured creditor that its customer continue to be able to purchase goods
and services on open account terms.

WORKING WITH FOREIGN BANKS

It is sometimes difficult to get a foreign bank to respond to a direct reference request submitted by the creditor company. Creditors considering a
foreign buyer's creditworthiness may find it helpful to arrange for their
bank to contact the customer's bank for a rating or reference on the customer in question [a bank to bank rating].

There is no way of knowing how cooperative a foreign bank will be,
and unfortunately the information received may not always be reliable.

WORKING WITH BANKS TO ACCELERATE CASH FLOW

The most important tool that the bank can offer its customers to accelerate cash inflows is a bank lockbox system. Over 80% of large companies and more than 60% of mid-sized companies currently use bank lockbox services. Lockbox services enable businesses to improve their cash flow by strategically locating collection points close to where their customers remit payments from. Here is a simple example of the lockbox concept in action:

The vast majority of the customers of a supplier located in Los Angeles, California are located east of the Mississippi. The supplier's bank is located in Los Angeles. That supplier could almost certainly reduce mail float on incoming payments by opening a lockbox east of the Mississippi rather than arranging for all payments to be sent to Los Angeles. The mail float associated with mailing the checks from the east coast to the west coast could easily add one or more days to DSO.

In this scenario, it may turn out that the supplier ends up with two lockboxes—one in Chicago and the other in Los Angeles. This process does not involve guesswork.

Banks have developed sophisticated software models to determine:

(a) how many lockbox locations a particular creditor needs, and

(b) where these lockboxes should be located.

For a nominal fee the bank or a third party specializing in this type of analysis will use sophisticated computer software combined with information from payment remittances to analyze the creditor's customer payment patterns and recommend how many lockboxes the creditor should have and where they should be located. There is a rapid payback on this type of study.

ADVANTAGES AND DISADVANTAGES OF LOCKBOX SERVICES

The main advantage of lockbox services is their simplicity. The supplier's customers are simply instructed to send payment to a P.O. box in a specific city. The customer might not even know the P.O. box is a lockbox. The bank empties that P.O. box several times a day, takes the payments to the check processing center, deposits them, separates the checks from the remittance advice and typically forwards a photocopy of the check along with the original remittance advice to the creditor company for cash application.

Some customers are reluctant to remit payment to a bank lockbox because they recognize that by doing so they will be losing the mail float on the checks being sent across the country. A small number of customers will consistently refuse to change their remittance address to reflect the correct bank lockbox address. In this situation persistence normally results in the correction being made, but it may take several reminders and requests before the buyer changes the remittance address in their accounts payable system.

Lockboxes have an added benefit—they tend to reduce the information delay between the time a customer's check is received and the time their check is posted. This is important because the sooner the information is available to the credit department, the sooner deductions and skipped invoices can be addressed. An additional and significant benefit involves the fact that, by presenting the creditor with remittance information more quickly, lockboxes allow the credit department to release more pending orders more quickly.

DISCOUNTING LETTERS OF CREDIT TO IMPROVE CASH FLOW

Another way to improve cash flow is to discount a time Letter of Credit. A time letter of credit is one that is payable at some point after negotiation—often between 30 and 120 days after presentation. Discounting is a process in which a bank at sight pays a time Letter of Credit that has been confirmed by a U.S.–based bank. The bank's profit on this transaction is the difference between the face value of the invoice and the discounted amount paid to the creditor/seller. Here is an example:

> The seller ships $100,000 to a foreign customer on a 120 day time letter of credit. The seller approaches the confirming bank [often its bank] and arranges to receive what amounts to an advance against the proceeds of the Letter of Credit. In this case, the seller might receive an immediate payment from its bank of $97,000 and at the end of 90 days when payment is due the seller's bank will keep the $100,000 received from the issuing bank in full and final settlement.

The bank may charge a hefty discount fee, but many creditors in need of instant cash are more interested in immediate access to the funds than the amount of the discount. If the confirming bank refuses to discount the letter of credit for any reason, the creditor may be able to discount the letter of credit using a trade finance company or another financial institution.

BANKS AND LETTER OF CREDIT DISCREPANCIES

When a Letter of Credit is payable at sight, if the seller's documents are found to have no discrepancies the seller can normally expect payment within seven days. Unfortunately, a discrepancy in the documentation submitted by the creditor company in support of their draft [their demand for payment] will result in payment delay and additional cost to the seller. It is also possible that a discrepancy may render the Letter of Credit valueless—in which case the creditor may find it difficult if not impossible to collect from the debtor. In either event, discrepancies delay payment.

Credit managers need to do their best to eliminate letter of credit discrepancies. Probably the most important and proactive thing the credit manager can do is to dictate the terms and conditions that must appear on the letter of credit. This can best be accomplished by providing the customer with a detailed, written set of instructions for them to use when they meet with their bank (the issuing bank) to arrange for the letter of credit to be opened.

It is far easier for the buyer and seller to agree on the letter of credit terms before the L/C is issued than afterward. It is also far less expensive to the buyer since the issuing bank will charge for each amendment that must be made. Even worse, if the Letter of Credit has been issued with unacceptable terms and conditions, then the shipment often must be delayed until the credit manager receives confirmation that the amendments have been made.

As a general rule, the seller's credit manager should not release any pending order for shipment until and unless the Letter of Credit is acceptable as presented, or until and unless amendments have been made and received by the seller to the original terms of the letter of credit making that L/C acceptable to the seller. Orders should not be released based on a commitment to amend the Letter of Credit.

TIP: Always consign your goods to the opening bank to try to prevent a situation in which a discrepancy exists and the buyer already has possession of the bill of lading. The bill of lading is the document that permits the buyer to take possession of the goods once they arrive at the port of destination.

BANKS AND DEBTORS

Normally, banks are secured creditors. As a secured creditor, the bank has a great deal of influence over the debtor company. When the bank becomes concerned about the debtor's ability to pay the secured debt and assuming the debtor is in violation of one or more of its loan covenants, the bank has these options:

- It can reduce the line of credit.

- The bank can withdraw the line of credit.

- It can demand payment in full of the outstanding balance.

- The bank can request that the debtor agree to allow the creditor to seize the company [assuming the bank has a security interest in essentially all of the assets of the company].

- The bank can "suggest" the customer make other banking arrangements.

- The bank can assess additional fees or include additional requirements or terms and conditions.

WHEN BANKS CALL THE LOAN [DEMAND PAYMENT]

Credit professionals need to know that when the bank, as a secured creditor, calls the note and demands payment in full, chances are excellent that the debtor company will file for bankruptcy protection. A bankruptcy filing does not necessarily impair the bank's security interest. The reality of a bankruptcy filing is that secured creditors such as the debtor's bank often receive payment in full at the expense of general unsecured trade creditors.

There are a number of ways that banks tell their customers that the bank no longer will support the debtor, including these:

(a) The bank may suggest or indicate that the customer should begin to look for a new lender.

(b) The bank may threaten to "pull the line" and to foreclose on the collateral because the debtor company is in violation of its loan covenants.

(c) The bank may reduce the debtor's line of credit in an effort to limit or to reduce the bank's dollar exposure.

(d) The debtor may be charged substantially higher interest on its borrowings

(e) The bank may request or even demand additional collateral as security for the outstanding debt.

(f) At its option, the bank may dishonor checks that it might otherwise have covered for the debtor using the debtor's working capital line or some other form of overdraft protection.

INDICATIONS OF A TROUBLED BANK RELATIONSHIP

A customer is unlikely to inform trade creditors directly about the problems that it may be having with its bank for fear of creating a problem in which both its bank credit and its trade credit begin to dry up at the same time. By periodically following up with a customer's bank loan officer, it is sometimes possible to get an indication of the bank's comfort level with the customer.

When a bank has decided that it is ready to walk away from its customer's business, it is highly unlikely the bank will inform trade creditors of this decision. Since trade creditors normally provide goods and services on an open account basis, banks want creditors to continue to ship to their customer since the assets delivered on open account terms increase the pool of assets available to the secured creditor if the debtors assets must be liquidated.

In this scenario, ideally the debtor will find another bank or financial institution to replace the secured creditor. The secured creditor bank will expect the new bank to pay off the secured debt in full. The trouble for the debtor is the same concerns and problems that made the original lender nervous about the account are the same problems that will make it difficult for that company to find another financial institution to "buy out" the original bank and take over the risk of doing business with the debtor.

THE TRADE CREDITOR'S RESPONSE

Any time a creditor learns that a customer is looking for a new bank, it is important for the credit manager to know why, to look carefully at the debtor company, and to determine under what terms and conditions [if any] sales to the customer can be made safely.

VALUE ADDED BANK SERVICES

Many banks offer a variety of value added services in addition to lockbox payment services. One example is information storage. Some banks store images of the front and back of checks received for future reference at the customer's request. Some banks can also place this information on microfilm for delivery to their customers.

Other banks use sophisticated imaging software to capture information and images from both the customer's check and its remittance advice. By scanning these documents the bank can provide an electronic version of the debtor's remittance advice capable of being used to automatically post against the accounts receivable ledger using software referred to generically as Auto Cash.

THE AUTOMATED CLEARINGHOUSE

The Automated Clearinghouse [ACH] is a rapidly growing alternative to paper checks. The ACH already handles billions of payment transactions annually and is used by more than 95% of the country's financial institutions. The ACH is most frequently used to process low dollar, pre-authorized repetitive payments such as direct deposit of payroll payments, social security payments, annuities, pensions, and other forms of payment.

The ACH system can be used by suppliers to extract payments from customer accounts. This is called a Direct Debit [sometimes referred to as a direct payment]. Direct Debits improve the vendor's cash flow, the credit department's DSO and the seller's ability to forecast cash inflows.

Direct Debits work this way:

- The customer authorizes the creditor to electronically collect a pre-authorized amount from a checking or a savings account. This can be a recurring amount, or a different specified amount for each transaction

- Once withdrawn by direct debit, the payment is forwarded from the buyer's bank to the seller's bank

WIRE TRANSFER PAYMENTS

Wire transfer payments are handled in the U.S. through the Fedwire Funds Transfer System. Fedwire payments are generated in real time. Foreign wire transfer payments are handled through the Clearinghouse Interbank Payments System [CHIPS] which is owned and operated by the New York Clearinghouse bank. Once received and verified, incoming foreign wire transfer payments are sent to the appropriate depository institution for deposit into the creditor's account using the Fedwire system for settlement.

FINANCIAL ELECTRONIC DATA INTERCHANGE

Financial EDI may well be the biggest key to improved productivity. Financial EDI reduces information float, which in addition to streamlining cash inflows is the greatest benefit of Financial EDI. Financial EDI [FEDI] involves the electronic transmission of remittance information to accelerate the posting process.

Some FEDI services provide a feature in which the bank helps the creditor to electronically match incoming lockbox payments with the creditor's detailed accounts receivable—through the use of what is called Auto-Cash software. FEDI promises to be one of the biggest changes in the future of cash payments from customers as more companies use automation to reduce overhead costs, track cash inflows and outflows, and improve efficiency.

CHAPTER 11

TRADE REFERENCES

It is impossible to make an informed credit decision without current and accurate information. One of the best sources of information about an applicant's creditworthiness is the applicant's trade references. Experienced credit professionals recognize that customers will always hand pick the company's they list on a credit application. Therefore, credit managers should always compare the way the applicant pays its best creditors to how the company pays the rest of its creditors. This can be done fairly quickly by comparing the payment history for references listed to the payment pattern shown on the credit report.

It is not uncommon for an applicant to have creditors that are paid right on time, and others that seem to be paid whenever the applicant gets around to paying them. Often, it is possible to spot a pattern that explains why certain suppliers are paid on time while others are not.

For example, the creditor might note that Original Equipment Manufacturers get paid on time while distributors are paid erratically. This would suggest that the customer is an opportunist... paying OEMs on time because that is the only way to assure the flow of goods—while paying distributors erratically because the customer can always find another distributor. One way to mitigate this problem involves addressing concerns about payment with the applicant before the decision to establish an open account is made.

WHEN TO CHECK TRADE REFERENCES

Typically, trade references are checked in the following situations:

(a) When establishing a new account

(b) During a regularly scheduled update of an existing account, or

(c) In response to an unusual event such as a large order being placed, or if an account were to become seriously past due.

Contacting trade references is labor intensive, making this process both time-consuming and expensive. Larger credit departments typically have at least one person whose primary responsibility is to gather trade references and respond to credit reference requests received from other creditors.

Selecting, training and retaining a person in the credit investigation position is important. Often, the position is entry level and is a springboard to other assignments in the credit department or elsewhere in the company. Unfortunately, unless the credit manager develops a strategy to retain the new employees in this position much of the time spent training the person is wasted.

CHARACTERISTICS OF A GOOD CREDIT INVESTIGATOR

When the credit manager is interviewing applicants for the position of credit investigator, he or she should look for some evidence of the following traits:

- A natural inquisitiveness

- A certain amount of assertiveness

- Persistence, combined with tact and courtesy

- Patience and self control, combined with politeness and initiative

---

Having to periodically hire and train people as credit investigators is a business reality for credit managers. The alternative to allowing employees to springboard from this position into other areas in the department is to hold back an employee capable of handling more complex tasks. Holding any employee back is demoralizing and a waste of a valuable resource—the capacity of the employee.

One strategy that seems to work well is to tell employees when they are hired that they must be in the position for one year before a transfer will be approved. [*Note:* This does not preclude the credit manager from promoting this person into a new position, it is an effort to ensure that the employee will be in the new account investigation position long enough to repay the credit department's investment in training.]

SUBSTITUTING TRADE CLEARANCE REPORTS FOR TRADE REFERENCES

Calling or contacting trade references for information is often a hit or miss proposition. Often, the caller will be referred to a voice mail system, and voice mail messages are often not returned. Often, when the call does get through the caller will be asked to fax or mail their inquiry. Occasionally, a creditor listed as a reference will make answering inquiries such a low priority that by the time the information is returned to the inquiring creditor it is too late to be of any immediate value.

For many creditors, there is an alternative to the process of calling each of the trade references listed. Many creditors are members of one or more industry credit groups. Most of these industry credit groups furnish trade clearance reports to members for a fee. These trade clearance reports typically contain much the same information, as creditors would get if they called the trade references listed on the application. Specifically, industry credit group trade clearance reports typically contain the following information:

- The reporting member's number—from which the creditor can determine who reported the information.
- The date the account was opened.
- The customer's high credit
- The current balance
- The terms of sale
- The average number of days to pay, and
- The aging of the accounts receivable [into aging buckets]

In many companies, the information from these trade clearance reports can be substituted for the information that would be obtained through direct trade reference checks.

THE CREDIT BUREAU REPORT ALTERNATIVE

Some creditors rely on credit bureau reports as an alternative to direct investigations of applicants for credit terms. Credit reports typically contain a great deal of information about the target company in addition to the trade payment information provided on a trade clearance report. The advantages of using credit reports rather than contacting the references [or using a trade clearance report] include all of the following:

- Access to credit reports is almost instantaneous. Contacting trade references is not.

- Given the quantity and the quality of information provided on a credit bureau report, many creditors find the use of credit bureau reports a cost effective alternative to the direct investigation process.

The disadvantage of using credit bureau reports is the fact that the creditor does not know who the trade creditors are who are reporting their experience to the credit reporting agency. As a result, the credit manager is not able to see how the applicant pays creditors their industry.

ANTITRUST ISSUES

Sometimes trade references must be requested from competitors. Federal courts have already decided the issue of whether or not sharing information about the creditworthiness of a customer is an illegal restraint of trade. The Courts have determined it is not; provide that the information shared is factual and historical. Federal laws specifically prohibit any discussion among creditors of future actions, including future terms, future prices, future marketing plans, distribution plans, new markets and future discounts—but have decided that there is a legitimate purpose and value to sharing historical credit information.

MISREPRESENTATION OF THE FACTS

Trade creditors are under no legal obligation to provide credit references to any other creditor. If they decide to share credit information with the party inquiring, there is no reason to "stretch" the truth in any direction. If the creditor has nothing good to say about a customer, but would prefer to say nothing bad about the company, then the creditor can simply decline to provide any information. Therefore, in theory, the creditor has these two options:

(a) Provide the requested information honestly and accurately, or
(b) Decline to provide any information about their customer.

If a creditor provides a reference containing false or inaccurate information, the creditor may be sued by the other party for providing false information. The lawsuit would arise because the creditor who relied on the false information suffered damages or lost money as a result of relying on the false statements.

THE RISKS OF TELLING THE TRUTH

Unfortunately, providing a factual trade references is not without risk. For example, if a creditor provides a truthful but unflattering trade reference about a customer and that customer "somehow" finds out what the creditor said then the customer may retaliate by taking its business elsewhere.

In theory, the creditor inquiring about a mutual customer should never reveal its sources of information, or what specific creditors said about the applicant. In reality, this breach of etiquette and trust occurs every day. Many credit managers know from bitter experience that many creditors do not respect the fact that trade references are supposed to be provided in confidence to the inquirer.

ONCE BITTEN, TWICE SHY

Without an assurance of confidentiality, creditors are often unwilling to provide credit references to anyone they don't know. Creditors need information in order to establish appropriate credit limits and terms, and yet certain trade creditors degrade their ability to get the information they need by violating the rules about confidentiality.

One lesson that credit managers learn after providing a credit rating and having the customer find out what was said is to make certain to respond only to written inquiries. There are several advantages of requiring written inquiries including these:

- The creditor will receive fewer inquiries because some companies are simply too lazy to request information in writing.

- The creditor will have a written record of the information that was reported.

- The response can be completed at a time that is more convenient to the creditor company.

- The creditor has a better idea about who is actually making the inquiry.

- The creditor can add a statement to the inquiry that the information is being provided in confidence to the inquiring party with the understanding that nothing in the credit reference will be revealed to the subject of the inquiry.

PROVIDING FALSE CREDIT REFERENCES TO COMPETITORS

A creditor might be tempted to provide a false, unfavorable credit rating on a customer either to punish that customer, or in an attempt to dissuade a competitor from establishing an account with that company. In either case, the creditor company may be sued for defamation if the customer learns of the false statements made about it, or it may be sued by the other creditor for unfair business practices.

WHEN IN DOUBT, SAY NOTHING

Creditors are not obligated by any rule or law to provide any information [including a credit rating] to any person or party inquiring about one of their customers. When in doubt about what to say or about who is asking, creditors always have the option of not responding.

Creditors submitting credit inquiries should expect only certain information. Only the following information should be requested, and provided:

- The date the account was opened
- The date of the last sale
- The customer's recent high credit [the largest open account balance in the last twelve months]
- The dollar amount owing at this time
- The amount past due, if any
- How far past due the account is at this time
- The creditor's terms of sale
- Whether or not the account is secured, and if so in what form that security takes
- The normal manner of payment of the customer—ideally the weighted average number of days the debtor takes to pay invoices

The key is that all of the information provided should be factual and historical data. A creditor might be excused for asking for more information, but the provider of the information must know what questions cannot be answered. Contrary to popular opinion, a debtor company's largest trade creditor is under no obligation to provide any more information than any other trade creditor.

TRADE REFERENCES AND DEFAMATION

Clearly, creditors can commit libel or slander while providing a trade reference. For this reason, credit managers should provide specific written instructions to their subordinates about how trade reference requests are to be answered.

The first rule should be that only designated persons may respond to credit inquiries. The second rule should be that all requests must be in writing, and submitted by fax or mail. The third rule should be that all requests received must be on the inquiring company's letterhead.

The personnel assigned to provide trade references should be carefully trained. One of the cornerstones of that training is one simple statement:

"Stick to the facts if you want to stay out of trouble."

Truth is a perfect defense against a claim of defamation. It is not defamation to provide an accurate but unflattering credit reference. Therefore, if a creditor only provides factual information about its customers they cannot get into legal trouble.

One of the biggest areas of potential credit exposure involves making so-called "off the record" comments about a customer. "Off the record" comments still subject the creditor company to liability since the laws relating to defamation do not recognize any special category of comments as being exempt from the prohibitions against libel or slander.

Similarly, creditors cannot recommend and should offer no comments about whether the party inquiring should offer the applicant company open account credit terms—and if they do under what terms and conditions, and at what credit limit. Often, the creditor might receive a relatively benign inquiry after the standard reference check. The party inquiring typically asks one of the following questions:

- Is this account satisfactory?

- How would you rate this account?

- What additional comments would you like to make about this company?

- What is your recommendation about this account?

The problem is that each of these is a trick question—and the trick is that each of the questions calls for a subjective, non-factual response. Let's take the first question as an example: "Is the account satisfactory?"

If they choose to answer at all to this question, a creditor would need to ask the party asking this question to:

- Define satisfactory
- Satisfactory to whom
- Based on what criteria
- In what specific areas
- Satisfactory now, or ever since the account was opened

The second question has the same problems: "How would you rate the account?" The questions the creditor would have to ask would include:

- How would I rate the account based on what criteria? Based on size? Financial strength? Purchase volume? Payment history? Profitability? Or perhaps a combination of all of the above, or possibly based on none of these factors.

THE RULE OF THUMB FOR RESPONDING TO CREDIT INQUIRIES

The rule of thumb in responding to credit inquiries is to assume that the customer involved will be told everything you say, or shown everything you write about them. If this mindset can be maintained, it makes it far easier for credit department personnel to remember to stick to the facts.

If the respondent treats every call and every inquiry received as if one copy were going to be delivered to the company's biggest competitor and another copy was going to be delivered directly to customer itself then each credit inquiry would probably be given the time and attention [and the caution] that it deserves.

SPECIFICALLY DELEGATE RESPONSIBILITY FOR PROVIDING RESPONSES TO REFERENCE REQUESTS

Credit managers should decide which of their employees is authorized to provide trade references. Most larger credit departments delegate the task to one specific individual—and provided the individual responding is well trained there should be no problems.

The training should be extensive, since mistakes as described above can be expensive. The person providing references needs to be told exactly how to respond to specific questions. The right person for this position is one that cannot be easily intimidated, and the person given this responsibility should not be overly chatty. The goal of the respondent is to avoid sharing more information than the creditor company wants or to reveal.

The respondent should be taught to deal effectively, courteously, professionally and firmly with callers. Here are some examples:

- If the company has a policy of rating by mail or by fax only, the respondent should state this policy when an inquiry is received by telephone. If the caller presses for a verbal rating, this statement should simply be repeated.

- In response to complaints, threats, and other attempts to intimidation the respondent into providing a verbal rating, the respondent should simply re-state the company policy.

- The respondent should be told that if the situation is becoming too difficult that the caller may be referred to the credit manager.

- The respondent should be told that if the caller becomes abusive or profane that they are permitted to hang up on the caller.

- The respondent will be told exactly what information he or she is permitted to give. The respondent should be told specifcally never to respond to *any* other questions such as: "How would you rate this customer."

- The respondent should be told never to guess at any fact presented in response to an inquiry. One common question is: What is the customer's high credit?" If the company's computer software only provides high credit for the last 12 months, that fact should be listed.

RATING BY TELEPHONE

If a creditor rates by telephone, it is a good idea to ask for the caller's telephone number and company name and call them back. Doing so reduces the likelihood that you are speaking to someone other than who they claim to be.

TIP: Many companies arrange for their switchboard operator to screen calls to the credit department. If the caller wants a credit rating, they are referred to a recorded message. The message instructs the caller to fax or mail their inquiry, and provides the relevant information for them to do so. This system works well provided that the inquiries are answered in a timely manner. If they are not, the credit department will have to contend with urgent follow up calls that are intrusive.

ASK FOR A RECIPROCAL RATING

It is always a good idea to ask the party requesting information about a customer for a reciprocal credit rating on the company. More often than not, the request for a credit rating is strictly routine. However, the request may come as a result of deterioration in the customer's payment pattern or financial condition. Asking the caller about the experience is a good way to gather up-to-date information about the customer in question.

THE LIMITATIONS OF TRADE REFERENCES

Some companies deliberately select a handful of vendors, pay them right on time, and use them again and again as trade references recognizing the need for open account terms and the competitive advantage of being able to purchase goods and services on open account credit terms. However, paying trade creditors on time is the exception rather than the rule for these companies.

It is important that creditors look beyond the list of references provided by the customer to get a less biased sample that is more indicative of the customer's payment pattern. One of the simplest ways to do so is to contact the customer and ask for additional references. Asking for additional references is also important when the first references provided contradictory information.

For example, rather than making a credit decision based on one good trade reference, one bad reference and one intermediate reference the credit manager should insist on additional trade references. If the customer asks why additional references are required, the best answer is the truth. That truth is as follows: the references provided certain contradictory information and additional trade references are needed to clarify the issue.

TIP: One of the most important factors for a creditor to consider as it relates to a trade reference is the length of time the reference has been doing business with the customer/applicant. Simply put, a long credit history with a supplier is better than a short one.

COMPETITOR REFERENCES

In addition to asking the customer for additional trade references, it is quite possible that the salesperson will be able to supply additional references based on either their conversations with the customer, their observations of the customer's operations. If nothing else, the salesperson should be able to tell the credit manager which competitor(s) the customer had been purchasing from.

While all the trade references are important, it is especially important to get trade reference in the same industry as the potential creditor. A reference from a competitor is important for two reasons. First, there is the possibility that the customer is coming to you because they have burned their bridges with their previous supplier—your competitor. The other reason that creditors should ask for a competitor as a reference is to find out how the debtor tends to pay companies in the creditor's line of business. For example, if your company sells a product that is seasonal and the debtor has a history of delaying payment to your competitor then chances are good that the debtor will pay your bills slowly, sooner or later.

PAYMENT PLANS

Customers occasionally contact creditors and ask them to accept an extended payment plan. These requests are a minefield of risk for the creditor. They should only be approved at the highest level in the credit department, and no one should be in a hurry to accept any payment plan. If the debtor submits a payment proposal, the credit manager should consider all of the following factors:

(1) The customer may simply be using the request to delay legal action or third party collection action by creditors - while the owners systematically liquidate the assets of the business and pocket the cash, or

(2) The customer may have every intention of paying creditors but find that they are unable to do so due to factors the debtor could not have anticipated.

(3) The customer may make a different payment proposal to every creditor. In this scenario, credit managers run the risk of accepting a payment plan only to learn after the fact that the debtor/customer has offered a better payment plan to other creditors—or worse to a competitor.

(4) The customer may be paying some of its trade creditors on time, and proposing an extended payment plan only to vendors it feels do not supply an essential product or service.

Credit managers should have the answer to all of these questions before agreeing to accept any extended payment proposal:

(1) Why didn't the custom ask its bank for short-term capital rather than asking your trade creditors to act as bankers by carrying the delinquent accounts receivable?

(2) If you the debtor asked its bank for short-term capital, what was their response?

(3) If the bank turned down their request, what reason or reasons did the bank give for that decision?

(4) From whom will the customers purchase goods during the extended payment period?

(5) How does the customer plan to pay for new merchandise the company needs to remain viable?

(6) Are they proposing exactly the same extended payment plan to every creditor?

(7) What other payment plans have been offered?

(8) What caused the company to have such severe cash flow problems that an extended payment proposal became necessary?

(9) What steps is the customer taking to make certain you never run into this problem again?

(10) Which creditors have agreed to extended dating proposal? Is there any reason that I cannot not call the companies to verify the facts?

(11) Has the customer considered a bankruptcy filing as an alternative? If so, is a bankruptcy filing still under consideration?

(12) Ask the debtor to describe its current relationship with its bank, or other secured creditor?

(13) What agreements if any have been reached with the secured creditor with respect to the money outstanding, both long term and short term?

Before agreeing to any payment proposal it is important that the credit manager speak to other creditors to confirm:

- The debtor has told them the same story

- The debtor has proposed the same payment plan to them

- The other creditor is not aware of any facts that would tend to cause the credit manager to question the customer's sincerity

- Other creditors are not aware of anyone else getting a better deal than the deal being offered to the creditor

CONFIDENTIALITY

One if the most basic requirements for the free and open exchange of credit information between and among trade creditors, banks and other creditors is that the information provided will be kept confidential. The credit department places confidentiality and its reputation at risk any time it shares information learned from trade references with anyone inside the company. Therefore, credit managers and their subordinates must resist the temptation to share information with other employees [such as sales department personnel] in an effort to explain or to justify their credit decision.

SUMMARY

Trade references are an inexpensive source of current information about a customer or an applicant. However, credit managers and their subordinates should be aware of the risks they run every time they respond to a credit inquiry.

One reason not to rate by telephone is that rating by mail and fax allows the credit department to schedule the work for slower periods. If the company rates by telephone, then credit department personnel will constantly be interrupted for credit references—often during the busiest part of the day when credit department personnel should be concentrating on improving the company's collection results, not on assisting other companies.

CHAPTER 12

Getting Information from Publicly Held Companies

SECURITIES AND EXCHANGE COMMISSION REPORTING REQUIREMENTS

Obtaining financial statements from publicly traded companies whose equity or debt are sold on any of the established exchanges in the United States [such as NASDAQ, the American Stock Exchange, or the New York Stock Exchange] is easy.

Under the reporting requirements set forth by the Securities and Exchange Commission [SEC], publicly traded companies with outstanding equity or debt are required to disclose their financial condition on a quarterly basis. The filing of financial statements with the SEC is a matter of public record. Consequently, one of the best sources of detailed financial information about U.S.–based publicly traded companies is the SEC.

Financial information is available on the SEC's web site, which can be accessed free of charge. The SEC's Electronic Data Gathering and Retrieval System [referred to by its acronym EDGAR] is located to: www.sec.gov. The EDGAR archives contains quarterly financial information for at least the last three years along with all of the other documents required to be filed electronically by the SEC for the same period of time.

AUDITED VS. UNAUDITED FINANCIAL STATEMENTS

The annual report [the 10-K] that the SEC requires all public companies to file must be audited by an independent CPA firm. Quarterly financial statements filed with the SEC are unaudited—but it is common that these statements are reviewed by the filing company's independent auditors before the filing.

Even though the quarterly financial statements submitted to the SEC on EDGAR are not fully audited, they are considered reliable because companies that file fraudulent financial statements with the SEC are subject to civil and criminal penalties under various federal laws including the Securities Act of 1933 and the Securities and Exchange Act of 1934.

CANADIAN FINANCIAL STATEMENTS

Getting financial statements from publicly traded Canadian companies is as simple as it is in the United States. The fastest, easiest and most economical way to gather quarterly financial information about a public company in Canada is by accessing Canada's SEDAR database on the Internet. SEDAR is an acronym for the System for Electronic Document Analysis and Retrieval.

The SEDAR web site is similar to EDGAR. It is a filing system for basic disclosure documents for public companies and mutual funds in Canada. Filing is required for all Canadian public companies, and these public filings generally become public within 48 hours of filing. Access to the SEDAR database is free. The URL for this web site is: http://www.sedar.com.

The SEDAR system contains a basic document called a SEDAR profile. It contains all of the following information about companies:

● Company name

● Mailing address and headquarters address

● Telephone and fax numbers

● Contact name

● Name of the independent auditor

● Stock exchange listing(s)

● Financial statements

DIRECT REQUESTS

Publicly traded Canadian companies will normally send individual investors, or creditors, a copy of their annual report at any time and at no charge in response to a direct request for this information. If the public Canadian company has a web site, chances are good that the web site will contain some information about the customer's financial condition and/or recent financial performance.

AUSTRALIAN FINANCIAL STATEMENTS

Financial statements on Australian public companies can be accessed directly from the company's web site in many instances, or it can be ordered through the Australian Stock Exchange. That URL is: http://www.asx.com.au under the heading Investor Select. A brief summary of information about publicly traded Australian companies can be accessed for free at this URL: http://www.asx.com.au/scripts/irxxxx.asp.

SOUTH AFRICAN FINANCIAL STATEMENTS

Financial statements on South African companies can be accessed on line. AFS online includes the annual financial statements of almost all listed South African companies. The site is continuously updated. The URL is: http://www.ventureweb.co.za/afs/main.html.

GERMAN COMPANY FINANCIAL STATEMENTS

Information about public companies in Germany is often available on their web pages, although not always in English. Certain information about publicly traded companies is also available on web site for the German stock exchange. That URL is: www.exchange.de/cgi-bin/sitemap.cgi.

OTHER SOURCES OF FINANCIAL INFORMATION

Most public companies whose stock or debt is listed on any of the major stock exchanges have informational web pages on the Internet. Credit managers interested in access to links to all of the major stock exchanges worldwide can find this information at the following URL: http://www/etc.com.au/fsi/stock_exch/welcome.html.

WEB SITES

Most public companies provide detailed information about the activities of the company on their web page, and many include a link that will allow a visitor to access the company's most current financial statements. Often, this information can be found on the web site under the heading "Company Information."

PRESS RELEASES OFTEN CONTAIN FINANCIAL INFORMATION

A web page also frequently contains access to the company's most recent press releases. When gathering information in order to monitor and manage credit risk, credit professionals should always scan the customer's recent press releases for information of interest to concern. On the Internet, press releases on public companies can be found at a number of different web sites. One of the most popular is the Press Release Newswire. Its URL is: http://www.prnewswire.com.

> Credit professionals can strengthen the bond between the credit department and the sales department by sharing information about a customer or applicant learned during the credit review process. It takes very little time and cost almost nothing to forward a copy of an interesting press release to the salesperson. Since information and knowledge are power, giving information to the salesperson makes them more effective.

OTHER WEB SITES

There are literally dozens of other web sites that contain financial information about public companies. Some of these web pages provide essentially the same information as the SEC's EDGAR web site.

Other web pages provide both the "raw" financial information and financial analysis including ratio analysis. For example, many brokerage houses are now offering on line access to financial data along with financial analysis including trend analysis, comparative analysis and ratio analysis.

Note: Some web pages charge an access fee for financial analysis. However, there are enough free sites that offer financial analysis and commentary for free that it is difficult to justify the cost to join a fee based Internet web site.

FREE FINANCIAL INFORMATION AND ANALYSIS

One of the best of these free web sites is The Market Guide Investor® at www.marketguide.com. The Market Guide Investor provides a vast amount of information about thousands of publicly held companies including:

(1) Historical financial information

(2) Current financial statements

(3) Trend analysis

(4) Ratio analysis (yes, the ratio analysis is done for you) and

(5) Comparative analysis

Another web page that contains financial statements as well as other information useful and helpful to credit professionals is The Public Register® located at URL: www.publicregister.com. In addition to financial statements, this web site offers the following free services:

- Financial profiles
- E mail link's to the company's investor relations department
- Free copies of annual reports
- Access to bulletin boards and other on-line discussion forums

ORDERING ANNUAL REPORTS ON LINE

If a creditor is interested in receiving a hard copy of a company or customer's annual report, there are any number of locations on line where these reports can be ordered. For example, annual reports on more than 1,100 companies may be ordered free from *The Annual Reports Service*. This company's URL is: www.annualreportservice.com.

Another on line web site that can be used to request free annual reports is the Public Registrar's Annual Report Service. This company's URL is: www.prars.com.

CUSTOMER WEB SITES

As mentioned earlier, one of the best sources of information is the company itself. It is relatively simple to request information directly from the customer once the creditor has located the customer's web page. There are any number of search engines that make this process easier. One of the most popular search engines is sponsored by Yahoo! Inc. The URL for that site is: http://www.yahoo.com.

DIRECT CONTACT WITH A PUBLIC COMPANY

When contacting the customer, the creditor should ask to speak to the investor relations department. Once in contact with investor relations, the credit manager should ask to be put on the customer's mailing list so that future quarterly updates will be sent automatically.

MORE CURRENT INFORMATION

More current information than is available from a company's quarterly financial statement filings may be available either from the company itself in the form of press releases, from one of the on-line sources of press release information, or from the SEC's EDGAR archives in the form of a Form 8-K filing.

Publicly traded companies are required to use Form 8-K to report the occurrence of any material events or corporate changes which are of importance to investors, security holders, creditors and other interested parties.

THE ANNUAL REPORT

Public companies generate annual reports to their stockholders and to other interested parties. Most annual reports contain optional items, however the US Securities and Exchange Commission mandates and requires that annual reports contain all of the following required elements:

- *The Report of Management.* This is a letter from a senior executive attesting to the validity and accuracy of the financial information contained in the annual report. The report attests to the presence of effective internal accounting and control systems that monitor operations, as well as the reliability of the financial reporting, and compliance with applicable federal laws.

- *The Auditor's report.* This report is a summary of the findings of an independent CPA firm indicating whether the financial statements as submitted are complete, and prepared consistent with generally accepted accounting principles [GAAP].

- *The management discussion.* Management discussion involves a series of detailed reports about the company's performance. The management discussion covers the results of operations, as well as the adequacy of liquid and capital reserves to fund ongoing operations.

- *Financial statements and notes provide readers of the annual report with information about the company's financial performance and recent financial history.* The SEC requires that public companies include in their annual reports (a) a statement of earnings showing sales revenues, expenses and net earnings or losses for at least the last three years, (b) two years of balance sheet data to allow for comparison, and (c) statement of cash flows, and (d) a set of related notes to the financial statements that provide explanations as well as additional and supplementary information.

- *Selected Financial Data.* This section summarizes the financial condition of the company and its performance over the prior five years. This data may be used for making comparisons over time about the company's financial performance.

THE PROSPECTUS

A company that is in the process of selling stock or debt to the public on one of the established exchanges must file a prospectus with the United States Securities and Exchange Commission. The prospectus describes the future plans of the business, presents relevant facts about the current operations, and provides information investors and others need to make an informed decision. Creditors can easily obtain a copy of a prospectus and use the information it contains—including financial data to support a credit decision about the company.

SUMMARY

There is no reason and no excuse for not having current financial information on a customer that is publicly traded. Even if the credit manager does not have access to the Internet, almost every publicly traded company in the United States will provide financial statements on request by contacting the company's Investor Relations Department. In many instances, the request is automated. The caller presses a few buttons on the telephone, leaves their name and address on a voice mail recording and the requested information arrives by mail a few days later.

Some credit professionals do not order financial information from public companies based on the assumption that because the company is publicly traded it is financially sound and stable. This is not necessarily the case. There are many instances of public companies that have run into serious cash flow problems, and even filed for bankruptcy protection. Given the minimal amount of effort required to obtain quarterly financial statements from publicly traded companies, there does not seem to be a good reason for any credit professional not to have this information on file.

Even if a creditor company elects not to bother its privately held customers with requests for financial information, there is no reason that these companies should not request statements from publicly traded customers. Often, these public companies are among a creditor's biggest customers, so having financial information only on these companies will improve the creditor's ability to manage risk.

CHAPTER 13

GETTING FINANCIAL INFORMATION FROM PRIVATELY HELD COMPANIES

There are approximately ten million businesses in the United States. Over 99% of these companies are privately held. These privately held companies include proprietorships, partnerships, and partnerships of all types including "C" corporations, subchapter S corporations and limited liability corporations. Publicly owned companies are corporations whose shares of stock can be purchased by the general public through any of the established stock exchanges including the New York Stock Exchange, and the American Stock Exchange. The financial statements of public companies are a matter of public record. There are any number of ways that creditors can obtain them including simply calling the company, asking for their investor relations department and arranging for the information to be mailed or faxed to your home or office.

On the other hand, a privately held proprietorship, partnership or corporation is under absolutely no obligation to release its financial statements to anyone [with the possible exception of federal, state and local taxing authorities]. Therefore, privately held companies are unlikely to release financial information to their unsecured trade creditors unless they are given a reason to do so. It is often difficult to persuade privately held companies to share their financial statements with general unsecured trade creditors because privately held companies have no legal obligation to do so. However, since privately held companies account for more than 99% of all companies in the United States, creditors are going to need financial information from at least some of these millions of privately held companies. Under certain circumstances, it will simply not be possible for the credit manager to approve the credit limit or terms requested without having the opportunity to review the customer's financial statements.

HOW FINANCIAL STATEMENTS ARE PREPARED

In a small company, generally a bookkeeper [possibly on a part-time basis] or the owner of the company, records information about the financial operations of the business. Some of the activities captured in these records would include:

- the purchase of inventory

- the sale of merchandise

- the purchase of machinery and equipment

- payment of wages and salaries

For small companies, financial activities are typically recorded on spreadsheets. There are a number of personal computer (PC) based spreadsheet programs available for this purpose. While the cost of these programs is minimal, the software programs are powerful and can compile, sort and document the information entered so that the software can generate financial statements including an Income Statement, a Balance Sheet and a Statement of Cash Flows.

As a company grows in sales volume and in complexity, normally the owner hires a full time bookkeeper, or even an accountant to help track the operations and the financial performance of the business more proactively. Financial statements [including the Balance Sheet, Income Statement and Statement of Cash Flows] are customarily prepared each quarter as well as annually for external use [for example, with the debtor's bank]. In addition, internal reports as generated monthly to help management evaluate and control internal operations. Examples of these internal reports would include daily sales volume reports, and monthly income statements.

FINANCIAL STATEMENTS FOR INTERNAL USE

Even though privately held companies are sometimes unwilling to share financial information with their trade creditors, almost all companies regularly prepare financial statements. Why? Because the management of any business needs a way to track and evaluate the overall performance of that business, and management needs detailed information about the company's financial and operating performance in order to make specific adjustments and corrections in order to maximize profits.

What this means to trade creditors is that customers normally have the financial statements the creditor needs; it is simply a question of whether or not the customer will release the data. No trade creditor will be 100% successful at getting privately held customers to share financial statements, regardless of the products they sell or the dollar amount of open account credit they are being asked to extend to the customer or applicant.

FINANCIAL STATEMENTS AND INVESTORS

In addition to the need for financial information to help internal management to assess the performance of the company, if a privately held company wants to attract outside investors [or already has outside investors that it needs to keep informed] the company will need to provide those investors with information about the performance of the business. Financial statements—since in a very real sense financial statements provide both a historical overview and a current scorecard of the company's performance for review by investors.

Typically, privately held companies' financial statements are not audited. This means that the statements are prepared without the oversight of a third party CPA firm. As a result, the accuracy of unaudited statements is always suspect. However, audits are expensive and unless there is a compelling reason to do so most privately held companies opt not to spend tens of thousands of dollars a year [on average] to have their financial statements audited by an outside CPA firm.

FINANCIAL STATEMENTS AND BANKS

If a privately held company has a borrowing relationship with its bank, they may be required to provide financial statements periodically to the bank. Typically, banks require their borrowers to provide a Balance Sheet, an Income Statement and a Statement of Cash Flows quarterly, and other reports about the bank's collateral monthly. The bank will use the financial statements and the monthly reports, [along with information gathered from other sources] to determine whether to increase the company's line of credit, to reduce it or to leave it where it is.

GATHERING FINANCIAL INFORMATION FROM THE CUSTOMER'S BANK

Occasionally, when a trade creditor is unable to gather financial information directly from the customer they are able to access the information they need by contacting the customer's bank. Normally, the only time the customer's bank officer will reveal anything about the customer's financial condition is when the customer or applicant has specifically authorized the bank to share this data.

A well-written credit application can include a statement authorizing the release of this type of information by the bank. Such a release would typically need to include two specific provisions before the banker would comply. First, the authorization to the bank to release financial information would need to be signed by an officer or an owner of the company. Second, the authorization would normally need to include an indemnification clause in which the customer agrees to hold its bank harmless for any information revealed to the creditor.

WHEN TO REQUEST FINANCIAL STATEMENTS

Depending on a number of factors, a trade creditor might request financial statements before extending credit, before offering extended dating, or before increasing the credit limit to a customer. Some of the factors in the decision about whether or not to request financial statements include:

- The size of the order or credit limit requested.

- The terms of sale offered or requested.

- The company's payment history, high credit and number of years as a customer of the creditor.

- The number of years in business, number of employees, and line of business.

Of course, there is nothing forcing customers to provide creditors with financial statements when they request them, just as there is nothing to prevent a creditor from deciding not to offer a company open account terms if that company refuses to share current financial statements with the creditor.

A privately held customer that is a candidate for a request for financial information is often one that:

(a) requests a relatively large credit limit

(b) elects not to share its financial statements with one or more of the national credit reporting agencies [credit bureaus] that gather this information

(c) is a relatively new customer requesting a substantial line of credit

(d) is a company that has not provided trade references in the dollar range it is requesting from the creditor company

(e) has a modest average bank balance relative to the credit limit requested

ONE REASON REQUESTS FOR FINANCIAL STATEMENTS ARE IGNORED

Occasionally customers will be surprised, even offended when a trade creditor requests financial statements in connection with their credit evaluation process. Many trade creditors do not request financial information from their customers, and it is possible for customers to consider this to be the norm—irrespective of how large an open account the customer is requesting.

As a general rule, if a privately held company is able to obtain credit without sharing its financial statements with creditors it will do so. With this fact in mind, if one creditor is willing to extend credit without financial statements but another trade creditor is not, all things being equal the company willing to extend credit without financial statements is likely to be given the order. For this reason, credit managers need to be judicious about when to request financial information, and when to insist on it as a pre-condition for extending credit.

Clearly, credit professionals could insist on receiving current financial statements from every applicant as a condition of offering open account terms. Most creditors do not do so because of competitive reasons. If the creditor is in the enviable position of having a unique product, or happens to operate in an environment in which demand for the seller's goods exceeds supply then that creditor can and should insist on receiving the customer's financial statements as a condition for considering the applicant company for open account terms. However, most creditors cannot afford to issue ultimatums to customers becuase they do not have the leverage to do so.

THE FINANCIAL STATEMENT CONTROVERSY

Most creditors do not require privately held companies to share financial information. These creditor companies are able to gather enough information from other sources to make the decision. Often, the customer wants a relatively small credit limit—making the decision to approve the credit terms without financial data an easy one.

Fearing that any request for financial information sent to a privately held company could damage the business relationship, some companies forbid their credit department from requesting this data. Similarly, some companies forbid their credit manager from requesting updated financial statements from active accounts out of concern about offending the customer by requesting this information.

Whether the request for financial data is being sent to an applicant or to an established customer, most companies are not offended by the request. In fact, many companies simply ignore the request. Becoming annoyed or angry about receiving a request from a creditor for financial statements is analogous to becoming offended by receiving junk mail.

However, there are a small number of accounts that will complain about a creditor's request for financial information. Any credit department that receives such a complaint, which is often directed to the credit department through the sales department, should answer it in the following manner:

- First, the credit manager, rather than a subordinate should respond.

- The credit manager should apologize for causing offense.

- The credit manager should state that the request was considered strictly routine—and not meant to suggest that the company under review represented a credit risk.

- The credit manager should indicate that they recognize that the company has a choice about whether or not to provide this type of information to its suppliers.

- If the customer refuses to do so, the creditor should note the file so that no follow ups requests for financial information are sent.

The fact that a complaint has been lodged should not change the process the credit manager goes through in evaluating a company for open account credit terms—except that the credit manager should be slightly more thorough in evaluating the non-financial factors before deciding whether or not to extend credit to the applicant. In other words, the fact that the customer complained about being asked for financial information, and the fact that the credit manager contacted the customer and apologized for offending them by doing so, does not change the fact that in certain situations it will simply not be possible to offer the customer the credit limit or the credit terms they requested without the customer's financial information.

USING SALESPEOPLE TO GET FINANCIAL STATEMENTS

Creditors should make the process of requesting financial information from new accounts seem as routine and as natural as possible. One way to create an environment in which a request by the credit department for financial statements does not come as a surprise to an applicant for the salesperson to tell the applicant that the credit department will "probably" be contacting them to request current financial statements. A little cooperation between the salesperson and the credit department will significantly increase the likelihood that the customer will provide the requested information. From the salesperson's perspective, the more information the credit department has on file the more likely the credit manager is going to approve the credit limit requested.

One way to reinforce the idea that financial statements are part of the regular credit review process is to financial statements on the credit application. Specifically, the credit application should state that that the customer's financial statements are expected to accompany the completed and signed credit application.

The credit department's goal is to be able to offer a customer the credit limit and credit terms they need and deserve. If a customer seems reluctant to share its financial statements with the credit department, the salesperson can sometimes help by using their personal contacts to convince the customer to send this information to the creditor. The salesperson can assure the customer that the financial information request is "strictly routine."

Sometimes, the best way to circumvent an uncooperative customer is to go through the salesperson and to the buyer to the salesperson. Both the salesperson and the buyer have a vested interest in setting the credit limit at whatever level the customer needs. The salesperson telling the buyer that the only way to get the credit limit needed is for the customer to release financial information may be the catalyst needed to get the information realeased.

TIPS TO IMPROVE THE CHANCES OF GETTING FINANCIAL INFORMATION FROM PRIVATELY HELD COMPANIES

Here are a few ideas that might increase the chances of getting information from a privately held company. None of these ideas are foolproof, and none will work in every situation:

- Contact a decision-maker, not a clerk with your request. The Controller or CFO is more likely to have the authority to share the company's statements than the accounts payable clerk, or even the accounts payable manager you normally deal with on a day-to-day basis

- Demand rather than request financial data only as a last resort. The initial "selling point" should be that the request for financial data is part of the company's normal review process.

- If the applicant expresses is concerned about the confidentiality of the information they might share, consider offering to sign a Confidentiality Agreement. If you do, remember that a Confidentiality Agreement is a contract and as a party to the contract the terms and conditions of that agreement strictly bind the creditor company.

- Be persistent. Some privately held companies make it a policy never to provide financial statements on the first or even the second request. These companies know from experience that a large number of creditors will not ask more than twice for financial statements. The reasoning is that if the creditor continues to follow up on their request for financial statements that the creditor is serious about getting them.

- When discussing the need for financial data from a customer or an applicant, the credit manager should remind the salesperson to stress to the customer that it is in everyone's best interest for the customer to get all the credit they deserve. One way to emphasize this is to tell the salesperson that in the absence of the necessary financial information the credit department has no alternative but to limit its credit exposure.

- If the customer refuses to provide a Balance Sheet, Income Statement and Cash Flow Statement, ask the customer to provide part of the requested information. Sometimes, a customer that is reluctant to share its Income Statement will reluctantly agree to provide a copy of its Balance Sheet.

TRY TO AVOID A SHOWDOWN

Sometimes, the creditor has no choice but to issue an ultimatum such as this: "Until and unless the applicant or customer sends me its financial statements, I cannot offer the company [or I cannot continue to offer the company] open account terms." Hopefully, it does not come to a showdown between the customer or applicant and the credit department. Using persistence, tact, courtesy, patience and professionalism it is often possible to get financial statements under difficult circumstances.

PERSONAL VISITS

One of the more effective ways to get financial information from privately held company is during a personal visit. While time and distance may make it impractical for the credit manager to visit every customer, occasionally a personal visit is the only way to solve a problem. if that problem involves the fact that the supplier will be unable to grant the credit limit or the credit limit increase until and unless the credit manager receives financial statements then that information can be delivered more delicately during the face to face meeting.

TIP: Your salespeople can be an excellent source of information about a customer or applicant. Normally, the salesperson will have met face to face with the customer, toured the customer's business facilities and had substantive discussions with the customer about its plans, needs and sales and growth projections. Based on the salesperson's experience and this first-hand information, they may be able to offer the credit professional information about the customer not available anywhere else.

ALIENATING CUSTOMERS

Most credit professionals are cautious about requesting financial statements from privately held companies for fear of alienating them. Sooner or later a customer or applicant will be insulted about receiving a request for financial information and complain about it. Experienced credit professionals realize that this type of complaint may be an indication of inexperience on the part of the applicant.

Sometimes, the customer's anger stems from confusion about why the creditor needs financial information. If they are given the opportunity to do so, the credit manager should patiently explaining why the information was requested, and emphasize that the request was strictly routine.

Sometimes, a company that is in serious financial trouble will decide that the best defense is a good offense. Rather than providing financial information they know would create concern on the part of a creditor, the customer or applicant will instead bitterly complain about how invasive the request for financial statements is the more a customer complains about a routine request, the more likely it is that there is some sort of problem that would be apparent on the financial statements.

REQUIRING FINANCIAL STATEMENTS

Occasionally, a creditor has no choice but to require financial statements from a company as a condition of sale. The typically happens at the beginning of the credit relationship, or when the customer's payment pattern has changed, or when the customer has requested a larger credit limit.

The decision about whether or not to require financial information as a condition for offering open account credit terms to a particular customer is a function of several factors, including:

(a) the amount of credit requested
(b) the creditor company's sensitivity to credit risk, delinquencies and bad debt losses
(c) the manner in which the customer pays other creditors
(d) the way in which this customer has paid this creditor in the past

One common excuse for refusing to share financial information is a statement that the customer is close to their fiscal year end. To some, this excuse seems reasonable. However, closer analysis will reveal some serious flaws. For example, the fact that the current year's fiscal year end financial statements are not complete does not prevent the debtor from sending the prior year's financial statements and at least one interim statement. Another option would be for the customer or applicant to send a draft of the current year's financial statements and follow up with the final copy once the year end statements are complete and are audited.

MAKE IT MANDATORY

Many companies have established a credit policies that an applicant wanting a credit limit above a specific dollar amount [for example $100,000 or more] must provide the creditor with financial statements (a) before the account can be established and (b) at least once a year every year thereafter.

It is useful to list this requirement on the credit application so there is no misunderstanding about the creditor's requirements and expectations.

ANNUAL UPDATES

Holding an order on an established account because the customer has not provided updated information when requested to do so is even harder to justify than refusing to establish an account until an applicant provides financial data. However, it is harder still to justify continuing to extend credit to a customer that has not provided financial statement as required—especially since companies in financial trouble are sometimes unwilling to provide creditors with updated statements.

AN ALTERNATIVE TO FINANCIAL STATEMENTS

If the customer is a proprietorship or a partnership and cannot provide a set of financial statements, it may be appropriate to request a copy of the owner('s) individual tax return(s). Information contained in the tax return(s) may be a reasonable substitute for a financial information requested.

A business that cannot produce a set of financial statements is a red flag to creditors. Without financial statements, it is difficult for the company's owners and senior executives to know how the company is performing and where it is going.

A NOTE ABOUT FOREIGN FINANCIAL STATEMENTS

For credit managers evaluating a foreign customer, a request for financial statements may be treated with surprise, concern, disappointment, bewilderment, and even hostility. Business norms vary from country to country, and in some parts of the world, creditors never ask for financial statements. Doing so is considered an insult to the business owner.

Even if foreign financial statements are received, the way they are formatted is often bewildering.

Even if the statements are received, they must be looked at with skepticism. The reasons for doing so include:

- Normally the creditor has no way to verify the credentials of the auditor
- The creditor normally does not know the rules relating to auditing standards, or how independent auditors are trained and certified.

INTERNALLY PREPARED DOMESTIC FINANCIAL STATEMENTS

Most privately held companies do not bother having their financial statements audited by a CPA firm. Therefore, creditors normally expect to receive unaudited or internally prepared financial statements from privately held companies. There are a number of risks associated with using unaudited financial statements to evaluate credit risk. When reviewing unaudited financial statements, credit professionals should adopt an attitude of professional skepticism. With unaudited statements, creditors should assume that the data provided is neither 100% accurate nor 100% inaccurate.

Unfortunately, there is little the credit manager can do to independently verify data provided in internally prepared statements. Experienced credit professionals know to look for obvious discrepancies and inconsistencies, but a creditor's ability to validate the information provided is limited at best. As a consequence of these issues surrounding unaudited financial statements, experienced credit professionals tend to evaluate them with a grain of salt.

CHAPTER 14

CREDIT SCORING

WHAT IS CREDIT SCORING?

Credit scoring software is one of a number of different types of software programs generically known as decision support software programs. Credit scoring software is designed to help credit managers to manage their portfolio of accounts more effectively. A credit scoring model is a scientific method involving the use of statistics to predict the creditworthiness of a consumer or a commercial credit applicant. Credit scoring has been around since the 1950's and since then it has primarily been used to evaluate individual applicants for consumer credit.

Credit scoring software programs continue to be used far more frequently in consumer credit than in commercial credit. The reason is simple: There are more than 150 million potential consumer customers, but there are less than 15 million commercial customers.

In the last ten years, commercial credit granters and programmers have begun to adapt this technology to their decision making process with significant success. There are a number of commercial credit scoring software programs now available on the market including Dun and Bradstreet's Risk Assessment Manager™ known by its acronym RAM.

The more sophisticated credit scoring software programs are Windows™ based and are designed to make the programs as user friendly, as intuitive, and as powerful as possible. Features of the more sophisticated credit scoring software programs include:

- Allowing users to develop their own customized credit risks score by adding new factors to the credit score, or changing the value of certain factors the software already evaluates
- A recommended credit limit based on criteria gathered from the credit manager
- The ability to generate reports about the quality of applicants reviewed by the software
- The ability to quickly calculate a credit score for applicants as well as active customers

Credit scoring software is a business tool. It is not intended to replace the credit manager or the credit decision making process. Credit scoring software makes recommendations that the credit manager may choose to accept or reject. As an evaluation tool, credit-scoring software can be used to monitor the credit risk associated with selling to existing customers.

The premise behind credit scoring is as follows: Credit scoring models begin with a large database of customers, some of whom have paid on time, some of whom have been chronically delinquent, and some of whom have either gone out of business of filed for bankruptcy protection. For each customer, specific data is accumulated. Examples of factors to be considered would include:

(a) the number of years in business,

(b) the total number of employees, and

(c) total annual sales.

Using statistical methods, the developers of credit scoring software will develop a model that indicates factors are statistically significant in identifying the creditworthiness of customers or applicants. For example, a statistical analysis might show that of the three factors listed above, only factors (a) and (b) are statistically significant when it comes to predicting whether or not an applicant or a customer will eventually become a problem account.

Once the factors that are statistically significant have been identified [many credit scoring software programs evaluate 30 or more factors] the software developers working in conjunction with statisticians will determine which factors have the most bearing on the future payment performance of a customer or an applicant. Then, a model will be developed by the statistician and coded by the software developer that allows the creditor company to input certain facts about a customer or applicant and have the software determine a credit score.

The most important concept underlying the use of credit scoring software is that combinations of certain characteristics or factors of an applicant or debtor are predictive of the customer's future behavior. An obvious example would be that an applicant that has consistently been slow in paying creditors in the past is likely to continue to be a slow payer. A less obvious risk factor would be the fact that the longer a consumer applicant has been at his or her present job and current residence, the lower the credit risk they present.

CONSUMER CREDIT SCORING

At the request of the subscriber, credit bureaus such as Experian, Equifax and Trans-Union can provide a numerical credit score for each consumer credit report they evaluate. Consumer credit scores work this way: The higher the score, the lower the credit risks. The advantage of credit scoring to consumers is that:

(a) Consumers are objectively evaluated, and

(b) Consumer applicants that score highly are likely to be approved quickly.

(c) Consumer applicants that do not score highly are not immediately disqualified. Instead, the applications are referred to a person for special consideration.

(d) Credit scoring software will identify the reason or reasons a particular applicant did not score highly.

Consumer credit reporting agencies score consumers on approximately 30 individual factors that are statistically significant indicators of the consumer's creditworthiness. In broad terms these 30 factors are in the following areas:

- The consumer's payment history
- Their outstanding debt
- The length of their credit history
- The number and the types of requests submitted for new credit
- The number of open accounts reported including bank credit cards, department store cards, and installment loans [such as car loans].

HOMEGROWN CREDIT SCORING PROGRAMS

Credit bureaus are not the only entities that generate credit scores. It is possible for an individual credit manager to create a scoring system using a predetermined list of factors that the credit manager considers important in the decision making process. Unfortunately, a "homegrown" credit scoring system suffer from several major limitations, including:

- A homegrown model is unlikely to have the statistical underpinning of a credit-scoring model developed by experts. As a result, the credit scores generated may or may not have a strong correlation to the creditworthiness of the applicant.

- Even if the credit-scoring model developed in house was statistically significant and valid when it was created, unless it is regularly updated it will become less valid over time.

- It is not enough simply to capture the variables that must be measured to evaluate creditworthiness; these variables do not carry equal weight. Therefore, in order to approximate the sophistication of commercially available credit scoring software programs, a home grown program must assign different weights to different factors or variables under review. Unless the credit manager is also a statistician, it is hard to imagine a homegrown system being anywhere near as accurate or sophisticated as a commercially available credit scoring software program.

Credit scoring is the fastest, most consistent and most accurate way to evaluate whether or not an individual applicant for consumer credit is likely to (a) be able to pay its bills, or (b) eventually default on payment altogether and file for bankruptcy protection. Consumer credit scoring models have been refined over the last thirty or more years to the point that they are uncannily accurate.

PREVENTING BAD DEBT LOSSES

Credit scoring is statistically relevant, but credit-scoring models do not prevent bad debt losses. Irrespective of their credit score, a certain number of consumer debtors will default on payment—often through no fault of their own. For example, a consumer that was considered an excellent risk could easily lose their job, or have a major illness in the family, or become the victim of a natural disaster.

Prior to the catastrophic event, the consumer might have been considered an excellent risk. Consumer credit scoring software obviously has no way of predicting these kinds of losses. Therefore, no matter how sophisticated consumer credit scoring software becomes, there will always be unexpected losses. In addition, given the competitive nature of certain industries and the demands made on the credit department by senior management, the credit department may be forced to lower its standards in order to help the company attract more customers even though by doing so the creditor company is assured of additional delinquencies and higher bad debt losses.

IGNORING THE CREDIT SCORE

Ignoring a weak credit score is hard to justify even if the consumer pays as agreed. There is always a risk for the credit manager who chooses to ignore the credit score and grant credit to a consumer applicant. The risk is that if the customer eventually defaults on payment that the credit decision will be second-guessed. While credit professionals are under no obligation to use the credit score to make their credit decision, most companies have internal policies that strongly encourage credit decision-makers to use the credit scoring tool available to them rather than relying on their instincts and intuition. Instincts and intuition are far less reliable than a statistically significant credit-scoring model.

REASONS TO OVERRIDE THE RECOMMENDATION

Credit managers can override the credit score and its implied recommendation at any time. Often, this is done for a specific reason and with the full knowledge and approval of senior management. For example, if a company is trying to increase sales or market share then the credit manager may be instructed to give greater consideration to applicants with lower credit scores. Credit managers owe it to themselves and to their company to document any discussion in which the credit manager is encouraged to liberalize the credit granting process.

Experience indicates that senior management occasionally has selective amnesia when it comes to issues such as this—especially when bad debt losses begin to mount.

CREDIT SCORING FLAGS HIGH RISK ACCOUNTS

Even after a consumer or commercial account has been approved for open account credit terms, the original credit score can be used by the credit manager to identify which customers should be given special attention. For example, applicants identified as marginal credit risks by the credit scoring software can be coded so that they are updated and reviewed more frequently, and are given less latitude when balances become past due. Here is an example of each of these risk management techniques:

(a) The credit manager approves applicant identified as marginal according to their credit score. If every customer's account is re-scored every year, the high-risk accounts could be re-evaluated every six months.

(b) Any account identified as marginal can be assigned a different protocol for follow up on delinquent balances. For example, if the typical delinquent consumer account does not receive a collection call until the account is at least 20 days past due, marginal accounts could be set up for calls once they become ten days past due.

CONSUMER CREDIT SCORING RISK FACTORS

Consumer credit scoring software typically lists at least the four most important factors in determining the credit score in the summary it presents. If credit has been denied, consumers have a right under the Equal Credit Opportunity Act to demand to know why their application was rejected. One of the biggest advantages of consumer credit scoring software is that it provides the creditor with specific risk factors. The risk factors identified by the software can be used as the basis for the explanation to the consumer.

Some of the most common factors that prompt credit-scoring software to indicate a consumer applicant is high risk include:

- The amount owed on accounts is too high relative to the applicant's take home pay.
- Creditors have reported delinquency on accounts.
- There are simply too many accounts with balances owing.
- The applicant is too new to rate.
- There have been too many accounts opened in the last twelve months.
- The length of the credit history is too short.
- There is a history of accounts placed for collection by other creditors.
- There is not enough information on file. Specifically, there are too few accounts with recent payment information.

FACTORS IN CONSUMER CREDIT SCORING MODELS

Consumer credit scoring software programs typically assign numerical scores to each of the following factors:

- Past credit payment history, including any late payments made

- Length of the applicant's credit history
- Types and dollar amounts of credit currently extended
- How many inquiries the credit bureau has received about the applicant
- The household income of the applicant(s)
- Whether or not the applicant owns or rents a home
- How many years the applicant has been at the same residence
- How many years the applicant has been at the same job
- The amount of disposable income the debtor has each month
- The applicant's age

Note: The law allows age to be used as a determinant in credit scoring software, but requires that people 62 years old or older must receive the maximum number of points allowed. This is in a sense reverse discrimination—but federal law requires that if age is used as a factor in the credit score that older Americans receive the maximum number of points allowed. The point to keep in mind is that consumer credit scoring software assigns or awards points based on each of these factors. Generally, the more points awarded the better the credit risk is perceived to be, and the more likely the applicant is to be approved for open account terms.

THE ADVANTAGES OF A PROFESSIONALLY DESIGNED CREDIT SCORING MODEL

One of the biggest advantages of credit scores generated by credit bureaus such as Trans Union is that the creditor company and the credit manager do not have to conduct any research or develop any ideas or models on their own. There is no technology investment required, and the credit manager does not need to become an expert in probability and statistics. The only thing the credit manager has to do is to request the credit bureau to provide the credit score along with the consumer credit report.

A distinct advantage of relying on the credit-scoring model used by the credit bureau is that the model is constantly being reviewed, refined and updated. Credit scoring software models constantly evolve in response to new information. As the database of information grows, the values and weights assigned to the specific factors change according to their statistical significance. For example, if the number of years an applicant has lived at his or her current residence is proven to be less statistically significant in predicting default or delinquency than it was the last time the model was reviewed, then that particular factor will be weighted accordingly.

SHARING CREDIT SCORES WITH CONSUMERS

Federal law does not require that creditors reveal credit scores to customers. Credit bureaus are not required to include a credit score on the reports they provide to consumers in response to requests received from consumers for access to their credit reports—in particular in response to a request for access to their consumer credit report in response to a decision by a creditor not to extend credit to the consumer/applicant.

This is not an attempt to hide anything from the consumer. Federal regulators have determined that the credit score need not be to consumers when they request the opportunity to review their credit reports for several reasons:

- The regulatory authorities recognize that credit scores are not necessarily the basis for any decision to deny credit. Typically, if a score falls outside of the acceptable range it will trigger a review by a human being rather than an outright rejection.

- Credit scores change over time as factors such as how a customer pays its bills from month to month change. Therefore, providing a current report may not be helpful.

- There is not a single, universally used credit score, so providing consumers with "a" credit score might only confuse them.

- The federal government does not believe that consumers would necessarily benefit from having access to their raw credit score. The raw number itself would be almost meaningless to a consumer—and the process of trying to explain the statistical methods used at arriving at a credit score would be difficult for the average consumer to follow.

The value of receiving a copy of their consumer credit report after being denied open account credit terms lies in seeing what the report says about the consumer—combined with the opportunity to review the credit report and dispute any inaccurate information.

LIMITATIONS OF CREDIT SCORING

A properly designed credit scoring system allows creditors to evaluate thousands of applications consistently, impartially, inexpensively, and quickly. Conversely, a poorly designed credit scoring software program can evaluate thousands of applicants incorrectly every time and recommend to the credit manager that the wrong decision be made every time.

Credit professionals using credit-scoring software must recognize all of the following limitations:

- Credit risk can never be measured precisely

- Credit risk can change literally overnight. A consumer that was a good credit risk might lose their job, and go from a good risk to a non-payer almost immediately.

- Credit scoring is a tool. A credit professional must make the final decision about which applicants qualify for open account terms.

- Despite the best efforts of the credit bureaus involved, there is a certain error rate on information reported on consumer credit reports.

- Credit bureaus gather information from their subscribers. Not every creditor can or will share credit information with every credit bureau. As a result, credit scores will vary from credit bureau to credit bureau.

WHO DEVELOPS CREDIT SCORING MODELS?

Credit scores calculated by credit bureaus are just one type of credit scoring system. Some creditor companies create their own credit scoring models for internal use. Unfortunately, these models may or may not offer statistically significant insights into the creditworthiness of customers and applicants. Private companies sell standardized or customized credit scoring software to companies of many sizes in many different industries, and the factors these systems measure are demonstrated to be statistically significant in prediction, delinquecy, and default.

CREDIT SCORING VERSUS HUMAN SCORING OF APPLICANTS

Credit scoring software is a tool. The ultimate decision to accept or deny credit is not done by credit scoring software. Credit scoring software is used to evaluate data quickly, efficiently, impartially, accurately and consistently. Credit-scoring software is superior to human credit scoring or credit evaluation because of these factors:

- Software does not discriminate. People do. People bring their own prejudices and biases to the process of evaluating an applicant for consumer or commercial credit.

- Software is consistent. It evaluates the same factors in the same manner every time it is used.

- Software does not forget to look at or for a certain fact. People do, and the decision or recommendation they make are weakened by the errors they make in the evaluation process.

- Decision rules established by the software itself and/or customized by the credit manager are followed consistently—meaning that inputting the same risk factors would result in the same credit score being calculated every time.

COMMERCIAL ACCOUNT CREDIT SCORING

Commercial credit scoring software programs are becoming more reliable because the database used to develop the credit scoring models is now large enough that important modifications and subtle improvements have been made over time, and each factor reviewed by the software is statistically significant. As a result, credit-scoring programs on the market are fast, user-friendly and relatively inexpensive—especially in comparison to developing and then maintaining a "homegrown" software program.

HOW ARE CREDIT SCORES USED?

Each company's credit department decides what credit score differentiates a low risk from a moderate risk, and a moderate risk from a high-risk customer or applicant. Typically, credit scores are used in commercial credit departments in the following manner with new applicants for credit:

(a) High scoring applicants [classified as low risk] can be approved with a minimum amount of review

(b) Applicants classified as moderate or marginal credit risks will be reviewed by the credit manager to determine whether or not the applicant qualifies for open account terms. Specifically, accounts whose score is in a specified range will be forwarded to the credit manager for further evaluation.

(c) A certain percent of applicants will be identified by the credit scoring software as being high risk. It is possible these accounts will be offered open account terms, but once again the decision is left to the credit manager and will be based on his or her skill and experience.

Typically, only a small number of applicants will be identified as being high risk based on their credit score. For this reason, the credit manager may simply elect to disqualify high-risk applicants from purchasing on open account terms unless additional assurance of payment [such as an inter-corporate guarantee can be obtained].

Accounts scored as low risk are normally approved with very limited review, applicants identified as high risk are rejected unless steps can be taken to moderate the credit risk, and the intermediate credit risk accounts are evaluated on a case by case basis to determine their eligibility for open account terms.

THE DIFFERENCES BETWEEN CREDIT SCORING SOFTWARE PROGRAMS

No two credit scoring software programs are alike. Each model may evaluate different factors, or assign different weights to the factors they look at in common. There are no universally used or applied rules for creating credit-scoring software, and the field is unregulated. This means that a software programmer with no expertise in statistics or statistical modeling could create and sell commercial credit scoring software. This makes selecting the right credit scoring software program a large part of the success or failure of that software.

Adding to the complexity of selecting the right software and then getting the software to provide scoring that the credit manager finds useful to his or her decision making process the fact that different companies have:

- different profit margins
- different expectations about the role of their credit department
- different tolerances for risk
- different short term and long term goals
- operate in different competitive environments

Given these factors, it is easy to see that credit-scoring software is unlikely to supplant the credit manager in deciding which applicants to accept and which to reject.

INTERNAL VS. EXTERNAL CREDIT SCORING

In consumer related credit, the big three credit bureaus and many of the smaller bureaus provide a credit score along with their standard credit report—for a slightly higher fee to the subscriber. The goal is to make it easier for the credit manager to arrive at his or her credit decision.

In commercial credit granting, none of the major credit reporting agencies offer this value-added service on line along with their credit reports at this time. At least one of the major credit reporting agencies, Dun and Bradstreet® offers credit-scoring software for commercial credit granters. This software interfaces with Dun and Bradstreet products, but the actual credit report is calculated by the creditor's computer system and not transmitted to the creditor by Dun and Bradstreet.

There are dozens of commercial credit scoring models available. Some are very sophisticated, and others are not. Some evaluate only new applicants, and others evaluate both active customers and applicants. There is no clear leader in this field, but there are approximately five companies that are clearly in the forefront in providing this type of software.

More and more frequently, credit professionals dealing with both consumer and commercial applicants and customers are coming to rely on credit scoring to evaluate both consumer and commercial credit risk. Some external credit scoring models provide the credit manager with an easy to read score. Internal credit scoring software programs typically present the credit manager with the raw score and an explanation of the most significant factors contributing to that score.

WHO MAKES THE DECISION?

Commercial credit managers are working in an environment in which downsizing is an unpleasant fact of life. Credit scoring can help credit managers by reducing the time it takes to evaluate every applicant and every active account, and by making consistent and objective recommendations.

However, given all of the variables that must be considered, and notwithstanding the speed, accuracy, sophistication and consistency of credit scoring models for the time being it is important that people and not software make the final decision about which applicants to accept and which customers to continue to sell to on open account terms.

SUMMARY

After getting off to a relatively slow start, the concept of commercial credit scoring is catching on in large and small businesses throughout the country. Commercial credit scoring is a "hot topic" at regional and national credit conferences. Credit managers looking for a way to reduce overhead, cut costs, lower risk, and control delinquencies more effectively are looking to commercial credit scoring software as a mechanism to accomplish all of these goals. Credit managers are coming to appreciate the flexibility of a product that can evaluate both new applicants and existing customers with equal speed and accuracy.

CHAPTER 15

RESTRAINTS AND RESTRICTIONS ON GATHERING AND DISSEMINATING CREDIT INFORMATION

In order for the economy to flourish, it is essential that suppliers be willing to extend credit to individuals and to businesses. One of the things that makes this possible is the ability to gather information from other creditors about a customer or about an applicant for credit.

The goal of credit granters is to gather enough information to make an informed credit decision. The process typically begins with the applicant completing and signing a credit application form. Most companies require applicants to provide at least three trade references.

Unfortunately, there are a number of barriers and restraints that may prevent creditors from gathering credit information from other creditors. Here are some of the most common restraints:

- Some creditors routinely refuse to rate their competitors.

- Other companies simply make it a policy not to rate to anyone.

- Some companies refuse to rate except by mail—recognizing that obtaining references is normally time sensitive, these companies know that by requiring references by mail they will reduce the number of inquiries they receive.

- It is quite common for companies to refuse to rate by telephone, although some companies that will not rate by phone will rate by fax

- Some creditors will only rate to companies that are members of their industry credit group.

Recognizing the importance of gathering credit references quickly, most credit investigators simply move to the next supplier on the list when they find a creditor that is unwilling to provide a credit rating to a fellow creditor.

CREDIT RATING RULES

There is no requirement under federal or state law that compels a company to respond to a credit inquiry. There is no doubt that credit information is valuable, and in that context it is relatively easy to understand why a creditor might elect not to share that information—in particular with a competitor. However, in the long run this decision is flawed.

Credit information is proprietary information and for this reason there is nothing improper, unprofessional, or unethical about refusing to rate to any company for any reason—or for no reason at all. Suppliers provide credit ratings to other creditors as a business courtesy. Creditors respond to credit inquiries because they understand that the free and open exchange of factual information about customers benefits all trade creditors in the long run.

DEFAMATION

Defamation involves an act of communicating a false statement that causes damage to an individual or a company's reputation. Defamation is a tort. Companies that defame a customer may be sued by that customer for monetary damages. One of the reasons that some creditors will not provide credit ratings is a concern about defamation. Any creditor that is willing to provide trade references must make certain that adequate safeguards are in place so that the person providing the rating does not defame the customer in the process. Out of concern about defamation, some creditors refuse to rate slow paying accounts. This precaution is unnecessary. it is not defamation to provide accurate factual information about a slow paying account.

The essential element in defamation is that the information provided in writing or orally must be false. If a creditor provides true and accurate, but unflattering information about a customer in a credit rating, then that rating is not defamatory—it is simply truthful *and* unflattering.

PREVENTING A CLAIM OF DEFAMATION

If a creditor elects to provide credit ratings, then they must be prepared to be asked questions that are clearly "out of bounds." Usually, responding to credit inquiries is a task delegated by the credit manager to a subordinate. If they want to avoid charges of defamation, then the credit manager must be certain the person delegated this task has been fully trained and is capable of responding to any inquiry in an appropriate manner. If the subordinate is not properly trained, chances are good that sooner or later something will be said or written that should not have been.

Two common area that inexperienced people often get into trouble with credit ratings is when they are asked to (a) rate the account or (b) provide additional comments. In both cases, the person providing the rating should not respond at all to these questions. Creditors that ask these questions are "fishing" for information. There is nothing illegal about asking the question, but there is no way to answer either question without putting the creditor company at risk.

LEGISLATION GOVERNING GATHERING CREDIT REFERENCES

Periodically, legislation is proposed at the federal or the state level that would limit the types and amount of information that business creditors could share with each other. This type of legislation is normally defeated because of its potential impact on business to business credit granting. Specifically, if laws were enacted that restricted creditors from exchanging credit information, then chances are excellent that applicants would find it harder to get for open account terms. Another disadvantage of any legislation of this type is that it would disproportionately affect relative new companies and relatively small companies. Why? Because public companies and well established companies don't benefit to the same degree as smaller, newer companies from the free and open exchange of credit information.

COLLUSION IS A PROHIBITED ACTIVITY

One of the most important limitations placed on creditors is that they may not collude with each other in any way that would tend to lessen competition or alter the free market forces of supply and demand. Thus, creditors cannot use the credit investigation process, and specifically the process of checking trade references, as a vehicle to conspire to violate the antitrust laws enacted by the Federal and State governments. It is *not* a violation of any federal or state law to provide a credit reference on a customer either in writing or orally - even if the party inquiring is a competitor. The key is to make certain that information provided is both factual and historical in nature.

Some trade creditors have elected not to list their terms of sale in responding to any request for a credit rating even though there is no specific prohibition against doing so. These creditors reason that if they do not provide any information about their terms of sale, they cannot be accused of conspiring to "fix" the terms of sale—which would be a violation of certain federal antitrust laws.

PROVIDING FALSE INFORMATION

A company anxious not to lose business to a competitor might be tempted to provide a false credit reference; a rating in which the creditor suggests that the customer is a worse risk than the customer actually is. For example, anxious not to lose a major customer, a company might be tempted to report that the customer pays invoices 90 days slow when in reality the customer pays an average of 9 days slow. Providing false references is unlawful. If a false credit reference such as this were provided orally, the creditor would be guilty of slander. If the false credit rating were provided in writing, then the creditor would be guilty of libel.

If a creditor wanted to help a friend or a relative by providing a credit reference when the company in question actually had never done business with the creditor company, that person would be guilty of fraud.

CREDIT INTERCHANGES AT INDUSTRY CREDIT GROUP MEETINGS

Industry credit groups are formed in order to facilitate the exchange of factual and historical data among creditors about common customers. It is not uncommon for suppliers to belong to two or more credit groups, to attend several credit group meetings a year, and to provide information to the group for publication once a month.

Industry credit groups often make corporate attorneys cringe. The reason is simple: Creditors choose to join industry credit groups in which they can gather as much information as possible about customers, and it is not uncommon for several direct competitors to be members of the same industry credit group. The credit groups' administrators are well aware of the potential for collusion among competitors. To limit the liability of the sponsoring organization, most group administrators go to great lengths to explain the following rules prior to every meeting:

- Creditors may only share factual information.

- Attendees may not discuss any future or planned actions.

- Creditors may not offer their opinions about a customer, nor may they speculate about the motives of a customer.

- Creditors may not collude or conspire to violate any antitrust law during or after the group meeting.

There are no laws prohibiting creditors from joining as many industry credit groups as practical. There is nothing wrong with creditors joining an industry group in which competitors are already members of the group. However, the presence of competitors should encourage credit professionals to be cautious.

Industry credit groups make it easy for credit professionals to get to know their counterparts at competitor companies. It may seem natural for a credit manager to socialize and to interact frequently with representatives of his or her competitors, but this is rarely a good idea. Even if no collusion is taking place, any private meeting between direct competitors gives the appearance of impropriety. Despite the fact that such meetings are not illegal, absent an intent to violate the antitrust laws by conspiring to work cooperatively to limit their mutual credit risk.

Tip: In many cases, creditors can "pay" for the entire cost of attending an industry credit group meeting by gathering one piece of information which allows the creditor to avoid a credit problem. Credit managers that believe industry credit group membership is a waste of their time are in the wrong credit group.

The problems associated with developing a personal relationship with a competitor's credit manager may include:

(1) The fact that familiarity breeds contempt. In this case, familiarity might eventually lead to contempt for and violation of federal and state antitrust laws.

(2) Developing personal relationships with competitors may give the appearance that the by-laws of the industry credit group and the various federal and state antitrust laws are being ignored or violated.

(3) Having personal relationships with one or more competitors may lead to divided loyalties—the credit manager may unwittingly become the source of leaks of sensitive information to the competition.

Credit managers should not avoid industry credit groups. Instead, they should exercise caution. Attendees are responsible for their own actions. By exercising reasonable care, creditors can enjoy the benefits of being a member of an industry credit group while limiting their risk. It is not a good idea to discuss credit terms or credit limits—especially not with competitors during group meetings. The key is to use discretion about everything you say and do.

DISCUSSIONS WITH COMPETITORS

Do not discuss your terms of sale [payment terms] with competitors. This can be the first step down a slippery slope that might end with an agreement about the terms of sale that competitors will offer—which would be a violation of federal law.

RULES FOR INDUSTRY CREDIT GROUP ATTENDEES

(1) Despite the assurances that attendees receive about confidentiality, never say anything that you would not want the debtor to hear—because they just might.

(2) Never say anything that you would be afraid to repeat in a court of law —because someday you may have to do so.

CONSUMER CREDIT REPORTS

Consumer credit reports are governed by the federal Fair Credit Reporting Act. Access to these reports is limited to companies with a legitimate business need for this information. This federal law is intended to protect individual consumers from unwarranted and intrusive invasions of their right to privacy.

The definition of what a legitimate business purpose is under the Fair Credit Reporting Act has been left deliberately vague. This was done to allow creditors as much latitude as possible while making it illegal for anyone to access a consumer credit report [other than their own] without a legitimate need for the information. Under this federal law, anyone who willfully and knowingly obtains a credit report under false pretenses may be fined or imprisoned. This important fact should be shared with anyone in the credit department who can request or who can pull a consumer credit report.

No one outside of the credit department should be allowed to order a consumer credit report. Regardless of who requests a consumer report, the ultimate decision about whether or not to order the report belongs to the credit manager.

CHAPTER 16

SAMPLE CREDIT APPLICATION AND INFORMATION REQUEST FORMS

A well-written credit application form is valuable to the creditor company during the entire life cycle of its business relationship with the customer. The credit application will or should:

- Initially assist the creditor in evaluating the creditworthiness of the applicant company
- Assist the creditor by identify the right people to contact to address and resolve problems that may arise from time to time, including the Chief Financial Officer, and the Purchasing Manager
- Help the credit manager if it should ever become necessary to refer the customer to a third party to collect an unpaid balance by specifying the venue for litigation, requiring that the loser pay the winner's reasonable attorney's fees, and providing for interest on any past due balance.

The customer is the best source of information about its operations. A well-written credit application provides the creditor with information that will make it easier to manage credit risk. A well-written credit application will include the following information:

- The credit limit requested
- A list of trade references
- A bank reference
- The names of officers or owners of the company

- An accounts payable contact name, telephone number and fax number
- Business affiliations with other companies [example: the names of parent companies, subsidiaries, d.b.a's, and affiliates]
- The applicant company's street address, mailing address and billing address
- The authorized ship-to location or locations
- A list of the people authorized to make purchases on behalf of the applicant
- A clause stipulating that if the creditor is forced to sue for payment that the debtor will pay interest on the debt and reasonable attorneys' fees and court costs
- A personal guarantee obligating the signer for the debts of the corporation
- An agreement to pay a specific returned check charge
- The granting of a purchase money security interest in the product supplied by the creditor, along with the Power of Attorney necessary to file and perfect the purchase money security interest.
- A clause requiring the customer to give the creditor written notice of an ownership change, or a change of address.
- An agreement about the venue for any lawsuit filed by either party. [Normally the seller would specify the venue of any litigation to be in the county and state in which the creditor is located rather than the debtor's location.]
- The signature of an officer of the corporation or the owner of a partnership or a proprietorship binding the applicant company to all of the terms and conditions listed on the credit application.

A credit application form is both a source of information as well as a contract between the buyer and the seller. Since the seller drafts it, the credit application should always favor the seller rather than the buyer. For example:

In order to make it easier to enforce the creditor's cash discount policy, the application should describe the discount terms and the potential consequences of taking unearned cash discounts. Specifically, the credit application form could state that a specific cash discount would be earned only if the creditor receives payment within 15 days of the invoice date irrespective of when the goods are received or inspected. The application might also state that any unearned discount will be charged back and must be repaid. It might also state that unpaid, unearned discounts can result in an immediate order hold.

THE CREDIT APPLICATION AS A CONTRACT

If the credit application is used as a contract rather than simply as a mechanism to gather information about an applicant, then as is the case with any other contract it must be signed. Specifically, it should be signed by someone with authority to bind the applicant to the terms and conditions contained in the credit application. In a corporation, ideally an officer or director should sign the application form. In a partnership or of a proprietorship, the owners should sign the credit application.

THE SHORT FORM CREDIT APPLICATION.

Customers occasionally complain that the creditor's application form is too long and too complex. In an effort to be seen as "customer friendly", some companies have reduced the size of their credit application to a single page. In effect, creditors have abbreviated their credit application forms so that

---

SHORT FORM CONSUMER CREDIT APPLICATION

A short form consumer credit application form might look something like this:

Application

Date:

Name:

Social Security #:

Residence Address:

How long?

Employed by:

How long?

Your bank name and address:

Account #:

Type of Account (Checking, Savings):

List of charge cards:

Name of creditor	Account #
Name of creditor	Account #
Name of creditor	Account #
Name of creditor	Account #

---

only the most essential pieces of information are included. The trouble with an abbreviated credit application is that by leaving out certain language or terms, the credit application provides less protection to the creditor. There is simply no way to shorten a credit application without reducing its usefulness to the creditor company.

GETTING BANK AND TRADE REFERENCES TO RESPOND

Creditors sometimes find it difficult to get the bank and trade creditors listed on the credit application to respond to their inquiries. One way to significantly increase the chance of getting a credit rating is to include a specific authorization from the applicant for the release of this information. Appropriate language would include the following:

> The Applicant hereby authorizes the _____ to contact the bank and trade references listed on this Application. The Applicant hereby authorizes the references listed to provide information to _____ and requests their prompt cooperation in providing this information to this creditor.

CUSTOMIZING CREDIT APPLICATIONS

There is no such thing as a "one size fits all" credit application. Different creditors sell different products in different competitive environments. Different companies offer differing terms of sale, and can demand varying levels of concessions and assurances of payment from applicants. For these reasons, creditors should design their credit application form with their unique requirements in mind. Credit managers should also periodically review and update their credit application form.

CREDIT APPLICATIONS AND CREDIT LIMITS

If the creditor company notifies customers of their credit limit and their terms of sale, then the credit application should state clearly that the creditor can change the terms of sale or the credit limit at any time, with or without notice to the customer and at the sole discretion of the creditor company. The appropriate language for the credit application might read as follows:

> "It is understood and agreed by the applicant that the seller can change the terms of sale or the credit limit offered to the appli-

cant at any time, at the seller's sole discretion, and with or without formal or written notice to the applicant."

UPDATING CREDIT APPLICATIONS

While it is not always possible to get, it is a good idea to ask that customers complete and sign a new credit application form periodically. Updated credit applications can be helpful to the creditor in managing credit risk and in collecting delinquent balances and resolving disputes. Asking customers to complete and sign new credit applications also ensures that the credit manager has on file the most current version of the contract outlining all of the terms under which the seller agrees to supply goods and services to the buyer.

PERSONAL GUARANTEES

Some credit application forms contain a personal guaranty that is made part of the application itself. Most experts recommend that the Personal Guaranty be a separate contract—but most creditors find it easier to get applicants to sign a Guaranty that is part of the application rather than presenting the applicant with a credit application form and a separate Guaranty.

Whether the Guaranty is contained in the body of the credit application or is a separate document, a personal guaranty is only valuable if the guarantor has the financial resources to pay if the debtor company defaults. Therefore, it is essential that creditors evaluate the creditworthiness of the guarantor before basing all or part of the decision to extend credit to a customer on the value of that guaranty.

Another point for creditors to remember is that Personal Guarantees must be signed as an individual. For example, a Personal Guaranty signed by John Smith; President is probably not enforceable against John Smith as an individual because John signed it in his capacity as the President of the debtor company.

Creditors should also be aware that Personal Guarantees may not be enforceable against assets of the guarantor held as community property in States with community property laws. Credit managers must factor this into their evaluation of the strength of the individual's personal guarantee. Creditors should also know that if the spouse is not active in the business, the creditor may not request that the guarantor's spouse co-sign the personal guarantee form in a community property state. In fact, the creditor must first deny the applicant's request for open account credit and the spouse's offer to co-sign a personal guarantee must be voluntary.

CHECKLIST FOR A PERSONAL GUARANTY

A Personal Guaranty is a contract between the seller and an individual who is an employee, owner or stockholder of the debtor corporation. The Personal Guaranty form itself should contain the following elements:

(1) The guaranty must be unconditional, and specific provisions should be included as to the manner and method in which the guarantor may withdraw the personal guaranty. For example, the contract might state that revocation of the personal guaranty must be made by certified letter, return receipt requested and delivered to the corporate headquarters of the creditor company and to the attention of the company President.

(2) The contract should state that revocation may not be retroactive.

(3) The guarantor must agree to pay all collection costs including reasonable attorney's fees should the matter have to be referred to a third party for collection.

(4) The guaranty should specify the venue should it become necessary to litigate in order to enforce the terms of the guaranty as signed by the guarantor.

(5) The document should state that the creditor need not exhaust all legal remedies against the debtor company or corporation before making demand for payment under the personal guaranty.

(6) As a contract, the guaranty itself should be notarized and a section included for the seal and signature of the notary.

Sample Short-Form Commercial Credit Application #1

CREDIT APPLICATION FORM

Customer name: _____

Address: _____

Phone #:_____ Fax#: _____ E-mail address: _____

Contact name: _____

Bill to address: _____

Ship to address: _____

Type of Business:

Corporation, Partnership, Proprietorship, or other: _____

Bank name: _____ Phone #: _____

Address: _____

Name of Account or Loan Officer: _____

D&B number: _____ D&B rating: _____

Credit References:

1. Name _____
   Address _____
   Phone _____
2. Name _____
   Address _____
   Phone _____
3. Name _____
   Address _____
   Phone _____

Authorization: I hereby authorize CREDITOR NAME to contact the bank and trade references listed above. I also authorize these references to provide CREDITOR NAME with information deemed relevant to this request for open account credit terms.

Signed: _____ Title: _____ Date: _____

Sample Short Form Commercial Credit Application #2

BUSINESS CREDIT APPLICATION AND AGREEMENT

Customer Name: _____

Address: _____

Name of Owner or President: _____ Business Phone #: _____

Date Business Started: _____ D&B#: _____

Trade references:

1. Name: _____ Address: _____

2. Name: _____ Address: _____

3. Name: _____ Address: _____

Bank reference: Name: _____ Phone#: _____

Account #:   _____ Bank officer name: _____

Credit limit requested?:   _____ Tax exempt: _____

[If yes, please attach State Tax Exemption Certificate]

The undersigned authorizes the creditor to conduct inquiries about this applicant company on the basis of this application. The Applicant acknowledges that the creditor may reduce or withdraw open account privileges at its sole discretion at any time without prior notification.

Signed: _____ Date: _____ Title: _____

Sample Credit Application Form #3

XYZ COMPANY STANDARD CREDIT APPLICATION

[Note: please complete all information on this form, and mail or fax this information as soon as possible to XYZ Company]

Company Name: _____

Address: _____

Phone#: _____ Contact: _____

Type of Company:

Corporation: _____ Partnership:_____

Proprietorship: _____ Other: _____ (please specify)

Date formed: _____

Banking Information:

Bank: _____ Phone #:_____

Contact: _____

Checking #: _____ Savings#: _____

Is there a borrowing relationship?: _____

Bank: _____ Phone #:_____

Contact: _____

Trade references:

Resale: Yes: _____ No: _____ Resale number: _____

Federal tax ID number: _____

Name: _____ Phone #: _____ Contact:_____

Name: _____ Phone #: _____ Contact:_____

Name: _____ Phone #: _____ Contact:_____

Officers' and owners' information:

Name: _____Position: _____

Home address: _____

Home Phone #: _____ S.S. #: _____

Name: _____ Position: _____

Home Phone #: _____ S.S. #: _____

Home address: _____

We have made an application to XYZ Company for open account credit terms. In accordance with their standard procedure, XYZ will be conducting an investigation based on the information we have provided on this credit application.

All information provided to XYZ Company will be treated in strict confidence. XYZ's sources and the results of their investigation will not be shared with us. Therefore, no responsibility or liability is attached to the bank or to the trade references reporting or providing information to XYZ Company.

Signed: _____ Title: _____ Date: _____

Applicant Company Name: _____

Sample Commercial Credit Application #4 [with Authorization to Obtain Personal Credit Reports on Individual Officers or Owners]

APPLICATION FOR CREDIT

Company Name: _____ E-mail address: _____

Address: _____

Telephone #:_____ Fax #: _____

Type of Business

Corporation _____ Partnership _____

Proprietorship _____ Other [specify] _____

State where registered or incorporated:_____

Nature of business: _____ Years in business: _____

Credit limit requested: _____

People authorized to purchase: _____

Ownership information:

President

Name: _____ S.S. #: _____

Home address: _____

Home phone number: _____

Vice President

Name: _____ S.S. #: _____

Home address: _____

Home phone #: _____

Commercial references:

Vendor name: _____ Account #: _____

Address: _____ Phone #: _____

Vendor name: _____ Account #: _____

Address: _____ Phone #: _____

Vendor name: _____ Account #: _____

Address: _____ Phone #: _____

Vendor name: _____ Account #: _____

Address: _____ Phone #: _____

Bank name: _____ Account #: _____

Contact name:_____ Phone #: _____

The undersigned warrants that the information contained in this contract is true and accurate, and agrees that the Applicant company will pay for all goods and services as they come due. The undersigned also understands a service charge of 1% per month is charged on past due balances unpaid. In the event the account is turned over to an attorney or to a collection agency for collection, the undersigned agrees to pay collection agency or attorney's fees and costs incurred in collection.

The undersigned authorizes **CREDITOR COMPANY NAME** to make inquiries with any credit reporting agency, bank or trade reference in connection with the extension of credit requested by the undersigned. The undersigned also hereby authorizes **CREDITOR** to obtain personal credit reports on the principals of the company that have signed below.

Signature of Owner/President: _____

Title: _____ Date: _____

Home Address: _____

Signature of Co-owner or Vice President: _____

Title: _____ Date: _____

Home Address: _____

Commercial Credit Application #5 (with a Personal Guarantee)

BUSINESS CREDIT APPLICATION AND AGREEMENT

Business Name: _____ Date: _____

Address: _____

Name of President: _____Co. Phone#: _____

How long in business: _____ D&B number: _____

Trade references:

Name: _____ _____Address: _____

Name: _____ _____Address: _____

Name: _____ _____Address: _____

Name: _____ _____Address: _____

Bank references:

Name:_____Phone#: _____

Account#: _____Bank officer name: _____

Name:_____Phone#: _____

Account#: _____Bank officer name: _____

Credit limit requested: _____ _____Tax exempt?: _____

[If yes, please attach State Tax Exemption Certificate.]

Personal Guarantee

As an inducement for CREDITOR NAME to, from time to time, and at the sole discretion of the Credit Department, extend credit to the company named in this Agreement, I agree to make myself liable and personally responsible for all and any indebtedness of the business whose name is listed below. I understand the debt may be on open account, by C.O.D. or by any other method of credit extension.

Signed: _____ Date: _____ Name:_____

Signature of guarantor

Full name of firm:

The undersigned authorizes the creditor to conduct inquiries about this Applicant Company on the basis of this signed Credit Application. The undersigned acknowledges that the creditor may reduce or withdraw open account privileges at any time.

Signed: _____ Date: _____ Title: _____

Officer's Signature   Corporate Title

Sample Credit Application #6 (with Credit Agreement)

CONFIDENTIAL CREDIT APPLICATION

Business Name: _____ Date: _____

Address: _____

Name of Co. President: _____ Co. Phone#: _____

How long in business: _____ D&B number: _____

Financial statements enclosed: Yes: _____ No: _____

[Note—Financial statements are required for any credit limit in excess of $10,000.]

Trade references:

Name: _____ Address: _____

Name: _____ Address: _____

Name: _____ Address: _____

Name: _____ Address: _____

Bank references:

Name: _____ Phone#: _____

Account#: _____ Bank officer name: _____

Name: _____ Phone#: _____

Account#: _____ Bank officer name: _____

Credit limit requested: _____ Tax exempt?: _____

[If yes, please attach State Tax Exemption Certificate.]

Credit Agreement

All invoices are due Net 30 days from the date of invoice. As a condition of sale, a monthly service charge of the maximum permitted by law will be assessed on all account not paid within terms. Goods are sold F.O.B. shipping point, with risk of loss or damage in transit passing at our docks to the buyer. CREDITOR may at its sole discretion and without any advance notice cease the further extension of credit. Applicant agrees to pay reasonable attorney's fees and other costs in the event of default. In support of this credit application, the Applicant authorizes CREDITOR to obtain personal and/or business credit reports.

Signed: _____ Title: _____ Date: _____

(Full name of firm)   (Owner/Officer Signature)

Alternative Closing Statements on Standard Commercial Credit Applications

(1) I certify the information provided in this Credit Application and Agreement is true and correct. I authorize CREDITOR NAME to verify the information provided and to contact the references listed.

Name: _____ Signature: _____

Title/Position: _____ Date: _____

(2) I certify the information on this Application is true and complete. I agree to furnish financial statements from time to time as requested by CREDITOR NAME, and to promptly notify CREDITOR NAME of changes in ownership, address, or financial condition.

Signed by: _____ Title: _____ Date: _____

(3) By submitting this signed and completed form, the undersigned certifies that all of the information on this form is correct, and agrees to make payment in accordance with CREDITOR NAME's terms of sale.

Signature: _____ Name: _____

Title: _____ Date: _____

(4) Signing below and submitting this form grants CREDITOR NAME permission to check the references and other information provided.

[Note: All applications require the signature of an owner or officer.]

Signed by: _____ Title: _____ Date: _____

(5) By signing below, we agree that that all purchases made on open account terms will be paid within thirty (30) days from the invoice date. We agree to pay a finance charge of 1.5% per month on any unpaid and past due balance and understand that orders are subject to credit hold at any time the finance charge is unpaid or ther account is past due.

Agreed and accepted by:

_____ _____

Signature: Date:

(6) The bank and trade references listed above are hereby authorized and requested by the undersigned to release financial and credit information to CREDITOR NAME concerning our account.

Applicant: _____

Signature: _____ Title: _____ Date: _____

(7) We certify that all of the information provided on this application form is correct, and that we fully understand your terms of sale and agree to pay all invoices as they come due.

Signed by: _____ Title: _____ Date: _____

(8) We understand that your terms of sale are Net 30 days from the date of the invoice. We acknowledge that a finance charge of 1.5% per month will be applied to all past due moneys. By signing below, we hereby authorize the bank and trade references listed to release credit information regarding our company to CREDITOR NAME. By submitting this form and signing below, I also certify that all the information provided is true and correct.

Signed by: _____ Print name: _____

Date: _____ Title: _____

(9) The above information is submitted for the purpose of obtaining open account credit terms from CREDITOR NAME. I hereby authorize CREDITOR NAME to investigate the information provided and to contact the references listed. I acknowledge responsibility, ability, and willingness to pay invoices within thirty (30) days of the date of invoice. I/we agree to be liable for reasonable legal and collection expenses should it ever become necessary to incur such expense for CREDITOR NAME to secure payment.

Name: _____ Title: _____

Officer/Owner Signature: _____ Date: _____

(10) The undersigned certifies that all the information on this form is true and correct. We fully understand your credit terms and agree to pay within these terms in consideration for the extension of open account terms.

C.O.D. terms are _____ are not _____ acceptable while you are reviewing this Credit Application.

Financial statements will ____ will not ____ be provided if required to approve the credit limit and credit terms requested.

Signed by: _____ Title: _____ Date: _____

(11) Applicant agrees the terms of sale are 2% 10 days, Net 31 days from the date of invoice. Exceptions to these terms must be made in writing, and signed by an officer of CREDITOR NAME. Both parties agree that the laws of the State of _____ shall govern this agreement. The Applicant agrees to pay reasonable attorney's fees and court costs should they be incurred to collect moneys owed to CREDITOR NAME or any division or subsidiary of CREDITOR NAME.

It is understood that cash discounts taken after the due date listed on each invoice will be charged back to the Applicant. Failure to repay within 30 days after being charged back may cause interruption of shipment until the unearned discount(s) are paid.

[Note: This application must be signed by the company owner, partner; or by an Officer if the Applicant is a corporation.]

Print name and title: _____

Signature: _____ Date: _____

(12) Applicant's signature below attests financial responsibility, ability and willingness to pay Seller's invoices in accordance with the terms stated below:

If open account terms are offered the terms of sale shall be Net 30 days from date of invoice. Monthly statements are sent as a courtesy only. Past due accounts are subject to a service charge of 1% per month. Any late charges assessed must be paid before additional open account sales will be made. Should it ever become necessary to assign the account balance to a collection agency or to an attorney due to payment default, the Applicant shall pay the Seller's legal fees and court costs.

_____   _____

Signature (owner or officer)   Name (typed or printed)

_____   _____

Title   Date

(13) The information in this application and in all the financial statements submitted in connection herewith are for the purpose of obtaining open account credit. The information provided is represented by the Applicant to be true, correct, and complete. The Applicant authorizes CREDITOR NAME to investigate all credit references and any other matters pertaining to its credit and financial responsibility. The undersigned authorizes its banks and trade creditors to provide CREDITOR NAME with complete information for the purpose of credit evaluation.

CREDITOR NAME Signature: _____

Title: _____   Date: _____

Print name: _____

Personal Guarantee: In consideration of any credit extended, the undersigned will personally guarantee full and prompt payment of all indebtedness of _____ incurred for merchandise provided by CREDITOR NAME in addition to any service charges or collection costs where applicable. This Personal Guarantee shall remain in force until the CREDITOR acknowledges its revocation in writing. Any such revocation shall not affect indebtedness incurred prior to receipt of written notice.

Individual Signature: _____ Date: _____

Home Address: _____

Home Phone #: _____ S.S. #: _____

(14) The above information is given for the purpose of extending credit, and is represented and warranted to be true, complete and accurate. CREDITOR NAME is hereby authorized to investigate the above listed references, each of which is authorized by the undersigned to provide all information requested by CREDITOR.

By signing below, I certify that I have the authority to bind the company to this agreement, and that I agree to CREDITOR NAME's terms of sale of 1% 15 days, net 30 days. I also agree and accept that the credit limit and credit terms may be changed or withdrawn at the sole discretion of CREDITOR NAME's Credit Department.

Applicant Company Name: _____

By: _____ Title:_____ Date: _____

Signature

(15) Authorization for Release of Information: For the purpose of being considered for open account credit terms by CREDITOR NAME, I authorize each of the trade references and bank references listed above to release information to CREDITOR NAME by telephone, fax or by mail.

Name of Officer: _____ Title: _____

Signature: _____ Business Name: _____

Date: _____

(16) Credit Agreement. Applicant understands that the Seller will conduct their usual credit investigation. The Applicant authorizes its bank, listed above, and the trade references listed above, to provide customary credit information to the Seller for the purpose of considering the Applicant for open account credit terms.

Applicant understands the Seller's terms are Net 30 days from date of invoice. Applicant also agrees that if the account becomes delinquent, and if it ever becomes necessary to place the account for collection that the Applicant will pay all reasonable fees and expenses incurred by the seller.

Signed by: _____ Title: _____ Date: _____

(17) The information given herein is offered as part of a request by the applicant for an extension of credit for commercial business use. We authorize the creditor to make inquiries into any and all matters set forth in this application; to obtain oral or written credit reports from any credit reporting agency, trade creditor, bank or any other applicable source of information for the purpose of evaluating our credit and financial responsibility.

We further authorize the references listed including our bank to provide to the Creditor any information concerning the financial status of this business.

Signature: _____ Title: _____ Date: _____

(18) This application must be signed by the owner of the company for a proprietorship or a partnership, by the general partner for limited partnerships, and by an officer if the applicant is a Corporation.

I certify that the above information, given for the purpose of obtaining credit from CREDITOR NAME is true and correct. By signing this Credit Application, I authorize CREDITOR to verify this information, provide information on this account to others seeking such information, and to obtain and review my personal credit report. I understand that late charges of 1.5% per month may be assessed on any balance remaining unpaid and more than 30 days past due. The Applicant agrees to pay attorney fees and costs if suit is necessary for collection. CREDITOR reserves the right to terminate the extension of credit at any time.

Signature of owner, partner,

General partner, or officer

Of the corporation: _____   Date: _____

Please print name: _____   Title: _____

(19) In consideration of CREDITOR NAME's extending credit to the Applicant, Applicant agrees to pay for all items delivered to or at its request within 15 (fifteen) days of receipt of goods. Applicant agrees that the terms of sale, the warranty on the product and Creditor's invoice shall be the term of the contract of sale between CREDITOR NAME and the Applicant.

Applicant agrees to promptly pay a monthly service charge on all sums that reach 30 days from receipt of goods. That service charge shall not exceed 1.5% per month, or the highest amount allowed by law. Waiver of one or more of these service charges shall not be deemed to be a waiver of all future service charges. If CREDITOR NAME must commence litigation or employ attorneys to secure payment of any sums due it from Applicant, the Applicant agrees to pay the Creditor's reasonable attorneys fees in addition to any other sums due.

Applicant agrees to notify CREDITOR in writing using Certified Mail and addressed to the Chief Financial Officer of CREDITOR NAME of any change in ownership or about a transaction covered by the Bulk Sale/Bulk Transfer laws. If written notice is not received at least ten business days before the Bulk Sale/Bulk Transfer or before the ownership change, all moneys owing will remain the obligation of the Applicant to the CREDITOR.

The undersigned warrants that he/she has the authority to bind the Applicant to the terms of this agreement, that he/she has read the agreement carefully and understands its implications.

Signature: _____ Title: _____ Date: _____

(20) In consideration of CREDITOR NAME extending open account credit terms to the Applicant the undersigned hereby agrees:

The credit limit and credit terms will be established at the sole discretion of CREDITOR NAME. All purchases will be made and governed by the terms of this agreement without regard to any conflict between documents. The terms of sale are Net 30 days from date of invoice. Applicant agrees to pay interest on any amount still owing and more than 30 days past due at a rate of 1.5% per month. Applicant agrees to pay any and all costs incurred if it should default on payment and CREDITOR would refer this matter to its attorney to litigate to collect any unpaid balance.

This agreement is governed and controlled by the laws of the State of _____. Any litigation required in connection with the sale of goods to the Applicant by the Creditor will be heard in Courts located in the County of _____, State of _____ without regard to conflicts that may arise as to the proper venue for litigation. Applicant agrees to pay a $25 service charge on any check returned to insufficient funds. Applicant agrees that by signing this agreement the Applicant is authorizing the bank and trade creditors listed to release information to CREDITOR NAME. This agreement can only be amended by written agreement signed by both parties.

Applicant warrants the information provided is true and correct. Applicant acknowledges that the information in question is being provided to help CREDITOR assess the Applicant for open account terms. Applicant authorizes CREDITOR to check Applicant's credit history, trade and bank references, and it authorizes banks and creditors to release this information to the creditor.

Applicant Company Name: _____

Signed by: _____ Title: _____ Date: _____

(21) The above information is submitted by the undersigned for the purpose of obtaining credit from CREDITOR NAME. The undersigned expressly agrees to the terms of payment of Net 30 days from date of invoice and any payment accepted after that 30-day period is not to be considered a change in terms. CREDITOR reserves the right to charge interest at the highest legal rate on past due balances.

The undersigned agrees to pay reasonable attorney fees and all other costs and expenses including but limited to applicable restocking, storage, insurance and freight incurred by CREDITOR in the collection of any obligation of the undersigned pursuant hereto.

It is understood that credit privileges can be revoked at any time without prior notice by CREDITOR NAME. This agreement shall become effective when accepted by CREDITOR. The undersigned shall not transfer or assign this agreement without the prior written consent of CREDITOR.

The undersigned agrees to notify CREDITOR immediately of any change in the information provided in this application.

Authorized Signature: x_____ Title: _____

Date Signed: _____ Please print name: _____

(22) By signing this application, I authorize CREDITOR to investigate my personal credit and financial records, including contacting my bank for information. As part of this investigation, I authorize CREDITOR to request and obtain consumer credit reports on me in connection with the opening, monitoring, renewal and extension of credit. I also authorize CREDITOR to contact the trade references listed above and for those creditors to report information to CREDITOR.

By signing this application, I acknowledge that I have personally guaranteed the debts and obligations of my business. I agree to make payments to your company as they come due.

Name: _____   S.S. #: _____

Home address: _____

Home phone: _____   Date: _____

Authorized signature: _____

(23) Terms and Conditions:

   (a)   CREDITOR shall establish, maintain or change the credit limit at its sole discretion.

   (b)   The Applicant agrees to pay all charges according to the payment terms established by each invoice.

   (c)   A signed purchase order is required on all purchases over $1,000.

   (d)   Applicant agrees to notify CREDITOR within five days of any change of ownership, address, or telephone number.

   (e)   Applicant agrees to pay interest on late payments at the rate of 1.5% per month.

   (f)   Applicant shall pay all costs and expenses including reasonable attorney's fees and court costs incurred by CREDITOR in exercising any of its rights or remedies or in enforcing any of the terms, conditions or provisions of this agreement.

   (g)   Applicant agrees that the CREDITOR'S terms as listed on each invoice shall control and govern over any conflict as to the terms of sale on an invoice.

   (h)   Risk of loss or damage shall pass upon delivery of the goods to the Applicant's (purchaser's) carrier, F.O.B. Seller's warehouse or other point or points of delivery designated by supplier as provided in these terms.

   (i)   These terms and conditions shall be governed and interpreted in accordance with the laws of STATE. Any conflict shall be litigated in the

Courts of COUNTY, STATE and Applicant agrees that these Courts shall have venue for the litigation of any disputes.

(j)   Product may only be returned with an authorized Return Merchandise Authorization ("RMA").

(k)   No modification shall be binding on either party unless such modification is in writing and signed by an authorized representative of both parties.

(l)   If any portion of this agreement is found to be unenforceable, then such unenforceability shall not affect the remainder of this agreement. The undersigned acknowledges that they have the Authority to bind the company to this agreement, and that thet understand and agree to the terms and conditions listed below.

Signed by: _____   Print name: _____

Title: _____   Date: _____

SUMMARY

Credit Application Guidelines

- If you intend for the customer to be bound by the terms and conditions listed on your Credit Application and Agreement, it must be signed by an individual in the debtor company able of binding the Applicant.

- If you have any doubt about the authority of the person who signed the Application to bind the Applicant, ask for a letter or a fax from that person stating simply that they have the requisite authority to sign the contract and to bind the Applicant.

- If you require a Personal Guarantee before granting credit to an Applicant corporation, recognize that in some States the guarantor's spouse's signature is also required on the Personal Guarantee to be enforceable. An attorney can provide you with all the information you will need to make Personal Guarantees enforceable.

- If and when an Applicant is approved for open account credit terms, the Credit Manager should send the new customer an approval letter that also restates the terms and conditions under which the terms of sale were granted.

- If the customer becomes past due, the collector should refer back to the signed Application and the terms and conditions under which open account credit terms were granted.

CHAPTER 17

An Overview of Financial Statement Analysis and Interpretation

The owners and managers of any business are interested in measuring how the company is performing. Banks and trade creditors are interested in knowing about the financial performance of their customers. Financial statement analysis is a tool suitable for the needs of each group. Financial statement analysis permits the analyst to evaluate a company's overall financial performance, to identify its strengths and weaknesses, to anticipate or forecast future problems, and to determine if the company under review is well managed.

For the credit professional, financial statement analysis can be helpful in determining whether an applicant is creditworthy and if an active customer remains creditworthy. In addition, financial statement analysis can help the credit manager to establish an appropriate credit limit and credit terms. Ultimately, financial statement analysis can be used to help the credit professional to decide if the company under review is a good credit risk in the long term and short term. Studying a company's historical the financial performance allows creditors to make better informed credit decisions that limit credit risk, lower delinquencies and reduce the risk of bad debt losses.

WHAT ARE FINANCIAL STATEMENTS?

At their most basic, financial statements are a scorecard of a company's performance. The Balance Sheet shows a company's financial position at a specific point in time. The Income Statement shows how the business performed over a specific period of time such as a year. The Cash Flow Statement shows how the business acquired cash and how it used cash over a specific period of time.

Evaluated together, these three financial statements tell a story about a company's financial position and they allow the analyst or credit manager to determine the customer's strengths and weaknesses.

TIMING OF FINANCIAL STATEMENTS

Company prepare financial statements at least once every twelve months if for no other reason than to calculate the taxes that it owes. Companies can elect to end their year on December 31st or they may choose any other date as the end of their fiscal year.

Interim financial statements are statements prepared between annual financial statements. Interim financial statements are customarily prepared quarterly. Many companies also prepare financial statements monthly for internal purposes only.

Financial statements provide the following information:

- The nature and value of what the company owns [assets]
- The nature and value of what the firm owes [liabilities]
- The amount the owners have invested in the company [equity]
- The amount of business the company has generated [revenues]
- How much the company has spent [expenses]
- How well the company has controlled the levels of cash inflows vs. out-flows [cash flow]
- The amount of profit generated

MANIPULATION OF FINANCIAL RESULTS

Financial performance is always subject to a certain amount of manipulation. Management is capable of making any number of subtle changes to the company's financial statements without violating any accounting rules or tax laws. For example, it is relatively easy to increase short-term profits by cutting discretionary expenditures. Discretionary expenditures might include expenditures on research and development, on advertising, on equipment maintenance and upkeep, or on travel.

American managers are often accused of focusing on maximizing short-term profits at the expense of long-term profits and long term competitiveness.

Since many senior executives are rewarded for increasing short-term profits, there is a natural tendency to focus on short term rather than long term objectives. There is also pressure to manipulate earnings to pull revenues and profits forward. Managers that try to manage the company for long term value rather than short term gains often find themselves replaced by stockholders more interested in short term than long term performance.

THE FOCUS OF TRADE CREDITORS

Trade creditors tend to extend open account credit to customers for a relatively short period of time—typically between 30 and 90 days. Since trade creditors normally extend credit on a short-term basis, their initial focus in examining a customer's financial statements is on the company's short-term debt paying ability. Specifically, creditors tend to focus on short-term liquidity rather than the degree of financial leverage the customer has chosen to utilize. Liquidity involves a customer's ability to pay its debts as they come due. Information about a customer's liquidity is found on the Balance Sheet and in the Cash Flow Statement.

This is not intended to suggest that trade creditors are not or should not be concerned about a customer's profitability. No company can remain viable if it continues to sustain losses over an extended period of time. However, it is true that most trade creditors are more concerned about short-term debt paying ability than they are about short-term profitability and long term viability.

STATEMENT OF CASH FLOWS AND NOTES

Credit managers typically receive only the Balance Sheet and the Income Statement from customers. Unfortunately, it is impossible to form a clear and comprehensive picture of a customer's financial condition without access to the Notes to the Financial Statements, and the Statement of Cash Flows. Even though they are unlikely to receive them, creditors should always request the Statement of Cash Flows and the Notes in order to do a comprehensive review of the applicant or customer. A complete set of financial statements provides unique insights into the strengths, resources, stability, management style, and strategies of the company under review.

Many trade creditors consider themselves lucky if they receive any financial data from their privately held customers. Trade creditors are often not in a position to demand other reports from the customers—especially when their competitors do not require them.

Financial statements are customarily prepared quarterly, but they are normally shared with trade creditors only once each year. If they are unable to get financial statements from customers, credit managers base their decisions on the following information:

- their credit experience with the customer

- the credit experience of other trade creditors

- the bank rating

- credit bureau reports, and trade clearance reports

Unfortunately, past payment performance may or may not be a good indicator of how a customer will perform in the future, and there are significant differences between bank credit and trade credit. A more accurate understanding of a customer's ability to pay bills as they come due can be achieved by combining information from the four sources listed above with financial statement analysis.

THE VALUE OF OUT OF DATE FINANCIAL STATEMENT.

The older the financial statement a creditor is reviewing, the less useful they become. Financial condition changes on a daily basis, as does the customer's ability to pay its debts. Depending on how long it has been since the end of the fiscal year, many creditors ask for copies of their customers' fiscal year end statements along with a copy of the company's interim financial statements.

ACCOUNTING METHODS

There are two accounting methods in common use—the cash basis and the accrual basis. Using accrual accounting, revenues are reported when they are earned rather than when payment is received. Similarly, using accrual accounting expenses are recorded when they are incurred and not when payment is actually made.

In contrast, cash basis accounting involves recording revenues when received, and recording expenses when they are paid.

PROBLEMS WITH FINANCIAL STATEMENT ANALYSIS

Financial statement analysis is widely misunderstood. There are numerous myths and misconceptions about financial statement analysis that will not go away. As a result of inadequate training credit professionals frequently misinterpret the information contained in the financial statements they receive from customers. This can result in the wrong credit limit or credit terms being assigned to a customer. It is critical that credit managers understand financial statement analysis and perform it properly.

All financial statements, including audited financial statements, are subject to a certain amount of window dressing. [Window dressing is intended to describe actions significantly short of fraud. Window dressing vs. fraud can be thought of as analogous to the difference between tax avoidance and tax evasion. One is perfectly legal but suspect, the other is false and illegal. Window dressing involves the manipulation of financial statements by the management of the company. For example, a company may delay payments near the end of the accounting period in order to record a large cash balance on the Balance Sheet. Recognizing that window dressing occurs will allow credit managers to review the statements they receive with the proper amount of skepticism.

BALANCING FINANCIAL ANALYSIS AND OTHER FORMS OF CREDIT INFORMATION

Credit managers sometimes place too much faith and emphasis on financial statements. By using financial analysis to the exclusion of non-financial factors, the credit managers are cutting themselves off from othere sources of relevant and valuable information.

For example, a customer whose financial statements indicate they have very limited cash reserves [tight liquidity] may be considered an unacceptable credit risk. However, the customer may have an untapped working capital line of credit already established to deal with the cash flow problem rendering the liquidity question mute. If a credit manager ignored the bank reference and based the decision on the customer's financial profile, the decision to reject the applicant or to offer a small credit limit might be the wrong decision.

Key non-financial performance standards include:

- historical payment performance with the creditor company
- historical payment performance with other creditors
- number of years in business
- management's business experience
- the debtor's access to outside sources of capital when required
- location, and the condition of the debtor company facilities
- conditions within the debtor company's industry
- size and breadth of the debtor company's customer base
- whether or not the creditor has a personal guarantee or other forms of collateral from the debtor

FINANCIAL ANALYSIS PHOBIA

Perhaps the biggest problem with financial statement analysis is the fact that some credit professionals are so intimidated by the complexity of financial statements that they do not use financial analysis to help control risk. This problem is preventable. There are numerous sources of information about financial statement analysis and interpretation including:

- Classes
- Seminars
- Books
- Speeches, and
- Home study courses

With the right motivation and the right instructor or book, anyone can learn how to use financial statements to evaluate credit risk.

FOOTNOTES TO FINANCIAL STATEMENTS

There are two separate and distinct kinds of footnotes or notes to financial statements. The first type describes among other things major accounting policies, and changes in these accounting policies over time. These notes are a part of the narrative section of an audited financial statement. The second type of footnote provides additional detailed disclosures about the operations of a business.

Footnotes are required reading for credit managers interested in understanding as much about a customer's business operations as possible because footnotes provide information and insight about a customer not available from any other source.

HOW TO USE FINANCIAL STATEMENTS MORE EFFECTIVELY

The goal of every credit manager is to find ways to perform all of their jobs more effectively and more efficiently. Here are some ideas for improving the effectiveness and the efficiency of financial statement analysis:

- Conduct a quick review immediately after receiving financial statements from customers. The goal is to identify customers that are in obvious financial trouble.

- If those statements reveal the customer is in trouble, the credit manager should conduct an in depth analysis of the financial statements as quickly as possible.

- Credit managers should request financial statements quarterly from publicly traded customers. This way, the credit department is unlikely to be caught by surprise by any significant changes.

- Follow up promptly on broken commitments by privately held companies to provide financial statements. Occasionally, the creditor may have to make several requests for financial statements before they are sent. Privately held companies sometimes wait to see if the creditor will give up and go away without financial data.

- Credit professionals should not rely too heavily on financial statements to assess risk and to assign credit limits to customers. The limitations of financial statement analysis are explained in detail later in this chapter.

- Credit managers should always request two or more years of financial statements. The goal is to have the prior years' financial results as a benchmark against the current year results.

- Recognize that even with audited financial statements the debtor company has a good deal of discretion in the way information is presented—and that so-called "Window Dressing" changes to the company's financial performance can have a significant impact on the results being reported.

- Be aware of the potential for fraudulent financial statements. Recognize that they will not be easy to spot. Ask yourself if the financial information presented makes sense given what you know about the debtor company.

THE BALANCE SHEET

A Balance Sheet reports the financial condition of a company at a specific point in time. It presents information about a company's assets, liabilities and equity on a specific date—but not about whether or not the company made money, and whether sales are growing or declining. Balance Sheets typically list assets on the left side of the Balance Sheet, and liabilities and equity on the right side.

Assets are things that a company owns or controls, while liabilities are things the company owes. Equity can be thought of as the owner's claims against the assets of the company after all liabilities have been paid.

THE BALANCE SHEET FORMULA

Assets = Liabilities + Equity

OR

Assets—Liabilities = Equity

Typical accounts on a balance sheet are shown in exhibit B.

EXHIBIT B—TYPICAL ACCOUNTS ON A BALANCE SHEET

Current Assets	Current Liabilities
Cash	Accounts Payable
Marketable Securities	Bank indebtedness due in less than one year
Accounts Receivable	
Inventory	Accrued Expenses
Prepaid Expenses	
Long Term Assets	Long Term Debts
Property	Bank indebtedness
Plant and Equipment	
Long Term Investments	Equity
Goodwill	Shareholder Equity
Total Assets	Total Liabilities plus Equity

Assets are presented on the Balance Sheet in a specific way. Assets are divided into three major categories:

• Current Assets.

- Noncurrent Assets, also known as Fixed Assets, sometimes referred to as property, plant and equipment.
- Other Assets.

Current assets. Current assets are those assets that are expected to be converted into cash within a year. Current assets are presented on the balance sheet according to their degree of liquidity. Liquidity refers to the ease or ability of the company to convert liquid assets such as accounts receivable into cash. The normal order of current assets, based on their degree of liquidity is as follows:

- Cash
- Marketable securities [sometimes called cash equivalents]
  - Accounts receivable
  - Notes receivable
  - Inventory [including raw material, work in process, and finished goods inventories]
- Other current assets

Tangible and Intangible Assets. Assets can also be divided into tangible and intangible assets. Tangible assets have physical form and substance. Intangible assets such as goodwill do not have any physical form.

Fixed assets. Fixed assets include property, plant and equipment. Fixed assets, except land, are depreciated over time. The matching principle mandates depreciation of over their useful life. The reason is fairly straightforward: If the entire cost of an asset were written off in the year it was acquired, this would tend to reduce net income in that year and to artificially inflate net income in subsequent years. The solution devised by accountants involves allocating a portion of the purchase price over the useful life of the asset. The two basic methods of depreciation are straight line and accelerated depreciation.

- *Current liabilities.* Current liabilities are debts of the company that are expected to be paid within the next 12 months.

  Noncurrent liabilities or "long term debts" are not due for at least 12 months.

- *Equity.* There are several different types of equity. Each is described elsewhere in this chapter. It is important to remember that equity the amount available to the owner(s) after all other obligations have been retired.

WHAT CONCERNS SHORT TERM CREDITORS?

Short-term creditors, including general unsecured trade creditors are normally concerned about the liquidity of current assets. The conversion of current assets into cash is the primary method by which debtors pay their short-term creditors. One important measure of liquidity is the current ratio, measured by dividing current liabilities. This might suggest that a high current ratio is a guarantee of payment. Unfortunately, things are not that simple. While it is possible that a high current ratio means that the customer is highly liquid, it is also possible the current ratio is abnormally high because the debtor company has an excess of idle cash, or worse, that it has accumulated slow moving inventory and/or slow paying accounts receivable.

FINANCIAL ANALYSIS TIP: Never allow financial statements received from a customer to be added to a pile for review before someone knowledgeable about financial statement analysis to review them briefly. A quick review will indicate whether or not the customer's financial condition is bad enough to warrant an immediate credit hold.

THE INCOME STATEMENT

The Income Statement is sometimes referred to as the Profit and Loss Statement. The Income Statement presents information about the Revenues, Expenses and Net Income [or net loss] a company incurs over a specific period of time—for example a fiscal year. If the Balance Sheet is described as a snapshot of the company's financial condition, an Income Statement can be thought of as a motion picture chronicling the company's activities over a specific period of time.

The Income Statement formula is: Revenues—Expenses = Net Income. If expenses exceed revenues, then the company would record a net loss.

Revenues and expenses can be further refined using the following explanations:

- *Gross sales* minus *sales returns and allowances* equals *net sales.*
- *Net sales* minus *cost of goods sold* equals *gross margin.* [*Cost of goods sold* are the expenses incurred to manufacture, to purchase raw materials, or finished goods inventories]
- *Cost of goods sold* minus *Selling, General and Administrative Expenses* equals *Operating Profit or Operating Income.*
- *Operating Profit or Income* minus *Taxes Paid* equals *Net Earnings after Tax.*

Unfortunately, Income Statement accounting is not quite that straight-forward. For example, using the accrual accounting concept, a company may record income when it sells goods or services regardless of when payment is actually received. Thus, it is possible for a company to record positive net earnings and a net profit based on accrual accounting and have insufficient cash on hand to pay debts as they come due. For example, to meet its revenue and profit targets the company might have to offer deals (such as extended dating) to customers to incentivize them to buy before the end of the accounting period.

THE IMPORTANCE OF THE CASH FLOW STATEMENT

The Cash Flow Statement [also called the Statement of Cash Flows] is a useful report for credit professionals. The analysis of a customer's cash flow is important to trade creditors. The Statement of Cash Flows reports the flows of cash into and out of a company in a given accounting period, along with the resulting changes in cash and cash equivalents. There are many instances in which a company failed not because it was unprofitable or because of lagging sales, but because the company ran out of cash.

A cash flow problem often occurs as the result of timing differences between cash inflows and cash outflows. Here is a simplified example:

A customer has current assets of $10,000 concentrated as follows: $1,000 in cash and $9,000 in accounts receivable. The same company has just $2,000 in current liabilities in the form of wages payable. The $2,000 in wages payable is due in 48 hours. The $9,000 in accounts receivable does not come due for 15 days.

This company has a serious cash flow problem despite the fact that the company has a current ratio of 5 to 1 caused by the timing of cash inflows and outflows. It needs $2,000 within 48 hours but has only $1,000 in cash. Unless the company can accelerate collection of its accounts receivable, or borrow $1,000 it will be unable to pay its employees' wages.

Another way to think about the importance of the Statement of Cash Flows is by using the following chain of reasoning:

Current liabilities cannot be paid with current assets, they cannot be paid with sales, or profits, or profit margins. Current liabilities cannot be paid with working capital, with retained earnings, or with quick assets. The only way current liabilities can be retired is with cash. Companies that cannot pay their bills as they mature are said to be insolvent, and insolvent companies represent a serious risk to creditors. Therefore, as a creditor it is important to pay attention to the Statement of Cash Flows in order to monitor a customer's ability to pay bills as they come due.

PROBLEMS INTERPRETING THE CASH FLOW STATEMENTS

The Cash Flow Statement intimidates many people because it is not easily understood. The Cash Flow Statement measures cash inflows and outflows. Cash flows normally involve collected sales revenues, repayment of money borrowed, money received in the form of equity investments, and money received from the sale of certain assets [other than inventory].

The major uses of cash [cash outflows] include the cost of raw material or inventories, operating expenses such as rent, wages and salaries, the repayment of money borrowed, money paid to the owners of the company in the form of dividends or distributions, and money used to buy capital equipment or other non-inventory assets.

OPERATING CASH FLOW

Of particular interest to credit managers in a Statement of Cash Flows is the figure for cash provided or used by operating activities. Operating activities represent the basic business of the company. If a company consistently fails to generate positive cash flow, sooner or later it will have a hard time remaining in business. This is not intended to suggest the negative cash flow from operating activities should result in the customer's open account being withdrawn. That would be far too simplistic.

FINANCIAL STATEMENT AUDITS

During an audit by a CPA firm, the auditors evaluate a company's internal procedures and controls, confirm the existence of certain assets, and test the financial statements prepared by the company to make certain the statements are complete, and that the company's accountants followed Generally Accepted Accounting Principles [GAAP] in compiling the financial statements. If the CPA firm finds no inconsistencies, errors, or variances from GAAP, the CPA firm will issue an Auditor's Opinion letter attesting to the fact that the statements as presented are a fair representation of the company's financial position. This is referred to as an "unqualified opinion letter." The word "unqualified" means the statements are being presented by the company without qualification [or exception] by the auditor.

TREND ANALYSIS

The problem with reviewing a single financial statement is the fact that the creditor is unable to establish a benchmark in order to evaluate trends in the customer's performance. Trend analysis refers to the process of reviewing a customer's financial statements for two or more accounting periods looking for patterns to emerge. For example, on the Income Statement one trend that would be readily apparent would be a trend towards increasing or decreasing sales. Trend analysis allows the creditor to see changes variances from accounting period to accounting period.

Similarly, if a particular customer's Selling Expenses increased significantly from one accounting period to the next but sales revenues decreased then these two facts taken together would be of concern to a credit manager selling to that company.

TREND ANALYSIS IN DOLLARS AND PERCENTAGES

Credit managers should perform trend analysis on the Balance Sheet and the Statement of Cash Flows using the raw dollar amounts, and perform trend analysis on successive Income Statements by analyzing both the raw dollar amounts and the numbers as percentages. [By using Gross Sales as the denominator and by dividing every other figure on the Income Statement by Gross Sales dollars, each amount can be converted into a percentage. For example, if Gross Sales are $120,000 and the Gross Profit is $80,000 then the Gross Profit percentage is .666 [66%]. This is calculated as follows:

$$\frac{80}{120} = .666$$

On the Income Statement, trend analysis using percentages can be particularly revealing. For example, trend analysis using percentages will answer each of the following questions:

- If net income grew, did it grow as quickly as net sales?
- Conversely, if net income dropped, did management react quickly enough to reduce expenditures or did net income drop more quickly than net sales dropped?
- If expenses grew, did they grow as quickly as net sales did?
- Which specific expenses seem to have been properly controlled, and which expenses seem out of control?

COMPARATIVE ANALYSIS

Comparison of financial statements provides creditors with important insights about customers' financial health. There are four main types of comparative analysis. They are:

(a) Comparison of financial statement for the company between successive years [or accounting periods] called trend analysis.

(b) Comparison of a company's financial performance to that of a specific competitor.

(c) Comparison of a company's performance to industry standards or norms.

(d) Comparison of a customer's performance to specific goals that it may have set for itself.

Comparative financial analysis has inherent weaknesses. For example, comparisons of financial performance between and among competitor companies may be meaningless to a company because of differences in the following areas:

• Inventory valuation methods

• Choice of method of depreciation

• Decisions to capitalize or to expense certain expenses

• The size and the age of the organization

• The existence or absence of extraordinary gains or losses

FINANCIAL RATIO ANALYSIS

Ratios are relationships between two numbers. The number of different ratios that can be calculated is limited only by the number of different combinations of variables listed on the Balance Sheet, the Income Statement and the Statement of Cash Flows. Used properly, financial ratio analysis can provide insights into the creditworthiness of a customer or applicant.

However, credit professionals should avoid overanalyzing financial statements. Calculating and reviewing too many financial ratios may actually make financial problems harder to spot than they would otherwise have been. Similarly, calculating ratios beyond two decimal places is unnecessary. When used properly, financial ratio analysis provides the credit manager with an overview of the customer's current and historical financial condition.

Myths and Misconceptions about Financial Statement Analysis

There are any number of widely held myths and misconceptions about financial statement analysis. Used properly, ratio analysis is an important part of a comprehensive credit risk monitoring and management process. Used incorrectly, the credit manager might:

(a) extend credit to customers that don't have the ability to pay even if they intended to do so, or

(b) might cause the credit manager to deny credit to accounts that are creditworthy.

Some of the more common errors and misconceptions about financial statement analysis, include:

MYTH: Receiving any financial information is better than having nothing on file. *Reality.* In reality, the more out of date financial statements are the less likely they are to bear any relationship to the current status of the account. As a general rule, creditors are at risk any time the financial data they review is more than a year old.

MYTH: Unaudited financial statements are better than nothing. Reality. Unaudited financial statements may or may not be better than nothing. If a customer or applicant submits unaudited, fraudulent financial statements, then the creditor company may be lulled into a false sense of security by the information received. Even if the customer is not engaged in outright fraud, honest mistakes made by someone without the necessary accounting skills may result in financial statements that present an overly favorable impression of the debtor company.

MYTH: Receiving and reviewing the notes to a customer's financial statements is a luxury, not a necessity. Reality. Receiving and reading the Notes to the financial statement is an essential part of any comprehensive financial statement analysis process. Notes not only explain certain items; they also outline changes in the way the financial statements were prepared. Notes also detail the results of those changes in accounting rules.

Credit professionals should:

• Read the Notes in their entirety, and

• Pay particular attention to contingent liabilities, special events, and changes in accounting methods

MYTH: Financial statement analysis should be used to establish credit limits. *Reality.* Financial statement analysis including trend analysis, comparative analysis and ratio analysis is only one tool that credit managers should use to evaluate credit risk and establish an appropriate credit limit.

MYTH: There are ideal financial ratios. For example, the ideal current ratio is 2 to 1. More than 2 to 1 would suggest the customer is keeping too much in current assets and not investing in assets for the long term. A ratio of less than 2 to 1 indicates the customer may not be able to pay its bills. *Reality.* There are no ideal ratios. Ratios are shortcuts for analysts, but every company and every industry is different. Therefore, it is not possible to have a single ideal financial ratio or series of financial ratios.

MYTH: Debt, and in particular long term debt is bad. Conversely, having little or no debt is good. *Reality.* From the perspective of the borrower, debt is neither good nor bad. What is true is that the more debt a customer has the harder it will be to borrow more, the more the customer will have to pay [in the form of interest] to borrow more, and the harder it will be to pay back. For these reasons, trade creditors are often concerned about customers with high levels of debt.

MYTH: Audited financial statements guarantee that the financial statements are reliable. *Reality.* Auditors use sampling techniques, and auditors rely on data provided by management and on the statements and representations made by management in arriving at their opinions. Audited financial statements are more reliable than any other form of financial statement. However, there are numerous cases of companies whose auditors have missed significant problems.

MYTH: Comparing individual customer performance to industry ratios and norms is a good way to evaluate a customer's financial performance. *Reality.* So-called industry norms are not necessarily indicative or reflective of the financial performance of the industry as a whole. Industry norms are gathered from sources that are anything but average. Typically, industry norms are generated from financial data provided by publicly traded companies, and from privately held companies that choose to share their financial statements with whichever reporting agency is gathering the data and calculating the norms. Thus, the industry norms almost certainly do not reflect the financial performance, weaknesses and strengths of an average company in that industry since public companies and well-performing private companies are not "average."

A better choice might be to benchmark the company's performance against a direct competitor of comparable size. A head-to-head comparison allows creditors to pinpoint specific strengths and weaknesses.

MYTH: A tight current ratio means that a customer or applicant will have trouble paying suppliers on time, and a high current ratio indicates the company will be able to pay short terms obligations as they mature. Reality. It is the timing of cash inflows and outflows combined with the amount of cash and marketable securities on hand that determine if a customer will be able to pay its suppliers as the bills come due.

Even if a customer or applicant has a "low" current ratio or quick ratio, that customer may be able to pay its creditors on time by either (a) timing cash inflows and outflows so there is cash on hand when it is needed, or (b) the customer can remain current with its suppliers by making arrangements with its bank to borrow money to make up for any shortfall in cash.

MYTH: It is difficult for customers to manipulate their financial statements, especially if those statements are audited. Reality. All financial statements are subject to a certain amount of manipulation. Even under Generally Accepted Accounting Principles, a company has some "wiggle room" relating to how its financial information will be reported.

For example, if a company wants to show at lot of cash at the end of its fiscal year, that company can simply stop paying vendors toward the end of the year. If a company wants to show higher profits, it can reduce or eliminate discretionary expenditures such as research and development, or on non-essential business travel.

MYTH: Audited financial statements are facts. Reality. Audited financial statements present financial data in a way prescribed by the Financial Accounting Standards Board. The dollar amounts listed on the financial statements may or may not be entirely reliable.

For example, fixed assets are recorded on the Balance Sheet at the original cost of the asset minus accumulated depreciation. The value listed on the Balance Sheet will never equal the "true" value or the fair market value of those assets.

MYTH: By demanding that an applicant their financial statement, creditors reduce the likelihood that the information provided is fraudulent. Reality. The rationale is that con men will not mail these documents because they are concerned about committing mail fraud. In reality, criminals typically break so many laws in committing credit fraud that it is unlikely they will be concerned about committing another offense. Even if the con man refuses to mail their financial statement documents out of concern about committing mail fraud, the criminal will have to commit either mail fraud or wire fraud to submit any order not hand delivered to the salesperson, such as an order placed by phone or fax.

THE LIMITATIONS OF UNAUDITED FINANCIAL STATEMENTS

Anytime a creditor receives unaudited financial statements from a customer, the accuracy of those statements should be questioned. Internally prepared statements are subject to all types of manipulation. Some of this manipulation may involve a deliberate attempt to mislead creditors. This is fraud.

The most common problem with unaudited, internally prepared financial statements is that the people responsible for preparing the financial statements do not understand [or do not follow] Generally Accepted Accounting Principles. The result is incorrect but not necessarily fraudulent statements. Internally prepared statements is they often fail to follow some of the most basic accounting assumptions, including:

- The conservatism concept—that the business will use measurement methods that have the least favorable impact on financial performance.

- The matching principle—that revenues will be properly matched with the expenses incurred to generate those revenues.

- The consistency rule—that financial statements will adhere to the same accounting treatment from one accounting period to the next unless the change is documented in the footnotes.

- The full disclosure concept—that companies will present all relevant data in their financial statements.

The real problem with internally prepared statements is that the credit manager is unable to determine whether or not the statements followed GAAP, and if not to what extent the statements varied from the GAAP rules. Most privately held companies do not have audited financial statements, therefore the credit manager must rely on the debtor's own assessment of its financial condition.

THE IMPORTANCE OF A QUICK REVIEW OF FINANCIAL STATEMENTS RECEIVED FROM CUSTOMERS

A financial statement should undergo a quick review by the credit manager as soon as it is received. Items of special concern would include:

- An Income Statement showing that the customer [or applicant] lost money during the reporting period

- A Balance Sheet showing the company under review had a deficit net worth [and is therefore technically insolvent], or a current ratio of less than 1 to 1 indicating that the company was illiquid.

- A Statement of Cash Flows showing the company had a significant decrease in Cash and Cash Equivalents—indicating that the company had negative cash flow.

- In the Notes to the Financial Statements, changes in accounting principals that significantly affected the financial statements presented, or where there are significant contingent liabilities that could devastate the company if they result in actual liability against the company under review.

A quick scan of each financial statement received from customers before it is placed into a queue for more detailed review can prove to be a very inexpensive way to avoid potentially significant problems. A cursory review can prompt immediate action to limit the creditor's risk and prevent bad debt losses.

THE GOING CONCERN CONCEPT

The "going concern" concept is an accounting principle which states that unless otherwise stated, it is implicit in the financial statements that a company will continue in business as a going concern. If, during the course of the auditor's review of a company's books and records, it discovers information suggesting the going concern assumption may no longer be valid, then that information must be disclosed. When this occurs, either the basis of the audit must fundamentally change or there must be appropriate disclosure about the going concern concerns found by the auditor.

FUNDAMENTAL ACCOUNTING CONCEPTS

Credit professionals should be aware of some of the more important accounting principles in order to fully understand and in order to properly analyze the financial statements customers present. In addition to the going concern concept described above, the following are fundamental accounting principles that influence or guide the compilation of financial statements:

(1) The business entity concept
(2) The concept of conservatism
(3) The consistency concept
(4) The matching concept
(5) The realization concept
(6) The money measurement concept
(7) The materiality concept

SUMMARY

One of the most serious errors a credit manager can make is to rely too heavily on financial statement analysis to evaluate credit risk. Financial analysis is part of a larger process of evaluating risk and establishing credit limits. Every company will ask its credit department to make credit decisions based on criteria that are important to that company such as sales or growth targets or market share goals, so financial analysis is only one part of the process of deciding whether or not to extend credit to an applicant.

There are many myths and misconceptions about financial analysis. These myths and misconceptions do not invalidate the use of financial analysis. Instead, they serve as a reminder to the credit professional to learn their craft so that they do not embarrass themselves by making a mistake that costs their employer money and themselves prestige.

CHAPTER 18

FINANCIAL RATIO ANALYSIS

One of the most popular and widely used forms of financial analysis involves the use of ratios. Ratio analysis is a useful method of tracking the performance of a business. By showing financial relationships in percentage form, it is normally easier to detect minor deviations that might be less apparent if the financial statements were left in dollar form.

Reducing the dollar amount on financial statements to percentages or ratios makes it easier for credit managers and financial analysts to evaluate the strengths and weaknesses of the customer's financial statements. For example, even if a customer doubles in size, the credit manager will still be able to compare ratios from one period to the next and the period to period analysis will remain relevant. In theory, by comparing financial ratios to benchmarks that are known [or at least thought to be good, fair, or poor] the credit manager can judge the financial health of the company and to make better informed credit decisions.

FINANCIAL RATIOS

Financial ratio analysis relies on comparisons between various Balance Sheet and Income Statement items. Financial ratios give the credit professional a method of making comparisons of a customer's financial performance over time. No single ratio can or should be used to judge the financial condition of a customer. Contrary to popular myth, ratios are not intended to be used to convey precise information about a company's creditworthiness. Instead, ratios provide the credit professional with a broad overview of a customer's financial position and condition.

Ratios are commonly written in several different formats. Each of them has the same meaning. For example, a company with current assets of $30,000 and current liabilities of $10,000 has a current ratio [defined as current assets divided by current liabilities] of three to one. A current ratio of three to one can be expressed numerically as:

- 3 to 1
- 3:1 or
- 3/1

USES RATIO ANALYSIS

Financial ratios can help company managers, as well as interested third parties including trade creditors to gain insights into a company's strengths and weaknesses. Ratios provide clues as to the financial strengths and weaknesses of the company being evaluated.

Every credit manager or credit analyst has a few favorite financial ratios they use to evaluate customers or applicants. It is important to remember that the best ratios to use are the ones that provide the analyst with the information needed to make informed credit decisions.

For example, a creditor considering shipping into a high fashion clothing boutique might place a heavy emphasis on the inventory turnover ratio. A creditor would want to see how quickly the clothing chain's inventory is turning over—since inventory turnover would be an indication of whether the company had selected the right product mix. A clothing boutique with slow moving inventory [as measured by the inventory turnover ratio and in comparison to industry norms] would suggest some poor purchasing decisions. This in turn could cause a cash flow problem or low sales and net losses.

Ratios are often compared to industry norms to determine if the financial performance of a customer is in line with other businesses in the same industry. Industry credit groups sometimes publish certain statistical information about the customers covered by the credit group. Another source of information is published by the Dun and Bradstreet Company is titled "Key Business Ratios." As the name suggests, the book lists financial ratios for hundreds of different industries, allowing the credit manager to perform "head-to-head" comparisons between the financial performance of their customers and industry norms.

CHOOSING THE RIGHT RATIOS

Most credit managers use a core group of financial ratios to evaluate customers' performance. The most common ratios used are:

- The current ratio
- The quick ratio
- The debt to equity ratio
- Net income as a percent of sales
- Gross profit margin
- Inventory turnover ratio, and
- The accounts payable turnover ratio

COMMON SIZE RATIOS

Creating common size ratios on the Balance Sheet involves comparing all the figures on the Balance Sheet to total assets. On the Income Statement, comparing all the figures to Gross Sales creates common size ratios. The use of common size ratios makes period to period, or company to company comparisons easier and more meaningful to the credit manager.

USING FINANCIAL STATEMENTS TO MANAGE CREDIT RISK

Relatively minor changes in a customer's financial ratios from year to year are almost impossible for a credit manager or a credit analyst to interpret. Therefore, credit professionals should not base changes in a customer's credit limit or credit terms on minor changes. Ratio analysis is intended to be used to identify significant changes in the financial performance of the company under review.

THE TYPES OF FINANCIAL RATIOS

Normally, ratios are divided into four categories, which are:

Liquidity ratios. Liquidity ratios measure a company's ability to meet its short-term financial obligations. Credit managers use liquidity ratios to assess whether an applicant or a customer is maintaining an appropriate level of liquidity. Too little liquidity raises the possibility of delayed payment, or more seriously the possibility of default on a debt payment, which might result in a bankruptcy filing.

Profitability ratios. Profitability ratios are a measure of how well the company did in an accounting period. These ratios measure how well a company does generating profits for its owners or investors, but they do not attempt to measure the amount of risk the company took in order to achieve the specific level of profits.

Leverage ratios. Leverage ratios [sometimes called solvency ratios] are used to measure the financial soundness of a company. Leverage ratios measure how dependent the company is on debt financing [borrowing] as opposed to equity investments. From the creditor's perspective, the lower the leverage ratio the greater the protection to general unsecured creditors. In contrast to liquidity ratios that tend to focus on a firm's ability to meet its obligations in the near future, leverage ratios tend to take a longer term view

Efficiency ratios. These ratios measure how efficiently a company operates, and has used its assets to generate sales and profits. Specifically, efficiency ratios show the relationship between the resources used and the level of productivity achieved.

Liquidity Ratios

Liquidity ratios are used in an attempt to measure a company's ability to pay expenses and meet any other cash obligations that come due during the current accounting period. Credit managers look at prior accounting period results to try to gauge the debtor's ability to retire its current obligations in the current accounting period as they become due.

The two most popular liquidity ratios are:

(1) The Current Ratio

Current assets
Current liabilities

The current ratio is one of the most widely used financial indicators of a company's liquidity. It is usually considered to be the best source of information about short-term liquidity. The current ratio measures the relationship between current assets and current liabilities; it measures the business's ability to meet its current financial obligations by liquidating [covering into cash] current assets.

In theory, the higher the current ratio, the better the debtor's ability to repay its current obligations as they come due because the greater the cushion between current assets and current liabilities. In other words, the higher the ratio the greater the protection to a short-term creditor.

What is considered an adequate current ratio varies widely from industry to industry. A high current ratio is not always a good omen. A high current ratio might also indicate slow moving accounts receivable and/or obsolete inventory since either of these would tend to increase the size of current assets without adding significantly to the prospects of covering those assets into cash. Thus, the composition and the quality of current assets are the critical factors in an individual firm's true liquidity.

Most creditors prefer not to see an unusually high current ratio. This might indicate that management was not managing assets in the most appropriate way. An unusually high current ratio might be an indication that cash might be better used as an investment in capital equipment.

A common misconception is that a current ratio of 2 to 1 or higher means that a customer will have adequate liquidity to pay debts as they come due. In fact, it is the timing of cash inflows and cash outflows that determines whether or not a company will have the cash on hand to pay bills as they come due. A high current ratio is an indication of liquidity but it is not a guarantee of payment.

A company's current ratio should be compared to several previous years to determine if there are any favorable or unfavorable trends.

(2)   The Quick Ratio

Quick assets
Current liabilities

The quick ratio [sometimes called the acid test ratio] measures the extent to which the assets that can most quickly be converted into cash can cover the current liabilities of a customer. As such, the quick ratio is a refinement of the current ratio because it is more a more sensitive measure of liquidity. The quick ratio excludes inventory because inventory is the least liquid portion of current assets. [Quick assets include cash + marketable securities + accounts receivable.]

Inventory may be slow moving and difficult to sell. For example, if the inventory on hand is obsolete, or if for some other reason demand for the product has dropped then it would be unreasonable to infer that the inventory could be sold quickly enough to meet current cash requirements.

As a general rule, the higher the quick ratio, the more liquid the customer is considered to be, and the better the short term credit risk.

There are exceptions to every rule. A high quick ratio could indicate a highly liquid customer, or it might indicate that the marketable securities and/or the inventory are of poor quality and are accumulating.

In summary, a low quick or current does not mean the debtor will be unable to retire debts as they come due. There are many companies with low current and quick ratios that have established borrowing relationships with their bank for use when the company needs cash in the short term. Conversely, a high quick and current ratio does not mean the debtor will be able and willing to pay bills as they mature. Financial ratios don't pay bills—only cash pays bills as they come due.

Profitability Ratios

Profitability ratios measure how profitability in the previous accounting period using various tests of profitability. Profitability is a scorecard for businesses. A company that is consistently unprofitable is unlikely to remain in business. The three most popular profitability ratios are:

(1) Net Profit Margin

$$\frac{\text{Net income}}{\text{Net sales}}$$

The net profit margin shows what percentage of each sales dollar that became part of the net profit for a company. Profitability ratios such as the net profit margin are an important indicator of the performance of the company and of its management team. A drop of even one or two percent in a firm's after tax profit is cause for concern for a careful credit professional.

(2) Return on Equity Ratio

$$\frac{\text{Net worth}}{\text{Net income after tax}}$$

Return on equity measures the rate of return on the owners' equity investment in the company. It is a good benchmark for the firm's overall performance. Generally, a high return on equity is one indication of efficient management performance and successful business operations.

Unfortunately, a high return on equity might also indicate the company is under-capitalized. A high return on equity can result from a high degree of financial leverage. Therefore, return on equity must be evaluated in conjunction with other financial ratios to form an overall opinion of the customer's financial situation.

(3) Gross Profit Margin

Sales – cost of goods sold
Net sales

The gross profit is the amount of revenue remaining after subtracting the cost of goods sold from net sales. Cost of goods sold represents the cost of labor and materials, along with the factory overhead required to bring to a marketable state the goods that were sold. Overhead, such as selling, general and administrative expenses are excluded from this calculation.

A higher gross margin is better than a low gross margin. However, if the company reduced costs by using inferior products or cutting costs during the production process itself, then a higher gross margin in the short term may result in long term problems such as defective returns, and lost customer loyalty.

Another issue that credit managers should be aware of in relation to gross margin is different methods of valuing inventory. Cost of materials is calculated by taking the difference between the beginning and ending inventory balances after adding in purchases. Inventory costs are a major component of the cost of goods sold. Each of the most common methods of inventory valuation can have a significant impact on the cost of goods sold and on the resulting profits reported.

Leverage Ratios

While liquidity ratios measure short-term solvency, Leverage Ratios [sometimes called solvency ratios] are concerned with the amount of financial leverage a firm has acquired. Leverage ratios attempt to answer this question: Does the company have the ability to meet its long-term principal and interest payments as they come due?

Highly leveraged companies are more vulnerable to business downturns than those with limited debts in relation to equity. Generally, a lower ratio of liabilities to equity makes it easier and less expensive for the company to borrow money in the future. Three of the most popular leverage ratios are:

(1) Current Liabilities to Net Worth Ratio

$$\frac{\text{Current liabilities}}{\text{Net worth}}$$

This ratio shows the relationship between total current assets [debts owed to creditors in the next 12 months] and the capital invested in the business by the owners or stockholders. An increase in current liabilities relative to the owner's investment in the company is a concern to credit professionals because it means the company is increasing its borrowings without a proportionate increase in ownership.

In theory, the smaller the net worth and the larger the liabilities, the higher the credit risk. A lower current liabilities to net worth ratio suggests the customer may be a better credit risk.

(2) Debt to Equity Ratio

$$\frac{\text{Total liabilities}}{\text{Net worth}}$$

This ratio measures the relationship between the amount borrowed to finance the business and the capital invested by the business owners. The higher the ratio, the greater the risk being assumed by creditors.

A firm with a high debt to equity ratio should not automatically disqualify an applicant from being offered open account credit terms. Instead, it should be one of the facts or factors considered in making an informed credit decision.

In addition to the total liabilities to owners' equity ratio described above, there are a number of other debt to equity ratios in common use. One is total debt divided by equity. Another is long term debt divided by equity. What is true for all of these ratios is that the greater the liabilities are relative to total equity, the greater the risk to creditors.

(3) Interest Coverage

$$\frac{\text{Earnings before interest and taxes}}{\text{Annual interest expense}}$$

This ratio is a measure of a firm's ability to meet its interest payments. It measures pre-tax earnings minus interest expense to total interest charges. In theory, the more times net income before tax can cover the annual interest expense the greater the company's ability to meet its interest obligations.

A high interest coverage ratio does not mean that a customer will pay its interest obligations as they come due. The ratio simply measures the relationship between the interest expense and the company's net income before interest and taxes. Whether or not the firm will pay interest payments as they come due is a function of:

(a) whether the firm has the cash on hand to make those payments as they come due, or

(b) if the company does not have the cash, whether or not it made arrangements to borrow the cash it needs, and

(c) even if a company has the ability to make its interest payments, the company must have the desire to make these payments

A high interest coverage ratio would suggest that a customer should have no trouble meeting its interest payments. This ratio is also a measure of a company's capacity to get and to manage additional borrowings. As a rule of thumb, an interest coverage ratio of 4 times is considered an adequate cushion.

From the customer's point of view, leverage is a mechanism to increase profits at the cost of increased risk. Assuming the company is able to make the principal and interest payments, a high level of financial leverage will be a higher rate of return on owners' equity. Creditors should expect every customer to have a certain amount of long-term debt.

There is a relatively large range within which a customer may be considered to have an appropriate level of financial leverage. It is also important to recognize that the nature a company's business impacts on the amount of debt that the company can carry safely. For example, a company with stable sales and steady cash flow is more likely to be able to manage debt repayment successfully than a firm that is highly seasonal with fluctuating sales and cash flow.

Efficiency Ratios

Every company wants to maximize profits, and to do so, companies must operate efficiently. Efficiency ratios assess the efficiency with which a company manages its assets and resources. Five of the most commonly used efficiency ratios are:

(1) Accounts Receivable Collection Period

$$\frac{\text{Net accounts receivable}}{\text{Average daily credit sales}}$$

This ratio measures how long it takes for a company to collect its account receivable—to convert an account receivable into cash. As such, it measures how efficiently the company manages its credit granting process, collection process, and terms granting process. The longer a customer's average collection period, the greater the likelihood the customer will have trouble paying bills as they mature due to lack of cash on hand.

Since most business to business transactions are conducted on open account terms, average collection period is a reasonably good measure of a company's efficiency in credit and risk management. The longer the dating the company being reviewed offers to its customers, the longer the accounts receivable collection period will be.

(2) Inventory Turnover

$$\frac{\text{Cost of goods sold}}{\text{Average inventory}}$$

The inventory turnover ratio measures the number of times inventory turns over [is sold] during the year—or the accounting period under review. It is an approximate measure of the total time it takes to acquire, to sell, and to replace inventory. The inventory turnover ratio is a measure of the efficiency of the purchasing department, the sales department, and the production control department in a manufacturing firm.

As a general rule, low inventory turns can lead to poor liquidity. In theory, the higher the inventory turnover the more efficient the company has been in its daily operations. However, inventory turnover rates vary significantly from industry to industry. For example, a retail dairy ideally will turn inventory fairly close to 365 times a year, while a variety retailer might be doing well to turn inventory 6 times a year.

However, as with most ratios there are no absolute good or bad measures. An extremely fast [high] inventory turnover ratio might indicate that the company is well managed and that the merchandise it sells is in high demand. However, a high inventory turnover ratio might also mean that the company keeps very little inventory on hand—resulting in stock outs, lost sales and lost customers.

A high inventory turnover also results in higher ordering costs, the loss of volume buying discounts, and a loss of leverage with key suppliers. Therefore, in an effort to maximize earnings and profits a company must find the right balance between the cost of buying and holding inventory against the costs associated with having an insufficient mix of inventory on hand.

In a manufacturing business, it is important to try differentiate between raw materials inventory, work in process, and finished goods inventory. If a creditor wants to evaluate the liquidity of a company's inventory, he or she really needs to know at what stage of the production cycle the inventory is in. Finished goods inventory is the most liquid and has the highest liquidation value. Raw materials inventory is the next most liquid, and work in process is third. Credit professionals need to be concerned if a customer has a disproportionately high percent of its inventory in raw materials. This may indicate the customer has overbought and has tied up its cash in raw materials. As a result, the company under review is less likely to be able to retire debts as they come due.

(3) Asset Turnover

$$\frac{\text{Net sales}}{\text{Average total assets}}$$

This efficiency ratio measures the relationship between sales and the assets employed. Specifically, this ratio shows how many dollars of sales were generated based on each dollar of assets employed to generate sales. This ratio is an important indicator of management's ability to properly use assets to generate sales. If a company has a low ratio in comparison to its competitors, this may mean that competitors have found ways to operate more efficiently with proportionately less assets employed.

(4) Fixed Asset Turnover

$$\frac{\text{Net sales}}{\text{Fixed assets}}$$

A high sales to fixed assets ratio reflects the efficient use of the company's investment in plant, equipment and other long term assets.

(5) Accounts Receivable Turnover Ratio

$$\frac{\text{Credit sales}}{\text{Average accounts receivable balance}}$$

The accounts receivable turnover ratio is a popular way for creditors to determine their customers' success in collecting its receivables. The

A/R turnover ratio shows the number of times the entire accounts receivable balance is paid in full. A low turnover ratio would indicate slow moving accounts receivable, which might result in a cash crisis. A low accounts receivable turnover ratio might simply mean the company under review offers its customers extended dating.

Accounts receivable is often one of a company's largest assets. As a general statement, the higher the accounts receivable turnover the better for the company and for its creditors. A fast turnover in A/R might indicate:

- The company has an excellent credit department, or
- The company can demand that customers pay on time because they enjoy a dominant market position, or
- The company has a stringent credit policy.
- The company has an overly restrictive credit and collection policy.

BENCHMARKING

There are two basic ways to benchmark a company's financial performance using ratios. The first involves a comparison between the current period's financial results compared to the ratios for prior accounting periods. This type of historical analysis will enable the creditor to discover favorable or unfavorable trends that may have developed gradually over time. It also allows the credit professional to focus on any ratio that has changed sharply in a short period of time.

The other type of benchmark used with financial ratios involves comparisons of the company's financial ratios to industry norms. Two of the companies that produce studies of industry norms are Dun and Bradstreet®, and Robert Morris Associates®. Simply put, creditors would prefer to see their customers' financial performance compare favorably to industry norms.

SUMMARY

Financial analysis is performed to assist the credit manager in making a more fully informed credit decision about the creditworthiness of a customer or an applicant.

There are industry norms available for most financial ratios. They are useful to some extent as a point of reference. However, each customer is unique, and credit managers must look beyond "rules of thumb" and industry norms to understand what is happening to their customers.

Credit managers should not allow themselves to get bogged down in the minutia of financial analysis. There are software programs that will spread a set of financial statements commercially available. These software programs produce detailed comparative analysis, and ratio analysis. The best part is that the software is simple to use—meaning that the task of inputting the raw data can be delegated by the credit managers —leaving the credit manager with more time for higher value added activities.

CHAPTER 19

IMPROVING CREDIT DEPARTMENT EFFICIENCY

In this chapter, a few of the many tools and techniques that can be used to improve the credit department's productivity will be reviewed.

SPEND LESS TIME IN MEETINGS

The average manager spends a great deal of time in meetings. Even worse, credit managers often must attend unproductive meetings and must make up for the lost time by staying late or by taking work home.

Credit managers should avoid formal meetings whenever possible. If the credit manager is "invited" to attend a meeting, they should ask why their attendance is required. If there is a specific reason for them to attend, they can ask if they could arrange to be called into the meeting right before their attendance is required and then leave right afterwards. Credit managers would be surprised at how often this request works, and as a result how much irrelevant information they don't hear and how many fewer meetings they will be invited to attend.

Credit managers can improve the meetings within their department by scheduling shorter meetings. Marathon meetings are boring. The topics discussed during marathon meetings tend to blur together and people come away from them not remembering what was said. Credit department meetings should be informal, the credit manager should have an agenda, and there should always be a time limit.

It is a good idea to appoint a timekeeper. If there is an agenda and a time limit, the meeting tends to stay focused and on track. If the meeting begins to wander off track, the credit manager must be the one to steer the meeting back on course.

When meetings are planned and an agenda is distributed, employees tent tend to:

- prepare in advance of the meeting, and

- make certain that they cover the points as quickly as possible, and

- spend less time on lengthy warm-ups and more time on the topics scheduled for review

INDUSTRY GROUP MEETINGS

A special note about industry credit group meetings: Anyone who does not feel that industry credit group meetings are not helpful to the credit department's efforts to manage delinquencies and minimize bad debt losses is probably in the wrong industry credit group. Membership in one of these groups usually includes a requirement that the company send a representative to a minimum number of meetings each year. As nice as it is to get out of the office, credit managers know that the work will normally pile up while they are away. With this in mind, credit managers should delegate the task of attending at least half of these meetings to one or more of their subordinates.

DELEGATION

Credit managers should delegate as much of their work as possible to subordinates. The rule of thumb for delegation of work is as follows:

> Work should always be delegated to the lowest level at which the task can be performed effectively.

The best way to delegate is to ask for volunteers. Volunteer is often someone who wants to demonstrate that they are capable of doing more than they are currently being asked to do. Before delegating, the credit manager must be certain:

- The person to whom the task is delegated has the skills necessary to complete it

- The person performing the work understands how important the task is\

- The person has the tenacity to do the job

- The person has the training to the job

- The person has the time to complete the assignment

- The person knows when the task is due, and the person knows to bring problems to the credit manager well ahead of the deadline.

DEALING WITH TELEPHONE INTERRUPTIONS

Credit managers and their subordinates should schedule work based on when it can be done most effectively. For example, mornings are usually the best time to make collection calls, and afternoons are the best time to return calls and to do any necessary research.

As it relates to telephone interruptions, the credit manager should block out a specific amount of time for making outbound calls then accepting inbound calls [or allowing other interruptions] tends to break collectors' concentration. It is easy to become sidetracked away from making the outbound calls scheduled. To increase overall efficiency, the credit manager should give the collectors specific instructions about when to schedule which activities. As important as it is to tell subordinates what to do, it is equally important to be specific about what not to do. For example, credit managers should tell subordinates not to do research in the morning except under extraordinary circumstances.

USING THE INTERNET

The Internet is a useful tool for business, and in particular for the credit department. It is also a toy and entertainment center for children and adults alike. It is for this reason that companies have been reluctant to give access to the Internet to everyone in the company with a PC at their desk.

Almost everyone in the credit department would benefit from having access to the Internet. The credit manager and the new accounts rep could do certain types of research on line. Collectors could use their Internet access to verify telephone numbers and other information about customers, and to send customers certain documents.

Information resources on the Internet are spread out over thousands of web-sites. To save time, everyone in the credit department that uses the Internet should "benchmark" specific web-sites that they use frequently. Because the Internet is also a playground, credit department personnel should be given a list of activities they may not engage in while on the Internet. The following activities are obviously inappropriate for a place of business:

- Playing on line video games.

- Visiting an adult entertainment site on the Internet [There are literally thousands of them.]

- Looking for a new job on the Internet [Definitely inappropriate, and a conflict of interest.]

- Downloading any executable file from the Internet including something as apparently harmless as a screen saver program [because of the risk of importing a computer virus].

- Conducting personal business such as managing stock trades while at work and on company time.

By establishing these basic rules up front, the credit manager has greater assurance that the time spent on the Internet will be spent productively.

IMPROVING COMMUNICATIONS WITHIN THE CREDIT DEPARTMENT

Most credit managers have more tasks things to do than time to do them in. As a result, credit managers sometimes forget to schedule time with their subordinates. To be fair, most credit managers will make time for subordinates when problems arise, but the goal of any manager and in particular the goal of a risk manager is to manage proactively, and not to manage from crisis to crisis. Regular meetings with subordinates are important for several reasons, including these:

- When communications break down, the result is a drop in both the quality and the quantity of work performed within the department.

- Poor communication results in higher absenteeism, lower morale, and more employee turnover

Therefore, scheduling regular meetings with subordinates is critical to maintaining an efficient and effective credit department.

SHOOTING THE MESSENGER

If the credit manager acts as if it an imposition every time a subordinate needs to talk to them, the credit manager is inadvertently discouraging subordinates from discussing problems with them. If the credit manager becomes angry every time a subordinate delivers some bad news, the messengers will quickly learn not to deliver any bad news—instead they will bury it where it will only get worse.

Credit managers must take the time to meet with subordinates, and to do so graciously. If they do not, subordinates will act make decisions on their own and sooner or later someone will make an expensive mistake. Here are a number of suggestions for improving communications with subordinates during these face to face discussions:

(a) Credit managers should take the time to explain why certain actions should be taken; not simply to issue orders that certain actions are to be taken.

(b) Remind subordinates that you are almost never too busy to meet with them or answer a question. If the question can wait, fine. If they need an immediate answer, you're ready.

(c) If a subordinate comes to you with a problem, solve the problem first and then worry about what went wrong first and who is to blame later.

(d) Set aside time each week for departmental meetings—even if it is only 15 minutes a week. It is important to hear from everyone in the department about what they are doing, what problems they have encountered and what help they need.

(e) Don't reserve private meetings just for criticism; give positive feedback and offer compliments both in private and in public.

(f) Build subordinates' self-esteem and self-confidence. If they come to you with a problem, ask how they would solve it. If their solution sounds reasonable, ask them to go ahead and to keep you informed of their progress.

IMPROVING COMMUNICATIONS WITH SALES

Improving communications with the sales department has a number of benefits for the credit department. Probably the most important benefit is that collection problems will be resolved more quickly. In many instances, salespeople are the source of problems with customers so it makes sense that salespeople would also be the solution to many of those problems.

IMPROVING THE NEW ACCOUNT INVESTIGATION PROCESS

The new account investigation process can be made more effective if the sales department can be convinced to provide the credit department with customer applications as soon as possible, an as long before orders are actually placed as practical. The best way to convince the salespeople to submit credit applications to tell them that in the absence of facts the credit department has no alternative but to make conservative credit decisions.

MAKING THE ORDER APPROVAL PROCESS MORE EFFECTIVE AND EFFICIENT

The order review and approval process can be made more effective if the credit department can convince the sales department to let the credit department know when any of the following events are likely to occur:

- A customer is going to place an unusually large order [or series of orders]

- The salesperson believes that the current credit limit is inadequate to support the buyer's current run rate on purchases.

- The customer is going to slow payments short term.

COMMUNICATING WITH CUSTOMERS

Effective communication with customers results in past due balances being paid more promptly. There are several ways to improve communications with delinquent customers, including these:

- Collectors should always try to speak with a decision-maker, and not with a clerk. If the individual they speak with is unable to make a specific commitment for payment, or if that payment proposal is unacceptable, the collector should ask to speak to whoever can give them the commitment they need.

- If a collector is given the option of holding to speak to a "live" person or leaving a voice mail message, the creditor should hold. Chances are good that any message left would not be returned.

- If the collector is offered the accounts payable department's voice mail by the company operator, they should ask to be placed on hold instead. If they are told they cannot hold, they should ask for the accounts payable manager.

- If their contact is not in or not available, the collector should ask to speak to someone "whoever is in charge."

USING MISTAKES TO IMPROVE THE PERFORMANCE OF SUBORDINATES

Credit managers can improve the effectiveness of the credit department by working with their subordinates to upgrade their skills. For example, credit managers have the opportunity every time a mistake is made to use it as an opportunity to coach and to re-train subordinates. Mistakes are inherently expensive and should be avoided whenever possible, but the most expensive mistake is one that is repeated.

The goal of any credit manager is to proactively avoid problems, not to reactively fix them after they occur. The credit manager should encourage subordinates to bring questions and problems to the attention. of the credit manager.

Another techniques involve in-house training sessions in which real problems or scenarios are described and discussed. The credit manager would present a scenario, and after a few minutes of discussion would describe how the problem could have been solved from his or her perspective.

REWARDING SUPERIOR PERFORMANCE

The credit department's success at controlling delinquencies and managing credit risk rests largely with the employees, rather than the credit manager. The credit manager and the company need to recognize and to reward superior performance otherwise turnover within the department. Long term employees bring consistency to the decisions made by the credit department. Long-term employees tend to build rapport with customers and salespeople, making them more effective as collectors and as risk managers.

INCREASING THE CHANCES OF COLLECTION ON A SERIOUSLY PAST DUE BALANCE

Often, the credit manager is in a difficult position when trying to negotiate with a seriously past due balance. The customer has the creditor's product and the creditor's money. Sometimes, despite the credit manager's best efforts it is simply not possible to extract an immediate payment from the customer or even a payment commitment. In this situation, some creditors elect to refer the account to a third party for collection. One way to improve the chances of collection before an account must be placed for collection is to get the customer to acknowledge the debt in writing.

Ideally, the customer will be willing to sign a Promissory Note acknowledging the debt, and a debt repayment schedule. Even if the customer is unwilling to sign a Promissory Note it may be possible to get the customer to acknowledge the debt in writing. Doing so has the following benefits:

- It minimizes the debtor's defenses if and when it becomes appropriate to place the account for collection [which might be the day after this acknowledgment is received].

- The acknowledgment gives the creditor a psychological advantage in future discussions and negotiations. For example, the customer is less likely to assert that the product was never received or it was defective.

USE A BINDING ARBITRATION CLAUSE

If a binding arbitration clause is included in a creditor's application a disputed balance be settled far more quickly and for less money than it would cost to sue the debtor.

Credit professionals should strive to create an informal environment in which questions and answers flow smoothly. However, the conversation should not be overly long or rambling. Credit professionals should have a group of questions they need answered, which would normally include the following information:

- the credit limit and credit terms requested
- information about the customer's present financial condition
- information about the company's relationship with its bank
- background information on the owners or officers of the company

---

REWARDS

Typically, goals are set on a monthly basis for the credit department. When these goals are met, it can be a morale booster for the credit manager to treat the entire department to lunch or to find some other way to celebrate the accomplishment. It is a common complaint in American business that employers and managers do a good of documenting when things go wrong, but do a poor job of acknowledging and rewarding employees when things go right. One of the tasks of a manager is to both manage and lead subordinates. Negative reinforcement is both demoralizing and de-motivating.

IMPROVING THE PROCESS OF ORDER PROOF OF DELIVERY

Many customers delay payment claiming they need proof of delivery in order to pay an outstanding and past due invoice. If the credit department carefully notes these kinds of problems, they are likely to see a trend emerging. If every time a customer requests proof of delivery the creditor company is able to prove clear delivery and yet the problem and the requests for delivery documents persist, there are two likely reasons which are:

(1) Because the customer needs additional time and is using the request for proof of delivery to increase float, or

(2) Because the customer's shipping and receiving department files and records are so disorganized that they really don't know whether a specific order was received

Credit professionals will never eliminate the need to provide proof of delivery. However, they can make the process more efficient by taking the following steps:

• Make certain to order proof of delivery before the deadline as specified in the contract with the shipper. Unless stated elsewhere in the contract with the carrier sellers normally have at most nine months to request a proof of delivery. However, contracts can list much shorter deadlines. For example, it is not uncommon for the overnight delivery services to list deadlines of between 15 and 30 days in their contracts. This short time line could cost the creditor a lot of money.

• Try to find a courier that allows its customers to order proof of delivery on line.

• Make arrangements in the contract that proof of delivery requests will be responded to within 24 hours, not when they get around to it. Creditors want to know when they can expect proof of delivery. The longer it takes to get the POD, the longer it takes to get paid.

ARRANGE FOR THE BANK TO CONDUCT A LOCKBOX STUDY

Many companies use lockbox services to accelerate deposits of incoming payments. However, many companies have only one lockbox location.

While it is possible that a company selling nationwide would need only one lockbox location, this is unlikely to be an ideal arrangement.

For a nominal fee, and in some cases at no charge banks will conduct with the creditor a lockbox study using a sophisticated computer software program. That study looks at the supplier's largest customers, where those customers remit payment from, and where their depository bank is located, and then recommend whether or not the supplier needs additional lockboxes and if so how many and where they should be located.

The purpose of increasing the number of lockbox locations [or relocating the lockbox site the company already has] is to reduce mail float. This in turn results in a reduction in Days Sales Outstanding which would benefit the credit manager and the company.

USE CREDIT SCORING SOFTWARE PROGRAMS TO EVALUATE NEW ACCOUNTS

Credit scoring software models can be used to evaluate applicants for credit. Credit scoring models predict both default [insolvency or bankruptcy] and payment delinquency. These software models use sophisticated statistical modeling to arrive at credit scores. These scores can be used to accelerate and standardize the credit review process. The software is uncannily accurate at predicting accounts that are likely to be slow paying customers at best, and default on payment at worst.

STREAMLINE CREDIT INVESTIGATIONS

The traditional credit investigation process involved receiving the customer's completed credit application and then contacting three or more of the trade references listed on the application form. For many reasons, many companies listed as trade references will no longer rate by telephone. Instead, these suppliers insist on receiving credit inquiries in writing. Credit managers can frequently streamline the credit investigation process by relying in industry trade clearance reports rather than contacting each of the trade references listed.

Industry trade clearance reports normally provide most of the same information as would be received if the new supplier were to contact the references listed. Specifically, trade clearance reports list:

- The creditor company name
- The high credit

- Terms
- Date account was opened
- Balance owed
- Amount past due
- Normal manner of payment

Using trade clearance reports will not necessarily eliminate the need to contact trade references, but it will certainly reduce the number of inquires the creditor must make.

ALLOCATE ACCOUNTS BASED ON RISK, NOT ALPHABETICALLY

Twenty years ago, credit managers routinely assigned accounts to collectors based on the account's alphabetical or geographic listing because that was the only practical way to sort accounts. Thanks to computer automation, accounts can normally be assigned to any collector, and accounts can be reassigned easily from one collector to another.

The most experienced collectors should be assigned to the most complicated accounts. Accounts requiring special handling should be assigned to collectors with the most skill at handling the particular problem. Accounts that only respond to a very firm and direct collection style should be assigned to the collector who possesses those collection skills.

CONCENTRATE YOUR THIRD PARTY PLACEMENTS

Credit managers should reduce the number of collection agencies they use a maximum of three third parties; for example two agencies and one attorney. By concentrating their account placements among fewer companies, the creditor becomes a more valued and important client to each company. This in turn assures the creditor company of more prompt attention to their placements, and to their inquiries about those placements. An added benefit is that by placing more accounts with fewer agencies, the credit manager has a better bargaining and negotiating position.

USE FINANCIAL ANALYSIS SOFTWARE

Many credit managers still perform financial statement analysis themselves. Often, they are the only person in the department capable of performing this analysis. Financial analysis is time consuming, and credit managers need to avoid time-consuming tasks if they can be delegated to someone else.

There are any number of off the shelf software programs that will perform financial statement analysis, including trend analysis and ratio analyses. The real advantage of purchasing this software is the fact that the credit manager can arrange for a subordinate to input the data. The credit manager can then concentrate on the value-added process of reviewing the results of the financial analysis in order to make better informed decisions.

CREATE AUTOMATIC WRITE OFF LIMITS

It is a mistake to charge back every deduction taken. There is a dollar limit for each type of deduction [with the possible exception of sales tax deductions] below which it simply does not make economic sense to create a chargeback. When one considers all of the costs associated with inputting the chargeback, printing the debit memo, forwarding it to the appropriate person, having that person review the debit memo and the supporting documentation and evaluate the deduction to see whether the customer or the seller was right, and then either issue a credit memo to clear the debit or contact the customer to arrange for it to be repaid, it is easy to imagine that the cost of this process could easily be $20 to $50 per transaction. If it turns out that the seller is wrong 50% of the time or more the actual threshold for write offs should be raised. For most companies, any deduction under $20 should be a candidate for an immediate write off.

Each credit manager should evaluate their own individual situation and recommend a write off level that is relevant toe their particular situation. Credit managers should always confer with their managers before making a change as fundamental to the cash application process as creating an automatic write off threshold.

ESTABLISH INDIVIDUAL PERFORMANCE GOALS FOR EVERYONE IN THE CREDIT DEPARTMENT

Computer automation makes it relatively easy to customize reports that document the results of work being performed by the employees of the credit department. Unfortunately, some credit managers have been slow to take advantage of the additional flexibility the new reports offered by creating specific goals for each subordinate. For example, the credit manager could create a standard that all delinquent accounts must be called within five days of becoming past due and then use automation to measure how far past due accounts actually get before the first collection call is placed. The credit manager could establish a goal that every order placed into the credit queue must be reviewed in 20 minutes or less. The credit manager could then order a report showing the average amount of time orders remain in the queue before being reviewed by people assigned to this task. The important point is that these reports could easily be customized to evaluate the performance of a specific employee.

Credit managers are always concerned about the big picture; about how the department is performing as a whole. What software and automation allow credit managers to do is to investigate the individual contributions of each person in the credit department. There is an old saying that a chain is only as strong as its weakest link. The reports described above would allow the credit manager to identify the weak link, and doing so is the first step in the process of bringing that person's performance up to the standard the credit manager needs subordinates to achieve.

SUMMARY

The performance of the credit department as a whole is made up of the performance of each of person and each function they perform. The ideas presented in this chapter are evolutionary, and not revolutionary. If the goal is to improve the overall efficiency of the credit department, the credit manager must be constantly looking for the new tools or new technique that will not necessarily move the credit department ahead by leaps and bounds, but through steady and incremental improvements. In baseball jargon, the analogy would be that a walk is as good as a single. It is great if the credit manager can hit the homerun once in a while but walks and singles win games far more often than homeruns!

CHAPTER 20

Factors to Consider in Consumer Credit

WHAT IS CONSUMER CREDIT?

Understanding the definition of consumer credit is important since various federal consumer protection laws attach to any transaction involving consumer credit.

Consumer credit is credit that is extended primarily for personal, family or household purposes. Goods acquired in consumer credit transactions are not intended for resale of further use in the production of other products. Consumer credit excludes business and agricultural loans.

Credit allows consumers to acquire goods or services without having to pay the full cost at the time of the transaction. There are a variety of federal and state laws that provide protection to consumers, and provide specific instructions to credit granters about how consumers' concerns must be addressed.

There are more than 180 million consumers in the United States with credit histories tracked by one or more of the big three consumer credit reporting agencies. Anyone who doubts the importance of consumer credit need only think back to the last time a credit card they were using failed to work.

Consumer credit takes a variety of forms, The most common of these are:

- credit cards
- store revolving charge cards
- home loans
- car loans
- guaranteed student loans

The ability to obtain credit is important to consumers. Conversely, the consumer's ability and willingness to pay promptly is important to creditors.

WHAT IS A CONSUMER CREDIT REPORT?

A consumer credit report is a factual record of an individual's credit payment history. It is obtained from a credit bureau. A credit bureau is a company that maintains credit reports on individuals and sells them to creditors and other interested parties for a fee. The purpose of a credit report is to help credit granters to make quick but objective assessment of a consumer's creditworthiness. Most of the information contained in a consumer credit report comes from the companies the individual does business with. Some information comes from other sources; such as public records.

Consumer credit reporting agencies make it possible in this highly mobile society for a consumer to move from Maine to Hawaii and to have their good [or bad] credit reputation follow them. It is in large part thanks to access to credit reports that American consumers enjoy the level of access to consumer credit that they do.

TYPES OF CONSUMER CREDIT

Consumer credit is either closed-end or open-end credit. An open-end credit transaction is one under which the consumer is allowed and is reasonably expected to make repeated purchases. In an open account credit arrangement, the consumer is given the option of paying the balance in full, or paying the balance in installments. The most common examples of open account credit accounts include:

- Bank credit cards
- Home equity credit lines
- Department store charge cards
- Service station credit cards
- Overdraft protection on a checking account

On open-end credit accounts, a finance charge may be added by the creditor on any unpaid balance provided that the finance charge was agreed upon in writing. Normally, the finance charge is part of the credit application form. Under an open-end credit arrangement, the creditor is required to notify the consumer in writing and in a single document and before the first transaction all of the following information:

- The conditions under which a finance charge will be imposed

- The grace period within which a balance may be paid and a finance charge avoided.

- How the finance charge is calculated, and the Annual Percentage Rate of the finance charge.

- If the rate is variable, the creditor must provide an explanation about under what circumstances the rate would vary.

- The minimum payment required in each billing cycle.

- In an annual fee is charged, the amount of that fee.

- A notice of the consumer's right to dispute billing errors under federal consumer protection law.

A closed end credit arrangement is one in which the consumer borrows a specific amount for a specific period of time on a fixed repayment schedule. No further purchases or loans may be added to the original amount without a further agreement between the consumer and the creditor.

Closed end credit includes all credit that does not fit the definition of open-end credit. In a typical closed-end credit transaction, credit is advanced for a specified period of time, and the following terms are defined between the creditor and the consumer:

- The amount financed

- The finance charge

- The schedule of payments

An example of a closed end credit transaction would involve the purchase of a car by a consumer. The consumer negotiates the amount to be financed, the annual percentage rate, the payment schedule, payment terms, any pre-payment privileges or penalties, and the disclosure of a security interest if title is to be kept in property as security. Another example of closed end credit involves the purchase of a home.

DENIAL OF CREDIT

A certain number of consumer applicants will not qualify for credit based on the specific creditors credit granting criterion. These applicants will be rejected. A certain number will want to know why their application was denied. Federal law gives consumers specific rights when they are denied credit. The Equal Credit Opportunity Act requires that creditors provide consumers that are denied credit either an explanation of the specific reason(s) for the denial, or notice that they are entitled to know the reason for the denial if they make a formal request for that data.

A denied applicant may request the specific reason(s) credit was denied within 60 days of their denial. The applicant has a right under this federal law to receive a written explanation within 30 days of receipt of their request for this information. For this reason, the ECOA requires creditors to keep consumer applications on file for a minimum of 60 days.

CONSUMERS AND BANKRUPTCY

In 1998, despite a robust national economy in its ninth consecutive year of expansion, and despite record low unemployment rates, and low inflation rates, there were a record number of consumer bankruptcies filed. Specifically, there were 1,398,182 consumer bankruptcies filed in calendar year 1998.

Experts forecast that the rate of increase may slow, but that consumers will continue to file bankruptcy at record rates. Of course, if the economy slows down, or unemployment and inflation rates rise, the number of personal bankruptcies could grow even faster.

Three of the most important reasons for the huge increase in the number of personal bankruptcies are:

(1) Bankruptcy filing does not carry the same stigma that it once did—despite the fact that the Bankruptcy will remain on the consumer's credit report for up to ten years.

(2) Changes in the US bankruptcy law have made filing faster and simpler. Amendments have increased the amount of personal property a bankrupt individual may keep. Advertisements from some law firms make it sound like there are few consequences for filing for bankruptcy protection, and the costs of a filing is relatively modest.

(3) Consumer debt is at an all time high and credit is easy to get—even for consumers with a spotty credit history. This makes it easier for consumers to get into financial trouble, and harder for them to work their way out of it.

For some consumers, personal bankruptcy has become a financial planning tool used to increase cash flow. About 70% of individuals filing for bankruptcy protection file for Chapter 7 liquidation rather than Chapter 13. That is significant because in more than 90% of Chapter 7 cases creditors receive less than ten cents on the dollar on pre-petition debt. Under a Chapter 13 bankruptcy, the personal property exemptions are larger than in Chapter 7 liquidation. This was done deliberately to encourage consumers to give more serious consideration to the Chapter 13 wage earner reorganization bankruptcy. Unfortunately for creditors, the vast majority of consumers choose to file for Chapter 7 liquidation rather than Chapter 13 reorganization.

BANKRUPTCY FRAUD

Many creditors feel that they are the victims of what amounts to fraud when a consumer files for Bankruptcy protection. A common scenario is one in which a consumer runs up a significant amount of debt over a relatively short period of time and then files for bankruptcy protection. Unfortunately, there is limited protection under the Bankruptcy Code for creditors in these circumstances—although changes to the bankruptcy code have been made to address the more obvious abuses.

EASY CREDIT MAKES BANKRUPTCY MORE LIKELY

Many consumer advocates blame the credit industry and in particular the credit card industry for the record number of filings. Credit card companies send out billions of credit card offers [solicitations] each year. Consumer advocates suggest that credit card companies are lending indiscriminately, and while that may be an overstatement what is true is when people already in financial trouble receive one of these solicitations it is like a life preserver that they grab onto as quickly as possible.

THE THREE Cs OF CONSUMER CREDIT

The three Cs of consumer credit granting are:

- Character
- Capacity
- Capital/Collateral

Character. Credit granters evaluate the character of an applicant for credit by looking at their existing credit relationships. This information comes primarily from a consumer credit report.

Capacity. A consumer's capacity to handle additional debt is measured by looking at the applicant's living expenses, current debts and other payments the consumer must make relative to their income. This data comes from the credit application and from the applicant's consumer credit report.

Capital/Collateral. If the loan is secured, or if the applicant will make a down payment and if so how large a down payment will all factor into the analysis of capital and collateral.

THE GOALS OF THE CREDIT GRANTER

The goals of creditors involved in granting credit terms to consumers are similar to the goals of their commercial credit counterparts. They are:

(a) to ensure that sales are made only to consumers likely to be able to pay for the goods or services supplied

(b) that profit will follow the sale, rather than a loss associated with an uncollectable account balance

(c) that the risks associated with selling to the portfolio of customers the creditor company sells should be consistent with the company's goal of increasing sales while minimizing risk and bad debt losses

(d) to ensure that future debt collection efforts can be administered with minimum cost

CONSUMER CREDIT DO'S AND DON'TS

● Do not hedge or equivocate when notifying an applicant that you are rejecting their request for credit terms. Instead, be decisive and forthright. Make decisions as soon as you have completed your investigation. Take full responsibility for the decision. Making reference to a supervisor being involved in the process only invites the applicant to call that person directly to appeal the credit decision.

● Don't look for perfection in the decision making process. No system of credit evaluation is error proof.

- Do not feel compelled to offer large limits to start out. As the creditor's experience and confidence build with the customer, the credit limit can be adjusted accordingly.

- Do have written permission from a consumer before obtaining a credit report. The Fair Credit Reporting Act does not require written authorization before obtaining a credit report when there is a "legitimate business purpose" in connection with a transaction initiated by the consumer. Despite the fact that this exception would seem to cover most trade creditors, it is a good idea to have the consumer's signature on file before ordering a credit report.

- Do not run a credit report on the President or the owner of a corporation without express written approval from that individual. This may be a violation of the Fair Credit Reporting Act.

- Don't fall into the trap of trying to explain to an applicant why one creditor offered the applicant credit and your company did not. All credit granters view facts and risks differently. Creditors make judgments about an applicant's creditworthiness—and applicants that meet one particular creditor's test may fail to meet another's minimum standards.

- Know your rights as a creditor. Despite any number of popular misconceptions, once an account is in default the creditor need not accept any payment plan or any amount short of immediate payment in full of the entire past due balance. However, creditors should consider any reasonable payment proposal as an alternative to placing an account with a third party for collection.

- Do not disclose or threaten to disclose to anyone without a legitimate reason or need to know the purpose of your call if you are calling to collect from a consumer. The only acceptable reason to contact a third party is to find out if the debtor still resides at the address listed on the account.

- Do not harass consumers for payment. Aside from being unproductive, it is illegal.

- Do contact a debtor at their place of employment to discuss a past due balance. Do not call again if the debtor informs you that their employer would prefer that you not contact them at work.

- Do not argue with debtors about the validity of an outstanding debt. Ask them to provide you with written documentation supporting their position. If they are unable or unwilling to do so, then you must assume that the debt is legitimately owed.

CONSUMER PROTECTION AND THE LAW

Arguably, the most important fact for trade creditors to remember about consumer credit is that consumer credit granting, is heavily regulated by both Federal and State laws. Many Federal and State laws overlap with minor variations—and it is up to the creditor to understand which "minor variations" apply to business transactions conducted in each State.

Antitrust Laws. Antitrust laws indirectly benefit consumers. Antitrust laws prohibit business practices that deprive consumers of the benefits of competition, resulting in higher prices and inferior products and services. Anti-competitive practices such as price fixing and bid rigging are illegal under Federal law because they provide no benefit to consumers and in fact they result in higher prices and fewer choices for the consumer.

The Sherman Act. The Sherman Act is an antitrust law written to protect consumers. It prohibits all contracts, combinations and conspiracies that unreasonably restrain interstate trade. Sherman Act violations are felonies and individual violators can be fined and sentenced to prison.

The Federal Trade Commission Act. The Federal Trade Commission Act prohibits unfair methods of competition in interstate commerce. The FTC uses civil enforcement actions to prevent unfair practices that tend to restrain interstate trade and to protect consumers against unfair, deceptive or fraudulent practices. The FTC's Bureau of Consumer Protection enforces a variety of consumer protection laws enacted by the Congress. Its actions involve individual company and industry-wide investigations. Its enforcement actions include administrative proceedings, and federal court litigation.

The Truth In Lending Act. All business engaged in extending credit to consumers should be familiar with the Truth in Lending Act. This Act covers any person or company that regularly extends credit used primarily for household purposes that is subject to a finance charge, or is payable by written agreement between buyer and seller. The goal of the Truth in Lending Act is intended to ensure that consumers receive from creditors meaningful disclosure about credit terms. The goals of these disclosures are to allow consumers to compare and contrast different offers they may receive from creditors. These disclosures must be made clearly and conspicuously.

The Equal Credit Opportunity Act. The Equal Credit Opportunity Act (the ECOA) prohibits creditors from discriminating against any customer or applicant on the basis of factors unrelated to creditworthiness. Illegal discrimination of any type is prohibited under the Act, and applicants have the right to sue creditors for damages if it can be demonstrated the creditor illegally discriminated against them. It is also illegal under the Act to discourage an individual from applying for credit because of one of these factors.

The ECOA states that consumer credit cannot be denied on the basis of sex, marital status, race, age, national origin, and religion or because a portion of their income is derived from public assistance income. This Act also provides that creditors must promptly inform consumers the reasons your application for credit terms was denied. The Act also prohibits creditors from discounting or refusing to consider the income of a woman of childbearing age based on an assumption that the woman might stop working to raise children. The Act also prohibits a creditor from asking about an applicant's plans relating to having children.

Under the Act, acceptable specific reasons for denial of credit to consumers include:

- the creditor received unfavorable trade references on the denied applicant
- the references received were adequate in nature but insufficient in number to authorize open account terms
- the creditor discovered a bankruptcy, or learned of delinquent obligations to other trade creditors
- the creditor was unable to verify the references provided

The Federal Trade Commission Credit Practices Rule. The FTC's Credit Practices Rule defines certain practices as being unfair to consumers. For example, the Rule defines as unfair the following practices:

- Requiring a confession of judgments as a condition of granting credit
- Requiring a stipulation permitting a wage assignment.
- Obtaining a non-possessor security interest in household goods other than those specified in a Purchase Money Security Agreement.

The Fair Credit Reporting Act. The Fair Credit Reporting Act [the FCRA] requires that a credit grantor such as a trade creditor provide notice to a consumer if the credit grantor takes adverse action [such as denying credit] based on the information contained in a credit report. The credit grantor is required to provide the name, address and telephone number of the credit reporting agency used to the applicant for consumer credit, and the credit grantor must also state that the credit reporting agency did not make the decision, and that the agency cannot explain the credit grantor's decision to the consumer. The credit grantor must inform the consumer of their right to receive a free copy of their credit report, and that the consumer has the right to dispute anything on the report that is inaccurate.

The FCRA requires credit-reporting agencies to exclude negative information after seven years, except for bankruptcies that may remain for up to ten years. This act also provides a specific mechanism that consumers can use to correct inaccurate entries on their personal credit reports, and if necessary the Act provides a mechanism for the consumer to dispute entries in writing. The Act also provides that if an error is found and corrected then companies that have ordered the report in the last year will be sent an updated version of the report noting the corrected information.

The Fair Credit Billing Act. The Fair Credit Billing Act [the FCBA] provides, among other features, for a step by step process for resolving billing errors on open-end credit transactions. The process begins when the consumer receives the erroneous information. The consumer has up to 60 days to respond. The creditor in turn must respond within 30 days, and formally address the dispute within 30 days. The FCBA was written to address the following types of billing errors:

- Charges appear on a consumer's account that were not authorized by that consumer
- Charges appear for goods that were not ordered or accepted
- There are computation errors
- There has been a failure to credit the account for returns

The Fair Debt Collection Practices Act. The FDCPA applies to people who collect consumer debts professionally—such as employees of collection agencies and collection attorneys. The Act prohibits certain collection practices that are considered unfair. Prohibited actions include:

- Using or threatening violence
- Using obscene language during collection calls
- Engaging a debtor in communications repeatedly and continuously
- Contacting the debtor at work when the debtor has made it clear that no collection calls are to be placed to the debtor.

HOW TO EVALUATE CONSUMER CREDIT RISK

One of the most common ways to evaluate credit risk when considering a consumer is by obtaining a credit report on the applicant along with a credit score. A credit report is any written or oral communication bearing on a consumer's credit standing, character, and credit capacity, personal characteristics or style of living. Such reports are compiled by consumer credit reporting agencies including Experian, Tran-Union, and Equifax.

In addition to the credit report itself, for an additional fee the "Big 3" credit bureaus will include a credit score the credit report. At its most basic, a credit score is a numerical summary of the information contained in the credit application. This score predicts how likely the debtor is to pay its debts.

Consumer credit scoring models have been in use for decades. These models typically consider twenty-five or more factors in arriving at a numerical credit score. The higher the credit score the less likely the individual is to default on the debt. Factors that affect an individual applicant's credit score include:

- the applicant's payment history
- the amount of outstanding debt
- the number of years the applicant has had credit relationships
- How many inquiries the credit bureau has received on the applicant
- The types of credit the individual has been granted

The Advantages of Credit Scoring over Individual Review of Credit Applications

Relying on subjective analysis in the high volume world of consumer credit granting is risky. Analysts differ in experience and expertise, and decisions made by individuals tend to be inconsistent. The use of credit scores to evaluate consumer credit applications actually benefits the consumer because credit scoring is:

- Precise
- Fast
- Unbiased

Credit scoring uses statistical models to assess an individual's creditworthiness based on their credit history and other data. At first glance, credit scoring may seem detached and impersonal. In reality, credit scoring results in decisions that are faster, more accurate, less expensive and less subjective that any other method used to evaluate consumer applicants.

Credit scoring is an important tool to minimize the number of accounts that are delinquent, in default, or end up being placed for collection or filing for bankruptcy protection. A credit scoring system assigns points to an applicant to each factor that had been proved to be statistically significant in predicting delinquency and/or default.

Another advantage of the use of credit scoring is that it permits the more experienced people to be re-assigned to other areas that require their skill and attention.

The use of credit scoring is largely regulated directly by the Federal and State governments at this time. Critics of credit scoring believe that it should be.

USING CO-SIGNER TO MANAGE RISK

Some creditors are willing to extend credit to an individual consumer credit applicant only if the applicant is able to find someone to co-sign for the obligation with them. In a sense, co-signers lend their good credit standing to the applicant. If the applicant fails to pay for any reason, the entire obligation becomes the responsibility of the co-signer. Creditors should be aware that the creditor is required to give the co-signer a written explanation of their obligations to the creditor in the event of default before asking them to cosign for a debt.

EVALUATING CREDIT RISK

As in commercial credit granting, creditors are concerned about financial risk when making a credit decision about an individual consumer applicant. Creditors evaluate three basic factors in making credit decisions, which are:

Character. Character is measured in many ways including personal stability, which creditors measure by looking at how long the applicant has been at their present and previous employers, and at their present and previous address. Creditors consider the financial character of an applicant by looking at the way the applicant has handled open account credit relationships in the past.

Capacity. Capacity refers or relates to how much additional debt the applicant can reasonably be expected to handle given their current income and present obligations to creditors.

Collateral and capital. Collateral refers to a situation in which a creditor is offered some form of security in return for the granting of open account terms. Capital refers or relates to the amount of money the applicant has in cash, and how much equity the applicant has in his or her home or other investments.

AN OUNCE OF PREVENTION

The best ways to safeguard the company's investment in accounts receivable is to be more selective in the credit granting process. This requires nothing more than establishing rigorous standards for credit approval. Once an account has been opened, the creditor may adopt a liberal or aggressive approach to collection of past due balances.

WRITE OFFS

If the credit manager determines that a consumer debt is uncollectable, then a bad debt write off should be initiated. Before writing off a delinquent debt, the credit department must take all appropriate steps to collect the debt including in-house collection efforts, and followed by referral of the debt to a collection agency or to a collection attorney. Normally, a write off will be approved only if one of the following conditions exist:

- A collection agency has been unable to collect the debt and has returned to debt with sufficient documentation to demonstrate that the debt is uncollectable.

- A judgment has been entered against the debtor and has failed to result in payment.

- Collection costs are estimated to exceed the amount recoverable

- The debtor has skipped, and the collection agency has been unable to locate them.

- The debt cannot be substantiated [for example, the debtor disputes the balance due and the documentation is either ambiguous or missing.]

- Evidence exists that suggests the debtor has no future ability to pay [for example, the debtor died, was sentenced to jail, or filed personal bankruptcy.]

One idea the creditor should consider is whether or not to report the debt write off to the Internal Revenue Service. Reporting bad debt write offs to the IRS has the effect of reporting the amount written off as income. Consequently, the IRS will require the debtor to pay taxes on that write off. This idea is controversial and should be reviewed with legal counsel and senior management before the idea is implemented.

SUMMARY

The rules and laws governing consumer collection are complex. The process is highly regulated, both at the Federal and at the State level. Adding to the difficulty is the fact that individual debtors tend to be relatively unsophisticated, and may not understand that the decisions made by the credit department and the actions taken by the collection department are not personal. In addition, many consumers are unaware of the rights of creditors and may be convinced that they (the consumer) have certain rights under the law which they do not in fact enjoy. In many respects, granting consumer credit, and collection from consumers is as complex or more complex than commercial (business to business) credit granting.

CHAPTER 21

Making the Credit Decision

Credit managers are hired for their ability to make decisions and solve problems. The ability to make important decisions quickly is rare. The ability to make important decisions quickly and with limited information is even more rare, and/or more difficult.

A credit manager's success is often measured in terms of his or her ability to make *accurate* credit decisions quickly, with limited information, and under pressure from the salesperson and the customer. It is not simply a question of making the right question most of the time. Credit decisions are expected to be uncannily accurate. For example, if the credit manager made the wrong decision one time in one hundred, then the company's losses would be 1% of sales. For most companies, an acceptable bad debt loss ration is in the .1% to .2% [meaning the credit manager can afford to be wrong in about 1 in every 1,000 decisions].

THE CASCADE EFFECT

Credit decisions, whether they are about establishing credit for a new account or releasing an order for an active account, have a cascade effect. For example, a good initial credit decision will normally result an account paying fairly promptly. The cascade effect of a "bad" initial credit decision involves additional work for the collection group and for the credit manager. Depending on how "bad" the credit decision was, the account might end up being placed for collection and eventually being written off as uncollectable.

FOLLOW THE LEADER

One way for credit decisions to be made is through a "follow the leader" process. Often, credit managers will base their credit decision on the credit decisions made by another creditor. The chain of reasoning in a follow the leader goes something like this:

> "Creditor ABC has been selling to this account for years on open account terms and reports no payment problems. Creditor ABC has a high credit of $xxxx dollars and reports no serious payment problems. This applicant only wants a fraction of that amount as an open account credit limit from us. If the customer is good enough for ABC, they should be good enough for us."

There is any number of flaws with this chain of reasoning. The first is the assumption that because a customer pays one creditor on time that customer will pay all creditors on time. The facts of the matter might be that ABC gets paid on time because ABC has a personal relationship with the customer built over years or even decades of business.

Another flaw with the follow the leader strategy is that the creditor is basing the credit decision on the actions of the customer in the past. Past payment history is not a perfect predictor of future performance. If it were, everyone would win in Las Vegas, and creditors would never lose a dime to bad debt write offs.

THE CONSERVATISM RULE

In credit management, the conservatism rule is as follows: "In the absence of adequate information, the credit department must take a conservative approach to credit granting. The credit manager will find little support for a decision that results in a bad debt loss for which the credit manager does not have a reasonable explanation. Decisions that result in bad debt losses and that are supported by documentation and evidencing due diligence on the part of the credit manager are likely to be dismissed as an unfortunate cost of doing business.

On the other hand, a bad debt loss that cannot be supported by relevant documentation will subject the credit manager to criticism. In the absence of information, the credit manager must act in a way that minimizes the credit grantor's risk.

SALESPEOPLE NEED AND DESERVE CONSISTENCY

A credit manager should be concerned if they hear a complaint about inconsistencies in the credit decision-making process involving their subordinates. For example, it is difficult to explain or justify to the salesperson why one employee opted to hold an order and another decided to release it. The credit manager needs to be concerned when their subordinates do not consistently apply the decision rules created to guide the credit decision-making process.

DECISIVENESS IS A TWO-EDGED SWORD

Every time the credit manager makes a decision to release an order pending, he or she is in effect betting that the customer will pay that debt. An indecisive credit manager would or will tend to create a huge bottleneck of orders in the credit queue waiting for approval.

Every credit manager gets stuck periodically with a truly tough decision. When this happens remember this statement:

> The importance of a credit decision and its value to the company are directly correlated to the courage it took to make that decision.

DEVELOP A SUPPORT NETWORK

One of the ways that some credit managers deal with the pressures of making the "close calls" is to describe the risk factors to a trusted colleague and ask their opinion. Often, another credit manager will be able to point to issues that the decision-maker had missed. The advantage of getting a second opinion is the other party can be completely neutral. He or she has no personal agenda, and no prejudice for or against releasing the order pending.

NOTE: It is easy to describe a credit risk in significant detail to a fellow credit manager without revealing any confidential information about the customer or applicant.

ACKNOWLEDGING PREJUDICES

- "South Florida is a hotbed for fraud operations."
- "Selling to anyone in New York on open account terms is like inviting them to pay you slowly."
- "Selling on open account into Mexico is like playing Russian roulette, but with five bullets in the gun instead of one."

Experienced credit managers have heard statements like these over and over again. Everyone has prejudices. Credit managers are often prejudiced against a certain type of business or a certain geographic territory because of previous loss experience. Credit managers owe it to the customer, to themselves and to their employer to acknowledge their individual prejudices, and then to lean over backward to make certain that a customer or applicants that happens to fit that profile is given special consideration. If there is a negative credit decision, it should be the result of facts gathered and evaluated and not based on prejudice and preconceived notions about the applicant or the customer.

SUPPORTING THE DECISIONS OF SUBORDINATES

One of the fastest ways to guarantee that the number of calls they receive each day will increase significantly is for the credit manager to get a reputation for overriding the decisions made by his or her subordinates. Doing so encourages the sales department to call any time they disagree with the decision made by the subordinate.

Credit managers should support the chain of command within the credit department. For example, if the credit administrator report to the assistant credit managers and someone in sales has a compliant about the actions taken by a credit administrator then the call should be referred to the assistant credit manager.

To the extent that the decision made by one of their subordinates is not seriously faulted, the credit manager should try their best to support that decision. It is humiliating and demoralizing for someone delegated credit granting authority to have their decisions overturned regularly. It undermines the confidence of the credit department employee, and it undermines the confidence of the sales department in the judgement and the expertise of the people in control of order approval on a daily basis.

Also, if the credit manager tends to hedge in his or her support of the decisions made by subordinates, they are likely to create a crisis in confidence between the sales department and their subordinates.

ALTERING CREDIT DECISIONS IN LIGHT OF NEW INFORMATION

No one is perfect. In their haste, the credit department personnel occasionally miss relevant facts, misread credit reports, or make other errors that directly affect the quality of credit decision-making process. A certain number of errors can be expected in any process this complex. With all of the decisions the credit department is required to make on a daily basis, incorrect decisions for and against the customer will be made every day. When the customer or the salesperson present new information, the credit manager has an affirmative obligation to either (a) make certain that the decision made was the correct one, or (b) change the decision based on the new information presented. Here is an example:

In response to a request for a $10,000 credit limit, the credit manager assigned a credit limit of $5,000 to the applicant because all of the references that responded indicated high credits in the $5,000 range. If the applicant then identifies the companies from whom they have received credit limits far in excess of $10,000 the creditor must not ignore the new information simply because doing so might be embarrassing.

When a mistake is made, the credit manager should make an immediate and sincere apology. Trying to cover it up, or trying to minimize the error and its implications is an insult to the customer's intelligence. Honesty is the best policy.

THE CREDIT DECISION-MAKING PROCESS

There are seven basic steps in the credit decision-making process. Those steps are:

(1) Identify or define the problem.

(2) Gather information.

(3) Evaluate that information.

(4) Consider options and alternatives

(5) Make a decision

(6) Act on that decision

(7) Move on to the next problem

This process is deceptively simple, but in several of these steps there are a series of options, obstacles and alternatives. In some instances, the options branch into a series of decisions that must be made before the process can continue. In reality, the process is anything but simple. Below is an examination of each of the seven steps in the credit decision-making process:

Step 1. Identify or define the problem. This is typically the easiest step. One of the most common problems is a situation in which an order is pending on an account that is past due, or over the established credit limit [or both].

Step 2. Gathering information. When gathering information the credit manager must normally answer all of the questions listed below:

- How long do we have to make this credit decision?

- How long have we had this company as a customer? What is their high credit? What are their average purchases? How much do they owe us now? How do they normally pay us?

- How important is this customer to the company?

- Is the credit file current, or out of date? If it is out of date, should a credit report be ordered? Should the customer's trade and bank references be contacted?

- Do we have the customer's financial statements? Do we need them to make this decision? If so, how can we get them and how long will it take? Do we have that long, or must we make a decision with or without financial information?

Gathering information also involves or requires that the credit manager separate fact from fiction, and myth from reality. The fact gathering process involves confirming the facts that the credit manager thought were true, and identifying anything that was believed to be true that is actually false.

Step 3. Evaluating information. There are all types of information the credit manager could consider in the evaluation process. There are two basic errors that credit managers can make when evaluating information. The first mistake is to wait for "perfect" information before acting. The credit manager has an obligation to the customer and to their employer to make a decision as soon as there is "adequate" information to do so. Gathering perfect information is extensive and often takes more time than the credit manager has available in which to make the decision.

The second trap that credit managers sometimes fall into is referred to as analysis paralysis. Analysis paralysis involves a situation in which credit managers continue to gather information and facts hoping to find one fact that will make the credit decision easy and obvious. In reality, additional facts do not always make the credit decision easier. Certain information received will contradict other information. There is a point of diminishing returns relating to gathering and evaluating data before making a credit decision.

Step 4. "All or nothing choices." One of the biggest problems that credit managers face is that they are often left with an "all or nothing" choice:

Release the order as submitted, or the order will be withdrawn. There is an old expression that half a loaf is better than none. If the credit manager is going to reject the order anyway, then there is little to lose by offering the customer alternatives. One option might be to sell the goods to the customer on COD terms with a cash discount. Another option might be to split the order in half, and ship the second half after the first half has been paid. Sometimes, a compromise can benefit both parties.

Step 5. Make a decision. Create a decision making grid if necessary. List the pro's and the con's, and make a decision. That decision should be documented in case the decision must explain it at some point in the future. Documentation is important to demonstrate that the credit department performed its due diligence, even if the decision resulted in a payment problem.

Step 6. Act on that decision. If the decision is to release the order, do so immediately. If the credit manager decides to hold an order pending or reject an applicant's request for open account terms then the customer and the salesperson should be notified promptly.

Like most people, credit managers do not enjoy delivering "bad news" to salespeople and to customers. However, it is necessary that negative credit decisions be delivered in a businesslike manner without equivocation or apology. Credit managers can take comfort in the fact that by the time they have made a negative credit decision that they have carefully studied the facts, considered possible alternatives, and concluded that this option is the most appropriate.

Step 7. Move on to the next challenge. There is an old Scottish saying. It goes like this: "You die if you worry, and you die if you don't, so why worry?" All too often, credit managers worry about past credit decisions but there is little they can do now about past mistakes. It is easier to say than to do, but credit managers need to put the past behind them and look ahead to the next challenge—because there will always be another challenge.

EVERY CREDIT DECISION IS INHERENTLY RISKY

Every credit decision carries a degree of risk. As a professional risk manager, there are going to be times when a credit decision results in an uncollectable balance but that does not necessarily mean the decision was wrong. Bad debt losses are an unavoidable cost of doing business with customers on open account credit terms.

This is not intended to suggest that credit managers should not look back on the decisions that they have made. There is an old expression:

"The most expensive mistake that anyone can make is one they continue to make."

The credit manager should look at collection problems and ask themselves what they missed or what they could have done differently. In some instances, the answer is that there was nothing the credit department could have done that would have made any difference. Sometimes, the credit manager will find a problem and can and must make the necessary corrections.

CONSUMER CREDIT DECISION MAKING

There is no accepted formula for determining a credit limit for a consumer account. Credit managers normally consider each of the following factors in arriving at a credit decision:

- Individual and family income
- Family size, number of dependents, and normal living expenses
- The size and the type of obligations currently outstanding
- The consumer's payment habits with their present creditors
- The consumer's high credit
- The consumer's estimated monthly purchases

DELEGATION OF AUTHORITY TO MAKE CREDIT DECISIONS

One of the most important decisions a credit manager can make is whether or not to delegate authority to a subordinate to release order or to approve new accounts. Most credit managers delegate some authority to one or more subordinates. When delegating this important task, credit professionals must make certain their instructions about order release and credit granting authority are unambiguous and clearly understood.

Training is critical. A credit manager who delegates this credit granting and order approval authority task to an untrained individual should know better and will likely suffer the consequences. Credit managers who find that the people they delegated to are not capable of doing these tasks properly should immediately withdraw the authority. The credit decision-making process is too important, and the consequences of making errors are too severe to delay the decision. For example, if the credit manager finds that an individual releasing is making poor credit decisions and when confronted about these decisions it seems apparent that the individual is caving in to pressure from the sales department or from the customer then that person's authority should be suspended immediately. Clearly, the individual was either not properly trained, or is ill suited for the task.

It is critical that anyone not expressly delegated authority to release orders be blocked from computer access to release orders. Failing to block access is simply inviting trouble. Each person with authority to release orders should have a password protected system log-in. The system should have a relatively short "time-out"—meaning that the pending order approval system will shut down if it is not accessed within a specified period of time—such as within 15 minutes. An unattended PC with an open port could be used by an unauthorized person to release orders pending.

DECISION SUPPORT SOFTWARE

Credit scoring software programs have been used for decades in consumer credit to handle the huge volume of credit applications that a creditor such as a credit card company might receive. Credit scoring software programs for use in commercial credit granting are becoming more popular.

The premise behind credit-scoring software is that certain customer characteristics are statistically significant in predicting whether the customer will pay its bills on time or will default on payment. Decision support software does not make the decision for the credit manager. Instead, it provides the credit manager with a tool that:

(a) Generates a numerical credit score intended to describe how good or how bad the credit risk is, and

(b) Allows the credit department to process new accounts more quickly.

(c) Permits accounts to be evaluated more carefully and more uniformly.

DELAYING CREDIT DECISIONS

Unlike a bottle of good wine, a difficult credit decision does not get better with age. In credit decision making, the longer it takes the creditor to make the decision, the more difficult it will be to justify the delay. [This is the case even of the decision is in favor of the customer].

Credit managers need to recognize that a decision to delay making a decision is in reality a decision to refuse for the time being to offer the applicant open account credit terms.

Refusing to make a credit decision can lead to accusations that the credit manager is indecisive. Conversely, making decisions too quickly and in the absence of adequate information could result in senior management considering the credit manager to be a "loose cannon." This is the knife-edge that credit professionals walk on a daily basis. An overly conservative credit policy results in criticism for because of lost opportunities for sales and profits. An overly liberal credit policy results in more delinquencies and defaults, which may cause senior management to question the credit manager's risk management and decision-making skills.

PERSONAL JUDGMENTS VS. BUREAUCRATIC RULES

In a commercial credit environment, companies want the type of credit manager that can successfully walk between increased delinquencies and lost sales opportunities. In order to properly balance out these two outcomes, the credit manager must exercise professional judgment. Commercial credit decision-making is dynamic. Attempts to restrict the ways in which credit professionals evaluate risks and make credit decisions tends to lessen the effectiveness of the credit manager, and to seriously reduce the credit department's ability to evaluate accounts and approve orders.

DECISIONS CREATE FURTHER QUESTIONS

Assume that a credit manager evaluates an applicant for credit and determines that the applicant is not creditworthy. Once that decision is made, a series of additional questions and options must be considered. For example, will the creditor agree to any of the following terms as an alternative to simply cancelling the order in question.

- Cash before delivery
- Cash on delivery in cash or certified check
- Cash on delivery in the form of a company check
- Cash with order
- Due on receipt terms

TIP: The term cash must be defined. Cash may involve actual currency, or a company check, or a certified check, or a cashier's check, a wire transfer or an ACH transfer. Defining term is one of the refinements that credit managers must make to operationalize their decisions.

SUMMARY

Credit management is not a popularity contest. Credit decision-makers that crave approval for the sales department or the customers are probably in the wrong profession. It is better for the company and for the credit department that the credit manager [and whoever else has credit granting authority] is to be respected by the sales department rather than being popular. Credit and sales are not in competition and are not opponents. Credit and sales are the two sides of a teeter-totter. They balance each other out. The "enemy" of the credit department and the sales department is payment delinquency and payment default.

CHAPTER 22

FACTORS TO CONSIDER IN COMMERCIAL CREDIT GRANTING

There are both costs and benefits inherent in offering customers open account credit terms. The benefits of being able to offer customers credit terms include:

- higher sales
- more repeat business
- the ability to remain competitive in a market in which credit terms are a selling point

There are also costs associated with offering commercial customers open account terms. These costs include:

- The carrying cost on the accounts receivable. Specifically, the cost of not having the cash in hand as would result from a COD shipment, and the "cost" of offering dating
- The cost of bad debts
- The costs associated with staffing the credit department, and with gathering the information necessary to make the credit decision
- The cost of collecting including people, phones, photocopies, faxes and account statements.

Most companies would agree that the benefits of offering qualified customers open account credit terms far outweighs the costs of doing so.

THE CHARACTERISTICS OF COMMERCIAL CREDIT GRANTING

Commercial credit granting involves sales from one business to another of goods and services not intended for individual or household use. Commercial credit is characterized by all of the following:

- The completion of a commercial credit application form.
- Recurring purchases from customers.
- Assignment of a specific credit limit and credit terms to each applicant.
- The extension of credit made on an open and unsecured basis for a relatively short period of time—with invoices due typically between 30 and 90 days from the invoice date.
- The delegation of responsibility for credit decision-making and collection to a credit manager and a subordinate staff.

CREDIT MANAGERS ARE RISK MANAGERS

In order to safeguard their company's investment in its accounts receivable asset, credit managers must constantly monitor and manage credit risk. Managing credit risk requires a diverse group of skills, knowledge and talents, including:

- A knowledge of accounting—in order to evaluate credit risk using financial statement analysis.
- Negotiation skills—necessary to reach the best deal possible with delinquent customers.
- People management skills—required to motivate subordinates to make credit department operations as effective and efficient as possible.
- Knowledge of commercial and bankruptcy law—needed to negotiate with customers from a position of strength.

In order to properly monitor and manage credit risk, credit professionals need to be part accountant and part detective. Most customers that find themselves with a cash flow problem or in financial distress are unlikely to inform their creditors about the problem.

Fortunately, there are a variety of tools available to the credit professional to help manage credit risk. Perhaps the most basic is the most effective—credit managers can look to their own payment history with a customer to determine if the customer's payments are slowing. Slow payments are a strong indication that the customer has cash flow problems.

Another simple tool most commercial credit managers should use to control risk involves periodically updating their credit files. Because of the rapidly changing business environment, it is a good idea to re-evaluate active customers at least once a year. If a customer has proven to be unreliable, or if it is apparent that the customer is in financial trouble, the credit file should be reviewed more frequently.

SELECTING THE PROPER CREDIT TERMS

Selecting the proper terms of sale is an essential element of any company's risk management program. Unfortunately, not every applicant will qualify for open account terms, and not every active customer will qualify to keep their open account credit terms. A creditor's willingness to offer customers open account terms is in effect a continuous balancing act between the need for sales and profits, and the fear of delinquencies and default.

If the credit manager offers terms of sale that are shorter than the terms available from other suppliers, customers will shift their business to the other suppliers. Conversely, offering extended dating terms tends to attract customers but with a concurrent rise in carrying costs, delinquencies, and ultimately in bad debt losses.

OFFERING THE PROPER TERMS OF SALE

There are many different terms of sale creditors might offer to customers. Some are relatively straightforward and uncomplicated [such as COD] and some are relatively obscure and limited to a handful of industries. Credit terms refers to the fact that the customer is to be offered a specific amount of time after taking ownership or possession of the merchandise in which to pay. Any time open account credit terms are offered to a customer, there is an element of credit risk. The primarily responsibility of the credit manager is to control that risk.

The customs and norms of the industry often determine the terms of sale a company will offer its customers. For example, the sale of perishable goods is often conducted on relatively short dating terms. Similarly, seasonal products such as Christmas decorations tend to carry longer dating terms—allowing the seasonal goods to be stocked and displayed for several months prior to the holiday.

Credit terms are normally fairly uniform within a specific industry, but can vary widely from industry to industry. As a general rule, the duration of the credit term is rarely longer than it will take for the buyer to either turn the raw materials into finished goods (if it is a manufacturer) or to sell the merchandise if it is already in its finished goods form.

There are a variety of influences on the duration of the terms offered to customers. Among the most significant is the impact of competition. In a highly competitive marketplace, companies may be tempted to use credit terms [and credit limits] as an inducement to attract customers and buyers. If, for any reason, it is a "seller's market" then credit terms tend to shorten, and seller's become more particular about the companies they are willing to do business with on open account terms.

The less creditworthy the credit manager feels the applicant is, the shorter the credit terms that are likely to be offered. If the risk is too great, open account terms should not be offered and the customer will be asked to consider paying cash.

HANDLING SPECIAL AND CUSTOM ORDERS

Some companies manufacture products for their customers based on the customer's unique requirements. In many instances, custom orders cannot easily be sold to another customer. As a result, credit managers must analyze the risk of selling a customized product far more carefully than a standard product.

The more unique the product, the better the credit risk must be. There are several ways that a credit manager can improve the sophistication of the credit risk profile of a customer ordering customized products, including these:

- The creditor can require current financial statements before releasing the order into production and/or

- The credit manager can require a down payment from the customer on the custom order and/or

- The seller can require that progress payments be made on the special order and/or

- The creditor can require the customer to provide a standby letter of credit.

THE USE OF CASH DISCOUNTS

Cash discounts are one component of the terms of sale offered to customers. The cash discount is expressed as a percentage of the invoice value. A cash discount represents the dollar amount the customer can deduct if the invoice is paid within the period from the seller's invoice date. Cash discounts are not offered in every industry. The decision about whether or not to offer some or all customers cash discounts is influenced by a number of variables, including:

- the actions of competitors
- the perceived risk of offering open account credit terms to each specific customer
- the seller's cash position—and specifically whether or not the seller needs cash quickly
- the seller's profit margin

UNEARNED CASH DISCOUNTS

Cash discounts are considered earned only if payment is received within the specified cash discount period. For example, cash discount terms of 2% 15 days means the customer is entitled to take 2% off the invoice value only if payment reaches the creditor within 15 days of the invoice date.

From time to time, customers will take unearned cash discounts. An unearned cash discount involves the customer taking a deduction after the discount due date. In response to receipt of a payment with an unearned discount, the creditor company may or may not charge back the unearned cash discount.

Creating chargebacks, administering outstanding deductions, and arranging for customer to repay unearned discounts is an expensive and time-consuming process. Often, the customer has a justification for taking the unearned discount. Since there may be legitimate reasons for a customer to take what appears to be an unearned discount [such as the fact that the account was in a credit balance up until the time that payment was made] the credit manager [or their appointee] must evaluate each reason given and make a decision about whether or not to allow the unearned discount.

One thing is certain, if a creditor is reluctant to invest the time and effort required to address unearned discounts, then customers are likely to continue to take them. In fact, without appropriate enforcement action on unearned discounts customers will probably continue—even accelerate—the abuse of the creditor's discount terms.

ANTICIPATION DISCOUNTS

Anticipation discounts are another element of selling terms in some industries or for some creditors. Anticipation discounts involve a process in which a customer elects to pay invoices before their due date and deducts a specific amount [approximately equal to the lost interest on the money plus a small premium] for each month or fraction thereof that the invoice is paid early. Here is a simple example of an anticipation discount:

A customer purchases goods on terms of 2% 60, net 61 days. The creditor offers a 3% anticipation discount if the customer will pay on delivery rather than at 60 days from the date of invoice. Thus, the customer is entitled to 3% + 2% = 5% in discounts.

A NOTE ABOUT SHORTENING CREDIT TERMS

Once a customer has been offered open account credit terms, it is difficult to change them—even when the creditworthiness of the customer has changed significantly. Credit managers may find themselves pitted against the customer and the salesperson if the credit manager tries to shorten the credit terms.

Another problem creditors frequently face is a situation in which a customer has been given special extended dating for a specified period of time, and now wants to keep the extended dating. Once the extended dating genie is allowed out of the bottle, it is difficult to get it back in.

THE PARENT–SUBSIDIARY RELATIONSHIP

It is always important that the credit manager know who owns their debtor's company. If the debtor company is a corporation, the credit manager needs to know:

- If the stock is publicly or privately held
- The ownership of the stock. For example, if another corporation owns the capital stock of one corporation a parent—subsidiary relationship exists.

Credit managers need to know the following information about subsidiaries:

- Typically, subsidiaries do not publish their own financial statements. Instead, the performance of the subsidiary is grouped together with the performance of the parent company and any of the parent company's other subsidiaries in a consolidated financial statements.

- Subsidiaries are separate legal entities from the parent company. This means that if the subsidiary gets into financial trouble its parent company may or may not choose to bail it out. The parent company has no legal obligation to do so absent a written commitment by the parent company, such as an inter-corporate guarantee.

PARENTS, SUBSIDIARIES AND INTER CORPORATE GUARANTEES

Companies are often unwilling to sign inter corporate guarantees. One of the advantages of incorporating is the fact that the corporation limits its liability. By signing an inter corporate guarantee on behalf of its subsidiary, the parent company is increasing its liability.

Credit managers should be aware that in most publicly traded companies, the corporation must have the approval of its Board of Directors before an inter corporate guarantee can be signed.

SUBSIDIARIES VS. DIVISIONS

Another fact credit managers need to know in connection with commercial credit granting is that while subsidiaries are separate legal entities divisions and branches are not separate or distinct. Selling to a division or the branch of a corporation is identical to selling to the headquarters. The creation of a division or branch or distribution center is an internal arrangement created for the convenience of the corporation. It has no legal or tax standing.

USING TRADE REFERENCES TO MANAGE RISK

Despite their limitations, trade references are an important source of information about an applicant or an active customer. Trade references are relatively inexpensive to obtain, normally provide up-to-date information and usually accurate information to a creditor.

As a result of downsizing, many companies no longer have the time to arrange for someone to contact the trade references listed on a credit application. Thanks to advances in computer automation, many companies can get the information they need on line from a trade clearance report offered by their industry credit group.

USING BROKEN COMMITMENTS TO MANAGE CREDIT RISK

Credit managers are usually looking for ways to improve their ability to manage risk. Every time a customer makes and then breaks a commitment for payment, the customer is sending one or more of these messages to their creditor—if a creditor is prepared to read between the lines:

- "Your account is not particularly important to us right now."
- "We are not concerned that you will hold orders—we are fairly certain that you will not do so."
- "Our accounts payable department is poorly organized."
- "We try to keep the payment commitments that we make but sometimes we fail."
- "We have serious cash flow problems and have decided not to tell anyone in the hope that we can work our way out of this problem."
- "We are not sure from day to day how much money we have and who we can pay. We are making payment commitments and hoping to keep these commitments."
- "You should not trust the commitments we make. Instead, wait for payments to arrive before shipping new orders."
- "We are high-risk."
- "It may be time for you to withdraw our open account terms—at least until we can work our way out of the financial abyss we have somehow gotten into."

HOW TO USE CREDIT LIMITS

Credit limits are established so that the credit manager does not have to review every order received. Instead, by using credit limits already established, credit managers and their subordinates are able to devote their time and attention to orders pending where the account is either past due or the order would put the customer over the established credit limit.

Credit limits should be established for every customer, including COD customers, to control credit risk

- They should be used as guidelines, not as arbitrary maximums

- Credit limits on active accounts should be reviewed at least once a year

- The credit department should change credit limits as condition change within the debtor company. For example, if payments slow significantly, the creditor should reduce the credit limit in response.

- The credit manager should be prepared to offer more liberal credit limits in response to changes in market conditions, or in response to a drop in demand for the products the creditor sells.

- Credit professionals should never use credit limits as an excuse not to ship an rder.

- The credit department should inform the salesperson when a customer is approaching its credit limit. If the creditor needs information from the customer—such as financial statements—in order to consider a larger credit line, then that information should be requested immediately.

- Credit limits should be raised or lowered whenever new information is received that would indicate the risk of selling to a particular customer has changed.

INCREASING CREDIT LIMITS TO RELEASE AN ORDER PENDING

There are few things more difficult for the credit manager than to receive an unexpectedly large, rush order for a customer that exceeds the established credit limit. Even worse is a situation in which the credit file is out of date. Further complicating this problem is the fact that many customers have gone to a just-in-time delivery system to reduce their investment in inventory. Because of this, the pressure to release orders on credit hold is constantly increasing.

The key to avoiding this problem is by managing credit limits. Credit managers need to work proactively and cooperatively with the sales department in order to gather the necessary information to approve an increase to the credit limit before the order is placed. This can be accomplished by:

- Giving salespeople access to viewing customers' credit limits

- Asking the sales department to give the credit department as much advanced notice as possible about the possibility that a particular customer will be placing an unusually large order—an order that would exceed the credit limit

- If, in the course of updating the credit file, the credit manager determines the customer will not qualify for the credit limit necessary to release the order, the salesperson should be informed immediately— and whenever possible the salesperson should be presented with options or alternatives.

RISK MANAGEMENT AND AUTOMATIC APPROVAL OF NEW ACCOUNTS

Some credit departments approve new accounts for relatively small amounts with little or no credit investigation. Basically, these companies have decided that it is simply not cost effective to do a full-scale investigation of a new account until there is some indication that the customer will need a significant credit limit.

Companies that adopt this approach are not unconcerned about bad debt losses. Instead, these companies have made a business decision that whatever losses they may take are not significant because the credit limits offered are minimal.

Automatic credit approval is not automatic. Most companies with this policy in place verify a few facts such as these: That the company has a credit report; that the phone number is connected, and that the application has been signed. While this approach to risk management is not for every company, it certainly frees up the credit department's time to work on higher profile applicants and to give these accounts more time and attention.

USING BOND RATINGS TO MONITOR CREDIT RISK

Bonds are debt instruments sold by corporations. Bonds can be secured by specific collateral, or bonds can be unsecured. Corporate bonds [both secured and unsecured] are rated. The two best known bond-rating companies are Standard and Poors and Moody's. Generally speaking, the lower the bond rating the higher the risk to bond holders.

Bondholders are creditors [rather than equity investors]. There are similarities between the risks facing bondholders and the risks faced by general unsecured trade creditors. With this in mind, credit managers can use bond ratings as one way to evaluate credit risk. The lower the bond rating, the greater the credit risk and more likely the debtor will default on payment to both its bond holders, and its trade creditors.

CREDIT LIMITS AND GUARANTEES

In a situation in which an applicant for commercial credit does not qualify for open account credit terms, the credit manager may want to consider using guarantees as a method to qualify the company. To the extent that guarantees, including personal guarantees and inter-corporate guarantees, provide creditors with additional assurance of payment in the event of payment default, they are useful to the credit manager and may be the added inducement the creditor needs to approve open account terms.

However, credit managers should not be lulled into a false sense of security because they have a personal guarantee or an inter corporate guarantee. In the case of a personal guarantee, if the company defaults on payment it is often not simply a matter of calling the guarantor and requesting they issue a check to clear the delinquent balance. In many instances, the seller must sue the guarantor for payment if they are unwilling to perform according to the guarantee.

Credit managers often have similar problems with inter-corporate guarantees. A guarantee is an additional assurance of payment—it is not a guarantee of payment. A guarantee does not represent a security interest or the pledge of capital.

It is important that a personal guaranty be signed by the obligor as an individual, and not in their capacity as an officer or director of a corporation. For example, a personal guarantee signed by "Fred Smith, President" is probably unenforceable against Mr. Smith because he signed the guaranty in his corporate capacity. Another important thing to remember is that some states, personal guarantees are not enforceable against assets owned as community property if the spouse did not sign the guarantee.

ACT IN HASTE, AND REPENT IN LEISURE

Credit managers cannot allow credit decisions to become so automatic or so rushed that mistakes are made. Credit managers should not allow themselves to be rushed by salespeople or customers into making a credit decision without adequate information.

CREDIT RISK AND NEW ACCOUNTS

There are few things more embarrassing than approving an order for a new account only to have the customer fail to pay for the very first order. Each of the factors listed below is an indicating that an applicant might not be able to pay for the first order.

- the company was founded less than a year ago
- there was a recent ownership change
- the company recently moved
- the credit bureau report shows a mixed payment pattern, with some creditors being paid promptly and others reporting serious delinquencies
- one or more vendors report the account has been placed for collection
- the bank reports the customer is a non-borrowing account
- the bank reports more than one NSF check in the last year, which is an indication the customer's bank is unwilling to put itself at risk by covering a check with insufficient funds
- the debtor and/or the officers of the company have filed for bankruptcy protection in the past

Approximately half of all new businesses fail in the first five years. Credit managers need to keep this important fact in mind every time they evaluate a request from a newly formed company for open account credit terms.

OFFERING CASH DISCOUNTS TO ENCOURAGE PROMPT PAYMENT

Often, companies are willing to offer customers cash discounts in return for prompt payment. If a cash discount is offered, it is a good idea for the invoice to list (a) the invoice due date, (b) the discount due date, and (c) the dollar amount of the discount. That way, there is less likelihood of confusion about the cash discount.

MANAGING CREDIT RISK ON MARGINAL ACCOUNTS

Credit professionals spend a disproportionate amount of their day managing marginal accounts in an effort to reduce risk and minimize bad debt losses. Marginal accounts can be identified by a variety of risk factors, including these:

- a poor payment history

- a trend toward slow payment

- a weakening or unbalanced financial condition

- a change in ownership or management

- tax liens filed, or judgments against the company made and recorded

Once a commercial account has been identified as being either marginal or high risk, the credit manager should take the following steps to minimize risk:

- Consider withdrawing the customer's open account terms

- Set credit limits more tightly

- Monitoring and modifying the credit limit frequently—as conditions with the debtor improve or worsen

- Shorten the terms of sale, even if it is necessary to offer a cash discount as an incentive to the customer to pay more promptly.

- Require the debtor to provide financial statements periodically as a condition of retaining the open account terms.

- Close any loopholes that might allow orders to bypass the credit department

- Require a personal guarantees or other forms of security.

- Arrange for senior credit department personnel handle collections on high risk account

- Require the person assigned to the account to notify the credit manager of any problems or broken commitments as soon as possible.

CREDIT RISK AND CHECKS

Commercial accounts normally pay for goods and services with company checks. If they are identified by the credit department as marginal risks, these companies may be asked to pay on or before delivery. Better credit risks will be offered open account terms commensurate with their risk profile. Checks are not cash. Checks are a written order to a bank to pay a specific sum on demand. Sooner or later, a customer will bounce a check.

If a customer presents a check that does not clear due to insufficient funds the creditor will remain at risk until that check clears or until the company check is replaced by another form of payment. Because of the risks associated with accepting company checks, under certain circumstances the credit manager may determine that more restrictive credit terms are in order. There are a number of options to choose from that represent less risk to the creditor. These terms include:

- Cash with order. Payment is required when the order is placed. This is sometimes used when the seller is manufacturing a customized product.
- Cash in advance. Payment is required in advance of shipment
- Cash before delivery. Payment must be made before shipment, but not necessarily before manufacture.
- Consignment terms. Under consignment terms, the "buyer" does not actually take title to the merchandise, they simply take possession of it. As the seller's merchandise is sold off the buyer expects immediate payment.
- Shipment against a standby letter of credit.
- Shipment against a documentary letter of credit.

NEGOTIATING PAYMENT PAYMENTS

Occasionally, a debtor company will present its creditors with a request that they accept installment payments on a past due balance. Current financial statements and a detailed explanation of what went wrong should accompany any request for an installment payment plan to substantiate the need for creditor assistance.

If the creditor agrees to the debtor's payment proposal, it should be supported by a contract that lists all of the terms and conditions of the agreement. The agreeement should also include an acceleration clause making the entire balance due and payable immediately if the debtor defaults on any of the progress payment for any reason.

When considering a payment proposal, the size and the frequency of payments in relation to the size of the debt must be taken into consideration. The creditor should always try to negotiate a plan that calls for payment to be retired in the current fiscal year so the debt does not have to be reclassified from a current asset.

LIMITING BAD DEBT LOSSES

Credit professionals are often evaluated in part on their ability to minimize bad debt losses. One reason is that bad debt losses are easy to calculate and monitor. Ideas to help reduce bad debt losses include the following:

- Evaulate credit insurance as a mechanism to limit losses

- Make certain subordinates understand they need to refer problem accounts to their manager promptly.

- Code specific accounts as high risk, and update those files more frequently than others.

- Add a personal guaranty to the credit application form if it does not already include one.

- Include a clause in the credit application that the customer must notify you in writing of a change in ownership or control in their company.

- Offer a particularly attractive cash discount to incentivize the customer to pay for goods on delivery.

- Stipulate in your credit application that disputes will be submitted to binding arbitration.

- Find out when it is, and then order proof of delivery before the common carrier's time limit expires.

ESTABLISHING AN ALLOWANCE FOR DOUBTFUL ACCOUNTS

One of the jobs of the credit manager is to establish an allowance for doubtful accounts to reflect the fact that a certain amount of the accounts receivable will be uncollectable. An allowance for doubtful accounts helps ensure that the company's trade accounts receivable are not overstated for financial reporting purposes.

The goal is to establish a realistic and reasonable allowance for doubtful accounts. These allowances rely on:

(a) historical loss data,

(b) the identification of specific accounts as problem accounts

(c) the experience and intuition of the credit manager.

MEMBERSHIP IN AN NACM AFFILIATE

The National Association of Credit Managers [the NACM] is a member owned association committed to enhancing, promoting and protecting the interests of trade creditors. The NACM has a large number of local affiliates. These affiliates provide their members with services including:

- Industry credit groups
- collection services
- credit reporting services
- credit groups for companies selling internationally

Credit managers normally join one or more industry credit groups each sponsored by one or more of the local affiliates, in order to gather information and gain insights about how to control credit risk with certain customers. It is not uncommon for industry credit groups to contain two or more direct competitors. Their membership in the industry group, and their participation in credit interchanges does not constitute any violation of the law. However, any time competitors are together there is always the possibility that a discussion of a mutual customer will cross over into collusion or a conspiracy.

THE LEGAL FORM OF THE BUSINESS

The legal form of the debtor's business has a significant impact on credit risk. Different forms of business convey upon debtors different rights and present different challenges to creditors. For example, if the owner of a proprietorship dies or becomes incapacitated then the business may not survive. If the President of a corporation dies or becomes ill, the corporation's Board of Directors will appoint someone to fill the open position and business will often return to normal fairly quickly.

The easiest type of business to establish is the sole proprietorship. Documentation and legal requirements for establishing a proprietorship are minimal. Normally, the business ceases when the proprietor dies. If the proprietor dies, trade creditors will typically receive nothing estate of the deceased.

From the creditor's perspective, some of the limiting factors of selling to a proprietorship include:

- Sole proprietors typically have limited access to capital markets [to raise venture capital and to attract equity investors].

- Proprietorships are limited by the management skills of the proprietor

- Proprietorships often have limited access to and are only marginally attractive to financial institutions for the purpose of borrowing for expansion, or for working capital needs.

A partnership is an association of two or more persons. Each partner has the right to take an active role in the operation of the business, and each partner has unlimited personal liability.

A limited partnership has two classes of partners: the general partner(s), and the limited partners. The general partner(s) control the management and the operations of the business. General partners have unlimited personal liability for the debts of the partnership. Limited partners risk only their investment in the limited partnership, but in return they forego any involvement in the management or day to day operations of the business.

A partnership normally can raise more capital than a proprietorship, but the limitation remains that partnerships have limited appeal to outside sources of capital.

Another form of business organization is the Corporation. A corporation is a legal construct. A corporation is organized under the laws of the State in which it incorporates. Corporations find it much easier to attract equity investors than do other business forms. Stock certificates are issued by the company evidencing ownership a portion of the corporation.

SUMMARY

This chapter describes some of the issues and problems facing commercial credit managers. The credit manager wears many hats and is responsible for all of the following areas:

- Establishing and maintaining the department's credit policy.
- Evaluating facts and making informed decisions about new accounts and active customers.
- Monitoring and managing credit risk.
- Controlling the collection process. Finding the right balance between assertive and aggressive collection techniques.
- Managing subordinates.
- Controlling and managing interactions with other departments.

CHAPTER 23

CREDIT INSURANCE

A credit insurance policy insures commercial accounts receivable against nonpayment. It is a guarantee that the seller will be paid for goods delivered or services rendered to a customer on open account credit terms in the event of a default by the customer—subject to certain limitations and restrictions.

As a product, credit insurance has been around in one form or another for about 100 years, however companies in the United States have a long history of self-insuring against bad debt losses. Accounts receivable is typically the only asset on the balance sheet of any size that is not protected by insurance—yet it often accounts for 40% or more of current assets. In the United States approximately one percent of sales are covered by credit insurance meaning that 99% of credit risks are self-insured.

Most credit managers know that a catastrophic bad debt loss could occur at any time, potentially throwing their company into a cash flow crisis and causing the credit manager's job to become at risk. Having an adequate bad debt reserve is not the solution to this problem. Bad debt losses impact cash flow—something that bad debt reserves do not address.

Purchasing credit insurance is one way for a company to protect itself against unexpected losses. Most credit insurance policies are sold through brokers. Insurance brokers "shop" the deal to several carriers, and bring back to the credit manager the deals that seem to offer the best service at the lowest cost.

THE BENEFITS OF CREDIT INSURANCE

Proponents of credit insurance point to the following benefits:

- Credit insurance protects profits, and cash flow.

- Credit insurance allows the seller to offer more attractive terms to less attractive customers.

- Lenders typically advance at a higher rate against accounts receivable backed by a credit insurance policy.

- Credit insurance will help companies increase sales and profits while dealing with the uncertainly associated with open account sales to marginal credit risks.

- Once credit insurance is purchased, the insured can often reduce its bad debt reserves resulting in a one time pick up on the income statement.

- The company and the credit department will control credit risk more effectively by working with the credit insurance companies underwriters who will identify deteriorating accounts to their clients.

COSTS

The cost of credit insurance varies based on a number of variables including these:

- The client's historical loss experience.

- The risk inherent in the portfolio of accounts for which the creditor seeks coverage.

- The spread of risk being offered to the insurance company.

- The seasonally of the creditor's business—which can cause spikes in the high credit and accounts receivable balance.

Credit insurance premiums for domestic accounts are usually a fraction of 1% of the annual sales covered by the policy. The actual premium is based on the type of business, annual sales, and the factors listed above, among others.

If the creditor wishes to insure its international sales, the international credit insurance coverage is likely to be significantly more expensive than the domestic coverage - especially if the creditor company wants both commercial risk and political risks coverage. The average premium to insure foreign accounts receivable is typically between 1% and 2% of annual sales.

COVERAGE

Domestic credit insurance policies cover losses that occur as a result of bankruptcy, an Assignment for the Benefit of Creditors, or simply payment default by the debtor. The typical policy runs for twelve months and covers losses shipped during the policy period, even if default on payment occurrs after the policy period.

Typically, credit insurance policies are designed to reimburse the creditor company for between 80% and 95% of covered losses. There are two reasons why insurance companies do not cover 100% of the loss. First, doing so would make the premium for coverage too expensive. Second, and probably more important, if a credit insurance policy covered 100% of the loss, the seller would have no motive to participate in the risk management process. In other words, if creditors received 100% coverage they would be far less discriminating about which customers they extended credit to.

Domestic insurance policies normally have two separate and distinct types of coverage limitations. The first is a specific schedule listing individual accounts that the insurance carrier wishes to underwrite individually. The insurance company's underwriters will typically assign a specific coverage cap on each of these accounts. Credit managers should know that sales in excess of that dollar cap are uninsured. The rest of the accounts receivable will be covered by so called discretionary credit limits. Discretionary Coverage typically provides a limited amount of coverage to accounts not specifically listed on the individual account schedule.

DEDUCTIBLES

Deductibles are designed to reduce premiums, while providing coverage for the types of catastrophic losses the creditor wants and needs coverage for. A typical domestic credit insurance policy is structured with an annual aggregate deductible. A policy might state that until aggregate bad debt losses for the year exceed $100,000 the policy will cover none of the losses.

In addition to the aggregate deductible, many policies come with a per occurrence deductible designed and intended to prevent to insured company from filing claims for small dollar losses. The per occurrence deductible is often between $5,000 and $25,000. The rationale is as follows: Credit insurance is intended to protect the credit against catastrophic losses, and not against small losses that are unlikely to harm the credit's overall liquidity significantly.

In addition to the deductibles, credit insurance coverage typically only pay a portion of the insured company's loss—typically between 80% and 95% of the loss. Here is an example to bring all three concepts together:

Assume that the aggregate deductible of $100,000 has already been reached and the insured suffers a bad debt loss of $50,000. The per loss deductible of $10,000 would reduce the claim to $40,000. Assume that the insurance company reimbursed the creditor for 80% of the covered loss according to the policy terms and conditions. The insured creditor would receive 80% of the eligible amount of $40,000 or $32,000 from the insurance company for this claim.

COVERAGE LIMITATIONS

Credit managers should be aware that domestic and export credit insurance policies almost never offer coverage for every customer the creditor wants to insure. In addition, policies written almost never cover the first dollar of loss. If a credit insurance policy did cover every risk and offered first dollar coverage, the premiums would be too high to be of any practical value.

Credit insurance companies would prefer to cover all of a company's accounts [with the exception of high risk accounts that the insurance company specifically excludes from coverage], but recently credit insurance companies have been more willing to look at insuring a reasonable spread of credit risks rather than the entire accounts receivable portfolio.

Selected insurers will even consider providing coverage for selected risks only—but credit professionals should know that they will not always be able to find special coverage for their specific unique credit risks. In addition, the premiums associated with single debtor or selected risk policies tend to be significantly higher than a credit insurance policy covering a broader spread of credit risks.

CLAIMS PROCESSING

The insured is required to notify the insurance company whenever a customer becomes insolvent. If a claim for reimbursement for a covered loss is being made, the insured company must provide the insurance company with copies of all relevant documents including invoices and proof of delivery.

The credit insurance company will process the claims in accordance with the terms and conditions of the policy. If there are no problems associated with the claim, the creditor can typically expect payment from the insurance company between 30 and 60 after submitting a claim with all necessary supporting documentation. Creditors can expect payment in 60 to 90 days against an international claim.

DISPUTED BALANCES

Credit managers should know that one of the biggest drawbacks to credit insurance is the fact that credit insurance policies typically do not pay the creditor on a claim involving a disputed debt. Instead, the creditor must have a "legally sustainable debt" before the claim will be covered under the terms of a credit insurance policy. In many instances, this means that the creditor must resort to litigating the dispute and must win judgment before the credit insurance coverage will "kick in."

For example, a customer might fail to pay claiming that the quality of goods delivered was unacceptable. The creditor might have had the shipment inspected before it was delivered and, after the delivery, tested samples of the goods and found them to be within specifications. Nevertheless, if the customer claims a legitimate dispute, then the credit insurance policy will normally exclude from coverage a disputed balance.

This coverage limitation is particularly serious when it is applied to export credit insurance coverage. If a foreign customer disputes the balance due, then the creditor typically must:

- File suit in the debtor's country against the debtor
- Hire local counsel at its expense
- Litigate the matter in the debtor country's court system, and
- Win the case

Until and unless this happens, under the terms and conditions of most foreign credit insurance policies state that the insurance company can deny coverage and withhold payment.

CLAIM DENIAL

Credit managers should also be aware that the insurance company will pay only those claims submitted that are in accordance with the terms and conditions listed in the insurance policy. For example, claims will not be paid if the creditor is in arrears on policy premiums, or did not submit the required monthly reports.

If creditors fail to provide the insurance company with the required monthly account monitoring report, or the report is not in the agreed format or does not contain all of the relevant documentation, then payment against a claim submitted may be denied.

MYTHS AND MISCONCEPTIONS ABOUT CREDIT INSURANCE

There are a number of myths and misconceptions about credit insurance. Some of the most common are the most pervasive, and include:

- The insurance company will allow you to borrow from them against covered accounts receivable.
- Credit insurance covers every loss.
- Credit insurance will cover every account.

COOPERATIVE CREDIT INSURANCE

Credit insurance is a cooperative venture between the insurance company and the creditor company purchasing the insurance. Coverage available today under credit insurance policies is far more flexible than programs available to creditors even a few years ago. The costs associated with cooperative credit insurance include:

- The annual insurance premium itself. [Premiums are typically less than 1% of the annual sales of the accounts covered].
- A per loss deductible.
- The co-insurance amount. [This is the amount of loss the customer must absorb. The amount may be assigned policy-wide, or on an account by account basis].
- A minimum claim amount sometimes referred to as the non-qualifying loss amount. [A claim may not be filed for less than the minimum claim amount].

- The risk or cost of self-insuring accounts the credit insurance company elects to exclude from coverage.

- The time and effort required to document the status of the A/R balance.

- Coverage limits on accounts. [Typically, above a specific dollar cap or limit, the insurance carrier will establish a specific coverage limit to each account it insures].

The goal of cooperative credit insurance is to make the creditor company careful about credit extensions. Without limits and restrictions, some creditors would extend credit to any customer that placed an order with them—knowing that in the event of a loss the insurance company would absorb the cost. Credit insurance should be thought of as a financial safety net rather than a bungee cord.

Some credit insurance policies include a collection clause in which delinquent accounts referred to the insurance company for reimbursement must be referred first to a collection agency affiliated with the insurance company.

COVERAGES

A credit insurance policy normally provides the seller with protection against the following types of risks and losses:

- a debtor filing for bankruptcy protection [voluntary or involuntary]
- if there is an assignment made for the benefit of creditors,
- if the secured creditor seizes the assets of the debtor company,
- when a buyer skips town without paying,
- if a sole proprietor dies, or is declared incompetent and the business closes without paying its creditors.

CREDIT INSURANCE AND CUSTOMERS

Until they insure their receivables, many credit managers have a limited understanding of how credit insurance companies help the credit manager to control risk. In many cases, credit insurance companies have access to information that is not available to trade creditors. For example, an individual creditor may be unable to persuade a privately held company to release financial statements. A credit insurance company that might represent dozens of creditor companies selling to that same company clearly has a better chance of getting financial statements—especially if the insurance carrier indicates that the alternative is for the insurance company will either withdraw or reduce the coverages it offers unless the company provides the requested data.

The advantages of purchasing credit insurance include:

- The fact that the creditor is protected against the majority of bad debt losses

- That once the claim has been paid the creditor does not need to concern itself with the collection process

- The fact that the insurance company will provide the creditor with reliable information and insights about changes in the creditworthiness of certain accounts on an ongoing basis. [The mechanism for this involves the fact that insurance companies will notify the creditor of changes in coverage on certain accounts. These changes in coverage suggest there has been a change in the credit risk associated with selling to the debtor.]

- The fact that the insurance company's underwriters are industry experts and constantly monitor covered accounts for potential problems.

- With credit insurance, borrowing capabilities are enhanced because banks recognize that insured receivables are more valuable than uninsured A/R. This often results in the seller's bank agreeing to lend the seller more money using the A/R as collateral.

- Creditor insurance allows a company to cap its bad debt reserves. Reducing bad debt reserves could have a positive one-time impact on the company's earnings if the company were ever reviewed .

- Credit insurance premiums are tax deductible immediately. Reserves for doubtful accounts are deductible only when a bad debt is incurred and is recognized.

- Credit insurance is less cumbersome than dealing with foreign customers on a letter of credit basis.

The disadvantages of credit insurance include all of the following:

- The cost of the policy itself. The cost of credit insurance varies by industry, and on the type of insurance purchased. A fairly reliable rule of thumb is that a company will pay between .25% and 1% of sales for credit insurance coverage.

- Another disadvantage is the fact that the insurance company may exclude certain accounts the creditor considers creditworthy.

- Still another disadvantage is the fact that a creditor may not be able to get full coverage on the higher risk accounts.

- To keep credit insurance in full effect, the seller must track invoices so those customers do not exceed their policy aggregates.

TYPICAL EXCLUSIONS

The following losses are typically not covered [excluded] by a credit insurance policy:

- Any loss below the non-qualifying loss amount

- Any loss above the coverage limit either (1) the customer-specific coverage limit, (2) the general customer account coverage limit, or (3) the policy coverage limit

- Accounts receivable owed by the customer that were 60 days or more past due at the time the application was submitted or approved.

- Disputed balances [until such balances have been legally adjudicated and the debt is determined to be owed to the creditor]

- In a bankruptcy case, any balance that is not allowed or scheduled by the bankruptcy court

- Accounts receivable owed to the creditor company by its subsidiary, or by its parent company, or by an affiliate company

- Losses caused by exchange rate fluctuations

- Losses caused by political events such as war, embargoes, and revocation of an import or export license—unless such losses are specifically included in the policy and an additional premium is paid.

- In the event that a customer cancels a contact based on provisions contained in the contract with the creditor—and the creditor suffers economic loss as a result of that cancellation.

- Non acceptance of merchandise upon delivery

THE SELLER'S OBLIGATIONS TO THE INSURANCE COMPANY

The seller has extensive obligations to the insurance company include:

- To promptly notify the insurance company of any covered account that is more than 60 days past due.

- To keep the detailed records as required in the insurance contract in order for the insurance company to determine whether or not a claim is bona fide and a covered loss.

- To provide detailed monthly reports to the insurance company.

- The seller must subrogate its legal rights to collect the debt to the insurance company when filing a claim with the carrier.

- Allow the insurance company to examine the creditor's books and records

- The seller may not make or accept any settlement offer with a delinquent debtor after filing a claim with the insurance carrier

- The creditor must give the insurance company documentation and reasonable assistance in the insurance company's efforts to collect on a claim placed by the creditor

EXPORT CREDIT INSURANCE

Basically, export credit insurance covers the risks of nonpayment of foreign buyers on shipments made on open account credit terms. There are two types of export credit insurance coverages offered: Commercial Risk, and Political Risks.

Thanks to a dramatic increase in international competition, companies that will not offer foreign buyers open account terms are at a serious competitive disadvantage. It is no longer the case that US based companies can demand that foreign customers pay in advance or provide the exporter with a Letter of Credit. Therefore, export credit insurance has an important role to play.

Most creditors are more uncomfortable about extending open account credit terms to foreign buyers than they are extending terms to domestic accounts. Requiring a foreign customer to provide a Letter of Credit may result in the sale being lost. In addition, Letters of Credit require a great deal of time and effort to administer properly, and failure to provide the issuing bank with the necessary and conforming documents within the time frame specified may result in the Letter of Credit being valueless. Export credit insurance is a viable alternative to Letters of Credit, allowing the seller to extend open account terms to a foreign buyer with confidence.

Export credit insurance is divided into two types of coverage. Commercial Risk insurance covers the buyer's failure to honor its payment commitment either because of insolvency and bankruptcy, or through protracted default. Political Risk coverage protects the seller from non-commercial risks that result in non-payment. Political risks protect the seller against non-payment caused by:

- War and riot,
- civil unrest,
- and changes in laws that prevent the buyer from paying the seller such as restrictions on the transfer of hard currency from the buyer's country

Most sellers choose to purchase export credit insurance against both commercial and political risk. This is referred to as comprehensive export insurance coverage. However, it is possible to un-bundle the coverages, and buy one but not the other.

The advantages of export credit insurance include all of the following:

- Creditors can sell more to existing foreign customers with greater assurance of payment
- Sellers can offer more competitive terms of sale to international customers
- The seller can make the deal more attractive to a foreign buyer by not requiring a letter of credit
- The seller will reduce risk
- The seller can have more confidence about selling to new customers in new markets because the insurance company and its experts will assist the credit department in assessing both the commercial and the political risk associated with selling to a particular applicant in that particular country
- If the customer is unable or unwilling to pay, the insurance company will have the expertise, the contacts and the resources to pursue the debtor for payment
- The seller will avoid unexpected losses

NOTE: For companies based in the United States, sales to customers located in Canada and in Puerto Rico are often considered to be domestic sales—covered under a domestic credit insurance policy. [However, credit managers should not rely on this general rule—they should review their policy to determine whether sales to Canada and Puerto Rico are specifically included or excluded from coverage under a domestic credit insurance policy.]

SOURCES OF EXPORT CREDIT INSURANCE

In 1961, the Foreign Credit Insurance Association [the FCIA] was created. This organization was made up of private insurance companies and the Export and Import Bank of the United States [the Exim Bank]. The private insurance companies offered coverages against default by the debtor itself, and the Exim Bank offered coverage against political risk that resulted in payment default. The FCIA still exists today.

In addition to export insurance coverage offered by FCIA members in association with the Exim Bank, many private credit insurance companies offer policies covering both the risk of debtor default [commercial risk] and political risk.

Creditors are more likely to be able to negotiate terms of an export credit insurance policy that is tailored to their needs. For example, in domestic credit insurance transactions, insurance companies often want to insure their client's entire portfolio of accounts. Export credit insurance policies often cover only a portion of the export accounts receivable—specifically sales to customer or countries that the credit manager is the most concerned about.

One of the forgotten benefits of export credit insurance is the fact that the insurance company will help to manage and underwrite the risk. Most export insurance companies have access to vast amounts of information, and they are often in a far better position to evaluate both the political risk and the commercial risk associated with shipping on open account terms to a buyer in a foreign country.

SUMMARY

Credit insurance coverage adds value to the company purchasing this product provided it is used properly. At its most basic, credit insurance is a financial tool that reduces the risk of an unexpected credit loss.

More fundamentally, companies that purchase credit insurance coverage reduces uncertainty, and increase peace of mind for senior managers and the owners of the company. Credit insurance gives companies the security of knowing that their accounts receivable are protected against unexpected and catastrophic bad debt losses.

Credit insurance also allows companies to sell more goods on open account credit terms. This benefits the buyer and the supplier. Without credit insurance, certain sales transactions would need to be done on a cash basis—or not done at all. Credit insurance is not necessary for some companies, and is not a practical option for others. Credit insurance limits an insured creditor's exposure to loss—it does not eliminate risk.

CHAPTER 24

GETTING CONSUMERS TO PAY THEIR BILLS

Consumer credit is an important element in the United States' economy. Unfortunately, millions of Americans have trouble paying their bills as they come due. Open account consumer credit extends the consumer's purchasing power, raises consumers standards of living, makes purchasing and travel safer and more convenient, and it make it possible for customers to satisfy their wants and needs more easily.

Unfortunately, the relative ease with which consumers can acquire credit makes it easy for consumers to become over-extended. Just as in commercial credit, the higher the level of debt an individual carries, the more susceptible they are downturns in the economy or to changes in their income—such as those that would be caused by a job loss.

Overspending involving the use of credit often leads to collection problems. The majority of consumers in serious financial trouble are:

- Middle income families,
- With jobs,
- Who are fundamentally honest and want to pay their bills and
- Who have relied too heavily on credit and now must repay the debts they have incurred but
- Are finding it difficult to do so.

INDICATIONS OF FINANCIAL DISTRESS

If the answers to one or more of the following questions are yes, a consumer may already be in serious financial trouble:

- Does the consumer routinely spend more money than they earn?

- Is the consumer regularly making only the minimum monthly payments on credit card debts?

- Does the consumer take cash advances against credit cards to pay down the debt on others?

STATISTICS ABOUT CONSUMER DEBT

Here are some sobering statistics about consumers and consumer debt:

- There were more than 1,398,000 non-business bankruptcies in 1998.

- More than 60% of consumer credit reports have negative information.

- Nearly half of all consumers in the United States have less than $10,000 saved for their retirement.

- Only 3% of homes in America are paid for.

- The average household debt, excluding mortgages, is almost $12,000.

- There are over 200 million separate consumers in the data base of the three largest consumer credit reporting agencies [excluding duplicated entries].

SECURED DEBT

The actions that a creditor can take against a delinquent consumer depends to a large extent on whether the debt is secured or unsecured. If a consumer pledges collateral as security for the debt, then in the event of payment default the creditor can in theory:

(a) Seize the collateral, and

(b) Sue the debtor for any shortfall when the collateral is sold

If the creditor is secured, in theory the creditor does not need a Court order or authorization to seize the collateral pledged to it. More precisely, a secured creditor has the right to "peacefully repossess" the collateral after making a reasonable effort to collect the debt. This does not mean that the creditor can simply walk into a debtor's home and seize the collateral pledged. However, if the creditor is invited into the home to repossess the collateral they may do so.

Default under a secured debt involves missing even one payment. Therefore, a debtor that is even one payment behind is at risk of being declared in default.

UNSECURED DEBT

The majority of debt incurred by consumers will be on an unsecured basis. If the creditor's in-house collection efforts fail to collect the balance due, the creditor has a number of options and alternatives, assuming the consumer has not filed for bankruptcy protection, including:

- Suing the debtor in small claims court.

- Placing the account for collection with a consumer collection agency

- Initiating civil litigation against the consumer/debtor over the unpaid balance.

CIVIL LITIGATION ON UNSECURED DEBT

In many jurisdictions, the Court will issue a summons to the debtor that is the subject of a lawsuit by a creditor. Typically, that summons will be delivered by certified mail or by an agent of the Court. The summons will tell the debtor when he or she must appear in Court, or by what date they must file a written response to the creditor's complaint.

If the consumer does not file a response and/or if the debtor does not appear in Court, then the creditor may be awarded a default judgment against the debtor. However, if the debtor appears at the preliminary hearing, or files a written response to the lawsuit, then the Court will set a trial date.

At trial, the plaintiff [the creditor] and the defendant [the debtor] will be given the opportunity to offer testimony and to submit into evidence any relevant documentation supporting their claim or assertion, and at the conclusion of the trial [and the deliberation process] a verdict will be entered.

Assuming the verdict is entered in favor of the creditor, the creditor then has several options about how to collect from the debtor. If the debtor indicates that he or she does not have the cash to pay the creditor, which is often the case, the judgment creditor can consider:

(1) The judgment creditor can apply to the Court to become a lien creditor. Once an Abstract of Judgment has been filed with the County

Recorder, it places a lien on any real property owned by the judgment debtor in that County.

(2) In some jurisdictions, a judgment creditor can apply to the Court for a Seizure Order. Once issued, a marshal or sheriff can seize and sell the personal property of the debtor to obtain money to satisfy all or part of the judgment.

(3) The Court can also compel the debtor and anyone who the creditor has reason to believe has custody or control of assets of the debtor to appear in Court to testify about the existence and location of those assets - including both real and personal property. The Court may direct or order the judgment debtor to tender custody of those assets to the judgment creditor or to the Sheriff for sale.

(4) If no real or personal property is found, the judgment creditor can apply to the Court to garnish the wages of the debtor. The creditor is typically able to attach up to 25% of a debtor's take home pay, with Court approval.

A creditor must always performed a cost benefit analysis to determine if it makes sense to file suit. If it is not cost effective to do so, the creditor many elect to simply write off the debt as uncollectable.

THE SMALL CLAIMS COURT OPTION

If a creditor is trying to collect a relatively small amount of money and finds that the only way to collect is to file suit, and assuming the debtor and the creditor are located geographical close together, then the creditor company might consider small claims court as an option. Each State establishes a jurisdictional limit for small claims court lawsuit. Typically, jurisdictional limits range from $2,500 to $7,500. [A jurisdictional limit is the maximum amount that may be awarded by the Court.]

The process used by creditors to sue in small claims court normally works this way [with some variations caused by local rules]:

● The creditor goes to the small claims court, fills out an application and pays a small filing fee to the clerk. The fee covers the cost of notifying the debtor of the pending action.

● The Court sets a trial date

● At trial, the creditor and the debtor offer testimony and documentation to the Court.

- The Court renders its opinion—often on the spot.
- If the debtor loses, he or she should pay immediately.
- If the debtor does not pay, the creditor may request that the Court authorize seizure of certain assets to satisfy the judgment.
- If the request for seizure of assets is approved, for a fee a sheriff or marshal will seize the assets identified, which will then be sold to satisfy the debt.

PREPARATION FOR SMALL CLAIMS COURT

In preparation for an appearance in Small Claims Court, the credit manager should:

- Document the relevant facts of the case.
- Make copies of all relevant documents including receipts, sales slips, monthly statements, NSF checks, and any other relevant supporting documentation.
- Bring with them any relevant witness, and all supporting documents.
- Mentally prepare for the process of having to testify in Court and to face the delinquent debtor [perhaps for the first time] face to face.
- Understand that in small claims court neither party may be represented by legal counsel.

UNDERSTANDING THE STATUTE OF LIMITATIONS

Most states have laws governing the amount of time a creditor has in which to file suit against a consumer over an outstanding debt. If the creditor does not bring action to collect on their debt within a specific statutory time frame, the creditor will be forever enjoined [prevented] from bringing an action in Court to collect that debt. The Statute of Limitations varies from State to State, but the various States Statutes of Limitation typically range between three and six year.

NEGOTIATION

The goal of every collector is to collect a past due balance from a delinquent consumer without having to resort to placing the account for collection. Even of the creditor has the pledge of security as collateral for the debt, a creditor company is normally far more interested in receiving payment [cash] than in seizing the collateral and then trying to dispose of that collateral in satisfaction of the debt.

Four other points to remember about litigation are these:

- Litigation is expensive and time consuming.
- It may take years for a civil suit to be scheduled on the civil court's docket.
- Win or lose, in most jurisdictions the creditor will have to pay their own legal costs.
- Even with what appears to be a strong legal position, the creditor might still lose a case.

That is why it is almost always better to reach a negotiated settlement than to litigate.

The more prepared the collector is before the collection call, and the more polished their negotiation skills are, the more likely the outcome of the conversation with the debtor will be successful. Successful negotiations with delinquent debtors don't just happen. The necessary steps in successful collection negotiations include:

- The collector must prepare mentally for the call.
- The collector must be certain they are speaking directly to a decision maker.
- The collector must have all the facts.
- The collector should try to convince the customer that it is better to work with the creditor now then an attorney later.

Negotiation with a delinquent consumer does not require that the parties like each other... it only requires that the parties understand the advantage to each of finding a negotiated settlement.

ALTERNATIVE DISPUTE RESOLUTION

The two most common and popular alternatives filing a lawsuit to resolving disputes with consumers involve mediation and arbitration. Mediation involves a process in which a neutral third party—the mediator—helps both the seller and the consumer to work toward a settlement of the dispute through a facilitated negotiation process. Mediation can take place in person on by telephone. In some situations when mediation does not result in a settlement, the matter will be forwarded to arbitration.

Arbitration involves the seller and the consumer presenting testimony and supporting documentation to an arbitrator. After reviewing the evidence presented, the arbitrator will make an award for the seller or the consumer based on the facts as presented. Arbitration may either be legally binding, or non-binding. A non-binding arbitration award is only enforceable if the losing party voluntarily agrees to accept the decision of the arbitrator. An award resulting from binding arbitration is legally enforceable.

In consumer related disputes, either the parties can agree to the use of alternative dispute resolution at any time. More frequently, the use of alternative dispute resolution is required by the Court prior to trial. The key advantage of alternative dispute resolution is that disputes are resolved more quickly and at a lower cost than they would be in a case heard in Court.

THE FAIR CREDIT BILLING ACT

The Fair Credit Billing Act is a federal law that creates procedures that require creditors to promptly correct billing mistakes. Specifically, if a customer complains in writing about a billing error, under this Act the creditor must:

- Acknowledge receipt of the letter within 30 days—unless the problem can be resolved within that same 30-day time frame.

- Within two billing cycles or 90 days [whichever is shorter] either the account must be corrected, or the debtor must be told why the creditor still believes the bill is correct as listed.

Credit professionals should know that if they break any of the rules in the Fair Credit Billing Act, the seller loses the disputed amount along with any finance charges on it—even if the creditor was able to prove at some point in the future that the debtor was wrong and that the creditor's bill as presented was correct.

COLLECTION UNDER A CONDITIONAL SALES CONTRACT

A conditional sales contract is a particular type of contract between a seller and a consumer. When a consumer purchases goods under a conditional sales contract, the contract stipulates that the creditor will own the goods in question until the balance has been paid in full.

The most common example of a conditional sales contract is the contract used when a car is purchased. The consumer who drives a car off the dealer's lot does not own the car. If even one payment is missed, the dealer can seize their collateral. The pink slip representing ownership of the car will only be sent to the buyer after the final payment is received. Until then, the seller can repossess "their" vehicle any time a payment is missed.

Because of the unique nature of conditional sales contract, it is far easier for the collector dealing with the debtor to collect any past due balance. The consumer knows that any significant delay in paying could result in the creditor seizing the pledged asset. If the creditor seizes the asset, sells it and is not paid in full in many States the creditor can sue the debtor after the fact for the shortfall.

BANKS, AND OTHER CREDITORS

In most States, if a debtor has an overdue loan payment and the debtor maintains a checking, a savings a certificate of deposit or a money market account with the bank, that bank has the right to setoff the cash in any or all of the debtor's accounts in full or partial settlement of the debt. [A bank cannot use a setoff to pay a missed credit card payment under Regulation Z of the Truth in Lending Act.]

A bank does not need the approval of a Court to do a setoff. The right of setoff is a statutory right, and contrary to popular opinion the bank:

- Does not need to give the customer any advanced notice.
- Does not have to leave any money in the account.

KEEP THE DISCUSSION ON TRACK

Discussions with delinquent debtors may need to be sidetracked. If the collector does not direct and control the conversation the time will be wasted. The more factual the collector is, the stronger the creditor's negotiating position will be.

KEEP ASKING QUESTIONS

Continuing to ask questions helps the collector to acquire the proper information and the proper perspective about how serious the debtor's financial problem has become. The questions should be specific and open-ended. Examples would include:

If the collector learns of a dispute, the collector should find out as much information from the consumer as possible. At a minimum, the collector should:

- Find out how much is in dispute

- Insist that the undisputed portion of the debt be paid immediately.

- Request as much detail about the nature of the dispute as is practical to get.

- If written documentation from the consumer is required to resolve the dispute, that request should be made immediately.

AVOID ARGUMENTS

Collectors must remain calm and professional. Arguments with a delinquent consumer are pointless, time wasting and unproductive. If the consumer refuses to address the past due balance reasonably and rationally, other alternatives must be considered including placing the account with a third party for collection.

PUTTING YOURSELF IN THE OTHER PERSON'S SHOES

Listen to what the consumer has to say. Allow them to do the majority of the talking. If the consumer's story sounds plausible, then the credit manager may want to consider making certain allowances or concessions. At least initially, credit professionals are expected to be neutral fact gatherers. They should not "look" for an interpretation of the facts that benefits their employer. They need to remain neutral.

START WITH THE FACTS

Before making a collection call, the caller should devise a plan of action. The collector should review the file and be familiar with the following facts:

- The name of the customer.

- How far past due the account has become.

- How much is past due.

- If any previous calls were made to the consumer and what if anything was said or promised in these calls.

Armed with this information, a collector can communicate more persuasively with a delinquent customer. The collector is less likely to be talked into accepting a payment proposal that is less than the debtor is capable of paying.

PERSISTENCE IS A KEY

Persistence is the real key to the collection process. Even when it appears that there is almost no possibility that the problem can be resolved amicably, a good collector will not give up until there is a clear sign that the collection process needs to be moved to the next step—specifically outsourcing the debt to a third party for collection.

COLLECTION PROCEDURES CAN BE STANDARDIZED

Here is an example of a standardized collection procedure:

(1) All accounts will be contacted by dunning notice if they are more than 15 days past due

(2) Customers will be called by a collector between the 30th day past due and the 35th day past due if the past due balance is in excess of $1,000

(3) Customers owing less than $1,000 will be contacted by telephone between 35 and 40 days past due.

(4) All accounts 45 days past due will receive a second dunning notice

(5) At 50 days past due, senior credit department personnel will review all accounts and a decision will be made about whether or not to place the account on hold.

(6) At 60 days past due, the credit manager will review any account with a past due balance of more than $1,000. Each account 60 days past due will receive a third dunning notice.

(7) The credit manager will review every account more than 75 days past due.

(8) Accounts that are more than 90 days past due without a payment commitment will be placed on hold and at the discretion of the credit manager may be placed for collection.

RESPONDING TO EXTENDED DATING REQUESTS

Sometimes a debtor will make a protracted payment proposal on a past due balance. Often, recommendations to negotiate directly with creditors come from self-help books, tapes and seminars. Sometimes, a creditor will accept the first offer made by the consumer—reasoning that a bird in the hand is worth two in the bush.

There is a better way to handle this scenario. Collectors should ask a series of questions before considering an extended payment plan proposed by a debtor. A list of relevant questions the creditor must ask is included elsewhere in this chapter. Creditors should remember:

- They normally have more experience and expertise than the debtor does.

- The collector should treat the customer's payment proposal as an invitation to negotiate even if it was intended as a best and final offer.

- It is unlikely any first order is a customer's best and final offer.

QUESTIONING DELINQUENT DEBTORS

One of the most important techniques in telephone collection involves asking questions. One of the most important questions you can ask is this: "Were you aware your account has a past due balance of $xxx which is up to XX days past due? The answer is that it may lead to a discussion about your company's credit policy and terms of sale, and about financial problems that your customer is having.

Often, a delinquent customer may have the ability to pay a creditor but fail to do so simply because they do not understand the terms of sale. This may seem unlikely to a creditor that offers one of the more standard terms of sale such as Net 30-day terms. However, if your company offers terms such as 2% 10th proximo, net 25th proximo then explaining your terms of sale is an important element in getting paid on time.

Asking questions forces the consumer to continue a dialogue with the creditor, and asking the right questions might cause the customer to pay the debt by making it uncomfortable for the debtor. For example, assume a collector calls a customer and is told that the consumer has no specific commitment for payment of the past due balance. The collector may want to follow up by asking these questions.

- Is this the correct billing address...?
- Did you receive my previous voice mail messages?
- Did you receive our statements and our past due notice(s) by mail?
- What are the specific reason(s) for the payment delay?
- Is there a check at this time?

- Is there something you can do to make sure that payments in the future are not delayed?

THE FAIR DEBT COLLECTION PRACTICES ACT

This Act applies to collectors who work for collection agencies. Collectors working for the creditor company itself may be prohibited from taking certain actions based on State law. Your attorney will be able to advise you of your rights and obligations under appropriate local and state laws.

COLLECTION TIP: Hostility and anger will only hurt the creditor's chances of getting paid by making them seem desperate. Disputes need to be resolved with facts, not in debates or arguments..

COLLECTION FROM NEW CUSTOMERS

Soft pedaling early in a credit relationship often creates a situation in which the debtor habitually abuses the creditor's terms of sale. For this reason, credit department personnel must make a special effort to be certain new customers are contacted on a more aggressive schedule than long term consumers are. Thanks to the level of automation used in many credit departments, it is normally quite simple to adjust the system so that newly opened customers are sent dunning notices more quickly and more frequently once the account becomes past due. Because it is so important to set the right tone early, the creditor company should also set a more aggressive collection call protocol for new consumer accounts.

DO NOT PUT A CUSTOMER ON HOLD DURING A COLLECTION CALL

Placing a customer on hold is discourteous. Placing a customer on hold in the middle of a collection call demonstrates indifference to the customer at best, and contempt at worst. Customers require and deserve the collector's undivided and uninterrupted attention during a collection call.

SUMMARIZE POINTS OF AGREEMENT

Summaries are an indispensable part of the collection process. Collectors should not wait until the end of the conversation to summarize the points of agreement—they should note them as agreements are made. Also, at the end of the conversation, the collector should summarize the commitments made.

SUMMARY

Consumer credit is a convenience for some, and overwhelming consumer debt is a source of financial ruin for others. American consumers seem to have a voracious appetite for debt. The average consumer has four credit cards, and many vocal critics blame creditors and in particular credit card companies for making consumer credit too easy to obtain. In a very real sense, this is analogous to blaming the victim for the crime. Creditors make credit available to consumers. It is up to the consumer to control their purchases and plan their spending based on their needs and their ability to repay the debt.

CHAPTER 25

Getting Commercial Accounts to Pay More Promptly

There is no single answer about how to get customers to pay more promptly. There are a variety of techniques which, used in combination, should result in more customers paying more invoices more promptly. It will never be possible for any creditor to eliminate delinquent accounts. Companies and credit managers should be satisfied if the credit department is able to limit delinquencies to predetermined levels.

PRIOR TO THE SALE

It is essential that the credit manager try to establish the rules early in the business relationship—ideally before the first shipment takes place. The creditor's terms of sale should appear in their credit application agreement. For this reason, it is important that new accounts always be required to sign the application form itself. Another way to create the ground rules before the sale is for the credit manager to generate a letter to a new customer; thanking them for their business, reminding the customer of the creditor's terms of sale, and making certain the creditor's payment expectations are clear.

That letter could also reiterate other policies that tend to cause problems for the credit department. For example, the credit manager's welcome letter could:

● List the creditor's terms of sale.

- Detail the cash discount policy.
- Describe how returns are to be handled on the account.

COLLECTING IN PERSON

One of the most powerful ways to demonstrate to a customer that you are serious about collecting a past due balance is by making a personal visit to collect it. Personal visits by credit professionals are rare. The sales department will often oppose a visit by the credit manager out of concern that the credit manager will somehow do permanent damage to the customer's relationship with the seller.

To be successful in collections during a personal visit, the credit manager must employ these skills:

- The credit manager must be persistent, but tactful.
- The credit manager must be firm and direct the discussion with the debtor
- The credit manager must act professionally at all times.

In addition, the credit manager should have the authority to make a deal or accept a payment plan, within limits, if that is in the creditor company's best interest. On the other hand, the credit manage must also have the authority to walk away from a bad deal and must have the experience to know when to make no commitment, and instead to gather information to present to senior management after returning from the business trip.

COLLECTION BY TELEPHONE

In consumer collections, creditor companies typically use a series of written reminders [dunning notices] to collect past due balances. There are two main reasons for using written reminders with delinquent consumer debtors. The first is that most creditors have so many consumer accounts that calling them early in the collection process would be impractical. The second reason is that since most consumer work during the day, finding and communicating with the debtor would be difficult, costly and time consuming even if creditors wanted to call customers.

In commercial collections, virtually the exact opposite logic applies. The use of dunning notices and monthly statements is normally used to augment the primary collection tool—the collection telephone call. In commercial collections, the telephone is an effective tool because a commercial customer is a stationary target and is likely to be there when the collector calls to discuss payment.

Also, because the average account balance for commercial accounts is typically significantly higher than a consumer account balance it is more urgent that the commercial account be contacted quickly. Finally, collations are handled by telephone because the telephone provides for two-way communication and two-way communication is essential for identifying disputes and deductions. Another advantage of the telephone over the mail is the fact that it is easy to ignore a past due notice or a monthly statement received by mail but a call is harder to ignore.

PREPARATION FOR A CUSTOMER VISIT

When the credit manager schedules a customer visit the credit manager should:

- Anticipate the excuses and arguments the customer will make
- Take copies of all relevant documents to the meeting including an account statement, invoice copies and proofs of delivery
- Bring a detailed explanation about the status of any outstanding deductions.

Having copies of all of the necessary supporting documentation in hand will make it harder for the customer come up with an excuse not to pay the visiting credit manager.

USING THE 80/20 RULE

In most companies, it is simply not possible for credit managers to review the status of every past due balances even once a week. Therefore, credit managers need to establish priorities. One way to do so is to arrange for the software system to list once a week the company's largest, and the largest past due customers. A second list should be created on a weekly basis listing outstanding deductions from the largest to smallest and oldest to newest.

ACCELERATE COLLECTIONS THROUGH THE USE OF A BANK LOCKBOX

Most companies large enough to use a bank lockbox service. Lockbox services speed up cash inflows by reducing mail float and check processing float. Under the lockbox system, customers remit payments directly to the creditor's bank's post office box, and that payment is deposited the same day it is received.

Lockbox systems reduce check float. Recognizing this fact some customers refuse to remit payments to a lockbox—instead they mail payments to the creditor's physical address knowing that this will delay the deposit of their check. In order to accelerate payments, the credit department must systematically address customers that mail payments to the wrong address. This process involves the following steps:

- Make certain the lockbox remittance address appears prominently on invoices, monthly statements and other correspondence.

- Track the customers that do not remit payments to the lockbox.

- Contact those customers and ask them to change their remit-to address.

- Track subsequently to make sure the customer's records have been changed.

- Follow up with any debtor that continues to send payments to the wrong address until the problem is resolved.

ACCELERATE CASH INFLOWS WITH SOFTWARE ENHANCEMENTS

Decision support software is being employed successfully by many companies to accelerate collections. Collection management software programs have become more powerful, less expensive, and easier to use, and it helps credit department personnel to plan their collection calls so that the most important to call are the customers called first. Collection management software programs benefit the credit manager because they provide the manager with a daily summary of the following information:

- The number of collection calls made per day by each collector.

- The number of accounts the collector was scheduled to call that they did not make.

Many of the most powerful collection management software programs offer the following features:
- Pop up payment reminders—reminding the collector to verify that payment was received.

- A program that creates customized collection notices.

- A report generator that allows the credit manager to create a series of customized reports sharing the status of the accounts receivable, and to evaluate the efforts and the performance of their subordinates.

THE SQUEAKY WHEEL CONCEPT

Every creditor is in competition with other creditors for money from debtors. Often, money is allocated to the accounts payable department and it is up to them to decide who to pay, but more often the decision about who is to be paid is made at a higher level. For example, the accounts payable department may be given instructions by the controller or CFO about which creditors are to be paid, and how much each is to receive.

One of the concepts that is widely accepted in collection is that the squeaky wheel that gets the grease. However, many collectors fail to understand that calling the accounts payable clerk several times a week for an update is unlikely to result in money being allocated to the creditor. In reality, the squeaky wheel concept only works if the collector is discussing the past due status with a decision-maker. The lesson to be learned is that persistence pays only if the collector persistently pressures the decision-maker for payment.

EXPECT EXCELLENCE FROM SUBORDINATES

The credit manager cannot be everywhere; that is why there is a credit department staff. Credit managers should expect excellence from their subordinates. Goals should be established for each collector. These goals must be relevant to the tasks assigned, and relevant to the current business realities. For example, if the company is not meeting its sales goals, it is unlikely that the credit department is going to be allowed to tighten the reins on credit in response to a slow down in payments.

ELIMINATE ROTTEN APPLES

Some customers are either unwilling or incapable of paying creditors on time. Even the most dynamic collection effort will not result in convincing every delinquent account to pay on time. Credit managers must eventually decide what level of delinquency the company can afford and accept, and what level of delinquency is unacceptable. Once that decision has been made, the credit manager actually is relieved of much of the burden of having to decide whether or not to withdraw open account terms offered to slow paying accounts. Once a threshold has been established, customers that consistently pay outside of the window should have their open account privilege withdrawn.

ADDRESS THE PROBLEM, NOT THE SYMPTOM

One of the most common mistakes that a credit manager can make is to address the symptoms of a problem, rather than the problem itself. Specific to collections, one of the most common problems involves failing to address the root causes of customer deductions. For example, if the credit department is constantly finding that pricing errors have been made, and these pricing errors result in payment delays, the long term solution to the problem is not to learn how to issue credit memos more quickly. Instead, it is to figure out why order entry is making so many pricing errors.

Therefore, one key to getting commercial accounts to pay more promptly involves effectively managing deductions by:

- Determining the most common type of error made by the company

- Documenting the problem

- Investigating the problem with the manager most directly involved with the problem

- Making specific recommendations to senior management about how the problem can best be addressed

- Making certain the necessary changes are made to the company's internal processes

- Following up to make certain that the expected improvements occur

- Once a specific problem appears to be under control, move to the next most serious or the next most common problem and address it in the same systematic manner.

Unless credit managers are willing to invest the time and energy necessary to identify, document and quantify problems, and then to follow through to make certain the necessary changes are implemented, the credit department is doomed to fixing the same types of problems month in and month out. Not only is this frustrating and unproductive, it slows payments unnecessarily.

STRICTLY ENFORCE CASH DISCOUNT TERMS

Creditors that want to get customers to pay on time should rigidly enforce their cash discount policy. A cash discount is an incentive for customers to pay invoices quickly. If a creditor allows customer to pay late and to take unearned discounts, the company is in effect encouraging the customer not to pay its invoices on time.

Credit managers concerned about unearned cash discounts should adopt the following rules relating to unearned cash discounts:

- Customers should be allowed a specific grace period on unearned discounts received.

- Beyond the grace period, the credit department should charge back every unearned discount taken.

- Rather than simply writing off a small unearned cash discount, the creditor might develop a letter to customers reminding them in the future payment must be received within the discount period or the unearned discount will be charged back.

If an unearned discount is charged back, the customer should be provided with this information:

(a) The discount due date
(b) The date the payment was received, and if possible the date that it was postmarked.

Creditors should remember that unless they have a vigorous policy of enforcing their cash discount terms, chances are good that customers will continue to test the discount policy and its enforcement resulting in payment delays.

ENCOURAGE CUSTOMERS TO TAKE EARNED DISCOUNTS FOR PROMPT PAYMENT

Cash discounts are intended to be an incentive to motivate companies to pay suppliers on time. The credit manager should try to reach a decision-maker such as the controller or CFO to make certain they are aware that: (a) a cash discount is available and (b) their company is not taking advantage of it. Often, it is a decision by the accounts payable department, or even the accounts payable clerk that results in payments not being processed quickly enough to take the cash discount. A quick call or a letter to the controller or the CFO might result in a change for the better in the customer's payment pattern.

SAMPLE CASH DISCOUNT LETTER

Dear _____:

Our terms of sale to your company are 1% 15 days, net 30 days. It has recently come to my attention that your company is not currently taking advantage of the cash discount by paying invoices within 15 days. Most of our customers find it financially beneficial to do so. I encourage you to review this matter and to consider whether or not this incentive for early payment would benefit your organization. Please call me if you have any questions.

Thank you. [Etc.]

BE DIRECT ABOUT COLLECTIONS

Some people consider calling and asking delinquent customers for money to me demeaning. Somehow they may equate calling for payment as begging. Needless to say, this is the wrong way to look at the collection process.

In commercial credit granting, the main reason that a collector contacts a customer is because the debtor has failed to honor its commitment to retire invoices as they come due. Rather than being embarrassed or apologetic about making this type of call, the collector should remember that their company is the injured party—not the delinquent debtor.

If a customer believes that they have leverage with a creditor, they will use it to their advantage by delaying payment. Tip: A collector can never allow a collection problem to deteriorate to the point where the delinquent debtor is dominating the discussion and demanding additional time and/or concessions from the seller.

A collector must help the customer to recognize that both the customer and the credit department have a vested interest in getting the past due balance cleared. People who fail to maintain the professional discipline necessary to deliver this message are likely to be disappointed with the outcome of their collection efforts.

BE STRICTER WITH NEW ACCOUNTS

In any new business relationship, buyers and sellers are trying to find out how the relationship can work best for them. From the buyer's perspective, one of the things that works best is for them to hold onto their cash for as long as possible. As it relates in particular to new accounts, any weakness or complacency about delinquencies or unearned cash discounts early in the business relationship will set the tone for the creditor's future relationship with the customer.

New accounts should be flagged for special care and attention. A new account that pays late on one or more of the first few orders placed is either (a) testing the creditor or (b) demonstrating that it is likely to a "problem" account. To accelerate collections, the credit manager should respond promptly and directly to any delinquency early in the business relationship. The credit manager should be prepared to quickly withdraw or change a new customer's open account terms if that customer does not pay as agreed.

USE A DIFFERENT OPENING LINE IN A COLLECTION CALL

Most creditors ask about the status of payment in about the same way. Specifically, most creditors begin a collection call like this:

> "This is ___ from the ____ Company. We show a past due balance of $xxx. Can you please give me an update on the status of that past due balance?"

This question is places control of the conversation largely in the hands of the delinquent customer. The collector would be far better off to start the conversation with a more unique, and a more direct question. Specifically, collectors should begin their calls by asking this question:

> "Is there a check in the mail to clear the past due balance of $xxx?"

This question may catch some customers off guard; even if it does not the question sets the tone for any discussion or payment negotiation that may follow it.

CONFIRM PAYMENT COMMITMENTS

If a customer agrees to pay immediately, it is a judgment call about whether or not to confirm that commitment in writing, unless:

(1) The customer has made and broken commitments in the past.

(2) The account is already seriously past due.

(3) There has been a serious deterioration in the customer's payment pattern.

If the creditor and the customer agree to make a compromise and settlement on a disputed balance, that agreement should always be confirmed in writing.

If the customer agrees to make progress payments until a balance due is paid, that agreement should be in writing and the creditor should ask the customer to sign a Promissory Note.

If the account is seriously past due, any commitment received should be confirmed in writing. Even if the commitment is for immediate payment of a seriously delinquent balance, the creditor should probably take the time to confirm the commitment in writing and send that confirmation to the customer by fax.

BE SPECIFIC ABOUT THE CONSEQUENCES OF DELAYED PAYMENT

Credit department personnel know that a certain number of customers with cash flow problems will instruct their accounts payable department to release payment only to creditors who indicate that others are on credit hold. If the credit manager has decided that an account is to be placed on credit hold the customer should be told. Some credit department personnel are reluctant to use this leverage, even when there is an order pending. Rather than beating around the bush, the collector or credit manager should try a more direct approach. The credit manager might state:

> "Your account is now on hold. There is an order pending for $xxx. There is a past due balance of $xxx. Neither of us wants to see this order. Why don't you pay us today so that I can release the order as soon as possible?"

HOLDING ORDERS

Whenever possible, the credit manager should give the salesperson advanced notice of a credit hold. Notice gives the salesperson the time and the option of contacting the customer to try to resolve the problem before a credit hold becomes necessary. At the very least, the notice is a business courtesy. Often, the involvement of the salesperson and the warning about an upcoming credit hold will result in payment being scheduled. In reality, the credit department has very little to lose and much to gain by providing the salesperson with this "heads up."

IF YOU WANT THINGS DONE RIGHT, BE PREPARED TO DO THEM YOURSELF

It is fair to say that most salespeople are not especially excited about handling the details necessary to resolve problems and to reconcile accounts. Recognizing this, it should come as no surprise that salespeople tend to give certain problems a relatively low priority. This is not intended to be a put down of salespeople.

It is often faster and easier and more efficient for the credit department to identify and to fix a specific problem rather than waiting for the salesperson to getting around to doing it. Credit managers and their subordinates should be prepared to roll up their sleeves and dig into a problem that the salesperson technically should handle in the interest of good customer service and to improve aging results.

SUMMARY

Right or wrong, fair or unfair, collection results are a convenient scorecard that can be used to evaluate the performance of the credit manager and the credit department. However, there is no single tool or technique that will work in every situation to accelerate payment.

The credit department does not exist in a vacuum. The credit manager does not have the luxury of rejecting every marginal account, or of holding orders to force delinquent debtors to address past due balances. Therefore, credit managers have no choice but to use a number of different tools and techniques before and after the sale to accelerate payment.

CHAPTER 26

H ANDLING DELINQUENT COMMERCIAL ACCOUNTS

Accounts receivable can be thought of as a reservoir of money that the credit department is responsible for managing and for converting into cash. The keys to collecting past due balances quickly and effectively are both mysterious and elusive. When any account becomes past due, creditors should make timely, appropriate and persistent and progressively more strident and insistent demands for payment.

The following actions will make it more likely that a customer will retire a past due balance quickly:

- The creditor company does not ignore late payments. The sooner a past due account is contacted, the sooner payment can be expected.

- Creditors should use orders holds when necessary to leverage payment from delinquent debtors. Credit holds also serve to put a cap on potential bad debt losses.

- Disputes and deductions often lead to delinquencies. Regardless of the type of dispute or deduction, the credit department should take the lead by gathering information and either doing the necessary analysis of the deduction, or making certain that someone else does so.

- Follow up periodically on past due and disputed balances to make sure that progress has not stalled.

- Send written payment reminders if customers ignore the collector's calls and messages.

- Always follow through on commitments. For example, if the credit department indicates that it will place an account for collection if the customer makes does not retire past due balance by a specific date, the commitment must be kept—otherwise the credit department loses credibility.

GOVERNING LAWS

The rights of the buyer and seller in a commercial sales transaction are codified in the Uniform Commercial Code as adopted by the various States. Credit managers should know that Federal laws may also govern certain aspects of the collection process. These federal laws generally protect debtors from unethical acts contemplated by a creditor company. Since ignorance of the law is not an excuse credit managers must familiarize themselves with the relevant federal and State laws that govern their actions.

For commercial credit managers, the good news is that the collection of commercial debts is not heavily regulated area. Legislators have come to realize that placing too many restrictions on the business to business credit and collection process will make open account credit harder to get. Since the economy of the United States is largely credit based, legislators have decided that over-regulation would injure buyers and sellers alike.

Nevertheless, certain federal and State laws cover commercial collections. For example, the U.S. Bankruptcy Code was created to protect insolvent debtors from actions of both secured and unsecured creditors, and the Uniform Commercial Code defines the rights and the responsibilities of debtors and creditors in every State.

IMPROVING COLLECTION RESULTS WITH DELINQUENT COMMERCIAL ACCOUNTS

Sometimes, it is the little things that a company and its credit department does or does not do that result in accounts becoming past due. Often, it is the cumulative effect of all of the changes made in the credit granting process and the collection management process that result in improved collection results. Credit professionals looking for one tool, one technique, one policy or one employee to significantly improve overall collection results are likely to be badly disappointed.

Here are some practical ideas that cumulatively will reduce overall delinquencies:

- The credit manager should make certain the credit application, the order confirmation form, the invoice and the monthly statement each list their terms of sale. That way, it will be difficult for the customer to claim they were not aware of this information.

- Be sure that the order entry department does not process any purchase order that lists the wrong price, credit terms, freight terms, etc. Doing so gives the customer a ready-made excuse to delay payment.

- Pay close attention to how the debtor treats other creditors by monitoring trade clearance reports. If the debtor pays your company on time, but pays other creditors slowly, chances are good that sooner or later the debtor will begin to delay payments to you.

- Update active credit files on a regular schedule. Don't wait for problems to surface or customers to want a larger credit limit to update credit files.

- Never allow the sales department to offer extended dating without the credit department's approval. Extended dating increases credit risk.

- Promptly research disputes and deductions. The longer a deduction is open, the less likely the deduction will ever be repaid. If creditor companies do not adequate resources into the deduction management and dispute resolution process, the process can easily spiral out of control resulting in significant write offs

COLLECTIONS FROM NEWLY FORMED BUSINESSES

Most credit professionals are aware that small businesses and new businesses fail surprisingly frequently. Statistics indicate that one out of two new businesses will fail within the first five years. Many new businesses fail is not because of poor sales; it is because of poor cash flow. New businesses often run out of cash and are forced to close, and at the very least are forced to delay payment to creditors.

Another problem for newly formed companies is that they often lack expertise in collecting their accounts receivable. Also, because new companies tend to be small they tend to have limited leverage with their customers they tend to be taken advantage of. Even if they have leverage with delinquent customers they are often reluctant to do so, for fear of losing that business. The following are also contributing factors:

- Some customers take advantage of the their smaller vendors by delaying payment—recognizing that the supplier probably needs them more than they need the supplier.

- Small companies often cannot afford to hire an in-house collection specialist. As a result, the task of collecting often goes to someone who may have no experience as a collector. As a result, the company's collection efforts are disjointed, disorganized and possibly ineffective.

- Even if the person assigned to make the collection calls is knowledgeable about the status of the accounts receivable and competent as a collector, they may dislike this type of work and postpone making the tough collection calls in favor of the easier ones.

- Business owners are often so busy trying to grow their business that they do not give collecting accounts receivable the attention it deserves until they run into cash flow problems. By then, it may be too late to rectify the problem.

Newer businesses must find the right balance between being accommodating to customers and being and easy mark for suppliers looking to delay payment.

COLLECTING FROM NEW ACCOUNTS

It is important that credit managers establish the right tone when they are calling a new account for the first time about a past due balance. New customers sometimes test new vendors to find their sensitivity to payment delays. Any delay in contacting the new customer about a past due balance, and anything short of a request for an immediate payment in full of the entire past due balance could be interpreted by a new customer as an invitation not to pay the supplier's invoices when they come due.

For this reason, it is a good idea to monitor new accounts closely. For example, if the supplier normally allows five to ten days before contacting a customer about a past due balance, that grace period should be shortened or eliminated with new accounts.

COLLECTING DURING PERSONAL VISITS

If a customer has a large balance due or past due, it is sometimes necessary to arrange for a personal visit to discuss the problem and hopefully to pick up the payment due. If this would be cost prohibitive to do so, credit managers should consider as an alternative using a courier service to pick up the payment.

PREPARING FOR COLLECTION CALLS

Collectors that take time to prepare before making a collection call will be more productive. Before a collector picks up the telephone, he or she should know the account history, including:

- how long the account has been active,
- the customer's high credit,
- if there are orders pending or on hold,
- the customer's normal payment pattern
- whether or not the customer has broken payment commitments in the past
- previous calls were made about the current past due balance.

Without preparation, it is easy for the collection call to be unproductive. Knowledge is power in collection situations.

HANDLING THE COLLECTION CALL

When calling a customer about a past due balance, the collector should speak to a decision-maker. Talking to someone about a seriously delinquent balance who does not have the authority to make a payment commitment is a waste of time. Collectors should ask for an immediate payment in full of the entire past due balance.

USING ULTIMATUMS AS COLLECTION TOOLS

Ultimatums can be an effective collection tool. Before issuing any ultimatum the collector should have specific approval from the credit manager for this action. An example of an ultimatum would be as follows:

> "Unless payment in full is received by Friday, your open account terms will be withdrawn for a minimum of 30 days."

This is not a decision or a threat to be taken lightly. Credit managers should reserve for themselves the authority necessary to make this type of decision.

PROFESSIONALISM AS A COLLECTION TOOL

During the call, a collector should at all times maintain a businesslike demeanor. Collectors should not debate with customers, or argue, or shout, or use profanity, or take the debtor's actions or statements personally.

It is important for the collector to maintain a positive attitude about their work. A collector that sounds bored or depressed is less likely to motivate a customer to take the time necessary to generate a payment.

AFTER THE CALL

After the call, the collector should make careful notes of commitments made and establish a follow up date. If no commitment was received, or the payment proposal made was unacceptable in the opinion of the collector, the collector should refer the matter to the credit manager for whatever additional action is deemed necessary.

CONFIRMING COMMITMENTS

In some situations and with certain customers it is important to take the time to confirm payment commitments. For example, if a customer has a history of making and then breaking payment commitments, then the collector probably should take the time to confirm the commitment in writing—preferably by fax or by e-mail. Similarly, if the balance owed is seriously past due or is a large dollar amount, it would probably be time well spent to confirm the customer's payment commitment in writing.

HOW TO NEGOTIATE WITH SERIOUSLY DELINQUENT DEBTORS

To negotiate successfully, the creditor must assume and act as if they are in a good bargaining position, even if in reality they are not. Without this mind-set, it is almost impossible to successfully negotiate on a seriously past due balance.

Negotiating involves gathering information from the other party. To negotiate the best deal possible, the credit manager needs to learn as must of the following information as possible:

(1) What caused the customer's financial problems?

(2) What the customer has tried up until now to correct the problem?

(3)   What the outcome of their efforts to date?

(4)   What additional steps does the customer plan to take to correct the problem?

(5)   Is the debtor's bank continuing to support the company?

TIP: It is critical that the collector gathers enough information from the debtor to differentiate between a short-term problem, and a serious—potentially fatal cash flow and/or financial problem. A candid, direct discussion between the debtor and the creditor is the key.

If the customer is unwilling to cooperate to the extent that they will take the time to answer specific questions, the credit department has no choice but to assume the worst and further restrict credit to the customer.

GOOD DEALS AND BAD DEALS

Experienced negotiators know that it is better to walk away with no deal than to make a bad deal. Credit managers are action oriented, but when it come to negotiations with delinquent customer sometimes the most appropriate action is to walk away.

One of the downsides of credit managers accepting a bad deal is that it is hard to explain or justify the poor decision made. Few Controllers of CFOs are going to accept a statement such as "You had to be there to know" as an excuse or justification for accepting an unreasonably long payment plan.

COLLECTION TIP: If creditors have a system in place to accept credit card payments, they should consider offering seriously delinquent customers the opportunity to pay their past due balance by credit card. This is a creative alternative. A certain number of customers will jump at the chance to clear a past due balance by putting the debt on a charge card against which they are only required to make a minimum monthly payment.**

A WORD ABOUT FIRST OFFERS

When negotiation with seriously delinquent customers, as a general rule creditors should not accept a customer's first offer. The first offer is often a "trial balloon." Many debtors are pleasantly surprised to see how many creditors will accept their first payment proposal. It is often fairly easy for creditors to negotiate a better deal simply by rejecting the first letter.

The credit manager must treat the payment proposal as an invitation to negotiate and not as the debtor's best and final offer. If the proposal is made in writing, some creditors write a counter-offer and invite the debtor to call to confirm that they accept the counter-offer.

If the debtor's payment plan is presented orally, the credit manager must think quickly. One suggestion is for the credit manager to indicate that they are not authorized to accept any settlement offer on the spot that does not involve immediate payment in full of the past due balance. This gives the credit manager time to study the debtor's proposal and to develop an appropriate counter-offer.

An example of a counter-offer or counter-proposal follows:

> The debtor proposes a ten week payment plan to clear a past due balance of $10,000, however the account balance is already 60 days past due. The creditor makes this counter-offer.

> "Since your account is already 60 days past due, a ten-week payment plan is unrealistic. We would agree to accept a written agreement that calls for payment of the $10,000 past due over the next five weeks, in five equal payments, provided the first payment is received by this Friday."

EVALUATING PAYMENT PROPOSALS

Any time a credit manager is considering a payment proposal made by the debtor, he or she must consider the following issues carefully:

(1) Will the debtor acknowledge the balance due in writing?

(2) Will the debtor sign a promissory note evidencing the debt?

(3) Will the debtor agree to pay interest on the unpaid balance?

(4) Will the debtor offer a personal guarantee or some other additional assurance to the creditor that this payment plan will be kept?

(5) Will the debtor agree that if any payment is late that the entire balance will become due and payable immediately?

(6) Will the debtor agree that they will not offer other creditors a better payment plan than the one you received?

If the answer to any of these questions is no, then the credit manager has every right to question how serious the customer is about resolving the past due balance amicably.

LIMIT AUTHORITY TO ACCEPT PAYMENT PLANS

If there is no specific policy in place, every credit department should create a policy that payment plans can only be approved by the credit manager. Similar to the policy about offering extended dating to customers, accepting a payment plan involves significant incremental credit risk. Therefore, the credit manager should have the authority to offer or accept such a proposal. [In some companies, even the credit manager does not have unilateral authority and such requests must be referred to senior management for review and approval].

TIPS FOR REDUCING DELINQUENCIES

Tips for reducing delinquencies quickly include:

(a) If you cannot get a delinquent customer to pay the entire past due balance, ask for asubstantial good faith payment. The reason is simple: half a loaf is better than none.

(b) Reduce or eliminate the grace period before beginning collection efforts. Many credit departments allow a specific number of days before calling on a past due balance. By calling sooner, past due balances will drop.

(c) If a creditor company tends to generate a relatively small number of large dollar volume invoices, consider implementing a collection policy in which customers are contacted before the invoices come due to make certain:

- The merchandise and the invoice were received
- The merchandise was found to be in good order
- That invoice is scheduled for payment on or near the due date.

Knowing when the customer has the invoice scheduled for payment allows the collector to follow up a few days after that date to make certain payment was received. Knowing the scheduled payment date also allows the creditor company to more accurately forecast cash flow.

(d) Credit holds tend to accelerate payments. If a delinquent customer refuses to acknowledge the past due balance, the account should remain on hold. Once a customer has acknowledged the balance due and made a good faith payment proposal, the creditor should consider selling on COD or COD Cash terms until payment is received.

Demanding that new shipments be paid in advance also tends to accelerate payment of the past due balance.

(e)   Given a choice of reducing the number of delinquent accounts and reducing the dollar amount of delinquencies most companies would choose to reduce the dollar delinquencies. Therefore, collectors must prioritize their collection efforts.

There will never be enough time to handle all accounts equally, so credit managers must devise different strategies for dealing with small dollar delinquencies and large dollar delinquencies. Unfortunately, some time and personal attention must be given to small dollar delinquencies because allowing them to get too old reduces the probability of collection significantly.

FINDING THE RIGHT CONTACT

Part of handling delinquent accounts properly involves finding the right person to work with in the customer's accounts payable department. For example, at the lowest level, the accounts payable clerk has virtually no decision-making authority. Since the objective is to get a specific commitment for payment, if the accounts payable clerk is not empowered to make that commitment, then the collector must proceed up the chain of command until someone makes a reasonable commitment for payment. For example, the creditor's representative might have to speak to the Accounts Payable Supervisor, the A/P Manager or even the Controller, before finding the person with the authority to make a specific payment commitment. It would be ill advised to contact the CFO or controller every time an account goes past due, but it would certainly not be inappropriate to elevate a negotiation to that level if the Accounts Payable Manager was unwilling to offer a payment proposal.

It is always more stressful to find and speak to the decision maker about a past due account rather than an Accounts Payable Clerk, but making the extra effort is well worth the time and effort. Collectors need to make the extra effort required to reach the right person instead of dealing with the wrong person.

HANDLING DIFFICULT CUSTOMERS

One of the most challenging aspects of collecting from delinquent commercial accounts involves dealing with customers who sometimes become belligerent. Experienced credit professionals know that a small number of customers use hostility as a strategy to delay paying bills. The strategy works this way:

(a) The more abusive and rude they are, the less frequently creditors will call for payment

(b) The less frequently creditors call for payment, the longer payment can be delayed

(c) Since delaying payment improves the debtor's cash position, delaying payment is good.

Credit managers should know that some accounts payable managers and purchasing agents are evaluated and rewarded based on their ability to delay payment to vendors. Provided that payment delays do not result in too many vendors placing the account on credit hold, companies are content to allow their purchasing manager and/or their accounts payable manager to control payments in order to maximize cash and to reduce accounts payable turnover.

Customers using this particular strategy often try to intimidate creditors. It is not uncommon for these customers to make statements similar to these:

- "Your collection efforts are out of control. You call every week for payment. We don't have time to deal with any vendors this often."

- "You are harassing us for payment, and if you don't stop we will take our business elsewhere"

- "I've already discussed this whole issue with your salesperson. Don't you people talk to each other?"

There are ways to counteract a strategy designed to intimidate creditors into waiting longer for payment. The following strategies work well in dealing with abusive customers:

- Let the customer talk, complain or yell without interrupting.

- When you sense they are done talking, apologize for having bothered them and explain that calling customers for payment is part of the normal collection process, and that it is not harassment.

- Never take what they are saying personally. Recognize it for what it is... a strategy to delay payment that has worked in the past and will continue to work in the future.

- Address the customer's complaints calmly, and one at a time. Take your time.

- Recognize that the customer does not believe what they are saying is true. Therefore, the customer cannot admit that their position is wrong.

Sometimes, when customers have no defense they simply go on the offense. For example, there is no defense for paying bills late, ignoring calls, and refusing to return messages left by creditors. Therefore, the strategy described above is used to try to shift the creditor's attention away from the central issue—that the account is seriously past due—and onto an irrelevant non-issue such as the suggestion that calling for payment somehow involves harassment.

COLLECTION TIP: When it comes to customers' commitments for repayment of seriously delinquent balances, when all is said and done a lot more is likely to be said than is ever done.

USING CREDIT HOLDS TO ENCOURAGE PAYMENT

At some point the credit department must consider placing the account on credit hold. A credit hold is a last resort, to be used only when the creditor is unable to convince the customer it is in their best interest to make a reasonable commitment for payment.

The credit manager should approve credit holds. It would be unprofessional not to inform the salesperson of the credit hold decision, just as it would be ineffective not to inform the customer of a credit hold. If an order is pending, the customer's accounts payable department should be contacted immediately and told the order in question is on hold until either (a) payment is received, or (b) a reasonable payment commitment is made.

Often, the fact that an order is on hold will cause the accounts payable department to release payment. One of the indications that the accounts payable department is being rewarded for delaying payments to suppliers is when a payment commitment is made as soon as the customer is told that orders are on hold. Another hint that the accounts payable department is trying to delay payment occurs whenever the customer's accounts payable representative asks specifically if there are orders on hold at the time.

WORKING WITH THE BUYER

Sometimes, companies allocate money to vendors based on advice from the purchasing department about which vendors are essential. Since credit managers do not normally work with buyers, if ongoing discussions or negotiations need to take place then the salesperson should be included in these discussions. Often, buyers are relying on "just-in-time" deliveries of product, and the salesperson knows how important the pending order is to the customer's production schedule. This information can be helpful in extracting payment from the debtor.

Tip: If a customer is delinquent enough to be placed on hold, the credit manager should evaluate the account to determine why the past due problem was allowed to become this serious before considering offering open account terms again. The credit manager should arrange for the credit file to be updated and should look for any obvious signs of deterioration in the credit risk profile. If the deterioration is serious enough, the credit manager may choose to lower or withdraw the open account.

BROKEN COMMITMENTS AS A RED FLAG

Every time a customer makes and then breaks a payment commitment, the credit manager should conduct a cursory review of the customer's credit file. If additional information is found that the customer is having serious financial problems, then the credit manager must consider withdrawing or reducing the customer's credit limit.

The "best" reason for a broken commitment is that the debtor's accounts payable department is poorly managed and does not keep track of the payment commitments it makes. Unfortunately, the most likely reason that a debtor makes and then breaks payment commitments is that the debtor's financial condition is so weak and their cash flow is so uncertain that the company cannot keep the commitments it makes from day to day.

NEGOTIATING DISPUTED BALANCES

One way to think of the credit department's role in dispute resolution is as follows: The credit department has no vested interest in doing anything but clearing the outstanding balance. If the evidence shows that the seller owes the buyer a credit, then a credit should be issued. If the evidence is overwhelming that the buyer needs to pay the creditor, then the creditor must be willing to go as far as necessary to collect the past due balance. If the documentation is ambiguous, the credit manager should recommend that the customer be given the benefit of the doubt, and that a credit should be issued.

USING ARBITRATION TO COLLECT DISPUTED BALANCES

Customer accounts often become delinquent because of a dispute between the seller and the buyer. If the matter cannot be resolved between the two parties directly, one dispute resolutio n process that creditors should consider involves Arbitration. Arbitration involves the submission of a dispute to one or more impartial third parties for a decision or determination. Arbitration may be either binding or non-binding. Non-binding arbitration is akin to mediation except the arbitrator renders a decision.

Unless required by applicable rules or laws, the parties to arbitration are not required to be represented by counsel. If the award is the result of finding arbitration, if necessary, a formal judgment can be requested by a Court having appropriate jurisdiciton based on the arbitrator's findings.

RESOLVING DELINQUENT BALANCES THROUGH MEDIATION

A mediator is a facilitator helping the buyer and the seller to work through their problems or disagreements.

Using a mediator may help to preserve some of the goodwill between the buyer and the seller. At least initially, a mediator may meet several times with each side, rather than bringing the parties together too quickly, which could result in an unpleasant confrontation. Mediators seek compromise, not a win for one party at the expense of the other. One key to successful mediation is that the mediator must be completely impartial, to have no vested interest in the outcome of the process.

The mediator will often recommend more than one possible solution to a problem. Creativity in resolving a dispute is one of the value-added services that a mediator offers. It is also the responsibility of the mediator to recommend that negotiations be terminated if he or she believes that resolution of the dispute is highly improbable.

EXTENDING COLLECTION CALLS

Frequently, delinquent customers want to end a collection call as quickly as possible having provided the creditor with as little information as possible. It is up to the creditor to control the collection call. It is a good idea whenever a collector calls a customer to discuss a past due balance to take a little extra time and do one or more of the following:

- Confirm the customer's billing address is correct in your system.

- Express concern about any trend involving a slowdown in payments that you may have noticed [if applicable]

- Ask if your account can be flagged for more prompt payment in the future.

- Ask why invoices are not being paid on time.

- Ask the customer to confirm your terms of sale.

- Flag your records for more frequent calls.

- If your company offers a discount for prompt payment, remind the customer of the advantages of taking the discount.

- If the collector is told the check was mailed, they should ask for the check number, and date, and when the check was actually mailed.

HOW TO WITHDRAW AN OPEN ACCOUNT

Delinquent customers are less likely to pay a past due balance if they know their open account terms have already been withdrawn permanently. Similarly, the salesperson is likely to be less helpful if they know the credit terms have been withdrawn. Therefore, it is a good idea for credit managers not to make any announcement until the past due balance has been paid.

One of the more difficult problems that credit managers face involves trying to collect a past due balance without revealing that the open account terms are withdrawn. The customer sometimes tries to negotiate with the credit manager by promising to pay a specific amount if the credit agrees to release an order on hold. The best way to handle this situation is refuse to negotiate with the customer.

If a customer asks directly whether they will be allowed to purchase on open account terms after the past due balance has been paid, the credit manager can respond as follows:

> "We will make a final decision about the status of your account after the account has been paid in full. It would be inappropriate for me to make any concessions or commitments while your account remains seriously past due at this time because it would be premature to do so, and we still do not have your payment."

Experienced credit managers who have tried not to make a commitment know that sometimes customers will not accept this vague response. The credit manager should not lie by telling the customer that orders will be released when the credit manager has no intention of releasing them. If the credit manager already knows the account will not be re-opened, the best response would be something like this:

> "I am not prepared to guarantee anything at this time. I am waiting to see if and when payment is received. I will not make any commitment or any final decision at this time. If you choose to pay the past due balance, great! If you choose not to, there is nothing that I can do at this time to force you to do so—but I think it would in your best interest to do so."

The larger or older the balance due, the higher up in the debtor organization the creditor should be prepared to go in order to obtain a commitment for payment.

USING PROMISSORY NOTES TO MANAGE DELINQUENT ACCOUNTS

Creditors sometimes require their customers to sign Promissory Notes in return for an agreement to accept an extended payment plan. A Promissory Note is a contract containing a written promise to pay a specific sum on a specific date [or on a specific payment schedule]. A Promissory Note may call for a single lump sum payment, or a number of progress payments, often equally spaced over a specified period of time. This is sometimes referred to as a serial Promissory Note.

Typical terms and conditions that a creditor would want to include in a Promissory Note would be:

- An acceleration clause: The clause provides that in the event the debtor misses even one payment that entire amount owed immediately becomes due.

- Carrying charges or interest: It is common that creditors ask their delinquent accounts to pay interest on the debt as part of an extended payment plan detailed in a Promissory Note.

Promissory Notes are not frequently used by unsecured trade creditors for the simple reason that unsecured creditors normally do not have the leverage necessary to demand that a delinquent customer agree to sign

WHAT TO LOOK FOR WHEN A SUBORDINATE REFERS A DELINQUENT ACCOUNT

Normally, credit managers want their subordinates to refer accounts to them that the collector feels that they are no longer making progress with the customer. Before the credit manager takes over one of these accounts, the credit manager should know:

- Whether or not the debtor company is still in business

- Whether or not the debtor acknowledges the debt is owed.

- Whether or not any portion of the debt is in dispute.

- What reason(s) the customer has given for not paying the debt.

- What specific payment commitment(s), if any, the debtor company has made, and which commitments have been kept and which were broken.

- When the next payment is scheduled, and how much is scheduled for payment.

- If the debtor has requested any documentation, and if so when it was sent and to whom.

- Whether or not the debtor wants to return inventory, and if so whether or not the company wants to accept the product back.

USING SALESPEOPLE AS COLLECTORS

The idea of using salespeople as collectors is controversial. Salespeople are not trained collectors and they are often reluctant to act in a capacity that they see as contrary to their role as an advocate for the customer. The disadvantages of using salespeople in collections include:

- Salespeople often have an aversion to collection work and may deliberately or accidentally do a poor job.

- If the past due balance is in dispute, the salesperson may be the source of the problem and may be reluctant to resolve it.

- The salesperson may choose to give collection a low priority

- Sales management may object to the use of their sales personnel in collections - since time spent collecting is time not spent selling.

- The salesperson may damage his or her long-term relationship with the customer by acting as a collector.

However, there are numerous advantages to using salespeople to help clear delinquent commercial accounts. The most obvious advantage the salesperson has is their personal relationship with the customer. Other advantages include:

- The fact that salespeople are located geographically close to the customer

- If the salesperson created a problem, they now have a chance to correct that mistake.

- In most collection situations, the salesperson can present themselves to the customer as an intermediary between the company and the customer.

GLOBAL OUT OF COURT SETTLEMENTS

Occasionally, a delinquent commercial account will notify its creditors that it is considering filing for bankruptcy protection, and as an alternative is considering an out of court settlement with its creditors. These out of court settlements normally involve the creditor accepting a fraction of the balance due in full and final settlement of the debt owed. How large a fraction of the balance due the customer is prepared to pay is the key to evaluating the proposal. Specifically, if the creditor believes there would be a larger recovery if the company were liquidated then the creditor should either (a) negotiate for a higher percentage or (b) force the debtor into bankruptcy.

Business consultants that bill themselves as "workout specialists" often present deals of this type. Any arrangement of this type is fraught with risk for the credit manager. Often, the workout specialist and the customer are cutting different deals for different creditors based on the importance of that creditor to the customer in the long term. With this in mind, it is important that before agreeing to any payment arrangement, settlement or compromise that the credit manager do their homework and find out what kinds of deals the customer is making with other creditors.

Another alternative to a bankruptcy filing is an Assignment for the Benefit of Creditors. [This process is explained in detail in Chapter 38.] The risks associated with an Assignment for the Benefit of Creditors and any other out of court settlement, include:

- The fact that there is no Automatic Stay of claims against the debtor—meaning that other creditors are free to pursue their collection efforts through the civil litigation process. The problem with this is the fact that if they win judgments they become judgment creditors instead of general unsecured trade creditors.

- There is nothing to prevent the debtor from offering better deals to creditors that are not impressed by the standard proposal.

- There is no creditors committee in an informal workout, and if there is one there is no statutory fiduciary requirement that the committee work in the interest of all trade creditors.

- In a bankruptcy, unsecured creditors are represented by legal counsel experienced in maximizing return to unsecured creditors. In an informal arrangement, creditors are normally only represented by counsel if they pay for it.

- In a bankruptcy, the debtor must present creditors with its financial statements and present information to the court under penalty of perjury and testify under oath. None of these requirements exist in an informal arrangement.

- In a bankruptcy, the debtor must submit financial statements to the Court and in reorganization must share current financial information with the Creditors Committee. This level of cooperation is not mandatory and therefore it is highly unlikely in an informal arrangement.

- In a bankruptcy, the creditors committee's attorney will normally work with the debtor to determine if there were any avoidable transfers such as insider preferences. In an informal arrangement, the debtor is less likely to provide this type of information to its creditors.

- In a bankruptcy reorganization, the debtor will not be permitted to make a sale that is not in the ordinary course of business without Court approval. In an informal arrangement, there are limited controls on the debtor's actions.

- There is nothing to compel the debtor company to cooperate with creditors in an informal arrangement, and no mechanism that requires the debtor to make the promised payments on time as there is in a bankruptcy.

- Typically, small claims in an informal plan are paid in full, or paid more quickly so that so-called nuisance creditors do not throw a monkey wrench into the effort to reorganize by suing or initiating an involuntary bankruptcy filing. While this may sound appealing initially, what it means is that certain creditors are being given preferential treatment over other general unsecured trade creditors.

The most that can be said in favor of an Assignment for the Benefit of Creditors, a workout, or any other informal debt restricting or settlement program is that the reduced expense of settling outside of the United States Bankruptcy Court can make these arrangements advantageous in certain situations.

PUTTING COLLECTION AGENCIES TO WORK

At some point, it may become necessary to issue a final demand and then to place an account for collection with a third party collection agency. The advantages of using a third party collection agency with an uncooperative or uncommunicative debtor include:

- A reputable third party collection agency employs experts in dealing with delinquent accounts.
- Placing an account for collection frees up resources in the credit department to work on resolving legitimate disputes and collecting past due balances
- The fact that the debtor has been placed with a third party can have a strong psychological effect—making it more likely the debtor will pay sooner.
- Third party collection agencies will recommend referral to a collection attorney that works on a contingency fee basis
- A collection agency will provide the creditor with periodic updates on their collection efforts. These reports can be used to document the fact that the credit department is actively and professionally pursuing payment of the delinquent balance.

THE ROLE OF CASH DISCOUNTS

Cash discounts are offered as an incentive to customers to pay invoices quickly. Therefore, offering cash discount discourages delinquencies among commercial accounts. For example, when inflation is low, a cash discount of 1% to 2% becomes a huge financial incentive for customers to pay their bills on time. Unfortunately, a certain number of customers will try to get the best of both worlds by paying the invoices beyond the discount due date but taking the cash discount [now unearned]. Allowing customers to consistently take these discounts defeats the whole purpose of offering a cash discount incentive to a customer.

There are a number of ways to address the widespread problem of unearned cash discounts, including these:

(a) First, the creditor's credit application, monthly statements and invoices should state the company's cash discount policy and indicate that unearned discounts will be charged back and must be repaid.

(b) Whenever an unearned cash discount is disallowed the customer must be notified in writing

(c) The accounts payable system should record the deduction as a unique open balance on the customer's account—and that balance due should appear on monthly statements until paid or resolved

(d) The creditor should save the envelope the payment was received in to show it was postmarked on or after the discount due date.

(e) Creditors should address unearned cash discounts as quickly as possible. The longer the delay between the time the unearned cash discount is taken and the time the creditor addresses the problem the less likely the debtor will repay the deduction.

(f) The less strident the protest against the unearned discount the less likely the customer will repay it. In fact, credit managers that do not vigorously protest unearned discounts may soon find that debtors become more brazen in their disregard for the vendor's cash discount terms.

USING PERSONAL VISITS TO ADDRESS DELINQUENT BALANCES

Experienced credit professionals know that it is difficult to ignore a creditor's payment request when the credit manager travels to meet with the debtor. Whenever it is necessary, credit managers should visit customers in person to address a past due balance.

They should be alert to the following indications that the customer is in serious financial trouble:

- Key personnel have recently left the company, or there has been a layoff.
- The business operation is unusually quiet.
- The customer seems to have little in the way of inventory.

CHAPTER 27

REDUCING CREDIT RISK

Credit managers have an obligation to manage and to minimize credit risk whenever practical. Two obvious but impractical ways to reduce credit risk are (1) sell on cash terms or (2) sell only to highly rated accounts. The study of economics reveals that unless the seller has already reached its production capacity, the seller can realize incremental sales and profits by shipping on open account credit terms to moderate credit risks. In certain circumstances, it may even be appropriate to sell to marginal credit risks on open account terms.

There are a number of practical steps that credit managers can take to reduce credit risk. The key point to remember is that risk management is not a once a year, a once a month, or even a once a week process. Risk management decisions must be made every day and at every level in the credit department, every time an order is placed into the credit queue, and every time an account becomes past due.

Unfortunately for credit managers, the ability to avoid 99 out of 100 problems that result in delinquency or default will probably not be good enough for senior management—especially if it can be demonstrated that the credit department should have and could have avoided that one in one-hundred loss.

A BALANCING ACT

Credit professionals are constantly striving to find the right balance between risk acceptance and risk avoidance. An overly aggressive risk avoidance policy will result in lost sales to accounts that should have qualified for open account credit terms. An overly liberal credit granting policy will result in higher delinquencies, and ultimately in bad debt losses that should have and could have been avoided.

Since the credit department makes credit decisions every day, the credit manager and his or her staff must always be alert to the question of balancing risk and reward. There are a number of actions that the credit department takes on a daily basis to manage and to monitor credit risk. The most obvious involves evaluating orders on credit hold to determine which can be released and which orders pending must be held. The order review process only works if the personnel assigned to this task are:

- well trained
- carefully selected
- knowledgeable
- take their jobs seriously
- understand the importance of the task they have been assigned, and
- do it to the best of their ability

It is up to the credit manager to select and train these subordinates carefully, and to make certain they do not lose sight of just how important this task is to reducing credit risk. People assigned to the task of releasing orders should be told never to guess about a credit decision. Instead, any tough decisions should be referred to the credit manager for his or her comments or instructions.

GETTING TO KNOW THE CUSTOMER

The process of reducing credit risk begins before the first sale is ever made. As a general rule the smaller the company the higher the risk of selling on open account credit terms. Similarly, the newer the company the greater the risk that the company will fail. Getting to know the customer is not intended to suggest that creditors fly off to meet with each new customer. Instead, getting to know applicants refers to a process of evaluating new accounts during which relevant information about the creditworthiness of the applicant is gathered and evaluated.

MONITORING PAYMENTS

Given a choice, every customer would prefer to pay its bills later rather than sooner. Once an open account has been established for an applicant, the credit department should pay close attention to the customer's payment track record for at least the first year. A cavalier attitude about collection during the first year of business will encourage a pattern of late payments that may last for as long as the companies do business.

It is not sufficient simply to review the customer's payment pattern with the new creditor company, it is important to know how the customer is paying its other creditors. For example, if a customer has a history of not paying some of its creditors on time, is likely get around to not paying every creditor on time sooner or later.

If payments from a customer get slower, the creditor needs a different approach. Often, the new approach is as simple as assigning the account to a new collector and telling that collector to turn up the heat on the debtor. The goal is to get the customer to recognize the need to place the creditor's invoices at the top of the "to be paid" pile.

Many companies that have not bothered to establish a borrowing relationship with their bank to help them over temporary cash flow problems. Instead, they prefer to rely on their trade creditors for temporary and interest free financing. Some companies place suppliers into four categories in their accounts payable system:

(a) Vendors that must be paid on time.

(b) Suppliers that should be paid on time, whenever possible.

(c) Vendors that can be ignored until it is convenient to pay them.

(d) Accounts that have been placed on payment hold.

Of course, the debtor does not place these specific descriptions next to each creditor... but most companies categorize suppliers based on their payment priority. No creditor wants to be in category C. Every creditor wants to be in category A, but most would settle for being a category B vendors.

COLLECT ACTIVELY, NOT PASSIVELY

It is simply not a good idea to make dozens of collection calls a day if half or more of the calls end up with the collector leaving a message on someone's voice mail system. The credit department's primary goal is risk management. Leaving a series of voice mail messages does not reduce credit risk, so this approach to collections is too passive.

It is relatively easy for collectors to understand the difference between passive and active collections. The goal of the collector is to motivate the customer to take action. The first roadblock is trying to find a way to contact the customer. The collector must learn to be more assertive and more creative in their approach to roadblocks that are deliberately placed in the way of their collection efforts. The rule of thumb for collectors should be as follows:

> If you encounter a roadblock in your effort to make contact with the customer to resolve a past due balance, you have several options: You can go around it; or go under it; or go over it; or go through it. The only thing you *cannot* do is allow the roadblock to remain in your way.

Specific to a scenario in which the collector is only able to reach the accounting clerk's voice mail system, the collector can remain passive and waste more time calling and leaving messages, or the collector can accelerate the process by calling the accounts payable manager or the controller to ask for status on the past due balance. On occasion a debtor will complain about this tactic, but the decision to elevate the problem to the next level is sound, ethical and practical. The goal of every collector is to get a commitment for payment. The collector must have the self-confidence and the authority to change their approach if the traditional approach of leaving messages in the hope that someone responds promptly does not work.

USING CREDIT LIMITS TO MANAGE CREDIT RISK

Contrary to popular myth, a credit limit is not cast in stone. If a customer is a good credit risk, the credit limit can be increased. The opposite is also true. If a customer has demonstrated that it is a poor risk by failing to pay invoices on time, by breaking commitments, by failing to make commitments, or based on its financial condition, then the credit manager should reduce the credit limit.

Reducing credit limits to slow paying accounts reduces credit risk only if the employees assigned to release orders understand the importance of holding customers to their assigned credit units. The credit manager should encourage anyone with authority to release orders to take that job seriously, and to disregard pressure from the salesperson and the customer when making a decision. Also, recognizing the importance of the order approval process, the credit manager must make it clear to anyone performing this duty that they can and should refer any order they are concerned about to their manager.

The fact that a customer is below the established credit limit does not automatically mean that orders should be released. Anyone given the authority to release orders needs to look at the "big picture" when evaluating an order pending. The fact that an account is below its credit limit, or that a payment commitment was given does not automatically mean that an order pending can or should be released. That is "cookie-cutter" thinking. They must look at the totality of the credit risk—and not at a single piece of information in making an informed credit decision.

For example, a decision to release an order pending against a specific commitment for payment for the entire past due balance might be appropriate for the majority of customers, but may be entirely inappropriate if the specific customer in question was:

(a) A new customer for which the past due balance represented their first order, or

(b) The customer in questions has a history of making and then breaking payment commitments, or

(c) The customer in question has already made and then broken a previous commitment for payment of this specific past due balance.

ESTABLISH A CREDIT LIMIT FOR EVERY ACCOUNT

The credit manager should make certain that a credit limit is established for every account, and that every active file is updated periodically—ideally at least once a year. Credit limits should be established for all accounts, including customers that purchase on COD terms, and even on accounts that purchase on COD cash terms.

For customers that buy on COD terms, it would be hard to explain why the creditor released an order for $20,000 on COD terms knowing the customer has a low 4 figure bank account balance... especially if the customer's check bounced.

A similar scenario occurs with customers willing to pay COD Cashier's Check for products. If the company is run by a con man, the criminal may agree to pay for a small opening order on COD Cashier's Check terms, and follow that small opening order a large second order for which the con man also agrees to pay cash. The trouble is that rather than paying with a valid Cashier's Check, the criminal pays the carrier with a forged check and disappears with the creditor's goods before the theft and fraud are discovered. By putting credit limits on COD, and COD Cash accounts the credit manager will be proactively reducing credit risk.

USING CREDIT TERMS TO REDUCE CREDIT RISK

The most obvious way that credit terms can be used to reduce credit risk involves eliminating a customer's open account credit terms. While the decision to withdraw a customer's open account terms certainly has its place in the credit manager arsenal of risk management tools, there are more subtle techniques that credit professionals can use to reduce credit risk. For example, if a credit manager simply wants faster payment, he or she could offer the customer a cash discount for early payment. If the cash incentive is large enough the customer will often take advantage of the offer.

If the credit manager wants to be sure to reduce the company's dollar exposure and credit risk, another way to do so is to cut the terms in half. For example, if the terms of sale were Net 30 days with an average balance of $10,000 and the credit manager reduced the terms of sale to Net 15 days, the credit manager could reasonably expect the average balance to drop proportionately to around $5,000.

PROPER COLLECTION TECHNIQUES HELP REDUCE RISK

An effective collection program reduces credit risk. Collection calls are typically placed dozens or even hundreds of times a day [depending on the size of the customer base and the size of the credit department staff]. Collectors need to be taught that their role is not simply to ask questions and take notes; the collector is expected to lead the discussion and to help the customer to understand the benefits of paying the past due balance along with the risks and costs of not doing so.

Because collection calls occur so frequently, collectors sometimes forget to inform their managers when a collection problem seems to be getting serious. Credit risk can be reduced by involving the credit manager sooner rather than later in complex collection problems. Every collector should be instructed to refer accounts to their manager whenever any of the following events occur:

- The customer makes and then breaks a payment commitment.
- The customer promises to pay one amount, and then pays a substantially lesser amount.
- The customer will not make any payment commitment.
- The customer makes an unreasonable payment commitment—for example, an offer to pay 5% of the past due balance per month.
- The customer will not take the collector's calls.

Collectors should be told not to be in a hurry to end a collection call, and not to allow the customer rush through it either. For example, if the customer has a cash flow problem, the more questions the collector asks the more information they will receive. The more information they receive directly from the customer, the more data will be provided to the credit manager and the more effectively the credit risk can be managed.

For example, if a customer indicates the past due balance has not been paid and is not scheduled for payment because their company is experiencing cash flow problems, the credit department representative would want to ask the following questions:

- Are any vendors being paid?
- If so, which ones?
- Are employees being paid?
- How long have you had this cash flow problem?
- What caused it?
- What steps have you taken—aside from not making payments to vendors—to address the problem?
- Are any creditors continuing to ship to you on open account credit terms at this time?
- If so, which ones?
- Have you contacted your bank to request a short-term loan?
- If so, what was their response?
- If you have not met with your bank, when do you plan to do so?
- Is the company considering filing for bankruptcy protection?
- If so, what steps have you taken to prepare for this?

The sooner a past due balance is collected, the faster the risk to the creditor company is eliminated. In most companies, there are far more past due accounts than time to call them on a particular day. For that reason, collectors must be instructed about how to prioritize their collection calls. There are several competing goals in establishing priorities for collection calls. They are:

- The company wants to collect as much as possible as quickly as possible. This suggests that collectors should concentrate on calling the largest past due customers first.

- Credit managers know that the longer a past due balance is left open, the harder it will become to convince the debtor to pay the balance due. This suggests that collectors should make certain that all balances are addressed, irrespective of how small the past due balance is.

- Small or large, if a customer has an order pending then that account should be contacted immediately. Often the credit manager needs to know the status of the past due balance before making a decision about whether or not to release the order.

Therefore, prioritizing calls involves the need to call accounts with large past due balances that are not particularly far past due, and find time to call customers with small balances that are seriously past due, and to call on any amount past due if an order is pending.

HOLD SUBORDINATES ACCOUNTABLE FOR THEIR MISTAKES

There are a few credit managers that take credit for everything that goes right but are quick to try to pass the buck any time something goes wrong. This is demotivating and demoralizing for the people who work in the credit department who deserve better. Subordinates deserve recognition for the tasks that they perform well and the things that they do that benefit the company. At the same time, subordinates need to be held accountable for the mistakes that they make—assuming of course that they were adequately trained and therefore should not have made the error.

Credit managers will reduce delinquencies and bad debts if they take the time to train subordinates properly, and then hold them accountable for their actions or inaction. Credit managers will reduce employee turnover and improve morale if they train subordinates, and share the credit with the entire department when things go right.

THE GOAL IS NOT TO ELIMINATE LOSSES; IT IS TO REDUCE RISK

Contrary to one popular myth, the goal of the credit department is to reduce credit risk, not to eliminate credit risk and bad debt write offs. Eliminating all credit risk would result in lost sales and lost profits. Another goal for the credit department is to eliminate unnecessary losses caused by poor planning, poor training, poor documentation, and poor execution of specific credit policies and procedures. This is a lofty goal. Nevertheless, it is a goal worth striving for. It requires the effort and participation of every person in the credit department.

TRY TO TRANSFER THE RISK

There are a number of mechanisms for transferring credit risk from the seller to a third party. The most obvious one involves the use of credit insurance. Another method to transfer most of the credit risk involves the use of factoring. Still another popular option involves the use of flooring [inventory financing].

Most credit professionals know how credit insurance works, and the process is covered in detail in Chapter 22. The two key facts to remember about credit insurance are:

(1) That credit insurance does not provide coverage against the first dollar of losses. The insurance company will use deductibles, co-payments, exclusions and other tools to make certain the creditor uses the policy as it was intended: to protect the trade creditor against catastrophic bad debt losses.

(2) A credit insurance company will exclude certain accounts from coverage, and will inform the creditor of its decision to limit coverage to other customers.

Factoring involves the purchase of a seller's accounts receivable by a factor, or a factoring house. The factor's fee or profit involves the fact that the factor will purchase the accounts receivable less a discount from the face value of the invoice. Factoring is one of the oldest forms of business financing available. Factoring is relatively expensive, and it is far more common in some industries that in others.

Working capital financing through "flooring" involves a three-sided transaction in which the customer, their supplier and a finance company each play a role. The finance company has established a perfected security interest in some or all of the assets of the debtor. The finance company gives the seller a specific shipment authorization, and agrees to pay the creditor when its invoice comes due. As with the factor, the finance company' profit results from charging a fee [typically in the 1% to 2% range] expressed as a deduction from the amount paid to the creditor for accepting the credit risk.

ACCEPTING SPECIAL, CUSTOMIZED ORDERS

A special order involves work done to a customer's exact specifications. A special order often results in the manufacture of products that have little resale value elsewhere. Therefore, special orders represent significant risk to the seller/manufacturer. When a special order is received, it is not uncommon for the credit department to be asked to evaluate the account and the risk associated with accepting the order.

There are several ways to limit the creditor's risk relating to special orders, including these:

- Refuse to accept special orders, or price them unrealistically high so that the customer goes to a competitor.

- Require the customer to make a partial payment when the order is placed. Doing so offers some protection against cancellation of the project.

- In addition to a down payment, require progress payments. Receiving progress payments makes it unlikely that the customer will cancel the order.

- Require the customer to provide a standby letter of credit—and refuse to accept the purchase order until and unless the standby letter of credit is provided and is acceptable to the seller and in particular to the credit department.

RECOGNIZE THE LIMITATIONS OF PERSONAL GUARANTEES AND OTHER ASSURANCES OF PAYMENT

Personal guarantees, promissory notes, and perfected security agreements often give general unsecured trade creditors a false sense of security. For example, assume a creditor selling to a corporation has the personal guaranty of the owner of the corporation. The question that must be answered is what that personal guarantee would be worth if the corporation filed for bankruptcy protection. It would not be unlikely for the individual guarantor to file for personal bankruptcy protection at the same time as his or her corporation filed for bankruptcy protection.

Similarly, a perfected security interest is beneficial to a trade creditor to the extent that the collateral pledged is valuable. For example, if a trade creditor has a perfected security interest in the debtor's finished goods inventory, it is possible that by the time the debtor is in serious financial the easily saleable merchandise will have been sold off leaving only the obsolete inventory for the secured creditor.

RECOGNIZING THE LIMITATIONS OF FINANCIAL STATEMENT ANALYSIS

Financial statement analysis has become the "holy grail" for some credit managers. They make repeated requests for the customer to provide them with current financial statements. If a customer is privately held, if the creditor receives anything they typically receive the following:

- Unaudited financial information
- For a single accounting period
- That does not contain any notes to the financial statements
- That does not contain the customer's Statement of Cash Flows

Despite the fact that most credit professionals understand that important data is missing, the credit manager will frequently complete the financial statement analysis and make credit decisions on the basis of this limited [and questionable] information.

USING OPEN ACCOUNT TERMS TO ESTABLISH NEW ACCOUNTS

Sometimes, one of the only ways to break into a new market is to offer customers open account terms. This strategy is fraught with risk. Specifically, lowering credit standards normally results in higher delinquencies and ultimately in more bad debt losses. In this scenario, open account credit terms are being used as an incentive to induce the customer to purchase from the creditor. The customer may be quite anxious to buy once the creditor company offers open account terms—because the customer recognizes that it is a poor credit risk and is not often offered the chance to buy on open account credit terms.

If senior management in the seller company has decided that offering open account credit terms to high risk companies to break into a new market, the credit manager must be certain that senior management is prepared to accept the payment problems that this concept will almost certainly produce. Provided that senior management is comfortable about the increased credit risk, the credit manager should document management's decision and move on. Even if the credit manager disagrees with the decision, the company will expect the credit department to play an active role in monitoring and in managing credit risk and the problems associated with doing business with the marginal accounts that the company has elected to sell to.

Even if management insists that orders be approved and released, the credit manager still has the opportunity and the obligation to try to manage collection risk and delayed payment by:

- Monitor payments carefully
- Recommend credit hold when an account already identified as high risk become past due.

- Review the high-risk accounts more frequently than other accounts.

- Keep senior management informed about any collection problems.

- Make certain that it is noted that the decision to sell was made by senior management over the objections of the credit manager

REDUCE RISK BY REFUSING TO BE RUSHED

Every credit manager recognizes the importance of being responsive to customers, and the need to evaluate applicants for credit as quickly as possible. In some instances, if the credit department is unable to process a credit application fast enough, the customer may give its business to a competitor company.

However, the credit manager cannot simply give in to pressure to make a quick decision without the information necessary to make an informed decision. One of the key elements of credit fraud is time. The longer the credit department has to make a decision about an applicant, the more likely it is that the credit department is going to find something that would indicate a serious problem. For this reason, con artists try to place significant pressure on the credit department to make a snap decision. In an effort to reduce credit risk, many experienced credit managers adopt this rule of thumb:

> "The harder a new account pushes for a fast credit decision, and the more pressure from the sales department and sales management for a fast decision, the more important it becomes to check and to double check the facts before approving the opening order."

BULLET PROOFING THE DEPARTMENT AGAINST CREDIT FRAUD

The topic of credit fraud is covered in depth in Chapter 31. However, in the context of reducing credit risk it is important for everyone in the credit department and throughout the rest of the company to acknowledge that there are people who will do their very best to separate creditors from their merchandise with no intention of making payment. The first step in preventing credit fraud is awareness. Awareness does not mean that credit managers or their subordinate should become paranoid about fraud and theft. It simply means that everyone in the credit department from the new accounts clerk would probably benefit from a degree of professional skepticism.

CONDUCTING AN AUTOPSY OF A BAD DEBT

The most expensive mistake a company can make is one that the company makes over and over again. In order to reduce the number of bad debt losses, the credit manager should conduct an autopsy after a loss has taken place to find out what, if anything, the credit department could have done to prevent or to reduce the loss the company took.

Sometimes, the answer to this question is that there was nothing that the credit department could have done to prevent the loss. For example, if the owner of a sole proprietorship dies unexpectedly and there is no one capable of running the business, then that company will probably fail and general unsecured trade creditors are likely to lose money. By performing the "autopsy," the credit manager can learn from their mistakes and find ways to reduce risk in the future.

SUMMARY

Reducing credit risk is not a one-time process restricted to establishing the terms and the credit limit for a new account. Customers are good at disguising the problems that they are experiencing. Credit managers and their subordinates can and must remain constantly vigilant to signs that a customer is in financial trouble. The decision about what to do about a developing problem should rest with the credit manager, but the credit manager must rely on the remainder of the credit department staff to point out the situations that require his or her attention.

CHAPTER 28

USING THIRD PARTY COLLECTIONS

One of the biggest challenges facing any credit manager is trying to find the right third party to use in when in-house collection efforts have failed to produce either (a) payment in full or (b) a reasonable repayment schedule backed by appropriate documentation.

A collection agency is a third party assigned the task of collecting past due debts from an unrelated third party. The ideal collection agent is one that combines all of the following traits:

- Their services are rendered professionally

- The agent is familiar with and in full compliance with all applicable federal and state laws including the Fair Debt Collection Practices Act.

- Collection is made on a contingency fee basis.

- The fees and any additional costs or charges are agreed on in writing before any collection process begins.

- The collection agent's contingent collection fees are competitive.

- If the creditor contemplates placing a large claim, the rates are negotiable.

- The collection agent remits payments received from collections a minimum of once a month.

- The collection agency is licensed, and bonded by an insurance company against the possible embezzlement of funds collected on behalf of the creditor company.

- The minimum size of the claim that the collection agency will handle is small enough to be relevant to the creditor company.

- Large and small claims alike are collected with professionalism and enthusiasm.

- The agent has industry specific collection experience.

- The third party selected has the geographic range necessary to be useful to the creditor company.

Typically, commercial credit managers use either collection agencies or collection attorneys as their third party collection agency. There are advantages and disadvantages to placing with one or the other, and there is no rule of thumb about when to use one rather than the other. One key is the third party selected must be cost effective, not simply the one that offer the lowest contingent collection rate quote.

COLLECTION AGENCY QUALIFICATIONS

There are literally thousands of collection agencies in the United States. In fact, at least one collection agency was selling franchises to people interested in getting into the collection business—complete with exclusive territories for each franchisee.

Many of the leading commercial agencies are members of organizations or associations interested in improving the standards of conduct and the professionalism of commercial collection agencies in the United States. For example, approximately 100 collection agencies are members of the Commercial Agency Section of the Commercial Law League of America.

COLLECTION AGENCIES ARE NOT CREATED EQUAL

There are thousands of collection agencies to choose from, and no two are alike in terms of rates, services, experience, professionalism, capability, capacity, and geographic coverage. Some collection agencies are well managed and professionally staffed, and others are not.

Creditor can expect to pay between 10% and 25% [or more] of the amount collected by the collection agency in collection fees. To some extent, the contingent collection fees paid by the creditor are a function of the volume of business the creditor gives to the collection agency, combined with the dollar volume of placements, combined with the skill of the credit manager in negotiating or demanding lower contingent collection rates.

THE TELEMARKETING COLLECTION AGENCY

Many credit managers are inundated with calls from collection agencies requesting their business. Some try to sell their experience and services, and a small number sell based on price alone. These so called telemarketing collection agencies make hundreds, perhaps thousands of calls a day to credit managers and other potential clients touting their low collection rates. If a credit manager is paying a collection fee of 15% then telemarketer offering a 10% contingent collection rate and nationwide coverage sounds good.

However, when credit managers look more closely they often find they get what they pay for. For example, the company offering a 10% contingent collection rate may do nothing more then send a series of demand letters followed by a couple of collection calls. If the agency collects, great. If they do not, the agency's investment in the process was minimal. This type of agencies plays the numbers game. It knows that a certain percent of delinquent customers will make arrangements to pay once their account has been placed for collection. The placements that are not recovered are simply "loss leaders" used to attract more business.

THE FAIR DEBT COLLECTION PRACTICES ACT

The Fair Debt Collection Practices Act [the FDCPA] is a federal law that governs the actions and activities of commercial collection agencies. The Federal Trade Commission administers the FDCPA. The FDCPA was written to protect consumers from abusive, deceptive and unfair treatment by debt collectors.

The FDCPA requires that:

- Debt collectors contact the debtor only in writing if the debtor requires it.
- The FDCPA also allows the debtor to require the collector to cease all collection calls and letters. [Doing so does not erase the debt, nor does it prevent a lawsuit from being filed to collect the debt].
- Collectors send a letter within 5 days of their first contact explaining the debtor's right to dispute the balance allegedly owed.

- The collector is required to report to any consumer credit reporting agencies involved if the debtor reports in writing that the debt is disputed.

- There are other state and federal laws that may also be relevant to the business of debt collecting.

The following practices as they relate to consumer debt are illegal under the Fair Debt Collection Practices Act:

- Debt collectors may not call the debtor about a consumer debt at work if it is inconvenient for the debtor.

- The collector may not call about a consumer debt at inconvenient times.

- The collector may not place an excessive number of telephone calls.

- The collector may not contact the debtor if legal counsel represents the debtor.

- The debt collector may not tell anyone else that the debtor owes money [such as your employer or manager]

- The debt collector may not threaten the debtor- in particular the collector may not threaten violence.

- The debt collector may not use profane or obscene language in communicating with the debtor.

- A collection agency cannot publish a list of customers that have not paid their debts

- A debt collector cannot threaten to take legal action unless the creditor intends to take such action

- A debt collector cannot falsely imply that he or she is a collection attorney or a government official

- A collection agency is prohibited from using postcards to collect, and may not place anything on the outside of an envelope to indicate the letter is from a collector

WHY ARE THIRD PARTY COLLECTORS NECESSARY?

Despite the best efforts of credit professionals, a certain percent of accounts will become uncollectable each year. Third party debt collectors are more likely to be able to devote the time and attention necessary to collect from an uncooperative debtor. Contrary to popular myth, reputable, professional commercial collection agencies do not use abusive or harassing tactics when contacting debtors. Doing so is unproductive, and illegal.

One of the reasons that collection agencies are successful in their collection efforts is psychological. Most debtors recognize that by the time a third party has been brought in that the problem is serious. Third party collection agencies are sometimes better disciplined than the creditor company's collectors to separate the delinquency from the debtor. Collection agencies typically begin the process by explaining that their role is to help both the debtor and the creditor by solving the collection problem—ideally by an immediate payment in full but if necessary based on an extended payment plan.

CONTINGENCY AND NONCONTINGENCY COLLECTIONS

Most collection agencies perform collections on a contingency fee basis—meaning that if there is no collection the creditor owes the collection agency nothing. Contingency fees typically range 10% of the amount collection to as much as 50% or more. There is no standard rate, and there are no laws that govern the amount of money a collection agency can charge. Therefore, it is critical that credit professionals evaluate every collection agency they use and understand the fee structure.

Another important fact about contingency fees is that the agency is entitled to their fee regardless of the amount of time and effort required collecting the debt. For example, occasionally a debtor will pay the past due balance as soon as they realize the account has been referred to a third party for collection. The collection agency may have placed one call or generated one letter, but once payment is received the collection agency is entitled to whatever contingent fee they have negotiated with the creditor.

Another common situation in one in which the delinquent customer calls the creditor company after being placed for collection and works out some sort of payment plan. Even though the collection agency did not negotiate the agreement [and may in fact know nothing about the payment arrangement] the collection agency is entitled to its contingent fee because payment occurred after the account was placed for collection.

In an attempt to limit the amount of contingent collection fees that the creditor must pay, most credit professionals use a collection agency that offers a free demand service. A free demand service is a program in which the creditor gives the debtor a ten day notice that if payment is not sent the account will be referred to a collection agency for immediate action. The ten-day demand often convinces a reluctant debtor that the creditor is serious and that the account is about to be placed for collection. This often results in payment, at no cost to the creditor.

Non contingent collection agencies charge a flat fee for their services irrespective of whether collections occur. Often, non-contingent collection agencies are, in effect, letter writing services. For a fee, these agencies send a series of progressively more strident collection letters. The credit department normally pays a relatively small fee for this service, which is due in advance and is owed whether or not the debtor pays the debt.

LOW COLLECTION RATES ARE NOT NECESSARILY THE BEST DEAL, AND HIGH RATES DON'T ALWAYS INVOLVE THE BEST SERVICE

When considering collection agency rates, the lowest quoted rate is not necessarily the best deal. Low rates may or may not result in a low impact collection effort. For example, an agency that offers a 5% contingent collection fee may do little more than send a series of letters to a delinquent debtor. Unfortunately, a collection agency that charges a 40% contingent rate may do exactly the same thing. It is a case of contingent collection fees, the rule of thumb is as follows: "Caveat Emptor:—let the buyer beware."

It is up to the credit professional to find out exactly what services a collection agency offers and exactly how much these services will cost. Often, but not always the credit professional will be able to negotiate a more favorable contingency collection rate from the collection agency [or agencies] the credit manager believes will be the best fit for the organization.

BEWARE OF UNUSUAL FEE ARRANGEMENTS

Occasionally, a collection agency will propose an unusual fee arrangement to its creditors. For example, a few agencies actually that creditors pre-paying certain fees. This tends to lock the creditor into using the collection agency irrespective of how successful they have been in their collection efforts.

Other debt collectors may propose an hourly fee arrangement rather than a contingency fee based collection effort. This is more common among collection attorneys than among collection agencies. Credit managers should be extremely cautious about accepting an hourly arrangement—keeping in mind the hourly fee is owed to the third party collector irrespective of whether or not collection takes place. The advantage of contingent collections is the fact that the creditor is making no additional "investment" in the delinquent debtor.

HOW TO SELECT A COLLECTION AGENCY

There are literally thousands of collection agencies operating in the United States. Only a small fraction can truly claim to offer service nationwide. Many agencies are small, "one man" operations working in a particular city or region. Because there is no standard method for collecting an outstanding debt, and no fixed schedule of fees for the services of a collection agency creditors must select an agency with care.

An inexperienced credit manager may select an agency simply because the company is persistent in trying to win their business. More experienced credit professionals prefer to use an agency that has been in business for at least five years [and preferably far longer], has competitive collection rates, and has a reputation of professionalism and results.

Collection agencies act as agents for creditors—meaning that the creditor can be held liable and legally responsible for any illegal acts performed by their collection agency.

TIP: Select a collection agency with experience in your industry. Knowing the industry and/or the debtor might give the collection agency a slight advantage over a collection agency without that experience.

OTHER FACTORS IN SELECTING A COLLECTION AGENCY

There are any number of other factors to consider when selecting a collection agency, include all of the following:

- The commercial agency's financial status

- Whether the agency is properly licensed and bonded [At least 33 states have licensing or registration requirements for collectors or collection agencies]

- Knowing the method that the collection agency uses in its collection efforts. For example, a series of collection letters is far less effective than a series of collection calls by telephone. A series of collection calls is less impactful than an unannounced visit by the collection agency's collection staff.

- The geographic territory the agency covers. For example, if a large fraction of a company's business is export business then the agency selected should have in place arrangements worldwide to provide collection services.

- How frequently the agency reports the progress that is being made.

- How and when the agency determines when to recommend placing an account with a collection attorney.

PROFESSIONAL COLLECTION AGENCIES

Collection agencies are important to the credit department. Some credit managers consider collection agencies to be an extension of their department.

There are a number of collection agency associations. It is a good idea to select an agency that is a member of one or more of the associations listed below:

- The American Collector's Association. More than 3,000 professional third party collection businesses are members of this organization. Membership requires members to agree to the ACA's code of ethics and business conduct.

- The Commercial Law League of America. There are more than 5,000 attorneys who concentrate their practice in the area of commercial law who are members of the CLLA.

- The International Association of Commercial Collectors. The IACC is a trade association of collection specialists and attorneys.

- The League International for Creditors is an association of independent debt collection agencies, law firms and credit reporting agencies.

REFERRALS

Normally a flat fee agency or letter writing service will be happy to refer the claim to a full service collection agency or to an attorney if the debt remains unpaid at the end of the collection letter cycle.

However, in some instances the affiliated companies to whom claims are to be referred if payment is not received an unusually high contingent collection fee. Some justify this high fees as being based on the prevailing rate for a so-called "second placements" of a delinquent debt.

Some critics of cut rate collection agencies suggest that the low rate is in fact a loss leader—a way to attract claims for placement with the affiliated full service collection agency or attorney.

DETERMINE THE MINIMUM SIZE CLAIM THE AGENCY WILL ACCEPT

The creditor should always ask about the minimum size claim the agency will accept. Some agencies are not interested in receiving claims valued at less than $1,000. In this scenario, if the average claim a creditor places is $500 the credit manager needs to find another agency that will actively pursue $500 claims. It may take some looking to find that agency, but the time spent finding the right agency will be time well spent.

HOW TO NEGOTIATE A BETTER RATE

One of the best kept secrets about commercial collections is that rates are negotiable. The collection business is extremely competitive, and established collection agencies must constantly deal with new competitors using lower contingent collection rates to attract new clients and gain market share.

The key is not to expect that a reputable, full service collection agency charging a 15% to 20% collection fee to match a 10% fee offered by a start up company. Instead, the credit manager can use a written quote of 10% as leverage to extract certain price concessions on contingent collections from their preferred collection agency.

The best time to discuss rates is before placing an account with an agency. On larger claims, it is a good idea to ask two or more agencies to bid for the claim. Doing so is neither illegal nor unethical, although the collection agency representatives will sometimes try to make the credit manager feel that their request for a bid is somehow inappropriate. Credit managers should not be surprised if one or more collection agencies refuse to get into a bidding war for a particular claim—but rest assured that with limited effort the credit manager will find a reputable collection agency willing to negotiate their contingent collection fee—especially as a way to invite a new client to try their services.

QUESTIONS TO ASK A PROSPECTIVE COLLECTION AGENCY

If the credit manager is seriously considering giving some business to a new collection agency, there are a number of questions that must be answered before making the decision. The most important questions are these:

(1) How often do you remit payments on money recovered from debtors? Often collection agencies remit payment once a month. For example, collection agencies might have the following policy: Funds recovered will be remitted to the creditor by the fifteenth day of the month following collection. This is a point the creditor might want to negotiate with the collection agency. Being paid once a month [on the fifteenth] means the agency is holding on to the creditor's money for an average of 22.5 days.

(2) How often will you make progress reports on the status of your collection efforts? A professionally managed collection agency will normally provide their clients with written summaries of their collection efforts on a monthly basis or as often as required.

(3) How do you collect accounts? Creditors need to know if the collection agency will send a collector to visit the debtor, or call the debtor or send a series of collection letters. A collection agency that does nothing more than write a series of collection letters is far less likely to collect than an agency that calls or visits the debtor personally.

(4) How long will you work on an account before recommending that the account be placed for collection? Different agencies have different schedules. You need to know the minimum and maximum amount of time the agency will devote to its own "in-house" collection efforts.

(5) If your in-house collection efforts do not work, what happens next with the claim? Normally, the collection agency will notify the creditor within 90 days of receiving a placement to indicate whether or not the agency believes the debt is collectable. If the agency cannot collect the debt, they will normally make a recommendation about whether or not the claim should be referred to an attorney. If the creditor wishes, the agency normally has a business relationship with collection attornies and can arrange to transfer claim to an attorney.

(6) How would funds received from your collection efforts on our behalf segregated from other cash? Ideally, the collection agency will maintain a separate trust account in which remittances from debtors are kept. Collection agencies are acting in a fiduciary capacity, and customers have a right to know how their money is being safeguarded.

TIP: Here are some ideas for dealing with unsolicited and unwanted calls from new collection agencies prospecting for new business.

(1) Interrupt the caller; tell them you aren't interested. Thank them, and hang up.

(2)   Ask if you can put them on hold and leave them on hold.

(3)   Instruct your subordinates not to forward calls from collection agencies to you.

(4)   Give your switchboard operators the same message.

(5)   Only speak with or meet with potential suppliers of collection services if you are dissatisfied with the current state of affairs and need to consider a new collection agency or collection attorney.

HOW TO EVALUATE THE PERFORMANCE OF A COLLECTION AGENCY OR COLLECTION ATTORNEY

Most collection agencies and collection attorneys will provide the credit manager with monthly updates. This information can be used to evaluate the progress the third party is making on current claim placements, and to help evaluate overall performance.

Typically, credit managers receive a quarterly report from their collection agencies and/or collection attorneys that provides the following information:

- The date the claim was placed
- debtor name
- amount of the claim
- amount collected to date
- status of the claim

No third party collector will be successful in collecting on every claim. There are a number of factors that determine the collectability of a claim placed with an agency, so it is difficult to measure head to head one agency's performance against another's. For example, if two different claims are placed the same day with two different debt collectors from two different debtors the fundamental collectability of those two claims will always be different.

WHEN TO PLACE AN ACCOUNT FOR COLLECTION

It is always difficult to know exactly when to place an account for collection. There is a natural tendency not to want to give up on a delinquent account—especially on a long term customer. On the other hand, credit professionals need to avoid falling into a trap of hoping that a delinquent debtor will somehow pull out of a financial dive at the last moment.

Some credit policies state that an account should be placed with a third party for collection when the credit manager feels that "they are no longer making progress toward clearing the past due balance." Unfortunately, that description is too vague, and may result in accounts being placed for collection too quickly or too slowly. Creditors can gauge whether or not to place an account for collection by using the following checklist:

A CHECKLIST OF WHEN TO PLACE AN ACCOUNT FOR COLLECTION

It is critical to know when to place an account for collection. The more of the following statements are true, the more appropriate it is to place an account for collection immediately:

- The customer has made and broken two or more payment commitments.
- The account is 90 days or more past due.
- The customer promised to pay one amount, but paid a lesser amount.
- After numerous conversations and commitments, the customer now disputes the validity of the balance due.
- Other creditors have placed the account for collection or have sued the company.
- Trade clearance reports show a significant slowdown in payments to all creditors.
- The customer has bounced at least one check, and has not replaced it.
- The customer indicates that it is "changing banks."
- The customer will no longer take your calls, and refuses to return your messages.
- You are unable to reach a decision maker and are forced to deal only with clerks.
- Key personnel within the debtor company are leaving.
- You learn the business is for sale, or that it was recently sold.
- The debtor company has filed a Bulk Transfer notice.
- The debtor offers a payment plan, but refuses to put the offer or their commitment in writing.
- The phone is disconnected, or the customer moved without telling you.
- The salesperson handling the account indicates they are unable to help you in any way to collect the outstanding debt.

THE POINT OF DIMINISHING RETURNS IN COLLECTIONS

Experienced credit managers know that at some point their collection efforts reach a point of diminishing returns in which trying to extract payment is no longer productive or cost effective. At that point, experienced credit managers know they must make their final demand for payment and if the debtor does not respond they must refer the account to a third party for collection.

The decision to place an account with a third party should be made only by the credit manager. Using third party contingency based collection agents is expensive. Companies can expect to pay at least ten percent of everything collected, and contingent collection rates of 20% or even 30% are not uncommon.

COLLECTION TIP: When a dispute arises with a customer, negotiate first and litigate last. Litigation is expensive and time consuming. Even if you are convinced your company is completely right and the customer is completely wrong, the credit manager must perform a cost/benefit analysis to see if a negotiated settlement is a better option than a lawsuit.

DISPUTED BALANCES

One of the biggest problems that collection agencies face is a situation in which a client places a debtor company for collection knowing that a dispute exists. A collection agency is not a mediator or an arbitrator. If a legitimate dispute exists, a collection agency is unlikely to be able to convince customers to pay a disputed balance. In addition:

- If the credit manager thought they would save the cost of hiring an attorney to litigate the dispute, they were probably mistaken.

- If the credit manager thought that the client would be intimidated into paying the legitimate dispute, they were probably wrong.

- If the company wanted to preserve any goodwill, but placed the account for collection anyway—despite knowing about the dispute—chances are good that (a) the matter will not be resolved with and through the collection agency, and (b) the customer will almost certainly not buy from the creditor again.

It is unwise to place an account for collection when a dispute exists. From the creditor's perspective, the outcome is normally unsatisfactory.

STEPS TO TAKE BEFORE PLACING AN ACCOUNT FOR COLLECTION

Before placing the account for collection, it is a good idea to take the following steps:

(1) Notify the salesperson and allow him or her to contact the customer's purchasing department, and to inform the purchasing manager that the account will be placed for collection unless the problem is resolved. Occasionally, the personal rapport the salesperson has with the customer will influence the customer to address and resolve a collection problem before it results in the account being referred to a third party.

(2) Before placing an account for collection, it is appropriate to send a letter to the President of the debtor company informing him or her of the collection problem, and inviting the company President assist in getting the problem resolved before a third party is involved.

CHOOSING THE RIGHT COLLECTION AGENCY

All collection agencies are not created equal. The kind of agency you choose to represent your company is a reflection on you as the credit manager. A professionally run collection agency will normally represent your company well, while an unprofessional, unethical, and unlicensed collection agency could damage your reputation as well as your ability to collect.

WORKING WITH YOUR COLLECTION AGENCY

It may seem strange or counter-intuitive, but one of the biggest complaints that collection agencies have is that some creditors fail to give the agency the information and the documentation they need.

For example, creditors may not respond promptly to a collection agency's request for invoice copies, proof of delivery or other documents. As a result, momentum may be lost. The solution to the "problem" is obvious. Give the collection agency whatever information or documentation they require (as long as it is not confidential) to assist the agency in its collection efforts.

DIRECT NEGOTIATIONS WITH THE DEBTOR

A creditor may actually undermine the collection agency's efforts by negotiating directly with the debtor after the account has been placed with the collection agency. Creditors often fail to realize the debtor may be engaging in yet another delaying tactic, and that it is highly probable that the only reason the debtor contacted the creditor was that the collection agency was having the desired effect. The solution is to refer the debtor back to the collection agency with whon the claim was placed.

WHAT ABOUT RETURNS?

Sometimes, a debtor placed for collection will propose that the creditor accepts a return of product in partial or full settlement of the outstanding balance. A reputable collection agency will present its client with this type of non-cash settlement proposal. Since collection agencies are paid on a contingency basis, most negotiate in advance to receive a portion [for example half] of their collection fee if the debtor returns goods in settlement of the debt.

Without this type of arrangement in place, the third party collection agency would not be motivated to negotiate settlements that called for anything other than cash payment.

CHAPTER 29

U SING COLLECTION ATTORNEYS

There is an old rule in credit management: "Always negotiate first and litigate last."

If a creditor determines it is unable to collect money legitimately owed by a delinquent debtor, the creditor has a handful of options that include:

(1) Placing the account to a Collection Agency

(2) Asking their corporate counsel to send a demand letter, or

(3) Filing a claim in small claims court, if the debtor is geographically close and the balance due is near or below the jurisdictional dollar limit,

(4) Referring the matter to an outside collection attorney

The use of a third party to assist with collections is always considered to be a last resort among professional credit managers. Experienced credit managers do not place an account for collection simply because the account has become a certain number of days past due. Instead, they consider the matter in its totality and look for reasons for and against placing the account with a third party. If the credit manager believes the debt cannot be collected any other way, then they have no alternative but to use a collection agency or a collection attorney.

**CHECKLIST FOR PLACING AN ACCOUNT
WITH A THIRD PARTY FOR COLLECTION**

The more of the following statements are true, the more likely it is that an account shoul be placed with a third party for collection:

- The customer has already made and then broken two or more payment commitments.
- The customer will not take your calls or return your messages.
- It has been more than a month since the account's last payment.
- Other vendors have already placed the account for collection.
- The customer's flooring company is no longer authorizing new purchases.
- One or more credit insurance companies have canceled coverage on the account.
- The customer is the subject of a "high risk alert."
- Key personnel are leaving the company.

SIMILARITIES BETWEEN COLLECTION AGENCIES AND COLLECTION ATTORNEYS

Most collection agencies and most collection attorneys work on a contingency basis—meaning that if there is no collection there is no fee to the creditor. As is the case with contingency based collection agencies, collection attorneys normally require no up front fees or membership fees. Attorneys' collection rates vary. Some collection attorneys' rates are in the 15% to 20% range, which is competitive with many collection agencies. Other collection attorneys have non contingent fees in the 30% range or higher.

Just as with a collection agency, the credit professional should not consider price to be the sole determining factor in selecting a collection attorney. As with most other purchases made by companies, the best choice is to select a cost effective collection attorney, not the lowest cost law firm. Just as is the case with collection agencies, some collection attorneys will negotiate rates for a customer that gives the attorney the majority of their collection business, or if the credit manager has a particularly large claim that they need to place.

Just as with a collection agency, there is nothing unethical or illegal about negotiating collection rates. If a lawsuit becomes necessary, the collection attorney will require that the creditor pay the suit filing fee. The objective of a suit filing fee, which the creditor company must pay, is to discourage commencement of frivolous lawsuits by attorneys.

QUESTIONS TO ASK A COLLECTION ATTORNEY

Before placing an account with any third party, there are specific questions the credit manager should ask or be given the answers to. As it relates to placing a claim with a collection attorney, the credit manager would need to know:

- The exact fee structure

- The process the attorney would use to try to collect the debt.

- At what point the account would be considered for litigation.

- Whether or not the creditor company would be contacted for permission to initiate a lawsuit.

- If litigation were recommended and were initiated, what additional fees would the creditor company be responsible for?

- What the minimum claim is that the attorney will accept and work actively?

- How frequently will the attorney report progress of accounts referred to him or her, and

- What, if any, alternatives are there to a contingency fee based collection arrangement.

Just as when the credit manager is purchasing any other good or service for the credit department, it is important to ask the right questions to enable the credit manager [as the buyer] to obtain the type of service that works best for the credit department and for the company.

USING IN HOUSE ATTORNEYS

The majority of companies in America do not have in-house counsel. However, many have on retainer or hired on an hourly basis an independent attorney. Whether a company works with an independent attorney or has in house counsel, it is always a good idea to refer collection issues to that attorney first. If the debtor is waiting to see what the creditor decides to do about a past due balance and receives a letter from an attorney rather than a call from a collection agency, the difference in approach may result in a different outcome—specifically the payment of the outstanding debt. Even using an independent attorney, the cost of generating what amounts to a form demand letter should be minimal. If the debtor does not respond within the time line specified in the attorney's letter, the creditor has no choice but to refer the account to wherever it can be handled most cost-effectively.

MISAPPROPRIATION OF RECOVERED FUNDS

One of the concerns that credit managers have is that their third party collector should promptly forward any recoveries to them [less their contingent collection fee]. There have been a number if instances in which a dishonest collection agency has recovered monies owed to its clients and simply kept the money. Credit managers should know that attorneys are required under their Rules of Professional Conduct to place payments received from debtors in a trust or escrow account.

While is not inconceivable, it is probably far less likely that a collection attorney would embezzle or misappropriate a recovery made from a debtor than it would be for a collection agency with the same number of employees to misappropriate money owed to their clients [the creditors].

WHAT EXACTLY IS A COLLECTION ATTORNEY?

Lawyers do not "major" in collection litigation in law school. Collection attorneys are attorneys who choose to specialize in protecting creditor rights. Any licensed attorney can initiate civil litigation over an unpaid debt. In fact, relative to some of the cases that attorneys handle, litigation over an unpaid debt for goods sold on open account credit terms is considered quite simple.

However, the Commercial Law League of America's Academy of Commercial and Bankruptcy Law Specialists has joined forces with the American Bankruptcy Board of Certification to form the American Board of Certification. This linkage has created approximately 1,000 attorneys in the United States certified in the area of creditors' rights, business bankruptcy, and consumer bankruptcy. On line access to the Creditors' Rights Section Member Listing for the Commercial Law League of America is available at no charge, on line, at URL: http://clla.org.crsmemberlist.html.

CREATIVE BILLING OPTIONS

A limited number of collection attorneys offer a creative billing approach. Rather than either a straight hourly charges; or a straight contingency fee for their professional collection services, a small number of attorney who specialize in commercial collection will offer some customers a hybrid collection fee. The hybrid collection fee involves offering clients a lower hourly fee plus a smaller than normal percentage of anything collected from a debtor placed for collection with the law firm.

THE LITIGATION THREAT

Litigation is not a panacea for a creditor's collection problems. Referring a delinquent account to an attorney does not guarantee payment, and it certainly does not guarantee a quick resolution to the problem. If it becomes necessary to file suit, the civil litigation process is lengthy, complex, time-consuming and costly. Also, any time a creditor files a lawsuit the debtor may file a counter claim or assert a defense. Even if the creditor believes they have an "open and shut case" the outcome of a case is never a certainly until the Court renders its verdict.

Having described some of the pitfalls of collection litigation, one of the advantages of placing an account with an attorney is psychological. For example, if a debtor has been contacted on numerous occasions by collection agencies in the past, they may feel fairly comfortable that they understand how collection agencies work. The debtor might assume that they have at least a month with the collection agency before the discussion with the collector turns to litigation. However, if a creditor company refers a debtor directly to an attorney, the debtor may not be able to predict the next step in the process and this uncertainty may result in payment.

THE TWO STEP LITIGATION PROCESS

When a collection agency cannot persuade a debtor to pay voluntarily, the collection agency has no choice but to recommend to the creditor company that:

- The account be considered uncollectable and written off, or
- That the delinquent account be referred to a collection attorney for appropriate action.

The disadvantage of using a collection agency is that a sophisticated debtor will understand that there is nothing that a collection agency can do to force a delinquent customer to pay its debts since the collection agency cannot initiate legal proceedings. Therefore, for the chronic slow pay account and for the customer in a financial crisis, it is simply a wasted step to place the account with a collection agency.

HOW COLLECTION ATTORNEYS WORK

Collection attorneys normally work this way: After receiving the claim from either directly from the creditor company, of in the alternative through a collection agency [and assuming the creditor and the attorney have agreed on a fee structure — hourly, contingency, or a combination of both] the attorney will contact the debtor. This is often done by certified mail. The attorney's letter will state:

- the attorney has been engaged by the creditor
- the amount of money owed according to the creditor
- that the amount due must be paid immediately
- that the debtor or its attorney is welcome to call the creditor to discuss the problem

Assuming the debtor does not pay within a short period of time [such as seven working days] the collection attorney would either issue a follow up letter — or a final demand letter. If the attorney sends a second reminder, that letter would also be sent by certified mail to the President of the company and it would normally state:

- the debtor failed to contact the creditor or the attorney
- the balance in question remains unpaid

- the debtor has apparently failed to pay, and/or failed to make any necessary arrangements to pay
- that a lawsuit is imminent and that payment must be received in 72 hours [or less].

If there is a third letter, it is normally the attorney's final notice. If that letter fails to generate payment, the attorney will then contact his or her client [the creditor] to:

(1) inform the creditor of their efforts to date, and the debtor's response [if any]
(2) recommend for or against filing a lawsuit
(3) present the creditor with a short list of options and alternatives
(4) review the costs of litigating the dispute from this point forward

THE ASSET SEARCH

Before spending a lot of time and effort preparing to litigate, an attorney might recommend that the creditor consider paying for an asset search to determine whether or not the debtor has the ability to pay the debt. The reason is simple - a judgment against a company or an individual that is no longer in business or has no assets is worthless. If a lawsuit were filed, the creditor [now the judgment creditor] might become a lien creditor, but unless specific assets found and targeted then the judgment against the defendant isn't worth the paper ii is printed on, and it certainly is not worth the filing fee, the court costs, the creditor's time, and the attorney's fees.

If no ssets are found, the decision about whether or not to go forward is relatively easy.

COURT COSTS

In the event that a creditor opts to file a civil litigation claim the creditor will have to advance the court costs and/or the filing fee. In many jurisdictions, attorneys are prohibited from paying court costs or filing fees. Legislators, many of whom are lawyers themselves, reasoned that requiring the plaintiff rather than their attorney to pay the suit filing fee would tend to reduce the number of frivolous lawsuits filed.

TIP:. Before sending an attorney Court costs and/or a suit fee, make certain that the debtor company is still in business. There is no use throwing good money after bad.

FACILITATING COLLECTIONS

If a creditor intends to use collection attorneys to supplement their own in-house collection efforts then the credit manager should make certain that the attorney has as much help as possible. The tools that can help in the attorney's collection efforts include:

- A signed credit application form including a signed statement about venue for litigation, and an agreement that the debtor / applicant will pay reasonable attorney's fees should it become necessary to litigate for the creditor to get paid. [The credit application is not simply a way to gather information about an application; it is [or should be] a contract that the seller and their attorney can use to their advantage if litigation becomes necessary.] In some States, a creditor may not recover attorney's fees in collection litigation. In others, the creditor may do so only if the attorneys fees are specifically included in the contract between the buyer and the seller [the credit application form is the contract].

- A personal guaranty from one or more of the individuals that own or manage the business. If a collection attorney is required to collect an unpaid balance the existence of a personal guaranty will make the attorney's call and correspondence more compelling to the individual(s) who signed the guaranty.

- If the debtor becomes delinquent and it is agreed that the debtor will be allowed to pay the creditor on an installment plan, that agreement should be documented in writing in the form of a Promissory Note. At the very least, the debtor should be required to send the creditor an acknowledgment of the debt on the debtor's company letterhead and signed by an officer or owner of the company. By reducing agreements to writing, it makes it far more difficult for the debtor to later assert some sort of defense or counterclaim if it becomes necessary to file a lawsuit to get paid.

- Make certain that the credit application, the invoices, dunning notices, statements and other documents generated all state the company's policy of charging interest on past due balances and a handling fee on returned checks. That way, if litigation becomes necessary the attorney can prove to the Court that interest on the past due balance was always contemplated as part of the contract between the buyer and the seller. The rate of interest that a creditor can charge varies from State to State.

- Keep photocopies of checks on hand to identify the customer's bank account in case it should become necessary to obtain a lien against that account.

- If the creditor has gone to the time and the trouble to obtain and to perfect a security interest, then the creditor must make certain that the security interest remains enforceable. For example, the creditor must file a continuation statement before the security interest expires, and must be certain to amend the financing statement if the debtor name changes or the pledged collateral moves. The goal is to make certain the creditor remains perfected in case the creditor's attorney needs to assert the company's rights as a secured creditor.

- Credit professionals must resist the temptation to hold onto an account for too long hoping that somehow the debtor will manage to turn around their financial problems and pay the creditor. Studies show that the longer a creditor holds a delinquent account in house [rather than placing it with a competent third party for collection] the lower the likely recovery will be. At about 90 days past due, the recovery percentage starts dropping off dramatically.

- Be aware that each State establishes a Statute of Limitations on debts—meaning that if a creditor company does not file suit to recover the past due balance within that statutory period that they will be prevented from doing so ever.

- If the case goes to trial, it will probably become necessary to prove that the debt is owed. That typically requires proving delivery of the merchandise. Credit managers should be certain to order proof of delivery against past due balances before time expires for them to do so. Typically, carriers allow shippers no more than nine months to order proof of delivery—and depending on their contract with the shipper this window could be far shorter than 9 months.

COMPARING COLLECTION ATTORNEYS TO COLLECTION AGENCIES

If a collection attorney were asked to explain why using an attorney is preferable to a collection agency, he or she would probably state that the creditor has a greater likelihood of intimidating the debtor into paying the debt by using an attorney. The attorney would probably also point out that if the collection effort is going nowhere the attorney has less of an incentive to keep working the debt and more of an incentive to file suit to collect. The implication being that collection agencies tend to hold accounts placed in house because they would prefer not to have to share the contingent collection fee with an attorney as they must do if their in house collection efforts fail.

The attorney would probably indicate that occasionally even a single demand letter from a law firm will change the debtor's mind about withholding payment.

Undoubtedly, collection agencies would point out that they sometimes get quick results as well. A collection agency would probably suggest that placing an account with an agency offers more flexibility and is more cost-effective. The collection agency would undoubtedly point out these facts:

- Using an agency causes less damage to the business relationship than using an attorney.

- In the event the collection agency is unable to collect from a delinquent debtor, with the creditor's approval the account will be referred to a collection attorney willing to work on a contingency basis.

- The collection agency continues to monitor and manage the process even after an attorney, and the collection agency will provide the creditor with periodic updates about the collection process.

Unfortunately, when an account is forwarded from a collection agency to a collection attorney the contingent collection rate normally goes up. This makes it difficult to measure a collection agency and a collection attorney's rates head to head. It would not be uncommon for the collection agency's rates to be below those contingent collection rates charged by attorney while the account was being collected in house, but for the collection agency's contingent collection rate or fee to be equal to or higher than an independent collection attorney's contingent collection fees if and when the collection agency refers that account to a collection attorney.

The only time an independent collection attorney's contingent rate is likely to change is if the debtor files a counter-claim. However, a collection agency's contingent rates also go up if the debtor files a counter-claim.

Credit managers are required to safeguard their company's investment in accounts receivable. Since no one can predict the future with certainty, the decisions that credit managers make every day will sooner or later result in an unpaid and uncollectable balance. When that happens, and consistent with the credit manager's goal of safeguarding the company's accounts receivable, the credit manager will have no choice but to place certain accounts with a third party for collection.

The credit manager does have a choice about which third party an account should be placed with. Before any decision is made, the company's in-house counsel or the company's independent counsel should always generate a final demand letter. This step is cost effective since it costs very little to generate a demand letter. Even if this process was effective in one situation out of twenty, for most companies the payback on such a simple idea as this would be tremendous.

Some credit managers develop guidelines or decision rules to determine whether an account should be referred to a collection agency or to a collection attorney. Some of those decision rules might include:

- If the account has an undisputed past due balance in excess of $25,000 refer the matter to an attorney for collection litigation on an hourly basis.

- If the debtor has an undisputed past due balance in excess of $20,000 supported by a Promissory Note and / or the personal guaranty of the owner of the company and the balance due is not in dispute then refer the mater to an attorney on an hourly basis, otherwise

- If the past due balance is past due and less than $20,000 and is not supported by any contract or writing then refer the account to a collection agency—except when the customer has indicated that a dispute exists in which case the account should be referred to a collection attorney on a contingent fee basis.

- If the account is out of business and owes less than $10,000 it should be referred to a collection agency. If it owes more than $10,000 it should be referred to a collection attorney.

These are examples of decision rules. This is not intended to be the comprehensive list. Each credit manager must create their own rules, which are unique to their firm and are based on the dollar amounts and other factors important to each firm.

SUMMARY

There is a lively debate among credit professionals about whether using a collection agency or a collection attorney yields the best results. Unfortunately, there has been no definitive study completed on this issue, and the anecdotal information makes it difficult to tell whether agencies or attorneys are the most cost effective.

What is certain is this: Each creditor company is unique, each debtor is unique, each set of facts surrounding a past due balance is unique and therefore every decision about whether to use an attorney or an agency depends on the facts surrounding that situation. The use of an attorney rather than a collection agency adds certain credibility to the collection process. However, whether that credibility justifies the higher contingent collection fees [assuming the attorney's contingent collection fees are higher] depends on whether the added credibility translates into more successful collection efforts.

CHAPTER 30

CREDIT AND THE LAW

Federal and state laws protect the rights of creditors to receive payment for merchandise delivered to customers. Federal and state laws also protect the rights of buyers and applicants for credit. In doing so, these federal and state laws limit the actions that can be taken by a creditor against a debtor.

The limitations on the actions and activities of the credit department are of particular concern to credit professionals. Under the American system of civil and criminal laws, ignorance of the law is not a valid excuse for breaking the law. For example, there are two federal laws that forbid sellers from participating in boycotts organized by foreign governments that the United States government does not support. The fact that the seller or the credit department was not aware of these laws does not change the fact that the seller broke the law and may be subject to penalties as provided in the Export Administration Act.

THE UNIFORM COMMERCIAL CODE

In the United States, every state has adopted the Uniform Commercial Code [UCC]; a codification of substantial portions of commercial law. The UCC involves a series of rules governing the sale and payment of goods. The UCC is divided into nine articles. They are:

Article 1. A general overview of the UCC

Article 2. Contracts for the sale and purchase of goods

Article 3. Commercial paper and other negotiable instruments

Article 4. Bank deposits and the collection of checks

Article 5. Domestic and foreign letters of credit and their negotiation

Article 6. Bulk transfers and the rights of creditors

Article 7. Warehouse receipts and other documents of title

Article 8. Securities

Article 9. Secured transactions, security interests and priorities among secured creditors

At least half of these nine Articles relate to the day to day operations of most credit departments. For this reason, most credit managers need to have a working knowledge of at least Articles 2, 3, 4, 5, 6, and 9 of the UCC..

DIRECT REGULATION OF THE COMMERCIAL CREDIT DECISION-MAKING PROCESS

Commercial credit granting and collection processes are far less carefully regulated than consumer credit and collection processes. Both federal and state legislatures have consistently rejected proposals to limit a creditor's discretion in determining whether or not to extend credit to another business entity—aside from requiring that the decision not be based on age, race, sex, religion, marital status or national origin of the owners of officers of that business. Experts have convinced lawmakers that over-regulating the process of business to business credit granting would result in fewer sellers offering open account terms.

The federal Equal Credit Opportunity Act (ECOA) requires that all credit applicants be considered on the basis of their actual qualifications for credit. The ECOA also forbids discrimination on the basis of certain personal characteristics such as marital status, sex, race, national origin or religion. The ECOA does not guarantee that a commercial or consumer applicant will be granted credit terms, it simply provides an assurance that the decision not to extend credit will not be based on preconceptions and prejudice.

Provided that credit granters do not discriminate against an applicant based on one of the characteristics or attributes protected by the ECOA, companies are free to establish their own standards about which applicants will and will not be offered open account terms. The law does not require any standardization in the credit decision making process. For example, a customer might apply to two suppliers who happen to be competitors. The customer might be asked to provide exactly the same information to each supplier, and after evaluating the application one supplier might offer the application open account credit terms while the other supplier might choose not to do so. No laws were violated. Creditors are free to establish their own policies about granting credit.

458

WHAT IS CONSUMER CREDIT?

Consumer credit involves loans or credit granted to individuals for the purchase of goods and services primarily for personal, family or household use. Laws governing consumer credit granting are far more complex than the laws governing the commercial credit granting process.

CREDIT AND ANTITRUST LAWS

Federal and state antitrust laws are intended to prevent businesses from price-fixing and other secret and illegal agreements that tend to circumvent the laws of supply and demand, giving companies engaged in these illegal activities a competitive advantage. Anti-competitive activities ultimately damage the consumer and result in higher prices, poorer quality, and a smaller selection.

Antitrust laws have existed in the United States for more than six decades. The four most important federal antitrust laws are:

(1)   The Sherman Act
(2)   The Clayton
(3)   The Robinson-Patman Act
(4)   The Federal Trade Commission Act

These laws promote and protect the competitive process. The U.S. Department of Justice, and the Federal Trade Commission share responsibility for enforcing laws that promote free and open competition. The Justice Department prosecutes serious and willful violations of the various federal antitrust laws using the criminal statutes. When criminal prosecution is not considered appropriate, the Justice Department may institute civil action seeking a court order forbidding future violations of the law, and requiring steps be taken to remedy the effects of past anti-competitive actions.

The Federal Trade Commission [FTC] was established in 1914 by the Congress to enforce the Federal Trade Commission Act as well as the Clayton Act. The FTC's Bureau of Competition seeks to prevent businesses from engaging in practices that unlawfully restrain trade in violation of federal law. The FTC's goal is to create a marketplace in which consumers are offered a larger variety of higher quality goods and services at a lower prices. Often, the FTC works with companies it suspects of unfair competitive practices to reach consent decrees in which the company agrees not to take certain actions in the future. The consent decree might also include requirements that the company make amends for past practices by taking certain affirmative steps—such as lowering its prices, or offering certain customers rebates.

THE SHERMAN ACT AND THE CLAYTON ACT

The Sherman Act was the first antitrust law passed by the federal government. It was written to prevent the establishment of monopolies and combinations that result in unfair restraints on trade. The Sherman Act outlaws "every contract, combination or conspiracy in restraint of trade." The Sherman Act makes it illegal for a company to monopolize, or attempt to monopolize trade or commerce.

Sellers should be aware that an express or implied agreement that limits or restrains trade, such as price fixing, is a per se violation of the Sherman Act. An agreement among two competitors that each will limit a delinquent customer to a $10,000 credit limit would almost certainly be a violation of the provisions of the Sherman Act.

The Clayton Act prohibits mergers and acquisitions when the effect may be to substantially lesser competition, or tend to create a monopoly.

THE ROBINSON-PATMAN ACT

The Robinson-Patman Act is intended to prevent discriminatory pricing arrangements. Specifically, the Robinson-Patman Act makes it illegal:

> "To discriminate in price between different purchasers of commodities of like grade and quality, where the effect of such discrimination may be to substantially lessen competition..."

Under the Robinson-Patman Act, price discrimination has been identified as including any of the following business practices:

- Offering different prices to purchasers of like grade and quality and quantity of products

- Offering "like" customers different credit terms [terms of sale].

- Offering "like" customers different allowances or programs when those programs or allowances result in price discrimination. Examples of such programs would include cash discounts, volume rebates, marketing allowance programs, slotting allowance programs, Spiffs, and co-op advertising programs.

- Any agreement among competitors to set or fix the terms of sale to a particular customer or group of customers constitutes illegal price fixing.

Specific provisions of the Robinson-Patman Act are applicable to the actions of the credit department. Here is a simple example:

Two "like" companies are offered Net 30-day term of sale. One is offered no cash discount. The other is offered a 5% cash discount. The company offered the 5% discount has in effect a 5% price advantage over the other company.

This may be a violation of the Robinson-Patman Act [the Act]. Credit managers should be aware that violation of federal antitrust laws carry both civil and criminal penalties are intended to dissuade companies from engaging in illegal activities. Many companies are either unaware of their duties under the Act, or choose to ignore the law.

One of the most common excuses heard is that they are not treating "like" customers differently because no two customers are exactly alike. That particular argument is not reasonable or rational. In point of fact, no two companies can or will ever be exactly alike.

There are a number of ways the seller can justify price variances between customers. For example, if the seller can prove that it was attempting to meet a competitor's price, then there is no violation of the Act. Similarly, if the price variances can be justified by documenting different costs of dealing with different customers then there is no violation of the law.

It is not illegal to offer different customers different terms of sale or different credit limits based on their creditworthiness. However, the decision about what terms of sale each customer will be offered must be based on the creditworthiness of the applicant, and credit terms cannot be used deliberately to give a competitive advantage to a favored customer.

THE FEDERAL TRADE COMMISSION ACT.

The Federal Trade Commission Act [the FTC Act] was passed in 1914. It is the most far reaching of the federal antitrust laws. The FTC Act states that all unfair methods of competition, and all deceptive acts and practices affecting commerce are unlawful. The FTC Act does not define the term "unfair." The kinds of activities that are "unfair" are left to the discretion of the FTC and the Courts.

DEFAMATION

Defamation involves an act of communication that causes someone to be ridiculed or shamed, to be held in contempt, or lowered in esteem, or to lose economic or employment status, or to otherwise suffer a damaged reputation. Defamation can occur orally, or in writing. Libel involves written defamation of character, while slander involves verbal defamation.

Credit managers need to recognize that credit inquiries are a ticking time bomb for the creditors providing the reference. If the creditor responds to a credit inquiry with incorrect information if the customer finds out about the mistake they are unlikely to be pleased. However, a far more serious situation can occur when a representative of the credit department defames a customer. A defamatory statement could be made jokingly. For example, the statements:

"This customer is as Dishonest as the day is long" or

"How do you know this customer is lying? His lips are moving!" might be meant in jest but are defamatory and actionable.

Defamation involves making a statement that damages the reputation of a third party. Defamation involves information that is:

- The information is delivered to a third party
- False, and the party disseminating the information knew it to be false
- Clearly defamatory, such as the statement above suggesting that the every word the customer utters is a lie.

Truth is a complete defense against a charge of defamation. Therefore, it would not be defamation to present a frank and honest credit rating that casts the customer as a poor credit risk. To protect the company against charges of defamation, creditors *must* only provide factual, historical information about the customer.

Irrespective of the pressure they may be under to provide additional information, or to make a recommendation for or against the applicant company, the person answering credit inquiries must be trained to provide only this information:

- The date the account was opened
- The customer's high credit [if the computer system provides this information—some systems do not]
- The terms of sale
- The balance owed
- The amount past due
- How far past due
- The normal manner of payment [ideally, a weighted average days to pay should be provided]
- Whether or not the debt is secured

Verbal defamation, slander, might occur during industry credit group meeting. Industry credit groups encourage the free and open exchange of factual information, but people can get carried away. Credit professionals should always obey the group rules and by-laws, and stick to the facts when speaking to the credit group.

DISCRIMINATION IN CREDIT GRANTING

The Federal Trade Commission enforces each of the following laws governing credit granting:

- The Equal Credit Opportunity Act
- The Fair Credit Reporting Act
- The Fair Debt Collection Practices Act

The Equal Credit Opportunity Act [the ECOA] was created to promote the availability of credit without regard to race, color, national origin, creed, sex, and marital status. The ECOA governs and controls both consumer and commercial credit granting. The Equal Credit Opportunity Act requires that if an applicant is denied credit terms and requests in writing the reason or reasons for their denial that the creditor must respond in writing to that inquiry within 30 days.

The Fair Credit Reporting Act [the FCRA] requires commercial credit reporting agencies to take reasonable steps to ensure that consumer credit reports are accurate. It also requires that consumers [as opposed to business credit applicants] be given specific information about their right to inspect and to correct any errors found in their personal credit report.

The Fair Debt Collection Practices Act [the FDCPA] describes the ways in which a commercial collection agency may attempt to collect a debt owed by a consumer.

RULES RELATING TO CO-SIGNERS

In an effort to protect individual consumers, The Federal Trade Commission requires that all potential co-signers be given the following notice before co-signing on behalf of an individual for a consumer debt:

"You are being asked to guarantee this debt. Think carefully before you do. If the borrower doesn't pay the debt, you will have to. Be sure you can afford to pay if you have to, and if you do indeed want to accept this responsibility. You may have to pay the full amount of the debt if the borrower does not pay. You may also have to pay late fees or collection costs, which increases this amount. The creditor can use the same collection methods against you as the borrower, such as suing you, garnishing your wages, etc. If this debt is even in default, the fact may become part of your credit record. Consider the following: some studies indicate that, with certain types of loans, three out of four co-signers are asked to repay the loan. You will be asked to take a risk that a professional lender will not take. And if you decide to co-sign a loan, be sure you get copies of all important papers and consider asking the lender to inform you if the borrower misses a payment, thereby giving you time to resolve the problem before it gets out of hand."

Typically, a co-signer is severally liable for the debt, meaning that the co-signer separately promises to pay the entire debt irrespective of the actions of the original debtor and/or the creditor's inability to collect from that debtor.

TITLE

Disputes that result in non-payment often arise involving goods lost or damaged in transit. The Uniform Commercial Code [UCC] addresses this issue in two ways. The first relates to title. The UCC provides that *if* the contract between the buyer and seller specifies that title passes from the seller to the buyer when the goods are delivered to the carrier then clearly the risk of loss or damage in transit belongs to the buyer. On the other hand, if the contract between the buyer and the seller states that title passes from the seller to the buyer when the goods are physically delivered then the seller is responsible for loss or damage in transit.

Because of these rules, it is important that the contract is specific about where title passes. If the seller is responsible for loss or damage in transit, then it may want to purchase transit insurance. If the buyer is responsible, it may want to purchase a transit insurance policy for itself, or the buyer may ask the seller to purchase coverage for the particular shipment through the common carrier with the cost of that coverage being added to the invoice.

The risk of loss or damage to goods in transit is also addressed in the commercially accepted shipping terms. In a contract for shipment, both title to the goods and risk of loss pass to the buyer when the goods are delivered by the seller to the common carrier under any of the following common terms:

- *C&F.* Cost and Freight
- *CIF.* Cost, Insurance and Freight

- *FAS.* Free Alongside
- *FOB.* Free on board

On the other hand if the contract of sale specifies or requires the seller to guarantee delivery, then the seller bears the risk of loss in transit. Common shipping terms designating that the seller is responsible for loss in transit include:

- Ex-Ship
- FOB Destination

OFFER AND ACCEPTANCE

Sellers frequently get into trouble because they fail to carefully examine the purchase orders received from customers. A purchase order is an offer from the buyer to the seller. Specifically, the buyer is offering to buy a specific quantity of merchandise, at a specific price and subject to specific terms and conditions listed on the purchase order. If the purchase order contains the wrong price, or certain terms and conditions of sale that are unacceptable to the seller, then the PO should be rejected and returned. If the seller accepts the PO without protest and ships against it, then chances are good that the buyer will have to accept these seller's terms or price.

Acceptance of a customer's offer may be express—such as sending the customer a written acknowledgment of the P.O. along with a scheduled shipping date. Acceptance of an offer can be implied, involving nothing more than shipping the order in response receipt of the P.O. To prevent the collection problems that arise when sellers do not challenge flawed purchase orders, people trained to do so must review each purchase order to determine if the terms listed by the buyer are acceptable to the seller. If the purchase order is not acceptable to the seller, the product ordered should not be shipped until a written amendment is received from the buyer.

DISPUTE RESOLUTION AND WARRANTIES

Credit managers and their department staff are often expected to resolve disputes with customers that arise as a result of the customer's claim that the merchandise delivered was defective. There are two types of warranties that sellers need to know about. The first is an express warranty. An express warranty describing exactly what the seller or manufacturer warrants or guarantees in connection with the merchandise being delivered. An example of a specific warranty would be as follows: " We warrant this product for one year from the date of purchase. If it fails during normal use within one year of the date of purchase, we will repair or replace it free of charge."

Creditors should also be aware that the law imposes a second type of warranty on sellers—an implied warranty. Specifically, unless excluded or modified all sellers warrant the products they sell are merchantable; that they are fit for the ordinary purpose for which the goods are used. For example, raincoats that are not waterproof would almost certainly violate their implied warranty of merchantability.

When evaluating a customer deduction involving an issue of warranty liability, the credit department must act as a neutral arbitrator. If the preponderance of evidence shows that an express or implied warranty applied, then a credit should be generated and submitted for approval. If there is not a legitimate issue of warranty liability, the credit manager should insist on payment.

CONFLICT OF LAWS

The laws in different countries vary, in some instances the laws in different states may be contradictory. Therefore, it is important for the buyer and seller to agree which law will control their business dealings. Determining which law controls the sale is important because that will determine where any lawsuit that must be filed will be heard.

Typically, the seller would prefer that any litigation occur in the county and state in which the creditor is headquartered. The buyer would like the same "home field" advantage. Often, "venue" is contractually agreed upon. Specifically, a well-written credit application form will include a provision about venue for litigation if litigation ever becomes necessary.

CREDIT FRAUD

Fraud is generally defined as an intentional misrepresentation of a material fact by one person or party, when such misrepresentation was made for the purpose of inducing another party to act. For fraud to exist, the damaged party must rely on the misrepresentation, and have suffered economic harm as a result.

Credit fraud is a generic term covering a variety of crimes. Some credit frauds are relatively unsophisticated, such as ordering goods on a COD basis and paying for the shipment with a valueless check. Some are far more sophisticated. For example, a bustout is a well financed fraud. To complete the fraud, the criminal must typically violate federal and state laws including committing both mail fraud and wire fraud.

Depending on the type of fraud committed, the criminal may be guilty of violating both federal and state laws. When discovered, the decision about whether to prosecute in federal or state court is made by the prosecutors—and not the creditors that were the victims of the fraud.

BECOMING A SECURED CREDITOR

The majority of trade creditors supplying goods do businesses do so on an open and unsecured basis. Any creditor can become a secured creditor. The mechanism for doing so is Article 9 of the Uniform Commercial Code [UCC] which codifies the rules for becoming and remaining a secured creditor.

A security interest is a lien on personal property that is subject to a specific and predictable system of creditor priorities. Security interests do not prevent losses; they reduce the likelihood of losses. The goal of any creditor is to obtain a security interest in the personal property of the debtor that is superior to any other claim that might be raised.

Becoming a secured creditor is a two-step process. The first step is called attachment, and the second is called perfection. Attachment occurs when the debtor signs a contract in which a security interest attaches [is granted] by the buyer to the seller. The contract that creates this security interest is called a security agreement. A security agreement will:

- Create a security interest
- Attach to the proceeds of the sale of the assets described in the security interest
- May grant the creditor a security interest in after acquired property

The second step involves perfection of the security interest. Perfection is the process of taking the steps necessary to insure the secured creditor's interest in the collateral listed in the security interest contract will withstand a challenge by other creditors to its validity. The most common way to perfect a security interest is by filing a public notice. This involves submitting a financing statement to the appropriate governmental entity. However, the first phase of this process involves a search of the public filings to determine if there are conflicting security interests. If there are pre-existing and perfected security interests on the assets the creditor wants to perfect a security interest in, then a trade creditor may want to consider filing a Purchase Money Security Interest rather than a security interest.

Perfecting requires filing or recording the lien. The general rule is that the date and the time the Security Agreement is recorded by the filing officer in the appropriate jurisdiction determine filing priority. A Security Agreement may secure old and new debt. To create an enforceable security interest, the following steps must take place:

(1) There must be an agreement in writing.

(2) The agreement must be signed.

(3) The debtor must have the right to the collateral.

(4) The secured party must give value [consideration] in return for the security agreement.

(5) Filing normally perfects security agreements. Perfection involves making the lien enforceable against other creditors so they cannot create rights to the property that are higher than the previously perfected liens.

Secured creditors generally receive payment before unsecured creditors. At the very least, having a security interest in personal property improves the creditor's position if the debtor files for bankruptcy or makes an assignment for the benefit of creditors. Section 9 of the UCC describes the process a creditor must complete in order to become a secured creditor.

If a debtor becomes insolvent and files for Bankruptcy protection, the secured creditor [at least in theory] may enter the debtor's place of business and repossess its collateral. The most common reasons that creditors do not secure their open account sales are:

- The cost of doing so in time, effort, and money.

- Because they do not have the leverage necessary to get customers to agree to allow the trade creditor to become secured.

- Because some creditors are not aware of their right to become secured creditors.

- Creditors often believe that there are so many prior perfected security interested that another one would be almost valueless.

- Because security interests create a false sense of security for the creditor.

Each State has a mechanism for recording financing statements, and each state may determine where the UCC-1 financing statement must be filed. Some states require only one filing be made with the Secretary of State. A handful of States require dual filings to record security interests, one with the Secretary of State and the other typically with the County Recorder.

A secured creditor must file an amendment to the financing statement when any of the following events occur:

- the customer moves
- the creditor moves
- the location of the collateral moves
- the debtor's name changes
- the creditor's name changes

The Uniform Commercial Code [UCC] provides a mechanism for creditors that provide goods to become secured creditors in the specific inventory they intend to ship irrespective of the fact that other creditors have a pre-existing perfected security interest in inventory and its proceeds. That mechanism involves perfecting a Purchase Money Security Interest [a PMSI]. To perfect a PMSI, the seller must:

- Conduct a search to determine which creditors have a pre existing and conflicting security interest.
- Notify each of the pre-existing creditors of its intention to obtain a Purchase Money Security Interest in its inventory and proceeds.
- The seller must then provide goods to the debtor within a specified number of days of perfection—typically within 20 days after perfection.

If the PMSI is properly perfected, it is valid against any and all previous, current or future filings of other creditors. A note of caution: A PMSI cannot be used to secure a pre-existing debt—and the PMSI will only supersede other secured liens if the creditor properly perfects the PMSI, including providing notice to pre-existing creditors before the debtor receives possession of the goods in question.

Contrary to popular myth, a creditor seeking to perfect a Purchase Money Security Interest does not need the approval of the pre-existing secured creditor(s). Instead, the creditor simply needs to notify those creditors before the debtor takes possession of the merchandise.

As a practical matter, many trade creditors are unable to obtain a PMSI because the debtor is precluded from signing them because of an existing contract with their secured creditors and in particular a loan covenant agreement with their bank. In other words, the secured creditor does not want its position eroded by the subsequent filings of Purchase Money Security Agreements and takes steps to ensure this does not happen.

CONSIGNMENT SALES

Consignment arrangements are often used in cases where a customer is not considered creditworthy, but is considered to be capable of selling the goods in question. A consignment involves the shipment of merchandise to a consignee without title to that merchandise passing to the recipient. Instead, under a contract called a Consignment Agreement, the recipient is obliged to pay the consignor of the goods when the goods are sold.

Shipping goods against a Consignment Agreement is one situation in which the consignor [the shipper and owner of the merchandise] would almost certainly want to perfect a security interest in "their" consigned inventory. In addition to requiring the consignee provide regular inventory reports and pay for goods as they are sold, the consignor will want a perfected security interest in the assets shipped on consignment so there is no misunderstanding about the rights of the consignor in the event the customer becomes insolvent.

PAYMENT DEFAULT AND PERFECTED SECURITY INTERESTS

In theory, a secured creditor is entitled to take possession of the collateral it holds a security interest in if the debtor defaults on payment, or is in violation of any other terms and conditions listed in the security agreement. As a practical matter, it is often difficult if not impossible for a secured trade creditor to convince a debtor to voluntarily turn over the collateral pledged. As a result, the true value of being a secured creditor results from the fact that a perfected security interest is relatively easy to enforce through civil action. Unfortunately, this means that a secured creditor often must file suit to recover its collateral.

Perhaps the biggest advantage of being a secured creditor involves the fact that if the debtor files for bankruptcy protection the secured creditor stands a good chance of recovering the collateral pledged or its cash equivalent.

BANKRUPTCY

Based on a provision in Article 1 of the United States Constitution, bankruptcies of individuals and of businesses are governed by Federal Law. Bankruptcy laws were written to help individuals and businesses that cannot pay their debts as they come due.

Under certain provisions of the U.S. Bankruptcy Code and insolvent debtor is required to surrender its assets to a trustee to be liquidated [sold] so that the proceeds of that sale can be distributed to creditors. This occurs in a Chapter 7 liquidation. Chapter 7 intended to give a bankrupt individual or business a fresh start. At its most basic, a liquidation works this way: All of the eligible assets are delivered by a third party, a trustee. The trustee sells the assets and the proceeds are distributed to creditors according to the order of priority established in the bankruptcy code.

In a bankruptcy, under the absolute priority rule, certain creditors are entitled to be paid in full before other classes of creditors receive anything. Under the absolute priority rule, inferior claimants will receive nothing if a superior claimant is not paid in full from the proceeds of the liquidation of assets.

In addition to Chapter 7 liquidation, there are two other major categories of Bankruptcy cases. These are:

- A Chapter 11 reorganization, suitable for large corporate debtors
- A Chapter 13 reorganization, suitable for individuals with a steady source of income.

Each Federal District Court has a bankruptcy unit that handles both individual and business bankruptcies. More than one million bankruptcy petitions a year are filed in the United States. Over 95% of these cases involve individual debtors rather than businesses.

Under the U.S. Bankruptcy Code, the trustee is entitled to recover assets that were transferred to a third party illegally. A fraudulent conveyance involves the transfer of property for less than fair market value for the purpose of delaying or hindering creditors.

THE AUTOMATIC STAY

When a bankruptcy is filed, it creates an Automatic Stay. This Stay prohibits creditors from engaging in actions or activities against the debtor or its property including placing collection calls and continuation of lawsuits to pursue payment. Violation of the Automatic Stay can result in the Court imposing fines and other sanctions.

Contrary to popular myth, the Automatic Stay does not affect a creditor's decision to halt shipments ordered prior to the bankruptcy filing that are in process or in transit at the time of the bankruptcy filing. Creditors may stop and arrange for the return of goods in transit.

Contrary to what some debtors are led to believe, there is no provision in the bankruptcy code that requires creditors to sell to a Chapter 11 debtor in possession on open account terms of sale. Creditors may elect to do so. Often, the decision about whether or not to sell is based on the following factors:

- Whether or not the debtor has arranged for financing [called debtor in possession financing]
- Whether or not other creditors are extending terms to the debtor
- Whether or not in the opinion of the creditor the company is likely to work its way out of bankruptcy or fail while trying
- The terms requested
- The credit limit requested

USING PROMISSORY NOTES TO DOCUMENT PAYMENT COMMITMENTS

Occasional, a delinquent debtor will ask a creditor for additional time to pay a past due balance. Rather than simply relying on that customer's commitment to pay the balance, creditors often ask customers to sign Promissory Notes. A Promissory Note is a written contract in which a debtor company promises to pay the creditor according to the terms listed in the note.

A Promissory Note normally includes an explicit acknowledgment listing a specific dollar amount as being owed and acknowledging that the debt owed is undisputed. A Promissory Note often includes a provision for payment of interest on the past due balance. Creditors often require that the debtor's signature be notarized so there is no debate or dispute about the signature if the creditor company must sue to recover the money owed.

A Promissory Note is evidence of the fact that a balance is due. Unfortunately, evidence of debt is sometimes confused with security for that indebtedness. A Promissory Note typically does not include a pledge of collateral; therefore a Promissory Note is not security for the indebtedness.

PARTNERSHIPS

A partnership is an association of two or more people who agree to enter a business venture together and to share the profits or losses of that business. In a partnership the partners are personally liable for the debts of the company. In a General Partnership, each partner has unlimited personal liability for the debts of the company. In a limited partnership, the limited partner(s) are personally liable for the debts of the company only to the extent of his or her investment in it. In a limited partnership, the general partner(s) [who are responsible for managing the day to day operations of the business] have unlimited personal liability for the debts of the company.

CORPORATIONS AS A SEPARATE LEGAL ENTITY

A Corporation is a fictitious entity that has legal rights and duties that are independent of the rights and duties of its stockholders. Individuals can become liable for the debts of a corporation if they sign personal guarantees on behalf of the corporation. In rare instances, individuals can become responsible for the debts of the corporation through operation of law; often because the individual acted or failed to act in a way that distinguished the rights and the obligations of an individual [such as the owner of 100% of the capital stock of the corporation] from the corporation itself.

Typically, only major stockholders of a corporation are willing to offer their personal guaranty in support of the corporation's efforts to obtain loans and/or credit. The "consideration" the guarantor receives in return for his or her guaranty is the fact that the creditor will extend credit [or additional credit] to the customer on the basis of the strength of the personal guarantee.

PREFERENCES

Preferences involve an insolvent debtor paying one or more creditors to the exclusion of other creditors. Under the U.S. Bankruptcy Code, preferences [or more properly Preferential Transfers] may be voided by the Court and are then recoverable to the estate of the bankrupt debtor. Trade creditors that received payments within 90 days of the date of the bankruptcy petition are at risk. Specifically, the trustee may challenge the payments, asserting they were preferential as defined in the bankruptcy code. The trustee may ask the court to issue an order demanding that the creditor disgorge [return] these payments.

VENUE

Venue is the legal and proper place where a particular dispute should be filed and the case heard. Every State has rules determining the proper venue for different types of lawsuits. In a dispute between a creditor and debtor over moneys owed, venue is an important consideration.

LITIGATION

When a delinquent debtor is unwilling to pay a creditor, it may be necessary for that creditor to file suit in order to recover the moneys owed. While the civil litigation process varies from State to State, civil litigation typically involves the following steps or processes:

- A lawsuit is filed in a Court with the proper authority to hear the case
- The defendant is notified of the lawsuit and given an opportunity to respond
- Assuming the defendant files a response, a court date is set
- Attorneys for the plaintiff and the defendant supply the other with requests for documents. Each party also serves the other with interrogatories. These are written questions to which the other party must provide written answers.
- After the interrogatories are received, depositions are taken. Depositions involve testimony about the facts of the case given under oath but outside of the court. Attorneys for both parties are present.
- The parties show up for the trial. The case is heard. A judgment is rendered either on the spot by the jury, or if it is a non-jury trial either immediately by the judge or after some review and deliberation by the judge.

SUMMARY JUDGMENT

After a lawsuit has been filed in a civil case such as a money dispute between a creditor (seller) and a customer (buyer), either party may petition the Court for a summary judgment. A motion for summary judgment asserts that the other party in the case has raised no genuine issues to be tried and asks the Court to rule in its favor.

For example, if during discovery the debtor company's representative admits under oath that no legitimate dispute existed or exists, but that the debtor "just doesn't have the money to pay for the merchandise" then the creditor (plaintiff) might petition the court for a summary judgment.

POST JUDGMENT COLLECTION

It often comes as an unpleasant surprise to a trade creditor that has sued a debtor and won to find that the debtor does not immediately pay the debt. An unsecured creditor holding a "money judgment" against a debtor company has a number of options and remedies.

One of those remedies involves becoming a lien creditor. Through a Notice of Judgment filing made with the Secretary of State, a lien creditor can place a lien on all of the personal property located in that State owned by the debtor company. Unfortunately, this somewhat passive method of collection may not result in immediate payment by the debtor.

A more aggressive approach is for the judgment creditor's attorney to conduct a judgment debtor examination. This is an interview conducted under oath in which the debtor is required to list what assets it holds and where they are located. The judgment creditor can then contact the sheriff in the County in which the assets are located and ask that these assets be seized. Creditors should be aware that seizure of these assets could be complicated by the fact that prior lien-holders rights take precedence. For example, if the debtor indicates that they own a car garaged in a particular city but title to that car remains with the seller [because it isn't fully paid for] then the car cannot be seized and sold because the rights of a secured creditor supersede the judgment creditor's rights to seize and sell assets.

If the judgment creditor cannot find sufficient personal property to satisfy the judgment, it can place liens against real property. To do so, the judgment creditor's attorney files an Abstract of Judgment with the County Recorder in each County in which the judgment debtor has real property. The judgment creditor can then either (a) wait for the property to be sold at which time the lien will become an obstacle to passing clear title resulting in payment to the judgment creditor or (b) request a judicial foreclosure. If there are existing liens on the property [such as a mortgage] then those prior liens once again take precedence.

If the Court does order the real property to be sold, the judgment creditor would only be entitled to payment if and when all superior lien-holders were paid in full. Therefore, the judgment creditor may want to determine how much equity there is in any real property before hiring an attorney to pursue a judicial foreclosure.

LITIGATION ALTERNATIVES

In an effort to avoid litigation which is costly and time consuming, some creditors have added clauses to their credit application contracts specifying that if a dispute arises between the buyer and seller the matter will be referred to a neutral third party to resolve the dispute. This process is called Mediation. Mediation is a non-adversarial process in which the mediator meets with the parties to try to find a settlement that both parties find acceptable. A mediator is a neutral third party skilled at bringing together parties involved in a dispute, and finding ways to help the parties work cooperatively to resolve their dispute.

ARBITRATION

Some creditors require in their credit application form that the buyer agrees to submit disputes to Arbitration. An arbitrator is a neutral third party that will hear evidence and review documentation submitted by both the buyer and the seller before rendering a decision. An arbitrator is often a lawyer, and may be a retired judge.

Arbitration can be either binding or non-binding. If it is binding, with few exceptions the losing party must accept the decision of the arbitrator and act accordingly just as if a judge or jury made the decision. If the decision of the arbitrator is non-binding, the parties can either agree to accept the decision, or pursue other legal remedies.

ASSIGNMENTS FOR THE BENEFIT OF CREDITORS

An alternative to Chapter 7 bankruptcy is a general assignment for the benefit of creditors. A general assignment is a method for liquidating a business enterprise. General assignments are created by contract. The contract provides that the assignor will assign all of its assets to an assignee who will then liquidate the assets. The proceeds of the liquidation of assets will be distributed by the assignee subject to certain priorities of claims. Often, the local credit managers association will act as or can recommend an assignee to handle the liquidation of assets and the distribution of proceeds.

RECLAMATION

The Uniform Commercial Code [UCC] provides that a creditor may reclaim [repossess] goods delivered to an insolvent buyer within a specific statutory period pursuant to section 2-702 of the Uniform Commercial Code. Under the UCC, insolvency is defined using one of two tests. The first is a situation in which the buyer's liabilities exceed its assets. The second test is the liquidity test. Failing the liquidity test simply means that the debtor is unable to pay its debts as they mature.

The UCC allows the seller of goods to retrieve all of their goods sold within 10 days prior to the seller's demand to the insolvent debtor for the return of goods. Typically, this ten-day window only covers a portion of the creditor's claim.

The UCC also provides that if a seller finds that a buyer is insolvent it may withhold goods scheduled for delivery and that it may contact the carrier and make arrangements for the return of any goods in transit.

SUMMARY

Business law is such a broad area that credit managers will not be able to memorize every fact. Credit managers need to concentrate on the basics and let competent attorneys handle the rest. The best credit managers are the ones that know when a problem needs to be reviewed by the company's attorney.

Sometimes, attorneys are not called often enough because they are expensive. This could easily become a case of the company being "penny wise and pound foolish." Credit managers are in a unique position to use they attorney to prevent problems and save the company money.

CHAPTER 31

COLLECTION AND BANKRUPTCY LAW

An individual or business debtor in financial distress may voluntarily seek relief under one of the chapters of the U.S. Bankruptcy Code subject to certain legal requirements and limitations. The creditors of an insolvent business debtor may file a petition with the appropriate Bankruptcy Court asking that the debtor be placed into an involuntary bankruptcy.

Federal law governs bankruptcy. The U.S. Bankruptcy Code is a subsection of the U.S. Code. The U.S. Code is a codification of the permanent laws of the United States and applicable in every State. Therefore, the U.S. bankruptcy court is a federal court. Every State has at least one federal judicial district, and each federal judicial district has at least one bankruptcy court.

There are two basic types of creditors in a bankruptcy case. The first is a secured creditor. A secured creditor holds a perfected security interest in asset(s) of the debtor company pledged to the creditor as collateral. The second is an unsecured creditor. An unsecured creditor has no security interest and no pledge of collateral from the debtor covering its claim against the debtor. Most trade creditors are general unsecured creditors.

TYPES OF BANKRUPTCIES

Trade creditors that extend credit from business to business typically deal with three types of bankruptcy. They are:

(1) The Chapter 7 Liquidation, and
(2) The Chapter 11 reorganization, and occasionally

For creditors that extend credit to consumers, the most common forms of bankruptcy are the Chapter 7 liquidation and as a distant second the Chapter 13 reorganization.

The Chapter 7 Bankruptcy

A Chapter 7 bankruptcy, sometimes called a "straight" bankruptcy, involves a liquidation of the individual or business debtor's assets. The goal is to liquidate the assets of the debtor, and then provide a fair and equitable distribution to creditors of whatever assets those assets could be sold for. The debtor is required to turn over all non-exempt assets to a bankruptcy trustee who then converts the assets into cash.

In a personal Chapter 7 bankruptcy, a certain dollar amount of personal is exempted from liquidation. In more than half of the Chapter 7 personal bankruptcy cases, no assets are turned over to the trustee to liquidate because the assets the debtor holds do not exceed the maximum dollar exemption value by category. Therefore, all of the debtor's assets are exempted and it becomes a "no asset" case. Exempted items involve a specific dollar amount or value of property in the following categories:

- Homestead exemptions

- Personal property

- Automobile equity

- Tools of a worker's trade

- Jewelry

- Pension, Social Security, Life Insurance and Alimony exemptions

In a Chapter 7 case, the office of the United States Trustee appoints a private trustee. The goal of the private trustee is to sell the assets and discharge debts quickly so that the debtor can be given a fresh start. However, certain types of debts such as child support payments and taxes owed cannot be discharged even in a bankruptcy.

After the private trustee provides the Court with an accounting of the assets liquidated and the cash received, the Court will approve distribution of the cash based on a list of priorities. After that cash is distributed, the debtor will receive a discharge of all dischargeable debts. The debtor will have a "fresh start" with the exception of the non-dischargeable debts, which include:

- Certain taxes
- Debts created through fraudulent conduct
- Debts not listed on the schedules that accompany the bankruptcy petition
- Alimony and child support
- Certain government guaranteed student loans

Some debts will be discharged unless a complaint to deny discharge of that debt is filed in a timely manner with the Court.

NOTE: In a Chapter 7 liquidation case, as a general rule claims filed after the Bar Date will not be accepted. Creditors should always file their Proof of Claim early enough to be able to confirm that the Clerk of the Bankruptcy Court received and properly recorded their claim.

The Automatic Stay Provision

Once a Chapter 7 Bankruptcy has been filed, all actions of creditors to collect the balances still owed are stayed [stopped]. The reference to an "automatic" stay refers to the concept that once a bankruptcy has been filed all creditors must stay or stop all collection actions. As a practical matter, creditors do not stop their collection efforts until they are notified of the bankruptcy.

Before any formal notice is sent, the debtor may tell creditors that a filing has taken place. At that point, the creditor should cease all collection efforts—at least until the creditor can confirm the fact that a filing has taken place. The fastest way to do so, short of arranging for the customer to fax evidence that the filing has been recorded is for the creditor to get the case number and the telephone number for the Court in which the case was filed and call to verify the filing did take place.

If a creditor continues to attempt collection after being notified of the bankruptcy filing, that creditor may receive a call from the debtor's attorney. If that does not work, the Bankruptcy Court may get involved. The Court may impose fines on any creditor that ignores its orders. The Automatic Stay is an order of the Court. Continuing to ignore the orders of the Judge may result in a charge of Contempt.

The Priority of Claims

In a Chapter 7 case, it is not uncommon for there to be nothing left from the liquidation of the assets of the debtor for any distribution to unsecured creditors. The requirement that secured and priority creditors' claims be paid first is codified in the U.S. Bankruptcy Code. Specifically, the Code specifies that certain classes of creditors have absolute priority over other classes of creditors. The absolute priority rule states that creditors with a higher priority claim must be paid in full before the next class of creditors receives any payment.

The Chapter 11 Bankruptcy

The Chapter 11 Bankruptcy is intended as a reorganization available to both individual and business debtors. The purpose of the Chapter 11 is to help the debtor to rehabilitate. Some corporations voluntarily file for Chapter 11 bankruptcy to protect an otherwise viable business facing temporary financial problems from its creditors.

An individual [or a married couple] may file for Chapter 11 protection if his or her secured debts exceed $750,000 and his or her unsecured debts exceed $250,000.

THE CHAPTER 7 PERSONAL BANKRUPTCY FLOW CHART

The bankruptcy is filed

The appropriate schedules are filed with the Court

A private trustee is appointed

The debtor delivers to the trustee all non-exempted assets

The trustee liquidates those assets

The trustee distributes the proceeds of the liquidation according to the priorities established under the Bankruptcy Code

The Court dismisses the remainder of the dischargable debts owed by the debtor to his or her creditors

The bankruptcy will appear on the debtor's credit report for seven years

---

A Chapter 11 bankruptcy allows the debtor the time required to rehabilitate, to reorganize and to pay all or only a portion of its pre-petition debts owed to its creditors. A Chapter 11 bankruptcy filed by a business allows the debtor to remain in control of the company and in possession of the assets of the business while preparing a plan of reorganization for creditors to consider.

The Exclusivity Period

In a Chapter 11 case, the business debtor is granted an exclusive period of 120 days in which to file a plan for repayment of its creditors. Bankruptcy Courts routinely extend this exclusivity period; or it may be shortened if an interested party cause show cause why the Court should do so.

Developing a Plan of Reorganization
In a Chapter 11 business bankruptcy, the debtor's goal is to create a Plan of Reorganization. A Plan of Reorganization divides creditors into categories and describes how each creditor class is to be treated. A creditor may be paid in full under the Plan, or may be an impaired creditor [meaning the creditor will not be paid in full based on the Plan as submitted]. Creditors vote about whether to accept or reject the debtor's Plan.

A Cram Down
If one or more classes of impaired creditors vote to reject the debtor's Plan of Reorganization as presented, the Court can accept this vote and instruct the debtor to draft another Plan for the creditor's review. Sometimes, the Court will intervene and force creditors to accept the debtor's Plan. This action by the Court is called a "cram-down."

Chapter 11 of the Code seeks to rehabilitate the debtor company by allowing the debtor in possession to reorganize its finances. In a case of fraud, gross mismanagement, or incompetence the Court may appoint a trustee to take over the business operations of a debtor in possession. The trustee may either continue to run the business for a short period of time in order to sell it as a going concern, or the trustee may elect to shut the business down and liquidate it.

Chapter 13 Bankruptcy

A Chapter 13 bankruptcy is a form of debt reorganization used by individuals and sole proprietorships [but not corporations]. A Chapter 13 bankruptcy is called the wage earner's bankruptcy, and provided the bankrupt individuals have a regular income, and provided there are less than $250,000 in unsecured debts and $750,000 in secured debts, the Chapter 13 rules allow the wage earner to propose a plan to pay creditors in full or in part over an extended period of time—typically over the next three years.

The U.S. Bankruptcy Court must approve and confirm the debtor's repayment plan. Individuals who do not have regular income cannot file a Chapter 13 case. Under a Chapter 13 bankruptcy, priority and secured creditors must be paid in full. A Chapter 13 bankruptcy [at least in theory] carries less of a stigma than a Chapter 7 bankruptcy.

To incentivize debtors to file Chapter 13 rather than Chapter 7 bankruptcy, people who elect to file Chapter 13 receive larger personal property exemptions than do people filing under Chapter 7 of the U.S. Bankruptcy Code. Despite this incentive, most personal bankruptcies are filed as Chapter 7 liquidations. The Congress is currently considering legislation that would limit the rights of wage earners to file under Chapter 7 rather than under Chapter 13 of the Code.

BANKRUPTCY STATISTICS

The statistics on bankruptcy are grim. For example:

- There were more than 1.42 million bankruptcies filed in 1998.

- Of those 1.4 million bankruptcies, over 71% were Chapter 7 liquidations.

- Non business bankruptcy filings accounted for almost 97% of the total bankruptcies filed in 1998.

- The total number of bankruptcies filed has broken the all time record for the last three years in a row.

- Over 75% of Chapter 11 reorganization converted to Chapter 7 liquidations in 1998.

- Approximately three times as many Chapter 7 liquidations are filed than Chapter 13 reorganizations.

FILING AN INVOLUNTARY BANKRUPTCY

At least three eligible trade creditors with combined unpaid and undisputed debts of $10,000 or more may file an involuntary bankruptcy petition against a business debtor. For unsecured creditors, this strategy is a double-edged sword. On one hand, an involuntary bankruptcy filing [or the threat of an involuntary bankruptcy filing] may force a delinquent debtor to address the issues that it previously ignored. On the other hand, an involuntary Chapter 7 bankruptcy filing may result in a smaller recovery to general unsecured trade creditors because of the complications of a bankruptcy, and the time and administrative costs of being a bankrupt company.

An involuntary bankruptcy filing is a drastic option, and the decision to place a creditor into bankruptcy must be made with great care. In certain circumstances, creditors may have no alternative but to force a debtor into bankruptcy. For example, an involuntary filing should be used when creditors have reason to believe that preferential transfers are being made, or that the debtor is engaged in fraud. In these scenarios, the trustee's power to recover asset transfers that resulted in preferential treatment, and the Bankruptcy Court's power to address and reverse certain other types of fraud, will often result in larger recoveries to general unsecured trade creditors.

BANKRUPTCY CODE AMENDMENTS

In 1994, the Bankruptcy Code was amended. One of the changes involved creating a special class of Chapter 11 bankruptcies, the small business bankruptcy. The purpose of the amendment was to make it faster and less expensive for a small business to reorganize under Chapter 11.

A small business was defined as a company with non-contingent liquidated secured and unsecured debts that do not exceed $2,000,000. The most important changes included:

(a) the fact that in a small business bankruptcy case no unsecured creditors committee is formed and

(b) the fact that the hearing to approve the disclosure statement relating to the debtor's Plan of Reorganization may be combined with a hearing on the confirmation of that Plan

THE VALUE OF PERSONAL GUARANTEES

Creditors should be aware that a personal guarantee for an officer or owner does not guarantee that a creditor company will be paid if the debtor corporation files for bankruptcy protection. For example, if the guarantor files a personal bankruptcy at the same time as the business bankruptcy is filed, then the personal guarantee may be almost valueless. This scenario is not unlikely if the guarantor is also the owner of the bankrupt corporation.

THE AUTOMATIC STAY PROVISION

The filing of a bankruptcy petition under any chapter of the Bankruptcy Code automatically operates as a stay against the commencement or continuation of judicial, administrative or other proceedings against the debtor involving pre petition debts. [Pre-petition debts are those debts that have arisen prior to the date of the filing of the bankruptcy petition.] Creditors are prohibited from taking certain actions including contacting the debtor to demand payment, taking action to collect money, attempting to seize property from the debtor, starting lawsuits, continuing lawsuits, or in the case of an individual garnishing or deducting money from the debtor's wages.

FILING A PROOF OF CLAIM FORM

In order to receive a share of a debtor's assets, creditors are normally required to file certain documents with the Court. The written statement to the Court setting forth the creditor's claim against the bankrupt debtor is called a Proof of Claim form. This form lists the creditor's claim against the debtor. Photocopies of all relevant supporting documentation should be mailed along with the completed and signed Proof of Claim form. If the creditor claims a secured status, evidence of the perfection of a security interest should be sent.

The Proof of Claim for should be accurate and complete since it is filed under penalty of perjury. Therefore, the person signing the document should verify the facts. Original documents should never be sent as supporting documentation for a Proof of Claim. Photocopies are adequate, since attachments can get lost and in the event of a dispute the creditor may be required to provide original documents to the Court.

Objections to Proof of Claims Filed

The debtor has a right to object to any Proof of Claim filed. Such an objection must be made based on a reasonable belief that the dollar amount of the claim is wrong, or that the creditor has identified an incorrect priority of claim.

For example, a debtor would object to a claim that a creditor has a secured claim when the claimant is in fact an unsecured creditor. Once the objection has been filed, the debtor and creditor can agree or settle the matter, or a formal hearing before the Court will be held to determine the validity of the Claim as filed by the creditor.

The Bar Date

The Bankruptcy Court establishes a deadline for creditors to file their Proof of Claim forms. This deadline is called the Bar Date. Creditors should make every effort to file far enough ahead of the Bar Date that they can request and receive from the Clerk of the Court a written confirmation that their claim was properly recorded.

If a creditor mails its Proof of Claim within a week of the Bar Date, they risk missing the Bar Date. A late filing might result in the claim being rejected, or the claim being given a lower priority by the Court. If the creditor is submitting a filing near the Bar Date, they should seriously consider using an attorney's delivery service. For a nominal fee, these services will deliver the creditor's Proof of Claim to the Court and return to the creditor written confirmation showing when the claim was filed.

RECLAMATION CLAIMS

One area of the Bankruptcy Code of particular interest to credit professionals deals with reclamation of goods. A reclamation claim involves an attempt by a pre-petition creditor to repossess goods delivered just before the bankruptcy was filed.

A demand for the reclamation of goods should specifically state that the seller does not intend to violate the Automatic Stay, but is submitting the request in compliance with the notice requirements for reclamation claims are provided for in the Bankruptcy Code.

Reclamation offers unsecured, pre-petition suppliers an important tool to recover assets that might otherwise be lost in the bankruptcy. Pre-petition creditors must take quick and decisive action since there is a limited amount of time in which a reclamation claim may be filed. Specifically, the law states that: "The seller may not reclaim any goods unless the seller demand in writing reclamation of such goods either:

(a) before ten days after receipt of such goods from the debtor or

(b) if the ten day period expires after the commencement of the case, then within 20 days after receipt of the goods by the debtor company."

Unsecured creditors should also know that the reclamation process has certain limitations. For example:

- A reclamation claim is only effective for goods in the debtor's possession. If the merchandise in question has been sold, then the seller does not have recourse against a good faith buyer of those goods.

- The seller does not have any reclamation rights with respect to the proceeds of the goods sold by the debtor.

- Reclamation rights are subordinate to the rights of a pre-existing security interest in the inventory of a debtor, and the existence of a prior perfected security interest in the inventory of the debtor is the most common reason that reclamation claims do not result in goods being returned to the seller.

In connection with reclamation claims, the Bankruptcy Court has the authority and the responsibility to balance the debtor's need for the goods with the seller's reclamation rights. The Court may order the goods returned to the seller, or at the discretion of the Court the seller may be denied reclamation but given an administrative expense priority, or a secured claim for the amount of the preference.

THE DEBTOR IN POSSESSION

In a Chapter 11 business reorganization, the debtor will remain in possession of the assets of the company during the case. This process may seem counter-intuitive to some creditors since it means that the same people who in many cases mismanaged the business into bankruptcy are still in charge of the business where they may still be making poor decisions.

In a Chapter 11 bankruptcy, a Debtor in Possession [DIP] is allowed to incur unsecured debt without prior approval from the Court provided it is in the ordinary course of business. The DIP is also permitted to sell assets in the ordinary course of business without Court approval and oversight.

THE ROLE OF A TRUSTEE

In all Chapter 7, 12 and 13 cases, and in a small number of Chapter 11 cases [in particular cases in which the creditors were able to convince the court the debtor was either not honest enough or not capable enough to run the business as a debtor in possession] a private trustee is appointed by the Bankruptcy Court. In every case, the trustee's job it to administer the estate and to make certain that pre-petition creditors receive as much as possible from the debtor.

If the Court is convinced to appoint a private trustee in a Chapter 11 bankruptcy, the trustee will be called on to either:

(a) Manage the business until a buyer for it can be found, or

(b) Liquidate the assets of the business if that is in the best interest of creditors.

A private trustee will only be appointed if creditors can demonstrate to the Court one or more of the following:

● The business is mismanaged or fraud is involved

● Management is incompetent or dishonest

● For any other reason deems satisfactory to the Court, provided it is in the best interest of creditors to appoint a trustee.

The Bankruptcy Code grants to the trustee the power to petition the Court to avoid certain transactions or transfers made prior to the commencement of the case that are classified as being preferential transfers or fraudulent conveyances. A fraudulent conveyance is a transfer of assets for less than fair market value. A preferential transfer typically involves a payment made to an insider within one year of the bankruptcy filing or a payment made within 90 days of the filing date to a noninsider.

Private trustees are not always attorneys. They do not work directly for the Bankruptcy Court. Private trustees' fees come from fees paid by the debtor in order to file for bankruptcy protection.

THE UNITED STATES TRUSTEE PROGRAM

The Office of the United States Trustee is part of the U.S. Department of Justice. As such, it is part of the Executive Branch and therefore separate from the Bankruptcy Court system. The primary role of the U.S. Trustee Program is to act in the public interest to promote the efficiency and integrity of the bankruptcy system. The Program works to secure fast and economical resolution of bankruptcy cases. The Program oversees various administrative functions for the Bankruptcy Court system. The U.S. Trustee also helps to identify and investigate instances of suspected bankruptcy fraud. In such cases, the Trustee will work cooperatively with the United States Attorneys, and the FBI to investigate and to prosecute such frauds.

The United States Trustees supervise the following cases filed under the U.S. Bankruptcy Code:

- Chapter 7 liquidations
- Chapter 11 reorganizations
- Chapter 12 family farm reorganizations
- Chapter 13 wage earner reorganizations

The U.S. Trustees assisting the US Bankruptcy Courts in a variety of ways including:

- Appointing and supervising private trustees
- Initiating investigations of suspected fraud
- Appointing a creditors committee in Chapter 11 business reorganizations
- Ensure that professional fees [such as the fees of the attorney for the official unsecured creditors committee] are reasonable

The U.S. Trustee's Office appoints and then monitors the performance of the private trustees working with the U.S. Bankruptcy Court. While the U.S. Trustee's Office does not administer cases itself, the Office can bring motions in the Court asking that:

- A case be dismissed,
- A debtor be denied a discharge.

STEPS TO TAKE AFTER NOTIFICATION OF A BANKRUPTCY

There are steps that every trade creditor should take to mitigate their loss once they are made aware that one of their customers has filed for bankruptcy protection. Those steps include:

- Contact freight carriers and arrange for the return of any goods in transit. [This does not constitute a violation of the Automatic Stay provision.]

- Zero out the credit limit and make certain no shipments are made until the credit department has decided under what terms and conditions a sale can be made safely.

- Review the credit file for personal guarantees, inter-corporate guarantees or other forms of security. [Creditors should demand immediate payment in full from any third party guarantor in a bankruptcy case].

- If goods were shipped and arrived within 20 days of the filing of the bankruptcy petition, the creditor should contact their attorney to discuss its reclamation rights.

- If any payment was received from, or any product was returned by the creditor within 90 days of the bankruptcy filing date, the creditor should consult with their attorney about Preferential Transfers and the creditor's possible defenses against a preference claim.

- The creditor should print a copy of the account statement as of the bankruptcy filing date, along with copies of all outstanding invoices.

- The creditor should order proof of delivery on all unpaid invoices in case it becomes necessary months or years into the bankruptcy to prove the goods were in fact shipped to and received by the debtor.

- The creditor should request a report from the debtor's accounts payable system showing their accounts payable balance.

- The creditor should consider whether or not to attend the first meeting of creditors—sometimes referred to as the "341 hearing."

THE FIRST MEETING OF CREDITORS

The debtor is required to appear at that the 341 Hearing and must answer questions under penalty of perjury. The hearing permits the trustee, or in Chapter 11 bankruptcies a representative of the United States Trustee's Office, to review the debtor's petitions and schedules, and to ask questions face to face with the debtor.

The 341 Hearing [or First meeting of creditors] is not an inquisition or a trial. The debtor may not be able or willing to answer the questions that creditors may want to ask. Most general unsecured trade creditors do not attend these hearings. A creditor who does not attend the hearing does not waive any rights they may have against the debtor [or the debtor in possession]

RECLAMATION CLAIMS

Reclamation involves a right of a seller to recover possession of goods delivered to an insolvent buyer. Under the U.S. Bankruptcy Code, reclamation claims are subject to significant restrictions. Notable among those restrictions is:

(a) a requirement that the goods in question were delivered in the ordinary course of business

(b) that the merchandise in question was delivered at a time when the debtor was insolvent according to the Balance Sheet Test [meaning that liabilities exceeded the realizable value of the assets]

(c) the seller made written demand for the return of the goods in question within ten days in most instances, or in twenty days in certain limited scenarios

(d) the product in question was in the possession of the debtor at the time the reclamation demand from the seller was received.

In order to reclaim goods, the merchandise in question must be in the possession of the debtor. A reclamation claim has no effect on a person or company that purchased the goods from the creditor's customer in good faith, a so-called holder in due course. An additional point to remember is that reclamation claims are not likely to be honored if there is a secured creditor with a prior perfected security interest in the inventory of the debtor.

DISCHARGE VS. DISMISSAL

An order dismissing a bankruptcy is very different from a discharge under the U.S. Bankruptcy Code. A dismissal of a bankruptcy petition ends a case. The dismissal of a case means that unsecured creditors may start to collect against pre-petition debts, and that secured creditors may proceed toward repossessing their collateral. A discharge will free the debtor from certain debts. A dismissal typically occurs when a debtor fails to file the required documents, or if the debtor fails to appear at the first meeting of creditors.

COMMON MISTAKES MADE WHEN FILING A PROOF OF CLAIM

Creditors frequently make mistakes when filing a Proof of Claim. These mistakes can invalidate their claim, resulting in unnecessary losses and write offs. Some of the most common mistakes creditors make include:

- Failing to file a Proof of Claim by the deadline set by the Court—the Bar Date. Filing a claim involves delivering a properly prepared, signed Proof of Claim form to the Clerk of the appropriate Bankruptcy Court.
- Failing to complete each section of the Proof of Claim form.
- Failing to sign and date the Proof of Claim form itself.
- Failing to include with the Proof of Claim the required supporting documentation evidencing the debt. [This is a common mistake.]
- Failing to ask the Court to send confirmation that the claim was received and recorded by the Court before the Bar Date.
- Failing a claim for the wrong amount—for example filing a claim for the gross amount due rather than the net amount due at the time of the bankruptcy filing.
- Failing to understand that Proof of Claim forms are filed under penalty of perjury, making falsification of the document a crime.
- Failing to amend the Proof of Claim when errors are discovered.
- Failing to file a Claim after the Bar Date if one is not filed before the Bar Date.

- Failing to notify a bankrupt debtor sending bankruptcy related notices to the wrong address to make the necessary address change.

Only "allowed claims" share in any distribution from a Bankruptcy. A Claim is deemed to be an allowed claim if a party in interest in the case files no objection to it, in particular the trustee assigned to the case. If in doubt, creditors should consult with their attorney about how to complete the Proof of Claim form.

THE OFFICIAL UNSECURED CREDITOR'S COMMITTEE

In most Chapter 11 Bankruptcy cases, the Bankruptcy Code provides for the appointment of a committee of unsecured creditors by the U.S. Trustee to represent the interests of all unsecured creditors before the Court during the case and while the Plan or Reorganization is being formulated. Usually, an unsecured creditors' committee has seven members selected from among the debtor's 20 largest unsecured creditors. The main functions of this committee are:

- To review the operations of the debtor company, and monitor the financial condition and financial reports of the debtor.
- To consult with the private trustee on matters relating to the case.
- To comment to the Court if they are not satisfied with the actions of the debtor in possession.
- To offer to the Court comments on the Debtor in Possession's disclosure statement.
- To offer a recommendation to the creditors identified as general unsecured trade creditors about the debtor's proposed Plan of Reorganization.

Advantages of Committee Membership

Membership and participation on a creditors' committee is strictly voluntary. Creditors are often puzzled about whether or not to volunteer to participate. The advantages of doing so include:

- The creditor will have the opportunity to closely monitor the debtor's activities. This can be quite useful if the creditor intends to continue to sell to the debtor post petition.

- Committee members direct the activities of an attorney hired to represent the interests of all unsecured creditors.

- Committee members have a vote about whether the committee should recommend for or against the debtor's Plan of Reorganization.

- Committee members can ask the Court to order the appointment of a trustee to liquidate the assets of the debtor company if they believe that the reorganization effort is failing or will fail.

- The committee can submit its own Plan of Reorganization as an alternative to the Plan submitted by the Debtor in Possession.

The Disadvantages of Committee Membership.

The disadvantages of volunteering for creditors' committee membership include:

- Membership requires a substantial time commitment, and may require out of state travel.

- This commitment may last for several years.

- Committee members are not compensated in any way for their time and efforts.

- The Committee members and their respective employers receive no additional payment or benefit relating to their claim in bankruptcy because they members of the committee.

The Small Business Chapter 11 Bankruptcy

One relatively recent reform to the U.S. Bankruptcy Code provided for the elimination of the creditors committee for "small business" Chapter 11 bankruptcy cases. A small business is defined by the Bankruptcy Code as a company with non-contingent liabilities of less than $2 million. Small business bankruptcies are [at least in theory] fast-tracked through the bankruptcy process.

CONVERTING A REORGANIZATION INTO A LIQUIDATION

If the debtor makes it through the bankruptcy process, their dischargeable debts will be discharged and the debtor will have the fresh financial start the bankruptcy code was intended to allow for. Unfortunately, more than half of business bankruptcies that start out as reorganizations [Chapter 11] end up as liquidations [Chapter 7].

In many instances, the debtor company simply informs the Court that it has been unable to find a way to make a profit, and will be unable to create a Plan of Reorganization that is satisfactory to its secured and unsecured creditors.

At that point, the debtor can either simply convert the case to a Chapter 7, sign over the assets to a court appointed trustee and walk away from the business. In either case, it will be up to the trustee to oversee the liquidation of the assets of the business and to distribute the proceeds in accordance with the rules governing the priority of claims under the U.S. Bankruptcy Code.

DISCHARGE OF DEBTS

In a bankruptcy, the debtor is entitled at the conclusion of the case to the discharge of all dischargeable debts. In most cases, a discharge means that creditors will never be permitted to attempt to collect the debt from the debtor. Certain debts are not dischargeable under the Bankruptcy Code.

Prior to discharge, creditors have the right to initiate a lawsuit if they believe that:

(1) the debtor is not entitled to receive a discharge under the Bankruptcy Code or

(2) if they believe the debt owed to them is not dischargeable under the Code.

SUMMARY

The United States Bankruptcy Code is a large and complex body of laws. Credit managers should be encouraged to consult with competent legal advice any time they feel they need to do so in connection with a bankruptcy case.

In the vast majority of cases, general unsecured trade creditors can expect to receive between 10% and 20% of the amount they were by the debtor company at the time of the bankruptcy filing.

CHAPTER 32

CREDIT FRAUD

Credit fraud involves a situation in which a customer [an individual or an organization] knowingly and willfully falsifies a material fact or makes false representations with the intent to defraud creditors out of goods and services. Any company that extends open account credit terms is at risk for becoming the victim of credit fraud. The goal of credit professionals should be to minimize the losses associated with credit fraud. It is almost impossible to eliminate this type of risk.

The most effective approach for credit managers is to be proactive in managing this type of risk. This involves first educating themselves about the various forms that credit fraud can take, and then educating subordinates about what they can do to try to prevent this type of loss from occurring.

Note: This chapter is not intended as a "how-to" manual for criminals thinking about committing credit fraud. Criminals are already familiar with all of the credit scams and cons described in this chapter. It is far more likely that the intended victims need information and education than criminals do.

THE CON MAN

The term "con man" is short for "confidence man." Part of the tools of the trade of a criminal intent on committing fraud is to gain the confidence of the victim. Normally, there are no outward clues to distinguish a legitimate customer from a criminal intent on committing credit fraud. Credit managers who believe they can somehow just tell the difference between an honest and a dishonest applicant have probably missed their true calling—as either a psychic or a homicide detective.

The victim of credit fraud is normally provided with false and misleading information, relies upon that information, ships product, and is never paid for the goods delivered. For fraud to occur, the victim must suffer an economic of financial loss as a result of the reliance on the false representation made by the buyer.

Credit fraud [and other types of fraud] can either involve

(a) Misrepresentation of relevant data such as an applicant providing phony trade references [references provided by co-conspirators], or

(b) In the concealment of a material fact.

FRAUDULENT FINANCIAL STATEMENTS

Credit fraud sometimes involves the use of fraudulent financial statements presented to the creditor in support of an applicant's request for open account credit terms. To be considered fraudulent, the financial statements must rise above the level of errors that creditors sometimes see on internally prepared financial statements when the prepared is not using Generally Accepted Accounting Principles. Fraudulent financial statements are created to deliberately misrepresent the true financial condition of the company. For a fraud to occur, the false financial statements must:

• be relied on by the injured party [in this case, a creditor company

• be material to the credit manager's decision to extend credit [material as opposed to trivial or irrelevant]

• must cause or result in economic injury or damage [in this case, a bad debt write off would be the most significant economic injury]

CREDIT CRIMINALS

Some individuals make their living by committing credit frauds. These are individuals who start businesses expressly to defraud creditors.

Occasionally, law enforcement authorities find businesspeople committing credit fraud who are generally honest but who are desperate to avoid bankruptcy and/or personal financial disaster. These businesspeople may be willing to commit one of the various forms of credit fraud in an effort to stay afloat. However, most of the large dollar frauds are committed by professional criminals, not by so-called white-collar criminals to try to salvage their business, and their personal finances.

MAIL FRAUD AND WIRE FRAUD

Section 18 of the United States Code makes it a Federal crime to use the United States mails to carry out a scheme to defraud. Section 18 of the U.S. Code also makes it a Federal offense to use interstate wire communications in carrying out a scheme to defraud. If a person knowingly and willfully devised a scheme to defraud, and that the U.S. mail or the interstate wire communications facilities were used to further that scheme to defraud, then that person is guilty of wire fraud or mail fraud. [The use of a fax machine to transmit an application, a purchase order, financial statements or any other documents in support of a scheme to defraud creditors would be considered wire fraud under federal statute].

It is hard to imagine a credit crime that does not involve or require that a criminal be willing to violate one or both of these federal laws. Even the simple act of placing an order with a seller almost certainly cannot be accomplished without using the mail or a fax or a telephone. The inescapable conclusion is that people prepared to commit credit fraud are not concerned about violating these federal laws.

CREDIT FRAUD NORMALLY INVOLVES A CONSPIRACY

For very practical reasons, many credit frauds involve a conspiracy to defraud creditors. Under Section 18 of the U.S. Code, a conspiracy involves an agreement among two or more parties in which the parties agree or conspire to commit another Federal crime. Many credit frauds involve a conspiracy by necessity because most credit managers would be somewhat reluctant to sell in large quantities to a "one-man" operation.

If the credit fraud involves providing the creditor with false trade references, then a conspiracy exists between the criminal running the scam and the people providing the false trade references by phone, fax or mail. It is not necessary for the party providing the false trade references to know all of the details of the credit scam, their willingness to provide false trade references to a potential creditor on behalf of another person creates a conspiracy... in this case a conspiracy to commit fraud. In addition to the crime of conspiracy, the person providing the false trade reference is almost certainly also guilty of either mail fraud or wire fraud.

HOW WIDESPREAD IS CREDIT FRAUD?

Accurate statistics about credit fraud are hard to obtain. If the credit fraud is truly successful, its victims will rarely be able to tell that a fraud has occurred. Credit fraud can never be eliminated given the competitive nature of American business and the pressure placed on credit professionals to make quick credit decisions.

Credit professionals can best serve their employers by being vigilant for signs of credit fraud. Credit managers need to make certain their company is not an easy target, and this chapter will describe steps credit managers can take to reduce the chances of becoming a victim of credit fraud in any of its many forms.

INDICATIONS OF THE POSSIBILITY OF CREDIT FRAUD

Indications of the possibility of credit fraud are not proof of fraud. Consider this scenario:

- The seller receives a rush order late on the afternoon on a Friday before a three-day weekend.
- The order is from a new customer, desperate for the product to ship.
- Willing to pay for the order on COD terms, and willing to pay for expedited handling for Saturday delivery.
- The buyer is not particularly concerned about price, product features or warranties.
- The credit department is unable to contact the company's bank which has closed for the day, and the credit reporting agency the creditor uses has no record of a company by that name at the location listed by the company.
- On the following business day the check is received and deposited.
- The check is returned two days later because the account was closed, and has been for more than a year.

Did a crime occur? The answer is maybe. Did the customer intend to pay for the shipment with a worthless check, or was it an honest mistake? There is not enough information to say. The creditor suspects criminal activity—but suspecting it accusing a customer of fraud are different. In this scenario, in a rush, late in the day, the customer might have simply picked up the wrong checkbook and written the check.

Creditors should to accuse anyone of committing credit fraud without absolute proof. Indications of fraud are not proof of fraud. Each of the following are indications of the potential for credit fraud:

- Receipt of a large, unsolicited rush order from a new account. [The key is the fact that the order is unsolicited. As most salespeople will tell you, new customers are scarce, unsolicited orders are scarce, and large opening orders are scarce. Putting all three together should be a red flag.

- A series of small initial orders paid on time, followed by an unexpectedly large order—or a situation in which the size of the order is out of proportion with the size of the company is an indication of trouble.

- The applicant is unknown to the creditor, and the credit bureau(s) that the credit department uses are unable to provide any information about the company.

- The applicant company has no references in the same industry as the creditor—and cannot explain from whom they purchased the goods they are now ordering from the creditor.

- The customer is known, but the buyer is not. A criminal will sometimes call a vendor pretending to be a buyer for a legitimate customer, order merchandise, arrange for it to be will-called, or shipped to an abandoned building or other location, will pick up the merchandise and disappear before the creditor even knows there is a problem.

- The seller has never shipped to the customer at the ship to location listed on the order.

- None of the trade references are companies that the credit manager is familiar with.

- None of the references listed are competitors.

- Without much protest, the customer agrees to provide the credit department with financial statements.

- The financial statements the applicant provides are not perfect, but they are surprisingly good.

- All of the trade references listed report the account was opened within in the last six months.

- The trade references contact go well beyond providing the normal facts and offer glowing opinions about the business, the owners, and the applicant's creditworthiness.

- The credit department finds itself pressed for a quick decision from all sides; from the customer, the salesperson, and sales management. Experienced credit professionals have learned that the harder they are pressed, the more cautious they should be with new customers.

AN INSIDE JOB

It is uncommon but not unprecedented that bad debt losses will occur because of the deliberate actions of one or more employees of the seller's credit department. This results from credit department personnel participating in decisions that do not conform to the "arms-length" principle. The company and the credit department should have a written policy that personal relationships may never influence the credit decision making process. Even better, the company should establish a requirement that employees reveal any potential conflicts of interest in writing to their employer, and that the company request updates to this written report at least once a year.

Occasionally, a customer or applicant will offer an employee of the credit department some type of bribe to extend credit or to release an order. The credit department should have a policy in place requiring that this offer be reported to the credit manager. When the credit manager receives such a report, he or she should document the conversation, suspend the account, update the file and determine what action should be taken. The credit manager must make a thorough study before approving any additional shipments on open account credit terms.

More frequently, an employee will have an undisclosed financial interest in a customer, and will base decisions about that customer on their personal financial interests rather than on the company's financial interests. Here is an example:

Assume the credit manager is an investor or a silent partner in a customer of their company. Even though the credit manager does not intend to defraud their employer, he or she may not employ the same degree of care in establishing the credit limit and in collecting delinquent balances as they would with a customer with whom they have no financial interest. The intent may not be to damage their employer—but by lowering the credit standards and slowed the collection process the credit manager has already done so.

Credit fraud involving an "insider" can be distinguished from bad credit decisions by the element of intent. A credit manager can make a decision that results in a bad debt loss and might be guilty of bad judgment, not of fraud. Determining when an insider is involved in committing fraud is difficult short of an outright confession. Even if the relationship between the employee and the customer were revealed or discovered, proving intent to defraud the company would be difficult. In this scenario, most companies would simply settle for the resignation of the employee involved.

BANKRUPTCY FRAUD—THE BUSTOUT

A bustout is a planned bankruptcy or insolvency. There are many variations on this basic theme, but a bustout normally works this way:

A criminal establishes a business with the intention of operating it for a short time. The criminal's goal is to quickly establish a reasonably good credit reputation, and then try to purchase large quantities of easily disposed of goods as quickly as possible—to sell the goods and pocket the cash. In a bustout, the criminal typically begins by buying small amounts of goods on open account terms and paying promptly. Current vendors are used as trade references to convince more companies to offer open account credit terms. Like a pyramid scheme, a successful bustout operator will order more and more goods from a larger and larger number of creditors. For a while, the criminal pays bills from the proceeds of selling the goods delivered by other creditors. Eventually, this becomes impossible. The Ponsi scheme collapses under its own weight. Credit dries up. Shipments slow down and once the criminal has sold as much of the inventory on hand as possible for cash the criminal either disappears or more frequently files for bankruptcy protection.

Prior to the liberalization of the U.S. Bankruptcy Code, a criminal engaged in a bustout had to "skip town" to avoid their creditors. Criminals now prefer to file for Chapter 7 bankruptcy and hope that their efforts to confuse and confound the trustee and creditors will work.

IN A BUSTOUT, TIMING IS CRITICAL

Sooner or later, the pyramid scheme involved in a bustout begins to crumble. The criminal realizes that it is time to order as much product as possible. Often, the bust-out occurs soon after a trade show. Armed with his or her best references and possibly a briefcase full of fraudulent financial statements, the credit criminal goes from booth to booth ordering product from every company willing to extend credit terms—regardless of product being ordered or the price being negotiated. As soon as these shipments arrive, the criminal sells as much of the merchandise in stock as possible, for cash and then:

(a) skips town with the proceeds of the sale and whatever merchandise that is left, or

(b) contacts a neutral third party and makes and Assignment for the Benefit of Creditors, or

(c) files for bankruptcy protection—typically under Chapter 7 of the U.S. Bankruptcy Code, hoping to shield the fact that the company's assets have been plundered from the creditors and the trustee.

A typical bustout operation will be in business for only a few months. Right up until the end the criminals will be looking for new creditors willing to sell to the company on open account terms.

BUSTOUTS DON'T JUST INVOLVE NEW ACCOUNTS

Bustouts often involve start up companies, but a popular variant on this model involve a change in control or ownership in which the criminal "buys" a business—but the change in control is not revealed to creditors. In this scenario, the original owner sells the business to the "new" owner for little or no down payment, but with a large balloon payment due shortly. The original owner might even be asked to stay on for a short time as a consultant. This adds to the outward appearance that it is business as usual. Under the cover of a legitimate business operation, the new owner will use the company's good credit reputation to order large quantities of product from existing creditors and from new ones. That merchandise is sold quickly, the proceeds are pocketed or they are embezzled from the company.

Of course, an unannounced change in ownership does not mean a credit fraud is involved or even contemplated. If the ownership change was concealed, the credit manager will probably want to know why. A change in ownership is simply another warning sign that an alert credit manager will take note of.

BANKRUPTCY FRAUD

The United States Trustee has dedicated significant resources to identifying bankruptcy fraud. The United States Trustee Programs works cooperatively with the Federal Bureau of Investigation and with the United States Attorneys in investigating and in prosecuting cases of bankruptcy fraud.

The Attorney General has stated publicly that she believes that only through aggressive law enforcement and criminal prosecutions can the integrity of the bankruptcy system be protected.

A private trustee has a fiduciary obligation to notify the U.S. Trustee if he or she suspects criminal wrongdoing in a bankruptcy case. The U.S. Trustee reviews all such referrals from private trustees to determine if enough facts exist to warrant additional investigation and referral to the U.S. Attorney.

ASSET CONCEALMENT

In Chapter 7 liquidation bankruptcies, asset concealment is the most common type of bankruptcy fraud. It is relatively simple to transfer [to convey] certain assets to a friend of relative "for safekeeping" in anticipation of a bankruptcy filing. Individual and corporate debtors that fail to list all of their assets on their bankruptcy schedules are guilty of fraud.

Because of the high volume of Chapter 7 bankruptcy filings [over 1 million in 1998] experts believe that most instances of asset concealment go undetected. Even in corporate bankruptcies, it is not uncommon for an individual to try to conceal and convert certain assets for their personal use or benefit.

ABUSE OF THE AUTOMATIC STAY

Another abuse of the Bankruptcy Code involves the abuse of the Automatic Stay provision. The Automatic Stay prevents collectors from attempting collection of pre-petition debts, from enforcing judgments, and from seeking orders that permit them to seize assets. In a bustout followed by a bankruptcy filing, occasionally a criminal may initially file under Chapter 11 of the Bankruptcy Code. The criminals will use the Automatic Stay provision to hold creditors at bay while they complete the liquidation of the assets of the company, or while they conceal or destroy as much evidence of their criminal activities as possible. Once their work is done, these credit criminals petition the Court to convert the case to Chapter 7 liquidation and disappear as quickly as possible—with the proceeds of the sales of the suppliers' inventory.

PIERCING THE CORPORATE VEIL

As mentioned earlier, many criminals prefer to incorporate to shield themselves from personal liability, and in order to create another layer of complexity between the criminal and the creditors of the company. In certain situations in which the creditors can demonstrate that the owner(s) of a corporation were engaged in a business created with the intent of defrauding creditors, creditors may be able to pierce the corporate veil. Piercing the corporate veil is a legal concept through which a corporation's stockholders, who are normally shielded from liability for the corporation's activities and debts, can and are held responsible for the losses resulting from the bustout.

CAN CREDITORS PREVENT BUSTOUTS?

Creditors cannot prevent bustouts, however there are a number of things that credit managers can do to reduce the chances that they will become the victims of a "bust-out." The first step involves having an understanding of the mechanics of a bustout. Once credit managers understand how bustouts work they can be alert to indications of problems and act appropriately.

Some of the more common defenses credit professionals use against bustouts include the following:

- Bustout operations are typically only in business for only a few months. Therefore, credit managers need to exercise caution when considering extending credit to a newly found company.

- Bustout operations tend to purchase in large dollar volumes relatively quickly. Customers normally grow slowly over time as the creditor company captures more and more of their business. Therefore, new customers that want to purchase large quantities relatively quickly are a potential problem.

- Bustout operations often buy products that do not make sense for their business when they are in the bustout phase of the operation. An example would be sporting goods equipment being delivered to a machine shop. Therefore, credit managers need to be alert to situations in which the product being ordered does not make sense for the business ordering it.

- In a bustout, the criminal will order in whatever quantity they can get on open account terms. An indication of a potential problem is a scenario in which the quantity of goods being ordered does not make sense. Credit professionals should consider whether or not the quantity of goods being ordered makes sense.

- Bustout operations typically do not welcome visitors. Another indication of a potential problem is a situation in which the salesperson has never been to the business location. Therefore, the credit manager should be sent copies of trip reports for their file. If a new customer has not been visited by the salesperson, the credit manager should be suspicious.

- Bustout operations develop a handful of legitimate credit references and use them as a springboard to convince other trade creditors to extend credit to them. These references receive numerous inquiries from other creditors—and the inquiries begin soon after the account is opened. Therefore, if the creditor is inundated with trade reference inquiries from other creditors about a new account, this should be a reason for concern and caution.

- Bustout operations often use "front men" to set up businesses. If the individual reported to be the owner or President of the company does not appear to have the business experience necessary or cannot explain where the capital came from to start the business, a red flag should go up.

- In the beginning of the bustout involving a relatively new company, criminals often falsify trade references to try to quality quickly to purchase from legitimate suppliers. Therefore, credit professionals should independently verify the trade references listed by:

  Calling directory assistance

  Checking the Dun & Bradstreet Æ reference book for a listing of the company

  Placing a call to the trade reference listed rather than accepting calls from the reference. [This way, you know the telephone number of the party you are speaking to]

DIVERSION OF SHIPMENT FRAUD

Diversion of shipment fraud is a relatively low tech, low risk type of credit fraud. Diversion of shipment involves an unauthorized change in the routing of a shipment in transit. The fraud works this way:

A criminal posing as a legitimate customer calls the creditor's sales department and places an order. The next day, the criminal calls and gets the tracking number for the shipment [Some creditor companies even offer access to this information on their web page as a convenience to customers.] The criminal calls the shipping company posing as a representative of the seller, and instructs the carrier to re-route the shipment to another location.

Once the goods are delivered, the criminal arranges for the merchandise to be picked and the merchandise and the criminal disappear. There is a low-tech way of preventing this type of fraud. Creditors can simply contact their freight carriers and establish written agreements about if, when, and how a shipment may be re-routed while in transit. Once this agreement with the carrier is formalized against this fraud.

If an agreement such as this is in place and in writing and assuming the shipment is somehow diverted, then the carrier should be liable for the loss instead of the shipper/creditor.

NOTE: Diversion of shipment fraud should not be confused with the crime of Diversion. Diversion involves the distribution of products into a market other than the one originally intended in violation of contract, law or regulation. A simple example of a Diversion would involve the purchase of high tech components by an end user that in turn diverts the shipment to a government or to a country to which such an export would be illegal under U.S. export law.

Often, a Diversion occurs because companies authorize price differentials on certain products for delivery into certain regions of the world. Unscrupulous businesspeople will capitalize on these legitimate price differentials by re-routing shipments to wherever they will receive the highest price for the merchandise.

Some might the scenario described above is the basis of capitalism and the free market, but in some cases suppliers have goals are not strictly profit driven. For example, some U.S. drug manufacturers are making available at or below cost certain drug treatments to countries that would otherwise be unable to afford the drugs. For these shipments to be diverted back to the U.S. and sold to the highest bidder defeats the drug companies' efforts to get their product where it is needed—at a price that local patients can afford. Diversion is not a victimless crime.

FRAUDULENT TRADE REFERENCES

One of the cornerstones of the new account investigation process involves contacting trade references. The theory behind this process is that past payment performance is a good predictor of future performance. Unfortunately, as much as 50% of all business frauds involve the use of fraudulent references.

Consider this scenario. A creditor company receives a credit application, orders a credit report and finds there is limited information. The creditor then contacts the trade references listed on the application. Each of the trade references indicates the applicant has been doing business with them for a relatively short period of time, but pays its bills on time and has never missed a single payment. In today's highly competitive business environment, the credit department would have a hard job justifying a decision to deny credit to the applicant. The applicant would probably be offered a modest to moderate credit line and monitored carefully.

However, if the creditor knew that one or more of the references contacted were fraudulent, specifically that the references were conspiring to help the applicant to secure open account credit terms, no credit would be extended.

Credit managers should make it a rule to deny credit any time they find an applicant has lied. Chances are excellent that there are additional lies the creditor has not discovered. Since the Character of the applicant is an important factor in considering the creditworthiness of the company, providing false information should automatically disqualify the applicant.

VERIFYING THE CUSTOMER'S TRADE REFERENCES

There are a number of ways to verify that an applicant has provided legitimate trade references and not fraudulent references from co-conspirators. The first method is the simplest. The creditor can check with directory assistance to verify the reference is listed, and equally important is listed at the telephone number provided. The credit department should always call the number provided by directory assistance rather than the one offered by the buyer.

Still another test of the legitimacy of a trade reference involves nothing more than looking up the company in a credit rating book. If the company name does not appear, this is a red flag.

CONTRADICTORY INFORMATION

If the creditor has any questions or concerns about the references listed, the credit manager should request additional trade references. For example, if the creditor learns contradictory information from the references, then additional trade references should be requested. For example, if one trade reference lists the applicant as slow and another lists the acount as prompt then more trade references are required. Other indications of potential problems with the references listed include:

- References that answer the telephone without giving the company name or the name of the department. Chances are good that a customer of another supplier is going to have another's supplier's credit department's telephone number.

- References listing only fax numbers. It is unlikely that an applicant would have the fax numbers for its suppliers' credit departments.

- All of the references listed are in the same area code. That scenario is not impossible, it is just unusual.

- The telephone number provided goes directly to the supplier's credit department and to the specific person that can provide the trade reference

FRAUDULENT AUDITOR'S OPINION LETTER

As noted above, criminals intent on committing credit fraud sometimes provide potential creditors with fraudulent financial statements. Occasionally, these fraudulent financial statements even contain a fraudulent auditor's opinion letter indicating that the statements were audited.

Unfortunately, criminals have learned from their past mistakes and are unlikely to make the same mistakes twice. For example, it is relatively easy to confirm that a CPA firm audited a set of financial statements. For this reason, criminals normally sacrifice the "seal of approval" that an auditor's opinion letter adds to a set of financial statements for the safety of not having to provide such an obvious problem discovered easily.

FRAUDULENT FINANCIAL STATEMENTS

Twenty years ago, a credit textbook might have suggested that if the credit professional finds glaring problems with an applicant's financial statements that the creditor would want to exercise reasonable caution against the possibility of credit fraud. Con men have learned from these mistakes and are unlikely to be sloppy enough to present financial statements with any of these problems:

- The balance sheet doesn't balance.

- The income statement shows extraordinarily high gross and net profit margins [for example, a distributor with a 25% gross margin and a 10% net profit margin.

- Assets and liabilities are listed in round figures [for example, accounts payable of $125,000]

Credit managers are likely to find more subtle problems if they find anything at all wrong with the financial statements. Examples of these subtle inconsistencies would include:

- Having a relatively new, privately held business with a relatively large retained earnings. This scenario is possible, but unlikely.

- Doing a comparative analysis and finding a relatively new company's financial statements are as good or better than industry norms.

- Reviewing a relatively new company's Income Statement and finding that the company's sales and profits have grown steadily since inception. This is not impossible, but it is unlikely since the company's more established competitors are unlikely to stand idly by while the new company takes market share and potential profits.

Therefore, credit managers must review a customer's financial statements in the context of whatever additional information they know about the industry or the type of business the company is in. If something does not make sense, the credit professional has an obligation to ask for additional information and continue to investigate the applicant until his or her concerns are confirmed or proved to be without merit.

BULK SALES AND FRAUD

A bulk sale or bulk transfer involves the sale of a major portion of a company's assets, when that sale is made in other than the ordinary course of business. A merchant contemplating a bulk transfer must notify its creditors at least ten days before the seller takes possession of the goods. The notification to creditors is required under Article 6 of the Uniform Commercial Code [UCC].

The goal of the bulk sale notice is to give creditors the opportunity to try to prevent the sale from being completed if the creditors are convinced that the buyer or seller may be conspiring to defraud creditors.

CHECK FRAUD

Check fraud is a growth industry. The Office of the Comptroller of the Currency estimates that check fraud losses exceed $15 billion a year—and that check fraud is growing at a faster rate than the growth in check volume. Check fraud is relatively low risk with potentially significant returns, and a good chance of success.

One popular check fraud scam involves the fact that creditors may be willing to sell to new accounts on COD terms with little or no credit investigation. Credit managers often mistakenly believe that a term of COD, and in particular COD cash terms cash eliminates credit risk. It does not. The use of counterfeit checks is on the rise. Criminals can defraud creditors by using a forged cashier's check to pay for a COD shipments. Forged cashier's checks are quickly and easily created using electronic image processing equipment, desktop publishing and a color printer.

THE FRAUDULENT CASHIER'S CHECK

A cashier's check fraud scam typically works this way: A new customer contacts the sales department and asks about placing a large, rush order. The customer indicates they are willing to pay by cashier's check on the opening order while the creditor checks out the company's references. The seller agrees to COD Cash terms. Delivery drivers are typically not allowed to collect cash, so COD Cash terms actually involves or requires payment on delivery by cashier's check.

When the goods arrive, the driver is given a forged cashier's check. Even before the carrier delivers the fraudulent check to the seller for deposit, the merchandise and the criminal have disappeared. Criminals know that it will take the several days for the carrier to deliver the forged check to the creditor, for the creditor to deposit the check and for the issuing bank to dishonor the forgery.

There are typically a number of red flags relating to this type of check fraud, including these:

- It is a rush order
- To a new account
- The company is willing to pay COD, even COD cash if necessary
- The creditor is not able to gather much information about the account [for example: no credit bureau report is available, or no bank reference is available]

A creditor can eliminate the risk of fraud by offering this simple alternative to COD cash terms: Since the customer has to go to its bank anyway, ask the customer to wire transfer payment rather than getting a cashier's check from its bank. Creditors should not release the order until their bank has received the wire transfer. Photocopies of documentation provided by the debtor that the wire transfer is on its way is insufficient because it can easily be forged. Instead, the creditor should simply wait for confirmation that payment has been received before releasing the pending order.

USING THE ACH TO BEAT CHECK FRAUD

Another way to beat check fraud involves requiring customers to remit payment via the Automated Clearinghouse [ACH]. The ACH prevents check fraud by eliminating checks. ACH transfers have the added benefit of eliminating check printing costs and mailing costs.

INDICATIONS OF A FORGED CASHIER'S CHECK

- There is no listing for the issuing bank with directory assistance.

- The issuing bank cannot or will not confirm it issued the check.

- The check is presented to the creditor after its bank has closed—in particular the day before a bank holiday or a three-day weekend.

- The check itself smudges when rubbed with a moist fingertip. The check has no watermark on the paper

- The check is printed on poor quality paper

- One or more words are misspelled

NSF CHECKS

Sometimes, a criminal will simply order goods for delivery on COD terms and issue a check drawn on an account with insufficient funds, or drawn on a closed account. What this scam lacks in sophistication, it makes up in boldness. As a negotiable instrument, a check only has value if the maker has funds available to cover the check.

Another scam that may be intended to defraud creditors or simply to delay payment by failing to sign the check, or by making the amount illegible, or by having one signature when two are required. What differentiates these acts or omissions as being fraudulent rather than accidental is the intent of the customer. If they intended to delay payment, they are guilty of fraud. If the customer made an honest mistake, then there is no fraud.

NSF CHECKS AND FRAUD

Receipt of a NSF check by itself is not proof of a fraud. However, returned checks may be strong indicators of a potential fraud if:

- The returned check represents the first payment the creditor has received
- The returned check represents the largest payment the creditor has received
- The return check was issued by a relatively new account
- The bank reports the returned check was drawn on a closed account
- The creditor company learns that other creditors have received NSF checks and have placed the account for collection
- When the creditor contacts the bank for an update, it learns there have been a substantial number of NSF checks
- The debtor acknowledges the NSF check, but refuses to replace it.

THE NAME GAME SCAM

A popular scam involves little more than claiming to be a subsidiary or division of a major corporation. There are many variations on the name game scam. One involves a new ship-to address for an established customer or for a nationally known company. This version of the name-game scam often works this way:

Late on a Friday, the sales department receives a call from an individual purporting to be the buyer for a major company. The "buyer" explains that his or her normal supplier has closed early for the weekend leaving the customer with insufficient product on hand for Monday's production schedule. The order is placed immediately. The credit department is notified and asked to release the order on open account terms. The credit department cannot verify any connection between the "buyer" and the creditworthy company. The salesperson contacts the "purchasing agent." The purchasing agent offers to pay COD company check or even COD cash as long as the goods ship for arrival on Monday morning. If and when the goods are delivered, the carrier is given a worthless company check or a forged cashier's check. The goods and the criminal promptly disappear. Beating this scam can be accomplished by:

- Requiring wire transfer payment in advance of shipment.
- Just saying no. Refusing to release the order until ownership can be confirmed.

- Refusing to release the order until the alleged parent company confirms the existence, relationship, as well as the billing and shipping address of their division or subsidiary.

- Arranging for someone to drop by or at least drive by the business to confirm its existence, and to verify it is a legitimate business address and not a mail drop, executive suite, or temporary facility.

Another form of the name-game scam involves setting up a company with a name similar to a legitimate company in the same city as the legitimate company -relying on the similarity in names to cause confusion. A hypothetical example of this version of the name-game scam might work this way: A criminal might establish a company in Los Angeles called Apple Tree Specialty Products Company in hopes of confusing creditors who think they are dealing with a legitimate business called Apple Tree Specialty Production Company. What criminals are counting on is that some creditors will recognize the name Apple Tree and will not bother to confirm that the applicant company is *the* Apple Tree company they are familiar with.

INTERNET FRAUD

Fraud on the Internet is a rapidly growing crime. Criminals have been quick to seize this new technology and find ways to beat creditors out of their money or their products. One of the most common problems involves a situation in which a company advertises its goods for sale on the Internet. Because of the anonymity of the Internet, criminals were quick to see the possibility of using stolen credit card numbers to order product offered for sale on the Internet. It is a difficult crime to defeat.

Many companies consider Internet based credit card fraud an unfortunate and inevitable aspect of dealing with credit card purchasers other than face to face. It is possible to use sophisticated software to compare the ship-to address with the credit card holder's bill-to address. If the credit card holder's bill-to address is in one state and the desired ship-to address is in another, a reasonable cautious creditor might be interested in this transaction and concerned about the possibility of credit fraud.

INTERNATIONAL FRAUD

International credit fraud is a growth industry. Certain countries have a higher incidence of corruption than others do, and this information must be taken into consideration any time a credit decision is being made. One source of on line ratings of the level of corruption in various countries can be found at www.tranparency.com.

Criminals rely on the fact that international fraud is hard to trace, expensive to prove, and difficult to prosecute. Even a successful prosecution is unlikely to result in payment to the creditor or the recovery of goods. In some countries, bribery of a foreign official or of company officers is not a crime. In fact, some countries allow such payments to be listed as deductible expenses on company income statements.

At this time, there is no international convention governing bribery and other unfair competitive practices such as those forbidden in the United States under the Foreign Corrupt Practices Act. The practice of using bribery to secure export business is widespread.

COMBATING INTERNATIONAL FRAUD

A number of organizations have been established to combat the increase of commercial frauds worldwide. Statistics indicate that international commercial fraud is growing faster than the growth of international commerce. International frauds tend to be more complex and involve larger sums of money than domestic commercial frauds. This is a good reason for credit professionals to be particularly careful and vigilant when considering international sales transactions.

One organizations intent on combating international credit fraud is the Commercial Crime Service—a division of the International Chamber of Commerce [the ICC]. The ICC has also established the International Maritime Bureau to deal with all types of crime, including fraud and cargo theft. The Commercial Crime Service [CCS] counsels member companies on fraud prevention and about working with law enforcement.

Another ICC division, the Commercial Crime Bureau [CCB] works proactively with police, customs and other law enforcement agencies to investigate cross-border commercial fraud and to make recoveries. The CCB maintains an extensive database on all aspects of commercial credit fraud. CCB members receive fraud warnings, special reports, and commercial crime summaries.

The International Maritime Bureau's practical services for members include recommending specific practices that reduce a seller's vulnerability to fraud, due diligence advice, investigation, seminars, special reports and alerts, confidential bulletins, and advice on claims and recoveries. The goal of the IMB is to prevent and to contain fraud and other illegal practices in international trade. To that end, the IMB investigates incidences of fraud and suggests avenues and procedures to help creditors to recover their products or their losses.

SUMMARY

Fraud is a cost of doing business on open account terms, just as bad debt losses are. Credit professionals must establish internal procedures and guidelines to reduce their vulnerability to credit fraud, and they must update these procedures regularly as criminals devise new schemes to separate creditors from their merchandise. No creditor can prevent credit fraud, and the costs associated with attempting to do so would be prohibitive.

CHAPTER 33

FRAUDULENT FINANCIAL STATEMENTS

Fraud involves an intentional misrepresentation of material existing facts made by one person to another. That misrepresentation is made intentionally with knowledge of the falsity of the information, and with the intent of inducing the other person to act in a way which results in injury or damage to that person. To constitute fraud, a misrepresentation must be false, and it must be material in the sense that it relates to a matter of some importance, and to constitute actual fraud the damaged party must have relied on the misrepresentation and suffered economic injury or damage as a result.

FINANCIAL STATEMENT FRAUD

Providing creditors with fraudulent financial statements as a way to induce them to ship goods on open account terms is fraud. It does not matter that the intent of the individual delivering the fraudulent financial statements might have been to pay for the goods when they came due. The act of delivering false financial statements in an attempt to deceive another into acting in a way, which creates economic benefit to the debtor and economic harm to the creditor, constitutes fraud.

For the purpose of this chapter, financial statement fraud shall be broadly defined as:

> Involving the publication and distribution of materially misleading financial statements with the intent of causing creditors to act

in a manner they would not do if the true financial condition of the company were revealed. Materially misleading financial statements are statements in which there has been deliberate manipulation of financial data including the omission of certain relevant information and significant distortion of other data.

Financial statement fraud is commonly accomplished primarily through the intentional misapplication of accounting principles in order to overstate profits, or assets or revenues. Another common device involves understating losses, expenses or liabilities.

However, as it relates to financial statement fraud involving an attempt to induce trade creditors to extend credit to an otherwise un-creditworthy company, the fraud may involve nothing less than the fabrication of an entire set of financial statements. Financial statements intended for use in perpetrating a credit fraud does not have to stand up to scrutiny for long. In most instances, the goal of the credit criminal is to get as much product delivered on open account credit terms as possible, to sell that merchandise and to disappear or file for bankruptcy protection before the trade creditor realizes there is a problem.

DELIVERY OF FRAUDULENT FINANCIAL STATEMENTS

According to Section 18 of the United States Code it is a federal offense for anyone to use the United States mails in carrying out a scheme to obtain money or property by means of false or fraudulent misrepresentations [18 U.S.C. 1341]. One prevalent myth about fraudulent financial statements is that a criminal who would use fraudulent financial statements to induce creditors to extend credit to a company would not send those financial statements by the U.S. mail.

The reasoning applied is that a criminal would be concerned about violating the federal mail fraud statute. It is probably fair to say that criminals willing to engage in a credit fraud involving a completely fabricated set of financial statements are not likely to be overly concerned about adding yet another offense to a list of offenses that would [probably] already include fraud, grand theft, conspiracy, and wire fraud. Therefore, the rule of thumb that suggested that financial statements received by mail were more reliable than financial statements that were hand delivered can probably be described as unreliable.

The entire discussion of how financial statements are delivered suggests or implies that the people in charge of these criminal enterprises are well educated, and in some sense criminal masterminds. They are not. Financial statement fraud is simple.

Anyone with a personal computer and even rudimentary knowledge of Lotus® or Excel® can create quite realistic looking internally prepared financial statements. The key to the success of most credit crimes is not the sophistication of the criminal, but the willingness of the criminal to commit a variety of crimes and risk being arrested in order to "con' credit managers into shipping goods on open account terms.

THE MYTH THAT CREDIT MANAGERS CAN SPOT FINANCIAL STATEMENT FRAUD

Fraudulent financial statements are normally intended to make a company's earnings look better than they actually are. Fraudulent financial statements may be created to cover up an embezzlement, or may be an attempt to cover up errors in judgment or changes in the marketplace that have caused the company to fail to reach its forecasts or targets. Some of the most common reasons people commit financial fraud include:

- To induce trade creditors to continue to extend credit.

- To induce banks to lend money, or to demonstrate the company is meeting the loan covenants on money already borrowed.

- To increase the stock price, or to induce investment in the company's stock by dispelling negative market perceptions about the company.

- To demonstrate that the management of the company has the requisite skills to manage the company successfully or to cover up mistakes made by management.

- To cover up an embezzlement of funds.

- To show the company was profitable when in fact it was not, in order to "earn" specific performance related bonuses.

- To defraud creditors into extending credit they would otherwise be unwilling to extend.

A prevalent myth is that credit managers have the tools at their disposal to spot financial statement fraud simply by carefully analyzing a customer's financial statements. It has been suggested that credit managers through their vigilance can differentiate between legitimate and fraudulent financial statements.

It is fair to say that:

(1) On occasion, a credit criminal engaged in financial statement fraud will make a mistake so glaring that a credit manager can spot a problem, but

(2) Financial statement fraud does not necessarily involve a complete fabrication of a company's financial statements, and

(3) Criminals do not frequently make glaring mistakes [like submitting balance sheets that do not balance], and

(4) Financial statement fraud often involves subtle manipulation of the company's financial statements, not wholesale changes that grossly distort the financial results as reported in the financial statements, so

(5) To spot financial fraud, credit managers would normally need unprecedented access to things that are simply not available. For example, in order to confirm the value of inventory listed the creditor would need to be able to perform physical inventory counts—and this is just one example of the steps the credit manager would need to "audit" a customer's financial statements and make an assessment of their accuracy.

In many instances, financial statement frauds have occurred even when an independent CPA firm audited the company's books. As described in the next section, financial statement fraud can exist even when the CPA completes a full annual audit, and performing quarterly updates in conformity with the reporting rules established by the U.S. Securities and Exchange Commission and the Financial Accounting Standards Board.

If financial statement fraud can occur with public companies whose financial statements are subject to review by independent auditors, by the SEC and by stockholders, then it certainly can occur in privately held companies not subject to anything approaching this level of scrutiny.

FRAUDULENT FINANCIAL REPORTING IN PUBLICLY TRADED COMPANIES

In early 1999, the Committee of Sponsoring Organizations [COSO] published a reported titled "Fraudulent Financial Reporting: 1987 to 1997. In that report, COSO summarized the findings of investigations conducted by the Securities and Exchange Commission of the United States [the SEC] into the problem of fraudulent financial statements issued by 200 publicly traded companies.

The COSO report presented a comprehensive overview of how financial statements were falsified; who is likely to be involved in creating fraudulent financial statements; and why people participate in financial fraud—especially given the fact that both civil and criminal penalties may apply to persons found in violation of the Securities and Exchange Act. Some of the more important findings of the COSO report are detailed below:

- The incidence of fraudulent financial statements was higher among smaller publicly traded companies than in larger publicly traded companies.

- The typical size of the companies committing credit fraud was less than $100 million in annual sales, with a high concentration with sales of less than $50 million annually.

- The majority of the companies [78%] were not listed on the New York or the American Stock Exchanges.

- 45% of the audit reports covering financial statements that turned out to be fraudulent contained a "going concern" statement by the Independent Auditor.

- In more than 83% of the cases the Chief Executive Officer and/or the Chief Financial Officer were participants in the fraud.

- In some cases, the pressure to falsify financial statements came from desire to meet Wall Street's profit expectations, or the corporation's own financial performance estimates.

- Fraudulent financial statements were more likely to be generated when the board of directors was made up of insiders.

- Fraudulent financial statements were more likely to be generated when the companies involved were reporting net losses, or were close to break even in the accounting periods prior to the financial fraud.

- Relatively few individuals involved in the financial frauds uncovered by the SEC's enforcement division served prison sentences for their crimes—although most were subject to significant civil penalties.

- Fraudulent financial statements were more likely to be reported in companies without an Audit Committee —or occurred in a company in which the audit committee met infrequently. In 65% of the fraud cases, no one on the audit committee was a CPA.

- Fraud was more likely to occur when the Board of Directors that was only nominally independent or was dominated by insiders.

The report also found that most financial frauds were not limited to a single financial period. This is because once a financial statement fraud has occurred, it is sometimes necessary that it be perpetuated over time. If it is not, the fraud may become evident.

The most common fraud techniques listed in the COSO report involved the overstatement of revenues and/or assets. In many instances, revenues were recorded prematurely. About half of the frauds also involved overstating assets by understating certain allowances for receivables, over-stating inventories, or overstating the value or property, plant and equipment. Approximately 50% of the companies in the COSO fraud study either ended up in bankruptcy or experienced a significant change of ownership [or both].

The financial statements of the 200 companies in this study were all subject to audit by independent CPA firms. The CPA firms were [presumably] given full access to the officers of the corporation and to the source documents supporting the financial statements as presented by management.

One of the implications of this report is that if a CPA located on site and charged with independently evaluating the financial statements over a period of several quarters and in some cases over a period of several years was unable to detect fraud, then it seems unlikely that a credit manager reviewing the end product, a customer's financial statement will be successful in identifying a financial statement fraud.

Of course, this assumes that the criminal involved in preparing the financial statements knows enough about accounting to prepare reasonably good financial statements—and does not make one or more glaring mistakes.

GLARING MISTAKES

Occasionally, a credit manager will be "lucky" enough to receive a set of financial statements from a customer or an applicant that are so obviously flawed that they lead the credit manager to believe that the statements represent an attempt by the customer to commit fraud. It is important that credit managers and their subordinates remember that indications of fraud are not proof that an applicant attempted to defraud the creditor. Some of the more obvious indications of the *possibility* that the financial statements the customer has submitted are fraudulent include:

- Randomly dated financial statements. Companies normally end their accounting periods at the end of a quarter and less commonly at the end of a month that is not also the end of a calendar quarter. Creditors should be concerned about randomly dated financial statements—for example, statements dated March 13th or September 23rd.

- Rounded figures. Most companies' financial statements do not contain any rounded figures. For example, a statement that lists inventory at $126,000 should be a red flag to creditors. Accounting rules do not permit rounding of this type—so the most charitable interpretation is that the person preparing the statements does not understand Generally Accepted Accounting Principles. This may be reason enough to discount the statements or to reject the application.

- The location of the CPA firm. Assuming the financial statements come with a auditor's opinion letter from a CPA firm, the credit manager would not be mistaken to be concerned if the auditor is not located in the same State as the debtor. It would be "unusual" to engage a CPA firm from another State. At the very least, this should trigger a call to the CPA firm to confirm they were engaged to perform the audit in question.

LOOKING FOR INCONSISTENCIES

Many times, it is not the obvious flaws in fraudulent financial statements that an alert credit professional will notice. Often, it is subtle inconsistencies that cause the credit professional to become more cautious. These more subtle inconsistencies would include:

- Inventory turnovers significantly higher than the industry norm

- Profit margins [gross or net] significantly higher than the industry norms.

- A relatively new company reporting a large net worth, and /or a significant amount in retained earnings.

- A balance sheet indicating the applicant has a lot of cash when this is inconsistent with the applicant's bank's average balance rating.

HOW TO FALSIFY FINANCIAL STATEMENTS

There are an endless variety of ways for companies to commit financial fraud. Unfortunately, many of them are undetectable to an outsider whose only insight into the financial performance of the company is the financial data that the customer presents. As credit professionals know, it is rare to get a fully audited financial statement from a privately held company. Often, the credit manager has to settle for a Balance Sheet and/or an Income Statement covering one accounting period.

It is not uncommon for financial statement fraud to involve several different methods for falsifying a company's financial performance. Some of the more common types of financial statement fraud involve:

- Recognizing revenues in the wrong accounting period

- Overstating assets such as inventory.

- Recording consigned inventory as owned inventory.

- Understating liabilities, including accounts payable

- Holding checks after recording them as being disbursed.

- Deferring the reporting of certain expenses that should not have been deferred according to Generally Accepted Accounting Principles

- Inadequate disclosure of related party transactions

Accelerating revenue recognition is relatively simple. It is often done by simply recognizing sales of merchandise that had not actually shipped as of the close of the accounting period.

Another way to manipulate revenues involves not recognizing customer returns in the proper accounting period, which is a violation of the matching principle. Some companies feel they are not "technically" violating the matching principle when the company simply refuses to issue return merchandise authorizations toward the end of a quarter, or near the end of the fiscal year.

Deferring discretion expenditures into the next accounting period is not financial statement fraud. It is a legitimate business strategy. Here is an example: A company might note that revenues were not as high as expected in the current period and in an effort to make certain that the company achieved its profit targets the company could mandate that discretionary expenditures be deferred. Discretionary expenditures might include certain types of off-site training, the purchase of certain new equipment, and certain types of business trips. Fraud occurs when a company deliberately delays the recognition of an expense [under the accrual accounting method] until the next accounting period.

A fraud involving overstating long term assets can be as simple as selling a piece of equipment, but failing to record the sale and to reduce the value of fixed assets.

Another form of financial fraud involves the failure to write down the book value of an intangible asset that is no longer worth what it is being carried on the books at.

CONDITIONS THAT CONTRIBUTE TO THE POTENTIAL FOR FRAUD

Certain factors increase the likelihood that a company will engage in financial fraud. Some of the most common factors that contribute to financial fraud include:

- When people in key positions do not have the proper background and education to detect and / or to prevent financial fraud.

- When employees that spot irregularities are not encouraged to report their concerns or suspicions, or when management makes it known directly or indirectly that it is more concerned about the results than they are about how the results were achieved.

- When the computerized management information system is not adequate for the company.

- When a good financial control system is permitted to deteriorate due to neglect or simply due to a lack of funds to upgrade the system.

- When internal controls are weak.

- When there is no external oversight of the firm's operations as is often the case with a small, privately held company that present internally prepared financial statements.

- Whenever the firm's financial statements are not audited.

THE INTIMIDATION FACTOR

One of the biggest factors contributing to the possibility of financial fraud involves a scenario in which the management of the firm is able to intimidate, manipulate or coerce the firm's internal auditors, or its independent CPA firm. Unless the CPA firm is able to maintain its independence, the resulting financial statements will be suspect. It is interesting to note that in the COSO report referenced above dealing with financial statement fraud investigated by the SEC, over 25% of the companies involved changed auditors during the period in which the fraud occurred. One way that management can deal with a CPA firm that asserts its independence is to fire the firm and hire another that will hopefully be more flexible.

Financial statement frauds sometimes occur because of the unique relationship between the firm and its outside auditors. Specifically, the CPA firm has a dual role as an independent contractor working for the firm and seeking to maintain good client relations, and an independent watchdog willing to challenge management's statements, assumptions and facts.

When the CPA firm cannot find the right balance between autonomy and accommodation, the quality of the financial statements being presented will suffer.

AUDITED FINANCIAL STATEMENTS AND FRAUD

There is a common misconception that audited financial statements are error free and fraud proof. Audited financial statements can be fraudulent. A description of some of the types of fraud that occur and some of the reasons fraud occurs are listed below:

- Fraud can be as simple as the intentional misapplication of one or more Generally Accepted Accounting Principles.

- Fraud may involve misrepresentation of the facts about specific transactions—which may in turn require the alteration of accounting records and documents.

- Related party transactions are not properly identified or recorded.

- Auditors offer an opinion about the accuracy of financial statements, not a guarantee

- Auditors rely on written and oral representations and explanations provided by management to specific inquiries during their audit. Misrepresentations made by senior management may result in the presentation of fraudulent or at best misleading financial statements.

- Often, executive management has a personal financial interest in the company's financial performance. Specifically, a significant amount of their compensation may be tied to the operating results of the company as reported in its financial statements. As a result, these executives may make inappropriate decisions in order to enhance the company's financial performance.

- It is relatively easy to improve the Income Statement by concealing losses and by lowering reserve requirements, or by reporting revenues and their attendant profits before the sale is actually made.

- Fraud perpetrated by the executive management team is often done in order to hide poor operating results; or in an effort to help the company meet sales or revenue forecasts made by senior management to its creditors and/or its investors.

- Internal controls designed to prevent fraud, such as segregation of duties are subject to inherent limitations such as the possibility of collusion among employees to defraud their employer.

- Another situation in which executive management may be tempted to engage in disseminating fraudulent financial statements is when management has personally guaranteed the debt(s) of a corporation

Audit risk involves the fact that errors may occur in a company's accounting policies and procedures, combined with the possibility that the auditor's sampling method may not discover these errors.

THE RESPONSIBILITIES OF INDEPENDENT AUDITORS

Certified Public Accountants are required under the Statement of Auditing Standard #82 [SAS 82] to plan and to perform an audit in such a way that they have "reasonable assurance" about the fact that financial statements they have audited are free from material misstatements, whether caused by error or by fraud. Based on this auditing standard for financial statements audited after December 15, 1997, credit managers have a reasonable but not an absolute assurance that the statements they receive do not contain any material misstatements.

SAS #82 requires that auditors specifically assess the risk of fraud, and it requires auditors to ask executive management if they are aware of any fraud that has taken place. SAS #82 provides auditors with a comprehensive list of fraud risk factors to evaluate. The goal of SAS #82 is to make audited financial statements more reliable.

TELLTALE SIGNS OF FRAUDULENT FINANCIAL STATEMENTS

Any time a creditor receives financial statements from a customer, unless the statements are audited by a CPA firm and the auditors have offered their unqualified opinion as the their accuracy the creditor must always wonder about how accurately the statements truly reflect the financial condition of the customer. As stated previously, one of the most important differences between fraud and simple error or incompetence is intent. If the party presenting knew the financial statements were fraudulent, then offering those statements to trade creditors in support of a request for open account terms constitutes fraud. On the other hand, many companies present financial statements that are internally prepared, are unaudited, do not follow Generally Accepted Accounting Principles (GAAP), contain errors and omissions and are not fraudulent. This chapter deals with the former situation—a deliberate attempt to obtain goods and services form a creditor by presenting that creditor with financial statements the customer knows to be fraudulent.

THE SECURITIES ACT OF 1933

The Securities Act of 1933 requires that investors receive financial and other relevant and significant information concerning securities being offered for public sale. The Act prohibits deceit, misrepresentations, financial fraud, and other fraud in the sale of securities.

The Securities Exchange Act of 1934 requires that investors have access to current financial statements and other information regarding securities. This Act also prohibits companies, securities brokerage firms and others from engaging in fraudulent and unfair business practices.

Both of these federal laws specifically address the issue of fraudulent financial statements. While these Acts do not prevent creditors from receiving fraudulent financial statements, the actions of the SEC's Division of Enforcement try to prevent this type of crime. The SEC vigorously urges the United States Attorney to prosecute deliberate violations of either of the two Acts listed above.

SUMMARY

Because of the risks associated with relying too heavily on financial statements, credit professionals would be well advised to carefully examine both financial and non-financial factors before granting credit to an applicant or significantly increasing the credit limit to a relatively new customer. Non-financial considerations in credit granting include:

- The five Cs of commercial credit. [Character, Capacity, Capital, Conditions, and Collateral]
- The background of the principals of the business.
- Information from trade references.
- Information from the bank reference—especially if the customer or applicant has a borrowing relationship with its bank.

Financial statement fraud is prevalent because the criminals know how the typical credit department works, the types of pressure the credit department is under to approve and release orders pending, and the kind of information that credit manager need to be comfortable releasing orders. For example, credit criminals know that a financial statement that shows a healthy net worth, revenue growth, shows the customer is making a profit and has positive cash flow will go a long way toward getting the open account terms and the credit limit the criminal is looking for. The fact that the sales, the assets, the retained earning, and the net income do not exist does not prevent them from appearing on paper giving the applicant the respectibility it needs and giving the credit department the justification that it needs to release the order pending.

CHAPTER 34

BULLETPROOFING YOUR ORGANIZATION AGAINST FRAUD

Credit fraud is a growth industry. Some people earn their living exclusively by committing credit fraud, and credit fraud is big business. Some of the techniques described in this chapter are absurdly simple [for example—ordering merchandise on a COD basis and paying with a worthless or NSF check].

Creditors lose billions annually, but there are no authoritative statistics about credit fraud because the best credit frauds are the ones in which the victim [the creditor] does not even know that they have been victimized.

Credit fraud involves stealth. The goal of anyone committing fraud is to get away without being discovered because the criminal penalties for fraud are severe. The criminal needs to make it appear to the company's credit managers that he or she simply made the wrong credit decision—a decision that has resulted in an uncollectable balance and a bad debt write off. The goal of the con man in most cons is to leave the trade creditor guessing about what caused the debtor company to fail—not trying to pursue the con man through the civil, criminal or bankruptcy court system. The best way to defeat a credit criminal is for the creditor not to stray from the normal process for reviewing and approving [or rejecting] applicants. Time, and the opportunity to perform due diligence are the enemies of credit criminals.

TIP: To reduce the likelihood that your company will become the victim of credit fraud, be leery of any attempt to convince the credit department to circumvent its normal checks in evaluating an applicant.

NOTE: The information in this chapter is not a How-To manual for con men and would-be criminals. Criminals already know about all of the scams and schemes described here. It is the potential victims of credit fraud that need a how-to manual in order to avoid becoming the victims of these crimes.

TIP: Vigilance is a key to preventing credit fraud. Credit department personnel should be encouraged and required to pass on their concerns or suspicions about an applicant or a customer to their superiors.

However, employees may not share their suspicions or concerns with anyone outside of the credit department until and unless clear and convincing evidence of a fraud is received. Even then, the supporting documentation should be forwarded to the creditor's legal counsel before any third party is notified.

WHAT IS CREDIT FRAUD?

Credit fraud is a term describing a wide variety of crimes associated with receiving goods without any intention of paying for them. In a credit fraud, the criminal's intent is to obtain goods from a supplier, and then sell them [often for pennies on the dollar] and pocket the proceeds. The criminal does not ever intend to pay the vendor for the goods the vendor delivers—which is why the criminal can sell the merchandise so quickly and so cheaply.

TIP: One of the first indications of a problem is when the creditor learns that a customer is selling its merchandise below cost, at cost or just above cost [but well below the standard mark up]. Often, this news comes from a competitor complaining about how cheaply the criminal enterprise is selling goods. Normally, the only way a company can sell below cost is because they do not intend to pay their creditor for the goods.

THE CRIMINAL MASTERMINDS

One of the misconceptions about credit fraud is that it is perpetrated by a criminal genius such as the charismatic con artist, Harold Hill, from the movie *The Music Man*. Most of the crimes described in this chapter are relatively simple, relying more on the willingness of credit professionals to ship merchandise than on the sophistication and the salesmanship of the con artist.

TIP: One way to protect your organization against credit fraud is to think small. It is far easier to con one hundred creditors into extending $1,000 in credit than it is to con one creditor into extending $100,000 in credit.

Con men recognize that the credit manager is almost certainly going to be the most difficult person in the organization to convince about a con. Con men do not try to match wits with the credit manager or with anyone else. Con men often try to avoid confrontations with the credit department by providing the credit department with whatever information or documentation they require, including trade references and financial statements [none of which, of course, are real].

TIP: Another way to bullet proof your company against credit fraud is to be leery of any customer or any applicant that has a ready answer to every question you ask. For example, it is unusual for a privately held company submit its financial statements to a new creditor without being asked to do so. The fact that unsolicited financial statements were provided by an applicant does not prove fraud, this fact simply encourages caution.

TIP: Con artists learn from their mistakes. They are unlikely to make the mistakes listed above twice. Instead, con men are likely to present creditors with fraudulent but convincing financial statements with no glaring errors, and nothing so obviously atypical that it would catch the creditor's eye as being "too good to be true."

A ONE-PERSON BAND

One person can perpetrate many of the credit frauds listed in this chapter. He or she only needs to be able to follow a plan intended to separate the supplier from their supplies without any cash changing hands.

TIP: Do not try to stereotype the types of people who may commit credit fraud. A credit fraud may involve an individual acting alone, or it may involve a conspiracy. The criminal may be well spoken and well educated, or the person may not seem particularly sophisticated. The criminal may have a broad understanding of the products you supply and their capabilities, or they may know nothing about the product. Stereotyping applicants does not prevent credit fraud—and may in fact lull the credit department into a false sense of security.

CONSPIRACIES

More sophisticated credit frauds may involve conspiracies to defraud as many trade creditors as possible. Accomplices are needed to support and perpetuate the misrepresentations made by the con artist to its creditors. The accomplices are employed to help convince credit managers to release the orders pending by answering the creditors questions, by reducing their fears and by filling in the blanks.

TIP: A credit fraud may involve a well-financed and fairly elaborate operation. There may be employees that are not a part of the conspiracy. Therefore, there is no business that can be automatically eliminated because it is too big to involve a credit fraud. Again, stereotyping does not prevent credit fraud—it makes it easier to commit.

HOW DO CON MEN FOOL SO MANY CREDIT MANAGERS?

Con men use their knowledge of how companies work to commit credit fraud. For example, con men know that salespeople will normally sell goods sight unseen to a new customer, and most credit departments are under tremendous pressure to establish new accounts and approve orders—especially large opening orders from companies that "appear" to be creditworthy.

TIP: If you receive a rush order on a new account, ask the salesperson a series of questions designed to find out whether or not the order in question was solicited or unsolicited, and about exactly how well the salesperson knows the applicant. The credit manager can ask:

- Who is your contact at the debtor company?

- What is their last name and title? [Not knowing their last name and/or their title should be a red flag to the credit department.]

- Why didn't you tell me about them before this order was placed?

- Where did you meet them?

- Have you been to their place of business? If so, when? Do you have a copy of your notes or of a call report?

- Were you given a tour of the customer's place of business? Who do they buy from at this time?

- Do you have a copy of the purchase order? If so, can you fax a copy to the credit department?

- Why have they decided to purchase from us? Why now?

In many instances, con men do not actually fool the credit manager. When asked about a loss that resulted from a credit fraud, many credit managers remember the transaction and will say that they felt something was wrong at the time but that they could not find the problem and could not justify holding the order. It is difficult for a credit manager to justify a negative credit decision based on a suspicion or a feeling about the buyer.

TIP: A credit manager walks a tightrope between being too liberal in credit granting [which results in higher delinquencies and higher bad debt losses], and too conservative in credit granting policy [which causes qualified applicants to be rejected]. Leaning too far in either direction can get the credit manager into trouble. If the company wants to be bullet proofed against credit fraud, then senior management must expect and accept that it will take longer to approve applicants for open account credit and that despite the credit department's best efforts some pending orders for some creditworthy customers will be held.

EDUCATING THE CREDIT DEPARTMENT STAFF

The most important step in preventing credit fraud is to educate everyone in the credit department about the various forms that credit fraud can take, and then asking them to be alert to potential problems. Any suspected fraudulent activity should be reported to and reviewed with the credit manager as soon as possible.

TIP: Like any worthwhile program, unless credit department personnel are regularly reminded about credit fraud and the need to report suspicious circumstances to the credit manager the program will slowly fade into obscurity.

STOP BLAMING THE VICTIM

Even if everyone in the credit department knows what to look for and is constantly vigilant, a certain number of frauds will still occur. The credit department operates within a larger business and competitive environment. Practical business necessity dictates that credit managers must accept a certain amount of credit risk in order to help the company to maximize sales and profits.

TIP: One of the techniques that con men use to get orders released is delay placing orders until it is likely that the credit manager may be out of town; for example by placing an order late in the afternoon on a Friday before a three day weekend. The con artist then works with the salesperson to exert pressure on whoever is in charge at the time to release the rush order. One way to bullet proof your organization against fraud is to make certain that everyone knows what their credit granting authority is, and that they do not exceed that authority regardless of the pressure exerted to do so.

In this particular scenario, if the credit manager were to have left early but had left an emergency contact number then a potentially serious problem might have been averted. For this reason, and in the interest of minimizing losses caused by fraud, the credit manager should be available by phone or pager whenever he or she is out of the office.

The credit department should become paranoid about credit fraud. The overwhelming majority of orders and applicants are creditworthy and honest. However, credit department employees cannot be faulted for having some professional curiosity. Curiosity and a dose of healthy skepticism are appropriate for credit department personnel.

Many credit fraud losses are not preventable. The credit fraud criminals know how to "beat the system." Losses of this type are a cost of doing business.

NACM'S LOSS PREVENTION DEPARTMENT

The National Association of Credit Managers is as concerned about credit fraud as its members. For this reason, the Loss Prevention department was formed. Working cooperatively with its members, with other credit professionals, and with local and federal law enforcement officers the Loss Prevention department works to reduce losses caused by credit fraud. It employs a three pronged approach to preventing losses.

First: The Loss Prevention department provides members with educational services including seminars and symposiums designed to teach credit professionals how to detect and prevent credit fraud.

Second: The Loss Prevention department sends periodic notices by e-mail or by mail about actual or suspected frauds being perpetrated.

Third: The Loss Prevention department works cooperatively with law enforcement to try to effect the capture and the prosecution of criminals involved in credit fraud.

TIP: Membership in NACM's Loss Prevention Department is less than $900 a year. It can be far more expensive not to join. Learning a technique that prevents one credit fraud should easily offset the entire cost of membership.

IF IT SOUNDS TOO GOOD TO BE TRUE...

Criminals sometimes start the process of trying to commit credit fraud by getting the creditor company's sales department excited about a large opening order—often at an unusually high profit margin. Con men are not concerned about the prices they are quoted since they have no intention of paying for the goods. With the salesperson on their side, the criminal has increased his or her ability to exert influence on the credit department to release the order on open account terms. The criminal is counting on the salesperson's greed as an ally.

TIP: Know the normal mark-up or profit margin on the products your company sells. Find out what the profit margin is on the rush deal. If the profit margin is unusually high, and there seems to be no particular reason why, then this is an indication that the credit manager needs to exercise caution.

RED FLAGS

There are a number of red flags that credit managers and their subordinates should look for when looking for credit fraud, including these:

Intimidation and threat. Sometimes, the criminal will put as much pressure as possible on the credit department to ship the order immediately. Time is the criminal's enemy and the creditor's ally. The longer the creditor has to investigate the applicant, the more likely they are to discover a fraud if one exists. An example of intimidation and threat would be a statement from a customer or an applicant that if the order pending is not released in the next ten minutes the customer will cancel the order and take its business elsewhere.

Experienced businesspeople understand that it takes time to establish an open account, and they do not wait until the last moment to place an order. Con men are seemingly always in a hurry to get orders shipped. They also always have a plausible explanation about why the order pending needs to be rushed and why they waited so long to place it. For example, the creditor might be told:

- The customer's normal supplier closed early, and
- The customer needs the order to ship for delivery the next morning so that the production line can be repaired

Occasionally, the criminal will solicit the help of the salesperson or even the sales manager in an effort to rush the credit department into making the wrong decision about an order pending. The con artist may on occasion call the credit manager directly and try to intimidate or threaten the credit manager into releasing the order pending—normally by suggesting that the credit manager's concerns are totally unfounded and stating something like this: No company has ever treated me this way before. If this is the way you treat your customers, then I am not sure I want to be a customer.

TIP: There are few things more embarrassing that being bluffed into releasing an order to a new account that ends up not paying. If the credit manager is pushed, they need to learn to push back.

If the credit department has not yet gathered enough information to make an informed decision about the order pending, then that is exactly what the customer and the salesperson should be told. There is no need to apologize for the fact that an order is being held while the credit department conducts its normal review. The credit department need not feel defensive about following standard procedures, nor should the credit department try to explain to justify the process of qualifying an applicant.

TIP: If the applicant/customer fails to understand why the credit department must evaluate the applican, then the applicant is either a poor or inexperienced businessperson, or a con artist.

The Invisible Customer. One of the tricks of the trade is that the con artist wants to have as little personal contact with any representative of the creditor company as possible—including the salesperson. The criminal does not necessarily want to meet anyone face to face, preferring instead to order merchandise by telephone, by fax or by mail.

A Bad Check. Often, one of the first indications of a fraud involves a returned check from a relatively new account. Credit managers normally have specific procedures for dealing with returned checks. They must be handled quickly, efficiently and professionally. For example, the procedure might include each of these steps:

(a)   Upon notification that a check is being returned due to insufficient funds, the account should be placed on credit hold and the salesperson notified of this fact.

(b)   If the NSF check is for more than $1,000 or this is the second time the check is being returned then the credit department should contact the shipping department and arrange for any shipment in transit to be stopped and the goods returned.

(c)   The customer should be contacted immediately and asked to make arrangements to have the check clear if and when it is re-deposited.

(d)   If the relatively new customer cannot or will not replace the NSF check with a cashier's check or a wire transfer [or if the check is drawn on a closed account] then the creditor company may be looking at a fraud and the credit manager should confer with legal counsel about what steps should be taken to protect the company as much as possible.

TO PREVENT FRAUD, CHECK THE SHIP-TO LOCATION

Even if a creditor has agreed to ship the merchandise on open account terms, the criminal is still in danger. He or she must take appropriate steps to make sure (1) the merchandise can be picked up without the criminal being identified and (2) the criminal must be concerned about a sting operation in which he or she picks up the merchandise and is then arrested on fraud charges. To limit their risk, many criminals use private mail boxes and arrange for the goods to be shipped to and from these locations.

One of the simplest cons involves nothing more elaborate than a criminal posing as a legitimate customer to place an order and arrange for it to be shipped to an address that does not belong to the customer. When the goods arrive, they disappear. When the invoice arrives, it is not paid because the customer never ordered it.

One way to bullet proof your company against this fraud is to establish a policy that third party drop shipments over a certain dollar amount must be confirmed with a faxed copy of the purchase order before they will be released by the credit department. This will not prevent all frauds, but it will prevent the majority of them.

There are often several cutouts, transshipments, and courier pick-ups before the criminal actually takes possession of the merchandise in question. Criminals prefer to have deliveries sent to:

- An inexpensive rental unit

- A mail box type service, but one in which the location is identified as a "suite" number rather than as a post office box, or unoccupied homes or business locations

TIP: Creditors should be aware of any instance in which a customer wants merchandise sent to a PO Box or to a "Suite." This fact alone does not indicate fraud, but it should alert the credit manager to take a closer look at the applicant.

BE VIGILANT AGAINST FRAUDULENT TELEPHONE OR FAX NUMBERS

It should come as no surprise that by using off the shelf technology a call to anywhere in the United States can be routed without the caller's knowledge to a single location. Therefore, it is possible for a criminal to list three trade references and one bank reference and then arrange for every call to the phone number or fax number listed to be re-routed back to him or to her. The criminal would then give glowing but totally fraudulent references about the company in an effort to defraud the creditor.

To defeat this type of fraud, creditors can independently verify the name and telephone number of one or more of the trade references listed on the application before contacting those creditors for a reference. It may seem like a lot of work, but if there is any doubt about the authenticity of the customer then this becomes an essential part of the risk management process. Two Internet web sites will help the creditor to look up trade references by names and telephone numbers are located at the URLs listed below:

Yahoo Yellow Pages. http://yp.yahoo.com

U.S. West Yellow Pages. http://www.uswestdex.com

WATCH OUT FOR COD CHECKS

A company check is not cash. A cashier's check is not cash. A certified check or a money order is not cash. Criminals intent on committing credit fraud are often happy to exchange a valueless piece of paper [such as a check] for valuable goods. COD terms do not prevent credit fraud, they encourage it. COD Cashier's Check terms [COD cash] is only slightly lower risk than accepting a company check. Unfortunately, desk top publishing software makes it possible to scan a legitimate Cashier's Check, make any necessary changes to it, print it out and have the check available for the seller's delivery service of choice.

DEFEATING INTERNAL FRAUD

Statistics prove time and again that the biggest risk that company's face involves theft and fraud perpetrated by current or former employees of the company. Current employees often have both the opportunity to attempt to defraud creditors and the skill to see the weaknesses in their company's safeguards against fraud.

One way to prevent fraud perpetrated by or with the assistance of an employee involves nothing more complex than obtaining a routine criminal background check on all new employees in addition to checking references.

TIP: In addition to a background check and employment verification, a pre-employment drug screening will help to round out the picture of the applicant. Due diligence in hiring reduces the likelihood of internal fraud.

USING PERSONAL VISITS TO DEFEAT FRAUD

Criminals intent on fraud do not welcome visitors, including salespeople. Often, they do not have an operation that would appear normal to a trained observer, so they try to transact business over the telephone, by mail, by fax and by e-mail whenever possible.

TIP: To be valuable and fully enforceable, credit managers should insist that credit applications be signed and that the person lists their title and affirms their ability and willingness to bind the company to the terms and conditions listed on the credit application agreement.

BUSTOUTS

Simply put, a bustout is a scheme devised to defraud suppliers through the use of a planned bankruptcy or other forms of business failure. The characteristics of a bust out scheme include the following:

- Initially, creditors are paid on time.

- Those creditors are used as references to obtain more open account credit.

- Fraudulent financial statements might also be given to potential creditors to convince them to extend larger amounts of open account credit.

- The debtor will delay payment to certain creditors, but continue to order from as many suppliers as possible. At the same time, the inventory on hand is being sold for cash and the money pocketed.

- Eventually, there are numerous suppliers with past due balances and credit begins to dry up.

- By this time, the supplier's inventory and the cash proceeds from the sale of that inventory are long gone.

- The bust out is normally a relatively new company that is growing by leaps and bounds.

- Once credit is established, the creditor immediately becomes a reference to other potential suppliers.

- The customer typically buys a series of small orders followed by a large order.

- Many of the trade references provided have done business for less than a year with the customer.

- A credit bureau report on the company provides little or no information about the company.

    If this pattern emerges, credit managers are urged to use caution.

SUMMARY

Credit managers can best combat credit fraud with information. Membership in the National Association of Credit Manager's Loss Prevention department gives members access to the NACM's on line database. The Loss Prevention department's educational seminars and educational publications keep the credit manager, and arguably the rest of the credit department staff, focused on bad debt losses and on loss prevention.

For as long as there is pressure on the credit department to make fast credit decisions with limited information there will always be the risk of credit fraud. Credit managers can either accept this risk, or become more cautious and possibly lose good accounts as a result. The credit department will always struggle with finding the right balance between accommodating customers and preventing losses.

CHAPTER 35

Managing Disputes and Deductions

In any long-term business relationship, disputes and deductions are inevitable. Even the best quality control system will not catch every error, and even if it did shipments can be lost or damaged in transit resulting in a dispute or a deduction. Some of the most common reasons for deductions include:

- Price discrepancies
- Unearned cash discounts
- Defective merchandise
- Short shipments
- Promotional allowances not given
- Damaged goods

The deduction management process can be very detailed and time consuming. The manner in which the creditor company addresses a dispute or a deduction determines if, or how quickly the problem will be resolved. If the seller's credit department has a somewhat disorganized and lackluster approach toward deduction management, then the customer is likely to assign the deduction problem and its resolution a relatively low priority.

On the other hand, if the credit department addresses the deduction promptly, provides the customer with any requested documentation quickly, and follows up periodically for updates on the status of the deduction, then the customer is likely to recognize several facts, including these:

(a) The deduction problem is not going to go away by itself.

(b) The creditor company is unlikely to allow the debtor to ignore the outstanding deduction indefinitely.

(c) Deduction management is obviously a priority for the creditor—even though this statement is obviously not true for all vendors based on other creditors' attitude toward outstanding deductions.

(d) Sooner or later, we're going to have to address and resolve this problem and it might as well be sooner rather than later because the creditor is likely to keep calling until this problem is resolved.

DEDUCTION MANAGEMENT REQUIRES TEAMWORK

Problems that result in unauthorized customer deductions are complex. Often, the underlying causes of customer deductions span departmental boundaries. The complexity of deductions, and the importance to the company of resolving them in a timely manner means that a team approach to deduction management is often the best approach to this problem.

For example, a customer's accounts payable department often needs the approval of the purchasing department to repay a pricing deduction taken in error. Often, the sales department would prefer that its credit department not communicate directly with the purchasing agent. Provided the credit department and the sales department can learn to work cooperatively so that the problem is addressed in a professional but forthright manner, and provided the salesperson is willing to handle the matter promptly and to report back to the credit department, then there is no reason that pricing deductions cannot be handled cooperatively.

Unfortunately, what often happens is that other departments in the creditor company do not have the same motivation as the credit department to address and resolve disputes as quickly as possible. As a result, a process that should take a few days to complete ends up taking weeks because the person the credit department is expected to work cooperatively with simply does not feel that the assignment needs to be given a high priority. To the extent that the collection specialist or the chargeback administrator is able put pressure on their co-worker to address and resolve the problem quickly, they should do so. However, if they are unable to convince the other party to make resolving the problem a priority the credit manager must be prepared to step in and make certain the process gets back on track.

PROACTIVELY MANAGING DEDUCTIONS AND DISPUTES

Studies show that at least 50% of the time customer deductions taken for things like short shipments, wrong product shipped, and pricing errors are legitimate. [Clearly, this is not true in every industry, for every seller and for every customer]. This means that customers are right more often than they are wrong when they take deductions. Every error a supplier makes provides a legitimate excuse for a customer to delay payment or to take a deduction. Deduction management is important to the cash flow and to the profitability of a company.

Credit managers can help themselves; can help their company's cash flow; and can improve the company's level of customer service by collecting information about the deductions taken by customers. If the information gathered can be summarized and then presenting it to senior management in a concise, objective and unbiased format, the credit manager will help to focus senior management's attention on a problem that deserves their attention. The credit manager's deduction management report should include the following information:

- The number of deductions taken each month.

- The total dollar value of these deductions

- A breakdown of the number and dollar value of deductions by reason code (example: pricing vs. short shipments).

- An analysis of the number of deductions cleared in the prior month, along with an analysis of specifically how they were cleared [Specifically, were they credited, written off, or collected?]

The credit department can help the company to develop picture of the of mistakes the company is making. This will help to identify problem areas, allowing the company to take corrective action that will improve customer service levels—and at the same time will reduce the number of errors made and consequently the number of deductions taken in the future.

Credit managers that choose not to take a leadership role in identifying problems that lead to disputes and deductions should remember this fact: The capacity of a company to create problems, to make mistakes that lead to disputes and deductions normally far exceeds the credit department's ability to resolve problems and to correct mistakes.

DEDUCTION MANAGEMENT SOFTWARE

One of the biggest changes in the area of deduction management involves the use of deduction management software. Deduction management software is designed to improve the productivity of the people in the credit department who handle deductions and chargebacks. Deduction management software typically provides the following functions or features:

- The ability to classify or reclassify chargebacks.
- The ability to produce customized letters or notifications about outstanding deductions or chargebacks
- Management reporting to help the credit department identify problem areas within the company.
- Rankings of customers by dollars of deductions outstanding
- Statistical data by customer about the number and types of deductions taken, and about the outcome of the credit department's efforts to clear the deduction [for example: was the deduction credited, written off, or repaid]

Deduction management software allows credit managers and their subordinates to track each step in the deduction review and resolution process. For example, as it relates to the process of reviewing and resolving a pricing deduction the deduction management software would document the following steps in the deduction management process:

- The software would establish a file on the deduction as soon as it is opened.
- If the reason for the deduction was not readily identified, the software may generate a request to the customer to identify the reason for the deduction and would list the reason code for the deduction as "unknown."
- As soon as relevant supporting documentation was received, someone in the credit department would change the reason code in the deduction management software from "unknown" to "pricing."
- The chargeback administrator would review the customer's debit and supporting documentation. If appropriate, a credit memo would be requested.
- If the collection specialist could not determine if the customer was owed a credit memo, the collection specialist would refer the matter to someone outside of the credit department for review—possibly the salesperson.

- The fact that the problem had been forwarded to the salesperson for review would be recorded in the deduction management software. A follow up date would be set.

- On the follow up date, the DM software would remind the collection specialist to follow up for a decision from the salesperson.

- If the salesperson were to approve a credit memo, that information would be recorded in the DM software, and another follow up date would be established to make certain that credit was issued.

- If the salesperson were to find that a credit was not due, that information would be noted and a request for payment would be generated.

- The software would then schedule periodic follow ups until payment was received to clear that pricing deduction.

Using the deduction management software, each step in this simplified example was documented. The follow up feature allows the collection specialist to stay on top of a deduction because a deduction management process that loses momentum damages the company's reputation for customer service as well as the credit department's reputation as problem solvers.

Deductions often arise as a result of a legitimate disagreement between a buyer and a seller. One of the things that credit managers can do to help their customers and their employer is to work to reduce ambiguity that often leads to customer deductions. Prevention is the key. Trying to resolve deductions after they have been taken has been likened to trying to hold back the incoming tide with a bucket.

PRICING ERRORS

One of the most common types of deductions involves pricing disputes. Often, the dispute arises because the buyer believes he or she was quoted one price, but the salesperson entered another price. One solution to this problem is to require that the buyer provide a written purchase order, or that the salesperson send an purchase order acknowledgment to the customer [in advance of the shipment] listing the agreed product, price and quantity.

Obviously, the process of carefully documenting the agreements reached between a buyer and a seller regarding the price and terms of sale on an order submitted is very different that the "standard" approach. The standard approach begins when a customer calls the salesperson, places an order verbally and waits for the merchandise to arrive. If the creditor companies are serious about reducing the number of pricing deductions and disputes, then the process of order "offer and acceptance" must be better documented.

UNEARNED CASH DISCOUNTS

The key question that each company that offers cash discounts to customers must answer is this: At how many days beyond the discount due date should an unearned cash discount be charged back. Credit managers must develop clear guidelines in this area for their cash application group. It should come as no surprise that if the decision to charge back an unearned cash discount is left to the collection specialist handling the account [or to the cash application department] then fewer unearned cash discounts will be charged back. Why? Because it is far easier simply to absorb an unearned cash discount than it is to charge it back and then to be responsible for collecting the unearned discount.

This is not to suggest that the credit department should be rigid and inflexible in light of information that would suggest that it would be appropriate to write off an unearned discount that was charged back. For example, if a customer delayed payment on an invoice because the account was in a credit balance it does not take much imagination to believe that it will be almost impossible to collect the cash discount. The point to keep in mind is that there will be situations in which it makes sense to write off a discount, but to do so during the cash application process or without relevant supporting documentation is probably inappropriate.

DISPUTING THE TERMS OF SALE

Disputes often arise as to the terms of sale offered by the seller to the buyer. For example, a customer may claim to have been offered 90-day terms on an order, while the salesperson entered the order might have entered it with the creditor company's standard 30-day terms. Unless the credit department can prove that the salesperson did not offer 90-day terms, it will be difficult to force the customer to pay the disputed invoice any sooner.

The solution requires additional work for the salesperson and additional discipline. In order to demonstrate that the agreed upon terms were not 90 days, the credit manager must be able to produce something more relevant than a copy of the invoice listing 30 days terms. For example, if the salesperson had sent an electronic purchase order confirmation then it would be relatively simple for the credit department to demonstrate that the buyer's records were wrong and for the collector to demand that the customer issue payment to clear the past due balance.

DISPUTED TERMS AND CONDITIONS OF SALE

Another problem area for many creditors involves the fact that the terms and conditions listed on the customer's written purchase order are often ignored by the person entering the sales order. A written purchase order is an Offer. Shipping against a purchase order without challenging an incorrect term [or price] could be considered "acceptance" of the buyer's "offer" under contract law. The receipt of goods and the promise of payment would constitute "consideration" under contract law. Thus, the creditor and the customer have all of the elements of a contract even if the purchase order submitted contains numerous, and serious errors. Here is an example:

Assume the customer's purchase order listed:

(1) terms of net 90 days from the date of receipt of goods, and

(2) stated that the buyer had unlimited return privileges for one year from the purchase date, and that returns would be credited at the full purchase price.

Assume the creditor's standard terms were:

(1) net 30 days from the date of invoice, and that

(2) returns were limited to the return of defective merchandise within 90 days for repair or replacement at the option of the seller.

Clearly, accepting the purchase order without requiring the customer to amend the two conditions listed above could result in a serious dispute about when the invoice was due—and could potentially result in another serious problem at some point if the buyer tried to return some or all of the merchandise for credit.

The problem in this scenario is not a lack of documentation; it is a lack of understanding about the importance of the terms and conditions listed on the customer's purchase order. The seller cannot afford to look only at the price, the quantity and the shipment date—but they often do just that. The purchase order should be reviewed to make certain that all the terms and conditions listed are acceptable to the seller.

ESTABLISH DEADLINES

Once a dispute or deduction becomes more than six months old, the chances of collecting it drop significantly. Once a deduction or dispute is allowed to age out over a year, the chances of collecting it are almost non-existent. For this reason, the credit manager should establish a specific deadline for resolving outstanding customer deductions. If six months seems appropriate, then within six months of a deduction being taken, the person in charge of the account should either:

- Recommend a credit hold to force the customer repay the deduction that the credit department has proven was taken in error, or

- Recommend that the credit department write off the deduction because the facts are "fuzzy" and it is difficult to know whether the seller or the customer is correct.

- Determine that the customer was correct in taking the deduction, and provide supporting documentation showing that a credit memo should be issued immediately to clear the deduction.

COMPROMISE

Even when the creditor proves that a deduction was taken in error, some customers will delay, deny and defer repaying the deduction. Credit managers need to recognize that certain customers, because of their buying power, will ignore the facts presented and try to avoid repaying any deduction. Credit managers must recognize in certain situations that it may be necessary to negotiate a settlement on outstanding deductions. The credit manager should know their dollar authority to settle deduction related disputes. If the balance due is large, the matter should be reviewed with senior management.

CONSIDER CREATING A CHARGEBACK SPECIALIST

If the credit department is large enough, credit mangers should give serious consideration to creating a position of chargeback administrator. The chargeback administrator would be a specialist with the primary responsibility for resolving, or more precisely for coordinating the process necessary to clear deductions.

Creating a chargeback administrator position would allow the collection staff to spend more time on collecting past due dollars—rather than diluting their efforts with attempts to reconcile discrepancies and resolve disputes and deductions. There is every reason to believe that collection specialists not being pulled away from their role as collectors will be far more effective since their focus will not be dissipated.

The chargeback administrator would work closely with the following groups and departments to clear deductions quickly and accurately:

- the customer
- the salesperson
- the shipping department
- cash application
- customer support
- the seller's returned merchandise area

There are many different sources or causes of deduction problems. One of the value-added services that a chargeback administrator will bring to the company is the ability to recognize patterns and to identify recurring problems within the company.

The key to winning the battle against chargebacks is proactively preventing problems—not being reactive to deductions and their underlying causes.

WARRANTY DISPUTES

A warranty is a contractual promise by a seller relating to the quality of the goods sold. A warranty can be express or implied. An express warranty is a written warranty that might appear on the back of the seller's invoice. In the absence of a written warranty, under the Uniform Commercial Code [UCC] there are several implied warranties. The most important is an implied warranty of merchantability. This means that in the absence of some disclaimer the goods are warranted to be what they state they are and be of commercially reasonable quality. There is also an implied warranty of fitness for a particular purpose—meaning that the goods sold will perform in the way they are expected to by a reasonable person.

It is possible [but unusual] for sellers to deliver goods in an as-is condition without any warranty whatsoever. This is accomplished through a specific disclaimer of warranty liability. Of course, selling goods in an as-is condition does not typically instill confidence in the purchasers of the product—nor does it encourage repeat business if in fact the product is of such poor quality that a disclaimer of warranty liability is necessary.

Assuming that goods are sold with a warranty, it is sometimes difficult for the customer to convince the salesperson to issue the return merchandise authorization, or to issue a credit in full for defective product. The credit department should always be prepared to intervene on behalf of the customer to expedite the credit or the return authorization. Ideally, the credit department will work to ensure that their company has a procedure in place so that there are no bottlenecks in the credit memo approval process. By doing so, the credit manager will reduce the number of disputes and deductions—and by issuing credit when credit is due, the creditor will create goodwill with its customers.

CREATING AN AUTOMATIC WRITE OFF FOR NEW DEDUCTIONS

No one wants to make it easy for customers to take deductions. Most credit managers want to charge back deductions, review the facts surrounding each deduction, determine which ones should be credited and which should be repaid, and then follow up on inappropriate deductions to make certain they are repaid. However, there is a point of diminishing returns below which it simply does not make sense to create chargebacks and to investigate the underlying deductions.

Credit managers should, with the express approval of senior management, create a tolerance level for deductions below which all deductions are written off during the cash application process. The logic behind this idea is fairly elementary: It does not make sense for the company and its credit department to spend $20 to collect a deduction of $10. One of the benefits of a process of automatically writing off deductions below a certain dollar threshold is that doing so frees up credit personnel to work on larger dollar problems.

ARBITRATION

Prior to establishing a business relationship or at any point thereafter, the buyer and seller can mutually agree by contract that all disputes, claims or controversies shall be resolved by binding arbitration. Binding arbitration is faster, less expensive, and less disruptive to the business relationship than litigation. For this reason, mediation, arbitration or binding arbitration clauses that are made a part of the standard credit agreement as part of the credit application can be used to resolve deductions without resorting to credit holds or to placing an account for collection. Arbitration works this way:

After hearing testimony and after reviewing the evidence presented by each party, the arbitrator will make a decision—called an award. If the arbitration clause stipulates the arbitrator's decision is binding, the parties agree to waive their rights to a trial, and must accept the decision of the arbitrator.

Despite the fact that a complex dispute will take time to hear and resolve even by arbitration, the advantage of arbitration are (a) the loser has limited recourse against an arbitrator's award, and (b) the use of arbitration rather than litigation may preserve some of the goodwill between the buyer and the seller and (c) the award is enforceable in court if that becomes necessary.

INTERNATIONAL ARBITRATION SERVICES

Disputes that arise as a result of international sales pose unique difficulties for the seller. Dispute resolution is far more complex than it would be in a domestic sales transaction. Typically, the parties are of different nationalities, make speak different languages, and may be distrustful of any attempt to mediate or arbitrate a dispute. Despite these limitations, international arbitration of disputes and deductions is a viable alternative to trying to sue a delinquent foreign debtor in the courts in the seller's country over a disputed balance —especially when one considers the language barriers, differences in law, travel costs, attorney's fees, and other costs associated with this type of litigation.

Probably the best known provider of international arbitration services is the International Court of Arbitration [ICA]—part of the International Chamber of Commerce [ICC]. The ICA's Rules of Arbitration provide a means for settling disputes quickly and at a relatively low cost. The decisions of the ICA are final and binding if the court's in the loser's country will accept and enforce the decision of the Arbitrator. Normally, the awards made by the ICA cannot be appealed, and more than 100 countries have agreed that they will be bound by the decision made by the ICA, and have agreed that a case will not be heard in their sovereign courts systems when the dispute is subject to an arbitration agreement.

The ICC also offers the service of mediators. The mediators seek an amicable and voluntary settlement of disputes. Mediation relies on the goodwill and cooperation of the parties, while binding arbitration does not. Arbitrators decide fact and render decisions. Their role is not as moderators and mediators.

OUTSOURCING DEDUCTION RESOLUTION

One of the more popular ways to manage customer deductions involves outsourcing the clean up of a backlog of deductions. There are many firms that for a hefty fee will assist the credit department in reconciling and resolving a backlog of deductions. These outsourcing companies may be attractive despite their high cost to companies that have a large number of relatively low dollar value deductions outstanding.

While it is difficult to justify pulling existing employees from resolving more current and higher dollar problems, it is often a fairly easy decision to outsource that portion of the outstanding accounts receivable that are not being addressed due to time and resource constraints. The logic of a decision to use an outsourcing agency can be described as follows:

> Getting 70% of something is better than ignoring these deductions and getting 100% of nothing.

SUMMARY

With the concentration of purchasing power in the hands of a smaller and smaller number of buyers, it is almost inevitable that customers' confidence in their power relative to their suppliers will grow, and that unauthorized deductions will become a more significant problem. Customer deductions are a growing problem for many companies, who are finding it increasingly more difficult to keep up with the workload.

Unless managing disputes and deductions is given the time, the attention, and the resources that it deserves, the result is likely to be a progressively larger write offs of disputes and deductions. Often, a supplier's biggest and "best" customers are also the biggest problem accounts in the area of deductions because:

(a)   these companies have the most leverage and buying power and

(b)   they are also the least likely to end up on credit hold over a deduction that they refuse to repay.

CHAPTER 36

An Overview of International Credit and Collection

Twenty years ago, most overseas sales were made by U.S.–based companies on a cash or a letter of credit basis. Whether out of habit, or fear of the unknown, U.S.–based creditors did not find it necessary or appropriate to offer open account terms to foreign customers. That situation has changed.

U.S. companies are now enthusiastic about exports, but foreign buyers are often no longer willing to allow sellers to dictate the terms of sale. Competition from other exporting countries has forced many U.S.–based companies to offer foreign customers open account terms—often for the first time.

EXPORT SALES STIMULATE GROWTH AND CREATE JOBS

International trade has been an important factor in stimulating growth in U.S. economy for the last fifteen years. International trade creates jobs and boosts economic growth. In the United States, it is estimated that over 12 million people owe their jobs to exports. The international market is more than four times larger than the U.S. domestic market. Growth rates in many foreign markets have dramatically outpaced U.S. domestic market growth.

INTERNATIONAL OPEN ACCOUNT TERMS

The sale of goods to any customer on open account terms, whether local, national or international, creates the possibility that the customer will default on payment. Selling on open account terms to a customer in a different country requires special processes, procedures, care and attention. The risks associated with offering foreign customers open account terms are significantly greater than the risk of selling to a U.S.–based company. The other side of the coin involves the fact that offering open account terms makes the seller's products cheaper and easier to buy, and more attractive to a foreign customer. The risks are significant, but with the right skills and the right tools the risks can be managed and moderated.

INTERNATIONAL TERMS OF SALE

International sales transactions are often governed by Incoterms. Incoterms is an abbreviation for the terms drafted by The International Chamber of Commerce. In an international sales transaction, Incoterms define the rights and responsibilities of the buyer and the seller as well as the documentation requirements for international sales transactions. Even though it technically is not part of the credit manager's job, in an effort to avoid problems and to simplify the department's collection efforts credit managers should give serious consideration to making certain that everyone in their company that has a role in an international sale and shipment understands the seller's responsibilities under Incoterms

Most experts agree that efforts must be made by governments around the world to ensure that the laws and regulations governing cross-border sales transactions are compatible. These steps are necessary to assure buyers and sellers that processes are in place that protect both parties. International commerce will not realize its full potential until and unless buyers and sellers both have faith in the integrity, safety and reliability of the transactions and the subsequent payments.

INTERNATIONAL RISK MANAGEMENT

Managing the risks associated with international trade requires the seller to be familiar with the documents, the trade terms, and the financing arrangements used in international sales. Equally important, in order to assess credit risk in international business transactions, the creditor must be able to assess country or sovereign risk. In many ways, assessing individual customer risk is far easier than trying to quantify country risk.

Selling on open account terms to a foreign country automatically increases credit risk, and creates additional problems for the credit professional. The risks of export trade for creditor companies are inherently greater than in domestic sales transactions. Compounding the problem is the fact that foreign shipments tend to be high in value, so the dollar risk to the exporter is also significant. In response to these factors, most credit managers are more cautious about selling internationally than domestically.

For a variety of reasons, export credit decisions must be more carefully analyzed than their domestic counterparts. There are far more factors to consider in making a credit decision, including:

- Country or political risk

- The risk of buyer default

- Whether or not to purchase export credit insurance

- How to accelerate payments on open account terms

- How to collect past due balances if the account becomes delinquent

- How to control foreign currency exchange risk

It is far more important to avoid problems with international sales than to try to resolve them after the sale. Often, resolving a problem with a foreign customer requires litigating the dispute in a foreign court. This is expensive, and often results in a disappointing outcome for the creditor. Credit managers should require the use of pro-forma invoices to deliver quotes to customers. On the pro-forma invoice, the creditor company's terms of sale including the shipping terms and payment terms should be tested. The customer's purchase order should match in all respects the product description as well as the terms and conditions listed on the pro forma invoice.

GATHERING INFORMATION

The less a creditor knows about a buyer, the more restrictive the credit terms must be. In order to feel confident about offering a customer open account terms, the credit department must have access to detailed information about foreign customers. Normally, the creditor being asked to make the decision will have less information than would be available on a domestic applicant. Another thing the credit manager needs to be concerned about involves the reliability of information received about foreign customers.

The key to managing credit risk internationally is access to current and accurate information. Often, credit reports on companies are prepared in response to specific requests from creditors. The advantage of receiving such a report is that it is current. The disadvantage is the fact that information is often not available immediately, and the cost of these reports are typically several times higher than domestic credit reports. Another problem with international credit reports is that they often do not contain the quantity or quality of information U.S.–based credit managers are used to receiving. For example, it is not uncommon for a foreign customer or applicant to decline to provide financial statements to the credit bureau, and credit bureaus often have trouble convincing local banks to provide information about their business relationships with their customers.

In spite of the problems associated with inability to gather the type, quantity and quality of information that it would like about its foreign customers, the credit manager must consider each of the following concepts before establishing the terms of sale and the credit limit:

The political climate. Information about the political and the economic climate of the country in which the customer is located is critical to make an informed decision about whether or not open account terms can be offered. The more unstable the political environment, the less important is the financial stability and the payment history of the applicant, and the more unstable the political environment the less likely that terms can and should be extended to the applicant.

Currency stability. If the economy, the currency or the government is unstable, the risk of offering open account terms is significant. An unstable currency on the foreign exchange market may make it difficult for the customer to pay the creditor. A significant change in the exchange rate between the U.S. dollar and the local currency between the time of shipment and the time that payment is due would make it less likely the debtor could pay as agreed. For this reason, if the currency exchange rate fluctuates significantly over time, them payment is less likely and the decision to approve for open account terms becomes more difficult.

Limited information about the applicant. It is sometimes difficult to purchase a credit report on a foreign customer at any price. Sometimes, they are unavailable on line and in real time. Often, the credit bureau must research the company before generating a report—putting pressure on the credit manager to make a decision in the absence of adequate information.

Reliance on financial statements. If the customer decides to provide financial statements to the creditor, they will be denominated in a foreign currency and will normally be in a foreign language. Most important, there will often be no way to gauge their accuracy. These statements are completed using different accounting rules, many of which may be completely unknown to the seller's credit manager.

The terms of sale. Foreign customers ofter ask for far better terms than they are likely to receive from the U.S.–based seller. Before open account terms are offered, the creditor must find out what terms other creditors are extending into this country given the political and currency risks they face by offering open account credit terms.

(1) Certain countries have established laws that require foreign creditors to offer a specific number of days dating when they export goods into that country. Credit managers need to know which countries require what dating before they can intelligently consider offering the customer open account terms.

(2) Credit professionals must understand the shipping terms in order to know if the buyer or the seller is liable for loss or damage in transit. Many exporters have been damaged financially by not realizing the risk of loss or damage was theirs and making certain that insurance was purchased to cover the shipment.

(3) The credit manager must understand the types of documents required for an export shipment. They must be sure that their company and/or their freight forwarder can provide those required documents.

(4) If open account terms are requested, the creditor must know if the foreign customer has had experience importing goods on open account terms. If not, the foreign customer may not be able to handle the complexities of making payments to foreign creditors.

(5) The shipping terms the customer has requested or expects.

ALTERNATIVE TERMS

Between the two extremes of requiring foreign buyers to pay for the merchandise on a payment in advance basis, or offering the customer open account terms are a number of alternatives and options. Some of those alternatives include:

- Using export credit insurance
- Factoring receivables
- Forfeiting accounts receivable
- Selling against a letter of credit, or a standby letter of credit

- Using sight drafts or time drafts rather than offering open account terms
- Consignment sales

CREDIT REPORTING AGENCIES OFFERING INTERNATIONAL CREDIT REPORTS:

- Dun and Bradstreet offers domestic and international business credit reports
- The FCIB [Finance, Credit and International Business] offer international business credit reports
- Global Scan is a company specializing in international business credit reports
- Graydon America also specializes in international credit reports
- Owens Online offers both types of reports also
- Veritas Business Information provides its clients with both U.S. and International reports

---

THE FCIB

As mentioned previously, the Finance, Credit and International Business [FCIB] offers access to international credit reports. The FCIB is the international arm of the National Association of Credit Management. Established in 1919, the FCIB provides a variety of services including:

- industry group meetings
- conferences, seminars and workshops
- publications about international business, including current trends and conditions
- information and reports about country or sovereign risk, and
- payment trend information

There is no contract required to order international credit reports from the FCIB. Another advantage is quick access to so-called country reports on more than 80 countries, including a risk rating, payment and collection information.

CONTROLLING EXPORTS

Often, credit professionals are expected to control all of the risks associated with export sales. Many of the potential problems associated with export sales are beyond the credit manager's direct control. However, there are things that an experienced credit manager can do to help the company export more effectively and more safely.

The key to effective collections is to make certain that everyone involved in the export transaction knows their job It is important that the sales department, the manufacturing department, the shipping department and the credit department all have written policies and procedures for handling export sales. Because of frequent changes in the rules, each company that is active in export sales should develop an in-house training program and should encourage employees to attend seminars to stay informed about changing policies, laws and documentation requirements.

INTERNATIONAL TERMS OF SALE

Cash In Advance

The most restrictive terms of sale a creditor can offer would involve pre-payment or cash in advance terms. These terms are not attractive to most buyers, but they offer the greatest security to the seller. One problem with cash in advance terms is the buyer bears all the risk that (a) the goods will arrive and (b) the goods delivered will be as ordered [in terms of quality and unit count.

Unless it is truly a seller's market, foreign customers are unlikely in this highly competitive global economy to agree to pay a vendor in advance. From the buyer's perspective, the risks and problems associated with cash in advance terms are significant and include:

- The possibility that the seller will not ship even after the payment is delivered in advance
- There may be political or economic uncertainties in the seller's country that make it impossible for the seller to export the goods. For example, the export license is revoked.
- By paying cash in advance, the buyer takes the risk that the product sent would not conform to the product specifications or the buyer's requirements.

DOCUMENTARY COLLECTIONS

At its most basic, documentary collections involves the seller arranging for a foreign buyer to create the appropriate document giving title of the goods to the buyer in return for either (a) an immediate payment or (b) a contractual promise to pay at a later date. Compared to the use of a letter of credit, documentary collections are relatively uncomplicated and inexpensive.

The use of Documentary Collections including sight drafts and time drafts involves significant risk to the exporter. The importer may decide not to pay its bank for the documents necessary to take title and possession of the merchandise due to cash flow problems, the unavailability of foreign exchange, the loss of their customer, or simply a situation in which the buyer changes its mind about the purchase or finds a better price [or better terms] elsewhere.

INTERNATIONAL LETTERS OF CREDIT

Most creditors would prefer not to offer foreign customers open account terms. One of the most popular ways to try to reduce credit risk is to require foreign customers to provide the seller with a letter of credit covering the shipment of goods. Letters of credit, whether domestic or international, are governed by the International Chamber of Commerce's Uniform Customs and Practices for Documentary Credits—abbreviated as the UCP. Letters of credit are explained in detail in Chapter 49.

ADVANTAGES AND DISADVANTAGES OF OPEN ACCOUNT TERMS

The advantages of selling on open account terms include the fact that the creditor does not need to be as concerned about documentation requirements. Another important advantage to the seller is the fact that offering open account credit terms should result in incremental sales to the exporter.

CONSIGNMENT SALES

Because of the risks inherent in international sales, a few creditors have developed a novel approach to controlling this risk. The use consignment. Consignment involves the delivery of merchandise without the transfer of title. This means that ownership of and title to the merchandise remains with the shipped. Foreign consignments typically work this way:

The merchandise in question is shipped to a bonded warehouse under the control of the seller, or a foreign bank or other trusted third party. Arrangements are then made for the release of merchandise from the bonded warehouse for delivery to the buyer when goods are needed and when money is available.

There are several problems with this process. One of the most important is that the seller has to pay demurrage [storage] charges while the merchandise in question is held in the bonded warehouse. The creditor needs a substantial margin in its products to make a consignment program work. Another problem is the fact that if the merchandise in question is not sold that the owner will need to arrange for the return of the consigned merchandise from the bonded warehouse and pay all of the costs associated with that return.

COLLECTIONS IN FOREIGN COUNTRIES

If the creditor elects to sell on open account terms, sooner or later one of the company's foreign customers will default on payment. If the credit department and the salesperson cannot get the customer to pay, then it may be necessary to use a third party collection agency. Using an in-country collection agency that is familiar with local laws, the local language and local customs may be more effective than using a U.S.–based company.

Another option involves retaining a local attorney to pursue payment through the court system. This may be a lengthy and expensive process, and unfortunately in parts of the world courts and judges are corrupt. Typically, foreign attorneys are not willing to take such cases on a contingency basis.

Less restrictive than requiring letter of credit terms involves the use of sight draft collections sometimes called documents against payment.

Under sight draft terms, the seller issues a draft, shipping documents, and an invoice to its bank. The seller's bank forwards these documents to the buyer's bank. The buyer's bank contacts the buyer once the documents and the merchandise have arrived. Once the buyer pays its bank for the goods, the bank releases the documents necessary for the buyer to take possession of the goods.

Always ask that your customer fax you a draft of the proposed letter of credit terms and conditions. This way, if there are obvious problems with it, changes can be made before the letter of credit is issued at which point the buyer must go to its bank to request a formal amendment to the letter of credit. The amendment process adds cost and may delay shipment by days or even weeks.

THE ROLE OF BANKS IN FOREIGN SALES

Banks offer their customers a wide variety of value added services that make it easier, safer and less expensive to export goods. For example, an experienced commercial bank can generate wire transfer payments, issue and process letters of credit, and facilitate collection against time drafts and sigh drafts.

FOREIGN FINANCIAL STATEMENTS

Foreign financial statements are normally formatted differently than U.S. financial statements. Accounting standards vary significantly from country to country. Foreign financial statements follow different accounting rules and concepts. U.S. Generally Accepted Accounting Principals are followed nowhere else in the world.

Foreign financial statements must be converted into U.S. dollars in order to be meaningful. It is easy to forget that exchange rates fluctuate on a daily basis. Often, a foreign currency will fluctuate within a narrow range relative to the dollar, but this is not always the case. Therefore, an additional step necessary gain a better understanding of foreign financial statements is knowning the exchange rate on the date the statements were generated and using that figure to convert the data into U.S. dollars.

Credit professionals should be aware that in parts of the world it may be uncommon, unprofessional or impolite to request financial statements from customers under any circumstances. In other parts of the world, it is not uncommon for companies to keep two sets of books—one to show the taxing authorities and another reflecting the true condition of the business. The most important thing for the creditor to remember is that the customer may interpret this request not as a routine request for information, but as a direct and negative statement about the creditworthiness of the applicant company. The credit manager must do everything possible not to accidentally or inadvertently convey this message.

Even if the customer is willing to share its financial statements with the creditor, the creditor's problems are only beginning. Why? Because the creditor must then try to interpret the financial statements. There are several pitfalls and obstacles to doing so, including these:

- the fact that the statements often are not presented in the same formats as U.S. financial statements, and therefore they must be interpreted and can easily be misinterpreted

- accounting rules differ from country to country and the creditor often cannot be sure whether the information presented is accurate, or is a fabrication
- the fact that creditor often does not have access to industry norms in the foreign country for comparative analysis

FOREIGN EXCHANGE CONSIDERATIONS AND HOW TO MANAGE CREDIT RISK

Non payment is not the only risk in selling internationally. Another significant risk involves volatility in foreign exchange rates. As a general rule, in an international sales transaction the creditor will be expected to assume the risk of depreciation or devaluation in the foreign currency exchange market.

Foreign exchange risk can be significant. Here is a simple example:

Assume a creditor exports products, the payment is to be made in sixty days in the buyer's currency, and the seller anticipates a pretax profit of 5% after paying the cost associated with exchanging the foreign currency for U.S. dollars. Assuming during the next sixty days the foreign exchange rate drops by 15% relative to the U.S. dollar. In this scenario, a company that anticipate a 5% profit would incur a 10% loss.

For this reason, creditors prefer to have international transactions quoted, billed and paid in their nation's currency. The buyer prefers the opposite.

Many credit managers are expected to understand and to manage is foreign exchange risk. Many factors influence fluctuations in currency rates. For example, a currency can become more or less valuable in reference to another currency because of factors including economic news, political events, and interest rate differentials and growth rate differentials.

There are a variety of ways to hedge against unfavorable swings in foreign currency exchange rates. Among these techniques are future contracts and future options. Foreign currency exchanges are either made at the spot rate [the current exchange rate] or sold for delivery in the future. A future contract is a specific commitment to buy a specific amount of currency at a specific date. A future option contract, as the name suggests, allows the purchaser the option of buying a specific quantity of the foreign currency at a specified exchange rate.

Creditors doing business internationally may opt not to hedge against foreign currency devaluation. Before any company elects to absorb this type of risk, it is essential that they recognize the scope of the risk, consider their options and alternatives, research the foreign currency, and understand or determine their company's tolerance for exchange rate risk.

EXPORT LICENSES

An export license is a document issued by a federal government agency that permits the licensee to export designated goods to certain approved destination. Depending on the product a U.S.–based company intends to export, the company may or may not need an export license. It is up to the exporter to determine if an export license is required.

Specific products may require an individually validated export license. This is the most restrictive type of export license. An individually validated export license is issued for a specific period of time, for a specific transaction covering specific product for delivery to a specific buyer in a specific country.

An individually validated export license is normally required for any merchandise deemed important to national security or critical to the foreign policy objectives of the United States. Dual use exports are the most common items requiring export license. Dual use exports are commercial items that could also have military applications. For example, certain types of high capacity computers could be considered dual use exports.

A company must classify its products against the Commercial Control List created by the Department of Commerce's Bureau of Export Administration. Fortunately, a relatively small percentage of exports require the submission of a license application, and in particular an individually validated export license.

Most license requirements are dependent on a product's technical characteristics. Other important factors include the country of destination, the intended end use, and the identity of the end user. The primary licensing agency is the Bureau of Export Administration. Other governmental agencies have regulatory jurisdiction over specific types of exports. For example, the Nuclear Regulatory Commission licenses the export of nuclear material and equipment.

Exporting companies can request an official classification of its exports from the Bureau of Export Administration. A commodity classification request requires the applicant to submit to the BXA an application along with the technical specifications of their product. Once the classification is obtained, the exporter knows for certain how to classify its products for export.

SHIPPING TERMS

Separate and distinct from the concept of credit terms are shipping terms. International shipping terms are published by the International Chamber of Commerce and are referred to as Incoterms. Shipping terms beginning with the letter C require the seller to both arrange and pay for the carriage and to deliver the goods to the carrier.

Shipping terms beginning with the letter D denotes that it is the seller's obligation to deliver the gods to the buyer's country. The group of Incoterms beginning with the letter E denotes the fact the buyer need not take delivery until the goods arrive at the buyer's facility. The letter F means the buyer is required to arrange and pay for carriage, storage, etc. and then deliver goods to a carrier such as a boat or a plane.

FOREIGN EXCHANGE RISK

A U.S. exporter ships product on open account terms to a foreign customer on 60-day terms. The invoice is denominated in the buyer's local currency, which we will call the Peso. Assume the present exchange rate is 10 Pesos to each 1 U.S. dollar [a 10 to 1 exchange rate]. The sale is worth $10,000 meaning the invoice is for 100,000 Pesos [P100,000]. When the invoice comes due, the foreign buyer sends payment of P100,000. However, suppose that during the intervening 60-day period, the value of the Peso has dropped and that the current exchange rate is 12 to 1. When the U.S. exporter presents the Peso for exchange, they receive only $8,300. The exporter has lost $1,700 because of foreign exchange [F/X] rate fluctuations.

FOREIGN EXCHANGE HEDGING

Exchange rates refer to the price of one currency in terms of another. Credit managers can help their companies to avoid losses that may result from exchange rate fluctuations through a process called hedging. There are four types of foreign exchange hedging; they are (a) the spot exchange, (b) forward exchange, (c) an option and (d) a swap.

> Spot foreign exchange contracts convert one currency into another based on the current exchange rate at the date and time the spot contract is executed.

> Forward foreign exchange contracts lock in a specified rate such as the current rate of exchange at a specific future date. The advantage of a

forward contract is that it allows the seller to be more certain about its future cash inflows.

Swap contracts involve the sale of one currency against another at a specific date along with the simultaneous repurchase from the same party at a different date.

As the name suggests, an options contract gives a company the option to buy or to sell a foreign currency at a specific date in the future at a specific rate.

Hedging contracts can be thought of as insurance for the seller against wide fluctuations in foreign exchange rates. Implementing a foreign exchange is time consuming, and the seller must be willing to pay certain fees and costs to hedge its risks. However, hedging can control costs and improve overall profits. The time and effort required to implement such a policy is normally more than offset by the fact that a foreign exchange strategy helps manage risk for the seller.

In theory, the cost of hedging should be added to the seller's cost. Because of the cost, and the complexity of hedging against F/X risk, many creditors decide to do without it. Credit professionals should always make sure that their managers aware of foreign exchange risk, otherwise they may be accused of failing to take into consideration the risks associated with foreign exchange rate fluctuations. The seller's bank should be able to offer advice on how to hedge one currency against another.

THE ROLE OF FREIGHT FORWARDERS

A freight forwarder is an independent business that handles export shipments for compensation. A freight forwarder's basic function is to help an exporter to get cargo from point A to point B at the right time and in one piece. Freight forwarders typically do not own any vehicles, ships or other conveyances for the cargo.

Freight forwarders provide a variety of value added services to exporters including information and assistance on U.S. export regulations, on required export documentation, as well as shipping methods and foreign import regulations and foreign import documentation requirements. Freight forwarders often prepare and present certain documents required before the exporter can be paid on open account terms or against a letter of credit.

SUMMARY

Export transactions are high risk. Foreign sales on open account terms are often high maintenance and high risk. Credit managers are expected to be able to handle domestic and international credit risk with equal skill.

Exporting is an attractive option for many U.S.–based companies interested in maximizing sales and profits. A credit manager who is an obstacle to this process will be seen as a hinderance to the company's growth. Therefore, credit professionals need to get whatever training they need to feel comfortable in this new role as a worldwide credit manager for their company.

CHAPTER 37

PREPARING FOR INTERNATIONAL CREDIT TRANSACTIONS

Export sales are an important part of many U.S.–based companies' growth plans. Over 90% of large U.S.–based companies already export products, and almost 75% of U.S.–based companies classified as mid-sized also export. Export sales offer the seller the opportunity to make use of excess production capacity, to increase sales and to generate more profits. Unfortunately, export sales also carry their own set of inherent credit risks.

Export sales transactions are far more complicated than domestic sales—primarily because of the additional documentation requirements for export sales. Because of intensified global competition, profit margins are shrinking. As a result, selling internationally has become even higher risk. If a foreign customer wants to purchase goods on open account terms, the credit decision is complicated by a number of factors including:

- Country risk associated with the political and economic stability of the country into which the seller plans to export goods

- Currency risk associated with foreign currency exchange rate fluctuations and/or the possibility that the buyer will be unable to obtain U.S. dollars to pay the seller, or

- The cultural differences between the seller and the buyer that might somehow reduce the likelihood of payment even if the merchandise in question was delivered on time and as ordered.

ESTABLISHING THE CREDIT TERMS

One of the most important steps in any export credit transaction is selecting the proper terms of sale for each customer. Favorable credit terms will make a company's products more attractive to the buyer. The two main elements of the process of establishing credit terms are (a) evaluating the risk associated with selling to the customer and (b) evaluating the risks associated with selling [exporting] into the country in which the customer is located.

Some exporting companies are not enthusiastic about the additional credit risk associated with open account international sales. These companies are content to require that customers pay for goods on Cash in Advance terms or require that the sale be covered by a Letter of Credit. Not surprisingly, these companies do not normally do a great deal of international business.

REASONS TO REQUIRE ADDITIONAL ASSURANCE OF PAYMENT FROM FOREIGN CUSTOMERS

It is not uncommon for companies manufacturing custom made products to require payment in advance and progress payments or a Letter of Credit.

LEARNING ABOUT INTERNATIONAL BUSINESS

Rather than simply jumping into the business of exporting, companies should spend time preparing to do business internationally. There is no need for a new exporter to reinvent the wheel. There are many sources of information available that can make exporting easier. There are a number of organizations that help prepare to export. Organizations such as the International Chamber of Commerce, and the World Trade Organization typically offer members the following types of services:

- Access to a local affiliate group. For example, the World Trade Centers Association has more than 300 local affiliates. The United States Chamber of Commerce has approximately 3,000 state and local chapters throughout the United States.

- An educational arm dedicated to increasing the skills, knowledge and productivity of members

- A division publishing magazines, pamphlets and books of interest to business professionals.
- Local networking opportunities

THE TRADE INFORMATION CENTER

The United States Department of Commerce's International Trade Administration funds the Trade Information Center. The Trade Information Center has a web page that is an excellent resource for any company thinking about exporting, and for any individual [such as a credit manager] who is being asked to take an active role on the export side of the business.

SELECTING THE APPROPRIATE CREDIT TERMS

Cash in Advance

Ideally, creditors would like foreign customers to purchase goods on cash in advance terms. However, the buyer will probably have a number of concerns about cash in advance terms, and will probably not agree to buy under these terms unless there are no alternative suppliers willing to offer better terms.

Assuming that the buyer agrees to pay in advance, if the buyer sends a check drawn on a foreign bank rather than a wire transfer payment then that check must be allowed to clear before the goods are shipped. It would be difficult for the credit manager to justify handling a check drawn on a foreign bank any other way.

Cash in Advance terms are recommended if:

- the buyer's country to politically or economically unstable, or

- the buyer is not creditworthy, or

- the product being sold is made specifically for the buyer and is not readily salable to anyone else.

- There is not enough information to make an informed credit decision.

CASH ON DELIVERY

This term is rarely if ever used in international business transactions. Cash on delivery is impractical and probably unenforceable.

There is simply no way to adequately protect the seller against these risks:

- The goods may be delivered but no payment demanded
- The goods may be delivered and payment collected but lost
- The goods delivered, the check collected, altered and then cashed by an intermediary

SIGHT DRAFTS

At first glance, sight drafts appear to be a relatively secure way to conduct business internationally. Unfortunately, there are any number of things that can go wrong with a sale made against a sight draft. For example:

- The buyer's bank makes no representations about whether or not the buyer will accept [will pay for] the sight draft.
- After the shipment has taken place , the buyer may decide that they do want the goods. [For example, they may have found a local source or a lower price].
- The buyer may want the goods, but not have the money to pay for them.
- The buyer may not be able to obtain enough hard U.S. currency through the official exchanges and the buyer may be unwilling to pay the black market price for the hard currency.

If the buyer does not want the goods, the seller must find another buyer, or pay to have the merchandise returned. If the exporter waits too long to decide what to do, the goods might be seized and sold by the foreign country's customs authority.

Another problem with sight drafts is that after the goods have arrived and before the buyer has signed the draft, the buyer may try to open negotiations about a lower price. The buyer recognizes that the seller must pay to insure and to store the merchandise until the buyer takes possession of the goods. Many buyers believe that this puts them in a good negotiating position.

A time draft is a variant of the sight draft. Instead of demanding that the shipping documents be released only after the buyer makes payment to the bank, the time draft specifies that the buyer must agree to return to the bank and pay for the goods a specific number of days after writing "accepted" on the draft and signing it in return for receiving title to the goods.

A time draft is similar in many ways to open account credit terms. The main difference is that rather than the debtor promising to pay the creditor a certain number of days after delivery, the buyer is making that payment commitment to its bank.

The myth and mystique about a time draft is the idea that the customer will return to its bank to pay the draft because to do otherwise would damage that company's reputation with its banker. In reality, the buyer may have:

(1) a non-borrowing relationship with its bank in which case the buyer is likely to be unconcerned about what the bank thinks about the status of the time draft; or

(2) A poor relationship with the bank; or

(3) May be far more interested in receiving the goods than it is concerned about what its bank might or might not think if the buyer does not fund the time draft.

Typically, time drafts are for periods ranging from 30 to 120 days. Because time drafts are similar to open account terms, many credit professionals are unwilling to offer or accept these terms. The time draft process is sometimes referred to as Documents against Acceptance, or D/A. The accepted draft itself is called a trade acceptance.

THE RISKS ASSOCIATED WITH DRAFTS

There are significant risks to the seller when drafts are used. One of the most serious risks is that the buyer's bank will release the documents to the buyer without requiring the draft to be signed and/or funded. Another problem is the possibility that the buyer signs the time draft but never returns to fund the draft. Even if the buyer's bank were prepared to act as an intermediary to help the seller recover payment against a time draft, all the buyer would have to tell the bank is that the goods in question were damaged or of substandard quality and the buyer's bank would probably not pursue it further.

For all of these reasons, credit managers should only agree to accept sight draft of time draft terms if:

● The seller has the expertise to assemble and to properly complete all of the documentation necessary to complete a sight draft or a time draft.

- The creditor has evaluated the customer's business reputation and credit history and found them to be willing and able to pay foreign suppliers' bills as they come due.

- Provided the foreign country is financially, economically and politically stable.

- Assuming there are no foreign exchange problems or restriction in effect—and none are contemplated, and

- In the event the buyer elects not to accept the goods for whatever reason, that the product in question is easily marketable elsewhere.

- The buyer would qualify for open account terms.

CREDIT CARDS

A few U.S.–based exporters are conducting business with foreign customers using credit cards. Trade creditors will find that the rules governing credit card transactions are different domestically vs. internationally. Using a credit card the creditor feels that it has received payment in advance. Unfortunately, international credit card transactions are fraught with risk to the exporter. For example, the credit card charge might be disputed. The merchant may or may not be permitted to dispute the buyer's version of the facts before the bank debits [removes the payment] from the seller's account. Often, the cardholder has a period of several months in which they can dispute a charge that has appeared on its bill.

In this scenario, the seller has very little leverage with the buyer. The buyer has the goods and the money—the best of both worlds. Credit cards are not recommended for international sales transactions.

SALES ON OPEN ACCOUNT TERMS COVERED BY EXPORT CREDIT INSURANCE

Export credit insurance has grown in popularity in the United States over the last decade for a number of reasons. Perhaps the most important reason is that creditors want to expand their business internationally, and recognize that they do not have the same access to information and the same expertise in managing credit risk as they do domestically. Therefore, companies interested in exporting safely are looking to export credit insurance to help them grow their international business.

There are two basic types of export credit insurance policies. Commercial credit insurance covers losses caused by the insolvency or default by the buyer. Commercial credit insurance coverage is similar to domestic credit insurance policies. It protects the seller against the default, bankruptcy or insolvency of the buyer.

The other type of export credit insurance coverage is for an entirely different type of risk—political risk. Political risk would include events that would cause a customer that would otherwise be willing to pay the creditor to be unable to do so. Examples of political risks that might prevent payment include:

- War

- Expropriation or confiscation of the exported merchandise by a foreign government.

- The inability of the customer or of the foreign government to obtain foreign exchange in order to pay the U.S. company.

- The inability to send payments out of the country due to governmental restrictions on foreign exchange transfers.

- U.S. government boycotts or restrictions.

SOURCES OF CREDIT INSURANCE

Foreign credit insurance coverage is available through both governmental and private agencies. The largest governmental source of export credit insurance is the Export Import Bank of the United States [the Eximbank]. The Eximbank is an independent federal agency whose mission is to support the export of U.S. goods and services through loan guarantees and insurance programs.

The largest non-governmental source is the Foreign Credit Insurance Association which is affiliated with the Eximbank. The FCIA is a private insurance association operating as Eximbank's agent. It provides export credit insurance to cover political commercial losses.

FACTORING

Factoring involves the sale of foreign receivable by an exporter to a factor [or a factoring house]. The factor buys the right to the proceeds of the seller's accounts receivable at a discount from the face value of the invoice. The discount represents the factor's profit.

Factoring works this way: The exporter transfers title to a foreign accounts receivable balance to a factoring house in return for immediate cash for an amount equal to the advance rate negotiated. Advances rates typically range from 75% to 90%. The remaining 10% to 25% of the value of the invoice minus the factor's profit [the discount] called the reserve or holdback will be paid to the creditor once payment is received by the factor.

Often, factoring of a foreign receivable is done without recourse— meaning the factor would absorb the entire loss if the foreign customer fails to pay the balance due. Factoring with recourse means that the seller must return the advance [or any amount paid by the factor to the seller] if the buyer does not pay the factored invoice within a specific time frame— regardless of the reason for the payment default.

A factor relies on the creditworthiness of the foreign customer to ensure payment. Because of this, factors can offer a creditor basically unlimited working capital without the seller incurring any additional debt provided that its customers are creditworthy. Improved working capital allows the seller to take discounts, purchase equipment, pay suppliers, and purchase inventory. Unfortunately, the factor's fee is relatively high making factoring impractical for many companies.

FORFAITING

Forfaiting is used infrequently. It involves the purchase of a series of notes [such as promissory notes] on a non-recourse basis. The forfaiter deducts interest at an agreed rate for the full period covered by the notes. Typically, a bank will guarantee the notes [or other debt instruments].

Forfaiting is similar to factoring in some ways, and dissimilar in others. Forfaiting is done without recourse. A forfaiting house would normally not handle transactions worth less than $100,000 and forfaiting normally covers medium term transactions in the one to ten year range. The fees or charges of a forfaiter depend on a number of different factors including:

- The credit risk of the bank guaranteeing the transaction
- The political risk of the country of destination
- The interest and inflation rate relevant to the currency of payment
- The cost of purchasing a hedge against exchange rate fluctuations.

Because many trade creditors do not sell in the dollar volume forfaiters are interested in working on, and because credit creditors typically do not offer the type of dating terms that forfeiters expect to see, trade creditors rarely use forfeiting.

SELLING ON LETTER OF CREDIT TERMS

A Letter of Credit is a conditional payment commitment made by the issuing bank. Specifically, the issuing bank agrees pay money to the seller of goods on behalf of the buyer. The conditions upon which the issuing bank's obligation to pay will be invoked are specified in the Letter of Credit contract.

A letter of credit allows the seller to demand payment for specified shipments of product provided that all of the required documents are presented, and provided those documents conform to a strict interpretation of the letter of credit.

Often, the seller's bank acts as an agent for the foreign bank that issued the Letter of Credit. In this capacity, the "local" bank will forward the documents submitted by the seller to the foreign opening bank along with a demand for payment. If and when the opening [the issuing] bank funds the Letter of Credit, the funds will be sent by wire transfer payment by the issuing bank to the seller's bank.

Letters of Credit [L/Cs] can be divided into two major types; (a) Documentary L/Cs and (b) Standby L/Cs. Documentary L/Cs are often used as a payment mechanism to support international trade. Standby L/Cs are normally used in domestic transactions and act as a payment or performance bond.

LETTER OF CREDIT TIP: For a nominal fee, the seller's bank will normally review the document for discrepancies prior to the seller submitting the documents to the advising bank to be forwarded to the issuing bank. If the issuing bank finds discrepancies, the creditor's bank will be notified and will inform the seller of the problem(s) found. Normally, the seller's bank will work with the seller to explain and if possible to help the seller to cure the discrepancy. The fee charged for this service is money that is well spent.

A Standby Letter of Credit [Standby L/C] is in a sense a mixture of open account terms and a bank guarantee. Standby letters of credit are used in conjunction with an open account. The seller ships the goods anticipating that the buyer will pay the seller's invoices as they come due. If for some reason the buyer does not pay as agreed, the seller can look to the issuing bank to honor its obligation to pay the seller.

Documentation requirements are very different between Letters of Credit and Standby Letters of Credit. For a standby L/C, the documentation requirements are minimal. They might include nothing more than a copy of the invoice, shipping documents and a demand notice signed by an officer of the seller stating that the invoice in question is past due and remains unpaid. Because the documentation required is so minimal, foreign buyers are normally reluctant to agree to offer a standby letter of credit.

A documentary Letter of Credit is a contract. Experienced credit professionals will provide the customer with a specific list of letter of credit terms that are acceptable and unacceptable to the seller.

The credit manager also should make certain that other departments within their company understand the requirements of the Letter of Credit. International shipments covered by a L/C often require special handling, and there are often unusual documentation requirements, as well as unique maritime insurance coverages needed. Unless everyone understands their unique responsibilities relative to the letter of credit, chances are good that a discrepancy will result.

Letters of Credit can benefit both the buyer and the seller. The seller looks to the issuing bank rather than to the customer for payment. The documentation requirements listed in the L/C are intended to reduce the buyer's risk of receiving faulty or defective merchandise. For example, the letter of credit may require the seller to provide a certificate of inspection, a certificate of origin, and proof of insurance.

LETTER OF CREDIT RULES

To ensure uniformity in interpretation, the International Chamber of Commerce has created a set of regulations for Letters of Credit titled "Uniform Customs and Practice for Documentary Credits" referred to as the UCP 500. Among other things the UCP says that only the language contained in the letter of credit is binding on the banks. The banks assume no responsibility for the authenticity or the validity of the documents—and do not concern themselves with the underlying documents. Instead, they look only at and to the documents submitted.

LETTER OF CREDIT DISCREPANCIES

A discrepancy is any documentation found not to be in accordance with the terms of the L/C. Often, seemingly trivial discrepancies between the terms and conditions listed on the letter of credit and the documents provided by the creditor will result in a discrepancy. For example, minor typographical errors having nothing to do with the underlying transaction may result in a decision by the issuing bank not to honor the letter of credit.

The exporter can remedy a correctable discrepancy by resubmitting documents prior to the expiry date and within the number of days permitted for presentation of documents. However, credit managers should be aware that the exporter cannot correct certain types of discrepancies. If the creditor is to be paid under a L/C containing a discrepancy that cannot be corrected, then the buyer, and the buyer's bank and the confirming bank [if there is a confirming bank] must approve waiving the discrepancy. Examples of discrepancies that cannot be fixed by the seller would include:

- Shipping after the last date of shipment.
- Making partial shipments when partial shipments are expressly prohibited.
- Transshipping when transshipments were prohibited.
- Inconsistencies between the descriptions of the goods on various documents submitted to the issuing bank.

COMMON LETTER OF CREDIT DISCREPANCIES

The most common discrepancies include:
- The letter of credit has expired
- The last shipping date as listed on the L/C passed before shipment was made
- There was late presentation of documents. Specifically, the documents must be presented within 21 days from the on board bill of lading date unless a shorter period is specified in the L/C
- The insurance documents are effective after the date of the on board bill of lading
- The draft and the L/C amounts do not match
- The draft is not completed, signed or endorsed properly
- The invoice does not show the same shipping terms as specified on the L/C
- The insurance coverage is insufficient or in a currency other than the L/C
- The shipment transited ports other than those specified by the L/C

BANKS AND THE UCP 500

Banks are in a unique position when evaluating documentation submitted in support of payment under a L/C. Banks drafted the UCP rules governing letters of credit; banks have sole discretion interpreting those rules as they relate to the documentation supplied by the creditor; and banks determine if and when to pay and how much to charge to "fix" the problems they discover. The most common [and serious] letter of credit discrepancies are:

- Documents are presented by the seller after the expiration of the L/C
- Insurance documents did not conform to terms required in the L/C
- Documents are presented more than 21 days after the date of the bill of lading

> A letter of credit cannot protect a seller from an unscrupulous buyer. If they look hard enough, an expert can almost always find a minor discrepancy, and often can find a major one.

- Shipment is made after the last allowable date
- There is an incorrect consignee on the bill of lading
- The description of the merchandise on the invoice differs from the description in the letter of credit
- One or more documents required by the L/C are missing

If a discrepancy cannot be corrected, the exporter has three options. It may:

(a) Request the non conforming documents be sent to the issuing bank on approval

(b) Request that the customer amend the letter of credit—assuming the L/C has not expired and the buyer has the time to do so

(c) Arrange for the returns of the merchandise assuming that it is still in transit

THE ROLE OF THE FREIGHT FORWARDER

A freight forwarder will be able to offer the company advice about the following topics:

- Proper packaging,
- Shipment options for on-time delivery,
- Local regulations, standards and certification requirements,
- Insurance coverage required, and
- Whether or not an export license is required, or whether trade sanctions apply.

The right freight forwarder will save the seller time and money. More importantly, a competent freight forwarder will help the credit department to avoid problems. Freight forwarders normally prepare many if not all of the documents exporters will need. Credit professionals should remember that a freight forwarder is not an employee of their company. Freight forwarders are independent contractors. The choice of freight forwarder is critical.

A freight forwarder should be :

- Reliable and honest
- Local
- Knowledgeable and experienced in handling the types of products your company manufactures.
- Cooperative,
- Patient, and
- One that understands its obligation is to you, the shipper, to help make certain you get paid on every transaction.

SHIPPING TERMS

Making certain the foreign customer understands and agrees to the credit terms is an important part of making certain the seller gets paid. It is also important that the buyer and the seller agree where their respective responsibility for loss or damage for goods in transit begins and ends. The three most common shipping terms are:

(a) CIF [Cost, Insurance and Freight]

(b) C & F [Cost and Freight]

(c) FOB [Free on Board]

Under shipping condition (a) listed above the seller is responsible to provide insurance and freight to the delivery point. Under C & F shipping terms, the cost of insurance is borne by the buyer. Under FOB terms as described above the seller's responsibility for the goods ends at the point that the goods are loaded on board the ship.

INSURANCE AGAINST LOSS IN TRANSIT

Credit managers should make certain that someone has purchased cargo insurance on international shipments. The reason is that under international law, common carriers have limited liability for missing or damaged merchandise while in transit. Depending on the shipping terms, either the buyer or the seller will be responsible for purchasing cargo insurance. In some cases, the exporter/seller will maintain cargo insurance on goods in transit just in case the buyer's insurance does not cover an entire claim if a claim is submitted.

Cargo insurance can be purchased one of two ways. It can be purchased (a) on an order by order basis, or (b) the exporter/seller can purchase a cargo or transit insurance policy from an insurance broker. Transit insurance policies are often "open" meaning all shipments of regular product are covered by it.

All risk insurance is the broadest form of coverage available, providing protection against all risk of physical loss or damage from any external cause. However, "all risk" insurance does not cover loss or damage due to delay or loss of market.

OPEN ACCOUNT TERMS

Some companies never offer open account credit terms to foreign accounts. Other creditors recognize that if the company is serious about expanding international sales then the company must accept more credit risk—possibly by offering open account terms to some foreign customers.

A well-written credit policy will include instructions about if or when open account terms are to be offered to foreign customers.

EVALUATING SOVEREIGN OR POLITICAL RISK

Sovereign or political risk deals with the fact that in an international transaction the creditor must be concerned about the debtor's ability to pay the debt and about the stability of the foreign country, its economy, and its currency. The country's central bank and its political system each play a role in determining whether or not an individual customer will be able to pay its bills as they come due. Delinquencies and defaults sometimes occur not because the debtor could not pay the debt but instead because the foreign government took action that made payment difficult or even impossible.

DEALING WITH FOREIGN LANGUAGES AND CUSTOMS

Credit managers should seriously consider hiring a collector that speaks the same language as the customer. It is also important to try to find someone who understands the customs and the business norms of the country they are contacting. For example, if the creditor offers a foreign customer open account credit terms they may learn that the customer does not understand the importance to a U.S.–based company of receiving payments within the terms specified on the invoice. Having a collector who speaks the customer's language makes it easier to explain the importance to the creditor of prompt payment, and the risk that the debtor company takes by not scheduling invoices for payment as they come due.

THE ROLE OF THE SALESPERSON

The sales department can be an important tool in convincing a delinquent export customer to pay its bills. Sales personnel dealing with foreign customers often have a personal relationship with one or more key executives within the debtor company. In many countries, business dealings are more focused on personal relationships than they are in the United States. Credit managers can use this to their advantage by involving the salesperson in the collection effort.

INTERNATIONAL SALESPEOPLE NEED INFORMATION TO HELP

The international sales department will be of more help to the credit department if the credit department provides each salesperson with an aging report on their accounts at least once a month. The theory behind providing this information is that with this information the salesperson can proactively contact their customers and keep them off credit hold.

COMMUNICATING WITH FOREIGN CUSTOMERS

In addition to language barriers and different business practices, credit professionals must remember that foreign customers are normally located in different time zones. This fact must be taken into account every time the creditor wants to contact the customer. Time zone differences are one of the primary reasons that creditors often use facsimile messages or e-mail to correspond with foreign customers.

Another advantage of making an electronic inquiry is that the customer can take their time to translate, and then to read the seller's question or comments.

ANTIBOYCOTT REGULATIONS

The United States has adopted laws that prohibits the participation of U.S. citizens, companies and their foreign affiliates in other nations' economic boycotts and embargoes. Antiboycott laws were adopted to encourage U.S. firms to refuse to participate in boycotts that the United States government does not sanction. The intent of these laws is to prevent U.S. firms from being used to undercut U.S. foreign policy.

Antiboycott laws apply to all foreign boycotts that are not sanctioned by the U.S. government. The most important of these boycotts is the Arab League boycott of Israel.

U.S. companies must report on a quarterly basis any requests they have received and any action they may have taken in support of an unsanctioned boycott to the Department of Commerce under the Export Administration Act. Reportable activities include:

- Agreements to refuse to do business with Israel or with any blacklisted company.

- An agreement to discriminate against persons or companies based on race, religion, sex, national origin, or nationality.

- Any agreement to furnish information about business relationship with or in Israel or any blacklisted country or company.

- Accepting or presenting letters of credit containing prohibited boycott terms or conditions.

Violations of the antiboycott provisions of Export Administration Regulations include both criminal penalties [fines and/or imprisonment], and administrative sanctions. Sanctions may include revocation of export license, the denial of all export privileges and civil fines.

SUMMARY

Creditors should never assume that the legal system in the country of export is the same or even similar to their own. Even if a contract between the buyer and seller specifically states that one country's laws will control the sale, the seller should assume that if delegation becomes necessary that it will be necessary to litigate in a court in the buyer's country.

The credit department's natural caution about offering customers open account terms is even more important when considering whether or not to extend credit to foreign credit applicants. Foreign customers are far more difficult to find and to collect from because of the differences in laws between countries. In addition to these problems, language barriers and the cultural, social and political environment in a particular foreign country may make it difficult, if not impossible, for a foreign creditor to win a judgment and collect an unpaid account balance.

CHAPTER 38

CREDIT AND COLLECTION AND INTERNATIONAL LAW

U.S.–based companies engaged in international trade face a confusing array of legal issues surrounding the process of exporting goods, and the right to be paid for those shipments. There are laws in the United States governing the types of products that can be exported and the countries that they can be exported to. There are laws in foreign countries that impose restrictions on the types of products that can be imported. In addition, there are rules governing the type of documentation that must accompany products being imported.

In addition to the laws that govern the process of importing and exporting goods, there are other laws governing payment for those shipments. If a credit manager elects to ship on open account terms into a foreign country, and the customer does not pay for the goods; the credit manager needs to know how to go about getting paid.

In this chapter, we will cover each of these three important issues:

- U.S. laws governing exporting
- Foreign laws governing the importation of goods.
- Mechanisms for securing payment.

THE CHALLENGE

The challenge for credit managers to know which laws and rules apply to which export transactions. There are an array of potential problems facing the credit manager who does not understand the laws governing export of goods.

EXPORT LICENSES

The U.S. Department of Commerce's Bureau of Export Administration issues export licenses. Most goods do not need a license to be exported. Licenses requirements are dependent on the item's technical characteristics, the destination, and the end user. In order to determine if an export license is required, the seller must know:

- What the product is
- Where it is going
- To whom is it being sold
- What do they plan to do with it
- What other activities are they [the end user or buyer] involved in

As a general statement, export license are required for certain high technology goods, or goods shipped into certain countries where the United States government feels that national security or foreign policy goals override the government's desire to assist U.S. companies to export their products.

An exporter can call or contact the Bureau of Export Administration [the BXA] to determine if they need an export license for their goods. It is also possible to access the BXA's web site to look up this information. In addition, the BXA holds seminars throughout the year to explain export licensing requirements.

For obvious reasons, certain products cannot be exported to certain countries because of overriding national security interests. Exporters should never assume that their goods do not require an export license. They must be certain that no license is required, and that requires knowing the BXA regulations. Exporters that ignore the BXA's licensing requirements in violation of the law subject to stiff fines. Companies and individuals that knowingly violate export licensing requirements may be subject to criminal prosecution.

THE FOREIGN CORRUPT PRACTICES ACT

The federal government has passed legislation that makes it illegal for an exporter to bribe a foreign government official in order to obtain or to retain business. The basic provisions of the Foreign Corrupt Practices Act make it illegal to:

(a) make bribes directly, or

(b) allow bribes to be paid by intermediaries

The Act specifically makes it illegal to make a payment to any person "knowing" that all or a portion of that payment will be offered as a bribe to a foreign official or foreign political party. "Knowing" includes the concepts of "conscious disregard" and "willful blindness" to the question of how the intermediary will use the payment made to him, her or it. The Department of Justice is responsible for all criminal enforcement of the Foreign Corrupt Practices Act.

COMPLIANCE WITH FOREIGN REGULATIONS GOVERNING IMPORTS

One of the most common questions that a credit manager must ask is what foreign regulations, standards or documentation requirements govern the export of the product my company sells into a particular foreign country?

Sovereign nations can impose any restrictions they wish on the import of goods into their country. For example, a certain Islamic Republic recently banned the importation of television sets into its country. One of the best sources of information about a foreign country's trade regulations can be obtained by accessing the Country Commercial Guides which are available through the U.S. Department of Commerce's Internet web site located at www.doc.gov. The Commerce Department's Trade Information Center is another source of information about foreign country regulations, standards, and documentation requirements.

Put simply, a U.S.–based company cannot and should not export goods into a foreign country without knowing the licensing requirements, documentation requirements and other standards. Failure to comply with local laws could result in the shipment being seized by local customs authorities. At best, a shipment found not to be in conformity with local laws will be delayed resulting in additional costs and additional risk to the exporter.

While none of this is directly the fault or the responsibility of the credit manager, the simple fact is that it will be the credit manager who will have to try to explain why an invoice was not paid. The fact that the documentation accompanying the shipment did not conform to local regulations will not change the fact that the invoice remains unpaid.

Typically, a foreign government may require that certain documentation accompany the shipment being exported. That documentation might include:

- A consular invoice

- An import license
- A certificate of origin
- A certificate of inspection

COLLECTION AGAINST FOREIGN OPEN ACCOUNT SHIPMENTS

If a credit manager ships goods on open account terms and the customer does not pay, the credit manager would prefer to sue that customer in the United States and be able to enforce judgments obtained in the Courts of United States in the buyer's country. Unfortunately, it doesn't often work that way.

Despite the fact that the United States has more than 200 bilateral trade agreements and is a signatory to any number of international conventions on trade, it is difficult to negotiate a provision in which a foreign national or foreign company is denied due process in their own country's Court system.

RECOGNITION AND ENFORCEMENT OF FOREIGN MONEY JUDGMENTS

Recognition and enforcement of foreign money judgments refers to a mechanism whereby a local court in a foreign country will compel compliance with a judgment rendered in a foreign judicial proceeding. For example, recognition and enforcement would be the mechanism by which a foreign customer would be required by a foreign court system to honor the judgment of the U.S. Court rendered in a dispute over money owed relating to a shipment made on open account terms.

As a general rule, a judgment rendered by a U.S. Court has no effect or direct force outside of the United States. Consequently, a judgment issued in favor of a U.S. exporter against a foreign buyer will be binding on a Court in that foreign country only if the foreign Court is willing to recognize and enforce the judgment. Recognition involves a foreign court recognizing that a claim or dispute has already been adjudicated in a foreign court—making additional litigation unnecessary.

Enforcement occurs when the foreign Court affirms the judgment of the U.S. Court and orders that relief be granted to the U.S. seller in the form of payment of the outstanding debt. While the United States Courts have been willing to recognize and enforce foreign judgments provided there was adequate evidence of due process, foreign courts have been far less willing to accept U.S. Court rulings with anything approaching the same ease and regularity.

Therefore, if an exporter needs a judgment against a foreign customer for non payment of debts, then the seller almost certainly going to have to litigate the matter in the foreign court. Many creditors who have sued in foreign courts have found to their surprise that judgment was entered for the debtor/defendant despite overwhelming evidence of the strength of the seller's case.

It should come as no surprise that in many parts of the world there is a good deal of anti-American sentiment. That prejudice against America and against American companies manifests itself in a variety of ways - including in the Court system. This is not to suggest that a U.S.–based exporter cannot get a fair trial anywhere in the world. It simply means that it is far more difficult when the plaintiff is a U.S.–based company and the defendant is a local company for the Court, and in particular for a jury, to find in favor of the foreign exporter and against the local importer.

IMPORT RESTRICTIONS.

Throughout the world, sovereign governments regulate their domestic economies to varying degrees. Some impose few barriers to imports, while others have a wide variety of rules and regulations governing imports. Credit managers need to know what limitations foreign governments have placed on imports in order to avoid potential problems when shipping merchandise ordered.

INTERNATIONAL LAW

International law falls into two broad categories, treaties and conventions. Treaties are formal agreements reached between two or more independent nations. Conventions are agreements or treaties that are sponsored by an international organization such as the United Nations and adopted by various nations voluntarily. The United Nations is by far the best known and most influential of what are called intergovernmental organizations. The stated purposes of the United Nations are:

- The promotion and the maintenance of peace and security throughout the world,
- The protection of human rights, and
- The promotion of economic and social cooperation.

THE UNITED NATIONS CONVENTION ON CONTRACTS FOR THE INTERNATIONAL SALE OF GOODS

This specific convention governs the formation of the contract of sale, and it defines the rights and the obligations of the seller and buyer that arise out of an international contract of sale. The parties are bound by any usage to which they have agreed, and by any practices that they have established between themselves.

Under this United Nations Convention, a contract of sale need not be evidenced in writing. In fact, this Convention does not specify any particular form that a contract must take. An offer becomes effective when it reaches the offeree. An offer may be withdrawn if the withdrawal reaches the offer before or at the same time as the offer. Similar to U.S. law, silence or inactivity does not signify acceptance. Also, if the reply to an offer contains changes or modifications to the contract then the other party has not created an acceptance—they have made a counter-offer.

The UN Convention on Contracts for the International Sale of Goods also specifies when and how goods are to be delivered to the buyer. The Convention addresses the issue of the quality of the goods, and the buyer's rights and obligations if it determines that the merchandise received is non-conforming.

COMPLEXITY IS A DIFFERENCE

International sales are more complex than domestic sales and more things can go wrong that would prevent payment. For this reason, credit managers need to work more closely with sales, manufacturing and shipping to make certain they understand that documentation requirements differ between domestic and international sales. If they do not help coordinate the exporting company's efforts to get the documentation right the first time, then the credit manager will pay the price later in the form of additional time needed to resolve problems in order to effect collection.

DISPUTE RESOLUTION

As with a relationship with a domestic customer, from time to time legitimate disputes arise between the buyer and the seller. Under international law, the seller has many of the same rights as a creditor in the United States has against a customer in the United States. Unfortunately, as costly as litigation and collection agency efforts are when dealing with delinquent domestic customers, the money and time and effort required to pursue a foreign customer through to collection is so high, and the outcome so uncertain, that creditors often elect to negotiate rather than to litigate. One avenue open to sellers and their foreign buyers is arbitration. Non-governmental organizations that provide international arbitration and/or mediation services include:

- The American Arbitration Association

- The International Chamber of Commerce

- The London Court of Arbitration, and

- The Spanish Court of Arbitration

THE UNITED NATIONS CONVENTION

Unless a different law is cited in the agreement between a buyer and a seller, and assuming the respective countries of the buyer and seller are signatories to the Agreement, the international sale of goods is governed by the United Nations Convention on Contacts for the International Sale of Goods which came into effect on January 1, 1988. The purpose of this body of laws [sometimes referred to as the Vienna Convention] is to provide a uniform body of law surrounding the formation of international sales contracts including creation and enforcement of those contracts. The UN Convention on Contracts for the International Sale of Goods contains the following rules, conditions and provisions:

- An international sale is defined as one in which the parties [the buyer and the seller] have their places of business in different countries.

- The parties may at their option and by mutual agreement opt not to be governed by the Vienna Convention.

- If the buyer and seller opt out, then the contract between them include a choice of laws clause.

- A sale is defined as the passing of title from the seller to the buyer.

- If the contract itself is silent on an issue or point of law, then the laws of the nation in which suit must be filed [typically the debtor's country] must be followed.

- A contract does not have to be in any specific form to be valid and enforceable.

- A contract occurs when there is both an offer and acceptance. The Convention requires no specific method in which an offer must be made and acceptance must be communicated.

- An offer is a definite proposal that describes the goods in sufficient clarity so that the parties know and understand what is being sold.

- An offer is irrevocable if the agreement says that it is.

- If the agreement does not state the offer is irrevocable, then the offer can be withdrawn unilaterally provided such a withdrawal occurs before the offer is accepted by the offeree.

- If a customer accepts the sellers offer but in doing so makes significant changes, then the seller has the option of filling the order and being bound by those changes, or the seller can choose to reject the customer' counter-offer.

- If one party fails to perform in a manner reasonably anticipated by the other party, then a fundamental breach of contract has occurred and the other party has the right to avoid the contract.

OBLIGATIONS OF THE SELLER IN AN INTERNATIONAL CONTRACT

The seller is required to deliver the specific quantity of goods ordered on time, and at the place agreed between the buyer and the seller in the contract, and required to insure that the goods delivered comply with the customer's specifications. The seller is entitled to demand that the carrier return merchandise that has not been delivered if it appears the buyer has or will commit a fundamental breach. The party damaged by a fundamental breach is entitled to reasonable damages from the breaching party.

THE BUYER'S OBLIGATIONS

The buyer is obligated under international law to pay for goods at the time and placed specified in the contract. The buyer must cooperate with the seller to facilitate delivery, and the buyer must inspect the merchandise in question as soon as practical to determine if any of the merchandise was lost or damaged in transit. The buyer is not obligated to take early delivery. The buyer is not obligated to accept delivery of more product than they ordered. If the goods are non-conforming, the buyer is entitled to a price reduction commensurate with the reduction in value of the goods at the time of delivery.

A buyer and seller may specifically reference the Vienna Convention in their Agreement, or it may be implicit. On the other hand, there is nothing to prevent the buyer and the seller from selecting the law of a specific country as governing the agreement. Creditors often find it helpful to list on their credit application or sales contract a so-called choice of law statement.

The parties to an international agreement may always insert and apply a "choice of laws" clause which indicates that even if an international law would cover and govern the sales transaction both parties agree that any litigation over the contract should be heard and adjudicated at (city), (state) and (country). If the buyer and seller have agreed that their contract should be governed by application of the laws in the nation -state in which the seller is located, then the Court shall apply those laws in settling the matter.

LICENSES

Many countries require that companies seeking to export goods into their country receive a license to do so. Licenses are required for a variety of reasons but they have the effect of limiting imports. Limiting imports may in fact be their primary purpose and benefit.

An exporter that makes the mistake of shipping without the appropriate export license might find their shipment seized by the exporting country's customs authority. If this happens, it is unlikely that the seller will ever get the product back. For this reason, exporters must carefully research the laws governing the export of their goods.

LABELS

Some countries require that products being imported be labeled in the language of the importing country. In addition, specific markings and labeling may be required on export shipping cartons or containers in order to ensure proper handling and acceptance at the foreign port.

Failure to include these labels may result in delayed payment, in misrouting of the product, or in seizure of the merchandise by the customs authority. Even if the credit manager is not involved in making sure the goods are shipped properly, he or she will certainly be involved after the fact in trying to clear up the problem so that the company can be paid.

Particularly on consumer products, foreign governments are often quite particular about labels, instructions and warranties. They often require these documents be in the buyer country's language. Failure to do so may subject the merchandise to seizure.

INSURANCE

Shipments for export are usually insured against loss or damage in transit. Depending on the terms of sale, the seller may be required to arrange to get transit [or cargo] insurance. Insurance protects the buyer and seller since rough handling or the theft of cargo is not uncommon, and damage or loss to the cargo may cause serious financial loss to the exporter.

Credit managers need to pay particular attention to this issue. In export transactions, different shipping terms dictate whether the buyer or the seller will be held responsible for getting insurance and for the cost of that insurance. Typically, the seller arranges for the coverage and pays for it. If the exporter's shipping department does not have the expertise to manage this process, the result may be uninsured loss.

Regardless of whether the loss or damage in transit was technically the responsibility of the buyer, the seller will find it difficult to collect. For this reason, no international shipment should be sent uninsured.

COMMON CARRIERS

When products are exported, sellers normally employ common carriers—although the use of charters and private carriers are not impossible. Common carriers are subject to extensive regulation in most nations, and multi-national carriers are also heavily regulated. The principal international convention governing the use of common carriers for export shipments is the United Nations Convention on the Carriage of Goods by Sea—sometimes referred to as the Hamburg Rules. Among other things, the common carrier is obligated to exercise due diligence. On the other hand, a carrier is normally not liable for damages that arise due to actions or activities beyond the control of the carrier including accidental fires, and acts of war.

Evan if the carrier is liable, as may be the case if the carrier loses the exporter's goods, the carrier's liability is limited. Depending on the value of the shipment, if the shipment is uninsured the amount the carrier pays for a lost shipment may be far lower than the value of the goods.

For this reason, many exporters elect to purchase maritime insurance. Maritime insurance covers goods in transit. Maritime insurance can cover either a single shipment, or a cargo policy can be purchased that insures all of the merchandise shipped by an exporter during the term of the policy. Maritime insurance policies commonly cover the following perils:

- Loss or damage while at sea
- Jettison of the cargo, or the sinking of the ship
- Explosion or fire, or
- Damage from the loading, unloading or transshipment of the cargo

ACCOUNTING RULES

Accounting rules and regulations vary widely from country to country. Even if a foreign the company's stock or debt is publicly traded in that country, a credit manager considering open account terms must carefully review the company's financial statements. Basically, there is no uniformity in the laws governing how and when financial statements must be generated and therefore many credit managers believe foreign financial statements [with some exceptions] lack credibility. There are also no worldwide auditing standards. As a result, credit managers have no guidelines against which foreign statements can be measured.

The International Accounting Standards Committee is trying to address this problem. The IASC is an independent private sector organization working to achieve more uniformity in the accounting principles used around the world through the widespread adoption of International Accounting Standards—a body of rules, procedures and laws governing financial accounting and auditing standards.

More than 100 countries are members of the IASC. The IASC works closely with national standards setting bodies such as the Financial Accounting Standards Board in the United States. While there are many similarities between the proposed IASC standards and U.S. Generally Accepted Accounting Principles, there are enough differences that the Financial Accounting Standards Board and the SEC will have a hard time accepting the IASC standards in their current form. Unfortunately, every change in the IASC standards that brings the standards closer to U.S. GAAP is likely to result in an objection from another IASC member.

The specific and stated goal of the IASC is for countries to allow publicly traded companies to use IASC standards in their financial reporting rather than the national accounting standards and rules. This change is already happening in the European Economic Community where certain countries already allow publicly traded companies to prepare financial statements in accordance with IASC standards instead of the national accounting rules.

CHAPTER 39

THE LETTER OF CREDIT PROCESS

A letter of credit is a written pledge of payment. That pledge of payment comes from a bank. More specifically, a letter of credit assures the seller of payment [subject to certain rules and restrictions] by substituting the credit standing of a commercial bank [called the issuing bank] for that of the buyer. Contained in the letter of credit is the issuing bank's promise of payment of a specific amount of money in return for receipt of specific documents, which must be presented within a stated maximum number of days, and by a specific date.

A letter of credit is not a guarantee of payment, it is a mechanism for requesting payment. Letters of credit are not without risk to the seller. In a very real sense, a letter of credit can be thought of as being a guarantee of non-payment unless the seller is able to conform to all of the terms contained in the letter of credit. However, if structured and handled properly, a L/C will protect the seller against the credit risk associated with doing business with a foreign buyer.

ADVANTAGES AND DISADVANTAGES OF A LETTER OF CREDIT

There are advantages and disadvantages to selling against a letter of credit. The obvious advantages of requiring foreign buyers to provide letters of credit include:

603

- Letters of credit are a way to reduce foreign credit risk
- L/Cs enhance cash flow by guaranteeing payment within a specific time frame.
- L/Cs allow sellers to make sales they would otherwise be unwilling to risk, and in turn make profits they otherwise would not have earned.

The disadvantages to the exporter [the seller] of L/Cs include:

- A letter of credit is not a guarantee of payment.

- Requiring customer to provide a letter of credit may make a seller's products less attractive to the buyer, resulting in lost sales opportunities.

- Setting up a letter of credit can be time consuming, and expensive.

- If the seller requires amendments to the L/C before shipment is made, there are significant costs involved, and the delivery date is often delayed.

- For the buyer, establishing a letter of credit normally carves out a portion of its borrowing base—making it difficult for the buyer to agree to offer a letter of credit unless no other options present themselves.

- 50% or more of letters of credit fail on first presentation.

- Some discrepancies can never be corrected—or cannot be corrected within the time left to do so under the letter of credit.

- Negotiating a letter of credit and receiving payment is complex; making the process inconvenient in comparison to open account terms.

THE LETTER OF CREDIT PROCESS

This is the normal flow for the letter of credit process used in international sales transactions, although some letters of credit may follow slightly different paths:

(1) The buyer and seller agree to do business under letter of credit terms.

(2) The buyer applies to its bank, the issuing bank, for a letter of credit based on the seller's instructions.

(3) The issuing bank prepares the L/C and sends it to the advising bank in the seller's country.

(4) The advising bank notifies the seller that the L/C has been issued, and forwards a copy to the seller.

(5) The seller carefully reviews the terms and conditions listed.

(6) If the seller discovers any problems, it contacts the buyer and asks that amendments be made to the letter of credit.

(7) If no problems are evident, or once the amendment has been received, the seller ships the goods, and then gathers the documentation required by the L/C.

(8) The beneficiary/seller checks the documents, and if they are in order the beneficiary forwards the documents to the advising or confirming bank.

(9) The seller's bank also reviews the documents, and if they appear to be in order the documents are forwarded to the buyer's bank for payment.

(10) If the documents are in order [meaning the seller must comply with every detail of the L/C terms and conditions, the issuing bank debits their customer's account and remits payment to the beneficiary's bank by wire transfer.

(11) Upon receipt of that payment, the beneficiary's bank notifies the seller/beneficiary and delivers to the buyer the documents necessary for the buyer to take possession of the goods.

RULES FOR PROCESSING LETTERS OF CREDIT

In processing Letters of Credit for payment, banks follow a standardized set of rules published by the International Chamber of Commerce [the ICC]. The current rules are the Uniform Customs and Practices for Documentary Credits, ICC publication number 500 [referred to as the UCP 500]. Credit professionals that want to increase the likelihood of payment under a L/C must be familiar with the UCP 500 rules.

THE DOCTRINE OF STRICT COMPLIANCE

The rules of the UCP 500 were drafted by and for the banking community. The strict compliance doctrine requires the bank to reject documents that do not exactly and specifically match the terms listed in the letter of credit and the rules as codified in UCP 500.

The strict compliance doctrine was created to protect banks from liability. In order to reduce their legal liability, banks exercise as little discretion as possible when comparing the documents presented by the seller against the terms and conditions contained in the letter of credit. If a bank pays against non-conforming documents then it may be financially liable to the buyer for this error. Specifically, if the issuing bank honors the letter of credit despite the fact that the letter of credit contains discrepancies, then the issuing bank may have to reimburse its customer for the payment made in error. For this reason, issuing banks carefully review the documentation submitted, looking for reasons to deny payment under the letter of credit.

There are numerous horror stories about apparently minor differences between the terms and conditions contained in the letter of credit compared to the documents presented that have resulted in the documents being rejected and payment being denied. A simple spelling error on an invoice or the letter of credit may prevent the seller from being paid.

Only the wording of the L/C and the terms and conditions listed in UCP 500 are binding on the bank. The bank has no obligation to verify the authenticity of the documents presented to it by the seller, nor is the bank required to be concerned with the quality or the quantity of goods received. This is referred to as the independence principle. The independence principle states that the letter of credit itself and the documents required under the letter of credit are completely independent from the underlying business transactions between the buyer and the seller. Specifically, the bank is only concerned that the documents presented by the seller conform to the documentary requirements as listed on the L/C.

AMENDMENT OF A LETTER OF CREDIT

If a seller finds an unacceptable term or condition contained in the L/C, the seller should require the L/C to be amended before shipment. The buyer must contact its bank to arrange for the amendment to be made. The buyer's bank notifies the advising bank once the amendment has been completed. The advising bank then notifies the seller and forwards a copy of the amendment(s) to the seller for review.

If for some reason the seller ships goods before a required amendment is received [which is never a good idea] the credit manager can make certain that the buyer does not take possession of the goods by making sure that the marine bill of lading [which is a title document] is consigned to the buyer's bank rather than to the buyer.

COMMON PROBLEMS WITH LETTERS OF CREDIT

The seller must know before shipping whether it is capable of presenting the required documents within the time limit specified, and if the other terms and conditions contained in the L/C are acceptable. If one or more required documents cannot be presented then the letter of credit will not protect the seller's right to payment. Therefore, before shipment, the letter of credit should be amended.

LETTER OF CREDIT CONSULTANTS

Certain companies provide exporters with consulting help intended to help the exporter reduce the risks associated with doing business via letter of credit; and to obtain faster payment. These consulting firms tend to be staffed by former bankers and other experts in the area of letters of credit. For a nominal fee, these firms typically provide assistance in the following two major areas:

(1) These consultants review the letter of credit as received and comment about any unusual terms or conditions that might make it difficult for the seller to provide conforming documents to the issuing bank.

(2) After shipment and before presenting documents for payment, the consultant reviews the package of documentation the seller has compiled to make certain there are no obvious problems.

Some consultants will actually negotiate on behalf of the seller with the buyer for less restrictive L/C terms and conditions. Others services offer even more comprehensive services including preparing pro forma invoices and gathering, reviewing and then forwarding the documentation required in support of the L/C to the issuing bank through the advising or confirming bank.

Fees for these services are modest—especially in light of the potential damage that could be caused by a discrepancy in the documents. Consultants help to prevent problems that delay payment at best, and render the L/C valueless at worst.

TIP: Experts on letters of credit, such as those who work for major banks will tell you that some letters of credit contain such unusual terms that a discrepancy is almost guaranteed. Credit professionals need to develop a close working relationship with the international department of their bank to reduce the chances of submitting documentation with discrepancies.

Credit professionals should attend at least one seminar a year to make certain they are aware of changes in this area.

LETTERS OF CREDIT ARE DATE SPECIFIC

Paying close attention to dates on a letter of credit is critical. Every L/C includes specific dates and deadlines that that must be met in order for the seller to have the right to collect payment. For example, the L/C may state that the goods must ship no later than a certain date. If the seller ships after that date, a major discrepancy is created and the letter of credit may be rendered valueless.

Another common time-specific discrepancy that results in documents being rejected by the issuing bank relates to the fact that if no specific time period after shipment to present documents is listed in the L/C, then under Article 43 of UCP 500 the issuing bank will not accept documents presented later than 21 days after shipment.

THE ROLE OF THE ISSUING BANK

The issuing bank is concerned only with whether or not the seller performed exactly as required under the terms of the letter of credit. Banks have found that by limiting their discretion in determining which letters of credit are accepted and paid vs. rejected and returned, the banks reduce the chances that they will be sued by one or both of the parties for exercising inappropriate discretion in evaluating documents presented against the letter of credit.

When negotiating with the buyer, the seller should try to get the buyer to use an issuing bank that has establishing and correspondent relationship with the seller's bank. This correspondent relationship tends to:

- Make it easier for the seller and the buyer's bank to work together

- Makes the transfer of documents easier and smoother

- It makes amendments easier to get, and minor discrepancies easier to get waived.

PROVIDING SPECIFIC LETTER OF CREDIT INSTRUCTIONS TO BUYERS

A seller's typical letter of credit instructions would typically include these requirements:

(1) The letter of credit must be irrevocable.

(2) The issuing bank must be acceptable to the seller, otherwise the letter of credit must be confirmed.

(3) The letter of credit should permit both partial shipments and transshipments.

(4) If the letter of credit is to be advised and confirmed, the seller should specify which bank is to perform this service.

(5) The letter of credit should be "available at any bank", and it should specify that it is governed by the rules contained in the UCP 500.

(6) The credit should show as the beneficiary the seller based on the exact name, address, city and state. The seller should not permit the beneficiary to be a d.b.a. for the seller.

(7) It should state that all fees are for the account of the applicant.

(8) The credit should allow 21 days from the date of last shipment for the presentation of documents at the counters of the issuing bank.

(9) The documentation required under the letter of credit should be the minimum number of documents the seller can negotiate.

(10) If the goods to be provided by the seller cannot be measured precisely, the words "about" or "approximately" should be used to make allowances for tolerances of up to 10%.

(11) The seller should never ship against a L/C containing boycott language, for example language supporting the Arab League's boycott against Israel, Israeli ports, and Israeli flagged ships.

LETTER OF CREDIT CONFIRMATION

The seller must determine whether or not to require the letter of credit be confirmed. If a L/C is simply advised through a U.S. bank, the advising bank is obligated to verify the authenticity of the L/C and then to forward this information to the exporter "without engagement." An advice does not obligate the U.S. bank to pay the seller in the even that the issuing bank fails to honor the L/C for any reason, or for no reason.

Many credit managers prefer that Letters of Credit be confirmed by a U.S. bank. In a confirmed letter of credit, the advising bank adds its guarantee to pay the seller in the event that the issuing bank fails to make payment against a L/C even though contained no discrepancies.

ADVANTAGES OF CONFIRMATION

From the seller's point of view, there are a number of advantages of having a confirmed letter of credit including:

- a payment guarantee from a domestic bank.

- a strong likelihood that the seller can discount the letter of credit if they need immediate cash.

- faster payment on the letter of credit.

SIGHT VS. TIME LETTERS OF CREDIT

A L/C may be "at sight" meaning it is to be paid immediately upon presentation or proper documentation. A letter of credit may be "at sight plus ___ days." This type of L/C will be paid at the indicated time in the future provided the proper documentation was received and no discrepancies were found.

DISCOUNTING A LETTER OF CREDIT

One advantage of having a confirmed letter of credit is the possibility of discounting the letter of credit. Under certain circumstances, the seller's bank will agree to discount a letter of credit. Simply put, this means the bank will pay the seller to surrender the letter of credit proceeds in the future in return for an immediate payment. The bank's profit for agreeing to discount the letter of credit include (a) a charge for discounting the letter of credit paid to the bank and (b) a processing or administrative fee.

TIP: If the country of origin of the letter of credit is less developed or politically unstable, the credit should insist the letter of credit be confirmed. Of course, it may be difficult to find a bank willing to confirm the letter of credit for the same reasons.

LETTERS OF CREDIT FROM MOST TO LEAST RELIABLE

An irrevocable, confirmed documentary letter of credit

An irrevocable, advised documentary letter of credit

An irrevocable unconfirmed documentary letter of credit

A revocable confirmed letter of credit

A revocable unconfirmed letter of credit

AVOIDING PROBLEMS CAUSED BY THIRD PARTIES

Many of the problems that arise when the seller requires the buyer to provide a letter of credit result from the actions of unrelated third parties. For example, many of the documents, which are required to be presented in support of a letter of credit, are prepared or handled by people not employed by the seller. For example, the freight forwarder must provide a variety of documents in support of a shipment made against a documentary letter of credit. The actions [or inaction] of others may create a discrepancy under the terms and conditions of the letter of credit that cannot be cured by the seller, or cannot be cured in the time before the letter of credit expires.

SPECIAL TYPES OF LETTERS OF CREDIT

There are special types of letters of credit used in certain unique situations. The following is a brief description of each:

- Back to back letter of credit. These letters of credit are normally opened by using the first letter of credit as collateral for the second. The back to back letter of credit may be used when a broker does not want the manufacturer to find out who the buyer is.

- A red clause letter of credit. This is a L/C in which all or part of the credit may be advanced to the seller—often to aid in financing production of the merchandise.

- A revolving letter of credit is one in which the issuing bank commits to restore the letter of credit to the original amount once the L/C has been drawn down. A revolving letter of credit typically specifies how many times the value of the L/C will be refreshed.

- A standby letter of credit. Standby L/Cs are created under the assumption that the buyer will pay the seller directly for the goods. A standby L/C is used as a backup payment method.

- A transferable letter of credit is one in which the beneficiary can transfer all or part of the proceeds of the L/C to another beneficiary.

SUMMARY

A Letter of Credit enables two companies that know very little about each other to reduce the risks associated with doing business with each other. A L/C assures the buyer that they will receive the merchandise ordered, and offers the seller additional assurance of payment but without a guarantee of payment. Creditors shipping against a letter of credit are never totally in control of the process and therefore they are never assured of payment.

The seller's bank plays a vital role in the L/C process. First, it validates the authenticity of the L/C when it is received. Second, the seller's bank normally handles all communication with the issuing bank and forwards all documentation to the issuing bank. Sometimes, the seller may fail to appreciate that their bank [the advising or confirming bank] is often the only party in the entire letter of credit transaction that will point out problems or help the seller's credit manager to avoid problems that result in payment delays or in payment default.

GLOSSARY

Absolute Priority: A provision of the bankruptcy code that senior creditors must be paid in full before junior creditors receive anything. In turn, junior creditors must be paid in full before stockholders receive any money from the bankrupt estate.

Accelerated Cost Recovery System: A method for accelerated depreciation of assets.

Acceptance: The drawee's act of accepting a draft calling for the drawee/buyer to pay its value at maturity. In contract law, acceptance refers to the act of agreeing to or accepting an offer.

Account Party (applicant): The party that instructs its bank to open a letter of credit, and on whose behalf the issuing bank agrees to make payment. The buyer.

Accounts Payable: The amounts companies owe to suppliers for goods and services delivered on open account terms.

Accounts Receivable (A/R): This represents money owed to the company by customers for goods sold or services provided or rendered on open account credit terms that has not yet been collected.

Accounts Receivable Turnover Ratio: Total Revenue for the last 12 months divided by Average Accounts Receivable for the last 12 months.

Address: The unique code assigned to each location on a network, or to each web page on the Internet.

Advice of a Letter of Credit: A notice from a bank verifying that an authentic letter of credit was issued by another bank, specifying the dollar amount of that letter of credit, the beneficiary and the other particulars.

Advising Bank: A correspondent bank of the issuing bank; the advising bank operating in the exporter's country receives a letter of credit or amendment(s) from the issuing bank. The advising bank notifies the seller of the existence and the authenticity of the Letter of Credit.

Affiliates: Business concerns that are affiliates of each other are related to the extent that (1) they exert power or control over the operations of the other company, or (2) a person or corporation has the power to control both companies. Corporations are often affiliated through common ownership.

Agent: One who performs services for another under an agreement that makes the agent subject to the control of the other person or company.

Agreement: An understanding reached between two or more parties regarding their rights and obligations relating to a specific subject matter.

Air Waybill [of lading]: A shipping document used by airlines for airfreight shipments. A signed receipt and contract to deliver goods by air. The air waybill contacts a description of the product, as well as shipping instructions. Generally, air waybills are not negotiable.

Allowance for Doubtful Accounts: When a creditor provides goods or services on open account terms it is inevitable that some debts will not be collected. An estimate of how much of the total A/R that is uncollectable is recorded in the Allowance for doubtful accounts.

Amendment: A document confirming a change to the terms or conditions of a Letter of Credit. The opening bank makes amendments at the request of the seller with the approval of all parties including the applicant; the issuing bank, the beneficiary, and the confirming bank [if one exists].

Annual Report: A report that a company publishes for its stockholders at the end of its fiscal year.

Antitrust: Federal laws prohibiting businesses from price setting, or other illegal activities that tend to circumvent the free market operations of supply and demand.

Antiviral Software Program: Software that monitors a computer for viruses in order to eliminate them before significant damage occurs.

Applicant: The buyer that opens a letter of credit through its bank.

Arbitration: A method of dispute resolution in which the disputing parties [such as a buyer and a seller] agree to submit their dispute to an impartial third party [the arbitrator] who will hear testimony and review evidence provided by both parties.

Arbitrator: A person selected to decide a dispute between parties, when that dispute is subject to an arbitration agreement or clause.

Asset: Anything of value that a firm owns or controls.

Asset Liquidity: The ease with which an asset can be promptly converted into cash.

Asset Turnover Ratio: An efficiency ratio, the asset turnover ratio is Total Revenues for an accounting period divided by the average Total Assets for that same period.

Assignment: An assignment [such as an assignment for the benefit of creditors] involves the transfer of property rights or title to another party by agreement—usually made in writing.

Audit: The systematic examination of the books and records of a company to ascertain whether all transactions were recorded properly.

Auditor's Opinion Letter: A summary of the findings of a CPA firm engaged to examine and to audit a company's financial statements.

Automated Clearinghouse: A facility used by financial institutions to distribute electronic debit and credit entries between member banks to settle such transfers.

Automatic Stay: In a bankruptcy, the automatic stay provides protection to the debtor filing bankruptcy against collection efforts including lawsuits.

Avoidance Powers: Avoidance powers grant the trustee in a bankruptcy the power to recover property that was fraudulently transferred, or involves a preferential transfer by the debtor prior to the bankruptcy filing date.

Award: The written document of determination by a Court or an arbitrator on the matter submitted for adjudication or review.

Balance Sheet: A report listing a company's assets, its liabilities and the equity at a specific date.

Bandwidth: A measure of the data transmission and receipt capability of a circuit or a system.

Banker's Acceptance: A banker's acceptance is a draft drawn and accepted by a bank.

Bankruptcy: A proceeding in U.S. federal court in which a debtor may be legally released from paying debts legitimately owed to others.

Bankruptcy Court: A division of the U.S. District Court System that deals exclusively with bankruptcy cases.

Beneficiary: The individual or company in whose favor a Letter of Credit is issued and who receives payment provided the terms and conditions of the L/C are met. The beneficiary of a Letter of Credit is normally the seller.

Bill of Lading: A document issued by a carrier to a shipper/seller evidencing the receipt of goods for shipment. A bill of lading is also a contract between the owner of the goods and the carrier. It is both a receipt for merchandise and a contract to deliver the merchandise as freight. In some forms, a bill of lading may also represent title to the goods.

Bond: A form of debt. A debt instrument issued by a government agency or a private company promising repayment of the original balance at a specific date along with periodic interest payments.

Bonded Warehouse: A warehouse authorized by local customs authority where goods are stored until the import duties are paid [if an incoming shipment is involved], or until the goods in question are exported.

Book Value: Book value, an accounting term, is the original acquisition cost of a fixed asset minus accumulated depreciation or amortization.

Bookmarking: A shortcut method of accessing one or more favorite web sites.

Cash Discount: A deduction allowed from the face amount of the invoice if payment is received within a specified number of days after the invoice date.

Cash Equivalents: Any short-term securities listed as current assets that can readily be converted into cash.

Certificate of Inspection: A document prepared by an independent third party that certifies the merchandise was in good condition immediately prior to its shipment. This is often used in connection with the sale of perishable goods.

Certificate of Manufacture: A statement issued by the producer/seller that the goods have been manufactured and are now available to the buyer.

Certificate of Origin: A document required by the customs authority of certain countries for tariff assessment purposes, verifying the country of origin of the goods to be imported. Sometimes countries use consular visas from their embassy or missions to certify the country of origin.

The country of origin is the country where the goods were grown, manufactured, mined or harvested.

Chapter 7: A bankruptcy proceeding involving the liquidation of the assets of the debtor for the benefit of its creditors. In a Chapter 7 filing, a trustee is appointed to collect and liquidate certain assets and then to distribute the proceeds to creditors according to a specific order of priority.

Chapter 11: Reorganization under the U.S. Bankruptcy Code typically used by corporations.

Chapter 12: A reorganization suitable for family farmers.

Chapter 13: A reorganization bankruptcy suitable for individuals with a regular income. The debtor pays creditors over a period of time [typically 3 to 5 years] according to a payment plan approved by the Court.

CIF: The acronym for Cost, Insurance and Freight, CIF terms mean that the seller has the same responsibility as under CFR but the seller also must contract for and pay for maritime insurance against loss or damage to the goods while in transit to the named port of destination.

Civil Action: In most jurisdictions, actions are divided into criminal and civil actions. Civil actions include lawsuits by and among private parties.

Class of Creditors: In a bankruptcy case, there are different classes of creditors. A class of creditors is a group of creditors entitled to the same treatment in the case under the U.S. Bankruptcy Code.

Claused Bill of Lading: A bill of lading that contains notations indicating the goods or the packaging were damaged in transit.

Clean Bill of Lading: A receipt for goods issued by a carrier with an indication that the goods were received in good condition with no damage apparent.

Collateral: Assets or property that is subject to a security interest, or property pledged to secure repayment of a debt or other obligation.

Collecting Bank: The bank that acts as an agent for the seller in collecting either payment, or a time draft from the buyer and forwarding it to the seller or the seller's bank.

Commercial Invoice: A commercial invoice acts as a bill for goods from the seller to the buyer.

Common Carrier: An individual, partnership, or corporation that transports goods in return for compensation. Carriers typically include steamship companies, trucking companies, overnight delivery services, airlines, and railroads.

Confirmed Letter of Credit: A letter of credit to which a second bank adds its pledge or guaranty of payment in the event of payment default by the issuing bank for reasons other than a discrepancy.

Consignee: The party to whom goods are shipped by the seller. The firm or person authorized to receive the cargo.

Consolidated Financial Statements: Financial statements on a company and one or more subsidiaries in which the financial performance of the related companies is consolidated rather than identified separately.

Consular Documents: A document such as a bill of lading, certificate of origin or other document such as a special, detailed invoice form signed by the consul of the exporting country—normally in the language of that country. Consular documents are used by customs officials in the importing country to verify the value of the shipment.

Conversion: In bankruptcy, the process of converting a case from one chapter to another. For example, a Chapter 11 reorganization is often converted to a Chapter 7 liquidation.

Corporation: A corporation is a form of business organization that may have many owners. A corporation is a fictitious legal entity that has rights and duties that are independent of the rights and the duties of real persons. A corporation can be either privately held or public. A corporation is owned by its stockholders, and it is created under the authority of state law.

Co-signer: A person responsible for repaying a debt if the borrower / debtor defaults on payment.

Cost and Freight [C&F Named Port]: All cost of goods and transportation to the named port are to be included in the price quoted by the seller to the buyer. The buyer is responsible for insurance while the goods are aboard the ship.

Cost of Goods Sold: The cost of producing finished goods including materials and labor.

Credit bureau: A company that compiles credit reports based on information it gathers from a variety of sources, and forwards this information to subscribers in the form of credit reports.

Credit History: A record of how a customer [a consumer or business customer] has paid credit accounts in the past.

Credit Interchange Group: A group of creditors who form an association to regularly share credit information about mutual customers.

Credit Report: A document that details a consumer or a company's credit history using information provided by banks, by trade creditors [including credit card companies and department stores], and from public records searches [such as those relating to bankruptcy filings or lawsuits].

Credit Reporting Agency: A company that gathers, files and sells information to creditors to facilitate their decisions about whether or not to extend credit.

Creditor: A creditor is any person, corporation or other entity to which a debt is owed. The term includes a general creditor, an unsecured creditor, a secured creditor, or a lien creditor.

CRF: An Incoterm requiring that the seller bear the cost and freight needed to deliver the goods at the named port of shipment. The risk of loss or damage one the goods have passed over the ship's rail passes to the buyer at that point.

Current Asset: An asset the company expects to convert into cash within one year.

Current Liabilities: Obligations of a company to creditors that are expected to be paid within one year or less.

Current Ratio: A measure of a company's ability to pay current liabilities as the become due. The Current ratio is calculated by dividing current assets by current liabilities.

Data Encryption: A process that transforms electronic messages into seemingly random streams of characters in order to protect the security of the data against electronic interception.

Debt: Money borrowed that must be repaid.

Debt to Equity Ratio: This is total debt for the most recent reporting period divided by total shareholders' equity for the same period.

Debtor: A person, corporation or other entity that owes a debt or debts to its creditor(s).

Debtor in Possession: In a Chapter 11 bankruptcy filing, the owner of the corporation is allowed to retain control of the company and to use its assets while reorganizing the company in order to present a plan to creditors for their consideration and vote. They are said to be "debtors in possession."

Depreciation: An accounting concept that allows the owner of an asset to record an allowance for the gradual diminishment in value of an asset over the estimated useful life of that asset.

DIP: A debtor in possession.

Disclosure Statement: In a bankruptcy case, a document prepared by the debtor that describes the terms of the proposed plan of reorganization.

Discrepancy: Any non-compliance of documents with the terms and conditions contained in the Letter of Credit [L/C] is a discrepancy. A discrepancy also exists if the documentation is presented after the deadline.

Discharge: The bankruptcy court order that releases the debtor from additional liability and prevents creditors owed these debts from taking further action against the debtor for collection.

Dividends: Cash payments from a company's profits [in the form of cash on hand] paid to stockholders.

Documentation Requirements: On a letter of credit, documentation requirements often include invoices, drafts, a bill of lading, certificates of origin, a marine insurance policy, inspection reports and/or statements from the shipping party.

Documents against Payment: Also referred to as a time draft, documents against payment involve instructions that a shipper gives to its bank that the documents attached to a draft are deliverable to the drawee [the buyer] only against a payment of the draft.

Download: To copy or transfer data from one computer to another.

Draft: A negotiable instrument that is used as a formal demand for payment.

Drawee bank: The bank listed as the payer under the letter of credit.

E Mail: A text message sent to an individual or group via the Internet. E-mail messages may include attachments.

EBIT: Earnings before interest and taxes.

EBITD: Earnings before interest, taxes and depreciation.

EBITDA: Earnings before interest, taxes, depreciation, and amortization.

Electronic Data Interchange: The computer to computer exchange of common business documents over telephone lines using a standardized electronic format.

Encryption: Changing a document into code that is not readable except by a person having an electronic key to decode the document.

Equal Credit Opportunity Act: A federal law that requires credit granters to make credit available without discrimination on the basis of age, sex, marital status, nationality, or national origin.

Equity: That portion of the company's assets that belongs to the stockholders after the creditors have been satisfied.

Exchange Rate: The number of units of one currency that must be exchanged for one unit of another currency.

Exclusivity Period: The 120 day time period authorized under Chapter 11 of the U.S. Bankruptcy Code in which the debtor has the exclusive right to develop and present a plan of reorganization. This 120 day period can be extended [or shortened] at the discretion of the Court.

Exempt Property: Property of a bankrupt debtor that the trustee and creditors are not permitted to seize and sell—unless a creditor has a security interest in the property.

Exim Bank: The export-import Bank of the United States.

Expiration Date: On a Letter of Credit, the expiration date is the last due to present documents.

Export License: A document issued in the United States by the Department of Commerce's Export Administration Bureau to authorize the export of certain products, in certain quantities to specified countries.

Factor: A company in the business of purchasing certain accounts receivable from a creditor company.

Factoring: The discounting of accounts receivable that does not involve a draft. The exporter transfers title of its accounts receivable to a factoring house in return for immediate cash.

Financial Accounting Standards Board [FASB]: An association of accounting professionals that establishes Generally Accepted Accounting Principles.

Financial EDI: An Electronic Funds Transfer transaction that contains payment related information.

Firewall: A type of security software or hardware that limits access to computerized data from any outside source.

Fixed Asset: Often referred to as Property, Plant and Equipment, fixed assets are any assetS a company uses for more than a year.

FOB: An Incoterm requiring that the seller clear the goods for export and load the goods over the rail and onto the vessel named by the buyer at the designated port of shipment.

Footnotes: Footnotes are notes to financial statements that explain certain events or facts or that document changes in accounting practices and their subsequent impact on the financial statements as presented.

Forwarder: An freight forwarder is an intermediary between the common carrier and the owner of the goods being transported.

Fraudulent Transfer: A transfer of an asset within one year of the date of a bankruptcy filing at less than fair market value done with the intent to hinder the rights of one or more classes of creditors.

Freight Forwarder: An international shipping specialist. Freight forwarders act as the seller's agent to help move cargo from origin to destination. A freight forwarder can offer advice, compile and control documents, and arrange for shipments.

Generally Accepted Accounting Principles [GAAP]: A set of rules and financial reporting requirements that companies follow that wish to have their financial statements audited.

Goodwill: The excess above fair market value that a company paid for assets acquired.

Gross Margin: Net sales minus Cost of Goods Sold equals Gross margin. Gross margin measures the amount of Gross Sales Revenues left after paying all direct production expenses.

Import Certificate: The certificate is a method by which the government of a country can exercise control over what is being imported into the country. In some instances and in some countries products cannot be imported without an import certificate.

Import License: A document required by some national governments authorizing the import of goods or commodities into the country.

Income after Tax: The amount remaining of after all expenses and taxes have been deducted from revenues.

Income Statement: A financial statement that presents the results of a company's business operations for a specific accounting period such as a fiscal year or a quarter. This document is sometimes referred to as a Profit and Loss Statement.

Incoterms: Standardized international trade terms devised with the intent of providing a common language and set of definitions for international buyers and sellers. The codification of certain terms by the International Chamber of Commerce to define which parties incur certain costs and at what point specific costs or risks are incurred.

Insolvency: The condition of being unable to pay one or more legal obligations [debts] as they come due.

Inspection Certificate: A certificate, usually issued by an independent third party, attesting that the goods to be shipped to the buyer conform to the order.

Intangible Asset: Any non-physical asset [such as goodwill, trademarks, and patents] that has value to the company.

Interest Coverage Ratio: Earnings before interest and taxes for a particular accounting period divided by interest expense for that same period.

Internet: An international network of computer networks that connects businesses, academic institutions, individual web pages, and government web sites to each other.

Inventories: Inventories consist of raw materials, work in process and finished goods inventories. Inventories are current assets.

Inventory Turnover Ratio: This ratio measures how quickly inventory is sold. It is defined as the Cost of Goods Sold divided by the Average Inventory.

Involuntary Bankruptcy: Creditors may petition the Bankruptcy Court to force a delinquent debtor into bankruptcy subject to the rules listed in the U.S. Bankruptcy Code.

Irrevocable Letter of Credit: A Letter of Credit that cannot be modified or canceled without the consent of the buyer, the seller, the issuing bank, the advising bank, and the confirming bank [if applicable]. An irrevocable L/C is one in which the buyer's bank must pay even if the buyer defaults.

Issuing Bank: The bank that issues the Letter of Credit and agrees to make payment in accordance with the terms of the L/C provided that the beneficiary submits documents that conform to the L/C requirements within the timeline described in the L/C.

ISP: A company that provides users with access to the Internet. An acronym for Internet Service Provider.

Judgment: The official court decision regarding an action or lawsuit.

Latest Date to Present Documents: Relating to a Letter of Credit, documents must arrive at the negotiating bank within 21 days from the latest shipping date but before the expiration date of the Letter of Credit.

Latest Ship Date: Relating to a letter of credit, the shipping documents must be dated on or before the latest ship date.

Lawsuit: A legal action initiated by a plaintiff against a defendant. A lawsuit is based on an assertion that the defendant failed to perform a legal duty resulting in harm to the plaintiff.

Letter of Credit: An internationally recognized contract drawn between a buyer, a seller, and the buyer's bank and issued at the request of the buyer.

Leverage: At its most basic, a company's use of debt rather than equity to support and to grow the business.

Liabilities: Liabilities include short and long term debts owed to both secured and unsecured creditors.

Libel: The defamation of an individual by statements made in writing.

Lien: The legal right to retain the lawful possession of the property of another until the owner of the property fulfills a legal duty to the person holding the property. A legal claim on the property of another.

Limited Liability Corporation: A form of business structure that is a hybrid between a partnership and a corporation. The members [stockholders] are shielded from personal liability, but the profits of the business are passed directly to the owners without the corporation paying corporate income taxes.

Limited Partnership: A business structure comprised of one or more general partners and one or more limited partners. The limited partners have no voice in the operations of the business and have limited personal liability. The general partners have unlimited personal liability and manage the day-to-day operations of the business.

Liquidity: The degree to which the assets of a company can be converted into cash to meet obligations.

Liquidity Ratios: These ratios measure the degree of a company's liquidity. Common liquidity ratios include (1) the current ratio, (2) the quick or acid test ratio, and (3) the inventory turnover ratio.

Long Term Debt: A debt a company will not have to repay for at least one year.

Long Term Debt to Equity Ratio: This ratio is total long-term debt for a fiscal period divided by total shareholders' equity for that same period.

Marine Bill of Lading: An insurance policy covering loss or damage to goods while at sea.

Market Value: The amount an unrelated party would be willing to pay for an asset.

Marketable Securities: Assets such as stocks and bonds that companies own and can readily convert into cash.

Negotiation: Relating to a Letter of credit, negotiation is the process of submitting documents to the bank to obtain payment under the terms of the L/C.

Net Change in Cash and Cash Equivalents: Taken from the Statement of Cash Flows, net change in cash and cash equivalents is calculated by adding cash from operating, investing and financial activities. The change can be positive or negative.

Net Income: Total revenues minus total expenses, where revenues exceed expenses. Net income is sales minus cost of goods sold minus operating expenses plus or minus extraordinary gains or losses minus taxes.

Net Loss: Total revenues minus total expenses, where expenses exceed revenues.

Net Profit Margin: This is calculated by dividing the Net Income after Tax by Revenue.

Net Sales: A company's Gross Sales minus returns and allowances.

Net Worth: The excess of assets over liabilities.

Newsgroups: Areas on the Internet reserved for discussions on specific topics. A newsgroup can be thought of as an electronic bulletin board where people with similar interests read and post messages.

Non-Exempt Property: Assets owned by debtors that are not exempt and may be seized and sold by the trustee to pay claims in a bankruptcy.

Ocean Bill of Lading: A B/L indicating that the exporter consigns a shipment to an international carrier for transportation to a specified foreign port.

Opening Bank: Relating to a letter of credit, the opening bank issues the letter of credit at the request of the buyer.

Operating Expenses: Costs associated with a company's operations but unrelated to the manufacturing process.

Packing List: A document that lists and describes to the buyer the merchandise contained in the box.

Payment on Sight, or at Sight: Payment on demand.

Plan of Reorganization: In a Chapter 11 bankruptcy case, the Plan of Reorganization must define the classes into which creditors have been grouped, a description of the treatment or recovery to each class of claim, a comparison of how each class of creditor would be treated were the debtor to liquidate, and an explanation of how the DIP plans to carry out the Plan.

Political Risk: In export transactions, political risk involves the possibility of expropriation or confiscation of assets, war, changes in tax policy or foreign policy, restrictions on the exchange of foreign currency, and other changes that heighten the risk of late payment or payment default.

Postpetition Claim: A claim arising after the date of the bankruptcy filing against the estate.

Pre-authorized Electronic Debits: PEDs allow creditors to debit the bank account of a customer based on a signed pre-authorization by the debtor. The Payer's bank normally sends payment of PEDs to the seller through the ACH clearinghouse system. PEDs are sometimes called ACH Debits.

Preferential Transfers: Certain transfers or payments made within 90 days of a bankruptcy filing may be reversed and recovered by the bankruptcy court on behalf of the debtor's estate. If the recipient is an insider, the 90-day period is expanded to one year. Payments or returns made to trade creditors are normally subject to a 90-day look back or preference period.

Preferred Stock: Preferred stock is senior to common stock. Most preferred stock pays a fixed dividend and preferred stock dividends must be paid in full before common stock dividends can be issued. Preferred stock does not normally have voting rights, and preferred stock has characteristics of both common stock and debt.

Prepackaged Bankruptcy: Before filing a bankruptcy case, the debtor and some or all of its creditors negotiate and agree to a Plan of Reorganization resulting in the Plan being pre-packaged.

Prepetition Claim: Any claim arising prior to the bankruptcy filing date.

Pre-Tax Margin: Net income before tax divided by total revenues.

Pro Forma Financial Statements: Financial statements intended to show what the financial results would have been if a company was structured in the past as it is structured now; or if it were structured differently in the future than it is now, or if a specific event did or did not occur.

Proof of Claim: A document submitted to and filed with the U.S. Bankruptcy Court that describes the basis of a creditor's claim, and the amount the debtor owed to the creditor at the time of the bankruptcy filing. A Proof of Claim form should be filed with the clerk of the bankruptcy court where the bankruptcy was filed before the Bar Date.

Quick Assets: Total current assets minus inventories

Quick Ratio: Cash plus Short Term Investments plus Accounts Receivable divided by Total Current Liabilities.

Ratio: A measure of the relative sizes of two numbers.

Reorganized Debtor: The entity that results from the confirmation of a Chapter 11 Plan of Reorganization under the U.S. Bankruptcy Code.

Replevin: The act of seizing an asset that the creditor has a security interest in to satisfy a debt.

Repossession: The surrender of an asset as a result of the customer's default on payment.

Retained Earnings: The total amount of net earnings of a company since its inception minus any dividend payments made to stockholders.

Return on Assets Ratio: This ratio is net income after tax for an accounting period divided by average total assets for the same period.

Revocable Letter of Credit: A Letter of Credit that can be changed [amended] at any time [even after shipment] by the buyer unilaterally without the approval of the seller/beneficiary. This type of L/C is rarely used because it is considered to be of little or no value to the creditor.

Secured Claim: A claim in a bankruptcy is secured to the extent that the creditor has a perfected lien on one or more assets of the debtor.

Secured Creditor: A seller, lender, creditor or other party in whose favor there is a security interest or lien.

Secured Debt: A debt for which a creditor holds collateral.

Securities and Exchange Commission: A U.S. government agency responsible among other things for ensuring that publicly held companies' financial reporting is accurate and timely.

Security Interest: An interest in property or other assets that secures payment or performance of an obligation. State law governs the process of lien creation and perfection.

Setoff: In a situation in which a pre-petition creditor also owes money to the bankrupt debtor, the creditor may setoff or offset their accounts payable balance by the accounts receivable balance — provided that both the accounts payable and accounts receivable occurred prior to the bankruptcy filing date.

Share: A share is a certificate of ownership in a company.

Shares Outstanding: This equals the number of shares issued minus the shares held as treasury stock.

Short Term Debt: Debt that comes due within one year.

Software Piracy: The unauthorized duplication of computer software programs.

Sole Proprietorship: Ownership of a business by one person who has unlimited personal liability for the debts of that business.

Standby Letter of Credit: A Letter of Credit typically used in conjunction with open account terms in which the demand for payment is made to the issuing bank in the event the debtor defaults on payment. A standby Letter of Credit is often used as a payment or performance guarantee.

Statement of Cash Flows: A financial statement that reports the firm's cash receipts and cash payments during a specific accounting period.

Stock Exchange: Organizations approved and regulated by the Securities and Exchange Commission. Stock exchanges were created to facilitate the exchange of certain stocks.

Stockholder: The owner of an equity share in a corporation.

Stockholders' Equity: The residual claims of stockholders against the assets of a corporation. Stockholders' equity is calculated by subtracting total liabilities from total assets.

Straight Bill of Lading: A straight bill of lading is a non-negotiable document in which the goods are consigned directly to a named consignee. The buyer can obtain the goods from the carrier by showing proof of identity.

Subordinated Debenture: An unsecured corporate bond.

Superpriority Claim: In bankruptcy, a superpriority claim is a post petition claim against which the court has granted a priority above other pre-petition and post-petition claims.

Terms of Sale: The conditions under which a firm offers to sell its goods or services to a specific customer.

Time Draft: A payment demand that matures and is payable at a stated future date. A time draft matures either a certain number of days after acceptance or [less commonly] a certain number of days after the draft's date.

Times Interest Earned: A ratio measuring earnings before interest and tax divided by interest payments.

Total Assets: The sum of all short term (current) and long term assets.

Total Asset Turnover Ratio: The ratio of net sales to total assets.

Total Debt: This is the sum of all Current Liabilities, Capital Lease Obligations and Long Term Debt.

Total Debt to Equity Ratio: A capitalization ratio comparing current liabilities plus long term debt to shareholders' equity. It is calculated by dividing Total Debt by Total Equity.

Total Equity: This is the sum of all of the individual equity line items listed on the Balance Sheet.

Total Revenue: Total sales and other revenues for a specific accounting period.

Transferable Letter of Credit: A transferable L/C is a credit which gives the beneficiary the right to make the credit available in whole or in part to one or more third parties.

Translation Exposure: The risk of adverse effects on a company's financial performance that results from changes in foreign exchange rates.

Transshipments: The transfer of goods from one ship to another for further transit.

Treasury Stock: Common stock that has been repurchased by the company and is now held by the company.

Trend: A pattern in a company's financial performance over time.

Trustee: An individual that administers a bankruptcy case. The Office of the United States Trustee appoints a private trustee in every Chapter 7, 12, or 13 bankruptcy case.

Uniform Customs and Practices for Documentary Credits: The UCP is a body of rules and guidelines governing international trade covered by letters of credit.

Unsecured Claim: A pre-petition claim that is neither a priority nor a secured claim. Trade creditors without security normally file an unsecured claim in a business bankruptcy.

Unsecured Creditor: A creditor that sells without benefit of collateral pledges or security in the form of a security interest or other forms of assurance of payment.

Unsecured Creditors Committee: The Bankruptcy Code allows for committees to act on behalf of various classes of creditors. The Official Committee of Unsecured Creditors acts in a fiduciary capacity to protect the rights and interests of unsecured creditors in a Chapter 11 bankruptcy.

URL: A Uniform Resource Locator, or URL, is a specific address that identifies a web site or other resource on the Internet. The URL contains four distinct sections to allow users to specify the exact location they want to visit.

Usance: The specified time between the signing of the draft and actual payment.

Usance L/C: A usance L/C provides for payment a specific number of days after the beneficiary presents the required conforming documents to the issuing bank.

Usenet: A Usenet is an Internet newsgroup or discussion group.

VAN: A VAN, or Value Added Network, is a third-party electronic mailbox service used by businesses participating in Electronic Data Interchange. VANs store messages, forward them, can track transmission and delivery, and offer translation services.

Web browser: A generic name for software that allows users to access information available on the Internet.

Wire Transfer: A method of transferring funds between banks. Wire transfers may be sent through a private bank wire system, or through the U.S. Federal Reserve's FedWire inter-bank electronic money transfer service.

X12: X12 or ASC X12 is the designation given to the standard electronic format by which companies exchange documents via Electronic Data Interchange.

10-K: An annual report required by the Securities and Exchange Commission each year from every publicly held company.

COMMON EXPORT TERMS

Amendment: The process of requesting a change to one or more of the terms and conditions of a letter of credit. The seller initiates the change. The seller's bank and the buyer's bank must both consent to the change before it can become effective.

Certificate of Inspection: A certificate issued by an independent third party attesting to the quality and the quantity of goods itemized on the commercial invoice.

Certificate of Origin: This document, normally endorsed by the Chamber of Commerce, attests to the origin of the goods.

Commercial Invoice: This is a bill for the goods from the seller to the buyer. It is used to determine the true value of the goods so that the importer can pay any applicable local taxes on the import.

Confirmed Letter of Credit: A confirmed letter of credit is one against which a bank in the exporter's company agrees to pay the seller if the buyer's bank defaults for reasons other than a non-conformity.

Consular Invoice. Required by some countries but not others, this documents is used to identify the goods being shipped [exported]. The country's consul or embassy must approve consular invoices.

Documentary Letters of Credit. A documentary letter of credit is a letter of credit issued by a bank guaranteeing payment of the specified dollar amount on behalf of its customer to a third party creditor provided that the terms and conditions of the letter of credit are fully complied with. The buyer is guaranteed payment only if the conditions stipulated in the letter of credit are fulfilled.

Free on Board [or F.O.B.]: A shipment for which the seller is responsible for transportation and shipping costs to the point where the goods are delivered to and loaded onto a carrier.

Ocean Bill of Lading: This is both a receipt for cargo and a contract for the transportation of that cargo between the shipper and the ocean carrier. The steamship company issues this document.

Pro-Forma Invoice: An invoice forwarded by the seller of the goods prior to shipment that advises the buyer of the details of the sale. A Pro-forma invoice may be required by the buyer in order to obtain an import license or a letter of credit.

Transshipment. Transshipment involves the shipment of merchandise from one country to another on more than one vessel or vehicle.

INDEX

631